T0277455

SHAKESPEARE ON PAGE AND STAGE

Stanley Wells is one of the best known and most highly respected Shakespeare scholars in the world. This volume presents a winning selection of the very best essays from his long and distinguished career. Wells's accomplishments include editing the entire canon of Shakespeare plays for the ground-breaking Oxford Shakespeare series, and over his lifetime he has made significant contributions to debates over literary criticism of the works, genre study, textual theory, Shakespeare's afterlife in the theatre, and contemporary performance. An introduction by Peter Holland is followed by thirty chapters, divided into themed sections: 'Shakespearian Influences', 'Essays on Particular Works', 'Shakespeare in the Theatre', and 'Shakespeare's Text'. An afterword by Margreta de Grazia concludes the volume.

Sir Stanley Wells C.B.E., described by Roy Hattersley as 'our greatest authority on Shakespeare's life and work', is Honorary President of the Shakespeare Birthplace Trust, Emeritus Professor of Shakespeare Studies of the University of Birmingham, and Honorary Emeritus Governor of the Royal Shakespeare Theatre. He is the General Editor of the Oxford and the Penguin Shakespeare series and (with Gary Taylor) of *The Oxford Shakespeare: The Complete Works*. His many books include *Shakespeare: For All Time*; *Shakespeare and Co.*; *Shakespeare, Sex, and Love*; *Great Shakespeare Actors*; and *William Shakespeare: A Very Short Introduction*. He was knighted in 2016 for services to Shakespeare scholarship. He lives in Stratford-upon-Avon.

The volume is edited by **Paul Edmondson**, Head of Research for The Shakespeare Birthplace Trust and Honorary Fellow of The Shakespeare Institute.

Further Praise for *Shakespeare on Page and Stage*

'His breadth and judiciousness are generously on view in an essay "On Being a General Editor," with advice that I have long taken to heart as to whether notes should appear at the foot of the page, how to keep the text as free as possible from algebraic signs, how to persuade individual editors in a series to absorb and act upon the advice they are given, and much more. These are only a few instances of enlightenment afforded by this immensely valuable collection of essays.'

David Bevington, *Renaissance Quarterly*

'Another collection poised at the intersection of theatrical practice and historical scholarship…The essays in this collection exhibit Well's extraordinary critical range, as well as his characteristic clarity, wisdom, and wit.'

Kevin Curran, *Studies in English Literature 1500–1900*

'[An] expansive, insightful essay collection…[Wells's] engagement with the material is lively enough that [readers will be inspired] to dust off their old editions of the plays from their school days and dive back in.'

Publishers Weekly

'At their best (and they are often at their best), these essays display the tough-minded wit that John Donne might have brought to, as well as found in, Shakespeare: wreathed, ingenious, supple, sophisticated—and delivered with a wink.'

Times Literary Supplement

STANLEY WELLS

SHAKESPEARE
ON PAGE & STAGE

SELECTED ESSAYS

EDITED BY
Paul Edmondson

OXFORD
UNIVERSITY PRESS

OXFORD
UNIVERSITY PRESS

Great Clarendon Street, Oxford, OX2 6DP,
United Kingdom

Oxford University Press is a department of the University of Oxford.
It furthers the University's objective of excellence in research, scholarship,
and education by publishing worldwide. Oxford is a registered trade mark of
Oxford University Press in the UK and in certain other countries

© In this volume Stanley Wells and Paul Edmondson 2016.
Introduction © Peter Holland 2016.
Afterword © Margreta de Grazia 2016.

The moral rights of the authors have been asserted

First published 2016
First published in paperback 2023

All rights reserved. No part of this publication may be reproduced, stored in
a retrieval system, or transmitted, in any form or by any means, without the
prior permission in writing of Oxford University Press, or as expressly permitted
by law, by licence or under terms agreed with the appropriate reprographics
rights organization. Enquiries concerning reproduction outside the scope of the
above should be sent to the Rights Department, Oxford University Press, at the
address above

You must not circulate this work in any other form
and you must impose this same condition on any acquirer

Published in the United States of America by Oxford University Press
198 Madison Avenue, New York, NY 10016, United States of America

British Library Cataloguing in Publication Data
Data available

Library of Congress Cataloging in Publication Data
Data available

ISBN 978–0–19–878654–2 (Hbk.)
ISBN 978–0–19–888456–9 (Pbk.)

Printed and bound in the UK by
Clays Ltd, Elcograf S.p.A.

Links to third party websites are provided by Oxford in good faith and
for information only. Oxford disclaims any responsibility for the materials
contained in any third party website referenced in this work.

PREFACE TO THE PAPERBACK EDITION

Since receiving his knighthood for his unparalleled services to Shakespeare in 2016, readers throughout the world have continued to enjoy the scholarship of Sir Stanley Wells. They know they will find there a rigorous and unflinching authority combined with a clarity of style. Stanley writes to be understood and can communicate his knowledge to audiences well beyond the university lecture hall or conference room. He has remained resolutely jargon-free throughout his whole career. He listens for the truth and speaks it.

Those who admire his work might like to know how he has continued to live out his life as a Shakespearian since the first appearance of this volume of essays.

Two energetic lecture series continue in his honour. The biennial series of Oxford Wells Shakespeare Lectures (established in 2008) have, since 2016, been given by John Kerrigan on 'Shakespeare's Originality', by Margreta de Grazia on 'Shakespeare Without a Life (1564–1616)', and by Bill Sherman on 'Decoding Shakespeare: How to Make Anything Signify Anything.' Since the first appearance of Stanley's selected essays, the annual Notre Dame London Shakespeare Lecture (established in 2011) has been given by Lois Potter, Gregory Doran, Michael Dobson, Russell Jackson, Peter Holland, Carol Rutter, and Simon Russell Beale. In 2020, Stanley himself took part—chairing a public conversation with his good friend Dame Judi Dench. All these occasions signify gratitude for what Stanley has given and continues to give to Shakespeare Studies. He himself honoured all these lectures by turning up to listen, and to take part in the conversations afterwards.

In 2020, Stanley's 90th year, The Shakespeare Birthplace Trust commissioned him to write his own brand-new lecture series. He took as his theme 'What was Shakespeare Really Like?' There were to have been four talks over four weeks in Stratford-upon-Avon, but alas the pandemic closed-down these easily sold-out events. Instead, I was able to make audio recordings of Stanley's talks which reached a far greater audience via the website of The Shakespeare Birthplace Trust. He has since revised and augmented them for publication, along with another essay 'Eight Decades with Shakespeare.' So, Stanley's latest book will appear in September 2023, stylishly framed with a foreword from one of his greatest fans, Stephen Fry.

In spring 2022, as part of a civic fundraising event to restore the statue of Shakespeare that David Garrick gave to the people of Stratford-upon-Avon in 1769, and which can be seen in a niche above the entrance to the Town Hall, Stanley took part in 'Shakespeare's Coming Home!', a sponsored reading of the complete works over twelve days. He turned up to read every day and his roles included Justice Shallow, Holofernes, Duke Senior, Nestor, and Prospero. Importantly and impressively the twelve days ended with the magical highlight of Stanley speaking Prospero's epilogue just before midnight.

Stanley continues to give talks and lectures at home and overseas: co-leading the annual Shakespeare retreat in the lovely Cumberland Lodge in Windsor Great Park, giving classes to students in Venice, taking part in podcasts, speaking on-line to international Shakespearian communities—for example his beloved Shakespeare festival in Stratford, Ontario—giving the key-note address for a conference in Brazil, the opening talk in the 'Shakespeare and Mediterranean' summer school in Verona, lecturing to a literary society in India, and attending the opening of the re-located Munich Shakespeare Library.

Fellow scholars and non-academics like Stanley because he listens and genuinely converses with them. And because he continues to listen to Shakespeare and finds his work to be life-giving. Just before I wrote this Preface, I reminded him of Cordelia's lines: 'Mine enemy's dog, though he had bit me, should have stood / That night against my fire' (*The Tragedy of King Lear*, 4.6.29-30). Stanley's eyes widened as he took in those words again. 'Oh', he said, 'Shakespeare just gets better and better.'

Paul Edmondson
The Shakespeare Birthplace Trust, 2022

EDITORIAL PREFACE

Rosalind appears at the end of *As You Like It* to tell us that just as 'a good wine needs no bush, 'tis true that a good play needs no epilogue'. The same might be said of this Preface, since I, like Rosalind, also find myself in the happy case of having 'to insinuate with you on behalf of a good play'.

Stanley himself selected the essays he wanted to include. Details about their first publication—some were written in tribute to friends and fellow Shakespeare scholars—can be found in the Acknowledgements towards the back of the book. The essays (like the plays in the Folio of 1623) have been thematically rather than chronologically arranged.

Apart from removing the occasional reference to their original context, no substantive revisions have been made to these essays, the better for them to exemplify their own age and moment, and to show the development of Stanley's own thinking and feeling, what Margreta de Grazia in her Afterword names his 'abiding openness'. The adverb 'recently' shimmers through the collection, and a variety of Shakespeare editions have been used for quotations over more than fifty years.

Perhaps, like vintage wine, these essays become even better with the passage of time. Recurrent themes emerge: we think of Shakespeare's plays as having act and scene divisions mainly because of the First Folio; there is the longing for experimentation with staging-practices at London's 'new' Globe; the final two essays in the volume are almost like mirror images of each other; and there are echoes and re-echoes of the insightful considerations which have beset one of the finest of all of Shakespeare's textual editors as well as, in the words of Peter Holland's Introduction, 'the work of one of Shakespeare's greatest critics.'

One of Stanley's earliest memories of reading for pleasure was as a young boy in Hull, hiding behind the family's sofa throughout the waking hours of one weekend, and laughing out loud at *The Pickwick Papers*. Shakespeare followed Dickens a few years later when Stanley's inspiring schoolteacher, Mr E. J. C. Large, introduced him to Sonnet 29, a poem which spoke profoundly and emphatically to Stanley's developing intellectual and literary tastes. That early infectious enjoyment of literature has fuelled Stanley's engagement with Shakespeare across a lifetime.

The publication of this volume happily coincided with Her Majesty Queen Elizabeth II honouring one of the most distinguished Shakespearians of the twentieth and twenty-first centuries with a knighthood in the 2016 Birthday Honours list—a tribute to him, as well as to the international field of Shakespeare studies he represents. Arise, Sir Stanley Wells.

PAUL EDMONDSON
The Shakespeare Birthplace Trust

CONTENTS

Introduction by Peter Holland   1

I. SHAKESPEARIAN INFLUENCES

1. Shakespeare: Man of the European Renaissance   11
2. Tales from Shakespeare   24

II. ESSAYS ON PARTICULAR WORKS

3. The Failure of *The Two Gentlemen of Verona*   49
4. *The Taming of the Shrew* and *King Lear*: A Structural Comparison   58
5. The Integration of Violent Action in *Titus Andronicus*   74
6. The Challenges of *Romeo and Juliet*   86
7. Juliet's Nurse: The Uses of Inconsequentiality   103
8. The Lamentable Tale of *Richard II*   117
9. *A Midsummer Night's Dream* Revisited   133
10. Translations in *A Midsummer Night's Dream*   148
11. The Once and Future *King Lear*   161
12. Problems of Stagecraft in *The Tempest*   178
13. 'My Name is Will': Shakespeare's Sonnets and Autobiography   192
14. Shakespeare Without Sources   205
15. Shakespeare and Romance   219

III. SHAKESPEARE IN THE THEATRE

16. Boys Should be Girls: Shakespeare's Female Roles and the
    Boy Players   247
17. Staging Shakespeare's Ghosts   255

18. Staging Shakespeare's Apparitions and Dream Visions   271

19. Shakespeare in Planché's Extravaganzas   288

20. Shakespeare in Max Beerbohm's Theatre Criticism   304

21. Shakespeare in Leigh Hunt's Theatre Criticism   319

22. Shakespeare in Hazlitt's Theatre Criticism   333

23. Peter Hall's *Coriolanus*, 1959   349

IV. SHAKESPEARE'S TEXT

24. On Being a General Editor   367

25. Editorial Treatment of Foul-Paper Texts: *Much Ado About Nothing* as Test Case   381

26. Money in Shakespeare's Comedies   396

27. To Read a Play: The Problem of Editorial Intervention   405

28. The First Folio: Where Should We be Without it?   425

29. The Limitations of the First Folio   438

Afterword by Margreta de Grazia   449
Notes   453
Select List of Publications   475
Acknowledgements   479
Index   481

Introduction

PETER HOLLAND

> For I am nothing if not critical.
>
> (*Othello*, 2.1.122)

What are the essential characteristics of the finest Shakespeare criticism? It is, of course, an impossible question to answer. For one thing, what is the very best for one kind of audience may not be right for another. Articles written to be read by the small group of scholars who are expert in a sub-field of Shakespeare studies can reasonably choose to use a kind of academic shorthand—some might call it jargon—that would make the argument incomprehensible to others. Some work is, from the start, aimed at a broad audience, made up of that sometimes apparently mythical beast called 'The General Reader', and therefore saying little that is new to expert Shakespeare scholars. Few critics have that wonderful knack of speaking comprehensibly to the latter while at the same time managing to say very many things that are new, intriguing, and persuasive to their academic peers. Stanley Wells is undoubtedly one of those few.

And, if the register of the critical language is a matter of choice, a choice whether to reach out to a wide audience or to a fit audience but few, there are other demands that one might make of Shakespeare criticism that are not simply matters of individual preference, demands that the most brilliant writing on Shakespeare's work seems always to aim at and achieve, qualities like a profound knowledge of the works themselves, equally deep appreciation of and generosity towards the work of other scholars, a sustained engagement with the plays as plays, not only or perhaps not even as literary texts to be read rather than seen and heard, an imagination responsive to the complexities of Shakespeare's language and to the power of its moments of complete simplicity, an ability to work in a wide range of disciplines such as book history, source-study, textual bibliography, theatre history, cultural history, historical linguistics, and so on.

If it seems simply unfair to ask so much of a single Shakespeare critic, then the articles that follow are the most distinguished demonstration that it can be done, for, for all the astonishing breadth of concerns in the practice of Shakespeare studies, there is hardly an area on which Stanley Wells's work, either in the selection gathered here or in the rest of his writings in monographs and editions, in articles in journals and collections (not to mention in theatre and book reviews, or in the more ephemeral forms of lectures or the newer forms of dissemination in blogs and tweets), has not touched with the fairness and fascinated engagement, the enthusiasm and acuity, and the stylish writing that the reader will find throughout this volume.

Representing more than fifty years of writing, these twenty-nine pieces are full of the wit and urbanity, the eloquence and delight that are hallmarks of his style, rich demonstrations that academic prose need not be dry to be scholarly and that the deep pleasure that Wells finds in his experience of Shakespeare, whether as reader, spectator, editor, or, simply, critic, can be and should be a part of his communication with his own readers. But Wells is also always the servant of his argument and the result is never self-regarding, never seeking to show off his knowledge and wisdom but always wanting, gently and entertainingly, to show us what wonders are to be found both in Shakespeare's works themselves and in the rich histories and geographies of the ways his plays and poems have been encountered and loved across centuries and across the world.

It is fitting, therefore, that the volume should begin with a section on 'Shakespearean Influences' and that the first article should be a consideration of Shakespeare as 'Man of the European Renaissance', an article that is not only a broad relocation of Shakespeare as European as well as English but also a piece that began its life as a plenary paper at the 9th World Shakespeare Congress in Prague in 2011, a keynote at a conference whose delegates thought widely about 'Renaissance Shakespeare' and 'Shakespeare Renaissances'. Defining Shakespeare not as a 'Renaissance man', someone who Alberti defined as able to 'do all things if he will', but as someone participating in 'those larger cross-national currents that link him with his European contemporaries', Wells sees Shakespeare as inevitably, like anyone who was formally educated, 'trained in the values and culture that we associate with the Renaissance'. So he describes the significance of Shakespeare's knowledge and use of Latin and Greek sources, and the ways in which his drama was part of the theatres' function as 'a forum for the circulation of both received and original ideas', not only scientific or political but also about religion as a matter for the individual and the state. The Shakespeare of this approach is 'of his age' as well as 'for all time' and exploring the connection between multi-panelled altarpieces and the structures of Shakespeare's plays leads Wells to ask 'whether there is any greater parallel to Shakespeare's portrayal of the suffering of King Lear than Masaccio's depiction of the expulsion of Adam and Eve'. Two of the greatest achievements of Renaissance art stand perfectly and powerfully aligned in their consideration of the pain of being human.

It may seem a long way from this to the subject of the next chapter, Wells's British Academy Shakespeare lecture of 1987 on 'Tales from Shakespeare', but it is really only a move to the ways in which, being 'for all time', Shakespeare is continually being remade for particular purposes. As Wells recognized then, and as is still true now, there has been little attention to prose narrative adaptations of the plays to compare with the attention to stage and screen versions. But the conjunction in 1807 of the publication of the first editions of both *The Family Shakespeare* by Thomas and Henrietta Maria Bowdler and *Tales from Shakespeare* by Charles and Mary Lamb is Wells's starting-point for a scholarly investigation both of the latter work and of alternative versions for young people, starting with J. B. Perrin's *Contes Moraux et Instructifs,... tirés des Tragédies de Shakespeare* in 1783 and ending with Leon Garfield's *Shakespeare Stories* (1985). Wells and Garfield would collaborate a few years later on the twelve episodes of *Shakespeare: The Animated Tales* (1992–4), for which Garfield wrote the screenplays and Wells acted as adviser. Typical of Wells's scholarship, not the least important part of the published version of the lecture is the extensive bibliography of dozens of editions of Lambs' *Tales* and of other versions, culled, I presume, from research in the holdings of the Shakespeare Birthplace Trust. And, equally typically, the lecture ended with Wells playing a recording of a version of *Romeo and Juliet* on a compilation called *One-Minute Classics*.

The second and much the largest section of the volume covers chapters on particular works, pieces that explore plays and poems on their own or in groups, a sequence that is both chronological across Shakespeare's career and across Wells's life, from a 1963 article on *The Two Gentlemen of Verona*, wryly titled as an exploration of its 'failure', to an article on the Sonnets as autobiography published in 2015 in *Shakespeare Survey*, the leading British Shakespeare journal which Wells edited with great distinction for nineteen years (from *Survey* 34 [1982] to 52 [1999]).

In *The Two Gentlemen of Verona* Wells explores its plot's 'peculiarities, limitations, and plain faults' ranged in three categories: 'the superficial, the technical, and the organic'. Shakespeare at the outset of his career is, for Wells, displaying 'an under-developed technique', prone to duologue rather than the greater complexities of multi-voiced scenes that this 'tyro in dramatic craftmanship' cannot yet create. When Shakespeare conceives Julia as a character of some depth, it only serves to 'expose the hollowness of Valentine and Proteus'. Balanced and cautious, Wells's view of the play accepts the problems: 'when we try to get below the surface of the play, we find it rests on shaky foundations' and so 'the best thing to do seems to be to come up to the surface again and examine that', valuing and relishing the play, as Dr Johnson did, for its local achievements rather than making a weak case for greater worth.

Here and elsewhere throughout these pieces, Wells is never afraid to show what Shakespeare cannot do, for his admiration for what Shakespeare does so magnificently is only intensified by his sharp awareness of the limitations here and there.

So, for instance, he can see moments in *Titus Andronicus* where 'Shakespeare fails to integrate violent action into the surrounding dialogue—or chooses not to do so'. But the recognition of this is not simply a matter of whether 'we regard this as a technical deficiency' but rather that it constitutes 'a feature of the play that has been largely responsible for its critical denigration' and, of equal importance for Wells, 'continues to cause serious problems to its theatrical interpreters', for Wells, impressed as he was by Deborah Warner's production of *Titus* at the RSC's Swan Theatre in 1987, still found that the play 'did not emerge as an unflawed masterpiece in this revelatory production'. But Wells also explores the dramatizing of violence across Shakespeare's writing for a further reason, beyond what he notes Alan Dessen calling '*Titus*-bashing', for comparison of the handling of such scenes may help with one of the most vexed of all Shakespeare conundrums: the chronology of the plays. The greater integration of violence in the *Henry VI* plays may be another fragment that shows *Titus* to be earlier than the histories. As always in Wells, the identification of weakness in Shakespeare proves to have rich rewards.

There is similarly thoughtful exploration of things that do not seem quite to go right in the dramaturgy of *Romeo and Juliet*, drawing on Wells's careful observation of successes in the many RSC productions (especially Terry Hands and Barry Kyle in 1976, Michael Bogdanov in 1986, Terry Hands again in 1989, Adrian Noble in 1995) in order to grasp how the play works with its moments of comedy or how a production explores Mercutio's sexuality ('intense but undirected' in Hands's 1989 version), as he moves towards 'the play's greatest challenge', its challenge to 'our notions of genre' as it requires that 'we abandon the idea that because it is called a tragedy it must centre on the fate of individuals and accept its emphasis on the multifarious society in which these individuals have their being'. Even a play written late in Shakespeare's life can show his ways of grappling with problems, as in Wells's study of stagecraft in *The Tempest*, a piece published as part of a celebration of Jan Kott's 80th birthday. The problems here are not 'simply practical' but ones 'that derive from features of [the play's] dramatic style', a style that Wells sets out to define precisely through these problems.

Wells is a superb guide to ways that individual plays are shaped, seeing, for instance, the ways in which *A Midsummer Night's Dream*'s concern with metamorphosis, 'of translation from one state to another', can be a route to open up the complex interconnectedness of its apparently disjunct elements—and Wells does this by seeing the wide range of meanings that the word 'translated' had in early modern English. Similarly, he finds in the frequency of laments in *Richard II* a vital clue to the ways in which 'its impression of poetic unity' is based on 'the dominance within its structure of emotional attitudes associated with lamentation'. The more one looks at a play's structure, the more surprising the results may be. I cannot think of another critic who would find reason to—or, indeed, dare to—compare *The Taming of the Shrew* with *King Lear*. But Wells achieves it as a means of demonstrating

Shakespeare's fascination with the relationship of mind and body from the 'fairly simple dualism' in *Shrew* to the expansion of the concept of 'mind' in *Lear*, even though '"body" will remain more or less constant'. The exposition of structural forms, simple in *Shrew* and 'exceptionally schematic' in *Lear*, proves a gateway to Shakespeare's profound thinking about the essence of being human.

It is always the case that Wells's analysis is based on thoughtful and open-minded close-reading of Shakespeare's language but, at times, he wants us simply to see and marvel at what Shakespeare can make dramatic language do, as in the way he sustains a brilliant exploration of the ways in which the inconsequentialities in Juliet's Nurse's long story about Juliet as a toddler create 'the illusion of spontaneity', an immediacy of speech that, for me, is one of Shakespeare's most extraordinary discoveries, for, as Wells shows, it enables 'the breakdown of linguistic control' in Lear on his 'revenges' or the cunning of Pompey's use of the device in the story of Master Froth and the prunes in *Measure for Measure*, or the revelatory depiction of the workings of Hamlet's mind in the soliloquies. In many of these essays, as in this example, he moves with ease and authority across the canon, showing how something found early by Shakespeare deepens its depth of possibilities later in a very different play, Shakespeare always remembering what he had done and learning from himself. The closer Wells engages with local achievements the more he is able to draw back and see the ripples years later, in another genre, a different world, a greater play.

And it is always the case that Wells's close-reading is shaped by his sensitivity to the plays in performance, not only in productions he has seen or ones of previous eras of which he has read but also ones his contemplation of the text reveals. Wells's interest in the conditions of early modern performance and of the subsequent histories of Shakespeare in the theatre forms the selections in the third section.

In 'Boys Should be Girls', Wells, critical of recent practice of casting adult males in female roles, as in *Richard II* at Shakespeare's Globe in 2003, is concerned that the practice 'is creating in many persons' minds the impression that this is ... a return to original practice'. Using the archival work of David Kathman, Wells explores the ages of Shakespeare's boy actors and the numbers of boys available to him as he wrote the plays (usually three but sometimes as many as six), in order to argue, against the growing audience expectation and occasional argument by scholars who should know better, that 'women's roles were always played by boys'. As, here, he shows 'Shakespeare's professional skill in cutting his coat according to his cloth', so he shows in two further pieces how ghosts, apparitions, and dream-visions were staged in early modern theatres and how Shakespeare's examples of these devices reveal him always to be remoulding conventions and not simply accepting them, testing out the experimental limits of the performative possibilities of a frequent stage event. These articles were written in honour of two fellow-scholars, G. K. Hunter and Philip Brockbank, whose scholarship Wells highly valued, a

Festschrift piece as a means generously to recognize the achievements of his friends and fellow-scholars.

Wells has long been fascinated by Shakespeare on the nineteenth-century stage in all its manifold forms. He edited a five-volume collection of nineteenth-century Shakespeare burlesques (1977), an extensive exploration of the phenomenon that Shakespeare scholars and theatre historians had too long ignored. In this volume, though, we have an earlier article, a study of Shakespeare in the stage extravaganzas of James Robinson Planché, published in 1963 and still the only substantial study of what Planché did with—or should that be 'to'?—Shakespeare in his spectacular 'whimsical treatment[s] of a poetical subject', as Planché himself defined his preferred form of show. But Wells is not only looking to remind us of a forgotten style of show, for he sees in Planché's work something that, in its higher concern for production standards than most of his contemporaries, 'served Shakespeare well' and shaped our own expectations for Shakespeare production.

Wells has, too, been an exceptional reviewer of Shakespeare, something one can see in, for instances, his three long pieces on Shakespeare performances in the 1980s for *Shakespeare Survey 41, 42,* and *43* (1989–91). Here we have selected a single example of his own reviewing, his lecture on Peter Hall's 1959 production of *Coriolanus* with Olivier as Coriolanus and Edith Evans as Volumnia, which first appeared in 1977 as the first of his four studies of Stratford productions in *Royal Shakespeare*, originally lectures at Furman University. The proud owner of a tape-recording of the production, made under mysterious circumstances but giving a chance to hear Olivier at his very best, Wells has also been known to give his own imitation of Olivier in the role, for the details of it have stayed fresh in his mind, so overwhelmed was he by the achievements of that production. As he writes of Olivier's dying fall,

> It was theatrical; but we were in a theatre. It was dangerous; but Coriolanus lived, as well as died, dangerously. It was the final shock for an audience that had been given many surprises, and it left me, at least, overcome with awe. I left the theatre, on the first night, profoundly impressed, and walked the streets of Stratford for twenty minutes before feeling I wanted to talk to anyone. That, I think, is what Aristotle meant by catharsis.

That is itself no empty gesture but a recognition that his experience explicates the central definition in Western thought of the nature of tragedy.

Wells has also been our finest guide to the history of reviewing of Shakespeare, especially in his carefully crafted collection of reviews, *Shakespeare in the Theatre: An Anthology of Criticism* (1997), which covers the long history of reviewing and also manages to include at least one review of every Shakespeare play. Three essays in this section show Wells at his best as he explores the writing of three reviewers he particularly admires: Max Beerbohm, Leigh Hunt, and William Hazlitt. One of the

6

demands Wells places on the reviewer—and makes sure his own reviewing always fulfils—is the description of the theatre event in such a way as to preserve the details of performance, not simply generalities of success and failure but a fixing of the moment. So he cherishes Max Beerbohm savaging an actor who, as Jaques in *As You Like It*, munched on an apple while speaking of the seven ages of man and thereby made the words inaudible, or Leigh Hunt on Kemble as Coriolanus speaking the word 'fair' which, 'instead of being a short monosyllable,...became a word of tremendous elongation. We can describe the pronunciation by nothing else than by such a sound as *fay-er-r-r*'. But he complains of Hazlitt's 'eulogies of Kean [which] tend towards the generalizing in their method':

> It is the kind of criticism that makes one wish one had seen the performance—which is something—but does not reach the excellence of almost making one feel one *has* seen the performance.

The last section of this volume brings together six articles on Shakespeare's text but, as one of the many threads that tie all the articles selected together, they can helpfully be read alongside 'The Once and Future *King Lear*', Wells's introduction to the collection edited by Gary Taylor and Michael Warren in 1983 that sought to show that the Quarto and Folio texts of the play, differing from each other in so many ways, large and small, were not two imperfect witnesses of a single original which can be seen in the 'conflated' text that was the norm in Shakespeare editions, but instead that these two versions show Shakespeare revising and rethinking the play. Wells and Taylor's 1986 edition of Shakespeare's works included separate editions of the Quarto, titled *The History of King Lear*, and the Folio, named *The Tragedy of King Lear*, and Wells went on to edit *Lear* (2000) from the Quarto for the Oxford series of individual play editions for which he was General Editor.

What precisely a General Editor does is the subject of the article I asked Stanley to write for the theme of 'Editing Shakespeare' for *Shakespeare Survey* 59 (2006), not least because no other General Editor has written about the task. But then Wells's work on Shakespeare's text has often involved clear-sighted investigation of the problems of editing, especially in his unprecedented study of the whole question of modernizing the spelling of Shakespeare's texts (*Modernizing Shakespeare's Spelling* (1979)) and his remarkable exploration of how to present the texts today (*Re-editing Shakespeare for the Modern Reader* (1984)). Textual study depends on complex analysis of the processes of early modern printing, an example of which is 'Editorial Treatment of Foul-Paper Texts' which uses *Much Ado About Nothing* as its test case. This is technical textual bibliography that minutely examines and subtly considers what the early published texts can show us of the printer's copy and print-shop practices—and it serves as a sample of the labours and demanding analysis that underpinned Wells's editing of Shakespeare.

The last two articles in the volume consider the most important of all Shakespeare publications, the 'First Folio' of 1623, the book that first printed a number of plays, whose monetary value is seen in the history of auction prices for copies, and whose cultural value is proved by the decision of the Folger Shakespeare Library to transport some of its copies around the United States so that a copy could be on display in each of the fifty states during 2016. Wells's understanding of the nature of F1 as a book, and Wells and Edmondson's thinking about strange contemporary beliefs in the extent to which F1 is witness to early modern performance practices, bring together book history and theatre history, the twin tracks through which Shakespeare is seemingly endlessly reproduced across time and across the world, returning us yet again to the concerns that opened this book: Shakespeare's reputation and influence.

From their original location in academic journals and *Festschriften*, collections and lectures, the articles stand now gathered together rather like some kind of First Folio collection of a scholar-critic's work. It is a fitting representation of the work of one of Shakespeare's greatest critics.

PART I
SHAKESPEARIAN INFLUENCES

1

Shakespeare:
Man of the European Renaissance

It was a very special pleasure and privilege to address the World Shakespeare Congress in Prague in July 2011. My previous visit had been during a British Council lecture tour in 1989. I had been invited at the instigation of my generous friend, Zdeněk Stříbrný, the doyen of Czech Shakespeare scholars whose presence at the Prague Congress was a great pleasure to us all. He greeted me on my arrival in 1989 with the news that there had been what he called 'a spot of bother'. A student had been beaten up and more trouble might follow. It did. My initial lecture, given to the Czech Academy, was punctuated by the chanting of the long line of protesters winding their way from Wenceslaus Square to the Presidential Palace. Afterward I stood with members of my loyal audience on a balcony to witness the seemingly endless procession stream by, the walkers waving up to the tall plate-glass windows of the National Theatre, whose actors, along with the students, had been prime movers in the protest. In the days that followed, my lecture schedule dwindled as what came to be known as the Velvet Revolution escalated. I still have the badge bearing the image of President Václav Havel that was thrown down to me from a window as I made my way to join a vast crowd in Wenceslaus Square. It was a deeply moving—and at times a rather scary—experience. Needless to say, without the liberating events of those fateful days, the World Shakespeare Congress in Prague could never have happened.

What follows, based on the plenary paper I gave in Prague, takes its cue from the overall title for the Congress, 'Renaissance Shakespeare, Shakespeare Renaissances', in having as its subject Shakespeare as a man of the European Renaissance.

At a conference in Venice some years ago, Patricia Parker made a simple but provocative remark that I found richly suggestive. We should think of Shakespeare, she suggested, not as a quintessentially English writer but as a European one. Perhaps this meant no more than that at the time Shakespeare was writing, educated Englishmen were the products of a civilization that was founded not on national values but on international ones: that he was in essence a man of the European Renaissance rather than a parochialized islander.

This set me thinking about ways in which Shakespeare's writings partake of and participate in those larger cross-national currents that link him with his European contemporaries. He was not of course a 'Renaissance man' in the Leonardo da Vinci sense, defined by Alberti as one who 'can do all things if he will', the kind of polymath embodied in the England of Shakespeare's time by Sir Philip Sidney, courtier, warrior, poet, prose writer, literary critic, ambassador, and patron of learning and the arts, embodiment of chivalric ideals to which Shakespeare's patron, the Earl of Southampton, appears also to have aspired. Nor was Shakespeare a versatile writer in the manner of a contemporary such as Francis Bacon, a courtier, philosopher, and essayist who wrote as fluently in Latin as in English, and whose work encompassed a wide range of genres. Considered in relation to many of his contemporaries, Shakespeare was circumscribed in both ambition and accomplishment. Unlike for example John Lyly, Christopher Marlowe, and Robert Greene, let alone Ben Jonson, Shakespeare was not versatile in the literary forms that he adopted in his own language. He wrote no prose fiction, no social pamphlets, no literary criticism, no plays for the private playhouses, no masques or pageants, not even any commendatory or memorial verses worth speaking of. He confined himself entirely to drama written for the public theatres along with a modest amount of non-dramatic verse. To this extent he was, among his contemporaries, unusually limited in generic range.

Nevertheless Shakespeare may properly be regarded as a man of the European Renaissance in the sense that he, like everyone else who received a formal education in his time, whether in England or elsewhere, was trained in the values and culture that we associate with the Renaissance, that is to say with the importance of ways of thought and of expression associated with the rebirth of classical learning and civilization originating in Italy, and above all in Florence. Though we have no direct records of his schooling, much about it can be confidently deduced both from the society of his time and from his writings. The very record of his baptism in 1564 is in a classical language: 'Gulielmus filius Johannes Shakespeare' [William, the son of John Shakespeare]—Latin not just because it was the language used in official documents of the time, but because it was written and even spoken both formally and informally by many of his fellow townspeople. Much of his schooling would have been conducted in that language, as we see reflected in Parson Evans's catechism of the boy William Page in *The Merry Wives of Windsor*, Act 4, scene 1. That scene—surely the most autobiographical in all the works—actually quotes passages from the textbook prescribed throughout the country for the teaching of Latin, William Lyly's *Short Introduction of Grammar*, authorized for use in schools in 1542 and a standard work for over three centuries. At school Shakespeare would have been required to write and even to speak in Latin from an early age, on the playground as well as in the classroom. His fellow townsman and relative by marriage Richard Quiney was a book lover who wrote letters to his Stratford colleagues in a mixture of English and Latin. We have a letter written in Latin by Quiney's son Richard before he was a teenager asking his father to bring back from London books of blank paper for his brother and himself, and in which he thanks his father for bringing him up 'in the studies of sacred learning'.[1] It is quite possible that if letters from Shakespeare are ever discovered, they too will be written in Latin. It was a lingua franca, used for example by English travellers in Europe when they were not familiar with the native language. The adventurous traveller Tom Coryate on a visit to France in 1608 records that as he walked from town to town he had a long conversation in Latin with a young friar 'on divers matters, especially of religion, wherein the chiefest matter that we handled was about the adoration of images'.[2]

As that anecdote suggests, modern languages are unlikely to have been taught in the schools of Shakespeare's time. But tutors and instruction books were available, including some written by John Florio, who taught French and Italian both to Southampton and to the Earls of Pembroke, and who may have taught Shakespeare too. Shakespeare clearly understood French by the time he came to write *Henry V*, and he had enough Italian to read Cinthio for *Othello*.[3] In *The Merchant of Venice* he causes Portia to make fun of her English suitor, Faulconbridge, because 'he hath neither Latin, French, nor Italian' (1.2.66–7).[4] I don't find it easy to think that Shakespeare would have written that if the same were true of him.

Greek is another matter. The only external evidence that Shakespeare had any familiarity with the language comes from Ben Jonson's snooty statement that he had 'small Latin and less Greek'. (Though it's interesting that two of the three classical personages named on his monument—Socrates and Nestor—are Greek; the other is the Roman Virgil.) But Greek literature certainly formed a standard element in humanistic education, and study of its language was on the curriculum in many English grammar schools, as T. W. Baldwin makes clear in his massive study *William Shakspere's Small Latine and Lesse Greeke*;[5] Greek grammar books were available to schools.[6] Stratford's is likely to have been among them.[7] But whereas Shakespeare's writings provide ample evidence that he understood Latin, there are so few traces of Greek in them that some scholars have concluded, in spite of Jonson's phrase 'lesse Greeke', that he knew no Greek at all. However, Andrew Werth, an Oxfordian (we must try not to hold that against him), has argued for a number of echoes of Greek literature and traces of Greek vocabulary in Shakespeare's plays.[8] Some of his arguments, such as those relating to *Titus Andronicus* and *Timon of Athens*, are vitiated by recent studies in Shakespeare as a collaborator, but in other respects they seem strong. In any case it's curious that the two most extended passages in all Shakespeare's works which are directly indebted to a work of classical literature that was not apparently available in translation in Shakespeare's time come from a Greek, not a Latin writer. These are Sonnets 153 and 154, both of which are direct versions of a single ancient Greek epigram by Marianus Scholasticus, a poet of the fifth and sixth centuries AD. In translation it reads,

> Beneath these plane trees, detained by gentle slumber, Love slept, having put his torch in the care of the Nymphs; but the Nymphs said to one another 'Why wait? Would that together with this we could quench the fire in the hearts of men.' But the torch set fire even to the water, and with hot water thenceforth the Love-Nymphs fill the bath.[9]

Shakespeare's Sonnets 153 and 154 clearly expand and play variations on this, but there are significant differences as well as resemblances. The poem is Latinized—its love god is Cupid, not Eros; his victim is a nymph of the Roman goddess Diana; and the plane trees prominent in Greek mythology are absent. In the first sonnet, it is simply one 'maid of Dian's' who takes advantage of Cupid, whereas in the second a whole troop of nymphs comes 'tripping by'. Shakespeare seems also to have introduced the numerous bawdy undertones that Stephen Booth expounds in his notes on these poems.[10]

What this amounts to is that the author of each of the English poems is both translating and exercising the power of *inventio* as well as variation. Margaret Downs-Gamble, in an article called 'New Pleasures Prove: Evidence of Dialectical *Disputatio* in Early Modern Manuscript Culture', has published a charming example of two similar English poems surviving in manuscript, one by William Strode, the other a free paraphrase of it.[11] Some scholars, reluctant to believe that Shakespeare read any Greek, have suggested that the last printed of the sonnets is indebted to a Latin translation of the Greek epigram, and Katherine Duncan-Jones, in her note on Sonnet 153, after a tortuous discussion of a variety of routes by which Shakespeare might have come to know the original, suggests that he might have depended on a hypothetical lost version by Jonson from a 1603 translation into Latin. This has obviously difficult implications for the dating of poems that Colin Burrow, Helen Vendler, and other scholars place among the earliest composed of the sonnets—as indeed does Duncan-Jones herself on another page of her edition.[12]

Other scholars who believe that Shakespeare knew no Greek have thrown up their hands in despair and fallen back on the hypothesis that these sonnets are not by Shakespeare at all. Is it not possible, however, that they may be schoolboy exercises in translation undertaken by a young man who was obliged to study Greek at school but did not take it much, if any, further than classroom level? The fact that both poems, unlike any others in the same collection, are identical in substance surely savours much of the kind of exercises in *imitatio* to which the Parson Evanses of Shakespeare's day subjected their pupils. Andrew Gurr's suggestion,[13] now generally accepted, that Sonnet 145, with its puns on 'hate' and 'away', represents Shakespeare's wooing exercise undertaken shortly after he left school opens the door wide to the possibility that the 1609 collection of sonnets is, as Paul

Edmondson and I have argued in our book on these poems, not so much a sequence as a collection which at times seems like a miscellany, even a ragbag of poems written over a long period of time.[14] It seems to me not unreasonable to suggest that these two sonnets, far from representing Shakespeare's personal reflections on his treatment in the city of Bath for venereal disease, as many critics have suggested, may literally be academic exercises thriftily preserved from his school notebooks and recycled—whether by him or by Thomas Thorpe—late in his career.

We have, of course, every reason to believe that Shakespeare's education did not proceed to the tertiary level. This is true also of Ben Jonson, but not of earlier contemporaries such as Christopher Marlowe, Robert Greene (who boasted himself master of arts of both universities), John Lyly, George Peele, and Thomas Nashe. These were the University Wits; they were already writing plays for both public and private theatres as Shakespeare embarked upon his own career—and, incidentally, all of them also wrote non-dramatic works of various kinds. At the Rose playhouse, and possibly as a member of the Queen's Men, Shakespeare was in direct competition with these university-educated writers. He undoubtedly learned from them, and indeed recent authorship studies suggest that in his early days as a writer he may well have collaborated with Marlowe, Peele, and Nashe. Their example; the stimulus provided by their writings, and probably by their company; their friendship; and their rivalry must have stimulated him to emulate them both in allusiveness to the classics and in technique. They formed a kind of surrogate university for him.

Shakespeare's participation in this intellectual community is witnessed in many ways. Like the Wits, he frequently chose to base plays on classical themes deriving from Plutarch and from Roman writers. One of his early plays, *The Comedy of Errors*, is closely indebted to a Roman comedy which he may have studied at school while also, in typically Shakespearean fashion, complicating the action and infusing it with romantic elements that relate it to medieval literature. His plays make extensive use of references to classical literature and history.

On a more detailed linguistic level, Shakespeare's classical education is demonstrated most obviously by his use of many figures of speech that he would have learned to recognize and to use from his schoolroom study of rhetoric, which, along with grammar and logic, formed part of the trivium that was at the root of the educational system and on which Sister Miriam Joseph and Brian Vickers, especially, have written illuminatingly. Rhetorical devices are most obviously apparent in his earlier work. The technical terms for some of them, such as metaphor, simile, litotes, hyperbole, and synecdoche, are still reasonably familiar to students of literature (though even so some of us may have to look them up); most of the others have forbiddingly difficult Greek names like zeugma, polyptoton, epanorthosis, and so on, reminding us of what Shakespeare makes Casca say of Cicero in *Julius Caesar*, 'for mine own part, it was Greek to me'. The modern reader, knowing little of this, may not even be aware while reading Shakespeare that specific identifiable rhetorical figures underlie familiar passages; and it would doubtless have come as a surprise to Pistol to learn that in his lines in *Henry V* to Nim beginning with the apparently straightforward 'Will you shog off' (2.1.39), as Sister Miriam Joseph remarks,[15] he mingles bomphiologia, soraismus, and cacosyntheton.

Even if the use of such devices passes us by, they are pervasive. They are most easily identifiable in the early writings, but Shakespeare uses them frequently, if decreasingly obviously, throughout his work. As Vickers has written, while '[t]he early poetry displays its rhetoric stiffly, the mature style absorbs it: therefore modern criticism has been able to ignore the rhetorical framework in the mature style and discuss the life and feeling direct. But it seems at least likely that an awareness of the forms of rhetoric can enlarge our understanding of the poetry, for in Shakespeare's time and in Shakespeare's poetry rhetoric and feeling were one.'[16] Vickers has also illuminated awareness of the extent to which Shakespeare's prose as well as his verse, so far from being improvisational and informal, is permeated with rhetorical devices.[17]

Readers untrained in rhetoric may easily be unaware of the self-conscious artifice that lies behind much of Shakespeare's writing. On the other hand his use of Latin tags and quotations is readily apparent. At a rough count based on the appendix to (earlier editions of) Onions's *Glossary*, there are about one hundred Latin phrases, sometimes whole sentences,[18] in plays written up to and including *Hamlet* but only about twenty-two in later plays.[19] Significantly, no doubt, it is during this period that he appears to have been working, at least in some plays, in collaboration with other, university-educated dramatists, such as Peele and possibly Marlowe and Nashe, whereas from the time that he helped to found the Lord Chamberlain's Men, in 1594, until around 1606, with the collaborative *Timon of Athens*, all his plays appear to be solo authored.

A similarly rough count of Shakespeare's use of Latin neologisms based on Bryan Garner's study of that name shows however that the language continued to influence his verbal inventiveness throughout his career.[20] The figure peaks with *Hamlet* (not entirely because of its length), closely followed, predictably, by *Troilus and Cressida*. It dwindles thereafter, rising somewhat with *King Lear*—'superflux', 'superfinical', 'reverbs', even the now-familiar 'paternal'—and *Coriolanus*, but noticeably fading with the final romances. Among the earlier plays, easily the most Latinate in vocabulary is *Love's Labour's Lost*, with around thirty-five neologisms compared with, for instance, only ten or eleven in its closest comparators.[21]

Of all Shakespeare's plays, this comedy, with its portrayal of the pedantic schoolmaster Holofernes, is the one most directly concerned with education. It reflects Renaissance educational practices not only in vocabulary and in references to and quotations from the classics but also, more fundamentally, in its dialectical structure. Shakespeare was working out his ideas in an almost formulaic manner. To this extent it reveals much about his thought patterns—I would use it as an argument against James Shapiro's contention in his book *Contested Will* that we can deduce nothing about Shakespeare from his works, though what we deduce here is a link with his inner life, his mental processes, rather than with biographical externals.[22] Its highly patterned main plot presents a dialectical conflict between reason and emotion in the lords' attempts to impose upon themselves a regime of austerity and self-discipline which is in opposition to their natural instincts. They prepare to withdraw for three years from all the pleasures of the world, including female society, and to start 'a little academe' in which '[t]he mind shall banquet, though the body pine'. (The word 'academe' appears incidentally to be one of Shakespeare's Latinate coinages. This is its first recorded appearance. Biron uses it again later in the play.) In parallel with this plot Shakespeare runs a dialectic between the fleshliness of the clown Costard and his paramour Jaquenetta and the sterile academicism of Holofernes and Sir Nathaniel. At the play's conclusion, its opposing elements rest in uneasy stasis as the lords impose upon themselves a new discipline which, if what has gone before is anything to go by, they may have difficulty in observing.

The dialectical patterning of *Love's Labour's Lost* makes it a seminal step in Shakespeare's artistic progress. Significantly and unusually, the plot is of his own devising, not indebted to existing literary sources. He is here working out in dramatic form a kind of template for ideas that would continue to inform his work to the end. The platonic opposition between discipline and flesh is central to the relationships between, for example, Prince Hal and Falstaff, Sir Toby and Malvolio, Angelo and Lucio, Posthumus and Cloten, Prospero and Caliban, and it underlies the debate between art and nature in *The Winter's Tale* and Prospero's pre-marital counsel to Ferdinand and Miranda in *The Tempest*. It figures too in the sonnets, most conspicuously in Sonnet 146, beginning, 'Poor soul, the centre of my sinful earth'. The process is adumbrated, too—if our chronology is correct—sequentially in the initially physical then mental taming of Katherine in *The Taming of the Shrew*, and is later fully developed in the parallel plot structure of *King Lear*, in which the King's mental sufferings are complemented by Gloucester's physical agony.[23]

The structure of Shakespeare's plays represents a great leap forward—stimulated in part not only by aesthetic and intellectual influences but also by developments in theatrical buildings and in the partly consequent size of acting companies—over that of medieval drama and of the plays written by his early contemporaries. At its most complex, it resembles that of some of the most elaborate paintings of the Italian Renaissance. I think for example of the wonderfully innovative *Romeo and Juliet*, of which T. J. B. Spencer memorably wrote that '[n]othing in European drama had hitherto achieved the organisation of so much human experience when Shakespeare, at the age of about thirty, undertook the story of Romeo and Juliet'.[24] In this brilliantly self-consciously constructed play, the three appearances of the Prince form points of rest from the hectic action of the scenes around them, creating a kind of arched structure in the manner of a Renaissance painting in which architectural blocks enclose a multiplicity of detail. You have only to walk around the Uffizi Gallery in Florence to see numerous visual examples of this kind of structure. This play too enacts a dialectical conflict between love and lust, based on the simple paradigm of lust without love in the opening dialogue of the servants and, at a more sophisticated level, in Mercutio and the Nurse; of love without desire in Romeo's pursuit of Rosaline; and in the combination of love and desire in the coming together of Romeo and Juliet.[25]

The subject matter of Shakespeare's plays based on classical narratives also forms another link between them and great Renaissance works of art. Andrea Mantegna's portrayal of momentous events of Roman history in his *Triumphs of Caesar* dating from the late fifteenth century adumbrates both the action and the verbal painting of Shakespeare's Roman plays.[26] The painting has a dramatic quality, with a sense of individual personality, of forward movement, of interaction among participants, and even of clamorous sounds suggested by the upraised trumpets, which would be paralleled by the musicians of the Globe. Like Mantegna, Shakespeare draws for his subject matter on Plutarch's *Lives*; and as one looks at Mantegna's painting one can imagine that a similar picture was conjured up in Shakespeare's mind as he conceived his drama, and perhaps even that he might have welcomed the scenic resources of late nineteenth-century theatre which would have made possible a more realistic staging of such episodes.

Shakespeare's participation in the culture and thought that we associate especially with the Renaissance is evinced too in the pervasive influence on his work of ideas about man and the universe such as E. M. W. Tillyard long ago expounded in his book *The Elizabethan World Picture* (1942). It is not necessary to suppose that Shakespeare subscribed to a simplistic view of the orders of creation for us to acknowledge the influence on his work of hierarchical theories of the great chain of being, the four elements, the four humours, and so on. Ulysses's 'degree' speech in *Troilus and Cressida* is of course a prominent exemplar. And we should give the audiences of Shakespeare's time credit for their willingness to perceive the theatre not only as a place of entertainment but also as a forum for intellectual stimulus where they could be put in touch with contemporary thought and philosophy. Shakespeare's plays could be, as the author of the epistle to the 1609 Quarto of *Troilus and Cressida* writes, 'commentaries of the actions of our lives, showing such a dexterity and power of wit, that the most displeased with plays are pleased with *his* comedies,' finding 'wit there that they have never found in themselves [...] feeling an edge of wit set upon them more than ever they dreamed they had brain to grind it on'.[27]

It is part of the greatness of the theatre of Shakespeare's time that it served not only to entertain and move its often underrated audiences but also as a forum for the circulation of both received and original ideas. In some ways the Marlowe who in, for instance, *Tamburlaine* and *Dr Faustus* brought into the popular theatre a restlessly enquiring concern with cosmology and religion, with the place of man in the universe, showed Shakespeare the way here. Shakespeare draws frequently on the concept of man as a microcosm, a little world, most famously perhaps in Hamlet's speech: 'What a piece of work is a man! How noble in reason! How infinite in faculty! [. . .] In action how like an angel! In apprehension how like a god!' And the historian Alison Brown relates this speech to the best known of all Renaissance images of man, Leonardo's great drawing known as *The Vitruvian Man*.[28] Hamlet's image, she writes, 'encapsulates the idealised image of Renaissance man as a microcosm, or little world, portrayed by Leonardo da Vinci as a perfect circle within the larger circle of the world; or by Michelangelo as the material through which the artist releases the divinity latent within it; or by Pico della Mirandola, in his famous *Oration* on man at the centre of the universe, free to decide his own destiny, either rising to the level of angels or sinking to the depths of animal bestiality.'[29]

There is a similar consonance between the revival in the Renaissance of ancient ideas about the influence on our psyche of cosmic harmonies and Shakespeare's invocation, most memorably in *The Merchant of Venice*, of the concept of the music of the spheres which can move human beings even though they cannot hear it.[30]

'Look,' says Lorenzo to Jessica,

> how the floor of heaven
> Is thick inlaid with patens of bright gold.
> There's not the smallest orb which thou behold'st
> But in his motion like an angel sings,
> Still choiring to the young-eyed cherubins.
> Such harmony is in immortal souls,
> But whilst this muddy vesture of decay
> Doth grossly close it in, we cannot hear it.
> (*The Merchant of Venice*, 5.1.58–65)

Shakespeare invokes the music of the spheres again in *Pericles*, where it is audible only to Pericles because of the 'extreme spiritual state' to which his reunion with Marina has brought him.[31]

Shakespeare often mirrors established notions of, for instance, the place of women in marriage, notoriously in Kate's big speech in the final scene of *The Taming of the Shrew*; he is capable also of challenging them, as he conspicuously does in Emilia's proto-feminist outburst on women's rights in marriage:

> But I do think it is their husbands' faults
> If wives do fall. Say that they slack their duties,
> And pour our treasures into foreign laps,
> Or else break out in peevish jealousies,
> Throwing restraint upon us; or say they strike us,
> Or scant our former having in despite:

Why, we have galls; and though we have some grace,
Yet have we some revenge. Let husbands know
Their wives have sense like them. They see, and smell,
And have their palates both for sweet and sour,
As husbands have. What is it that they do
When they change us for others? Is it sport?
I think it is. And doth affection breed it?
I think it doth. Is't frailty that thus errs?
It is so, too. And have not we affections,
Desires for sport, and frailty, as men have?
Then let them use us well, else let them know,
The ills we do, their ills instruct us so.

(*Othello*, 5.1.85–102)

This speech is particularly interesting in that it is present in only the revised version of the text, as if Shakespeare felt strongly enough about the issues that Emilia raises to take the trouble to insert it as he reworked the play. He, as well as Emilia, here makes a deeply felt contribution to a contemporary moral and intellectual debate.

In this passage he does so in an incidental fashion. But his concern with debate extends itself more fundamentally to the kind of questioning of basic issues of human life that appears to have renewed itself in the Renaissance and which is observable among the thinkers, including other dramatists of his time about politics and religion. Marlowe, we are told, along with other prominent figures such as Sir Walter Raleigh and the Earl of Northumberland, propagated heterodox opinions about the divinity of Christ. We have no reports of Shakespeare's personal attitude to such topics, but his plays show a deeply probing concern with ontological issues, a concern which evinces itself not only within individual plays but from one play to another, creating the sense of an ongoing debate within his mind.

I see this at a deep level in for instance the differences in attitudes to religion between *Hamlet* and *King Lear*. Neither play is explicitly concerned with religious issues in the manner of earlier miracle plays; indeed the theatrical use of biblical subject matter was prohibited by statute. Nor are there any narrative links between them. Nevertheless I see an interrelationship between both tragedies which enables us to think of them as parallel contributions to thought about man's place in the universe. *Hamlet*, with its courtly setting and language, and with its numerous classical allusions and Latinate vocabulary, is a pre-eminently Renaissance play. Hamlet himself is the nearest Shakespeare comes to portraying a Renaissance prince. The tragedy is also one in which Shakespeare makes extensive use of a Christian frame of reference. The appearance of a ghost early in the action immediately raises questions about the possibility of life after death. As the tragedy continues we are constantly reminded that we are in a Christian environment by a long sequence of allusions to Christian themes including Marcellus's lines about 'the season [...] wherein our saviour's birth is celebrated'; the information that Hamlet studies at the strongly Protestant University of Wittenberg; his invocations of 'the Everlasting', of 'Angels and ministers of grace', of the 'host of heaven', of 'St Patrick', and, frequently, of a singular God; his anxieties about whether the ghost may be a devil, and his fears about the afterlife. Christian belief and ritual underlie more extended episodes too, such as the scene showing the King at prayer, the Gravedigger's as well as the Priest's discussion of the propriety of allowing Ophelia a Christian burial, and Horatio's final invocation of 'flights of angels' to sing Hamlet to his rest.

In *King Lear*, on the other hand, Shakespeare seems self-consciously to have abjured a Christian frame of reference even though in the early play on the same theme which he used as a source the pre-Christian narrative is heavily Christianized. W. R. Elton wrote that '[i]n contrast to *Hamlet*, a Christianized version of the pre-Christian Amleth story, *Lear*, in Shakespeare's hands, becomes a paganised version of a Christian play'.[32] Whereas characters in *Hamlet* frequently swear by or allude to a single, Christian God, characters in *King Lear* swear by Roman deities, Apollo, Juno, and so on. There is only a single point at which the word 'god' could be thought to refer to a single deity, and that is in a phrase—'gods spies'—where the absence of an apostrophe in the early texts means that it too could be construed as a reference not to the Christian god but to pagan deities. Stripped of the consolations of received religion, the play gains in mystery, in the sense of life as a battle with the elements, a struggle for survival against wind and rain in a world where humanity has to compete with animal forces both within and outside itself.

To say this is not to deny that *King Lear* can promulgate Christian values or that it draws at many points on the language and associations of Christianity, as it manifestly does in the portrayal of, especially, Cordelia, Kent, Edgar, and the Fool. But Shakespeare was clearly anxious not to place the action within a specific philosophical or religious context, as he so consciously does in *Hamlet*. The point was well made long ago when S. L. Bethell suggested of *King Lear* that we may 'suspect Shakespeare of deliberately intending to present a world without revelation, in order to determine how far human nature could penetrate its mysteries and achieve religious and moral order apart from the gift of supernatural grace'.[33] We may make what we will out of the fact that, as it seems to me, the Christianized *Hamlet* is the most consoling of the tragedies, and the pagan *King Lear* the bleakest.

The strong contrast between the two tragedies means, I suggest, that we can see them as Shakespeare's deliberate attempt to work out a tragic vision first with and secondly without a religious frame of reference. To this extent they may be seen as different portals to Shakespeare's imagination. Like *Venus and Adonis* and *The Rape of Lucrece*, works that were clearly conceived as a pair, one complements and contrasts with the other. This kind of fundamental interrelationship between superficially very different works helps us to discern a unifying mind at work within different parts of the canon, and to justify the importance we give to the belief that, give or take a few collaborations, Shakespeare's plays are the product of a single mind and imagination. The fact that one mind tackled fundamental matters of life and death from opposing perspectives increases our sense of the magnitude and interrelatedness of Shakespeare's achievement.

During Shakespeare's writing life of some twenty-five or so years, the world around him changed with exceptional speed. The theatre became less preoccupied with classical themes with the introduction from 1598, with William Haughton's *Englishmen for My Money*, of citizen comedy, rapidly followed by a stream of London-centered plays by Thomas Dekker, Ben Jonson, Thomas Middleton, and others. Shakespeare veered briefly in the same direction at around the same time with *The Merry Wives of Windsor*, though characteristically that play, in spite of its English setting, is indebted to Italian sources, and in subsequent comedies he returned to the more romantic mode of his earlier manner. Although the direct, identifiable influence of his schooling went gradually underground as time went on, as we have seen in his decreasing use of classical allusions, of readily identifiable rhetorical figures, and of Latinate vocabulary, his overall playwriting mode did not keep up with the times, which is why Jonson, in the prologue to *Every Man in His Humour*, could mock Shakespeare's continuing use of increasingly outdated dramatic fashions, and could later (in his 'Ode to Himself') deride *Pericles* as a 'mouldy' play.

Shakespeare continued to use romantic stories in *Pericles* and *Cymbeline*; and *The Winter's Tale* adapts a romance written by his old enemy Robert Greene some twenty years earlier. In *Antony and Cleopatra* and *Coriolanus*, Shakespeare reverts to explicitly classical themes. His final solo-authored play, *The Tempest*, is neo-classical in structure like the early *The Comedy of Errors*. Maybe John Fletcher helped to bring him closer to contemporary dramatic fashion in the pastoral tragicomedy of *The Two Noble Kinsmen*, but the world around him was changing: Neo-classicism would continue to exert a strong influence for another century and a half, but the Renaissance world into which Shakespeare was born was yielding before the Scientific Revolution, and Latin receded into the realm of dead languages. The entry of Shakespeare's death in 1616 is written not in Latin, but in English: 'William Shakespeare, gent.'.

The theme of the Prague conference invited us to think about Shakespeare Renaissances as well as about Renaissance Shakespeare. Shakespeare is constantly being reborn, reconstituted in a dazzling range of new configurations. In Stratford in 2011 one could see an RSC production of *The Merchant of Venice* in which the action was transferred from Venice to a casino in Las Vegas, and in which the entertainment included songs performed in the style of Elvis Presley. I had not yet seen it when I spoke in Prague, but my prejudices were fully formed. When I expressed them in the presence of a teacher of English, he asked if I was a purist, rather in the tone of voice in which he might have asked 'Are you a rapist?' I don't think I am;

indeed I'm far from sure that I know what 'purist' means. I have enjoyed productions, adaptations, and versions of Shakespeare in a wide range of styles, some of them far removed from the original texts and from the conventions of the theatre of his time. I realize that the fusion of the Elizabethan text with later theatrical conventions and forms of entertainment may create thrilling experiences for modern audiences, at least if they happen to like the songs of Elvis Presley. But then I wonder what may be lost, whether perhaps we may gain as much by seeking to enter into Shakespeare's world as by re-creating it in our own image.

In Florence earlier in 2011, nobly undertaking a research trip on my readers' behalf, I visited the Uffizi and the Bargello and the Convent of San Marco, joining the throngs of visitors who were admiring and taking pleasure in the creations of the great visual artists of the Renaissance. As I joined them in doing so, I thought of the analogies between the structures of three- and five-panelled paintings, many of them altarpieces, with the structures of Shakespeare's plays; I thought of the parallels between the exquisite intricacy of their visual detail and the rhetorical patterning, the interrelated imagery, and the stylistic complexity of Shakespeare's verse and prose; I thought of the resemblances between the depth of individual characterization in many of the paintings and sculptures of Florentine citizens of the Renaissance with the richness of Shakespeare's portrayal of characters within his plays. I asked myself too whether there is any greater parallel to Shakespeare's portrayal of the suffering of King Lear than Masaccio's depiction of the expulsion of Adam and Eve from the Garden of Eden.[34]

We know of course that the visual arts are fixed while drama is infinitely changeable, responsive to the fluctuating demands of its audiences, reflecting and responding to the society of the age in which it is performed. But the crowds that throng the Uffizi, the Accademia, the great galleries and churches of Florence and Venice and Paris and London and Los Angeles, and all the other places to which works of Renaissance art have travelled don't go there for purely antiquarian or scholarly reasons. They go because they can derive a living pleasure from the art of the past, because it can challenge and feed their imaginations, because it can extend and enrich their experience of life beyond the present. Perhaps we should admit at least that it is legitimate to take pleasure in those aspects of Shakespeare's art, too, in which he was of his age as well as those in which he was for all time.

2

Tales from Shakespeare

Some coincidences seem more coincidental than others. It is surely rather a manifestation of the spirit of the age than pure chance that 1807 saw the publication of two adaptations, each of twenty Shakespeare plays, designed to make those plays both more accessible to young readers and more suited to what their elders thought the young should be reading; chance may, however, be held responsible for the fact that both adaptations were undertaken by the less distinguished sisters of more distinguished brothers, and that over the years the brothers have received more than their fair share of credit for their sisters' work. One of the adaptations, published anonymously, was *The Family Shakspeare*, offering (literally) bowdlerized texts.[1] In its second edition, of 1818, this work was ascribed to Thomas Bowdler, MD; he is still frequently held responsible, though in 1966 it was shown that his sister, Henrietta Maria, undertook the initial task of expurgation, and that Thomas was responsible only for the plays added in the second edition.[2] This adaptation, now relegated to library basements and mentioned only to be derided, enjoyed many years of success; Jaggard records some thirty-five editions between 1807 and 1900.[3]

The other adaptation, *Tales from Shakespear. Designed for the use of young persons*, was ascribed on its first publication to Charles Lamb; not until the seventh edition, of 1838, was his sister's name added to the title-page, though Charles had made it quite clear in letters to his friends that Mary wrote fourteen of the tales and that he had contributed only six—the tragedies—along with 'occasionally a tail piece or correction of grammar … and *all* of the spelling'.[4]

The Lambs' letters give a charming picture of the process of composition, the brother and his mentally unstable sister (she had already stabbed her mother to death) writing, as Mary says, 'on one table (but not on one cushion sitting) like Hermia & Helena in the Midsummer's Nights Dream, or rather like an old literary Darby and Joan. I taking snuff & he groaning all the while & saying he can make nothing of it, which he always says till he has finished and then he finds out he has made something of it …'.[5] Mary, too, groaned, complaining, according to Charles, 'of having to set forth so many female characters in boy's clothes'.[6] She gets stuck (understandably) in *All's Well*; Charles writes to Wordsworth that he encourages her with flattery, and we know that the flattery succeeded because a few days later Mary writes to Sarah Stoddart that she is 'in good spirits' because Charles has told her that *All's Well* is 'one of the very best' of her stories.[7]

The *Tales* were composed for The Juvenile Library, published by William Godwin and his second wife, Mary Jane, known to the Lamb circle as 'the bad baby', and execrated by Lamb for her inept choice of topics for illustration, which included a picture of Hamlet with the grave-diggers, even though the scene 'is not hinted at in the story, & you might as well have put King Canute the Great reproving his courtiers'.[8] Payment was at the rate of three guineas per tale, and initial publication was in two volumes, though eight individual tales were also issued separately in chapbook versions which are now, according to David Foxon, 'probably the greatest rarities of more recent English literature'.[9]

The Lambs' Preface contains a modest statement of their aims and methods. The *Tales* are intended to introduce young readers to the study of Shakespeare, whose own words are used whenever possible; in narrative passages, 'words introduced into our language since his time have been as far as possible avoided'. The *Tales* are 'faint and imperfect stamps of Shakespear's matchless image ... because the beauty of his language is too frequently destroyed' by the need to change verse into prose; even where, 'in some few places', 'his blank verse is given unaltered, as hoping from its simple plainness to cheat the young readers into the belief that they are reading prose', it still suffers by being taken out of context. The *Tales* are written mainly for 'young ladies ... because boys are generally permitted the use of their fathers' libraries at a much earlier age than girls are'; and boys are encouraged to explain the hard bits to their sisters, and even to read pleasing passages from the original plays to them, 'carefully selecting what is proper for a young sister's ear'. When the young readers are old enough to turn to the plays for themselves, they will discover many surprises not hinted at in the *Tales*. And the last paragraph of the Preface— written by Charles—expresses the wish that in the future 'the true Plays of Shakespear' will prove 'enrichers of the fancy, strengtheners of virtue, a withdrawing from all selfish and mercenary thoughts, a lesson of all sweet and honourable thoughts and actions, to teach you courtesy, benignity, generosity, humanity: for of examples, teaching these virtues, his pages are full'.

Though the principal aim is clarification and simplification, there are hints also of a certain moral protectiveness; fraternal selection of 'what is proper for a young sister's ear' is precisely akin to Miss Bowdler's expunging of 'any thing that can raise a blush on the cheek of modesty'.[10] There is, too, an implied assurance that reading Shakespeare is good for you; an assurance that may have been particularly welcome to parents at a time when the child attending the theatre might be, as Wordsworth had recently put it,

environ'd with a Ring
Of chance Spectators, chiefly dissolute men
And shameless women...
While oaths, indecent speech, and ribaldry
Were rife about him... (*The Prelude* (1805), vii.385–90)

Both Mary and Charles reduce the plays' complexity, concentrating where possible on a single story-line. The Gloucester plot disappears almost entirely from *King Lear*; *The Merchant of Venice* loses the caskets and, almost, Lorenzo and Jessica. Theseus makes only a fleeting appearance at the opening of *A Midsummer Night's Dream*, and all that remains of the mechanicals is a nameless clown 'who had lost his way in the wood' and who stands in for Bottom in the episode with Titania. Low comedy episodes and characters—Christopher Sly, Juliet's Nurse, Paroles, Cloten, Touchstone and Jaques, even Sir Toby, Sir Andrew, and Malvolio—all disappear entirely or are reduced to the merest ciphers. Humour suffers greatly, as Lamb admits in his Preface; many of the comedies are brought closer to the romance tales on which they are founded.

Shakespeare's own tendency to idealize his sources is heightened: the bed trick in *All's Well* becomes a 'secret meeting', and Helena is not pregnant at the end; in *Measure for Measure*, Claudio had simply 'seduced a young lady from her parents' (though Isabella does speak to Claudio of Angelo's demand that she 'yield' her 'virgin honour'). There are no bawds or brothels in either *Measure for Measure* or *Pericles*, and bawdy language is almost totally expunged. In those pre-Partridge days, however, Mary Lamb—like Miss Bowdler—could retain Graziano's closing couplet about 'keeping safe Nerissa's ring'.

Along with omission and reduction there is also a little elaboration. The narrative mode encourages additional exposition, comment, and even interpretation. Some additions are purely explanatory: 'In those times wrestling, which is only practised now by country clowns, was a favourite sport even in the courts of princes' (*As You Like It*); 'though it is not the custom now for young women of high birth to understand cookery, it was then' (*Cymbeline*). There are some gently humorous comments—'fathers do not often desire the death of their own daughters, even though they do happen to prove a little refractory' (*A Midsummer Night's Dream*)—some moralistic ones—Antigonus' ursine death was 'a just punishment on him for obeying the wicked order of Leontes' (*The Winter's Tale*)—and some aphoristically generalizing ones that have won the praise of commentators.[11] Some additions reveal preconceptions about the characters and their actions, sometimes with important interpretative consequences: Prospero is 'an old man', and it is as a result of 'his magic art' that Miranda fell in love so suddenly; and Antonio's silence at the end of *The Tempest*, always interpreted by modern critics as a sign that he is unrepentant, suggests to the more generous-minded Mary Lamb that he was 'so filled...with shame and remorse, that he wept and was unable to speak'. Interpretative elaboration is particularly prevalent at the ends of stories: Mary Lamb is in no doubt that, after the events shown in Measure for Measure, 'the mercy-loving duke long reigned with his beloved Isabel, the happiest of husbands and of princes'; nor is there anything tentative about her conclusion to All's Well that Ends Well: Helena 'at last found that her father's legacy was indeed sanctified by the luckiest stars in heaven.' But Charles is even more apt than Mary to offer explicit interpretation; indeed, his elaboration of the role of Kent in King Lear has caused Jonathan Bate—who finds that Charles's Tales 'form a kind of creative commentary' on Shakespeare to suggest that perhaps Lamb 'saw himself as a Kent-figure, characterized by loyalty and honesty, a willingness to remain in the shadow of the great souls around him, a preference for plain language, prose to the verse of Wordsworth and Coleridge'.[12]

The reception of the Tales on publication was in general lukewarm, with one notable exception. There are seven reviews, all anonymous, mostly very brief.[13] Criticism centres on moral purpose. In spite of the Lambs' efforts to avoid causing offence, the Literary Panorama regretted that 'morals...' had not 'been deduced from such incidents as afford them'. Though The Anti-Jacobin Review thought that the Tales were told 'as decently as possible', it did not consider them 'very proper studies for female children'; and the Lambs had properly put their foot in it by telling girls that there are parts of Shakespeare that they should not read till they are older: 'This only serves as a stimulus to juvenile curiosity, which requires a bridle rather than a spur.' The only really enthusiastic praise of the Tales is in a notice in the Critical Review which places the volume firmly in the context of the current debate about children's literature, a debate with which Lamb was himself concerned. In a letter to Coleridge of 1802 he had complained that didacticism was supplanting imagination in children's books: 'Science has succeeded to Poetry no less in the little walks of Children than with Men.... Damn them. I mean the cursed Barbauld Crew, those Blights & Blasts of all that is Human in man & child.'[14] The writer in the Critical Review is entirely of Lamb's mind: 'We have compared it [the Tales] with many of the numerous systems which have been devised for rivetting attention at an early age, and insinuating knowledge subtilly and pleasurably into minds, by nature averse from it. The result of the comparison is not so much that it rises high in the list, as that it claims the very first place, and stands unique, and without rival or competitor, unless perhaps we except Robinson Crusoe.' The Tales 'will effect more than all the cant that ever was canted by Mrs Trimmer and Co. in all their most canting and lethargic moments'.

For the rest, the highest praise comes from The Gentleman's Review, saying that the 'very pretty Tales...may interest the mind at an age when the plays themselves cannot be properly appreciated'. 'Very pretty Tales' has seemed apt enough to later ages as a description of what the Lambs produced. These Tales are generally undemanding; their literary quality is modest. They have been praised for narrative clarity, for ease of style, for an understanding of the needs of a child's imagination. They have been seen as a manifestation of the Romantic interest in childhood, and as a blow on behalf of the arts in the education of the young.[15] But, as even so sympathetic a critic as Lord David Cecil wrote, their success 'is a little surprising; for the tales are told in a gentle undramatic manner, unlikely, one would have thought, to excite children in Lamb's day, let alone many years later'.[16] Nevertheless, A. Hamilton Thompson, writing (in 1915) in *The Cambridge History of English Literature*, claimed that 'the collection forms one of the most conspicuous landmarks in the history of the romantic movement'.[17]

This initially surprising claim may be supported by consideration of the volume's publishing history. During the Lambs' lifetime, it enjoyed a modest success. It was reprinted in 1809 and 1810, and appeared in three more editions by the time Charles Lamb died, in 1834. By the time Mary died, in 1847, there had been five more editions, making eleven in all. After this, edition succeeded edition with increasing, and increasingly astonishing, rapidity. To chart their progress fully would require a bibliographical study which so far as I know has not been undertaken, and which would be difficult to prepare accurately, because even the copyright libraries seem to have wearied of giving shelf-room to the full spate of editions and reissues. The British Library has many that are not in the Bodleian; the Bodleian has some that are not in the British Library; the picture is complicated by the existence of selections, simplified versions, reprints of individual tales, foreign reprints in English, and translations. With that proviso, let me say that I have evidence of close on 200 editions in English, and of at least forty translations extending beyond the major European languages to Burmese, Swahili, Japanese, Macedonian, Chinese (in 1905, the first Chinese translation of Shakespeare in any form), Hungarian, and the African dialects Ga and Ewe. I won't bore you with the detailed statistics (painfully though these have been acquired), but some indication of the periods of greatest popularity may be of interest. Reprints of English versions continue steadily after Mary Lamb's death until 1873 (by which date there had been fifteen, in sixty-four years). Then—doubtless under the influence of Forster's Education Act of 1870—they accelerate rapidly. 1879 was a bumper year, with seven editions, three of them in Calcutta. There are sixteen editions in the 1880s, ten in the 1890s, and thirty-six in the first decade of the twentieth century. From 1910 to 1920 there are twenty-six, and then numbers dwindle a bit: eleven in the 1920s, twelve in the 1930s, eleven in the 1940s, thirteen in the 1950s, fourteen in the 1960s. I have no reliable figures for more recent years, but *Books in Print* reveals ten editions currently on the market.

I adduced these figures initially to support Thompson's assertion of the volume's importance 'in the history of the romantic movement'. They show that the *Tales* became a classic with a popularity matching that of *Alice in Wonderland*. I say 'a classic' rather than 'a children's classic' because it is clear that the *Tales* (like *Alice*) is both read by adults and chosen by adults as a book suitable for children, not necessarily by children as a book that they are anxious to read for themselves. Indeed, its very title—unlike, say, *Charlie and the Chocolate Factory* or *Five on a Treasure Island*—requires knowledge, or information, along with cultural aspirations. Thompson's own support for his assertion is that the *Tales* 'is the first book which, appealing to a general audience and to a rising generation, made Shakespeare a familiar and popular author and, in so doing, asserted the claims of the older literature which, to English people at large, was little more than a name'.[18] But this gives too much weight to the volume's declared function of serving as an 'introduction to the study of Shakespeare'. In fact there is a sense in which the *Tales* supplanted Shakespeare, becoming an object of study in its own right, a book that itself required to be introduced and explained to young readers, and on which they could expect to be examined, sometimes in conjunction with a few extracts from the plays on which it is based, sometimes as an independent text. This can be seen by looking at some of the more important editions, which fall into two main streams: those intended for a general readership, and those specifically presented for use in schools.

In the early period particularly, it is not always easy to distinguish between the two. As early as 1843, a reprint is furnished with a Chronological Table (beginning with *Pericles*, 1590, and ending with *Twelfth Night*, 1613); and Charles Knight's edition of 1844, whose Advertisement states that the *Tales* 'have become as attractive to adults as to those for whose use they were originally intended', seems aimed at the more earnest kind of general reader; he adds 'a few *Scenes*'—such as the dagger soliloquy and murder scene from *Macbeth*—'which may be advantageously read after the perusal of the Tale, to furnish some notion of the original excellence of the wonderful dramas upon which the Tales are founded'. These extracts are lightly annotated with explanatory glosses. An edition of 1879 in Macmillan's Golden Treasury series includes an admirable Introduction by Canon Alfred Ainger (author of the volume on Lamb in the English Men of Letters series), setting the background of the *Tales* and offering an appreciation of the Lambs' methods, especially Mary's 'casual and diffused method of enforcing the many moral lessons that lie in Shakespeare's plays'. This, says Ainger, is why 'these trifles, designed for the nursery and the schoolroom, have taken their place as an English classic. They have never been superseded, nor are they ever likely to be.' Thus the volume was canonized. An edition of 1893, attractively presented in four slim, elegant volumes, provides 'a continuation by Harrison S. Morris', unmoralistic retellings of the sixteen remaining plays carefully done and including characters that the Lambs would certainly have dropped, such as Costard and Jaquenetta (in *Love's Labour's Lost*) and the Clown in *Antony and Cleopatra*.

Alfred Ainger had stressed the value of the *Tales* as an introduction to Shakespeare. Andrew Lang, in an Introductory Preface to an edition of 1894, disputes this, arguing that children 'are best introduced to Shakespeare by Shakespeare himself', that they 'do best to begin with the plays themselves, afterwards Lamb's Tales may bring them back to the originals'. (Does he mean, I wonder, that because they don't understand the plays they will read Lamb, and will then be able to understand the plays?—If so, why not start with Lamb?) Although Ainger's was not specifically a school edition, he had stressed that 'a knowledge of Shakespeare' was more and more 'coming to be regarded as a necessary part of an Englishman's education'. Not so, says the disputatious Lang: 'Alas, it is not Shakespeare, but the notes of Editors that are now a necessary part, not of an Englishman's education, but of an English boy's "cram", for the purpose of examiners.' We should read for pleasure: 'It is a misery to turn classics into schoolbooks.' Lang's essay, clearly not intended for young readers, is consciously anti-academic; he doubts whether 'the exquisite English of Lamb and his sister will attract the infants of today', and regrets the omission of the comic bits. One is left with the impression that Lang wishes he had not agreed to write this Introduction.

The most physically impressive of all editions of the *Tales* is that prepared by F. J. Furnivall and published by Raphael Tuck in 1901. The two handsome volumes, bound in gilded white cloth, are adorned with a portrait of Shakespeare and a full-page photograph of the bushy-bearded, sage-like Furnivall (who at least had the decency to reserve himself for the second volume). This, one feels, is an edition for the rich man's library, one that might stand beside the New Variorum Shakespeare. It is, boasts Furnivall in the full flush of late-Victorian materialism, 'the grandest and most costly ... ever issued'. (It sold for 31s. 6d., with a cheaper issue at 22s. 6d., in a year when other editions were published for between 2s. 6d. and 7s. 6d.) Beyond being grand and costing a lot, its aims are uncertain. Furnivall writes characteristically quirky introductions on various topics, supplies a chronology (omitting *Titus Andronicus*, because 'Its story is too repulsive to be told in a book for boys and girls'), and sketches the stories of six plays omitted by the Lambs while declaring that 'for the Histories ... readers must turn to Shakspere's works', and opining that *Measure for Measure* is 'the gloomiest and most unpleasant of Shakespeare's comedies'. Furnivall is at his most sympathetic in his comments on the Lambs' reduction of Shakespeare's comedy: 'The odd thing is, that two such humourful folk as Mary and Charles Lamb were, two who so enjoyed Shakspere's fun, made up their minds to keep all that fun (or almost all) out of his plays when they told the stories of them to boys and girls who so like fun too ... I can't help thinking that most boys would like the fun put into the Tales, and the stories cut shorter; but they can easily get it all in the plays themselves, so there's no harm done' (Volume 1, p. xi).

Furnivall's edition is expensively illustrated with indifferent pictures by H. Copping; and a number of less elaborately presented editions have been newly illustrated. Indeed, some seem primarily intended as vehicles for the work of particular artists. Routledge's Sixpenny Series in 1882 had forty quite striking engravings by Sir John Gilbert. In 1899 Dent's Temple Classics for Young People had twelve illustrations by Arthur Rackham; transferred to Everyman's Library in 1906, this edition is still in print; the Rackham illustrations are not as fine as those he did for *A Midsummer Night's Dream*, but it's a pity that the most interesting of them—a coloured one of Ariel and Caliban—is omitted at least from the paperback reprint, and that the delicacy of line which gives some of them a Beardsleyish quality has become much coarsened in successive reprints. Heath Robinson illustrated an edition of 1902, and the Oxford edition of 1905 has sixteen illustrations unadventurously chosen from the Boydell Gallery; the same year saw a reprint in the Hampstead Library with a sensible introduction by George Sampson praising the Lambs for sounding 'no jarring modern note, nothing that causes the mind to forget the master-author upon whose plays the work is based'. In 1909 Mrs Andrew Lang came upon the scene, introducing a handsome, gift-book style edition which sold for five shillings. Her 'Life of Shakespeare' condescends to the young reader in a manner that makes us appreciate the Lambs' refusal to do so: 'Many a posy William picked for his mother, of "daffodils that come before the swallow dares"...'. An edition of 1911 adds additional tales by one Winston Stokes whose composition seems to have weighed heavily upon him: 'The writing', he says, 'has presented untold difficulties; and to portray in foreign form the shifting battle-scenes of "Henry the Sixth", and guide the thread of an unbroken narrative among the horrors of "Titus Andronicus", must forbid an equal literary merit with Lamb's Tales, even if this had been attempted.' At any rate it was enterprising of him to include *Titus*, even though he glosses over what happens to Lavinia—she was 'subjected...to cruel tortures'—and no pie is served at the feast. Many of the more recent editions have no special features, as if publishers had regarded them as self-propelling, non-copyright volumes assured of a steady sale with very little effort on their part. The Bantam edition of 1962 has an introduction by Elizabeth Story Donno which treats the *Tales* with a kind of cynical expectation that they will be used mainly as a crib to Shakespeare: she writes a historical introduction to Shakespeare's life, times, and stage without even mentioning the Lambs, provides an index of characters, and tells the stories of plays not treated by the Lambs in compressed synopses of about two pages each. J. C. Trewin balked the challenge of *Titus* (and of *Henry VIII*) in the twelve gracefully told tales that he added to the beautifully printed Nonesuch edition of 1964. His method resembles that of the Lambs except that he includes undisguised passages of verse at certain points. In 1979 O. B. Hardison briefly introduced a handsome paperback version illustrated with nearly a hundred pictures—some rare and fine, others rare and boring—selected from the Folger art collection.

The first edition of the *Tales* that seems explicitly intended for schools appeared in 1862, when Gordon's School and Home Series published sixteen of the *Tales* in four parts costing threepence each. A popular but unambitious Pitt Press edition of 1875 adds an 'appendix of speeches from three of the plays...for the use of teachers who may wish to play the part of the elder brother of the Lambs' Preface, and to introduce their pupils at once to Shakespeare himself'. As might be expected, moral considerations are stressed in Victorian school editions; *Measure for Measure* is dropped from one of 1883 because 'teachers find objection to it'. The 1888 version in John Heywood's Literary Readers, edited by Alfonzo Gardiner, Headmaster of the Little Holbeck Board School (Leeds School Board), states as one of its aims 'to give such needful explanations as shall make the language and the allusions intelligible to young readers', and as another 'to show the many moral lessons that Shakespeare's plays enforce'. The glossarial notes include '*Immortal Providence*—The goodness of God to us, which never ceases'; there are Lists of Spellings, and vile illustrations. William P. Coyne's forbidding edition of 1895 numbers the lines of the tales in fives, offering them as fodder for a method of instruction that has little to do with the imagination and that illustrates the danger of confusing Lamb with Shakespeare: the volume 'may be of practical service in offering themes for the always valuable class-exercise of paraphrase and analysis, and may supply the teacher with apt and admirable materials for, say, a contrast of the dramatic and narrative styles of writing, for an occasional discourse on the merits of Lamb's methods of criticism, or for an historical reference to the qualities of idiom and diction, which make the language of Shakespeare a model of strength, pith, and brevity'. This kind of didacticism is exactly the attitude of mind that Lamb thought he was combatting by retelling the *Tales* in the first place. Like other editors of this period, Coyne stresses the moral value not merely of the *Tales* and of Shakespeare but of the lessons to be learned from Charles Lamb's 'self-annihilating devotion...to the care and tutelage of his sister', which 'affords...one of the most touching and noble incidents in the range of literary annals'.

A number of editions around the turn of the century illustrate the growth of character criticism: one of 1899 provides 'Sketches of the Principal Characters', as does the Oxford and Cambridge edition of 1904. Such preoccupations are apparent too in the questions with which pupils are presented: 'Name three men whose characters you admire, and give your reasons...' (1899); 'What do you admire most in the characters of...' (1899); 'Can you justify Desdemona's choice of a husband?' (1904). The 1904 edition is particularly suggestive as to the educative methods applied to the *Tales*: 'short character sketches...will be found to contain... all the leading features of each character'; passages from the plays 'will afford useful practice in paraphrasing, in parsing, and in analysis; many of them are also suitable for committing to memory'; there is a section on 'Lessons to be derived from the Tale', and a statement that the editors 'have expunged without ceremony whatever seemed unsuitable for juvenile readers'. The detailed annotations are a curious mixture of the naïve and the over-sophisticated; the young reader who needed to be told that a dragon was 'a fabulous monster' might have been daunted when faced with the gloss 'peculiar, special, particular: from Old Fr. peculier: Lat. peculiaris, one's own'.

Later school editions are less ambitious. A much used one is in Dent's King's Treasuries of Literature series (1920); it has eight tales with extracts from the plays and simple 'Literary Exercises', such as 'Which of the plays would you call tragedies?', 'Who is the jolliest person in the stories?', and—continuing the moral emphasis on Charles Lamb's treatment of his sister—'What was there heroic about Charles Lamb's life?' In 1934 A. C. Ward wrote: 'Only in the present generation has the repute of [the Tales] suffered a serious decline, under the influence of a new scholastic conviction that paraphrased and pemmicanised classics are a hindrance more than an aid to literary appreciation.'[19]

I hope I've said enough—and I fear I may have said too much—to indicate something of the function that the Lambs' Tales have fulfilled since their publication. Their work has undoubtedly become a classic, and if it is less used as a Shakespeare substitute in schools than it used to be, it still serves as a crib even to distinguished performers of Shakespeare: the actress Gemma Jones writes in Players of Shakespeare (1985) that, invited to play Hermione in The Winter's Tale at Stratford, she tried to read the play but, finding difficulty in understanding it, resorted to Charles and Mary Lamb, who, she says, 'tell me a tale'.[20] This pinpoints one of the attractions of the Tales: even an actress, accustomed to working with playscripts, acknowledges the easier comprehensibility of a third-person narrative.

Although the title 'Tales from Shakespeare' instantly evokes the Lambs, the classic status of their volume has not gone unchallenged; and I should like now to turn to some of the alternative versions that have been offered. Most are long-forgotten. Some may well have fallen virtually dead from the presses; others had a life that is now expired; some of the more recent ones have a vitality that may carry them alive and kicking into the next century—though by then, of course, they may have more competitors.

Although the Lambs may not have known it, fourteen of Shakespeare's plays had already been turned into short stories, in French. In 1783, J. B. Perrin, a London-based teacher of French to the English nobility and gentry, had published Contes Moraux et Instructifs, à l'usage de la Jeunesse, tirés des Tragédies de Shakespeare. Subscribers to the volume included David Garrick's widow, who took six copies, and the tales—which include histories and Cymbeline as well as tragedies—are based on theatrical versions, including Garrick's adaptation of Romeo and Juliet. Presumably Perrin worked from Bell's recently published theatre edition. His Preface is predictably preoccupied with the unities, and Titus Andronicus is declared fit to be performed only before cannibals. The principal function of this volume was later to be fulfilled by the many foreign-language translations of Lamb.[21]

Two rival volumes appeared during Charles Lamb's lifetime. One, Tales of the Drama by Elizabeth Wright Macauley, published in 1822, is interesting partly because its author was (in her way) both a poet and an actress. Her collection, drawing on the current theatre repertoire, includes tales based on plays by Massinger, Shirley, Rowe, Steele, Goldsmith, and Mrs Cowley, as well as six by Shakespeare. A publisher's Preface declares that she has attempted 'to preserve all the colloquial wit and scenic effect' and, above all, 'to render the whole strictly obedient to the most refined ideas of delicacy, subservient to the best purposes of morality, and conducive to the highest sense of religious awe, and love for a beneficent Providence'. Again one notes the purificatory function; and Miss Macauley's theatrical affiliations make it even clearer than in the case of the Lambs that she is trying, as her publishers say, to extend knowledge of the stage even 'to family circles where the drama itself is forbidden'. This curious volume is decorated with many pleasing little engravings, and the plots are both treated with some freedom—*The Winter's Tale*, for instance, begins with the episode of Antigonus and the bear and tells the preceding part of the story in retrospect—and also elaborated with verse passages written by Miss Macauley herself: thus, *The Merchant of Venice* includes an original verse invocation by Portia to 'the spirit of her venerated father', and ends with Miss Macauley's poetical thoughts on friendship. Lest there should be any danger of confusion, verse quotations from 'our immortal Avonian Bard' are marked with asterisks. The tone throughout is highly moralistic. This volume, never reprinted, might repay investigation by students of the theatre.

The principal interest of *The Juvenile Shakespeare, adapted to the Capacities of Youth* published in 1828 by Caroline Maxwell, a minor novelist, is that, including only plays with a historical basis, such as *Cymbeline, Titus*, and *Lear*, she nevertheless omits the major English historical plays while including the apocryphal *Thomas Lord Cromwell* and *Sir John Oldcastle*. This is an introductory volume, designed to tell the stories of the plays 'in the most simple and easy style...and to introduce in the course of the narratives, some of the most beautiful passages which each contain, for study or recitation...'. Again, moral purpose is rammed home: 'on no occasion has the fair purity of the infant mind been for one moment forgot...'. (Presumably Caroline Maxwell, like Macbeth, had no children.)

Around mid-century, Duncombe's Miniature Library published a series of Dramatic Tales, brief narrative versions of dramas, melodramas, extravaganzas, and pantomimes performed in London's minor theatres. These tiny volumes, each illustrated with a crude, often coloured engraving, sold for twopence each. Presumably they were on sale at the theatres, just as editions of the text as acted in grander performances could be bought at the Theatres Royal. The Library includes over twenty tales from Shakespeare, retold by a minor—indeed, minimal—playwright, Joseph Graves, which could be had either individually or in bound volumes accompanied by a Life of Shakespeare. Like Perrin's *Contes Moraux*, these tales are based on theatrical adaptations. At the end of *Richard II*, the Queen dies 'upon the corse of her unfortunate husband', as in Richard Wroughton's version acted by Kean in 1814 (and published in 1815). *King Lear* has its tragic ending, but, as in Tate, there is no Fool, and Edgar is in love with Cordelia; though he becomes King, he 'never afterwards formed any attachment; but devoted the remainder of his days in [*sic*] sorrow and mourning'. Most curiously, at the end of *A Midsummer Night's Dream* Theseus delivers an encomiastic defence of the drama as a beneficent moral and ethical influence, and instructs Philostrate to 'further its interests whenever opportunity offers'. This appears to be a flight of Graves's own fancy rather than a reflection of a theatre version.

After this, the Lambs' supremacy was unchallenged until 1880, when Mary Seymour published *Shakespeare's Stories Simply Told*, in two volumes. These are simple, sometimes simplistic versions, perhaps influenced by the Lambs—at any rate, making some of the same omissions—though including all the plays. Although the author is not over-moralistic for her time, she exercises some ingenuity in avoiding moral awkwardnesses: 'Claudio ... had for some time been leading a very bad life, which was quite forbidden by the laws of the city'; no mention is made of Juliet's pregnancy, Angelo is actually married to Mariana, but has 'cast her from him', and the bed trick becomes 'another interview'. All ends well, 'for Claudio became reformed in character, and when Isabella was made Duchess of Vienna her influence over the people was sufficient to exterminate the vices to which they had for so long been prone, and the state became once more prosperous and glorious'.

A sweetly pretty fancifulness characterizes Adelaide C. Gordon Sim's *Phoebe's Shakespeare*, of 1894, very clearly intended for little girls—or presumably for one particular little girl, since the Preface is addressed to 'My Dear Little Phoebe' and signed 'Auntie Addie'. 'Once upon a time ... there lived a most wonderful man called Mr William Shakespeare. No one before he lived ever made up such beautiful stories ... Mr Shakespeare wrote some stories that even children can read and understand; and I have written these down for you, and made them into this book, because I want you to learn to know them, and to love them, while you are still a little girl.' It's all very sweet and charming; the plots have passed through an imagination and come out far more heavily romanticized than by the Lambs, though not totally lacking in moral fibre—Romeo 'should have been a little more patient and less selfish, and [have] remembered that he had no right to kill himself just because he was unhappy'. Like other, later writers, Adelaide Sim brings Shakespeare himself into the picture: 'Mr William Shakespeare was a poet, and a poet is a person who *can* see fairies, and one lovely summer night, when he was lying under the trees on the soft moss in the woods, he heard and saw some wonderful things, and wrote them down and made this story ...'. Though the plots are simplified in structure they are sometimes elaborated in detail, as in the way *The Tempest* is rounded off: 'sailors tried to discover' Prospero's island, 'but they have never found it to this day, and I don't think they ever will, for, after Prospero and Miranda left, I believe the fairies gave it to the mermaids, who took it down to the bottom of the sea and used it for a palace, and Caliban went down with it. He'll never be able to do any more mischief.' A similar level of readership is envisaged by E[dith] Nesbit in *The Children's Shakespeare* of 1897, which is prettily if kinkily illustrated with paintings and drawings in which children are portrayed in grown-up roles: we see a 4-year old Romeo embracing a little dimpled Juliet, a tiny Hamlet histrionically banishing a diminutive Ophelia to a nunnery, and an innocently merry little Malvolio with a suitably haughty young Olivia.[22]

By contrast to this kind of little-girlishness, there is a hearty, self-conscious young-manliness about A. T. Quiller-Couch's *Historical Tales from Shakespeare*. The volume appeared in 1899, during the last years of Queen Victoria, when English soldiers were fighting in South Africa. Patriotic fervour ran high, and Quiller-Couch regarded patriotism as the 'great lesson' of Shakespeare's history plays: indeed, they 'might almost serve as a handbook to patriotism, did that sacred passion need one'. Unfortunately there was one serious lapse: the portrayal of Joan of Arc (in *1 Henry VI*). Again the issue was exacerbated by topicality: this was the period during which Joan was being groomed as a candidate for canonization. Quiller-Couch would like to believe that Shakespeare 'was always fair and just', that he 'had no hand in the slanderous portrait of Joan of Arc sent down to us under his name'. In any case, 'no writer with a conscience could repeat that portrait for the children in whom are bound up our hopes of a better England than we shall see … here they will not be given the chance; since today, if ever, it is necessary to insist that no patriotism can be true which gives to a boy no knightliness or to a girl no gentleness of heart.' In the play, you will remember, Joan, condemned to death as a sorceress, disowns her poor old father, claims to be of royal birth, and at first proclaims her virginity, but then, finding her captors unmoved, confesses she is with child, and claims first that the father is Alençon, then that it is René, King of Naples; she is led cursing to execution. Quiller-Couch's version is much closer to that with which we are familiar from Bernard Shaw: 'A pile of faggots was raised in the market place of Rouen, where her statue stands today. The brutal soldiers tore her from the hands of the clergy and hurried her to the stake, but their tongues fell silent at her beautiful composure. One even handed her a cross he had patched together with two rough sticks. "Yes!" she cried, "my voices *were* of God!" and with those triumphant words the head of this incomparable martyr sank on her breast. "We are lost", muttered an English soldier standing in the crowd, "we have burned a saint".' This is adaptation in the service of propaganda; and Quiller-Couch is even more blatant in some of his footnotes. Of the closing speech of *King John* ('This England never did, nor never shall, Lie at the proud foot of a conqueror … ') he writes that 'the lesson of this "troublesome reigne" is summed up for us in the wise, brave, and patriotic words of Faulconbridge—lines which every English boy should get by heart'; and John of Gaunt's speech on 'this royal throne of kings' is an 'incomparable lament', which 'may only be rendered in

Shakespeare's own words, which no English boy, who is old enough to love his country, is too young to get by heart, forgetting the sorrow in it'.

In his Preface, Quiller-Couch disclaims the attempt 'to round off or tag a conclusion' to the Lambs' 'inimitable work', and indeed his method is very different from theirs. In keeping with a movement of thought that I noticed in school editions of Lamb at this time, he says that he stresses 'the *characters* in these plays'. He adds a considerable amount of historical detail and background—Falstaff, for example, was 'a poor gentleman shaken loose from the lower degrees of feudalism when that edifice began to rock and totter'—and draws attention to important changes of history. He reproduces and paraphrases much dialogue, and tells the stories at considerable length with that narrative flair that made him, in his time, a highly successful novelist. The volume had two new editions, in 1905 and 1910.

Quiller-Couch pays tribute to the 'easy grace' of the Lambs' style, but Sidney Lee, in his somewhat heavy-handed Introduction to Mary Macleod's *Shakespeare Story-Book* of 1902, complains that Mary Lamb 'had little of her brother's literary power' and claims (reasonably enough) that her omissions, in particular, justify the 'endeavour to supply young readers with a fuller and more accurate account'. In conclusion he stresses the tales' exemplary value: 'of both stories and characters proffering the counsel to seek what is good and true and to shun what is bad Shakespeare's pages are full'. Mary Macleod herself was a successful children's writer; her books include adaptations of Malory, Froissart, and Spenser, and *A Book of Ballad Stories* introduced by Edward Dowden, along with *Hilda at School* and *Tiny True Tales of Animals*. The *Shakespeare Story-Book* had a fourth edition in 1911 and appeared in Spanish translation the following year. She writes vigorously, provides some historical placing (beginning *Macbeth* with information about witchcraft, for example), and is capable of incisive comment: 'when trouble arose, the nurse's shallow, selfish nature became apparent, and poor Juliet was soon to learn that she must rely solely on her own strength and judgement in the sorrows that overwhelmed her.' Like Beerbohm Tree in his then-current production, she ends *Hamlet* with the flights of angels that sing the hero to his rest; and at times in her narrative passages she makes a strong attempt to convey a conception of the play in performance: 'And what was left for Shylock to answer? Baffled of his revenge, stripped of his wealth, forced to disown his faith, his very life forfeited—a hated, despised, miserable old man—he stood alone amidst the hostile throng. Not one face looked at him kindly, not one voice was raised on his behalf. Twice he strove to speak, and twice he failed. Then, in a hoarse whisper through the parched lips, came the faltering words: "I—am—content".' 'Shylock', said *The Spectator*, 'is Mr Irving's finest performance, and his final exit is its best point... the expression of defeat in every limb and feature, the deep, gasping sigh, as he passes slowly out, and the crowd rush from the Court to hoot and howl at him outside, make up an effect which must be seen to be comprehended.'[23] It is difficult not to feel that Mary Macleod was influenced by Irving's interpretation.

I pass quickly over the relatively undistinguished versions of Lois Grosvenor Hufford (an American) in 1902, R. Hudson, an elementary and highly selective version of ten plays in 1907, and of Alice Spencer Hoffman (1911), and alight briefly on those of Thomas Carter, a Doctor of Theology who made his contributions to Shakespeare scholarship with *Shakespeare, Puritan and Recusant* (1897) and *Shakespeare and Holy Scripture* (1905), and who also, under a pseudonym, wrote improving books for boys, such as *Jeffrey of the White Wolf Trail* (1912), *Sinclair of the Scouts* (1911), both published by the Religious Tract Society, *The Stolen Grand Lama: An English Boy's Adventures in Wild Tibet* (Boy's Own Paper, 1917), and *Yarns on Heroes of India: A Book for Workers among Boys* (Church Missionary Society, 1915). Dr Carter did not seek to abandon his more scholarly persona when he came to publish *Stories from Shakespeare* in 1910, and *Shakespeare's Stories of the English Kings* in 1912. I wonder if you can guess, for example, which play is being introduced here: 'On the great plain of Attica, watered by the Kaphisos and the brook Ilissus, and circled by its hills, Parnassus, Hymettus, Pantelicon, and Lycabettus, there stands the famous city of Athens. Not many miles away, the sunlit waters of unconquered Salamis, the Bay of Eleusis, and the bold Saronic Gulf enclose the land in a belt of purple sea.' That is how Thomas Carter seeks to lead his young readers into the world of *A Midsummer Night's Dream*. The didact is evident in, for example, the distancing of the opening of *Macbeth*: 'The great story of Macbeth is an illustration of the powers of imagination of conscience, working in a sensitive and highly-strung mind.... To feel the power of the story you must know its setting.' Carter elaborates detail in a manner that seems at times to anticipate the worst excesses of psychological criticism: 'Death had early taken away his [Shylock's] wife Leah; and his daughter Jessica, too careless and too selfish to strive to learn the secret of a proud man's heart, had allowed his home to grow into a place of suspicion and coldness and bickering, wherein the strife of the world outside was carried within its walls, and dishonesty and treachery allowed to make havoc of its peace.' And at times he seems to occupy the pulpit rather than the story-teller's chair: 'as he [Lear] passes from our sight in a passionate agony of yearning for the peace and light and love which dwelt for him in the pure and holy heart of Cordelia, we feel that the great writer in the words "Look there, look there!" lifts up the dark curtain for an instant that the light of the Eternal may shine through and speak of hope Beyond.' Carter makes immensely worthy, earnest attempts to turn the plays into improving short stories; it seems no accident that the copy of *Stories from Shakespeare* that I picked up in a second-hand shop had been presented as a school prize. Nor is it entirely surprising that when four of the verbose Carter's stories were reissued in 1937, they were 'adapted and rewritten within the thousand-word vocabulary'.

The batch of tales of which I have just been speaking, published from 1893 to 1914, coincides, you may have noticed, with the period during which the Lambs' *Tales* were at the height of their popularity. The new versions, in other words, seem not so much to have been driving the Lambs off the market as to have been supplying an alternative demand—partly (though only partly) by providing versions of plays that the Lambs had omitted. As reprints of the Lambs' *Tales* dwindled, so, for a while, did alternative versions. Even so, there are more than I can spare time to mention. There is a *Shakespeare Tales for Boys and Girls* dating apparently from around 1930 whose attitude to the events of *Measure for Measure* suggests a major shift in moral values: Claudio had been condemned 'for an act of rash selfishness which nowadays would only be punished by severe reproof'. Even so, there is no bed in the bed trick. Friars, we are told, 'are as nearly like nuns as men can be', and Claudio had 'a queer friend called Lucio' who was finally 'condemned to marry a stout woman with a bitter tongue'. At the end 'She [Isabella] was his [the Duke's] with a smile, and the Duke forgave Angelo, and promoted the Provost.'

Much more interesting is a forgotten volume of 1934 which I confess to regarding as something of a find. Called *Six Stories from Shakespeare*, it boasts as authors John Buchan, Hugh Walpole, Clemence Dane, Francis Brett Young, Winston Churchill, and Viscount Snowden.[24] Each tells a different tale. I wondered if Churchill might have chosen *Henry V*; in fact his play is *Julius Caesar*. He displays a politician's shrewdness in his analysis of Brutus's arguments in favour of the assassination: 'Caesar must not be allowed even the chance of going wrong, the seed of potential tyranny must be killed outright, like a serpent in the egg. One could hear the sigh of relief and release with which he finally persuaded himself to acquiesce in this sophistry.' And in the Forum scene Churchill stands apart from the tale with a comment on the oratory: 'It can scarcely be necessary to remind the reader of what [Antony] said, for no speech in the history of the world is more famous, none better known. "Friends, Romans, countrymen . . . " . . . the words are alive on every tongue, and custom cannot stale them.' There Churchill treats Shakespeare as history, and comments on it (in 'custom cannot stale them') with a half-submerged quotation from Shakespeare himself.

But the most aesthetically interesting of these tales are those told by the professional novelists. Hugh Walpole creates a great sense of awed wonder in the narrator of the Lear story. John Buchan's narrative of *Coriolanus* is told at a tangent from Shakespeare's play, with old Publicola as the central character; as he takes his ease in various parts of Rome, the events are narrated to him by characters including the tribunes, Menenius, and Flaccus, with the result that the story acquires a distanced, retrospective quality. It ends with Flaccus telling Publicola of the hero's death:

'He died like a Roman', said Menenius.
'He might have been the Volscian king, but he was too noble', said Flaccus.
But old Publicola flung a fold of his cloak over his head and looked on the ground.
'It is as I feared', he said. 'He had no part in Rome. He had gone barbarian.'

And in *Hamlet* Francis Brett Young takes his cue from Hamlet's request that Horatio 'draw [his] breath in pain | To tell my story'. Again, the tale is told in retrospect; as narrator, Horatio is also (validly) a commentator, who sounds as if he had read, as well as met, *Hamlet* at Wittenberg: 'if the mere act of vengeance appeased [Hamlet's] devotion to his father's memory, I believe that the artist in him took pleasure in the complicated hazards against which it must be wreaked; I believe he took pains to contrive his vengeance as a work of art…'. Paradoxically enough, here, as in Buchan's *Coriolanus*, the narration of the drama's events by an involved participant rather than a detached, omniscient story-teller restores something of the dramatic mode. The best of these *Six Stories* seem to me to float free from their models and to acquire value as fully realized short stories in their own right.

Very different is the unemphatic, even laconic tone of the scholar G. B. Harrison in his two volumes of *New Tales* of 1938 and 1939. Not for Harrison the rhetoric of Thomas Carter at Lear's death—though there is a reflection of Bradley: 'So they gathered round, watching Lear as he feebly knelt beside Cordelia. The little life left in him began to flicker. Suddenly he thought that her lips moved, and with a cry of joy he fell over her body.' Harrison's generally phlegmatic tone may be not unfairly represented by the ending of his composite story 'Sir John Falstaff', of which the last words are 'So that was the end of Falstaff'. 'Nothing is here for tears…'.

As the Shakespeare quatercentenary of 1964 approached, so, as if in anticipation, the number of new tales from Shakespeare increased. In 1960 appeared Marchette Chute's version, summary in style and making no real attempt at imaginative reconstruction. Irene Buckman's *Twenty Tales from Shakespeare* of 1963, nicely produced with excellent photographs of recent productions, has a short foreword by Peggy Ashcroft saying that, whereas the Lambs' *Tales* 'were for the nursery and the fireside', these are for 'the young playgoer and the young playgoer's parents'. But these too are relatively summary in manner.

There is more life in Roger Lancelyn Green's two volumes (twenty tales) of 1964. Christopher Fry, in a brief foreword, remarks that Green had acted many of the minor roles himself, and certainly he has theatrical touches. There seems, for example, to be a direct echo of Clifford Williams's 1962 production of *The Comedy of Errors* in Green's '"Are you pleading with me, fair lady?" asked Antipholus, looking behind him to see if she was talking to someone over his shoulder.' The action is occasionally updated in the manner of modern-dress productions—Dr Pinch is a psychiatrist, though his methods of treatment sound a little archaic: 'Both your husband and your servant are suffering from schizophrenia: I know the symptoms only too well. They must be bound and laid in a dark room.' There are other fanciful additions—Leontes gave the old shepherd 'lands in Sicily where he settled down as a gentleman-farmer, and was able to employ Autolycus as a bailiff'; and Lady Macbeth helpfully tells Macbeth 'I know what it is to be a mother, for I had a child by my first husband.' But Green's tales are ultimately reductive because of a failure to match up to the emotional demands of the story, nowhere more evident than at the end of Shylock's trial: after the Duke has said that Shylock must sign a deed, we are told simply 'So Shylock went off home'!

More successful is Ian Serraillier's *The Enchanted Island: Stories from Shakespeare*, of 1964. Serraillier creates alternative titles: 'A Wild-Cat for a Wife', 'Bottom the Actor', 'Murder at Dunsinane', and so on. He does not aim to be comprehensive—there is, for example, no Viola plot in 'The Love-Letter' (based on *Twelfth Night*); Cesario *is* Orsino's page. There is no casket story in 'The Pound of Flesh'—Bassanio simply woos Portia nor are there any young lovers in 'Bottom the Actor'. The tone is straightforward and clear, but uncondescending. Action is successfully visualized, though not necessarily in stage terms. We might once again take the ending of *King Lear* as a sample:

> The field between the two camps was crowded with soldiers, Kent and Albany among them. Suddenly the ranks broke and in the silence a tragic figure stumbled forward. It was Lear, clasping Cordelia's limp body and crying out in a voice of anguish, 'She's gone for ever. She's dead as earth.'
>
> Yet somehow he could not believe that she was really dead. He asked for a mirror to hold close to her mouth to see if there was any breath to mist the glass; then for a feather to see if it would stir on her lips. For a moment it seemed to stir—but only in mockery.... All he could grasp w₂ ʾhat Cordelia was in his arms, that she was dead and would never come to him again.
>
> A moment later he too had gone, his ˙ʾing martyrdom ended at last. Death had come as a blessing, for he could endure no ₁ ˙re.

The tone is unsentimental, unmoralistic, and the₂ ˙s no condescension.

One has the sense in Serraillier's volume, as ₁ ˙ome of the others I have mentioned, that these stories are not primarily intrₑ ˙ctions to the study of Shakespeare, or even introductions to Shakespeare in perₑ ˙nance, but the result, in however minor a way, of an interaction between the authₑ ˙ imagination and Shakespeare's; the stories have their own independent interest, ˙ʾeply indebted though they are to Shakespeare.

There may come a point in such a process at which tales cease being v₂ ˙ons, or reinterpretations, of Shakespeare and assume a virtually independent life ₍ ˙heir own. Such a point, approached in Serraillier's work, is reached and passed in Bernard Miles's popular *Favourite Tales from Shakespeare* of 1976 and *Well-Loved Tales from Shakespeare* of 1986. These are free, idiosyncratic fantasies on plays rather than retellings of them.

But it is pleasant to record that the most recent—or almost the most recent—of the retellings that I have traced is one that, in my opinion, brilliantly succeeds in translating both the substance and the effect of Shakespeare's plays into the narrative medium. In *Shakespeare Stories*, of 1985, Leon Garfield adopts a crisp, sharply metaphorical style, often employing bold images: Juliet stares down from her balcony 'with her willow hair weeping'; when Kate, the shrew, stormed through her father's house in a bad temper, 'doors kept going off like exploding chestnuts'; in Illyria, thatched cottages are 'neat as well-combed children'. Though Garfield's prose is not unmannered, it succeeds remarkably in providing an acceptable alternative to Shakespeare's poetry. Like the Lambs, Garfield omits some episodes—the Porter from *Macbeth*, the Nurse's introductory scene from *Romeo and Juliet*, the Pedant from *The Taming of the Shrew*—but he displays a mastery of the plays' structural principles that enables him to transmute their essential features into the medium of the short story. This is apparent in, for instance, his use of analytical parallels to effect transitions: 'While one Harry was idly dreaming of the glory that would be his, the other Harry was much concerned with the glory that *was* his'; and 'Even as the casket that Jessica had thrown down from Shylock's window had contained her father's treasure, so one of the three closed caskets in Belmont contained another father's treasure.' Such comments put criticism to creative use.

The essential difference, it seems to me, between Garfield's method and the Lambs' is that where the Lambs provided a simplified reading experience as a preparation for a more complex and difficult experience of the same kind, Garfield seeks to convey in prose narrative the experience, not of reading the twelve plays that he includes, but of seeing them performed. Sometimes he visualizes action that could be used as stage business: Falstaff 'sat down and regarded his countenance in the diminishing bowl of a spoon' before saying 'why, my skin hangs about me like an old lady's loose-gown'; Polonius reads his list of entertainments offered by the actors who visit Elsinore 'from the company's extensive advertisement, which reached down, like a paper apron, almost to his knees'; and after the enraged Claudius has stopped the play and stormed out of the chamber, 'the bewildered Player King crept back to recover his tinsel crown. Then he went away, sadly shaking his head. The performance had not gone well.' It might almost be Hazlitt writing about Kean—and there is a Shakespearean touch in the sudden recognition of the Player's point of view. Garfield is best known as a writer for teenagers, and his volume is presented in a manner that seems intended primarily for young readers, but his transmuting power gives his stories a wider appeal; they are not pale reflections of Shakespeare, not introductory studies, but fully imagined re-creations with a life of their own.

I have, I know, given only a superficial survey of a literary subgenre which, though minor, has been too popular to be adequately considered within a single lecture. In recent years, theatrical adaptations of Shakespeare from the Restoration onwards have been much reprinted and studied. Prose adaptations have been almost entirely neglected, yet they have been immensely popular, and are often no less radical in their revisions and reinterpretations.[25] I don't suggest that I have identified an important new growth area in Shakespearean studies; but I hope I've said enough to suggest that the successive retellings of Shakespeare's stories offer a body of material that permits an interesting exploration of narrative techniques, that—like stage adaptations—they can reflect changing critical and moral perspectives on Shakespeare himself, that they are of sociological interest, especially in relation to the history of education, and that some of them are not negligible as prose fictions in their own right.[26]

Editions cited

(a) Charles and Mary Lamb

Tales from Shakespear. Designed for the use of young persons... By Charles Lamb. Embellished with copper-plates. 2 vols. (London, 1807).

Tales from Shakespear. 2 vols. (London, 1809).

Tales from Shakespear. 2nd edn. 2 vols. (London, 1810). (Duplicates the 1809 edition, except that this has a new title-page and the engravings of the first edition, and lacks the 'advertisement' of 1809.)

Tales from Shakespear, 6th edn. (London, 1838).

Tales from Shakspeare... To which is added, the Life of Shakespeare (London, n.d.; *c.*1843).

Tales from Shakspeare by Mr and Miss Lamb. A New Edition. To which are now added, Scenes Illustrating Each Tale. 2 vols. (London: Charles Knight and Co., 1844).

Tales from Shakespeare. 4 Parts (Edinburgh and London, 1862). (Gordon's School and Home Series; reprints sixteen tales.)

A Selection of Tales from Shakspeare. Edited with an Introduction, Notes and an Appendix of Extracts from Shakspeare by J. H. Flather, M.A. (Cambridge, 1875). (Pitt Press; six tales.)

Tales from Shakspeare. Edited, with an Introduction, by the Rev. Alfred Ainger, M.A. (London, 1879).

Lamb's Tales from Shakspeare: with 40 illustrations by Sir John Gilbert, R.A. (London, n.d. [1882]). (Part of Routledge's Sixpenny Series.)

Tales from Shakspere. With Illustrative Extracts from Shakspere's Plays (Annotated), and a Picture to each Tale (London, 1883). (Marcus Ward's Educational Literature; omits *Measure for Measure* 'to which teachers find objection'.)

Tales from Shakspeare. Ed. with explanatory notes, &c. for the use of schools, by A. Gardiner (Manchester, 1888). (John Heywood's Literary Readers; selected tales.)

Tales from Shakespeare including those by Charles and Mary Lamb with a continuation by Harrison S. Morris. 4 vols. (London, 1893).

Tales from Shakspeare. Introductory Preface by Andrew Lang. Illustrations by R. A. Bell (London, 1894).

Tales from Shakspeare. Edited with introduction and notes and chronological tables by William P. Coyne M.A., 2nd edn. (Dublin and London, 1895). (Browne and Nolan's English Texts; selected tales. British Library records only the 'second edition'.)

Tales from Shakespeare with twelve illustrations by A. Rackham (London, 1899). (Dent's Temple Classics for Young People; reprinted in Everyman's Library, 1906, etc.)

Tales from Shakespeare. With Introduction and Notes by C. D. Punchard B.A. (1899, etc.) (Eight tales.)

Tales from Shakespeare. With Introductions and Additions by F. J. Furnivall...Founder and Director of the New Shakspere and other Societies. 2 vols. (London, 1901).

Tales from Shakespeare. With 16 full-page illustrations by W. H[eath]. Robinson (London, n.d. [1902]).

The Oxford and Cambridge Edition of Tales from Shakespeare for Preliminary Students, with Introduction, Notes, Examination Papers, Extracts from the Plays, etc. Edited by Stanley Wood M.A., Editor of Dinglewood Shakespeare Manuals, etc., and A. T. Spilsbury, M.A., Senior Classical Master at the City of London School. 2 vols. (n.d. [1904, 1909]). (Selected tales.)

Tales from Shakespeare...With sixteen illustrations (London: OUP, 1905)

Tales from Shakespeare, edited, with an Introduction and Notes, by George Sampson. Illustrated by J. A. Walker (London, 1909). (Hampstead Library.)

The Gateway to Shakespeare for Children. Containing A Life of Shakespeare, by Mrs Andrew Lang, A Selection from the Plays, and from Lamb's *Tales*. With Sixteen Coloured Plates and many other Illustrations (London, n.d. [1909]).

All Shakespeare's Tales. Tales from Shakespeare by Charles and Mary Lamb and Tales from Shakespeare by Winston Stokes. Illustrated by M. L. Kirk (London, 1911).

Lamb and Shakespeare: Selected Tales with Extracts from the Plays (London, n.d. [1920]) (Dent's King's Treasuries of Literature; eight tales).

Tales from Shakespeare...expanded...to include the complete plays, with essays on the Elizabethan theater and Shakespeare's life and times. Edited and with an introduction by Elizabeth Donno (New York, 1962).

Tales from Shakespeare. All those told by Charles and Mary Lamb with 12 others newly told by J. C. Trewin (London, 1964).

Tales from Shakespeare. Foreword by O. B. Hardison (Washington, DC: Folger Books, 1979).

(b) Other authors

Six Stories from Shakespeare. Retold by John Buchan [*Coriolanus*], Hugh Walpole [*King Lear*], Clemence Dane [*The Taming of the Shrew*], Francis Brett Young [*Hamlet*], Rt Hon. Winston Churchill [*Julius Caesar*], Rt Hon. Viscount Snowden [*The Merchant of Venice*] (London, 1934). (Eight illustrations by Fortunino Matania)

Anon., *Shakespeare Tales for Boys and Girls* and 'When Shakespeare was a Boy' by Dr F. J. Furnivall, M.A. (London, n.d.; c.1930?).

Buckman, Irene, *Twenty Tales from Shakespeare*, with a Foreword by Dame Peggy Ashcroft (London, 1963).

Carter, Thomas, *Stories from Shakespeare*...With sixteen full-page illustrations by Gertrude Demain Hammond (London, 1910). (Eleven plays.)

Carter, Thomas, *Shakespeare's Stories of the English Kings*...With sixteen full-page illustrations by Gertrude Demain Hammond (London, 1912).

Chute, Marchette, *Stories from Shakespeare* (London, 1960). (All the plays.)

Garfield, Leon, *Shakespeare Stories*. Illustrated by Michael Foreman (London, 1985).

Grave, Joseph, *Dramatic Tales founded on Shakespeare's Plays*, to which is added the Life of this Eminent Poet, by Joseph Graves. Embellished with Superb Engravings (London, n.d. [1850?]). (Duncombe's Miniature Library; the tales appeared both individually and in various combinations.)

Green, Roger Lancelyn, *Tales from Shakespeare*, with a foreword by Christopher Fry. 2 vols. (London, 1964). (Twenty plays.)

Harrison, G. B., *New Tales from Shakespeare* (London, 1938). (Seven plays.)

Harrison, G. B., *More New Tales from Shakespeare* (London, 1939). (Five plays.)

Hoffman, Alice Spencer, *The Children's Shakespeare*, Being Stories from the Plays with Illustrative Passages (London, 1911). (Twenty plays; illustrated by Charles Folkard.)

Hudson, R., *Tales from Shakespeare* (London, n.d. [1907]). (Ten plays, retitled (e.g. 'Rosalind and Celia', 'The Story of Perdita') and told in elementary fashion.)

Hufford, Lois Grosvenor, *Shakespeare in Tale and Verse* (London, 1902). (Fifteen plays.)

Macauley, Elizabeth Wright, *Tales of the Drama* founded on the Tragedies of Shakespeare, Massinger, Shirley, Rowe, Murphy, Lillo, and Moore, and on the Comedies of Steele, Farquhar, Cumberland, Bickerstaff, Goldsmith, and Mrs Cowley by Miss Macauley (Chiswick, 1822). (Includes *King John, The Winter's Tale, Richard II, The Merchant of Venice, Coriolanus*, and *Julius Caesar*.)

Macleod, Mary, *The Shakespeare Story Book* with Introduction by Sidney Lee. Illustrations by Gordon Browne (London, 1902). (Sixteen plays; reprinted 1911.)

Maxwell, Caroline, *The Juvenile Shakespeare, adapted to the Capacities of Youth* (London, 1828). (Includes only plays with a historical basis (e.g. *Cymbeline, Timon of Athens, King Lear*, but omits e.g. *Henry IV, Henry V, Richard III* while including *Thomas, Lord Cromwell* and *Sir John Oldcastle*.)

Miles, Bernard, *Favourite Tales from Shakespeare* (London, 1976). (*Macbeth, A Midsummer Night's Dream, Romeo and Juliet, Twelfth Night*, and *Hamlet*.)

Miles, Bernard, *Well-loved Tales from Shakespeare* (London, 1986). (*The Tempest, As You Like It, Othello, The Merry Wives of Windsor, Julius Caesar*.)

Nesbit, E[dith], *The Children's Shakespeare* (London, n.d. [1897]).

Perrin, J. B., *Contes Moraux Amusans & Instructifs, à l'usage de la Jeunesse, tirés des Trágedies de Shakespeare* (London, 1783). (*Hamlet, Coriolanus, King Lear, Romeo and Juliet, Othello, Macbeth, Julius Caesar, Antony and Cleopatra, King John, Richard II, Henry IV, Henry V, Richard III, Cymbeline, Timon of Athens*.)

Quiller-Couch, A. T., *Historical Tales from Shakespeare* (London, 1899). (Reprinted 1905, 1910)

Serraillier, Ian, *The Enchanted Island: Stories from Shakespeare* (London, 1964).

Seymour, Mary, *Shakespeare's Stories Simply Told*, 2 vols (London, n.d., [1880]). (Includes all the plays; reprinted 1883; German translation, 1890.)

Sim, Adelaide C. Gordon, *Phoebe's Shakespeare*, arranged for children (London, 1894).

PART II

ESSAYS ON PARTICULAR WORKS

3

The Failure of *The Two Gentlemen of Verona*

*T*he *Two Gentlemen of Verona* has not been a favourite of the critics. Not all have been as damning as that uninhibited lady, Mrs Charlotte Lennox: 'This Play every where abounds with the most ridiculous Absurdities in the Plot and Conduct of the Incidents, as well as with the greatest Improprieties in the Manners and Sentiments of the Persons.'[1] But Coleridge, in making a chronological table of Shakespeare's plays, dismissed it as a 'sketch'; Hazlitt, who was not altogether unappreciative, used similar terms: 'This is little more than the first outlines of a comedy lightly sketched in'; E. K. Chambers considered that no other play of Shakespeare's 'bears upon it such obvious marks of immaturity'[2] and T. M. Parrott found it 'full of faults'.[3] Sketchy though it may be, its inclusion in Francis Meres's list suggests, perhaps that it was acted, and at least that it was regarded as a completed piece of work; so it may fairly come up for critical examination. On the other hand, it is not amenable to those techniques of modern interpretative criticism which are applied to fully developed and highly organized works. There is, perhaps, some danger of underrating it simply because it is not as good as other plays in which Shakespeare used similar materials. It contains, as has often been remarked, many anticipations of later plays, such as *The Merchant of Venice* and *Twelfth Night*; but to consider this too deeply has its dangers. It may lead to a too easy dismissal on the grounds, not that the play is unsuccessful in itself, but that it does not provide the critic with what he wants, and finds elsewhere. It may on the other hand lead to over-interpretation, such as John Vyvyan's theory[4] that the outlaw scenes represent in parable-form Valentine's need to learn control of his baser instincts.

A more helpful approach is probably that through earlier literature, such as H. B. Charlton adopts in a chapter of *Shakespearian Comedy* (1938) which remains perhaps the most extended critical discussion of this play. Charlton clearly demonstrates Shakespeare's dependence, in the play's more serious aspects, upon the conventions of romantic love as derived from the medieval tradition and its modifications by Petrarch and the neo-Platonists; and he adduces some close parallels of idea. In discussing the use Shakespeare made of these conventions, Charlton comes to the conclusion that something went wrong. His thesis is perhaps fairly summed up in his penultimate sentence: 'Clearly, Shakespeare's first attempt to make romantic comedy had only succeeded so far that it had unexpectedly and inadvertently made romance comic.' In order to test the truth of this, it is necessary to look at the methods used by Shakespeare to project and organize his raw material.

The plot—I use the word in a fairly wide sense, to refer both to the actions and to the methods of narrative presentation—seems to me to exhibit a number of peculiarities, limitations, and plain faults, which for convenience I divide into the superficial, the technical, and the organic. The superficial ones can be passed over with little comment. Dr Johnson drew attention to the play's peculiar geography, and to the fact that it is not even self-consistent; but this might almost be regarded as a normal feature of romance. Johnson's further complaint that, at the end of 2.4, Shakespeare 'makes Protheus, after an interview with Silvia, say he has only seen her picture' is probably answered by the fact that 'picture' could mean 'appearance' (cf. *Hamlet*, 4.5.86 and *Merchant*, 1.2.78) and here implies only superficial acquaintance. In any case, these peculiarities are neither more numerous nor more striking than those to be found in many other, greater plays.

The technical limitations of the plot are, I find, more interesting and revealing. It is a curious fact that Shakespeare's technique in this play is limited almost exclusively to three devices: soliloquy, duologue, and the aside as comment. Thirteen of the twenty scenes go no further than this: they are 1.1, 2, and 3; 2.1, 2, 3, 5, 6, and 7; 4.2, 3, and 4; and 5.1. Moreover, several other scenes, including three of the play's longest (2.4; 3.1; 5.4), escape inclusion in this list only by virtue of a few lines of more complicated dialogue. The climax of this structural method is reached in 4.2, in many ways the best scene. It begins with a soliloquy from Proteus, followed by a dialogue between him and Thurio, with the musicians in the background; then the Host and Julia enter and speak together unheard by the others; their conversation is broken by the song; it is followed by a brief passage between Proteus and Thurio, after which Sylvia makes her appearance; her conversation with Proteus is commented on in asides by Julia, and the scene ends after Proteus's exit with a few lines between Julia and the Host. The patterning is simple but effective. The silences of the Host and Julia are, of course, explained by their situation; those of Proteus and Thurio offer some difficulty to the producer, but can be partially covered by the preparations for the serenade and by the continuance of instrumental music after it. There is no reason to wish that Shakespeare had attempted anything more complex: the limited technique justifies itself; it could be entirely deliberate.

However, what happens when Shakespeare steps outside these limits may well suggest that they are the consequence of an underdeveloped technique rather than a deliberately restricted one. Several times a character is left in unnatural silence when the dialogue switches from him to someone else. 1.3, for instance, begins with a duologue between Antonio and Panthino. When they have come to a decision, Proteus enters 'in good time' and Panthino stands silently by during the conversation between Antonio and his son until he is haled off by Antonio. In 3.1, a feeble effort is made to keep Launce in the picture after he enters with Proteus at line 188, but he soon drops out and says nothing for forty lines. In the next scene, where a truly three-cornered dialogue might well have been expected, Thurio speaks only two of the twenty-eight speeches uttered when he is on stage with the Duke and Proteus.

2.4 gives a notable illustration of the author's failure to think in terms of a number of characters at once. Valentine, Sylvia, Speed, and Thurio are on stage. Sylvia addresses Valentine, but they are interrupted by Speed who has a very brief conversation with Valentine. This ends at line 7, and Speed is heard no more for the rest of the scene—editors give him an (unmotivated) exit. After this Sylvia tries again to talk to Valentine, but again there is an interruption, this time from Thurio, and again Valentine is diverted into two-handed back-chat. Sylvia makes a few interjections, replied to by Valentine. On the Duke's entrance, attention is switched entirely to him and Valentine; the others are silent while we hear of Proteus's arrival at Court. Having given his news, the Duke departs. There follows a short duologue between Sylvia and Valentine, with one twitter from Thurio. On Proteus's entrance we have a brief passage of three-cornered dialogue, which does not extend beyond presentations and compliments. Thurio poses problems here; either he is silent on-stage during this passage, in which case his next line, 'Madam, my lord your father would speak with you', is apt to sound like clairvoyance; or else he must slip off during the presentations, to return a few lines later with his message. Sylvia takes him off with her, and the rest of the scene passes easily in duologue and soliloquy. A crowning insult is offered Thurio in 3.1, where he is dismissed speechless in the first line. The failure of the outlaw scenes, where the ability to deal with a group of characters is of prime importance, is too obvious to require further notice.

Of the entire play, no scene has given rise to more unfavourable comment than the last; it has been emended, rewritten, reviled, and rejected. The difficulties here are complex: both technical and organic. On the latter I reserve comment until later; for the present, it may be worth noticing the inflexibility of technique displayed. Though six important characters as well as a band of outlaws are on-stage, the scene ends with a long duologue between the Duke and Valentine. Thurio has two speeches in the entire scene (admittedly, he enters late), and Sylvia says nothing at all while she is first donated by Valentine to Proteus, then rejected by him in favour of Julia, then claimed by Thurio, only in his next breath to be renounced by him, and finally handed back to Valentine by her father. Was ever woman in this humour won?

The basic technical failure of the play, I suggest, arises from the fact that Shakespeare is still a tyro in dramatic craftmanship: he has not yet learned how to manipulate more than a few characters at once. This explains the complete failure of that chaste wraith, Sir Eglamour, and of Thurio, since the dramatist did not consider them important enough to be given soliloquies or a foil; and it also goes a long way towards explaining the failure in the last scene to develop a tricky situation in a way that would have achieved a fully articulate emotional resolution. And it is this more than anything else that gives the impression of sketchiness. It does not ruin the play: along with, and partly because of, the sketchiness, there is a wholly charming simplicity and directness: what Hazlitt called 'a careless grace and felicity' 'through-out the conduct of the fable'; but there is not that density and harmonic richness which come where the characters of a play have a subtle complexity of cross-relationships such as we find in *Twelfth Night* and would, to some degree, have been desirable here.

Before going on to discuss the more 'organic' deficiencies of the play, I may be permitted a few more general considerations arising from this discussion of a technical aspect which has not, so far as I know, been previously remarked.[5] First, the particular technical limitations of which I have been speaking are characteristic, not only of many Tudor interludes, but also, and to a marked degree, of a play Shakespeare knew very well: Gascoigne's *Supposes*. Secondly, I find it difficult to imagine how a dramatist with a technique of character-manipulation as limited as this play reveals, not only in scenes, such as the last, where he had to wrestle with thematic complexities, but also in straightforward scenes of exposition, could, unaided, have plotted, for instance, the last scenes of *The Comedy of Errors* and *The Taming of the Shrew*, and much of *Richard III*: plays often thought of as earlier than *The Two Gentlemen of Verona*. The problem of chronology is of course exceedingly complicated, and cannot be solved simply by considering the flexibility of character-manipulation; but it is a consideration that seems to have been neglected. Thirdly, I suggest a possible fallacy implicit in many discussions of the chronology of Shakespeare's early plays: the idea stated (though not necessarily endorsed) by Geoffrey Bullough: 'Since it [*The Two Gentlemen of Verona*] replaces the dry hardness of *A Comedy of Errors* and *The Shrew* with some of the warmth and eloquence, the surplusage of word-play, found in *A Midsummer Night's Dream* and *Love's Labour's Lost*, the play probably belongs to the same group, though it may be earlier than these, for it treats its romantic theme with a somewhat jejune absence of self-criticism hardly possible after their delighted mockery of Love.'[6] It seems to me equally possible that a young writer should begin with 'warmth and eloquence' and only then, discovering in himself technical deficiencies, restrain these qualities at the risk of 'dry hardness' in order to acquire greater formal discipline.

The organic deficiencies of the play are the result of Shakespeare's failure to devise a plot which will enable characters conceived within the conventions of romantic love to behave in a manner compatible with these conventions. We are, for instance, invited to sympathize with Valentine; he is the attractive, intelligent young courtier whose love for Sylvia is seriously and forcefully presented; the man who at the end is capable of the grand romantic gesture of offering to sacrifice love to friendship. But the exigencies of the plot require this intelligent young man to behave in a manner not merely unrealistic, but downright stupid. Realism, of course, we have no right to expect; the trouble is that Shakespeare cuts across the convention by using his romantic hero as a vehicle for a type of comedy which deprives him of his whole basis of existence. The scene in which Valentine fails to realize that the letter he is writing on Sylvia's behalf is addressed to himself might perhaps have been acceptable as a tenderly absurd illustration of the lover's traditional blindness: the wit made weak with musing; but when the humour of the situation is explicitly pointed for us by Speed, who here shows much more intelligence than his master, the tenderness is in great danger of being lost in the absurdity. A later scene that quite deflates our confidence in the young man is that in which he ingenuously reveals to the Duke his plan for eloping with the Duke's daughter. If the person concerned had been Thurio, all would have been well; but as it is, the situation is at variance with the character.

A somewhat similar difficulty arises with Proteus. Again our first impressions are sympathetic. Before long, not merely is he behaving in the most caddish manner imaginable, but he is inviting our sympathy in what he takes to be a moral dilemma. It must be admitted, I think, that his soliloquy at the beginning of 4.2 comes near to redeeming him as a dramatic character, for he shows quite powerfully his awareness of his falseness to Valentine, his injustice towards Thurio, and his worthlessness in comparison with Sylvia; he grows in depth when he tells how, 'spaniel-like, the more she spurns my love, | The more it grows and fawneth on her still'. The mature Shakespeare could have done much with this obsessed lover (witness Angelo); but at this stage he has not yet learned to maintain this depth of characterization, and in a few seconds Proteus goes on to perform with no apparent difficulty the treacheries he has just been deploring. The result is a loss of moral coherence; it is paradoxical that this would have been less evident if Proteus had been more shallowly presented throughout.

In these characters we see the strain imposed by a discrepancy between plot and convention. This aspect of the play has been brilliantly handled by G. K. Hunter, who finds that its 'Lylian kind of structure will, however, only work when the characters are as simple as are Lyly's'. As he says, in Valentine we see the matter at merely intellectual focus, whereas in Proteus 'we have a psychological dimension as well'.[7] A further strain is imposed by the juxtaposition of these figures with the much more realistically conceived Julia. Her letter scene (1.2) is true comedy infused with genuine feeling; in technique it might fairly be considered an anticipation of Shakespeare's use of blank verse to show us the thought-processes of the Nurse in *Romeo and Juliet*; and throughout, the character is consistently, economically, and touchingly presented. The misfortune is that this exposes the hollowness of

Valentine and Proteus. As Madeleine Doran says, 'too much "character" in Julia has fouled up the conventional lines of Shakespeare's story'.[8]

These difficulties reach their climax in the passage of the last scene which has become the most notorious literary and dramatic crux of the play: when Valentine, impressed by Proteus's repentance, says:

> And, that my love may appear plain and free,
> All that was mine in Silvia I give thee. (5.4.82-3)

This has provoked many different reactions. In J. P. Kemble's acting edition,[9] it is materially altered. After Proteus's molestation of Sylvia (toned down from the original), she and Valentine are given a brief conversation (italicized below):

> VALENTINE ~~Thou friend of an ill fashion!~~
> PROTEUS Valentine!
> VALENTINE *Comrades, lay hold on him.—*
>   *[The Outlaws seize Proteus,—Julia runs to him.*
>   *My dearest Silvia!*
>   *Indulgent Heaven at length has heard my prayer,*
>   *And brought again my Silvia to my arms;*
>   *No power on earth shall ever part us more.*
> SILVIA *It is delusion all,—Alas, we dream,*
>   *And must awake to wretchedness again.*
>   *O, Valentine, we are beset with dangers.*
> VALENTINE *Dismiss those fears, my love; here I command:*
>   Thou common friend . . .

Valentine's forgiveness of Proteus is postponed till after the recognition of Julia, Proteus's penitence is expanded, and Valentine's gift to him of Sylvia is omitted. Other alterations include the provision of extra speeches for Sylvia and Thurio, and of a final speech for Proteus:

> *Thanks, generous Valentine:—and I myself*
> *Will be the trumpet of my Julia's worth,*
> *Her steadfast faith, her still-enduring love,*
> *And of my own misdoings.—Pardon me,*
> *Ye who have ever known what 'tis to err!—*
> *And be this truth by all the world confess'd!*
> *That lovers must be faithful to be bless'd!*

These are a theatre-man's attempts to make the scene workable in his own terms. It has given equal trouble in the study, where doubts have been cast upon both its authenticity and its textual integrity. Dowden, rejecting arguments for 'duplicity of authorship', yet believed that 'If the fifth act came from Shakespeare's pen as it now stands, we must believe that he handed over his play to the actors while a portion of it still remained only a hasty sketch, the *denouement* being left for future working out'.[10] Dover Wilson and Quiller-Couch could not stomach it at all, and propounded an elaborate theory of playhouse interference, tentatively adopted and modified by Parrott.

On the other hand, attempts to justify the scene as it stands have been made, for instance, by drawing parallels with the Sonnets, and even (by Masefield)[11] with a real-life situation between Shelley and Thomas Jefferson Hogg; and Allardyce Nicoll calls the renunciation 'a testimony to love's perplexing and unassailable power'.[12] There can be no doubt, I think, that, whatever our opinion of the rest of the scene, its climactic situation in itself would have been perfectly acceptable to an Elizabethan audience. As M. C. Bradbrook has written: 'The school-boy cries of "cad" and "scoundrel" with which Valentine is pelted by critics, the epigrams of Q ("By now there are *no* gentlemen in Verona") would have struck Shakespeare's audience as simply a failure in understanding.'[13] And John Munro very pertinently observes that 'in the "Brotherhood" stories (on which the Valentine–Silvia–Proteus romance is based), of which...[M.] Leach examined some eighty-six closely related versions, one of two men woos and wins, or is won by, or even weds, a woman, only to transfer her to his beloved companion in the all-dominating urge of sworn friendship. Shakespeare should perhaps have disembarrassed himself of this incident in the plot; but he let it stand, bent at this stage on adhering to the tale. At a later stage, interested much more in character, as against plot, he would, no doubt, have acted differently'.[14] My only objection to this is the implication that Shakespeare was here more 'interested' in plot than in character. The trouble is twofold: partly that he had not *enough* interest in the plot to see how it should have been moulded to synthesize with the other elements of the play; and partly sheer inadequacy in the mechanics of his craft, which rendered him incapable of manipulating his characters in a convincing way.

The comic characters, as I have suggested, at times impinge inappropriately upon the serious ones; but they are more often used to provide a wholly successful comic implied commentary on the romantic agonies of the lovers. When Speed comments on the letter scene between Valentine and Sylvia, he makes Valentine look an ass; he does not simply comment on the romance: he (at least momentarily) destroys it. On the other hand, when he and Launce discuss Launce's requirements of his girlfriend, they provide an attitude that can co-exist with the other: they are not mutually incompatible, but mutually illuminating. The first does, as Charlton says, inadvertently make romance comic; the second provides a perfectly legitimate comic counterpoint to the romance.

In its overall organization, then, I see this play as a failure. It shows Shakespeare accepting dramatic conventions with one hand and throwing them overboard with the other. He fails, partly because he puts more into the framework than it can hold, and partly because he still has much to learn about the mechanics of his craft. But the play is very far indeed from being a total failure. There are partial successes even in its attempts to be an integrated poetic comedy. Already Shakespeare is making some use of recurrent and significantly placed imagery to prepare us for the turns of the story; we may notice for instance the emphasis on the blindness of love, on the way it 'metamorphoses' a man, so that he wars with good counsel, and his wit is made weak with musing; and the two developed images of the transitoriness of love (2.2.200–2, 3.2.6–10). These go some way towards preparing us for Valentine's partial blindness and for the shift in Proteus's affections: though they do not make them completely successful, they erode the frontiers of our disbelief. Even the word-play, mechanical as it often is, sometimes takes on anticipatory depths, as in the passage between Julia and the Host:

HOST	How now! are you sadder than you were before?
	How do you, man? the music likes you not.
JULIA	You mistake; the musician likes me not.
HOST	Why, my pretty youth?
JULIA	He plays false, father.
HOST	How? Out of tune on the strings?
JULIA	Not so; but yet so false that he grieves my very heart-strings.
HOST	You have a quick ear.
JULIA	Ay, I would I were deaf; it makes me have a slow heart.
HOST	I perceive you delight not in music.
JULIA	Not a whit, when it jars so.
HOST	Hark, what fine change is in the music!
JULIA	Ay, that change is the spite.
HOST	You would have them always play but one thing?
JULIA	I would always have one play but one thing. (4.2.54-72)

Julia's answers are misunderstandings, but being functional, they are not comic: they stress her isolation and loneliness. There is wit here, but its effect is not one of hilarity; it serves rather to sharpen the poignancy of Julia's situation.

The very tenuousness of the plot, and the shadowiness of some of its characters, help us to accept the situations as it were on a hypothetical basis, and to follow with interest the ways in which they are developed. In this the play resembles the prose romances of the period, in many of which the story exists merely as a machinery to place the characters in interesting situations; then rhetoric takes over, and the emotional ramifications are developed at great length. The parallel does not hold entirely, for there are clear signs that Shakespeare was trying to do more than this; but at least it may help us to see where to look for the play's virtues. And the looseness of action does above all allow Shakespeare to bring in the estimable figure of Launce and the silent Crab, who are much more relevant thematically than structurally, and who show how marvellously creative Shakespeare's imagination already was when given a free rein. Again, though I have stressed the limitations of dramatic technique in this play, it must be repeated that Shakespeare is often wholly successful within the limits of a single scene. And the most important reason for the play's successes is that, however immature he may be in other ways, he is already completely assured as a writer of comic prose, of lyrical verse, and even sometimes of genuine dramatic verse. When we try to get below the surface of the play, we find that it rests on shaky foundations. In these circumstances the best thing to do seems to be to come up to the surface again and examine that; then we may return to Johnson: 'It is not indeed one of his most powerful effusions, it has neither many diversities of character, nor striking delineations of life, but it abounds in γνῶμαι (wise sayings) beyond most of his plays, and few have more lines or passages which, singly considered, are eminently beautiful.'[15]

4

The Taming of the Shrew and *King Lear*: A Structural Comparison

In this essay, I wish to suggest that, in writing two of his plays, Shakespeare was more than usually aware of the sometimes complementary, sometimes opposing functions of the mind and the body in human life; and that this awareness may be discerned in the layout of the narrative—the overall design—in the characterization, and in the language: not simply the diction, but also the choice of sentiments to be uttered. I do not suggest that a reliance on these concepts accounts for every aspect of the plays' structure, nor that Shakespeare may not have had other guiding principles, too. But I hope that an analysis of the plays with these ideas in mind may tell us something about how they are made; I hope, too, that the juxtaposition of two essentially very different plays may also be fruitful.

The relationship between mind, or soul, and body was a common topic in Renaissance writings about religion, philosophy, morality, and physiology.[1] There is, to give just one example, an essay about it in Plutarch's *Moralia* which, interestingly enough, first appeared in English translation (by Philemon Holland) in 1603, shortly before the composition of *King Lear*, though I can find no evidence of direct relationship. Shakespeare has many glancing references to the theme, and some longer treatments of it. The plays with which I am concerned are not the only ones to which, I believe, it can provide a useful critical approach. I have chosen them for two main reasons. One is that in them the theme is exceptionally evident in verbal details, so that the critic is less susceptible to the charge of reading between the lines; the other is that the juxtaposition of an early play in which design is relatively close to the surface, and a late one, in which the technique is far less readily apparent, seems to me to provide an insight into Shakespeare's creative processes.

In writing of *The Taming of the Shrew*, I shall be concerned with a fairly simple dualism of mind and body. But in *King Lear*, though 'body' will remain more or less constant, 'mind' will need to be extended to a range of meanings stretching as far as those usually signified by 'soul'. This appears to be justified by Shakespeare's own usage. Sometimes in him, as in other writers, we can discern a clear distinction between 'mind' referring to purely intellectual powers, and 'soul' referring to purely spiritual ones. But at other times the concepts merge: one of *OED*'s definitions of 'mind' is 'the soul as distinguished from the body' (III, 17), and one of its definitions of 'soul' is 'Intellectual insight or spiritual development; high development of the mental faculties', with a first quotation from *Othello* ('these fellows have some soul': 1.1.54). So in *Love's Labour's Lost*—which, indeed, might be regarded as an extended treatment of the topos—we have 'The mind shall banquet, though the body pine' (1.1.25), a statement which has its spiritual counterpart in the metaphysical Sonnet 146: 'Then, soul, live thou upon thy servant's [that is, the body's] loss, | And let that *pine* to aggravate thy store'. But in the grossly physical Sonnet 151, *soul* seems to encompass intellectual as well as spiritual powers: 'My soul doth tell my body that he may | Triumph in love; flesh stays no farther reason . . . '. And in 2 *Henry IV*, 'soul' could be substituted for 'mind' in the lines

> . . . the Bishop
> Turns insurrection to religion.
> Suppos'd sincere and holy in his thoughts,
> He's follow'd both with body and with mind. (1.1.200–3)[2]

Of all Shakespeare's plays the early comedies are those in which structural patterns can be most readily discerned. We think of the double quartets of lovers in *Love's Labour's Lost*, the two pairs of twins in *The Comedy of Errors*, the master–servant juxtapositions of *The Two Gentlemen of Verona*, and the double pairs of lovers in *A Midsummer Night's Dream*. *The Taming of the Shrew* is a little more difficult to discuss in these terms because of a textual problem. We cannot be certain whether the episodes involving Christopher Sly form a framework enveloping the main action, or whether that action emerges from them, like a butterfly from a chrysalis, never to return. But in any case, there is undoubtedly a relationship between these episodes and the play proper. Let us look at this for a moment in the light of the concepts of the mind and the body. These concepts are very prominent in the opening action. Initially, Christopher Sly is seen very much as a body, unanimated by a mind, scarcely even by breath:

> What's here? One dead, or drunk? See, doth he breathe? (Induction, 1.29)

The trick that the Lord devises to play upon him will work, by means of mainly physical properties, upon his mind. 'The beggar' will then be made to 'forget himself', to suppose that the body which he inhabits belongs in fact to someone else, 'a mighty lord'. The actors who help to put the trick into execution are, in doing so, obliged to exercise their own minds to control their bodies; indeed, as their leader reminds the Lord, they make a speciality of this:

Fear not, my Lord; we can contain ourselves,
Were he the veriest antic in the world. (Induction, 1.98–9)

They are professionals. Bartholomew, the Lord's page, is only an amateur. In case his mind cannot produce the requisite changes in his behaviour and appearance, he is to have external help:

An onion will do well for such a shift,
Which, in a napkin being close conveyed,
Shall in despite enforce a watery eye. (Induction, 1.124–6)

In these episodes we are shown something of the power of art to deceive the mind and thus to influence the body, and this underlying basis of the action is made explicit in a curious image. The Lord and his servingmen offer to show Sly pictures which will seem like reality. All will be 'As lively painted as the deed was done'; indeed, it seems, the reality of the painting will not merely deceive Sly, but will affect the characters within the paintings themselves; they will show Sly

...Daphne roaming through a thorny wood,
Scratching her legs, that one shall swear she bleeds
And at that sight shall sad Apollo weep,
So workmanly the blood and tears are drawn. (Induction, 2.55–8)

Once Sly's metamorphosis is complete, the transition to the play proper is made in terms which again emphasize the power of mind over matter: Sly's doctors think it proper for him to see a comedy.

Seeing too much sadness hath congeal'd your blood,
And melancholy is the nurse of frenzy.
Therefore they thought it good you hear a play
And frame your mind to mirth and merriment,
Which bars a thousand harms and lengthens life. (Induction, 2.129–33)

These terms are interestingly like the claims made in preliminaries to Elizabethan works, such as the Epistle to Dekker's *The Shoemaker's Holiday*, in which, it is said, 'nothing is purposed but mirth. Mirth lengtheneth long life...'. So, perhaps consciously, we are prepared to see what follows as a work of art in itself. At any rate, the power of art to work on the body as well as the mind is re-stated at the beginning of the play-within-the-play, when Tranio advises Lucentio that, while it is all very well to 'admire | This virtue and this moral discipline', he should also use 'music and poesy' to 'quicken' him (1.1.29–30, 36).

It is, however, in the 'taming' plot itself that the concepts of mind and body are most clearly of structural importance. Petruchio is mentally independent, so confident in his self-knowledge that he declares himself impervious to physical imperfections in his wife:

> Be she as foul as was Florentius' love,
> As old as Sibyl, and as curst and shrewd
> As Socrates' Xanthippe or a worse—
> She moves me not, or not removes, at least,
> Affection's edge in me, were she as rough
> As are the swelling Adriatic seas. (1.2.7–72)

(The same idea is reinforced, in more generalized metaphors, at 1.2.196 ff.: 'I think you a little din can daunt my ears ...'.) But Petruchio, in approaching Baptista with his request for permission to woo Kate, claims that he is moved mostly by mental qualities:

> I am a gentleman of Verona, sir,
> That, hearing of her beauty and her wit,
> Her affability and bashful modesty,
> Her wondrous qualities and mild behaviour,
> Am bold to show myself a forward guest
> Within your house... (2.1.47–52)

And initially, in soliloquy, he announces his determination to overcome her expected resistance to him through an exercise of his mind:

> Say that she rail; why, then I'll tell her plain
> She sings as sweetly as a nightingale.
> Say that she frown; I'll say she looks as clear
> As morning roses newly wash'd with dew.
> Say she be mute, and will not speak a word;
> Then I'll commend her volubility,
> And say she uttereth piercing eloquence. (2.1.169–75)

This is, I take it, a key speech, placed as it is immediately before the first of the wooing scenes, and giving the audience insight into the way that Petruchio's mind is working. It provides an important perspective on the action, inclining us to see the taming process primarily from his point of view. And at this stage there is no suggestion that he will work on Kate by physical means. Except for a mild scuffle or two, his wooing is carried out in a combat of wits. Kate succumbs to it with unexplained ease—again the dramatic perspective favours Petruchio—and not until he is in church does he begin to exercise physical violence, as we hear in

Gremio's description of the wedding. By now it is, surely, not merely easy but essential for the audience to understand that this is part of an act that Petruchio is putting on, just as the Lord and his gentlemen had put on an act to transmogrify Christopher Sly, and as the Lord had instructed the actors to behave before Sly. This it is that enables Petruchio to retain our sympathy. The physically aggressive behaviour stems from mental calculation of a good-humoured and benevolent kind.

The taming process itself, which begins with the marriage, takes place in two major stages, one of them aimed at subduing Kate's body, the second at taming her mind. That this has, so far as I can tell, been little remarked may be simply because it surely needs little demonstration. In the first stage, Petruchio carries Kate bodily away from her father's home; he causes her to undergo the physical tribulations, memorably catalogued by Grumio, of the journey to his home; and he knocks his servants around in her presence, throwing food and dishes at them. Again, the action is put in a perspective favourable to Petruchio by a soliloquy—or more properly, perhaps, a monologue addressed to the audience—in which he reminds us of the calculatedness of his behaviour—'Thus have I politicly begun my reign' (4.1.172–95)—in which he compares Kate to a falcon which he is taming, outlines the next stage of his campaign, and claims the audience's sympathy by saying

> ...amid this hurly I intend
> that all is done in reverend care of her

and by asking, disarmingly,

> He that knows better how to tame a shrew
> Now let him speak; 'tis charity to show.

The next stage of the taming story continues the physical process. Kate ruefully sums up the technique before it begins:

> ...I...
> Am starv'd for meat, giddy for lack of sleep;
> With oaths kept waking, and with brawling fed;
> And that which spites me more than all these wants –
> He does it under name of perfect love. (4.3.7–12)

After these recapitulatory and anticipatory passages, the taming begins again, as Kate is deprived first of food, then of new clothes; and this stage in the process comes almost to its end with the long speech of Petruchio, addressed to Kate, in which he draws a moral in terms which bring the ideas that I have been tracing explicitly to the play's surface:

> Well, come, my Kate; we will unto your father's
> Even in these honest mean habiliments;
> Our purses shall be proud, our garments poor;
> For 'tis the mind that makes the body rich;
> And as the sun breaks through the darkest clouds,
> So honour peereth in the meanest habit. (4.3.165–70)

The tone is different from Sonnet 146, but the idea is the same: 'Within be fed, without be rich no more.'

Petruchio continues in this vein at some length, stressing the importance of inherent qualities rather than superficial ones. His long speech marks a turn in both the action and Petruchio's technique. In the coda of the scene, Shakespeare gently prefigures the next stage, as Kate contradicts Petruchio's statement that ''tis now some seven o'clock', and receives her warning from him:

> I will not go to-day; and ere I do,
> It shall be what o'clock I say it is. (4.3.190–1)

Hortensio's closing line—'Why, so this gallant will command the sun'—is also deliberately anticipatory. Now Petruchio is to work on Kate's mind and, even more importantly, on her imagination. He calls the sun the moon, Kate contradicts him, and he gives orders to return; but Kate is beginning to learn how to deal with him:

> Forward, I pray, since we have come so far,
> And be it moon, or sun, or what you please;
> And if you please to call it a rush-candle,
> Henceforth I vow it shall be so for me. (4.5.12–15)

It is a spirited reply, in its acknowledgement of absurdity. Petruchio puts her through her paces:

> PETRUCHIO I say it is the moon.
> KATHERINA I know it is the moon.
> PETRUCHIO Nay, then you lie. It is the blessed sun.
> KATHERINA Then, God be bless'd, it is the blessed sun;
>   But sun it is not, when you say it is not;
>   And the moon changes even as your mind.
>   What you will have it nam'd, even that it is,
>   And so it shall be so for Katherine. (4.5.16–22)

There is a new-found articulacy in Kate's style here; and is there not something of a dig, not wholly submissive, at Petruchio in 'the moon changes even as your mind'?—it was, after all, women's minds that were proverbially as changeable as the moon.[3]

But Hortensio, at least, feels confident enough to congratulate Petruchio—'the field is won'—and the next episode reveals Kate not merely concurring with her husband in patent absurdity, but entering with full imaginative commitment into what now seems more like a game than a display of the results of brainwashing, as she addresses old Vincentio as 'Young budding virgin, fair and fresh and sweet...' (4.5.36). This time she agrees immediately when Petruchio contradicts her, claiming that she has been 'bedazzled with the sun', and the episode passes off harmoniously. It remains simply for Kate to demonstrate her affection for her husband in public, and this she does, after a momentary flinching, with 'Nay, I will give thee a kiss; now pray thee, love, stay' (5.1.133).

Behind my remarks lies a purpose which is to some degree secondary; to demonstrate that the 'taming' process is one which brings Katherine to a full realization of her potentialities as a woman[4] rather than, as some interpreters would have it, being analogous to a process of brainwashing, crushing her into cowed submission. But my primary purpose has been, perhaps, a simpler one, a demonstration of what may well seem entirely obvious: that the structuring of this process can objectively be stated to be based on a design which has as its basic components the body and the mind, and that this finds its reflection also in other parts of the play.

I move with trepidation from the relatively simple pattern of *The Taming of the Shrew* to the far more complex structure which is *King Lear*; but I take encouragement from the fact that the tragedy has generally been thought to be exceptionally schematic, at least by comparison with most of Shakespeare's other, later plays. It is, we are often told, his only tragedy to have a fully developed subplot; the action is stylized; the characters divide with unusual patness into the good and the bad. A. C. Bradley summed it up by saying that in *King Lear* Shakespeare's imagination tended 'to analyse and abstract, to decompose human nature into its constituent factors, and then to construct beings in whom one or more of these factors is absent...'. This is, as he says, 'a tendency which produces symbols, allegories, personifications of qualities and abstract ideas; and we are accustomed to think it quite foreign to Shakespeare's genius, which was in the highest degree concrete. No doubt in the main we are right here; but it is hazardous to set limits to that genius.' Bradley is here commenting on the bases of Shakespeare's portrayal of character in this play, but he goes on to extend his observation to refer to the imagery, in particular to 'the idea of monstrosity' and to 'the incessant references to the lower animals and man's likeness to them'. The influence of such a technique is, says Bradley, 'to convey to us...the wider or universal significance of the spectacle presented to the inward eye'.[5] In suggesting that in *King Lear*, as in *The Taming of the Shrew*, Shakespeare was exceptionally aware of the dualism of mind and body,

I am pointing to another manifestation of the same overall tendency that Bradley discerned in this play, and one that has the same overall effect.

The presence of the dualism in the play has been often enough remarked. Richard David, for example, states it as a commonplace: 'Lear, who has erred in judgment, loses in consequence his reason, the light of his mind, while Gloucester, whose error was physical and sensual, loses his eyes, the light of his body'.[6] That is an acknowledgement of the importance of Shakespeare's basic decision to juxtapose the story of a man who goes mad with one who is blinded; and it was, we must feel, a decision made with a purpose. W. R. Elton, discussing the double plot, lays more emphasis on character than action: 'Among . . . explanations for the double plot is that which identifies in Lear and Gloucester traditional aspects of the sensitive soul: the irascible and the concupiscible matching the protagonists' anger and lechery.' He points to examples of this dualism in some of Shakespeare's immediate predecessors, and finds that Lear and Gloucester receive traditional forms of punishment: 'Lear's intellectual error of anger receives the conventional punishment of madness (ira furor brevis), and Gloucester's physical sin of lechery the conventional retribution of blindness.'[7]

Clearly, then, the fact that 'Gloucester's struggles are largely physical, in contrast to Lear's 'spiritual trials' is 'a commonplace',[8] and the contrast-within-resemblance between them is very apparent in the fact that the crisis of Gloucester's suffering comes when he is blinded, of Lear's, when he goes mad. I want to suggest that the contrast evident in these facets of the play's action is merely the most obvious aspect of an exploration of the relationship between mind and body which may be held to underpin the structures of the entire play. I should say immediately that the connotations of these terms are enormously greater in King Lear than they were in The Taming of the Shrew. In particular, they expand into their moral counterparts, so that the body becomes associated with the values of sensuality and materialism, and the mind with virtue and spirituality. So in speaking of this play I shall use these and similar terms without feeling a need on every occasion to refer back to my basic terminology.

The play's opening lines emphasize Gloucester's physicality in the chatting about the 'whoreson', Edmund. Lear, too, in his opening speech, is concerned with the body, in his case, with its decay—he is dividing the kingdom that he may 'Unburdened crawl toward death'. In the love-contest that follows there is a juxtaposition of material and spiritual values in which we see that the mind needs to find expression through the body, and that in the process, the truth may be distorted: Cordelia's 'love's | More ponderous than [her] tongue'—she cannot 'heave | [her] heart into [her] mouth'—that is, her body is an inadequate representative of her mind, yet she is glad not to have her sisters' 'still-soliciting eye' and tongues; and Kent wishes that her sisters' tongues may utter 'large speeches' which their 'deeds' will 'approve', while obviously fearing that they will not; here 'deeds', physical in their action, are seen nevertheless as reflections of the mind's truth. Lear condemns Cordelia to receive her 'truth' as her 'dower': an ironical betrayal of the falseness of his own scale of values, since, as the play is to show, in spiritual terms, this is the best dowry she could have. The King of France understands this—Cordelia 'is herself'— that is, without the material bounty that her sisters have gained—'a dowry', so, he says, 'Thee and thy virtues here I seize upon.'

The first scene thus establishes an opposition between material and spiritual values, the false and the true. Of course, Shakespeare is not portraying a total opposition between mind and body, because the mind, whether virtuous or not, must operate through the body. This is, and is seen to be, one of man's basic limitations. What Shakespeare can do, and does, is to suggest a possible disjunction between mind and body, so that some people consciously make the body's functions misrepresent their mental attitudes—they are hypocritical—and other people may be more or less successful in discerning this. Goneril and Regan exercise their tongues to misrepresent their mind's truth; Cordelia finds her tongue inadequate to represent her mind's truth; she cannot heave her heart into her mouth. Lear fails to discern the mind through the body; the Duke of Burgundy cares more for material than for spiritual good; but Kent and the King of France can see through the body's false appearances to the truth that lies within. It is perhaps a paradox that Goneril and Regan, too, can see where truth lies; indeed, this completes our sense of the consciousness of their evil: 'He always lov'd our sister most,' says Goneril, 'and with what poor judgment he hath now cast her off appears too grossly.' And Regan replies: ''Tis the infirmity of his age; yet he hath ever but slenderly known himself' (1.1.287–93).

Lear's confusion of values in relation to his daughters is mirrored in Gloucester's attitude to his sons, and in similar terms. Reading the letter purporting to be written by Edgar, Gloucester asks 'Had he a hand to write this? a heart and brain to breed it in?', and Edmund says 'It is his hand, my lord; but I hope his heart is not in the contents' (1.2.53–4, 64–5). It is a complex variation on the situation in the first scene; for Edmund, pretending to hope that Edgar's hand does not convey the truth of his heart, is in fact himself dissimulating in a manner that causes us to associate him with Goneril and Regan, Edgar with Cordelia. And Edmund's rationality, too, in his denial of supernatural influence on man's actions, also aligns him with the wicked sisters, whereas Gloucester's attribution of significance to 'These late eclipses in the sun and moon' (1.2.99), though naively superstitious in tone, at least suggests a mind open to persuasion.

The short first movement of the play is over by the end of the third scene. This is the exposition, of ideas as well as action. With the fourth scene, Lear's troubles begin. They seem trivial at first, merely the insolence of the servant, Oswald. But as Lear's sense of outrage increases, two characters emerge as important to him. One is Kent, his body now disguised, and determined to 'serve' where he does 'stand condemn'd'. The idea of relationship between the heart, or mind, or intention, whatever we like to call it, and the body's appearance is taken a step further. Though Kent wishes to act as his mind prompts him—that is, virtuously—he can do so only by disguising his body's reality. Goneril and Regan had looked other than they were for evil purposes; Kent does so for good. It is significant to the play's design that Kent offers practical services: 'I can keep honest counsel, ride, run, mar a curious tale in telling it, and deliver a plain message bluntly' (1.4.32–3). Kent, we may say without excessive over-simplification, offers Lear bodily help; and, before long, he performs it in tripping up and beating Oswald. As soon as this is established, the next phase of the scene begins, with the entrance of the Fool, the paradoxically intellectual character who works entirely through his mind, who refers to himself as 'Truth'— a 'dog' that 'must to kennel' (1.4.110)—and who immediately gives an extended demonstration of his ability to work obliquely, through parable and paradox, on Lear's mind.

Shakespeare's conscious design is apparent behind the scene's vivacious naturalism. The design is related to that of *The Taming of the Shrew*, but it is subtler and more complex. The influences on body and mind are present simultaneously, not consecutively; and Lear's problems are greater than Kate's.

An early reaction of Lear's to the discovery that his daughters may use against him the power with which he has endowed them is the suspicion that either his mind or his body is beginning to fail him; he says of himself,

> Either his notion weakens, or his discernings
> Are lethargied. (1.4.227–8)

In fact, of course, his mind is being forced into unaccustomed activity. The effort to restrain his anger against Cornwall and Regan pushes him to suppose that Cornwall may be unwell, and here he explicitly uses the terms with which I am concerned:

> ... we are not ourselves
> When nature, being oppress'd, commands the mind
> To suffer with the body. (2.4.105–7)

The statement is more interesting in relation to the man who makes it than to its subject. Lear is beginning to learn about man's limitations, the inevitable interdependence of mind and body—a lesson that is rubbed harshly home by Regan:

> O, sir, you are old;
> Nature in you stands on the very verge
> Of her confine. (2.4.144–6)

But his self-control is short-lived, and in the curses into which he erupts, his images are again of different parts of the body: Goneril had 'struck' him 'with her tongue...upon the very heart'; her 'eyes are fierce', but Regan's 'Do comfort and not burn'. He is astonished that his body can contain his emotion: 'O sides, you are too tough' (2.4.158–9, 171–2, 196). Nevertheless, he will commit himself to his emotion, even though to do so also means that he must make great demands upon his body; he will

> ...abjure all roofs and choose
> To wage against the enmity o' th' air,
> To be a comrade with the wolf and owl (2.4.207–9)

rather than betray his mind's truth by returning with Goneril. His intransigence, which is in some ways deplorable but is seen nevertheless as an essential facet of his integrity—as Cordelia's had been—resembles that of an even more fixedly intransigent character, Coriolanus, who expresses his refusal to compromise in terms of a conflict between mind and body:

> ...I will not do't,
> Lest I surcease to honour mine own truth,
> And by my body's action teach my mind
> A most inherent baseness. (3.2.120–3)

The result of Coriolanus's intransigence is that for a while he lives 'Under the canopy ...I' th' city of kites and crows' (4.5.38–42). Lear, too, is forced, by both external and internal pressures, to ever-increasing dependence on his own body, uncushioned by ritual, ceremony, and the comforts of the court. The process makes him question the need for such 'superfluity'—Goneril's gorgeous clothing, for instance. (Kate had been subjected to similar criticisms.) But his reiterated expressions of fear that he will go mad show his concern that the body shall continue to be guided by the mind.

Though his hundred knights melt away, Lear is never destitute of loving companionship. We could if we wished see Kent and the Fool as projections of two aspects of Lear himself: his physical strength and his striving after the truth; but to do so would reduce the play's humanity, for Kent and the Fool are individuals whose loyalty to their master shows some of the better aspects of human nature. So on the heath they remain true to their natures, and thus to Lear, the Fool labouring 'to outjest | His heart-struck injuries' (3.1.16–17), Kent offering more practical help. The Fool has the more difficult task: for though Lear suffers in body, his mental anguish is greater and, paradoxically, reduces his physical pain:

> ...When the mind's free
> The body's delicate—

that is, when one has an untroubled mind one is particularly conscious of bodily sensation—but

> ...this tempest in my mind
> Doth from my senses take all feeling else
> Save what beats there. Filial ingratitude!

Again, the offence is imaged through parts of the body:

> Is it not as this mouth should tear this hand
> For lifting food to't?

Lear's sense of having been wronged increases his determination not to submit:

> ...In such a night,
> To shut me out! Pour on; I will endure. (3.4.17–18)

And he is brought to a feeling of kinship with the 'Poor naked wretches' who depend on body alone. His exposure has taught him to 'feel what wretches feel'—bodily sensation is affecting the imagination—and he recognizes the need for a fairer distribution of 'the super-flux'.

Plot and subplot begin to merge with the reappearance of Edgar, whose physical disguise for good motives parallels Kent's, whom he also resembles in his ingenious practicality. The Fool prophesies that bodily suffering will afflict their minds: 'This cold night will turn us all to fools and madmen' (3.4.77)—and although Lear strives to retain his grasp upon reality in his contemplation of Edgar's 'uncover'd body' it is at the moment that he determines to become, like Edgar, 'the thing itself', 'a poor, bare, forked animal' (3.4.101, 105–7), that his mind deserts him. Now he can receive only physical help, so the Fool fades out of the play. Kent's comment implies that the mind has been to some extent dependent upon the body:

> ...Oppressed nature sleeps.
> This rest might yet have balm'd thy broken sinews,
> Which, if convenience will not allow,
> Stand in hard cure. (3.6.97–100)

And Lear is taken to Dover, by Gloucester, Kent, and the Fool. As they go out, Edgar comments, in gnomic couplets that draw attention to their own function, on the relativeness of mental suffering, and on the fact that it can be alleviated by companionship and by comparison:

When we our betters see bearing our woes,
We scarcely think our miseries our foes.
Who alone suffers suffers most i' th' mind,
Leaving free things and happy shows behind;
But then the mind much sufferance doth o'erskip
When grief hath mates, and bearing fellowship.
How light and portable my pain seems now,
When that which makes me bend makes the King bow. (3.6.102–9)

The action turns immediately from the mental to the physical; from the maddening of Lear to the blinding of Gloucester. This is the area of the play in which the dualism of mind and body is most readily apparent. Paradox, so prevalent in *King Lear*, is dominant here. As soon as Gloucester loses the power to see literally, he begins to do so metaphorically. The fact that he learns the truth about his sons immediately his second eye has been put out makes Shakespeare's intention transparently obvious. Like Lear, Gloucester is learning through deprivation:

Our means secure us, and our mere defects
Prove our commodities. (4.1.21–2)

Like Lear's, his new knowledge extends from the particular to the general. Lear had learnt to 'feel what wretches feel' and wished to 'shake the superflux to them'; Gloucester, in lines of complex nuance, expresses the need in man for a proper balance of physical and mental qualities: the 'superfluous and lust-dieted man'—he who is excessive in both material possessions and sensual gratification—is he who 'will not see | Because he does not feel' (4.1.69–70): the complexity lies in the pun on 'see', coming from the newly blinded man who would still have been able to see literally if through proper feeling he had been able to recognize truth, followed by the use of 'feel' in a metaphorical sense rather than the literal one that might be expected to follow from 'see'.

Of course, Shakespeare's design is not so crude that Gloucester's suffering is merely physical; otherwise he would be no more than one of the animals so frequently evoked in the play's language. The physical and mental suffering that lead him to attempt suicide do not, however, drive him to madness; indeed, he wishes they had:

The King is mad; how stiff is my vile sense,
That I stand up, and have ingenious feeling
Of my huge sorrows! Better I were distract;
So should my thoughts be sever'd from my griefs,
And woes by wrong imaginations lose
The knowledge of themselves. (4.6.279–84)

The idea that physical suffering can bring mental revelation—that people will not begin to see until they learn to feel—is repeated by Lear in his madness, in vividly physical terms: 'When the rain came to wet me once, and the wind to make me chatter; when the thunder would not peace at my bidding; there I found 'em, there I smelt 'em out' (4.6.100–3). And Gloucester's paradox is repeated, too, as if to drive it home:

> LEAR ...Your eyes are in a heavy case, your purse in a light; yet you see how this
>   world goes.
> GLOUCESTER I see it feelingly.
> LEAR What, art mad? A man may see how this world goes with no eyes.
>
> (4.6.146–51)

The Dover beach scene shows the play's central characters at the nadir of their fortunes; yet it shows them, too, in spite of their afflictions, as in some senses wiser and better men than they had been at the beginning of the action. Wretched though their state is, Shakespeare has already shown us a counter-action designed to alleviate it. Cordelia's return to the play is reported before we see her, in a scene (4.3) omitted in the Folio text and sometimes accounted unnecessary and sentimental. Certainly it presents Cordelia as a radiantly idealized figure. In her reactions to the letter bearing news of her father, she has displayed an ideal balance between mental control and physical response:

> ...It seem'd she was a queen
> Over her passion, who, most rebel-like,
> Sought to be king o'er her. (4.3.13–15)

And the idealization is reinforced by what follows. As the play enters its last phase, its polarities become more extreme. Cordelia's virtues take on something of a transcendental quality. She herself associates her compassion with

> All blest secrets,
> All you unpublish'd virtues of the earth,

asking that they may

> Spring with [her] tears; be aidant and remediate
> In the good man's distress. (4.4.15–18)

(The unobtrusive adjective 'good' there is one of the subtle ways in which Shakespeare is guiding us towards total sympathy with Lear himself.) Lear, awaking from sleep and madness, sees her as 'a soul in bliss' and 'a spirit'; he speaks of them both as if they were somehow untouchable by time:

> [We'll] take upon's the mystery of things
> As if we were God's spies; and we'll wear out
> In a wall'd prison[9] packs and sects of great ones
> That ebb and flow by th'moon. (5.3.16–19)

Kent and Edgar are seen as entirely selfless and compassionate; Albany develops from weakness into a strong upholder of the right, and speaks of the surviving characters of the play in morally absolute terms:

> ...All friends shall taste
> The wages of their virtue, and all foes
> The cup of their deservings. (5.3.302–4)

If 'mind' seems only vaguely appropriate as a term for one of the polarities in the last phase of the play, it surely can be claimed that 'body' is entirely appropriate for the other, in two of its important aspects. One is the sensual. The scene in which the virtuous Cordelia reappears is preceded and followed by ones in which Edmund's physical involvement with both Goneril and Regan is made known to us. Lear, in his madness, speaks of adultery, copulation, and luxury in a terrible diatribe against female sexuality. Goneril and Regan's competition for Edmund becomes increasingly sordid, and causes Goneril to encourage Edmund to kill Albany. Edgar, speaking to the defeated Edmund, attributes their father's suffering to his sensuality: 'The dark and vicious place where thee he got | Cost him his eyes': a moralization which, though Edgar's tone is conciliatory—'Let's exchange charity'—also invites us to link Edmund's present plight with *his* moral crimes.

Even more prominent in the play's closing passages is the sense and sight of a body as a corpse. Edgar kills Oswald; Lear believes that he has been taken from a grave; we are reminded of Cornwall's death; Regan is poisoned by Goneril; Edgar describes Gloucester's death; we hear that Kent is near to death; a Gentleman enters with the 'bloody knife' which Goneril has used to stab herself; her body and Regan's are brought on to the stage; Lear carries in the dead Cordelia, and boasts 'I kill'd the slave that was a-hanging thee'; we hear of Edmund's death; and Lear dies.

The play's closing moments throw an appalling emphasis on the dead human body. Granville-Barker's comment on Lear's entry 'with Cordelia in his arms' is often quoted. 'What fitter ending to the history of the two of them, which began for us with Lear on his throne, conscious of all eyes on him, while she shamed and angered him by her silence? The same company are here, or all but the same, and they await his pleasure. Even Regan and Goneril are here to pay him a ghastly homage. But he knows none of them—save for a blurred moment Kent whom he banished—none but Cordelia. And again he reproaches her silence, for

> ...Her voice was ever soft,
> Gentle and low, an excellent thing in woman.

Then his heart breaks.'[10]

That is a fine perception. But is it positive enough? Does Lear do no more than reproach Cordelia for her silence? Is it not important that now, in a total reversal of the crisis of the first scene, all his attention and all his love are focused upon Cordelia, that now he truly sees and acknowledges the beauty of her truth? And would it be entirely far-fetched to suggest that Lear's self-fulfilment is like Kate's in that both have been brought about through a complementary interaction of bodily and mental influences?

Cordelia's intensity of his emotion over her body is the play's final paradox. Bewildered, despairing, nakedly true to his emotions, giving out pure and merited love, he is at his best; he is, if we wish to use the theological term, redeemed. Through feeling, he has been brought to see. 'Look there, look there.' Whether or not it is expressive of delusion, it shows sight well directed, and reminds us of what goodness has achieved. Fully human, Lear dies. The play ends by asserting the spiritual values which human beings can enshrine while also acknowledging the frailty of the individual human body. Thus, it seems to me, Shakespeare brings to a culmination his exploration within the fabric of this play of the relationship between mind, or soul, and body, and does so in action which has sometimes been thought to go distastefully beyond the requirements of plot, but which is essential to its structure of ideas.

5

The Integration of Violent Action
in *Titus Andronicus*

For centuries *Titus Andronicus* was either rejected from the Shakespeare canon as being unworthy of its author's genius, or vilified as a terrible aberration committed perhaps as a concession to the tastes of barbarous audiences. Now at last it is undergoing both theatrical and critical rehabilitation. Deborah Warner's 1987 production for the Royal Shakespeare Company at the Swan Theatre in Stratford-upon-Avon was hailed as revelatory confirmation that the play could exert just as powerful an effect in an uncut text as it had in Peter Brook's no less revelatory but heavily adapted and abbreviated version in which Laurence Olivier achieved one of his greatest triumphs in the Royal Shakespeare Theatre itself in 1955. Eugene Waith's Oxford edition, published in 1984, before the Swan production, offers a guarded defence: 'However inferior this first of Shakespeare's tragedies may be to its successors, it is not the inchoate essay that it is sometimes thought to be.'[1] Alan Hughes, in his New Cambridge edition of 1994, and Jonathan Bate in the Arden (Third Series) of 1995 use both the Brook and the Warner productions as evidence for their claims that the traditional condemnation of the play is unjust. Hughes describes it as 'the work of a brilliant stage craftsman' which 'does very well' in the theatre when sensitively handled.[2] Bate writes of it with more enthusiastic approbation, concluding his Introduction with an unequivocal reference to 'the greatness of *Titus Andronicus*'.[3] All three editors, of course, built not only upon the evidence of successful productions but also upon an increasing number of critical studies that, if they are not necessarily wholly admiring of the play, at least take it seriously. Things have changed a lot since T. S. Eliot wrote of it as 'one of the stupidest and most uninspired plays ever written'.[4]

Objections to the play have centred on its use of violence, and critics writing in its defence have accepted this as their sternest challenge. In particular they have experienced a need to counter the charge that the violence is 'gratuitous'—which I suppose means that it is there for its own sake, as a source of titillation rather than as a function of the plot essential to what the critic discerns as the dramatist's serious artistic purposes. So Waith argues that 'Brutal violence, occasionally tinged with comedy, serves several artistic purposes. It represents the political and moral degeneration of Rome when Saturninus becomes emperor. It also plays a major part in the presentation of the hero's metamorphosis into a cruel revenger. While no artistic device can be called inevitable, one can say with some assurance that Shakespeare's use of violence in *Titus Andronicus* is far from gratuitous. It is an integral part of his dramatic technique.'[5]

I should not disagree with this. What I wish to argue in this essay, however, is that at a number of points Shakespeare fails to integrate violent action into the surrounding dialogue—or chooses not to—and that, whether or not we regard this as a technical deficiency, it is a feature of the play that has been largely responsible for its critical denigration and that continues to cause serious problems to its theatrical interpreters. Before examining *Titus Andronicus* in any detail, I should like to offer a couple of examples from later plays by Shakespeare in which violence seems to me to be thoroughly and successfully integrated.

First, the blinding of Gloucester, in *King Lear*. This is generally agreed, I suppose, to be the most uncompromisingly horrifying episode in any of his other plays. Many people would like to evade it, many of us regularly shut our eyes when it happens, it has even been played (as for example in Jonathan Miller's Old Vic production) off stage, but it is never accused of being gratuitous. This is partly because of its overall thematic appropriateness in a play that is deeply concerned with the paradoxes of seeing and not-seeing: Gloucester's loss of the ability literally to see parallels Lear's loss of his reasoning power, but both men gain by their loss: Gloucester's insight into his misjudgement of Edmund and Edgar follows with calculated patness upon the loss of his second eye.

More pertinent to my purposes is the structure of the scene itself. 'Pluck out his eyes' says Goneril even before Gloucester enters; the cruelty with which he is treated gathers in intensity as successively he is forcibly bound to a chair, then Regan plucks him by the beard, then he is subjected to a vicious interrogation during which he expresses suffering—'I am tied to th'stake, and I must stand the course'— and anticipates his own fate in saying to Regan that he has sent Lear to Dover 'Because I would not see thy cruel nails | Pluck out his poor old eyes'. As the blinding becomes imminent Gloucester utters a plea for help and a cry of protest, a servant intervenes and is killed as a result, and after the plucking-out of Gloucester's second eye he has another expression of suffering. The entire episode is a model of the art of how to lead up to, sustain, and modulate away from an episode of violence.

For my second example I should like to take one that is even more relevant to *Titus Andronicus*: the sequence of deaths in the final scene of *Hamlet*. I must treat this in even more summary fashion than my example from *King Lear*, but it should be enough simply to point to the thoroughness of the preparation for the deaths of Gertrude, Laertes, Claudius, and finally Hamlet himself, and to the steadiness of the pacing by which these deaths are spaced out: some sixty-five lines are spoken between the Queen's drinking the poisoned cup and Hamlet's last words.

The relevance of these two examples will, I hope, become apparent in my discussion of *Titus Andronicus*. The most notorious episode of violence in this play takes place off stage, no doubt both because it involves rape and because the victim would originally have been played by a boy. The original direction reads (modernized) '*Enter the Empress' sons with Lavinia, her hands cut off, and her tongue cut out, and ravished.*' The subsequent brief dialogue between the brothers Chiron and Demetrius makes her plight explicit, in case it has not been immediately apparent. It is summed up by Demetrius:

> She hath no tongue to call, nor hands to wash,
> And so let's leave her to her silent walks. (2.4.7–8)

This is entirely workable. More problematic is Marcus's subsequent speech, forty-seven lines in length, in which he meditates on Lavinia's plight. The speech is admirably written, but its extreme artificiality, with its elaborate use of rhetorical devices and of classical references, and above all the improbability, conceived in naturalistic terms, that anyone would spend so long describing Lavinia's suffering instead of trying to do something about it, has been a stumbling block. Peter Brook omitted it altogether, other directors have shortened it; yet, as is apparent from Alan Dessen's discussion of this episode in his valuable book in the Shakespeare in Performance series,[6] it can be made to work with no extraneous business, and, played uncut, formed one of the most profoundly moving and disturbing episodes in Deborah Warner's production.

Criticism and performance together have vindicated Lavinia's shocking entry and its aftermath as a piece of dramatic craftsmanship that needs no apology. The entry of the mutilated Lavinia has been adequately prepared for in the preceding episode in which Tamora has urged her sons to 'satisfy their lust' on her; the horror of her appearance contrasts ironically with the callous brutality of the way in which the brothers speak of her, and this in turn leads to the stunned compassion of Marcus's reactions which, though they do not fall within the conventions of naturalistic drama, have nevertheless proved themselves to be acceptable if played as a heightened representation of thoughts that take far longer to articulate than to experience. As Alan Dessen writes of the Warner production, 'we observe Marcus, step-by-step, use his logic and Lavinia's reactions to work out what has happened, so that the spectators both see Lavinia directly *and* see her through his eyes and images. In the process, the horror of the situation is filtered through a human consciousness in a way difficult to describe but powerful to experience (so as to produce what many observers felt to be the strongest single moment in the show).'[7]

Nevertheless, the play also contains a number of on-stage representations of violence which, it seems to me, have not yet been successfully defended. I am not arguing that they are gratuitous in the sense that the play could make its tragic effects just as effectively without them. On the contrary, the violence represented in all of them is just as integral to this play as, say, the stabbing of Polonius, the smothering of Desdemona, the blinding of Gloucester, or the killing of Macbeth are to theirs. What causes problems in the episodes I have in mind is, as I have suggested, Shakespeare's failure to integrate the representations of violence into the dialogue that precedes and follows them. His imagination, that is to say, has not projected the presentation of violence in terms of the actions and reactions of the perpetrators and their victims. As a result, it seems applied rather than organic, rather as if at these points the dramatist were thinking of the composition of the play's dialogue and the arrangement of its actions as two separate tasks.

The highly literary quality of *Titus Andronicus* has often been remarked. Waith, for example, commenting on an image in Marcus's long speech which is identical with one that appears also in *Venus and Adonis*, notes 'the close connection between *Titus* and Shakespeare's narrative poetry'.[8] What I see as the failure to integrate dialogue and action is, I suggest, characteristic of a playwright whose mastery of the art of verse composition has outstripped his command of dramatic construction, and is paralleled by, for example, certain features of another early play, *The Two Gentlemen of Verona*.[9]

Before attempting to substantiate my allegations about Shakespeare's technical competence in *Titus Andronicus* it seems necessary to acknowledge that in this, as in all his plays, he draws on conventions of dramatic representation which demand from readers and theatregoers of today an exercise of the historical imagination, and that the generic relationships of this play are particularly demanding in this respect. I want, that is to say, to try to distinguish between, on the one hand, features of dramatic craftsmanship which are entirely acceptable in terms of the conventions of the age in which they were written, even if they may be unfamiliar to us, and, on the other hand, passages that seem likely to have made exceptional demands upon interpreters and audiences even at the time the play was first performed.

Dumbshows provide obvious examples of the former. To take the best-known example, it is clear that dramatists of the time could write directions such as that which precedes the play within the play in *Hamlet* in the full expectation that they would be adequately understood and that they would be successfully realized in performance. There is no instance of comparable elaborateness in *Titus Andronicus*, but the direction for Titus's first entrance has something of this quality. '*Sound drums and trumpets, and then enter two of Titus's sons and then two men bearing a coffin covered with black, then two other sons, then Titus Andronicus, and then Tamora the Queen of Goths and her two sons Chiron and Demetrius, with Aaron the Moor, and others as many as can be, then set down the coffin, and Titus speaks.*' So reads the quarto. This is a pageant-like entry, the kind of thing that made a French member of one of the play's earliest audiences, at a private performance on New Year's Day 1596, value it rather for the spectacle than the content ('le monstre a plus valu que le sujet').[10] The dramatist is relying upon his interpreters (whom of course he may well have been directing) to realize the effect called for within the conventions of the period. Modern interpreters have no special difficulty in translating the direction into stage actions appropriate to the conventions of their own productions.

Other plays believed to date from the late 1580s and the early 1590s, written both by Shakespeare himself and by fellow dramatists, present action in a similarly stylized, sometimes wordless fashion that clearly represented a convention acceptable to the age. This is particularly true of fights. From Shakespeare we may instance, in *The First Part of the Contention* (2 *Henry, VI*), the opening of 4.3: '*Alarums to the fight, wherein both the Staffords are slain. Enter Cade and the rest*', and at 4.7, '*Alarums. Matthew Gough is slain, and all the rest. Then enter Jack Cade, with his company.*' Marlowe's *Edward II* offers a parallel: '*Alarums, excursions, a great fight, and a retreat*'.[11] Shakespeare himself in later plays frequently has directions for alarums and excursions for which the precise action must be invented in rehearsal, and in very late plays, such as *Pericles* and *Cymbeline*, reverts to an earlier mode with directions for wordless action even more elaborate than those in his early plays.

For all this, the fact that certain types of action could be represented in stylized form does not absolve the dramatist from the responsibility of presenting in a plausible manner moments of action which necessarily spring out of the dialogue, and, perhaps even more importantly, of ensuring that the actors have the opportunity to convey to the audience some sense of the significance of what has happened to the characters involved. Or, to put it less judgementally, the dramatist runs the risk, if he does not both adequately prepare the audience's minds for what is to happen and give his actors words that will enable them to portray appropriate reactions, of placing himself too much at the mercy of his interpreters, who may fail to convey the significance of what happens or may find themselves obliged to resort to excessive and embarrassing mugging in the absence of suitably expressive words. And when the action portrayed is horrifically violent, the result is likely to be that kind of discrepancy between action and reaction, between what happens and what is said, that creates a sense of absurdity resulting in inappropriate laughter. The effect will approach that of burlesque or parody rather than tragedy: and it is an effect that has characterized inadequate performances of *Titus Andronicus*.

There are a number of points at which the text is particularly vulnerable to accusations of courting this effect, and it is necessary to my purposes to give a brief account of those that seem most conspicuous.

In the opening scene Tamora's son Alarbus is forcibly carried off by two of Titus's sons to be slaughtered (1.1.129); he says nothing; indeed, he is a totally speechless character. The awkwardness of this might be overcome if he were gagged from the moment of his entry, but there is no direction for this.

Later in the same scene Lavinia is forcibly abducted; she says nothing. Moments later, Titus attacks and kills his son Mutius; the only words given to Mutius are 'Help, Lucius, help!', and his brother Lucius's reaction is distinctly bathetic:

> My lord, you are unjust; and more than so,
> In wrongful quarrel you have slain your son. (1.1.288–9)

Later in the play, both Demetrius and Chiron stab Bassianus, who dies. Bassianus says nothing (2.3.117). In the same scene Quintus and Martius make no verbal reaction on being dragged, along with Bassianus's body, from the pit into which they have fallen even though Saturninus has ordered:

> .. drag them from the pit unto the prison.
> There let them bide until we have devised
> Some never-heard-of torturing pain for them. (2.3.283–5)

As the action progresses, horrors accumulate in number and, still more important, in intensity. In Act 3, scene 1 Titus has no direct verbal reaction to the cutting off of his hand by Aaron. The words he speaks immediately after his mutilation are the matter-of-fact

> Now stay your strife. What shall be is dispatched.
> Good Aaron, give his majesty my hand.

Only later does he open up into eloquent utterance. After the great speech—it is no less, even by Shakespeare's highest standards—in which he laments his and Lavinia's plight, a messenger enters 'with two heads and a hand':

> Here are the heads of thy two noble sons,
> And here's thy hand in scorn to thee sent back.... (3.1.235–6)

Again, Titus has no direct reaction; indeed, the next speakers are Marcus and Lucius. It might be suggested that the horrors piling up on Titus drive him speechless; perhaps his great line when at last he does speak, 'When will this fearful slumber have an end?', is all the more powerful for the silences that precede it; and the laughter with which he responds to Marcus's invitation to express himself in words, provoking Marcus's question 'Why dost thou laugh...?', leads to one of the play's potentially most poignant lines: 'Why, I have not another tear to shed.' In my experience of the play in performance this is its most moving scene, but Shakespeare has taken great risks in leaving so much unsaid at crucial points in its action.

Later in the play, yet another character, the Nurse, dies apparently without speaking, though howls of protest are suggested by the mockery with which her assassin describes the consequences of his action: after killing her, Aaron says '"Wheak, wheak"—so cries a pig preparèd to the spit.' There are two subsequent points at which failure to react to deathly violence is entirely explicable: Chiron and Demetrius have been bound and gagged before Titus cuts their throats, and the tongueless Lavinia clearly has no capacity to react in words as Titus kills her. But the failure to integrate violent action into the dialogue reaches its potentially most ludicrous extreme in the sequence of killings that follow shortly after this. First Titus stabs Tamora with little verbal preparation—''Tis true, 'tis true, witness my knife's sharp point' is all he says—and with no verbal reaction from his victim. Instantly Saturninus kills Titus: 'Die, frantic wretch, for this accursèd deed.' Titus has no dying words. No less rapidly, Lucius takes revenge for his father's death:

> Can the son's eye behold his father bleed?
> There's meed for meed, death for a deadly deed.

He kills Saturninus, who also remains silent.

Understandably the rapid sequence of deaths in this episode—so different in its handling from that of the last scene of *Hamlet*—has provoked writers on the play to irony. Dessen writes of the problem for the director in dealing 'with the staccato murders so as to avoid an unwanted audience reaction', and cites Gordon Crosse's account of Robert Atkins's 1923 Old Vic production in which 'at the end some of us fairly broke down and laughed when the deaths of Tamora, Titus, and Saturninus followed each other within about five seconds, as in a burlesque melodrama'.[12] Nevertheless Dessen and other writers on the play have been at pains to emphasize how directors of the more successful productions have overcome the problems of this and other episodes. Some directors have, quite simply, cheated, either by omitting the most difficult actions or by presenting them in a stylized manner that evades the implications of the original directions. Brook, for example, had the severed heads 'concealed in black cloths and steel baskets' (Dessen, p. 22), and Chiron and Demetrius were murdered off stage.

More interesting in relation to attempts to defend the play as written are productions in which the challenges of the text have been successfully faced and overcome. The earliest of these, we must assume, were the performances given in Shakespeare's own time, since the play is known to have been exceptionally popular. We have too little information about them, but there is at any rate one variation between the quarto and the Folio texts with some bearing on the matter, even though it does not occur in an episode of violence. At the end of the first episode of the opening scene, Saturninus and Bassianus are directed in the quarto to '*go up into the Senate House*' (1.1.63.1); Shakespeare is clearly thinking in terms of the fiction rather than of the theatre, and the instruction is regularly interpreted as a direction for them to ascend on to the upper stage to join Marcus and those Tribunes and Senators who are already there. Later Marcus proclaims Saturninus Emperor (237), after which Saturninus makes a speech. The quarto has no direction at this point, but the Folio, in which a direction for a '*Flourish*' is added before the direction for the ascent, here adds '*A long flourish till they come down.*' The word 'long' draws attention to the fact that Shakespeare has provided no dialogue to cover either the ascent or the descent—in other words, has failed to integrate the action with the dialogue—and shows his original interpreters (perhaps guided by him) helping him out with sound effects.[13]

Later interpreters, too, have resorted to numerous devices designed to increase the plausibility or the effectiveness of moments in the script to which I have drawn attention. For example Brook, 'to accompany the cutting-off of Titus's hand ... produced "a throbbing effect" by playing "two alternating chords quite slowly on the piano within which was a microphone"; he then "over-recorded the result, and slowed it down to make it deeper."'[14] In Gerald Freedman's New York production of 1967, 'Titus's killing of Mutius ... was done in slow motion, with a frightened and apparently prescient Mutius calling for help in advance'; 'no severed heads were visible'; and the triple killing in the last scene was heavily stylized.[15] In a 1974 production at the Oregon Festival, 'the severed heads in III.i were lifelike, but the audience did not see the severed hand; rather, after the amputation, they saw an object covered with a white cloth that had upon it not a bloodstain but a snowdrop pattern of red rhinestones' (p. 29); in a later Oregon production of 1986 'the three murders were done rapidly, but, just as some spectators began to titter at the staccato action, soldiers wafting red banners appeared to cover the bodies and cut off the laugh—a stunning stage effect' (p. 30), and in a 1977 production at the New Jersey Shakespeare Festival 'All the violence was done symbolically or ritualistically' (p. 32). Even in Jane Howell's BBC television production, described by Dessen as 'the most "realistic" *Titus* one is likely to see', the death of Mutius was played in slow motion (pp. 44–8).

Until Deborah Warner directed the play at the Swan in 1987, all productions of the play had used a script that was to some degree, often considerably, shortened and rearranged. Boldly, Warner used a complete and virtually unaltered text. The violence was not shirked. Only the fact that Titus's chopped-off hand and his sons' severed heads were represented by stuffed cloth bags lessened the physical representation of horror. The staging was so simple that it could have transferred to a reconstruction of the Globe—or the Rose, where we believe the play was acted in 1594—with little change. It was nevertheless skilful, even cunning, in its manipulation of audience response so as to evade the unwanted laughter that has often marred performances of this play, and it did this partly by exploiting all the genuine comedy that is latent in the text, along with a little that is not. As Michael Billington wrote in a review, the director's 'wiliest tactic is to pre-empt possible laughter at the play's grosser cruelties by launching them in a spirit of dangerous jocularity' so 'the horror when it comes is all the greater' (Dessen, p. 61). In the last scene she permitted herself a wordless interpolation: servants whistled a merry tune modelled on 'Heigh-ho, heigh-ho, 'tis off to work we go', from *Snow White*, as they carried on the furniture for the Thyestean banquet. I should never have imagined that the subsequent stretch of action, in which Titus kills his own daughter and then, within the space of a few lines, kills Tamora and is himself killed by her husband, who is then killed by Titus's son, could have been so chillingly effective. The chorus of servants played its part, squatting in ranks to each side of the stage before the pie was served, stretching forward in horror at the death of Lavinia, bending as Titus killed Tamora, gasping as Saturninus killed Titus, and finally rushing off through the audience as Lucius killed the Emperor. This choric action both directed and channelled off the audience's reaction.[16]

The success of Warner's production compelled a revaluation of *Titus Andronicus*, which (as I wrote in a review) 'emerged as a far more deeply serious play than its popular reputation would suggest, a play that is profoundly concerned with both the personal and the social consequences of violence rather than one that cheaply exploits their theatrical effectiveness. I was impressed as never before by the art of its structuring: its twin climaxes of violence, one directed at Titus, the other directed by him; by the force of the counteraction, led by Lucius; and by the part played within the whole by details of language, such as the recurrent, increasingly horrific emphasis on "hand" and "hands" (between them, the words occur some seventy times). The production increased my respect, too, for the play's first audiences; groundlings who made this play popular, if they experienced it in full, were not merely seeking cheap thrills. It did not emerge as an unflawed masterpiece in this revelatory production, but subsequent directors will have far less excuse than before for evading its problems by textual adaptation or by evasive theatricalism.'

After that it may seem churlish of me to insist that the points in the play to which I have drawn special attention are flaws rather than straightforward aspects of the play's dramaturgy which, however problematic they may have appeared in the past, have now been vindicated by the demonstration that they can be made to work in a skilful production. After all, it may be argued, every dramatist depends upon the collaboration of his interpreters; a play is as good as it can be made to seem in performance. This is a fair point of view, but we may nevertheless argue that the playwright needs to give his interpreters every possible help and can be faulted for aspects of his technique that are persistently seen as obstacles rather than as helps to successful interpretation.

In any case, my purpose in discussing this particular aspect of Shakespeare's technique is not simply to indulge in what Dessen calls *Titus*-bashing[17] but, among other things, to suggest that comparison of Shakespeare's presentation of violent action in this play with that adopted in other of his early plays may provide us with clues to the chronology of these works. This is of course a highly problematic area of investigation. It would be simplistic to suggest that Shakespeare necessarily progressed in linear fashion from more 'primitivist' conventions to ones that seem more characteristic of his later plays. On the other hand, it seems reasonable to suppose that he learned from experience, so if it is agreed that the episodes I have identified may have caused difficulty in his own theatre as well as to later interpreters, it may be useful to see if there are other early plays in which comparable action is handled in a less problematic manner.

The obvious plays for comparison are the early English histories, traditionally known as the First, Second, and Third Parts of *Henry the Sixth*. Unfortunately the order of composition even of these plays is disputed: the Oxford editors reflect the views of some earlier scholars in placing Part One after the other two. I shall adopt this as a working hypothesis and look first at Part Two, which was first printed in 1594, as *The First Part of the Contention*...This includes no on-stage violence to match the worst excesses of *Titus*, though there are certain comparable episodes. In 2.1, the whipping of Simpcox is well prepared for but is followed by no verbal reaction: the direction reads '*After the Beadle hath hit him once, he leaps over the stool and runs away* ...'. But of course this is a comic rather than a horrific episode, and in the brief sequence that rounds it off we hear Simpcox's wife's defence: 'Alas, sir, we did it for pure need!' At the opening of 2.3 several characters are sentenced to death; they say nothing, but this may seem in keeping with the legal formality of the proceedings, and anyhow they are taken off-stage for punishment. Later in the same scene comes a fight in which '*Peter hits Horner on the head and strikes him down*'. Horner, unlike comparable characters in *Titus*, says something before dying: 'Hold, Peter, hold—I confess, I confess treason.' The opening of Act 3, scene 2 shows the smothering of Duke Humphrey; he says nothing, but the presentation of the action is akin to that of a dumbshow. The following scene opens with a parallel tableau in which Cardinal Beaufort is revealed '*in his bed raving and staring as if he were mad*'; later, as King Henry says, 'He dies and makes no sign', but no violence occurs. In the first scene of Act 4 Suffolk is taken off-stage (line 140) to be decapitated, and the third scene opens with a dumbshow in which '*the Staffords are slain*'. Later (4.6.8) an unnamed Soldier is killed with no reaction. At the beginning of 4.7 comes the dumbshow I have mentioned in which '*Matthew Gough is slain, and all the rest of his men with him*'. Later in the scene Lord Saye, like Suffolk before him, is taken off-stage to be killed; his head, and Sir James Cromer's, are later carried in '*upon two poles*'. Two scenes after this the death of Jack Cade at the hands of Sir Alexander Iden is thoroughly prepared for, and he is given a proper dying speech (4.9.72–5); Iden later enters with Cade's severed head as a gift for the King (5.1.63). The death of Somerset is presented in dumbshow at the opening of the brief 5.2, and the last killing in the play comes in battle when, after 'alarums', '*York killes Clifford.*'

It seems reasonable to suggest on the basis of the evidence presented here that *The First Part of the Contention* shows its author to be more conscious than in *Titus*

Andronicus of the desirability either of keeping violent action off-stage or of giving his actors the opportunity to express appropriate reactions, or of integrating it with the surrounding dialogue.

No one disputes that *The Second Part of the Contention* is later than the First. Although the narrative calls for a lot of killing and decapitation there is little sudden violent action, and its presentation seems to me to show the same process as can be observed in the earlier play. Richard Plantagenet shows Somerset's severed head in the opening episode, but decapitation has occurred before the play begins. The killing of the young Earl of Rutland in 1.3 is well prepared for, and he has a dying speech—of, admittedly, only one line, in Latin. The lead-up to the death of his father, the Duke of York, in the next scene, is one of the most theatrically powerful episodes in all these plays, and after York has been dispatched by both Clifford and Queen Margaret he has a two-line speech:

> Open thy gates of mercy, gracious God—
> My soul flies through these wounds to seek out thee. (1.4.178–9)

In the last Act Warwick enters wounded and eventually dies, but there is no violence and he has a two-line speech. Perhaps the closest approach to the manner in which violence had been presented in *Titus Andronicus* comes with the death of the young Prince Edward, who is stabbed almost ritualistically by King Edward, Richard of Gloucester, and the Earl of Clarence in succession; he has no dying words. Henry VI dies in the play's penultimate scene, stabbed to death by Richard; like Warwick, he has a formal death speech.

Although *Henry the Sixth Part One* calls for many fights, skirmishes, and the like, it presents little sudden violent action, so regrettably offers little evidence germane to my purposes. Joan la Pucelle's fight with the Dauphin in 1.3 is relatively unintegrated, but not conspicuously difficult to present. Salisbury and Gargrave are both mutilated in 1.6, but not in cold blood: chambers are shot off, the two men '*Fall down*', each reacts with a cry to God for mercy, and it is Talbot who tells us what has happened:

> One of thy eyes and thy cheek's side struck off? (1.6.53)

This is horrible enough, but does not require such direct presentation as, for example, the cutting off of Titus's hand. Later in the play Bedford, who has been carried on sick, dies on a five-line speech.

Overall it is my impression that all three of the plays about Henry VI present violence in a more integrated fashion than *Titus Andronicus*. If my contention that this shows a Shakespeare in the process of learning from experience is accepted, it may serve as a crumb of evidence to be placed in the scales along with all the other factors that bear upon the dating of the play to indicate that it precedes the Henry VI plays. The dating of *Titus Andronicus* is exceptionally complicated, as can be seen from the large amount of space devoted to it in the 'Canon and Chronology' section of the Oxford *Textual Companion*.[18] Gary Taylor there tentatively assigns the composition of all but the 'fly' scene to 1592, immediately after 1 *Henry VI*, but concedes that a 'feasible alternative would be to assume that *Titus* belongs to the very beginning of Shakespeare's career, and hence that it was written in 1590 or before'. As it happens, this coincides with Ernst Honigmann's view, based largely on biographical evidence, that this is Shakespeare's first play, though not necessarily that it dates from as early as 1586.[19] Personally I still reserve that honour for *The Two Gentlemen of Verona*,[20] but I am quite prepared to believe that *Titus* followed close upon its heels.

There is one scene of violence in *Titus* that I have not mentioned. In this scene one of the play's characters, Marcus Andronicus, commits an act of violence upon a living creature and kills it. Titus asks what creature it is that has died, and Marcus's reply is followed by a lengthy discussion of the deed and of its consequences for the innocent victim. At first Titus is full of sympathy for the victim, but Marcus's self-justification so convinces Titus that he not only pardons Marcus but declares that he will himself 'insult on' the victim's corpse, which he proceeds to strike twice with Marcus's knife. The victim is unable to express suffering because it is a fly; but the episode is painstakingly, indeed beautifully, integrated into the action.

This fact may surely support the general (though not universal) view that 3.2 is a later addition to the text. It looks forward not only to the last Act of *Hamlet* and the blinding of Gloucester, but to such other subtly integrated, and often symbolically central, episodes as the death of Mercutio, the killing of Cinna the Poet, the murder of Desdemona, and the deaths of Lady Macduff and her children. Like them, it shows us a Shakespeare for whom the portrayal of violence is not simply the pretext for theatrical titillation but a stimulus to meditation on man's place within the chain of being, on the significance and value of human life.

6

The Challenges of *Romeo and Juliet*

The story of Romeo and Juliet—one of the great myths of the Western world—first appeared fully formed in an Italian version of 1530, and since then has had a vigorous afterlife, not all of it deriving from Shakespeare. It has been frequently reincarnated and recollected in a multitude of forms and media—prose narratives, verse narratives, drama, opera, orchestral and choral music, ballet, film, television, and painting among them. Besides being presented seriously it has been parodied and burlesqued; there are several full-scale nineteenth-century travesties of Shakespeare's play,[1] and its balcony scene in particular has often formed the basis for comic sketches. Romeo is a type name for an ardent lover, and Juliet's 'Romeo, Romeo, wherefore art thou Romeo?' is often jokily declaimed even by people who have never read or seen the play.

Already when, around 1594, Shakespeare decided to base a play on the story, he was able to consult more than one version. He worked closely from *The Tragical History of Romeus and Juliet*, by Arthur Brooke (who, like the hero and heroine of the story, himself died young), first published in 1562 and reprinted in 1587. Brooke had used a moralistic French adaptation, by Pierre Boaistuau, of a story by the Italian Matteo Bandello, and Shakespeare probably also read William Painter's translation of Boaistuau in his *Palace of Pleasure*, of 1567.

Brooke's style is, to say the best, uninspired, but he provided Shakespeare with both a well laid-out story and much valuable detail. Brooke treated the events as historical, ending his poem with the statement that

> The bodies dead removed from vault where they did die
> In stately tomb on pillars great of marble raise they high.
> On every side above were set and eke beneath
> Great store of cunning epitaphs in honour of their death.
> And even at this day the tomb is to be seen,
> So that among the monuments that in Verona been
> There is no monument more worthy of the sight
> Than is the tomb of Juliet, and Romeus her knight.

These lines clearly influenced the end of Shakespeare's play, in which the effect of the lovers' deaths is to some extent alleviated by the consequent reconciliation of their feuding families; and the alleged historicity of the tale continues to be of value to the Veronese tourist industry.

For most people at the present time Shakespeare's play embodies the classic version of the story. But, although it is widely read and frequently performed, it has itself undergone adaptation, sometimes slight, sometimes substantial, in ways that are implicitly critical of the original. The play's ending has proved especially subject to alteration. In a lost version by James Howard performed shortly after the restoration of the monarchy in 1660, the tragedy was endowed with a happy ending (or perhaps one should say an even happier ending: one of my old professors, responding to a lady who said, after seeing a performance of Shakespeare's play, that she wished it ended happily, mischievously asked 'O, don't you think it does?'). The result was that (as the prompter Downes wrote) 'when the tragedy was revived again 'twas played alternately, tragical one day and tragicomical another for several days altogether'.[2] Not long after this, in 1680, Thomas Otway wrote a new play, *Caius Marius*, borrowing much of Shakespeare's dialogue. Apparently Otway was dissatisfied with Shakespeare's conclusion, in which R᷈ before Juliet recovers from the sleeping potion given to her by the Friar. Otway, clearly—and perhaps rightly—thinking that Shakespeare had missed a good opportunity for an affecting passage of dialogue, conceived the notion of causing his heroine to wake before her lover expired, and gave them a touching duologue. When Theophilus Cibber came to adapt Shakespeare's play, in 1744, he incorporated passages from Otway, including the death scene, with only minor changes, and around the same time David Garrick, in a version that follows Shakespeare's text more closely, nevertheless seized upon Otway's basic idea, while writing a new duologue for the lovers in which they go successively mad. This was accepted into the theatrical tradition, and although the American Charlotte Cushman (playing Romeo) returned to Shakespeare in the mid-nineteenth century, Garrick's version appears not to have been completely abandoned until Henry Irving put on the play in 1882.

Garrick's death scene is easily guyed: 'Bless me! how cold it is!' says Juliet on waking, and later, 'And did I wake for this!'; yet Francis Gentleman, writing in 1770, praised it highly: 'no play ever received greater advantage from alteration than this tragedy, especially in the last act; bringing Juliet to life before Romeo dies, is undoubtedly a change of infinite merit. The whole dying scene does Mr Garrick great credit.'[3] In its day, and for long afterwards, it must have been highly actable—and it gave the performer of Romeo a stronger death scene than Shakespeare had provided. Bernard Shaw, writing in 1894, described his first experience of the play, 'in which Romeo, instead of dying forthwith when he took the poison, was interrupted by Juliet, who sat up and made him carry her down to the footlights, where she complained of being very cold, and had to be warmed by a love scene, in the middle of which Romeo, who had forgotten all about the poison, was taken ill and died'.[4] No modern director would be likely to interpolate Garrick's words into Shakespeare's text, but in more than one production the terrible irony of the situation has been pointed by Juliet's showing signs of life as Romeo dies which are visible to the audience though not to him.[5]

In the twentieth century English-speaking productions have at least taken Shakespeare's original text as their point of departure, though the denouement was radically altered in one of Stratford's more iconoclastic versions, the one directed by Michael Bogdanov in 1986. This modem-dress production came to be known as the *Alfa-Romeo and Juliet* because of the presence on stage during part of the action of a bright red sports car. Characteristically of this director, it had a strong political slant which manifested itself especially in his handling of the ending. Academic critics have suggested that when Montague and Capulet say that they will 'raise the lovers' statues in pure gold' they are revealing false, materialistic values.[6] Bogdanov translated this suggestion into theatrical terms. His text came to a halt with Juliet's death; the dead lovers were covered with golden cloths and then, during a brief blackout, they sprang to attention and stood as their own statues, the final episode became a wordless media event, as reporters and photographers flooded the scene, the survivors posed in attitudes suggestive rather of a desire to have their photographs published in *Hello!* magazine than of either true grief or reconciliation, and the Prince spoke part of the prologue—omitted at the start—transposed to the past tense.

In this essay I want to concentrate on the text as it has come down to us in editions based normally on the 'good' Quarto of 1599 (though often incorporating stage directions, and occasionally other readings, from the 'bad' Quarto of two years before) and on some of the challenges faced by directors who try to translate this text into terms of modern theatre. I do not intend to be judgemental about this text; indeed, I shall deliberately refrain from expressing my own opinions about its theatrical viability. Theatre history clearly shows that lines, speeches, whole episodes that were unacceptable in other ages, and in other theatres than those of today, have been restored to theatrical life in more recent productions. Even so, the programme for Adrian Noble's, in 1995, admitted to the omission of about 564 lines—getting on for 20 per cent of the complete text. That presumably represented Noble's judgement of what could be made to work by his particular actors in the Royal Shakespeare Theatre before the audiences going to that theatre in the theatrical conditions pertaining in 1995. It did not, I take it, claim to present an absolute judgement on the text's theatrical viability. Different textual cuts might be made in different circumstances even at the present time; it will be interesting to see if a full text will be presented in the new Globe, and if so, how it will work.

As I have said, twentieth-century productions, at least since John Gielgud's of 1935, in which he and Laurence Olivier successively played Romeo and Mercutio, and which also had Peggy Ashcroft as Juliet and Edith Evans as the Nurse, have tended to play fuller and purer texts than those of earlier ages; the BBC radio production by the Renaissance Theatre Company, available on audio cassette, uses a full text, but that is a special case, and it has to be admitted that even in our time some of the most theatrically exciting productions, including those of Peter Brook at Stratford in 1947 and Franco Zeffirelli at the Old Vic in 1960, have cut and otherwise altered the text extensively, presenting their vision of it in terms of the theatre of their time rather than offering text-centred performances. Indeed, both the directors I have named explicitly rejected engagement with the text's literary values; Brook declared that 'To come to the theatre merely to listen to the words was the last decadence', and Zeffirelli is reported to have 'said repeatedly that he had no use for [the play's] verse'.[7] And even directors who have been less radical in their treatment of the text than Brook and Bogdanov have made extensive cuts. Later I shall try to identify some of the main areas that have presented problems, and to suggest some reasons why they have done so.

The modern director's task is complicated by the fact that, since Shakespeare wrote, the story of the fated lovers has attracted many other creative artists, some of whom have drawn exclusively on Shakespeare, some on other versions of the tale, and others who have mixed the traditions. There is no reason, for instance, to suppose that Tchaikovsky went beyond Shakespeare for his immensely popular fantasy overture of 1869 (later revised), or Prokofiev and his choreographers for their ballet, first performed in 1938; on the other hand, Bellini's opera *I Capuleti ed i Montecchi* (1830) appears to owe nothing to Shakespeare (though its double death scene bears a suspicious resemblance to Garrick's), and the librettists of the only other successful opera based on the story, Gounod's *Roméo et Juliette* (1867), incorporated Garrick's tomb scene into their work, as does Berlioz (wordlessly) in his dramatic symphony of 1839.

The existence and popularity of symphonic, operatic, balletic, filmic, and other offshoots is relevant to the performance history of the play itself because they create images that superimpose themselves on the Shakespearean text, forming expectations in the imaginations of the play's interpreters and audiences which subtly affect our response to efforts to translate that text into performance. In the wonderful *scène d'amour* in Berlioz's work, long-breathed phrases accompanied by rhythmical pulsations speak eloquently of passionate yearning in a manner that would not lead listeners to expect the humour that also lies latent in Shakespeare's dialogue; and Berlioz's musical depiction of the gradual dispersal of the masquers into the night, apparently strumming their guitars and humming snatches of half-remembered song, is not only theatrical as well as musical in its effect but appeared to be reflected, whether consciously or not, in one of the more sensitively directed episodes of Michael Bogdanov's production with the dying away of the sounds of motorbikes as revellers left the Capulets' ball. In a different way, the long tradition of scenically spectacular productions, aided and abetted by the popularity of Zeffirelli's film, with its beautiful Tuscan settings, may lead theatregoers to expect visual splendours.

Also relevant to modern theatrical interpretations is the play's complex literary background. Although the often incandescent quality of its verse is responsible for much of the admiration that the play has evoked, at the same time its self-conscious literariness has repeatedly been implicitly or explicitly criticized as detrimental to its theatrical effectiveness. 'It is a dramatic poem rather than a drama', wrote Henry Irving, 'and I mean to treat it from that point of view.'[8] For all that, he omitted a lot of its poetry while succeeding, according to Henry James, only in making 'this enchanting poem' 'dull ... mortally slow' and 'tame' by 'smothering' it 'in its accessories'.[9] The history of critical and theatrical reactions to the play demonstrates the fact that Shakespeare worked in a far more literary mode than has been fashionable in the theatre of later ages, and that its literariness has often been regarded as a theatrical handicap.

In a memorable tribute, T. J. B. Spencer wrote that 'Nothing in European drama had hitherto achieved the organisation of so much human experience when Shakespeare, at the age of about thirty, undertook the story of Juliet and Romeo.'[10] The manner in which the play organizes experience is highly self-conscious and deeply indebted to a variety of literary traditions. Many devices of parallelism and repetition create an almost architectural sense of structure. This structure is defined by the appearances of the Prince of Verona. Some productions bring him on to speak the Prologue, appropriately enough since his three appearances within the action have something of a choric function. We first see him in his own right as he enters to exercise his authority at the height of the brawl between the followers of Montague and Capulet in the opening scene; he makes one formal though impassioned speech, and his departure marks a turning point from the public to the private action of the play as Benvolio, after recapitulating what has happened in lines that are usually abbreviated, describes the symptoms of Romeo's love-sickness for Rosaline. The Prince's second appearance comes at the climax of the play's second violent episode, culminating in the killing of Tybalt and Mercutio, which provokes him to another display of authority as he banishes Romeo, the principal turning point of the action; and he reappears in the final scene to preside over the investigation into the lovers' deaths and to apportion responsibility. His are the closing lines which round off the play, returning it to the condition of myth:

> For never was a story of more woe
> Than this of Juliet and her Romeo.

The formality evident in the appearances of the Prince recurs in many other aspects of the play's design. Shakespeare is still sometimes regarded as an inspired improviser, and perhaps in some plays he was, but it is impossible not to feel that before he started to write the dialogue of this play he worked out a ground plan as carefully as if he had been designing an intricate building. One could point, for example, to the parallels in function between Mercutio and the Nurse, both of whom are almost entirely of Shakespeare's creation: he a companion and foil to Romeo, she to Juliet, he consciously mocking Romeo's romanticism with high-spirited, bawdy cynicism, she no less earthy but less aware of the sexual implications of much of what she says, each of them involuntarily failing their companion in their greatest need, he through his accidental death which turns the play from a romantic comedy into a tragedy, she because of the limitations in her understanding of the depths of Juliet's love which leave Juliet to face her fate alone. There are parallels too in the design of scenes: the Capulets' bustling preparations for the ball (1.5) are echoed in those for Juliet's marriage to Paris (4.4); and each of the play's three love duets—one in the evening, at the ball, the second at night, in the garden and on its overlooking balcony, the third at dawn, as the lovers, now married, prepare to part—is interrupted by calls from the Nurse.

These features of the play's structure create an impression of highly patterned formality; they may be regarded as dramatic strengths; and in any case a director can scarcely avoid them without rewriting the play, but there are others that have often suffered under the blue pencil. For example, at a number of points characters recapitulate action that has already been enacted before us. In the opening scene, Benvolio spends ten lines satirically describing Tybalt's intervention in the fray between the servants of the Montagues and Capulets; later, after the fight in which both Mercutio and Tybalt are killed, Benvolio again recapitulates what has happened, this time in twenty-three lines of verse; and in the closing scene the Friar, notoriously, after claiming 'I will be brief', recapitulates the full story of the lovers in one of the longest speeches of a play that is not short of long speeches. 'It is much to be lamented', wrote Johnson, 'that the poet did not conclude the dialogue with the action, and avoid a narrative of events which the audience already knew.'[11]

This technique of recapitulation can be, and has been, defended; for example, Bertrand Evans remarks that, 'far from being a repetitious exercise best deleted on the stage, the Friar's speech is an indispensable part of the total experience of the tragedy; not to be present when some key participants learn how their acts resulted in the pile of bodies in the Capulet tomb—Romeo's, Juliet's, Tybalt's, Paris's—would be to miss too much'.[12] Certainly these speeches constitute a challenge that should be accepted by directors concerned to present the text in its integrity; for the actors, I take it, the challenge is to seek out a psychological subtext that will help them to deliver the lines not merely as a summary of what has gone before but as utterances emanating naturally and spontaneously from the characters as they have conceived it. Performers of Benvolio can portray his summaries of the action as the reactions of a well-meaning but puzzled man desperately attempting to make sense of what has happened; the Friar's long speech has been played in more than one production less as a judicial apportioning of blame (which it unequivocally is in Berlioz, where the role of the Friar encompasses some of the functions of Shakespeare's Prince) than as the frightened reactions of a man who fears he has betrayed his responsibility; the reactions of the other on-stage characters as he reveals the secrets, previously unknown to them, of the marriage and the potion are no less important than his own state of mind as he speaks. Nevertheless the speech has been implicitly criticized by directors concerned to streamline the action; Peter Brook and Michael Bogdanov omitted it altogether,[13] and all twelve of the Stratford productions since Brook's have shortened it, some considerably.

The deliberation of the play's structure is of a piece with its self-conscious, even ostentatious literariness and intellectualism. 'Now is he for the numbers that Petrarch flowed in. Laura, to his lady, was a kitchen wench', says Mercutio of Romeo, whom he believes to be still in love with the 'pale, hard hearted wench' Rosaline, as if to draw attention to Shakespeare's indebtedness to the Petrarchan tradition, well established in England at the time he was writing, of the besotted lover sighing in vain for an unresponsive beloved—a situation that he was to dramatize directly in the figures of Silvius and Phoebe in *As You Like It* and that is also related to that of the chaste young man with no interest in ensuring his own posterity who is addressed in the first seventeen of Shakespeare's sonnets. The explicit reference to a major literary influence on the play—also omitted in most modern performances—is a counterpart to the appearance on stage of a volume of Ovid in *Titus Andronicus*.

The literary form most strongly associated with Petrarchism was the sonnet. The Argument to Brooke's poem is in sonnet form, and *Romeo and Juliet*, written during the ten or so years when the amatory sonnet cycle was enjoying a vogue greater than ever before or since, makes direct use of the complete form in the Prologue, in the rarely performed Chorus to Act 2, and, famously, in the shared sonnet spoken between the lovers on their first meeting. At a number of other points, too, such as the speech by the Prince that ends the play, Shakespeare uses the six-line rhyming unit ending in a couplet that forms the final part of the sonnet form as used by Shakespeare and which is also the stanza form of his narrative poem *Venus and Adonis*, of 1593. Other well established literary conventions, less obvious to the modern playgoer, that influence the play include the epithalamium, reflected in Juliet's great speech beginning 'Gallop apace, you fiery-footed steeds', and the dawn-parting, or 'alba'—one of the most universal of poetic themes—which provides the basic structure for the entire scene of dawn-parting between Romeo and Juliet.[14]

The play's creative use of conventions of lyric poetry is responsible for much of its enduring popularity as perhaps the greatest of all expressions of romantic love; it is complemented and to some extent counterbalanced by an intellectualism manifesting itself especially in complex wordplay that has stood the passage of time less well and has often been censured (and, in recent times, defended) by literary critics as well as being subjected to the more practical criticism of being excised from acting texts. David Garrick, in the Advertisement to his 1748 adaptation, states his 'design... to clear the original as much as possible from the jingle and quibble which were always thought the great objections to reviving it'. 'Jingle' refers to Shakespeare's extensive use of rhyme, regarded by neo-classical critics as indecorous in tragedy; Garrick's modifications—which included reducing the sonnet form of the lovers' declaration to two quatrains—reduced the play's range of poetic style.

'Quibble' is, if anything, even more integral than rhyme to the effect of the play as Shakespeare wrote it. Wordplay extends from the bawdy of the servants' comic opening dialogue, through the self-conscious jesting of Mercutio and the often involuntary double entendres of the Nurse, up to passages of quibbling wordplay spoken in wholly serious, even tragic circumstances by Romeo and Juliet them-selves. Modern performers and audiences have been educated into an easier accept-ance of wordplay than Garrick, partly as a result of its serious use in post-Freudian literature, above all by James Joyce (whose 'stream of consciousness' technique is anticipated by the Nurse), and also by studies encouraging a historical awareness of its prevalence in uncomic writings by Shakespeare and his contemporaries, such as John Donne. Even so, cuts made in acting versions of the present day suggest that the quibble is still more easily regarded as an ingredient of comedy than as a vehicle of tragic effect. This springs, perhaps, from too limited a notion both of what Shakespeare may encompass within the portmanteau definition of tragedy, and of the language appropriate to the form—if, indeed, it can properly be called a form. It has often been observed that for much of its considerable length *Romeo and Juliet*—especially if, as in Bogdanov's production, the Prologue is omitted—comes closer to our expectations of romantic comedy than of such a tragedy as the one that immediately precedes it in Shakespeare's output, *Titus Andronicus*, to which *Romeo and Juliet* might be regarded as a deliberately contrasting companion piece. If directors are to realize this script in its full richness they need to free themselves of the conventional connotations of tragedy and to play each episode in its own terms. And if audiences are to meet Shakespeare on his own terms they must find room in their responses not only for the direct if poetically heightened expression of heartfelt emotion that has caused the balcony scene to be valued as perhaps the most eloquent of all depictions of romantic love, but also for the contrived artifi-ciality with which Shakespeare endows even the lovers' language at some of the most impassioned points of the play's action. This is not only a 'most excellent and lamentable tragedy', as the title-page of the 1599 quarto puts it, it is also, in the terms of the title-page of the 'bad' quarto of 1597, 'an excellent conceited tragedy'—which I suppose might be paraphrased as a tragedy notable for the ingenuity of its verbal expression. Under the surface of the play's poetry lies a complicated network of rhetorical figures that are rarely recognized by even the more erudite among the play's modern readers. This poses great problems for the actors, as Bernard Shaw recognized when he wrote 'It should never be forgotten in judging an attempt to play Romeo and Juliet that the parts are made almost impossible except to actors of positive genius, skilled to the last degree in metrical declamation, by the way in which the poetry, magnificent as it is, is interlarded by the miserable rhetoric and silly lyrical conceits which were the foible of the Elizabethans.'[15] The conceit with which Juliet imagines her and her lover's fate after death, with its hidden wordplay on the sexual sense of 'die', is as extreme as anything in metaphysical poetry:

> when I shall die
> [or 'he shall die', according to the unauthoritative fourth
>   quarto and some later editors]
> Take him and cut him out in little stars,
> And he will make the face of heaven so fine
> That all the world will be in love with night
> And pay no worship to the garish sun. (3.2.21–5)

Even more difficult, I take it, are the play's several extended passages of dialogue in which characters are required, on the basis of misunderstanding or of false information, to act out emotions that, as the audience knows, the true situation does not justify. One such passage comes just after the lines I have quoted. Juliet's Nurse enters with the cords designed to make a rope ladder to give Romeo access to Juliet at night. 'Wringing her hands', as the bad quarto's direction and the good quarto's dialogue tell us, she bemoans Tybalt's death, of which Juliet has not heard, but in such a way that Juliet thinks Romeo, not Tybalt, is dead. In a sense the episode is an extended piece of wordplay on the pronoun 'he':

> Ah, welladay! He's dead, he's dead, he's dead!
> We are undone, lady, we are undone.
> Alack the day, he's gone, he's killed, he's dead! (3.2.37–9)

So says the Nurse, speaking of Tybalt, but Juliet takes her to refer to Romeo, and even when the Nurse speaks directly of Romeo—

> O Romeo, Romeo,
> Who ever would have thought it Romeo? (3.2.41–2)

Juliet takes her to mean that Romeo is the victim, not the killer. The misunderstanding continues through a long episode in which Juliet again resorts to complex wordplay:

> Hath Romeo slain himself? Say thou but 'Ay',
> And that bare vowel 'I' shall poison more
> Than the death-darting eye of cockatrice.
> I am not I if there be such an 'Ay',
> Or those eyes shut that makes thee answer 'Ay'.
> If he be slain, say 'Ay'; or if not, 'No'.
> Brief sounds determine of my weal or woe. (3.2.45–51)

Not until the Nurse resorts to plain statement is the misunderstanding clarified:

> Tybalt is gone and Romeo banishèd.
> Romeo that killed him—he is banishèd. (3.2.69–70)

And even then Juliet launches into a highly mannered lament, full of the oxymorons that are a conspicuous feature of this play's style. This scene has regularly been abbreviated in post-war Stratford productions, every one of which has omitted or shortened the wordplay on 'I', and most of which have abbreviated the oxymorons.

The artifice both of situation and of style in this scene is bound to have a distancing effect; it displays wit on the part of both Shakespeare and Juliet, yet for Juliet the situation is tragic. She needs to speak her lines with a high degree of intellectual control which may seem at odds with the spontaneous expression of deeply felt emotion. But perhaps this is the point: M. M. Mahood regards the puns on 'I' as 'one of Shakespeare's first attempts to reveal a profound disturbance of mind by the use of quibbles'[16] and Jill Levenson too regards Juliet's withdrawal from emotional expression as psychologically plausible: 'Juliet's prothalamium quickly shrinks to mere word-play and sound effects as she glimpses calamity in the Nurse's report, the swift reduction implying that absolute grief has arrested Juliet's imagination.'[17] Those are, I think, subjectively interpretative rather than objectively descriptive comments, but they suggest ways in which the performer may face the need to hold emotion in suspense, as it were, so that we appreciate the paradox of the situation while retaining sympathy with Juliet's plight.

Juliet faces a rather similar situation a little later, when her mother mistakes her grief at Romeo's banishment for mourning for her cousin Tybalt's death combined with anger at his killer, Romeo. She dissembles her true feelings in a series of quibbles and paradoxes:

> Indeed, I never shall be satisfied
> With Romeo till I behold him, dead,
> Is my poor heart so for a kinsman vexed.
> Madam, if you could find out but a man
> To bear a poison, I would temper it
> That Romeo should, upon receipt thereof,

Soon sleep in quiet. O, how my heart abhors
To hear him named and cannot come to him
To wreak the love I bore my cousin
Upon his body that hath slaughtered him! (3.5.93–102)

Johnson comments that 'Juliet's equivocations are rather too artful for a mind disturbed by the loss of a new lover',[18] and they are shortened or cut in the promptbooks of all the productions I have mentioned except one;[19] but perhaps the cleverness of style here is more encompassable than that in the previous scene as an expression of Juliet's bewilderment as she tries to respond to her mother's misplaced sympathy without actually perjuring herself; perhaps, indeed, it should teach us that wit is not incompatible with tragic effect.

The play's most notorious instance of discrepancy between what characters can be expected to be feeling and the manner in which it is expressed is the scene of mourning following the discovery of Juliet's supposedly dead body. The keening starts with the Nurse's words 'O lamentable day!', and is taken up successively by Lady Capulet, Paris, and Old Capulet in a formalized liturgy of grief whose repetitions culminate in the Nurse's

O woe! O woeful, woeful, woeful day!
Most lamentable day! Most woeful day
That ever, ever, I did yet behold!
O day, O day, O day, O hateful day,
Never was seen so black a day as this!
O woeful day, O woeful day! (4.4.80–5)

These lines take us into the world of Pyramus and Thisbe; indeed, one of the reasons for the hypothesis that *A Midsummer Night's Dream* dates from later than *Romeo and Juliet* (about which I am doubtful) is the suggestion that Bottom's expressions of grief over the corpse of Thisbe burlesque the Nurse's over Juliet. But it is all too easy for the lines to burlesque themselves. The classic objections to the passage were put by Coleridge:

As the audience knows that Juliet is not dead, this scene is, perhaps, excusable. But it is a strong warning to minor dramatists not to introduce at one time many separate characters agitated by one and the same circumstance. It is difficult to understand what effect, whether that of pity or of laughter, Shakespeare meant to produce;—the occasion and the characteristic speeches are so little in harmony![20]

Over a century later Granville-Barker remarked that 'even faithful Shakespeareans have little good to say of that competition in mourning between Paris and Capulet, Lady Capulet and the Nurse. It has been branded as deliberate burlesque.' He attempts a defence, but admits that 'The passage does jar a little.'[21] Most attempts to justify the scene have proposed that the blatant artificiality of the mourners' expressions of grief represents a deliberate distancing effect, forcing the audience to recall that Juliet is not actually dead even though these people believe her to be so. These defences tend to seem half-hearted and lame.[22] Scholarship came to the aid of criticism when Charles Lower, observing that the passage is particularly inadequately reported in the first quarto, proposed that this is because the lines were delivered simultaneously in the performance on which that text is putatively based: in other words, that the speeches were intended to convey a generalized impression of mourning, not be listened to in their own right.[23] The Oxford editors, while not accepting that this was Shakespeare's original intention as represented in the 'good' quarto, nevertheless (in keeping with their aim of representing the plays so far as possible as they were acted) print the direction '*Paris, Capulet and his Wife, and the Nurse all at once wring their hands and cry out together.*' Whether this represents Shakespeare's own solution of a problem with which he had presented himself, or merely an evasion of it, we can't tell. The scene of mourning, and the episode with the Musicians that follows, have often been omitted and, I think, always abbreviated, even in recent times. Nevertheless, at least one director had anticipated the editors: Peter Holding records that in Terry Hands's 1973 Stratford production this episode, so far from being ridiculous, was

Perhaps the most affecting...successive speakers picked up the tone of lament from their predecessor, overlapping with some of the final phrases and then developing the cry with appropriate personal embellishments. The emotion of the lament was sincere but kept at a certain distance, while allowing the audience simultaneously to enjoy the fact that of course Juliet was still alive.[24]

The scene was handled in similar fashion in Adrian Noble's production.

Holding's comment reminds us that these texts, for all their undoubted literary quality, are, fundamentally, scripts for performance, and that at too many points we simply lack information about how their author intended them to be realized on the stage. A successful surmounting in any given production of problems that have previously seemed acute may vindicate Shakespeare's judgement, but equally may simply demonstrate the ingenuity of the interpreter. All criticism must be provisional.

Although there are uncertainties about tone in various passages of the play, perhaps its greatest glory is the wide range of its literary style in both prose and verse, encompassing the vivid, frequently obscene colloquialisms of the servants in the opening scene and elsewhere, the more elegant witticisms of the young blades, the fantasticalities of Mercutio, the controlled inconsequentialities of the Nurse, the humane sententiousness of the Friar, the dignified passion of the Prince, the lyricism of the lovers and also the increasing intensity of their utterance as tragedy overcomes them. Even as one attempts to characterize the play's stylistic range one is conscious of the inadequacy of the attempt to do so within a brief compass, but it may at least be worth insisting that the play is not simply, as the novelist George Moore described it, 'no more than a love-song in dialogue'.[25] No play that Shakespeare—or anyone else—had written up to this date deploys so wide a range of literary expressiveness, and very few later plays do so, either. And it is partly as a result of this stylistic diversity and richness that the play offers so wide a range of opportunities to actors. Performers of minor roles such as Samson and Gregory, Peter, and even the Apothecary—who speaks only seven lines, though he is also picturesquely described by Romeo in lines that provide a challenge to the make-up department—can create a strong impression within a short space. On the other hand, some of the more important characters may seem, at least on the printed page, to lack individuality—by which I suppose I mean that their speeches seem more important for what is said than for who says them. Obviously this is true of the two speeches given to the anonymous Chorus, in which the authorial voice is most apparent. Johnson regarded the second chorus as pointless: 'The use of this chorus is not easily discovered, it conduces nothing to the progress of the play, but relates what is already known, or what the next scene will show; and relates it without adding the improvement of any moral sentiment',[26] and it has almost always been omitted in performance. The obvious functionality of the speeches of the Prince puts them in a similar category, which no doubt is why some directors have had him speak the opening Chorus while, conversely, Peter Brook gave his closing lines to the actor who had spoken the Chorus (who also played Benvolio). The Prince is an authority figure who quells the opening brawl with passionate indignation, exiles Romeo for killing Tybalt, and takes command in the final scene; but we know nothing about him personally except that he is a kinsman of both Mercutio and Paris, and feels some responsibility for their deaths:

> And I, for winking at your discords, too
> Have lost a brace of kinsmen. (5.3.293–4)

It is just enough to create a sense of personal involvement, and his response—'We still have known thee for a holy man'—to the Friar's offer of himself as a sacrifice can be moving, but does not invite detailed characterization. Paris is a relatively undercharacterized role, hard to bring to life, and Benvolio—who is more interesting as satirized by Mercutio (3.1.5–33) than in his own right—vanishes without trace soon afterwards. Tybalt is potentially more interesting—in Bogdanov's production he was having an intralineal affair with Lady Capulet—in spite of Shaw's view that 'Tybalt's is such an unmercifully bad part that one can hardly demand anything from its representation except that he should brush his hair when he comes to his uncle's ball (a condition which he invariably repudiates) and that he should be so consummate a swordsman as to make it safe for Romeo to fall upon him with absolute abandonment...'.[27] If these roles constitute challenges to their performers, it is in remaining content with being cast as lay figures: 'don't do something, just stand there'. The composition of the play requires relative colourlessness from some of its constituent parts.

In other roles the challenge lies mainly in suggesting that the lines of the play have not been just learned by the actor, but spring spontaneously from the character he is playing. Friar Laurence has some characteristics in common with the Prince in the relative impersonality of his many sententious, generalizing remarks, but he has a longer role, plays a crucial part in the play's action, and is far more personally involved with a number of the characters. Though the role is not an obvious gift to an actor, it offers opportunities for suggesting a warmly human, compassionate, and even vulnerable man beneath the clerical garb, as Robert Demeger showed in the Bogdanov production when, looking exhausted after his efforts to rouse Romeo out of his almost suicidal depression, he watched Romeo go off and then, sighing with relief, produced a cigarette from beneath his scapular and took a quick drag on it. And in Adrian Noble's 1995 production Julian Glover virtually stole the show as a Friar who kept a chemistry set on a bench in his cell and, as Michael Billington wrote, 'work[ed] up Juliet's death potion from old chemistry books to her fascination'.[28]

If the challenge to the actor in the role of the Friar is to seek out a humanizing subtext, with other roles the problem lies rather in discrepancies of behaviour or of style which the actor may leave unresolved but, at least if he has been trained in the school of Stanislavski, may otherwise seek to reconcile into some semblance of psychological consistency. For much of the action Capulet seems an amiable old buffer genuinely fond of his daughter; when we first see him he expresses the fear that she is too young to be married and declares

> But woo her, gentle Paris, get her heart;
> My will to her consent is but a part,
> And, she agreed, within her scope of choice
> Lies my consent and fair-according voice. (1.2.14–17)

Yet when it comes to the point he reacts with uncontrolled violence to Juliet's prayers that she be not forced into a marriage which we know would be bigamous, in a display of angry indignation that culminates in threats of physical violence.

> An you be mine, I'll give you to my friend.
> An you be not, hang, beg, starve, die in the streets,
> For, by my soul, I'll ne'er acknowledge thee,
> Nor what is mine shall never do thee good. (3.5.191–4)

Is Shakespeare simply careless of consistency, providing his actor here with a strong set piece, regardless of what has come before? Or is he expecting his actor to lead up to this passage by making what he can of earlier signs of tetchiness in Capulet, as for instance in his harsh words to Tybalt at the dance (1.5.75–87), or even by suggesting, as Bogdanov did, that Capulet is more concerned that his daughter should advance his family's social status than achieve personal happiness? Perhaps modern audiences are more conscious of inconsistency of characterization than those of Shakespeare's time; although I found Bogdanov's capitalist monster a caricature, I was also disturbed by the absence of transition in the Adrian Noble production.

If Capulet's rage is a concerted set piece such as might form the basis for an impressive bass aria in an opera by Handel or Rossini, Mercutio's Queen Mab speech is a solo set piece that actually forms the basis of a tenor aria in Berlioz's dramatic symphony; in fact his scherzetto is Mercutio's only verbal contribution to the work, and—along with the Friar's impressive concluding exordium—the only part of it to use words at all close to Shakespeare's; Berlioz apparently regarded the speech as so important, or at least so appealing, that he also composed an orchestral scherzo, 'Queen Mab, the spirit of dreams', which opens Part 4. Within the play it complicates the role of Mercutio in a way that may help to account for the fascination that it has held for actors, audiences, and readers. Mercutio's role—like Shylock's, which also encompasses elements so diverse that they have sometimes been held to be incompatible—has been accused of having taken on a life of its own that endangers the dramatic balance; indeed, according to Dryden, Shakespeare 'said himself that he was forced to kill him in the third act, to prevent being killed by him'.[29] This is nonsense, I think; Shakespeare developed the role from a hint in his sources as a foil to Romeo and a counterpart to the Nurse, and Mercutio's death is an essential element in the plot. But the Queen Mab speech has been regarded as a charming excrescence, a piece of self-indulgence on Shakespeare's part that is difficult to integrate into both the play and the role—to Granville-Barker, 'as much and as little to be dramatically justified as a song in an opera is';[30] and more recently Edward Pearlman has proposed that Shakespeare interpolated the speech after completing his first version of the play, remarking that 'without the Queen Mab speech, Mercutio is consistent and coherent; once the speech is added, his character is incoherent on the page and must be reinvented by the collaboration of performer and audience or by the ingenuity and faith of stage-literate readers.'[31] It has also, of course, been defended.[32] Richard David wrote that 'its main purpose ... is to create a gossamer sense of uneasy mystery so that Romeo's supernatural forebodings do not fall on altogether unprepared ground'.[33] That may be true in terms of the play but probably would not be of much use to an actor trying to reconcile its fancifulness with Mercutio's mocking obscenity else-where. But audiences rarely feel it as a problem—or even actors, because for all the accusations of irrelevance this speech generally survives the blue pencil. Mercutio's wordplay, bawdy as it is, marks him as a clever man, and there is a cerebral quality to Queen Mab that is in line with this. In any case the speech is moving into obscenity in its closing lines, when Mercutio's fancy seems in danger of getting out of hand and

Romeo halts him in his tracks as if to save him from his over-heated imaginings, provoking Mercutio to deny their validity:

> I talk of dreams,
> Which are the children of an idle brain,
> Begot of nothing but vain fantasy,
> Which is as thin of substance as the air,
> And more inconstant than the wind... (1.4.96–100)

in terms that demonstrate the very 'fantasy' that he is denigrating. The role seems to me to be one of fascinating complexity rather than of irreconcilable discrepancies; but it certainly faces the actor with challenges in the handling of verse. In recent times it has become complicated by psychological interpretations of subtext proposing that the evident homosociality of the young men verges on, or even merges into, homosexuality. In Terry Hands's Swan Theatre production of 1989 the actor conveyed in both gesture and body language an intense but undirected sexuality that motivated the bawdy; a sense of male bonding not quite amounting to direct homosexuality was conveyed in one of the character's bawdiest passages (2.1), full of fantasies about Romeo's sexuality, in which he leapt on Benvolio's back and groped his crotch as if impelled to mock the absent Romeo by the pressure of repressed impulses within himself. Later he kissed Romeo on the lips, heartily if not lingeringly.

Perhaps the most complete character in the play as written is that of the Nurse, one of Shakespeare's few (if unknowing) gifts to actresses who are no longer able to play young women. The main danger here, in my experience, is sentimentalization. I remember a production at Stratford by John Barton and Karolos Koun in 1965 in which the role was sensitively played by a deeply sympathetic actress, Elizabeth Spriggs, but in which she made what seemed to me to be the mistake of suggesting that the Nurse's attempts to reconcile Juliet to the thought of marrying Paris went against the grain, as if she was doing her duty by the parents while identifying with the desires of the daughter. It was interesting but implausible.

The roles of which I have spoken so far are all ones that can be played by what are known as character actors. Romeo and Juliet themselves come firmly into the category of romantic lead, with all the challenges and problems that the term implies. For one thing, there is the matter of age. Juliet is emphatically and repeatedly stated to be not yet 14. This may not have caused difficulties when the role was played by a highly trained boy; now that women have taken over, it is often said that actors with the experience to encompass the technical difficulties of the part will inevitably be too old to look it. But recent directors seem to have more difficulty in casting plausible Romeos than Juliets. His exact age is not given, but too many actors, Ian McKellen among them, in 1976, when he was, I believe, 35—and, I should say, Kenneth Branagh in the sound recording—try too hard to look and/or sound younger than their years.

Henry James wrote that 'it is with Romeo as with Juliet; by the time an actor has acquired the assurance necessary for playing the part, he has lost his youth and his slimness'.[34] Though the role is a passionate one it is not heroic, which may explain why it has appealed to women. By all accounts the most successful Romeo of the nineteenth century was Charlotte Cushman, playing to the Juliet of her sister Susan. Admittedly the text was tailored to emphasize the role. And I think this is a crucial pointer to the principal challenges offered by the title roles. *Romeo and Juliet* does not accord such prominence to its tragic lovers as Shakespeare's other double tragedy, *Antony and Cleopatra* does to its, especially at its end. Even more to the point, Romeo and Juliet are not as vividly characterized as the later pair, or, still more importantly, as other roles in the same play, notably Mercutio and the Nurse. Though I spoke of these characters as foils to the lovers, there are times when the actors playing the lovers may feel that it is they who are acting as foils to the supposedly subsidiary characters: Peter Holding remarks that 'Productions have occasionally been dominated by Mercutio or the Nurse.'[35] This no doubt helps to explain why actors go to some pains to find comic touches in the lovers' verse: in the balcony scene, for instance, Peggy Ashcroft got a laugh on 'I have forgot why I did call thee back',[36] and in Bogdanov's production there was comedy in the lovers' self-absorption, their wonder at each other—'She speaks', said Romeo, as if it was a remarkable achievement for Juliet to have acquired the skill at such an early age. This is entirely legitimate, but theatrical changes that have been made at the end of the play, and indeed some critical reactions to it, betray a dissatisfaction with the original script that seems designed to make it conform to expectations that may derive from conceptions of tragedy other than those that were in Shakespeare's mind as he wrote. Garrick, we have seen, expanded the lovers' death scene; Peter Brook, like most directors, severely shortened the last scene; in some performances he even went so far (like Gounod's librettist) as to omit the reconciliation of the houses.[37]

In part the alterations to the last scene result from practical considerations of staging; it is notoriously difficult to work out exactly how it would have been played in the theatres of Shakespeare's time. Perhaps Shakespeare was not in this play a complete master of practical stagecraft. Perhaps too some of what I have, somewhat neutrally, described as challenges to be faced might more properly be regarded as weaknesses that have to be overcome. I don't want to imply that *Romeo and Juliet* is in every respect a perfect specimen of dramatic craftsmanship. But I find it interesting that many of the criticisms and alterations to which the play has been subjected over the centuries bring it closer in line with expectations of romantic tragedy, perhaps derived in part from Shakespeare's own practice in later plays; they do not face up to the challenge of interpreting the text as written. They suggest, in short, that perhaps the play's greatest challenge is to our notions of genre. The script can be interpreted in all its richness and diversity only if we abandon the idea that because it is called a tragedy it must centre on the fate of individuals, and accept its emphasis on the multifarious society in which these individuals have their being.

7

Juliet's Nurse:
The Uses of Inconsequentiality

LADY CAPULET   Thou knowest my daughter's of a pretty age.
NURSE   Faith, I can tell her age unto an hour.
LADY CAPULET   She's not fourteen.
NURSE   I'll lay fourteen of my teeth—
    And yet, to my teen be it spoken, I have but four —
    She's not fourteen. How long is it now   15
    To Lammas-tide?
LADY CAPULET   A fortnight and odd days.
NURSE   Even or odd, of all days in the year,
    Come Lammas Eve at night shall she be fourteen.
    Susan and she—God rest all Christian souls!—
    Were of an age. Well, Susan is with God;   20
    She was too good for me. But, as I said,
    On Lammas Eve at night shall she be fourteen;
    That shall she, marry; I remember it well.
    'Tis since the earthquake now eleven years;
    And she was weaned—I never shall forget it—   25
    Of all the days of the year, upon that day;
    For I had then laid wormwood to my dug,
    Sitting in the sun under the dove-house wall.
    My lord and you were then at Mantua.
    Nay, I do bear a brain. But, as I said,   30
    When it did taste the wormwood on the nipple
    Of my dug, and felt it bitter, pretty fool,
    To see it tetchy, and fall out with the dug!
    Shake, quoth the dovehouse. 'Twas no need, I trow,
    To bid me trudge.   35
    And since that time it is eleven years;
    For then she could stand high-lone; nay, by th'rood,

She could have run and waddled all about;
For even the day before, she broke her brow;
And then my husband—God be with his soul!   40
'A was a merry man—took up the child.
'Yea,' quoth he, 'dost thou fall upon thy face?
Thou wilt fall backward when thou hast more wit,
Wilt thou not, Jule?' And, by my holidam,
The pretty wretch left crying, and said 'Ay'.   45
To see, now, how a jest shall come about!
I warrant, an I should live a thousand years,
I never should forget it: 'Wilt thou not, Jule?' quoth he;
And, pretty fool, it stinted, and said 'Ay'.
LADY CAPULET   Enough of this; I pray thee hold thy peace.   50
NURSE   Yes, madam. Yet I cannot choose but laugh
To think it should leave crying and say 'Ay'.
And yet, I warrant, it had upon it brow
A bump as big as a young cock'rel's stone —
A perilous knock; and it cried bitterly.   55
'Yea,' quoth my husband, 'fall'st upon thy face?
Thou wilt fall backward when thou comest to age;
Wilt thou not, Jule?' It stinted, and said 'Ay'.
JULIET   And stint thou too, I pray thee, nurse, say I.

(*Romeo and Juliet*, 1.3.11–59)

The style of the Nurse's speeches in Act 1, scene 3 of *Romeo and Juliet* makes a vivid impact on both readers and spectators. It is described by Nicholas Brooke as 'something altogether new, both in this play and, in fact, in Shakespeare's output'. He finds its 'nearest antecedent', not in verse, but in 'the prose of I, i'. While 'it goes far beyond that', nevertheless 'its characteristic is that it is close to prose, or rather to prosaic speech, developing its own rhythmic momentum'.[1] By the time that Shakespeare wrote *Romeo and Juliet* he had written much dialogue that approximates to prosaic speech rather than to literary prose; and I should like to begin this essay by examining some of the characteristics of the Nurse's utterance which may account for the claim that it represents 'something altogether new'.

It is easy to point to aspects of the style which create the illusion of spontaneity. There are colloquial expressions such as 'Come Lammas Eve at night', 'Shake, quoth the dovehouse' (so personal as to be obscure in meaning), 'stand high-lone', and 'broke her brow'. The diction is familiar, even vulgar: 'dug', 'tetchy', 'trudge', 'waddled'. There are emphatic or asseverative expressions, including 'Well', 'as I said', 'marry', 'Nay', 'I trow', 'by th'rood', 'by my holidam', 'I warrant'. Some of these words and phrases, and others, are repeated or slightly varied in a manner that would be avoided by a literary artist but which helps to bind the speech together and to give the impression that they are idiosyncratic to the speaker: 'God rest all Christian souls!'...'God be with his soul!': is this sententiousness or piety?—the performer may decide; 'I remember it well...I never shall forget it...I never should forget it'; 'pretty fool...pretty wretch...pretty fool'; and 'To see it...To see, now...'.

These devices might equally well be discerned in the racy prose dialogue of Act 1, scene 1, or in individually longer prose speeches, such as Launce's principal soliloquies in *The Two Gentlemen of Verona* (2.3, 4.4). More individual to the Nurse is the structure and argument of the speech (or, in effect, its denial of structure and argument): the sequence of ideas and images, and the aim to which they are applied. Coleridge referred to them in an 'Essay on Method in Thought'[2] as an example of Shakespeare's exhibitions of 'the difference between the products of a well disciplined and those of an uncultivated understanding'. He remarks that 'the absence of Method, what characterises the uneducated, is occasioned by a habitual submission of the understanding to mere events and images as such, and independent of any power in the mind to classify or appropriate them'. One very obvious symptom of the 'absence of Method' in the Nurse's disquisition is the frequency with which she interrupts herself. Sometimes this is because she follows an associative train of thought irrespective of its relevance to her listeners:

> I'll lay fourteen of my teeth
> And yet, to my teen be it spoken, I have but four—
> She's not fourteen.

Is her self-interruption here a conscious playing with 'four' and 'teen', or rather the subconscious struggle to clear her mind of verbal entanglements? Again, the performer may choose.

Part of the comedy of the Nurse's utterance lies in the fact that what she interrupts has in itself no logical sequence. The information that she has to convey in her main speech is entirely contained in its second line:

> Come Lammas Eve at night shall she be fourteen.

This fact might well be pointed by stage business, Lady Capulet endeavouring to resume the conversation after this statement. But the Nurse's well of recollection has been tapped, and the flow cannot be quenched. Coleridge parallels this speech of the Nurse with one of Mistress Quickly. In answer to Falstaff's question 'What is the gross sum that I owe thee?', she replies

> Marry, if thou wert an honest man, thyself and the money too. Thou didst swear to me upon a parcel-gilt goblet, sitting in my Dolphin chamber, at the round table, by a sea-coal fire, upon Wednesday in Wheeson week, when the Prince broke thy head for

liking his father to a singing-man of Windsor—thou didst swear to me then, as I was washing thy wound, to marry me and make me my lady thy wife. Canst thou deny it? Did not goodwife Keech, the butcher's wife, come in then and call me gossip Quickly? Coming in to borrow a mess of vinegar, telling us she had a good dish of prawns, whereby thou didst desire to eat some, whereby I told thee they were ill for a green wound? (2 Henry IV, 2.1.81–94)

Here, Coleridge remarks that 'the connexions and sequence which the habit of Method can alone give have in this instance a substitute in the fusion of passion'. The Nurse lacks Mistress Quickly's vituperative passion of self-righteous indignation, but her recollections, too, are grounded in emotion, provoked by the memory that she had had a daughter of the same age as Juliet. The very fact that Susan's relationship with the Nurse is not explicitly stated is itself an aspect of Shakespeare's dramatic style here. It tells us obliquely of the Nurse's intimacy with the family in which she lives, an intimacy which the performers can use by suggesting a sympathetic, if bored, acceptance that once the Nurse has embarked on this tack, she must be indulged. And it engages the audience by requiring them to make the inference. The death of an infant has an inevitable poignancy, and one which must link the Nurse to the Capulets since Juliet has thriven on the milk which should have reared Susan. And we may recall that the shadow of infant mortality has already darkened the play, in Capulet's 'Earth hath swallowèd all my hopes but she' (1.2.14).

The Nurse's recollection that Juliet and Susan 'Were of an age' is interrupted by the pious commonplace 'God rest all Christian souls!', leading us to infer that Susan is dead, and is followed by two more clichés: 'Susan is with God; | She was too good for me.' The ordinariness of these expressions is surely part of their point; they come naturally from the mouth of a simple-minded woman. To say, as G. I. Duthie does in the New Cambridge edition,[3] 'She knows she has faults. When she declares that little Susan was too good for her, she is speaking partly jocularly but partly, for a second, seriously, with self-knowledge', is surely to ignore the stereotyped quality of the assertion.

After her digression, the Nurse's pulling herself up with 'But, as I said', and coming full circle with

On Lammas Eve at night shall she be fourteen,

marks another point at which she might have concluded. But her recollections have a self-generating momentum, and as she goes on, she becomes increasingly self-absorbed. Coleridge's 'Method' implies consideration for the listener (or reader), an ordering of statements requiring the application of fundamental brainwork such as is associated with literary artistry or conscious rhetoric, and is thus outward-looking; the 'absence of Method', on the other hand, implies a delving into the subconscious which produces the kind of monologue that achieves communication rather by accident than by design. The Nurse makes no pretence that her ramblings are relevant to the situation. They are a form of self-indulgence which is also a form of both self-investigation and (when conducted in public) self-revelation, so the response of listeners is a measure of their response to the speaker's character. The Nurse's listeners allow her to continue; whether they do so with complete indulgence or with some degree of indifference, and with attempts to interrupt, is open to interpretation. The Nurse's repetitions of 'But, as I said' may be regarded as a method of staving off interruption, or they may be less outward-looking, her own method of attempting to exert some control over her discourse.

After concluding the first paragraph of her speech, she marks time for a moment with 'That shall she, marry; I remember it well' before embarking on another paragraph whose beginning also is to reappear as its ending. And from the recollection of one landmark—Lammas Eve as the time of the infant's birth—she passes to another—the day of 'the earthquake' as that on which Juliet was weaned. That Shakespeare was here considerately making a topical allusion in order to help scholars of the future to know when he wrote his play is improbable. An 'earthquake' is chosen as the kind of event which would be significant in the lives of all who experienced it, an episode certain to engrave itself upon the collective memory. It serves again to link the masters with their servants. The coincidence of Juliet's being weaned on the day of the earthquake is stressed in the phrase 'Of all the days of the year', and seems to confer importance upon the event; but always, as these facts emerge, they are linked and given significance by being shown as part of the life-experience of the woman who recollects them. It is her memory in which they dwell—'I remember it well', 'I never shall forget it'; and it is her body with which they are associated.

So far we have had only statements; now, as she becomes more immersed in her topic, she becomes anecdotal. The absence of intellectual logic in what she says is apparent in the false connective 'For'—'For I had then laid wormwood to my dug'—but the sudden sequence of nouns in this and the succeeding line—'wormwood...dug...sun...dovehouse' and 'wall'—helps to create a vivid picture of peaceful normality which gains in credibility by its association with a violently abnormal event. Yet another association obtrudes—'My lord and you were then at Mantua'—and the pressure of recollection becomes so great that the Nurse returns to the present in wonderment at her own mental powers—'Nay, I do bear a brain.'[4]

She resumes her anecdote, losing herself again in memories which allow no acknowledgement that the baby of whom she speaks is the girl who stands beside her. Her style is not expository but exclamatory, deepening the suggestion that she is reliving the experience:

> pretty fool,
> To see it tetchy, and fall out with the dug!

This exclamation is followed by another, elliptical and slightly obscure,[5] which recalls the earthquake's shocking disruption of normality—'Shake, quoth the dove-house.' Again she is jolted back to the present as she recalls her hasty flight and rounds off the second paragraph with a return to the statement with which it began: 'And since that time it is eleven years.'

The final part of the speech again begins with a false connective, and has no logical link with what precedes it, nor even any obvious associative one, unless it is that the Nurse's memory of her need to 'trudge'[6] leads from her own legs to Juliet's, and thus to the recollection that Juliet was able to *stand* by herself. The second anecdote features another newly introduced character, the Nurse's husband; the touch of sadness that he is dead is offset by her memory of him as 'a merry man'. For the first time now she quotes direct speech, in her husband's somewhat bawdy, familiar remark to the child 'Jule'. The Nurse's own, self-absorbed delight in her recollections is evident in her repetition of the anecdote. Whether she has carried her stage audience along with her is again a matter for interpretation. Lady Capulet's interruption,

> Enough of this. I pray thee, hold thy peace

appears to demonstrate impatience, yet it can be played against its sense, in full enjoyment of the comedy of the tale. Coleridge referred to the Nurse's 'childlike fondness of repetition in her childish age—and that happy, humble ducking under, yet resurgence against the check—

> Yes, madam! *Yet* I cannot choose but laugh.'[7]

And she adds the circumstantial and bawdy detail of the 'bump as big as a young cock'rel's stone' before winding herself to a standstill with her fourth telling of the tale.

I have written of the speech so far as if it were composed in prose, not verse. I have referred to the 'prose' characteristics of its diction and structure, and to the fact that it quotes a passage of (supposedly) prose speech. Although in modern editions we read the speech as verse, it is a curious fact that it was printed as prose in all the early editions: the bad quarto (1597), the good quarto (1599), and the First Folio (1623). It is less surprising that verse should appear as prose in the memorially reconstructed bad quarto than that most of the Nurse's speeches in this scene are set in italic type in both quartos. There is evidence that in Q2 the first thirty-four lines of the scene are reprinted directly from Q1,[8] and it is likely that this fact influenced the Q2 compositor to go on setting these speeches as prose even though they were presumably written out as verse in the holograph from which he is believed to have set the remainder of the scene. Not until Capell's edition (1768) were the Nurse's speeches arranged as verse. In the meantime Thomas Otway had adapted and amplified them, while retaining their substance, in unmistakable prose in his *Caius Marius* (1679). Garrick, naturally, set them as prose in his adaptation of 1748, followed, in spite of Capell, in John Bell's acting edition (1774). At least two nineteenth-century editors—Staunton (1857) and Keightley (1865)—did the same, and so does Frank A. Marshall in the *Henry Irving Shakespeare* (8 vols., 1888–90), with a note condemning 'the modern editors who have tried to make verse of what was surely never intended for it', and asking: 'Why should Shakespeare be made to violate every rule of rhythm and metre, for the sake of trying to strain this conventional prose into blank verse?' (i. 240). Irving's acting edition of 1882, however, prints the expurgated remnants as verse.[9] G. B. Harrison reverted to prose in his Penguin edition (1937), and even Dover Wilson wrote that 'editors have never been able to make anything but very rough verse out of these speeches and it is quite possible that Shakespeare intended them to be rhythmical (i.e. easily memorized) prose'.[10] But this statement is impressionistic rather than accurate. G. Walton Williams (p. 107) analyses the scene carefully and shows that the earlier section of the Nurse's long speech 'is marked by irregular verse': the nineteen lines include one four-syllable line (35), three hypermetrical lines with unaccented final syllables (18, 22, 31), and five hypermetrical lines with accented final syllables (23, 25, 26, 28, and 32); these are not violent irregularities, and several of them may be explained as contractions in pronunciation; the remainder of the scene, Williams finds, is 'in smooth verse' with minor exceptions. Minor rhythmic irregularities may be expected in verse which is so clearly intended as this is to represent 'prosaic speech'; as Kenneth Muir says, 'Shakespeare obtains some subtle effects by the verse rhythm underlying the apparently colloquial speech.'[11] Little more than a glance is needed to show that in both the inauthentically and the authentically derived sections, the ends of lines are almost invariably also the ends of sense-units: the only enjambment in the main speech is at lines 31–2 ('the nipple | Of my dug...'). There can be no question that Shakespeare was fully conscious that he was writing verse, nor, to my mind, that he was going further than ever before in the experiment of combining the diction, rhythms, and even the mental processes normally associated with prose utterance within the overall rhythms of blank verse. The speeches would be remarkable enough as an exhibition of the 'quick forge and working-house of thought' if they had indeed been in prose; it is the fact that in them prose rhythms are counterpointed against a verse structure that makes them 'something altogether new, both in this play and... in Shakespeare's output'.

I should like now to draw back from a close focus on the speech itself to a broader consideration of its function in the play as an aspect of Shakespeare's dramatic style. *Romeo and Juliet* is often dated 1594–5, a fact that it has in common with *Love's Labour's Lost*, *The Two Gentlemen of Verona*, *The Comedy of Errors*, *The Taming of the Shrew*, *A Midsummer Night's Dream*, *The Merchant of Venice*, *Richard II*, *King John*, and *Titus*

Andronicus. Obviously the composition of these plays must have been spread over a period of several years, but it is fair to regard *Romeo and Juliet* as one of a group of early plays in which Shakespeare shows an experimental interest in verbal style. *King John* and *Richard II*, along with the earlier 1 and 3 *Henry VI*, but like no other plays in the canon, are written entirely in verse. In them Shakespeare seems to be deliberately limiting his stylistic range, seeking intensity rather than diversity. In other plays he seems rather to be seeking a wide range of stylistic variation. Part of the effectiveness of the Nurse's speech derives from the fact that, though it occurs no later than the opening of the third scene, it has been preceded by passages written in very different styles, including the sonnet form of the Prologue; the colloquial prose of the opening dialogue of the servants; Prince Escalus's dignified blank verse; the more lyrical blank verse of Benvolio's description of the lovesick Romeo; Romeo's own rhapsodic verse, which includes rhyming couplets and has some of the qualities associated with metaphysical poetry; the comic prose of Capulet's servant; and sonnet-type sestets from both Benvolio and Romeo.

This rich stylistic diversity has helped to establish verbal style as a guide to character, and has encouraged us to respond to verbal effects. We know that this is to be a play in which plot is not all-important, and this is essential, since in terms of plot the whole of Act 1, scene 3 could exist without the Nurse. Her big speech is a set-speech in more senses than one. It is an extended show-piece for the performer, and also for the Nurse herself. This is, we may well suspect, an oft-told tale. Do we not feel, as soon as she says 'I can tell her age unto an hour', that she is about to give us every detail? And may we not feel, too, that her on-stage audience has heard it all many times before? This seems to me to be suggested by the line, completing a verse couplet, with which Juliet almost succeeds in bringing the Nurse's recollections to an end. 'And stint thou too, I pray thee, nurse, say I.' What is the tone? Is Juliet embarrassed or bored? indulgent or irritable? imploratory or imperative? Again, there is room for variety of interpretation.

If the Nurse's speech is irrelevant to the plot, we may ask how Shakespeare came to write it, and why he was disposed to lavish so much of his artistry on it. Is it merely an exuberant exercise of virtuosity, a set-piece for the author as well as for the actor and the character? Is it an inartistic irrelevance, a fanciful embroidery of the situation unnecessarily pursuing a hint suggested by the source? There is, indeed, some basis for it in Arthur Brooke's *Tragical History of Romeus and Juliet*,[12] which may provide pointers to the style in which the scene should be played as well as help to explain the style in which it is written. One vexed question relates to the Nurse's age. Brooke clearly thought of her as old: he calls her 'an auncient dame' (line 344), an 'olde dame' (line 345), an 'auncient nurse' (line 689). Yet 'in her youth' she 'had nurst' Juliet 'with her mylke' (line 345). Brooke's Juliet is 16, more than two years older than Shakespeare's; but this still leaves some awkwardness about the Nurse's having been able to suckle the infant Juliet, and have a child of the same age herself, and yet now being 'auncient'. In a narrative poem, the point may pass unnoticed; on the stage it is more obtrusive. Thus St John Ervine, reviewing Edith Evans's legendary perform-ance in 1935, remarked that though the character was 'superbly played' she was 'made to totter as if her legs had been racked with rheumatism for half a century'.[13] Terence Spencer attempts to reconcile the discrepancy, suggesting that she is not 'to be imagined as an aged crone but as, perhaps, in her early fifties'.[14] But perhaps the performer is best advised to ignore logic and to play for effect.

One function of the Nurse's repetitiveness is to lay great stress on Juliet's age, which has created a different problem. Shakespeare makes her younger than either Brooke or Painter (who says that she is 18). Geoffrey Bullough suggests that this is intended 'to emphasise the charm of her girlish directness, the pathos of her passion and resolution'. Charles Armitage Brown (quoted in the New Variorum edition) had a more practical suggestion: 'Juliet's extreme youth was, at the time, an apology to the audience for the boy who played so arduous a part.' Whatever the truth of this, actresses playing the role have frequently chosen not to include among its ardours the effort to look 13. Theophilus Cibber (1744) offers what might have been classed as an emendation if it had not occurred in a mere acting edition: Lady Capulet says: 'She's but fifteen', and the Nurse replies 'She's not fourteen' (but Cibber spoils the impression of thoughtfulness by then having her say 'come Lammas-Eve at night shall she be fifteen'). In Garrick's acting text (followed by Bell) Juliet is 'not yet eighteen' (with appropriate alterations to the number of the Nurse's remaining teeth and to other figures); Benson, like Garrick, relieved his leading lady from the strain of attempting to look no more than a fortnight under 18.

These are considerations that relate to the style of acting the Nurse's role. Shakespeare also derived hints from Brooke for the style in which he wrote it. Brooke's 'prating noorse', too, is repetitive and anecdotal; she makes a 'tedious long discoorse'. The crucial lines are worth quoting:

> And how she gave her sucke in youth she leaveth not to tell.
> A prety babe (quod she), it was when it was yong,
> Lord how it could full pretely have prated with it tong,
> A thousand times and more I laid her on my lappe,
> And clapt her on the buttocke soft and kist where I did clappe.
> And gladder then was I of such a kisse forsooth,
> Then I had been to have a kisse of some olde lechers mouth.
> And thus of Juliets youth began this prating noorse,
> And of her present state to make a tedious long discoorse. (lines 652–60)

Here, as in Shakespeare, we have prosaic speech cast into the form of verse. Shakespeare's diction is related to Brooke's ('prety babe', 'quod she', 'it' for 'she', 'thousand'). So also are the mode and tone of the Nurse's discourse. The comic earthiness of 'clapt her on the buttocke soft and kist where I did clappe' is reflected in the Nurse's unabashed acknowledgement of the physical details of breast-feeding and in the bawdy implications of the anecdote about her husband. Needless to say, this was not to the taste of the Victorians. Bowdler (1818) omitted the whole of the anecdote about falling backwards; he retained the breast-feeding while altering 'dug' to 'teat'. Lacy's acting edition of about 1855 outdoes Bowdler in purification, omitting even the breast-feeding, reducing the major speech to only eleven lines (compared with Bowdler's twenty-two), and entirely omitting the following speech. Henry Irving's acting edition of 1882 is even more brutal, and results in nonsense. Mary Anderson, at the Lyceum four years later, allowed Mrs Stirling her anecdote, but Forbes-Robertson, in 1895, omitted the bawdy, while curiously retaining the lead-in to it, as if to encourage the audience to recall (or imagine) it if they will:

> 'Yea,' quoth he, 'dost thou fall upon thy face?
> Thou wilt—'
> LADY CAPULET   Enough of this.

To show that Shakespeare found some suggestions in his source for both the content and manner of the episode is not, of course, to provide artistic justification for it. But if it is irrelevant to the plot, it is far from irrelevant to the greater entity which is the play. Terence Spencer has remarked that the 'momentous and breath-taking four days' to which the play's action is confined 'are given a context in the passage of time much larger and longer', and that 'Old Capulet and the Nurse, in particular, carry the mind outside the framework of the play to events and emotions which nevertheless put Juliet and her Romeo in perspective'.[15] The Nurse's ramblings do indeed give us a sense of the past; and they do so in a particularly poignant context. The stage situation shows us a girl poised on the brink of womanhood. We have not met her before, and one function of the Nurse's speeches is to engage our sympathetic interest in the play's heroine. As the Nurse talks, her memories not only throw our minds back to the infancy of this girl, they also recall a prediction made at that time of how Juliet would react when she had 'more wit' and came 'to age'. The child who is talked about as an innocent infant is now before us, the subject of marriage plans. She retains the vulnerable innocence of the baby that 'stinted and said "Ay"', as we see in her reaction to the question 'How stands your dispositions to be married?' 'It is an honour that I dream not of', says Juliet. This is in naïve contrast to the sexuality of 'Thou wilt fall backward when thou hast more wit', and it partakes of the infantile naivety of Juliet's earlier response: 'Ay.' Thus the Nurse's delving into the past recalls an anecdote which looked forward to beyond, but only just beyond, the present in which she speaks. The temporal complexities of the situation are subtle and ironical.

One function of the episode is, of course, to establish the Nurse's personality, and in this it has succeeded so notably as to have become a classic instance of Shakespeare's genius for character portrayal. Nicholas Brooke finds that her utterance here 'offers a very telling contrast to the hollow courtliness of i.ii: earthy, sentimental, warm-blooded, bawdy, repetitious. At all levels delightful, and most refreshing in its unselfconsciousness' (p. 93). And G. I. Duthie goes further in sketching a personality on the basis of what she says here: 'despite all her crudities, we can never forget the essential good-heartedness of this old woman who, vulgar and earthy as she is, looks back on past days and compresses precious memories into words which, while brief, suggest a loving and happy married life, with sorrow philosophically endured' (p. xxxvi). These comments testify to her credibility; but this is not enough. Coleridge, replying to suggestions 'that her character is the mere fruit of observation', spoke of it rather as a 'character of admirable generalisation'.[16] He betrays an implicit concern that the dramatic character should relate, at least, to recognizable characteristics of certain types of human beings. 'Let any man conjure up in his mind all the qualities and peculiarities that can possibly belong to a nurse, and he will find them in Shakespeare's picture of the old woman: nothing is omitted.' Some of these qualities are admirable, some not; so he finds in her 'all the garrulity of old age, and all its fondness...the arrogance of ignorance' and 'the pride of meanness at being connected with a great family', and 'the grossness, too, which that situation never removes' (p. 145). These observations are, of course, elicited by the Nurse's behaviour in all the scenes in which she appears, but it is significant that most of her qualities can be discerned in her initial speeches. The appeal that she exerts is as a 'character' in the sense that we speak of someone as 'a great character': one, that is, who is so self-consistent, so roundedly and immutably himself, so much of a fixed point in a landscape, that we can delight in his idiosyncrasies without needing to declare judgement on him. So Shakespeare, we feel, gives us the Nurse in her totality on her first appearance; she is herself a landmark, a constant against which the changes and developments in other characters can be measured. And here we come to those aspects of Shakespeare's portrayal of the Nurse which make her not just credible as an individual and recognizably representative of a class, but of essential importance to the play in which she is found. The 'fondness' for Juliet which she clearly conveys draws us to Juliet as well as to the Nurse. And her limitations, suggested here, will later be tragically relevant to Juliet. Nicholas Brooke follows his expression of pleasure in the Nurse's character by saying that: 'It is also, humanly speaking, shallow enough in its own way, and this will be sharply exposed later; but here, the judgement is withheld.' Judgement comes, of course, when (only a few days later in the play's time-scheme) Juliet, a bride, is shown to have passed far beyond any understanding that the Nurse can offer. Then she becomes in Juliet's eyes 'Ancient damnation! O most wicked fiend!' (3.5.236). To this extent she is seen as a foil for Juliet, a rounded, developed but static character that serves as a measure of the speed and extent of Juliet's spiritual and emotional development. These opening speeches lay the groundwork of this relationship.

I have written of the Nurse's speeches in relation to their verbal style, and also to what we may call Shakespeare's theatrical and dramatic styles. Many aspects of the speeches can be admired; the one that seems most original, and most important for Shakespeare's later development, is their exploitation of inconsequentiality. By a carefully controlled representation of utterance which is characterized by an absence of linguistic control, Shakespeare creates interstices which can be filled with nuance. This is a splendidly theatrical mode, because it leaves something to the performer, who, by means of gesture, movement, facial play, and subtlety of intonation, may create an appropriate physical realization of all that the speech implies.

And such realizations may be very different from one another. As long ago as 1902, a theatre critic remarked that 'By tradition of the stage this is a comic character, the confidential retainer, rustling with silks and rattling with keys, interfering in everything, prone to take offence at imaginary slights, tyrannizing over those she nominally serves, and all the time English to the finger-tips. Mrs Stirling [who played with Ellen Terry in Henry Irving's production, and with Mary Anderson] was a perfect embodiment of that type. Miss [Tita] Brand [who played in the Ben Greet production under review] gives us a very different person. Here is an Italian crone, just such a figure as may be met by the dozen in the streets of Rome or Naples; a southern face, with parchment skin and hairy growth, and the four teeth to which the owner confesses much in evidence....'.[17] Such openness to interpretation is surely a mark of the truly theatrical conception.

As well as leaving something to the actor, the role no less importantly leaves something to the audience. Allusions, oblique references, incomplete logical connections, implications, half-concealed trains of thought require the audience's intelligent collaboration to be wholly meaningful. The audience is, as it were, drawn into the speaker's mind, engaged with a lively intensity which can be much greater than response to a harangue composed with complete 'Method'.

Whether Shakespeare derived the style of the Nurse's speech from sources in literature and life we cannot say.[18] Arthur Brooke contributed suggestions for their effect, but no model for their method. I suspect it is relevant that, at about the time the play was composed, Thomas Nashe was demonstrating his capacity in what he calls the 'extemporal vein'. What is clear is that, having, as it were, learnt the trick, Shakespeare, as we should expect, went on to develop and vary it. The Nurse's inconsequentiality arises from the fact that her mental processes are too feeble to create an adequate syntactical structure; or—to look at it from her creator's point of view—in the Nurse Shakespeare employs broken syntax and inconsequentiality to suggest a mind that is naturally lacking in intellectual control. He does something similar, though in prose, with Mistress Quickly, as we have already seen. The Nurse's speech patterns are related to those of Justice Shallow, in whom they suggest the effects of senility. All these characters give the impression of complete spontaneity. Lacking the power to order their thoughts and control their expression, they display no disjunction between the impulse to speak and the terms in which their thoughts are formulated. This gives them a kind of innocence. Pompey, in *Measure for Measure*, may seem rather to be using these tricks of language to pull the wool over his interlocutors' eyes than to be incapable of greater coherence:

> As I say, this Mistress Elbow, being, as I say, with child, and being great-bellied, and longing, as I said, for prunes; and having but two in the dish, as I said, Master Froth here, this very man, having eaten the rest, as I said, and, as I say, paying for them very honestly; for, as you know, Master Froth, I could not give you three pence again. (2.1.94–100)

These are speakers of prose. In verse, Shakespeare learnt that inconsequentiality could be a powerful means of portraying mental anguish, the overthrowing of a noble mind. Hamlet's soliloquies—like the Nurse's speech—encompass familiar diction, exclamations, repetitions, self-interruptions, and broken syntax within a verse structure:

> Why, she would hang on him
> As if increase of appetite had grown
> By what it fed on; and yet, within a month —
> Let me not think on't. Frailty, thy name is woman!—
> A little month, or ere those shoes were old
> With which she followed my poor father's body,
> Like Niobe, all tears—why she, even she—
> O God! a beast that wants discourse of reason
> Would have mourned longer—married with my uncle,
> My father's brother; but no more like my father
> Than I to Hercules. (1.2.143–53)

In *King Lear*, too, the breakdown of linguistic control is used to high emotional effect:

> No, you unnatural hags,
> I will have such revenges on you both
> That all the world shall—I will do such things—
> What they are yet I know not; but they shall be
> The terrors of the earth. (2.4.277–81)

And the same play exhibits at its most powerful Shakespeare's technique of counterpointing speech rhythms with a verse structure:

> And my poor fool is hanged! No, no, no life!
> Why should a dog, a horse, a rat have life,
> And thou no breath at all? Thou'lt come no more,
> Never, never, never, never, never.
> Pray you undo this button. Thank you, sir.
> Do you see this? Look on her. Look, her lips.
> Look there, look there! (5.3.305–11)

It seems to me that the Nurse's speeches in Act 1, scene 3 of *Romeo and Juliet* show Shakespeare to be suddenly the master of a technique that enabled him greatly to extend the expressive resources of dramatic language.

8

The Lamentable Tale of *Richard II*

In Act 5, scene 1 of *Richard II* the King, addressing his Queen, advises her in the future to think of him as dead:

> In winter's tedious nights sit by the fire
> With good old folks, and let them tell thee tales
> Of woeful ages long ago betid;
> And ere thou bid goodnight, to quite their griefs
> Tell thou the lamentable tale of me,
> And send the hearers weeping to their beds. (lines 40–5)[1]

It is a characteristic piece of self-dramatization, with a strong element of self-pity. It is also one of those passages, not uncommon in Shakespeare, in which the audience is made aware of the play as a mimic representation, in which they are conscious of the play as play, the actor as actor; for the performers are in fact enacting the 'lamentable tale', and the audience are the hearers who, if the actors succeed, will go 'weeping to their beds'. It is the adjective 'lamentable' that I wish to emphasize. The play is full of laments. It seems to me to owe its impression of poetic unity not only to what R. D. Altick[2] calls its 'symphonic imagery'—important though that is—but also to the dominance within its structure of emotional attitudes associated with lamentation. Like the words, these attitudes form a pattern which helps to give the action a more-than-documentary significance, and I want to concentrate on this aspect of Shakespeare's poetic and dramatic technique in the hope that to do so will help to define something of the play's individuality.

Lamentation is, of course, appropriate to tragedy, and we should expect it to occur, at least after the tragic climax, as in, for example, Marlowe's choric lament for Dr Faustus, 'Cut is the branch that might have grown full straight'. In fact, W. H. Clemen shows, in *English Tragedy Before Shakespeare*,[3] that the set-speech of lamentation had become a regular dramatic convention by the time that Shakespeare was writing. Indeed, Clemen's estimate of its importance is so great that he devotes an entire section (Chapter 14) of his book to 'The Dramatic Lament and its Forms', selecting the lament as 'a particular type of set speech that is employed by almost all the playwrights' (p. 211). 'The note of lamentation', he writes, 'resounds throughout the whole of pre-Shakespearian tragedy. With what frequency are English tragedies described in their titles as "lamentable" or "most lamentable"! And pitiable and lamentable indeed is the fall from high estate which, perpetuating the medieval conception of "tragedye", provides the basic theme of so many of these plays' (p. 214). This is indeed the central situation of *Richard II*, and, adopting a standard theme, Shakespeare adopts also some of the conventional ways of treating it. It does not seem too much to suggest that he has so laid out the action of his play that lamentation is appropriate not merely at the ending, but almost throughout. We can see this in the overall design: Thomas of Woodstock has died before the action begins; the first Act is concerned with retribution for his murder; John of Gaunt dies in Act 2; the middle stretch of the play shows Richard's fall; and the last Act shows his death. And if we look at the action in more detail, we can see that Shakespeare has manipulated historical events, and added to them, so as to create a high concentration of situations that are provocative of lamentation.

Let us remind ourselves of the more important. In the opening scene, Boling-broke's accusation that Mowbray plotted Thomas of Woodstock's death incorporates a brief lament for the murdered man. This in turn provokes from Mowbray a lament for the slander on his reputation. The second scene—which begins, fittingly, with the word 'Alas'—is a conversation between John of Gaunt and Woodstock's widow, the Duchess of Gloucester, consisting largely of a lament for Woodstock and expressions of despair from the Duchess. Shakespeare invented this scene. In the following scene of the lists, he invents lengthy laments for both Mowbray and Bolingbroke on their banishment, and also for John of Gaunt on the fact that he is unlikely to see his son again. In the first scene of the second Act, also invented by Shakespeare, John of Gaunt speaks his great lament for the shameful state of England under Richard. Gaunt's subsequent death is notable for the brevity of lamentation from Richard—

> The ripest fruit first falls, and so doth he.
> His time is spent, our pilgrimage must be.
> So much for that. (2.1.153–5)

Here, Richard's inadequate observation of the convention is itself significant. The Duke of York rapidly, and lengthily, laments Richard's callousness and his rash seizing of Gaunt's possessions. Towards the end of the scene, too, Northumberland, Ross, and Willoughby lament the state of the kingdom under Richard. The following scene (2.2) opens with another of Shakespeare's inventions, Richard's Queen's grief at the King's departure. Act 2, scene 4 is the choric lament by the Welsh Captain—developed from just a hint in Holinshed—on the fear and foreboding in the country, followed by Salisbury's lament on Richard's falling fortunes.

Act 3, scene 2—the Berkeley Castle scene—is particularly interesting for the way in which Shakespeare has rearranged his historical material, creating a pattern which permits an exploration of the polarities of Richard's confidence and despair. In Holinshed, the events take place over a considerable period of time, partly at Berkeley Castle, partly at Conway; but Shakespeare places it all at Berkeley in a single action based upon a conventional design, that in which a sequence of messengers brings increasingly bad news. Shakespeare had used the convention in, for example, the opening scene of 1 *Henry VI* and Act 4, scene 4 of *Richard III*. Here, it serves admirably as a stimulus to lamentation. Richard is given a supreme expression of confidence in the divine protection of his kingly state; the news that the Welsh army has fled provokes a lament; his confidence returns, and he hears of Bolingbroke's success in raising troops. Shakespeare avoids monotony by making anger, not lamentation, the reaction to this; but then Richard learns that Bushy, Green, and Wiltshire are dead, and this provokes the first of his great laments, 'Of comfort no man speak...' (3. 2.144–77). Shakespeare's only hint for this in Holinshed was the statement that Richard, 'hearing how his trusty counsellors had lost their heads... became so greatly discomforted that, sorrowfully lamenting his miserable state, he utterly despaired of his own safety...'.[4] The following scene, at Flint Castle, repeats the contrast between exaltation and despair: Richard's defiance of Bolingbroke, expressed in the confidence that

> God omnipotent
> Is mustering in his clouds on our behalf
> Armies of pestilence (3.3. 85–7)

is rapidly followed by Richard's long, anticipatory lament—'What must the King do now?'—culminating in his great comparison of himself to 'glistering Phaëton'. This is all of Shakespeare's creation; all that Holinshed reports Richard to have said in this situation is 'Dear cousin, I am ready to accomplish your will so that ye may enjoy all that is yours, without exception.'[5] In this part of the play laments about Richard are spoken not by others, but by himself. As Robert Ornstein puts it: 'In earlier scenes Gaunt, York, and Northumberland served as choruses to the King's wantonness. Now that his princely education has begun, Richard can act as his own chorus.'[6]

Another choric scene, entirely invented by Shakespeare, and consisting of little but lamentation, follows: that in which the Queen expresses her melancholy to her ladies, and in which the gardeners deplore the state of the kingdom. Act 4, scene 1 includes an interestingly unmelancholy response to the death of Mowbray, on which I shall comment later. It also has Carlisle's prophetic lament for the state of

England if Bolingbroke becomes king (this is based on Holinshed, though all the prophetic and lamentatory aspects of it are Shakespeare's); then we have Richard's laments of renunciation, what he himself calls the

external manner of *laments*

which

Are merely shadows to the unseen grief
That swells with silence in the tortured soul. (4.1.295–7)

These are the play's climactic laments; but in the last Act we still have the scene of lamentation between Richard and his Queen (again invented by Shakespeare, though with some possible influence from Samuel Daniel). In the following scene, York laments Richard's fall. In the next one, it is Bolingbroke's turn to lament, as he complains of his son's unprincely behaviour; and the play ends with his lament for Richard's death and for his own guilt.

I have spoken of the lament so far without attempting a definition; nor is any rigid definition possible. There is no set form or content for a lament, as there was for a sonnet, a funeral elegy, and an epithalamium, for example. Nor would such rigidity have been welcome to Shakespeare; its absence enables him to move unobtrusively in and out of lamentation, integrating these submerged set-pieces within his dramatic structure. Two elements, however, are essential. One is grief for something lost, or in danger of being lost; the other, consequent upon this, is a sense of the value of what has been lost. This in itself creates a tension which can be poetically and dramatically exploited. At various points in *Richard II*, especially in the early part of the play, Shakespeare implants an impression of an ideal state whose destruction or loss would inevitably be lamentable. So, early in the first scene, Bolingbroke and Mowbray salute the King with an expression of what he may ideally hope for: as both king and man.

BOLINGBROKE   Many years of happy days befall
My gracious sovereign, my most loving liege!
MOWBRAY   Each day still better other's happiness
Until the heavens, envying earth's good hap,
Add an immortal title to your crown! (1.1.20–4)

This establishes a value against which what happens to Richard throughout the play may be tested. In the second scene, the Duchess of Gloucester expresses her sense of the value of her murdered husband by depicting royal descent as part of an order of nature:

> Edward's seven sons, whereof thyself art one,
> Were as seven vials of his sacred blood,
> Or seven fair branches springing from one root. (2.2.11–13)

This passage, too, presages much that is to come, most obviously the imagery of England as a garden which may be well or ill tended. Best known of all the play's assertions of positive value is John of Gaunt's praise of England—'This royal throne of kings, this sceptred isle, | This earth of majesty, this seat of Mars...'—expressed in a single long sentence which appears to be a panegyric until, after nineteen lines, the appearance of the main verb reveals that it is in fact a lament, since 'this dear dear land...Is now leased out...Like to a tenement or pelting farm' (2.1.40–60). As I have already said, assertions of the value of kingship occur notably in the second and third scenes of Act 3, where they are ironically undermined by messages of bad news, so that Richard's confidence turns to despair.

It is when we turn to look at the ways in which Shakespeare actually presents the grief of the loser that we can appreciate both the imaginative variety with which he endows the lament and the success with which he relates individual sorrow to the general state of man, developing his particular, historical narrative in ways that link it with some of the central themes of literary expression.

At its simplest, lamentation can consist merely of complaints, a recital of wrongs or woes, such as we hear from Ross, Willoughby, and Northumberland as their impatience with Richard II grows:

> The commons hath he pilled with grievous taxes,
> And quite lost their hearts. The nobles hath he fined
> For ancient quarrels, and quite lost their hearts (2.1.246–8)

—and so on. These are laments for a state of affairs in which the speakers share, but which is scarcely 'a fee-grief | Due to some single breast' (*Macbeth*, 4.3.196–7).

Somewhat similar, if on a larger scale, are those plaints which find expression in a sense of the breakdown or violation of order, such as York's

> Take Hereford's rights away, and take from Time
> His charters and his customary rights;
> Let not tomorrow then ensue today. (2.1.195–6)

This is the theme, too, of the most generalized lamentations for England, those of the Welsh Captain, 'The bay trees in our country are all withered...' (2.4.8 ff.); of the Gardeners (3.4.43–5)—

> ...our sea-wallèd garden, the whole land,
> Is full of weeds, her fairest flowers choked up,
> Her fruit trees all unpruned...

and of Carlisle, in his prophetic lament for the state of England—

> Peace shall go sleep with Turks and infidels,
> And in this seat of peace tumultuous wars
> Shall kin with kin, and kind with kind, confound.
> Disorder, horror, fear, and mutiny
> Shall here inhabit... (4.1.139–43)

Those who lament mainly on their own behalves often express a sense of the worthlessness of life, and of the imminence of death. Sometimes it is expressed sententiously, with no great personal emotion. So Mowbray declares that men whose reputation is tarnished are 'but gilded loam, or painted clay' (1.1.179); later, under sentence of banishment, he speaks his lament (1.3.159 ff.) that

> The language I have learnt these forty years,
> My native English, now I must forgo—

a lament of particular importance in this play which is, as R. D. Altick (p. 113) says, 'preoccupied with the unsubstantiality of human language'. Other characters in the earlier part of the play become particularly conscious in grief of their own approaching deaths. John of Gaunt's refusal to avenge the murder of Woodstock seems to bring Woodstock's widow, the Duchess of Gloucester, closer to her own death; and she memorably describes her home in terms which create a vivid sense of desolation:

> ...what shall good old York there see
> But empty lodgings and unfurnished walls,
> Unpeopled offices, untrodden stones,
> And what hear there for welcome but my groans?
> ....
> Desolate, desolate will I hence and die,

she says, and does (1.2.67–73). John of Gaunt's case is similar. Grieving for his son's banishment, he foresees that he himself will die before it is over, and expands into reflections on the relentlessness of time's passage and the superiority of its power over the King's:

> Thou can help time to furrow me with age,
> But stop no wrinkle in his pilgrimage. (1.3.229–30)

Later, lamenting Richard's 'unkindness' to himself, he feels stronger premonitions of death:

> Convey me to my bed, then to my grave.

The theme reaches its climax with Richard himself in his lament following the deaths of Bushy, Green, and the Earl of Wiltshire:

> Let's talk graves, of worms, and epitaphs
> . . . .
> —nothing can we call our own but death
> And that small model of the barren earth
> Which serves as paste and cover to our bones.

Really beginning to enjoy himself, he adopts what Clemen (p. 232) calls the 'lugete-topos'—the convention by which the speaker calls on others to help him to lament—

> For God's sake let us sit upon the ground
> And tell sad stories of the death of kings...

And his speech reaches its climax with his classic expression simultaneously of the glory and the vanity of kingship,

> ... within the hollow crown
> That rounds the mortal temples of a king
> Keeps death his court; and there the antic sits,
> Scoffing his state and grinning at his pomp... (3.2.154–63)

Such a fusion of celebration with lament makes direct contact with the traditional theme of 'sic transit gloria mundi', which can be discerned at many other points of the text, most directly perhaps in Salisbury's

> Ah, Richard! With the eyes of heavy mind
> I see thy glory like a shooting star
> Fall to the base earth from the firmament, (2.4.18–20)

and in Richard's own wonderfully and strangely excited and exhilarating version of the same image, which seems to create the blaze of a falling star even as it charts its descent:

> Down, down I come like glistering Phaëton,
> Wanting the manage of unruly jades.
> In the base-court—base-court, where kings grow base
> To come at traitors' calls, and do them grace.
> In the base-court. Come down—down court, down King,
> For night-owls shriek where mounting larks should sing. (3.3.178–83)

The theme sounds with a more plangent lyricism in the ritualistic repetitions of the deposition scene:

> With mine own tears I wash away my balm,
> With mine own hands I give away my crown,
> With mine own tongue deny my sacred state,
> With mine own breath release all duteous oaths.
> All pomp and majesty I do forswear. (4.1.206–10)

We hear it again in Richard's meditations on the looking-glass:

> ...Was this face the face
> That every day under his household roof
> Did keep ten thousand men?—
> ....
> A brittle glory shineth in this face.
> As brittle as the glory is the face,
> For there it is, cracked in an hundred shivers. (4.1.280–8)

It recurs more elegiacally, and more objectively, in Richard's vision of the folk-image of himself, when men of far-off times will speak of him when they tell 'sad stories of the death of kings'; then

> ...some will mourn in ashes, some coal-black,
> For the deposing of a rightful king. (5.1.49–50)

In speaking of the ways in which Shakespeare establishes the value of the thing that is lost, I pointed to some passages which offer a more or less pure expression of an ideal. Oddly enough, one can do the same for Shakespeare's portrayal of grief, in that there are some passages which seem almost to offer a quintessential distillation of grief. They are associated particularly with the female characters. There are only three women of any importance—the Duchess of Gloucester, Richard's Queen, and the Duchess of York—and the first two do practically nothing but lament. The Queen is particularly pure in grief. In her first important scene (2.2), she feels about herself as T. S. Eliot felt of Hamlet: that her emotion is 'in excess of the facts as they appear'. She suffers from what she calls a 'nameless woe', which serves to create foreboding, and to show that someone of whom we know no ill can love Richard. But perhaps the dominant effect of this scene in the play considered as poem is its establishment of the vocabulary of lamentation. The 'sad' Queen suffers from 'life-harming heaviness' and an 'unborn sorrow'. The most important word of all is 'grief'. The word and its derivatives appear forty times in the play—considerably more often than in any other of Shakespeare's plays. More importantly, the concept is bodied forth with such vividness that it almost acquires a life of its own, and might be added to the list of dramatis personae. The Duchess of Gloucester had personified it as her companion; Boling-broke, after his banishment, felt that he was 'a journeyman to grief'; now grief is the Queen's 'guest' in the sense that an unborn child is a guest in its mother's womb; and the imagery of the scene brings the baby to birth; the Queen feels that

> Some unborn sorrow ripe in fortune's womb
> Is coming towards me,

and then finds that the 'nothing' which is her sorrow

> ...hath begot my something grief.

Green is the 'midwife' to her 'woe', and Bolingbroke her 'sorrow's dismal heir'; thus hath her 'soul brought forth her prodigy', leaving the Queen 'a gasping, new-delivered mother'. Later in the play, too, the Queen sees 'hard-favoured grief' as a guest lodging in the 'beauteous inn' which is Richard (5.1.14–15). In the scene (3.4) with her ladies and the gardeners, too, the Queen's inconsolable grief is presented almost in its own right. Her last appearance is in the sad parting with Richard (5.1), which makes us more conscious of why she should grieve, though again she is portrayed rather as a stylized emblem of grief than as an individual.

* * *

In lyric poetry, and even in dramatic choruses, lamentation can be self-contained. A dramatist may make occasional use of self-contained laments, but if he is going to integrate them into a continuous action he will look for ways of moving his characters out of lamentation into some other state of mind. Clemen (pp. 240–1) says that 'With the tragic heroes of the Elizabethan age great suffering is seldom associated with the gentler feelings... more often it gives rise to rage, rebellion, and frenzy... Lament turns into accusation.' Richard II, however, is more passive than most tragic heroes. His principal lament in Act 3, scene 2—'Of comfort no man speak...' (lines 144 ff.)—ends with one of those rhetorical questions which Clemen finds characteristic of the form:

> I live with bread, like you; feel want,
> Taste grief, need friends. Subjected thus,
> How can you say to me I am a king?

Onward movement is made possible by the Bishop of Carlisle:

> My lord, wise men ne'er sit and wail their woes,
> But presently prevent the ways to wail.

Aumerle joins in with some practical advice, and Richard is roused, if not to 'rage, rebellion, and frenzy', at least to the resolve

> ...Proud Bolingbroke, I come
> To change blows with thee for our day of doom.

But his resolve is undermined by a new message of bad news, and he chides Aumerle:

> Beshrew thee, cousin, which didst lead me forth
> Of that sweet way I was in to despair,

and declares that he will 'pine away'. The scene ends in hopelessness:

> Discharge my followers. Let them hence away:
> From Richard's night to Bolingbroke's fair day.

Of course, passive despair is most conveniently presented, as here, at the end of a scene. So in the Duchess of Gloucester's only appearance, in Act 1, scene 2, the design is somewhat similar, except that her lament arouses in her the desire for revenge, and it is she who does the inciting:

> ...To safeguard thine own life
> The best way is to venge my Gloucester's death. (lines 35–6)

It is her failure to arouse John of Gaunt to take vengeance that casts her into the despair with which the scene ends.

The desire for vengeance is a natural issue of lamentation, and there are several instances of it in *Richard II*. Indeed, the emotional terms in which Bolingbroke, in the opening scene, phrases his desire for vengeance on Gloucester's murderer cause his statement to be simultaneously a lament; Gloucester's blood

> ...like sacrificing Abel's, cries
> Even from the tongueless caverns of the earth
> To me for justice and rough chastisement. (1.1.104–6)

Like Bolingbroke, Mowbray turns naturally from grief to desire for revenge:

> I am disgraced, impeached, and baffled here,
> Pierced to the soul with slander's venomed spear,
> The which no balm can cure but his heart-blood
> Which breathed this poison. (1.1.170–3)

Even Richard acknowledges this sentiment while declaring that he cannot act upon it; bidding farewell to Bolingbroke before the intended combat, he declares:

> Farewell, my blood—which if today thou shed,
> Lament we may, but not revenge thee dead. (1.3.57–8)

And in his lament at Flint Castle, one of the possible courses of action that he suggests to Aumerle is a curiously oblique method of vengeance:

> We'll make foul weather with despisèd tears.
> Our sighs and they shall lodge the summer corn
> And make a dearth in this revolting land. (3.3.161–3)

(This, I suppose, may be regarded as a transmutation of the appeal to the elements which Clemen (pp. 233–5) classes as a conventional feature of dramatic laments.)

When a character is himself to blame for what he grieves over, the natural issue is repentance followed by some form of expiation, and this is what we see in Bolingbroke after Richard's death, at the end of the play.

An alternative to the desire to take positive external action about a cause of lamentation is an attempt to find consolation (or, in the play's vocabulary, 'comfort') through a change of mental, internal attitude to it. Bolingbroke demonstrates this with apparent stoicism on receiving his sentence of banishment:

> Your will be done. This must my comfort be:
> That sun that warms you here shall shine on me... (1.3.144–5)

But he softens after the King has left, and admits to 'the abundant dolour of [his] heart'. Roles are reversed as his father, John of Gaunt, who had lamented the banishment to the King, now urges his son to take a more positive attitude to what has happened:

> Think not the King did banish thee,
> But thou the King. (1.3.279–80)

The long, formal exchange between father and son about the power of the imagination to alleviate mental suffering is one of Shakespeare's most explicit and extended statements of a theme which is of fundamental importance not only in this play but in his work as a whole. It recurs in the philosophical discussion between Bushy and the Queen (2.2) about her sadness at parting with Richard:

> Each substance of a grief hath twenty shadows
> Which shows like grief itself, but is not so.
> …So your sweet majesty,
> Looking awry upon your lord's departure,
> Find shapes of grief more than himself to wail,

urges Bushy. 'It may be so,' replies the Queen, 'but yet my inward soul | Persuades me it is otherwise.' The thought that, as Bushy says, ''Tis nothing but conceit' is of no help to her.

If you fail to cheer yourself up by looking on the bright side, you can try consoling yourself with the thought that human values and emotions are insignificant in the light of eternity. This is the traditional theme of *contemptus mundi*, obviously related to that of *sic transit gloria mundi*, to which I referred earlier. It is adopted by Richard in his attempts to stave off despair in Act 3, scene 2; fearing, correctly, that Scroop brings bad news, he declares:

> Mine ear is open and my heart prepared.
> The worst is worldly loss thou canst unfold.
> Say, is my kingdom lost? Why, 'twas my care;
> And what loss is it to be rid of care?
> . . . .
> The worst is death, and death will have his day. (lines 93–103)

But the most impressive version of the theme comes in the following scene, when Richard prepares himself to be deposed.

> What must the King do now? Must he submit?
> The King shall do it. Must he be deposed?
> The King shall be contented. Must he lose
> The name of king? A God's name, let it go.
> I'll give my jewels for a set of beads,
> My gorgeous palace for a hermitage,

My gay apparel for an almsman's gown,
My figured goblets for a dish of wood,
My sceptre for a palmer's walking-staff,
My subjects for a pair of carvèd saints,
And my large kingdom for a grave,
A little, little grave, an obscure grave. (3.3.143–54)

Ernst Kantorowicz, in his justly admired treatment of the play in *The King's Two Bodies*,[7] says of this passage: 'It is a lonely man's miserable and mortal nature that replaces the king as King.' I think this is a slight distortion. The image that Richard chooses for himself is not that of an outcast but of one who has voluntarily adopted the way of life of a religious hermit, in the belief that this will earn for him eternal life. It may be an empty piece of self-dramatization, and it is followed, here and elsewhere, by much talk of the grave without immediate reference to a life beyond it; but it includes an element of self-consolation.

In this respect, I suggest, it links up with a series of references which offset the lamentation of the play with something more positive. I referred to an ideal of kingly happiness expressed almost at the beginning of the play by Mowbray: he caps Bolingbroke's wish that 'Many years of happy days' may befall Richard with

Each day still better other's happiness
Until the heavens, envying earth's good hap,
Add an immortal title to your crown! (1.1.22–4)

This adds particular interest to the Bishop of Carlisle's report of Mowbray's death, a passage which expresses confidence that Mowbray himself has achieved the ideal which he wished for Richard:

Many a time hath banished Norfolk fought
For Jesu Christ in glorious Christian field,
Streaming the ensign of the Christian cross
Against black pagans, Turks, and Saracens,
And, toiled with works of war, retired himself
To Italy, and there at Venice gave
His body to that pleasant country's earth,
And his pure soul unto his captain, Christ,
Under whose colours he had fought so long. (4.1.92–100)

News of the death of Mowbray, that is to say, is reported not with a lament, as might have been expected, but with a tribute and an expression of satisfaction in both a life well spent and a death that deserves what Bolingbroke wishes for him:

> Sweet peace conduct his sweet soul to the bosom
> Of good old Abraham!

This emphasis on the fate of the soul after death, and on the hope of salvation, is found elsewhere, too. In challenging Mowbray, Bolingbroke had said that what he speaks

> My body shall make good upon this earth,
> Or my divine soul answer it in heaven. (1.1.37–8)

After the combat has been forbidden, he says

> By this time, had the King permitted us,
> One of our souls had wandered in the air,
> Banished this frail sepulchre of our flesh. (1.3.194–6)

That he goes on to advise Mowbray not to bear along

> The clogging burden of a guilty soul

stands in ironic contrast to his later wish. Green, before his death, comforts himself with the thought

> …that heaven will take our souls
> And plague injustice with the pains of hell. (3.1.33–4)

Richard, parting from his Queen, returns to the notion of the religious life and its rewards:

> …Hie thee to France,
> And cloister thee in some religious house.
> Our holy lives must win a new world's crown
> Which our profane hours here have thrown down. (5.1.22–5)

And apparently he thinks he succeeds; because, as he dies, he says

> Mount, mount, my soul. Thy seat is up on high,
> Whilst my gross flesh sinks downward here to die. (5.5.111–12)

To this extent, at least, the note of lamentation which forms so important a part of the play's structure and tone is counterpointed with the hope of consolation, a hope that after the passing of the world's glories, contempt of the world may earn a share in heavenly glory.

* * *

The aspects of *Richard II* on which I have been concentrating seem to me to be ones which engaged a major share of Shakespeare's poetic interest as he wrote. They are, I think, largely responsible for the poetic pleasure that we experience: the satisfaction and exhilaration that come from a sense that emotion has been given full expression. Of course, they do not constitute the entire play. I have omitted much; though not, I hope, for the reason implied by A. P. Rossiter when he wrote that 'most commentators direct attention to parts of the play which they can manage, and tacitly divert it from "misfits" they cannot'.[8] The way in which I have chosen to talk about the play is more relevant to the Richard of Acts 3 and 4 than to the Richard of Acts 1, 2, and 5. I referred ironically to the pleasure that Richard takes in his lamentations; and he is often thought of on this account as a self-indulgent wallower in emotional excess. Nicholas Brooke, in his chapter on the play in *Shakespeare's Early Tragedies*, is at pains to destroy the popular image of 'a petulant, effeminate Richard, swooping gracefully to the bare earth, but looking embarrassed every time…that someone remarks how like his father the Black Prince he looks'. He shows that 'no hint' of Richard's 'weakness as a man' is given until his return from Ireland, and also that even in the scenes of his fall, Richard demonstrates a forcefulness which can embarrass Bolingbroke. Remarking that at the end Richard 'still has the energy to make a dramatic last stand against his murderers', Brooke comments that 'it is no mere dreamer we are to remember'.[9] Neither, we may add, is it as a mere lamenter that we are to remember him. Whether Richard's prison soliloquy raises him to the status of a tragic hero is open to debate. At least, I suggest, it shows a progression in him from lamentation to a more constructive form of thought; if we were to put it in poetic terms, we might say that he has developed from a lyrical to a metaphysical poet. But if Richard ends in assertion, the play does not. Structurally, it ends with another variation on the traditional 'messenger' scene. To Richard, messengers had brought bad news; to Henry, the news that they bring is, apparently, good. First Northumberland brings reports of the capture and execution of the King's enemies; then Fitzwalter does the same. Harry Percy brings in another of the enemies, the Bishop of Carlisle, in person, captive; finally Exton enters not merely with the news that Richard, the greatest enemy of all, is dead, but, all improbably, with the corpse itself. This should represent a moment of great triumph for Henry; but he does not respond with the gratitude that Exton might have expected.

> The guilt of conscience take thou for thy labour,
> But neither my good word nor princely favour.

The glory of kingship has turned sour on him, and in the play's closing lines, which are also its final lament, he, in turn, calls on others to lament, and promises to show contempt of the world:

> Come mourn with me for what I do lament,
> And put on sullen black incontinent.
> I'll make a voyage to the Holy Land
> To wash this blood off from my guilty hand.
> March sadly after. Grace my mournings here
> In weeping after this untimely bier.

9

A Midsummer Night's Dream Revisited

The edition of *A Midsummer Night's Dream* which I edited for the New Penguin Shakespeare appeared in 1967. During that time it has been reprinted some twenty times and has sold well over 320,000 copies, which have certainly been used by many students and schoolchildren, and have formed the basis for a number of productions of the play, including the famous one by Peter Brook. It is, of course, like all other editions, gradually going out of date; and I hope it may be of interest to look at some of the more outstanding developments in the play's fortunes that have occurred since I prepared the edition, not simply in order, as it were, to bring its Introduction up to date, but also as a sample of the changes that can occur in attitudes to a Shakespeare play over a comparatively short period in its after-life. During this time there have been new editions, including two with detailed annotations—the new Arden (1979), edited by Harold F. Brooks, and the New Cambridge (1986), edited by R. A. Foakes—and one—the Oxford (1986)—with significant textual innovations.[1] There have been new scholarly investigations; there has been much new criticism, including the first full-length book to be devoted to the play; there have been new offshoots, extending as far as Woody Allen's film *A Midsummer Night's Sex Comedy*; and of course there have been many new productions of the play itself. A bibliography published in 1986 lists well over 1,500 items (including performances), most of them dating from 1940 to 1982; its authors, D. Allen Carroll and Gary Jay Williams, estimate that during this period 'There has been, on average, a published comment on the *Dream* (excluding reviews of productions) every ten days and a production of the play, by conservative estimate, every six weeks'.[2] It would be boring and unproductive to attempt a complete survey of all these developments; what I want to do is rather to select a variety of the most significant ones, and I will begin with investigations of the occasion of the play's first performance.

In 1967 many writers on *A Midsummer Night's Dream* accepted as orthodoxy the view that the play was written for a noble wedding, and that this supposed fact accounted for some of its features, especially the presence in the cast of an exceptional number of roles that might be played by children, and the epithalamic nature of its ending, with the fairies' blessing of the house in which three newly married couples have retired to bed. At least eleven court weddings, ranging in date from 1590 to 1600, have been suggested as the occasion for the play's first performance. (No one has discovered a triple wedding that might have been relevant.) In editing the play I felt it necessary to take this hypothesis seriously, for a number of reasons, most obviously that if we could establish for certain that the play was written for a particular wedding we should also establish for certain its date, about which also there has been much conjecture. This might seem to be of limited interest to the reader of a semi-popular edition, like the New Penguin, which was not intended primarily as a contribution to scholarship; but the wedding theory seemed of fundamental importance, above all because those who accepted it were inclined to underrate the play as a result of it: there was an implication that because some of the play's features could be ascribed to the demands of the occasion its artistry was thereby the less. So I felt obliged to investigate evidence for the theory; and I was not convinced by what I found. In 1967 I wrote:

> There is no outside evidence with any bearing on the matter. The theory has arisen from various features of the play itself. It is, certainly, much concerned with marriage; but so are many comedies. It ends with the fairies' blessing upon the married couples; but this is perfectly appropriate to Shakespeare's artistic scheme, and requires no other explanation... A *Midsummer Night's Dream* (like *Love's Labour's Lost*) appears to require an unusually large number of boy actors. Hippolyta, Hermia, Helena, Titania, Peaseblossom, Cobweb, Moth, and Mustardseed would all have been boys' parts. Puck and Oberon too may have been played by boys or young men. But the title page of the first edition, printed in 1600, tells us that the play was 'sundry times publicly acted by the Right Honourable the Lord Chamberlain his servants'. If Shakespeare's company could at any time muster enough boys for public performances, we have no reason to doubt that it could do so from the start. Thus the suggestion that the roles of the fairies were intended to be taken by children of the hypothetical noble house seems purely whimsical. The stage directions of the first edition, which was probably printed from Shakespeare's manuscript, show no essential differences from those in his other plays; a direction such as '*Enter a* Fairie *at one doore, and* Robin Goodfellow *at another* (II.1.0) suggests that he had in mind the structure of the public theatres. Furthermore although noble weddings in Shakespeare's time were sometimes graced with formal entertainments, usually of the nature of a masque, the first play certainly known to have been written for such an occasion is Samuel Daniels's *Hymen's Triumph*. This was performed in 1614, some twenty years after the composition of *A Midsummer Night's Dream*. By this time the tradition of courtly entertainments had developed greatly; and *Hymen's Triumph* does not appear to have been played in a public theatre.[3]

The scepticism expressed there has won converts. S. Schoenbaum, for instance, quotes this entire passage with approval in his *William Shakespeare: A Documentary Life*

(1975); R. A. Foakes is distinctly sceptical of the wedding hypothesis in his New Cambridge edition; and in the opening chapter of a forthcoming stage history of the play, Gary Jay Williams will subject the theory to the most rigorous criticism it has so far received and conclude that there is nothing 'within the play that compels us to believe that it was created for a court wedding at which Elizabeth was present or any other wedding'. Nevertheless, the view persists and is given credence particularly by the attention paid to it in the influential new Arden edition of 1979, whose editor declares that 'Most scholars are agreed that the *Dream* was designed to grace a wedding in a noble household'; Stanley Wells is cited among 'The one or two sceptics'. I raise the matter here because of two contributions to scholarship which have a bearing on the matter. One is an article by William Ringler, 'The Number of Actors in Shakespeare's Early Plays', published in 1968 but not referred to by the Arden editor, which demonstrates that the fairies can be doubled with the mechanicals, and so weakens the argument that the play needs an exceptional number of boy players.[4] It also raises the intriguing possibility that the fully grown male performers that Peter Brook was to use in his production in 1970, two years after Ringler's article appeared, were more authentic than has generally been supposed. The critical consequences of this doubling have been supported by Stephen Booth, who argues that it 'mirrors, underscores, and comments on the comically troublesome philosophic implications of the "doubling" of Flute, Snout, Starveling, and Snug—four "real" people—with Thisby, Wall, Moonshine and Lion—the complexly and variously unreal creatures they personify in the play staged within the fiction'.[5]

The Arden editor rules out a number of marriages proposed for the original performance of the play, and alights on the two favoured by E. K. Chambers: that between Elizabeth Vere and the Earl of Derby, on 26 January 1595, and that between Elizabeth Carey and Thomas Berkeley, over a year later—it took place on 19 February 1596. Each bride was among the many god-daughters of Queen Elizabeth. Harold Brooks favours the latter wedding—the one between Elizabeth Carey and Thomas Berkeley—on the grounds partly that the bride's grandfather, Henry, Lord Hunsdon, was the Queen's Lord Chamberlain and patron of the company of actors to which Shakespeare belonged. This is beguilingly plausible; and one scholar has followed up the hypothesis with an article arguing that the play is full of topical allusions to the Careys.[6] But the danger of building on ill-constructed foundations is demonstrated in a brief, modest article by Marion Colthorpe, in which she draws on a contemporary history of the Berkeley family written by John Smyth, a contemporary of the bridegroom and a long-standing family retainer.[7] It is clear from Smyth's account that the marriage was celebrated with no remarkable festivity, and certain that the Queen was not present.

In demonstrating that *A Midsummer Night's Dream* was not performed at the marriage regarded by the Arden editor as its most likely stimulus, Marion Colthorpe does not of course totally demolish the wedding play hypothesis; but she does diminish the evidence in its favour. When I look back on my own attitude over the years I find that I am still as sceptical as ever. It would take really hard evidence— external, documentary evidence—to convince me; and if such evidence turned up, it would require me to readjust my basic conception of Shakespeare as a professional playwright. At the same time I should be prepared to admit that my scepticism was provoked partly by a somewhat romantic attitude to the relationship between the author and his work such as has been questioned by much recent critical thought. I was anxious to see the play as the product of a single imagination. More recent criticism sees a more organic relationship between the play and the circumstances of its composition, as an emanation that is, of currents of thought and of social attitudes of which Shakespeare was a product as much as a cause. I do not deny the validity of such criticism; in particular, I think it is quite legitimate, and valuable, to relate the play to contemporary marriage customs, as has been done by Paul Olson and, more recently, by François Laroque in a paper in which he relates elements in the play to those of masque and antemasque as employed in both courtly and popular entertainments.[8] Laroque remarks that 'il existe dans le texte même de A *Midsummer Night's Dream* tout un ensemble d'éléments qui servent à rappeler l'éxistence d'un cordon ombilical reliant la naissance de la comédie au contexte général des cérémonies nuptiales'. I can find this entirely acceptable while reiterating my conviction that even a play very profoundly concerned with marriage does not need to have been written for a marriage.

Proponents of the wedding-play theory have been apt to suppose that the text of the play as first printed, in the 'Fisher' quarto of 1600, incorporates revisions relating to its dual function as a play for both private and public performance. They do not, however, explain why the text incorporates also some of the revisions that, according to their hypothesis, would have been required for public performance. Dover Wilson's demonstration that Theseus's speech on the imagination at the opening of Act 5 incorporates additional lines written after the initial act of composition has been generally accepted, and the Complete Oxford edition offers a reconstruction of the passage as it was originally drafted. More contentious has been the suggestion that the quarto incorporates alternative endings. The theory is stated by Harold Brooks: 'If ... the play was composed originally for a wedding in a noble household, there would hardly be a long delay before its revival on the public stage, when it is likely that the fairy masque would have to be omitted. Puck's epilogue presumably took its place, and it may be that the expansion in V.i. 1–83 was undertaken at that juncture, partly to help compensate for the shortening.' This strikes me as pure guesswork. In the first place, I see no reason why 'the fairy masque would have to be omitted' in public performance. It is fully integrated with the play's fiction. (Nor, properly speaking, is it a masque.) In this it is totally different from the only passage in the whole of Shakespeare's works which clearly does relate to a particular performance, the lines alluding to the festival of the order of the Garter in

The Merry Wives of Windsor. There is no trace of these lines in the 'bad' quarto of that play, which appears to be based on actual performance, and they have regularly been omitted in later performances. Here, for once, Shakespeare was very much 'of an age'. In *A Midsummer Night's Dream*, on the other hand, the fairies' blessing on the house is found in both the quarto and the Folio texts, and has regularly been performed with no sense of redundancy or incongruity. Even in Benjamin Britten's opera, which reduces the play's lines by about 50 per cent, the episode is included and is the occasion for one of the most beautiful passages in twentieth-century opera.

Furthermore, there is general agreement that the first quarto of *A Midsummer Night's Dream* was printed from Shakespeare's own original manuscript. Brooks, writing on what he regards as the play's alternative endings, cites W. W. Greg's view, 'There would be nothing surprising in finding both in the foul papers, and we should expect to find them in the order in which they were written', but this seems to me an extraordinary aberration on Greg's part. Though his statement has been cited in support of the wedding-play hypothesis, it appears not to have been subjected to scrutiny, nor do I believe it can withstand such scrutiny. For one thing, the 'fairy masque' has been anticipated at the moment of Oberon and Titania's reconciliation, when the fairy King says:

> Now thou and I are new in amity
> And will tomorrow solemnly
> Dance in Duke Theseus' house triumphantly,
> And bless it to all fair prosperity.

There is nothing in the quarto to suggest that these lines had been marked for omission when the play was performed in public playhouses. I find it difficult to believe that if Shakespeare in his original manuscript had been trying to provide simultaneously for both private and public performance he would simply have written an alternative ending for public performances which as it happens dovetails perfectly with that provided for private performance; nor do I think that the so-called alternative ending does in fact make the play more suitable for public performance. To my mind the play including the fairies' blessing would end baldly without Robin Goodfellow's epilogue, which is surely as suited to private as to public performance; and I think that this epilogue would come awkwardly after Oberon's final lines if the other supernatural figures, too, had not made a reappearance. Furthermore, if the change had been made, I should have expected some sign of it to have been found in the Folio, which it is generally agreed was influenced by a promptbook used in public performance.

It is in relation to the status of the text of the play printed in the 1623 Folio that attitudes have most drastically shifted during the past twenty years. It has generally been agreed that the Folio printers used a copy of a reprint of the quarto which had been annotated in consultation with a promptbook used by Shakespeare's company. Thus, for example, Foakes writes: 'It looks very much ... as though the Folio text was somewhat carelessly set up from a copy of Q2 that had been rather haphazardly corrected and expanded by an editor who was able to compare it with a manuscript marked up for use in the theatre' (p. 139). The Folio editor made several corrections to the dialogue (such as supplying a word accidentally omitted in the quarto, at 3.2.220) which most later editors have accepted, but he also made a number of other, more specifically theatrical, changes, which have customarily been dismissed but which are accepted in the *Complete Oxford Shakespeare* of 1986. Previous editors—including myself in 1967—preferred the quarto because it was closest to Shakespeare's first thoughts, but in recent years scholars (including me) have become more willing to concede that a playscript reaches full fruition only in the theatre, that Shakespeare was above all a man of the theatre working in the closest possible collaboration with a single company of actors, and that we may therefore reasonably pay heed to the evidence of how his texts were played in his own theatre, and print a version of the play which reflects changes made during the process of rehearsal and performance rather than, or as well as, one which reflects the dramatist's earlier, untested intentions.

There is a minor example of this in 3.1. Bottom and his companions are rehearsing their play. Robin Goodfellow (as I think he should properly be called, rather than 'Puck') enters with the words 'What hempen homespuns have we swaggering here ... ?' The Folio text has a duplicate entry for Robin some fifteen lines previously, as the mechanicals are discussing how to present moonshine. The Arden edition regards this as a straightforward error, but it is one that requires explanation since there was no need for the annotator to make any alteration to his copy. In my New Penguin edition I suggested that the entry may reflect Elizabethan stage practice in bringing Robin on stage to watch the mechanicals before he speaks, and R. A. Foakes agrees with this in his New Cambridge edition, but only the Complete Oxford edition goes so far as to mark an entrance for Robin at this point.

The most substantial Folio alteration affects the staging of the opening of the last Act of the play. The alterations remove a number of the lines from two different speakers and give them to two other speakers, and they cannot be accidental. Essentially they fall into two groups: those that replace Philostrate by Egeus, and those that allocate to Lysander lines spoken in the quarto by Theseus. I will take the second first. In line 45 in the quarto text Theseus has a speech lasting seventeen lines in which he both reads the titles of the entertainments offered for his nuptial ceremony and comments on them. In the Folio this speech is shared between Lysander and Theseus: that is, Lysander reads the titles, and Theseus offers his comments. As Foakes says, 'This was perhaps an arrangement designed to make the passage more dramatic, and to give more involvement in the action to at least one of the lovers, who otherwise stand silent through the first part of the scene; possibly it was always played in this way' (p. 141). Most editors have retreated to the safety of the quarto, as I did in my 1967 edition, but the Complete Oxford edition follows the Folio, and this seems to me right if we are to give priority to theatrical values. It seems undeniable that the change was made by Shakespeare's own company, and probable that it had his approval.

A more fundamental change in the same area of the play reassigns most of the lines spoken in the quarto by Philostrate (who has a non-speaking role in the play's opening scene) to Egeus, father of Hermia. Again, the change is clearly deliberate. Philostrate remains in the scene to speak only lines 83 to 87; he could be implicitly included among the 'Lords' mentioned in the scene's opening direction, but it seems more likely that the annotator simply failed to cancel one of the quarto's speech prefixes and that these lines too should be spoken by Egeus. The theatrical and dramatic consequences of this change, which also is accepted in the Complete Oxford edition, are explored and defended in Barbara Hodgdon's article 'Gaining a Father: The Role of Egeus in the Quarto and the Folio', published in the same year as the Oxford edition.[9] The usual assumption has been that the substitution of Egeus for Philostrate was designed to save an actor, and that it may have been made purely as a theatrical exigency. But the fact is that it does not save an actor: it would be difficult for a single actor to double Philostrate and Egeus in the play's opening scene, since only four to six lines separate Philostrate's exit from Egeus's entry; and in any case if the Folio's ascription of a few lines in the last scene to Philostrate is correct, separate actors are required for both Philostrate and Egeus. If, on the other hand, Philostrate in the last Act had been required to speak all the lines ascribed to him in the quarto, the role could still have been undertaken by the actor who had previously played Egeus since only one of the two characters would have been required to appear in the final Act. The simplest way of effecting an economy, if this had been required, would have been to alter the name of Philostrate in the play's opening episode; then the two roles could easily have been doubled with no need for the major surgery involved in transforming Philostrate to Egeus.

If we accept, as I think we must, that the last Act change of Philostrate to Egeus may have been made for artistic rather than for practical reasons, then our inter-pretation of certain aspects of the play, and particularly of the role of Egeus, must be altered. In the quarto, Egeus appears twice: in the opening scene, where he forbids Hermia to marry Lysander, and in the scene of the lovers' awakening, where he maintains his objection, only to be overruled by Theseus:

> Egeus, I will overbear your will. (4.1.178)

The Folio offers opportunities to develop Egeus's attitude to Lysander. Egeus, it would seem, hands to Lysander the 'brief' listing the wedding entertainments. As

Barbara Hodgdon remarks, 'Either Lysander is reading over Egeus's shoulder or he takes, or snatches, the paper from Egeus. Whichever, the Folio text clearly gives Lysander an action to play, one which can show either that Lysander now has Egeus's approval or that... he uses this opportunity to deny Egeus's voice and assert his own... Either possibility recalls the tensions and accusations both at the play's opening and in 4.1 and, lightly, either heals or continues them' (pp. 538–9). There are, as Hodgdon also points out, further possibilities for theatrical exploration in the exit of Theseus and his train, which can suggest either that Egeus is reconciled to his daughter's marriage to Lysander or that he continues to oppose it. What is perhaps most interesting about the changes is that they extend the role of a character— Egeus—who is integral to the play's action at the expense only of one— Philostrate—who is peripheral to it.

Barbara Hodgdon's article is interesting partly because, it seems to me, its combination of bibliographical expertise with subtle thought about theatrical interpretation means that it could only have appeared within the last ten or fifteen years. Reinvestigation of the play's textual origins is associated with a rethinking of its theatrical possibilities not in post-Shakespearean adaptation but in relation to its text as originally written and as performed by Shakespeare's own company. This is a healthy sign. A similar concern activates a more purely critical study of the role of Hippolyta conducted by Philip McGuire in his book *Speechless Dialect: Shakespeare's Open Silences*, published in 1985.[10]

McGuire points out that in the play's opening scene Hippolyta speaks only 4½ lines—the ones beginning 'Four days will quickly steep themselves in night'—which form the second speech of the play. After this:

> When Theseus says that, having conquered her in battle, he will now make her his wife 'in another key, | With pomp, with triumph, and with revelling', Hippolyta says nothing, and she maintains that silence the rest of the time she is onstage. The defeated Queen of the Amazons becomes a mute observer as the man who 'won' her love by doing her 'injuries' (line 17) rules that a young woman who is one of his subjects must die or live a life cloistered among women if she does not obey her father and enter into a marriage that she does not want. (p. 1)

McGuire's subsequent analysis of the scene is an admirable demonstration of the developing technique of performance criticism. First he examines the words of the text in the 'attempt to clarify the meanings and effects of [Hippolyta's] silence' (p. 2), paying particular attention to Theseus's and Hippolyta's disparate attitudes to time—Theseus comments 'how slow | This old moon wanes', but for Hippolyta 'four days will quickly steep themselves in night...'. Though their opening exchange 'permits us to see their differences as facets of an underlying harmony', it can also, 'without distorting the words of Shakespeare's playtext, just as plausibly be taken as reflecting a conflict between Theseus and Hippolyta. If the nuptial hour approaches so slowly for Theseus because he desires it so much, then perhaps it approaches so quickly for Hippolyta, the newly conquered queen of a society of women who had long resisted male domination, precisely because she desires it so little.' The ambiguity cannot be resolved from the text; Hippolyta's silence 'is capable of having meanings and effects that are not fixed by those words and that take on distinct form and shape only during performances of the play'.

From this, McGuire goes on to examine from four specific productions 'the range of meanings and effects that Hippolyta's silence can generate without contradicting the words of Shakespeare's playtext'. His conclusion is that Shakespeare 'has assigned to those who perform A *Midsummer Night's Dream* the power to give Hippolyta's silence shape and local habitation' and that 'the exercise of that power can bring forth from Hippolyta's silence meanings and effects that differ, sometimes profoundly, yet remain compatible with the words that Shakespeare did pen'. Hippolyta's silence means that the play can 'change significantly while retaining identity and coherence': for example, it can respond to the concerns of feminism 'because Hippolyta's silence allows for the possibility that she, like Hermia, does not submit to male authority'.

In this chapter, McGuire's approach is centred on the text, not on the author. He explores that text much as a theatre director might, and he is searching, not for evidence of authorial intention, but for evidence of the multiplicity of meaning that the unadapted text may legitimately yield. This approach is characteristic of modern 'theoretical' criticism, but the virtues of a more traditional approach are exemplified in a book that appeared in 1966, while my edition was in the press. David P. Young's *Something of Great Constancy: The Art of 'A Midsummer Night's Dream'* is, I believe, the first full-length book to be devoted to the play, and it is written with missionary zeal in an attempt to communicate the author's conviction that A *Midsummer Night's Dream* is one of Shakespeare's 'most important plays and a touchstone for the understanding and interpretation of others'.[11] The book is valuable for excellent analysis of the play's style and structure and for a subtle discussion of its concern with dreams. But at the heart of the author's argument is his discussion of the part played by imagination in A *Midsummer Night's Dream* and his concern 'to emphasize its significance as a source of our knowledge of Shakespeare's own attitude toward drama, poetry, and the imagination'. This attempt to see the play in relation to Shakespeare's own ideas about his art is related to an essay of my own, 'Shakespeare Without Sources', published in 1972, in which I discuss A *Midsummer Night's Dream* along with *Love's Labour's Lost* and *The Tempest* as plays in which Shakespeare is exploring his own artistic preoccupations.[12]

Championing the play as an 'expression of contemporaneous intellectual issues', David Young declared a 'hope for productions of the play which do not treat it as a kind of Elizabethan *Peter Pan*'. The subsequent work of scholar-critics such as

Barbara Hodgdon and Philip McGuire with a strong and serious interest in the play's theatrical realization helps to bridge the gap between the study and the stage, though I fear that the world of the theatre, which for long mocked academics for lacking a sense of theatrical values, has been slow to profit from the ever-increasing interest that academics have taken in the theatre in recent years. But directors of *A Midsummer Night's Dream* have been treating the play with increased seriousness, re-examining well-worn traditions of performance, and sometimes even adopting textual variants. Bill Alexander's RSC production brought on Egeus instead of Philostrate in the last Act; so did John Caird's (1989), in which also the Hippolyta of the opening scene was a distinctly reluctant bride, visibly sympathizing with Hermia, though fully reconciled to marriage after her experiences in the person of Titania in the forest. Productions both in the theatre and on film and television have continued to stimulate interest in the play, to spread enjoyment of it, to reinvestigate its theatrical possibilities in ways that have often been related to those employed by academic critics and that have continued to stimulate this work, both consciously and unconsciously. When I wrote my Introduction to the play, its most historically significant production, at least in the twentieth century, seemed to be that of Harley Granville-Barker given at the Savoy Theatre, London, in 1914. I remarked that this production 'represented a thorough re-thinking of the play which effected a healthy clearance of conventional accretions...Since Granville-Barker's time the desire for simplicity of presentation has slowly won ground over the desire for visual elabor-ation.' With hindsight, this seems to represent an overly simplistic, evolutionary view. The pendulum has continued to swing, now in the direction of simplicity, now in that of elaboration. And of course there has been a production that has been as revolutionary, and controversial, in its time as Granville-Barker's was in the early years of the century.

Peter Brook's production of *A Midsummer Night's Dream* for the Royal Shakespeare Company in 1970 was characteristic of its time in being influenced by a piece of literary criticism, the chapter on the play in Jan Kott's book *Shakespeare our Contemporary*, which had appeared in a British translation in 1964,[13] while I was working on my edition, but I ignored it both in my Introduction and in my list of 'Further Reading', doubtless for reasons which I expressed in a book published in 1970, where I wrote:

> Jan Kott...has worked in the professional theatre as a producer, yet he can write about *A Midsummer Night's Dream* in terms that seem quite incapable of realization in theatrical terms. This is, he says in *Shakespeare our Contemporary*, 'the most erotic of Shakespeare's plays.' He imagines Titania's court consisting of old men and women, toothless and shaking, their mouths wet with saliva, who sniggeringly procure a monster for their mistress. He finds Oberon is determined that his Queen shall sleep with a beast of a kind which represents 'abundant sexual potency...Bottom is

eventually transformed into an ass. But in this nightmarish summer night, the ass does not symbolise stupidity. Since antiquity and up to the Renaissance the ass was credited with the strongest sexual potency and among all the quadrupeds is supposed to have the longest and hardest phallus.'[14]

And he goes on: 'I visualize Titania as a very tall, flat and fair girl, with long arms and legs, resembling the white Scandinavian girls I used to see in rue de la Harpe, or rue Huchette, walking and clinging tightly to negroes with faces grey or so black that they were almost indistinguishable from the night.' Kott finds it a matter of surprise that 'the scenes between Titania and Bottom transformed into an ass are often played for laughs in the theatre'. And I remarked that 'even the Pyramus and Thisbe scenes weigh heavily upon him ... Kott ... uses the play as a stimulus to his own imagination and, by selecting certain aspects of the text, produces a bizarre falsification of it.' There is a world of difference between McGuire's scrupulous re-examination of the text for meanings that are compatible with its dialogue and Kott's flights of fancy which, taking off from the text, rapidly leave it far behind.

In suggesting that Kott's vision of the play was 'incapable of realization in theatrical terms' I was, I now realize, underestimating the capacities of, for example, the German expressionist school of theatrical production, as may be seen merely from a glance at the illustrations to Maik Hamburger's article 'New Concepts of Staging A Midsummer Night's Dream'.[15] And in failing to mention Kott's chapter I was shutting my eyes to a piece of essentially belle-lettrist criticism which, much as I continue to dislike it, has exerted a strong influence on thought about the play, for better and for worse, and by reaction as well as by agreement. Kott's sensationalist mode of writing, along with the fact that he had genuinely interesting things to say about some of Shakespeare's plays, caused his book to reach a wide audience. His chapter on A Midsummer Night's Dream provoked much comment. As D. Allen Carroll writes in the Garland Bibliography, it is 'the most distinctive piece on the play in our era', and though 'most critics have dismissed Kott's reading as wrong in its single-mindedness and urgency' yet 'Kott has made a difference. For a full decade some reaction to him was obligatory, and the result has been, on the whole, that we see more in the play than we saw before.' Kott has helped people to see that the play is not, as Derek Traversi had written in 1954, 'barely more than a delicate, tenuous piece of decoration' (a view which Traversi considerably modified after Kott's piece appeared), though my own feeling is that G. Wilson Knight had gone quite far enough in drawing attention to the sinister side of the fairy world in a seminal treatment of the play published in 1932 in his book The Shakespearian Tempest. This view had already reached the stage in George Devine's 1954 Stratford production, in which, as Richard David wrote, the director sought to emphasize the fairies' 'distinction from human kind, their strangeness, their remoteness from normality, and, with his designers, had seen as a symbol of this quality not the dainty midget, the tutu fairy, the decorative butterfly of recent tradition, but a bird, creature of freaks and passions that sometimes appear very like our own, and yet closer akin to the reptiles than to man' (*Shakespeare Survey 8*, 138).

If George Devine anticipated Peter Brook in having 'decided that the conventional prettinesses were to be avoided at all costs' (p. 136), the time was not yet ripe for him. His production achieved nothing like the impact made by Peter Brook in his revolutionary and triumphant RSC production of 1970, which, opening in Stratford-upon-Avon, was seen also in New York, Boston, and London in 1971 and went on a world tour in 1972 to 1973. Brook's production was a consequence of the liberations of the 1960s; it was visibly influenced by Jan Kott's essay, but happily Brook is independent enough in his genius not simply to have transferred Kott's vision of the play to the stage but to have made selective and creative use of it. I shall not attempt here a detailed description or critique of the production, but I should like to make a few points about it which seem relevant to the play's continuing impact.

It is necessary first to remark that Brook used a complete, virtually unadapted text. The production was revolutionary not because of any textual adaptation but because of the attitudes that Brook took towards the text. To a certain extent it was—like Granville-Barker's production before it—a critique of, and a reaction against, earlier productions, and against the play's stage history in general. I mentioned earlier that Brook used fully-grown male performers for the fairies; and they were not prettified: one of them, indeed, was aggressively fat and hairy. This was a clear reaction against the use of charming child actors in these roles. Of course, it goes against the text's description of the fairy attendants: but, as I wrote in my New Penguin Introduction, even the smallest human actor could not impersonate these fairies on stage as they are represented in the dialogue; 'Shakespeare seems deliberately to draw attention to the discrepancies between what we see and what is described...the audience is required to use its imagination in order to make the play possible' (p. 19). Ringler's work on doubling suggests the possibility that the small fairies were played by grown actors in Shakespeare's time, and it is arguable that the demands that Brook made on our imaginations are more in line with Shakespeare's artistry than attempts to make the fairies correspond as closely as possible to the text's descriptions of them.

These adult fairies were involved in the most obviously Kottian moment of the production, which came just before the interval. The moment is described by Roger Warren in his useful little book about the play in the 'Text and Performance' series:

> Titania's 'Be kind and courteous' speech-song was repositioned to follow the dialogue between Bottom and the fairies, and her line 'To have my love to bed and to arise' was repeated at the end of the song, with 'arise' interpreted in such a way that the song could lead directly into a wild orgasmic conclusion. The fairies hoisted Bottom on to

their shoulders; one of them thrust a muscular arm up between Bottom's legs like a grotesque phallus; Oberon swung on a rope across the stage, and the rest of the cast threw paper plates and streamers like confetti over Bottom and Titania as the Mendelssohn Wedding March blared out.[16]

I have referred to this as a Kottian moment, and this is true of its sexual suggestiveness, pointing to a far more physical relationship between Bottom and Titania than the more idealized one that has traditionally been inferred from the text. But it was unKottian in its joyfulness: there was a theatrical elation about this moment in performance which was worlds away from the sordid vision of lust and prostitution presented by Kott.

The use of a snatch of Mendelssohn's Wedding March also made this a theatrically self-referential moment. Mendelssohn's marvellous overture and incidental music for *A Midsummer Night's Dream* have been associated with the play ever since they were composed in the first half of the nineteenth century, and they are ineradicably linked with the romantic style of presentation. Only such a style could sustain the use of a wedding march lasting over six minutes. Granville-Barker had deliberately broken with the tradition of using Mendelssohn's music in 1914, when he employed English folk songs. But in 1954, the year of George Devine's production, another elaborately nineteenth-century-style production using Mendelssohn's score and performed jointly by the Old Vic Company, the Sadler's Wells Ballet, and a full symphony orchestra was played in London and New York; and, of course, the wedding march has a life of its own in churches rather than in theatres. So Brook's use of it here was a complex one, in part cocking a snook at the romantic style of presentation, but also drawing on the joyful associations of the music to form a climax to the first part of his production.

The theatrical self-referentiality of Brook's production links it to a strain in criticism that has been much apparent in recent years in which the play has been seen as 'metatheatrical' in its mode, as a work in which Shakespeare is in part concerned with his own art and with the art of the theatre in general. This aspect of the production, or the critical mode that it reflects, may have influenced a later Stratford version of the play, directed by Ron Daniels in 1981, which set it in Victorian times, playing the woodland scenes 'not even in front of a Victorian representation of a wood, but on the deserted stage of a Victorian theatre at night, strewn with theatrical properties, including scenic flats with their wooden frames, not their painted sides, facing the audience'.[17] As Roger Warren writes, some spectators 'enjoyed the performance out of a sense of nostalgia for traditional nineteenth-century stagings of the *Dream*', but more subtly Daniels appeared to be suggesting that we do better to acknowledge that our conception of the play is conditioned by its later stage history than to attempt to resist or exorcise this.

SHAKESPEARE ON PAGE AND STAGE

Even more influential on more recent stagings of the play has been Peter Brook's doubling of certain characters. Some of the doublings seemed to have no great interpretative significance, though I suppose that Philostrate's equation with Robin Goodfellow may have encouraged us to see both of them as Masters of court revels. More important was the doubling (not actually initiated by Brook) of Theseus with Oberon and of Hippolyta with Titania, as if to suggest that one of each pair is the alter ego of the other—or, as Roger Warren puts it, 'that the events in the wood represented the dark animal fantasies beneath the public front which Theseus and Hippolyta present to the world' (p. 56). The dispute about whether this double may have been intended by Shakespeare or carried out in his theatre is indicative both of the uncertain state of our knowledge of Elizabethan theatrical practice and of the attempts to explore the extent of our own ignorance by questioning the fundamental assumptions on which scholarly investigations have been based. William Ringler, writing a few years before Brook directed the play, had denied the possibility of this doubling on the grounds that as soon as the fairy King and Queen have left the stage after their reconciliation, Hippolyta has to re-enter with Theseus and his courtiers. This denial was based on the assumption that after leaving the stage in one persona, an actor needs a short period of time to recostume himself before re-entering in a fresh guise. But Peter Brook showed that the immediate transformation could be successfully effected simply by causing the actors who had walked up to doorways as Oberon and Titania to don cloaks, turn round, and immediately walk downstage again as Theseus and Hippolyta; so, as Stephen Booth writes, 'the entrance that caused Ringler to say that the kings and queens could not have been successfully doubled delighted audiences, and also seemed to delight the two actors (who strode back through the doorway grinning in apparent triumph at the transparent theatricality of their physically minimal metamorphosis)'. Booth argues that 'most of our thinking about Elizabethan casting is still based on the assumed universality of Ibsenian practices', showing 'a narrowmindedness improbable in a century that accepted Charlie Chaplin as monochromatic, silent, twenty feet high, and flat'.[18]

The dispute about the theatrical authenticity of the doubling is paralleled by that about its aesthetic validity. For some critics, such as Stephen Booth, it is revelatory. Citing the passage in which Titania glances at Oberon's 'credit with Hippolyta', while he makes aspersions about Titania's 'love to Theseus', Booth finds that the lines 'suggest that they were written to capitalize on and intensify the effect of planned theatrical doubling'. But doesn't theatrical doubling run the risk of drawing the audience's attention to the resemblances between the characters at the expense of ironing out their differences? So John Russell Brown suggests, complaining that Brook's doubling operated 'as if the actors' task was to make what likeness exists between the pairs as obvious and inescapable as possible, and to minimize the very considerable differences'.[19] To cite a parallel in which doubling (or trebling) would be possible only by using the trickery of film or television, everyone agrees that there are significant resemblances between the situations of Hamlet, Laertes, and Fortinbras, but to have a single actor play the three roles would not necessarily be advantageous.

Although, as I have said, Brook's production has exerted considerable influence over later theatrical realizations of the play, it is characteristic of the way theatre works, and also symptomatic of the play's openness to variety of interpretation, that the next major British production, by John Barton at Stratford in 1977, did not adopt Brook's doubling and reverted to a generally more romantic style of presentation which also characterized the BBC's television version. The theatre operates partly by a process of action and reaction, and this is also true, to some degree, of criticism and even of scholarship. Though we may seek for certainties, we often have to rest content with provisional solutions, with ultimately unprovable hypotheses, and we may favour now one, now another. The text of *A Midsummer Night's Dream* is less than 2,200 lines long, but in writing those lines Shakespeare unconsciously created a generator for an astonishing quantity of human activity of many different kinds. I have indicated only a small amount of that activity during a period of little more than twenty years. Undoubtedly, more is yet to come. I do not want to be prophetic about the form that this activity will take. The text itself will shift slightly as the result of further editorial activity. There will certainly be more scholarship, more criticism, more productions, probably more derivative offshoots. What is most important is that what Shakespeare wrote will continue to give delight, to stimulate imagination and to satisfy imaginative needs in the theatre. If we study the text alone, we are like musicians studying a score. It can tell us much. But it is only in the theatre that the text achieves realization, and only there that, however imperfectly, the visions of which Robin speaks in his epilogue can appear.

10

Translations in *A Midsummer Night's Dream*

Midsummer Night's Dream* is profoundly and constantly—though also delicately and humorously—concerned with processes of change, of translation from one state to another, and its audience is frequently made aware that for human beings translation—any kind of translation—is likely to be a difficult process requiring that obstacles be overcome, and that it may involve loss as well as gain. The most prominent, and most frequently discussed, aspect of translation in the play is from the unmarried to the married state. In no other play by Shakespeare is the process of courtship leading to marriage so central a concern. Almost all his comedies portray attempts to overcome obstacles to marriage, but at the end of most of them marriage is deferred, not accomplished. This play, however, opens with preparations for marriage, continues with the story of wooings at first thwarted but then successfully concluded, and ends with the celebration of not one but three marriages. But the transition from the unmarried to the married state is not the only form of translation with which the play is concerned, and I shall consider the idea less in relation to the lovers than to the labourers, or mechanicals, and especially Bottom. 'Bless thee, Bottom, bless thee', says Peter Quince at a climactic moment, 'Thou art translated' (3.1.113). But Bottom is a translator as well. I shall look at both roles, and I start with the passive rather than the active.

At the moment of his translation, Bottom's appearance wearing an ass's head comes to Quince and his fellows as a total, and unwelcome, surprise. It is a surprise for the audience, too, though one for which there has been, in Shakespeare's usual manner, a good deal of subtextual preparation. We know of Oberon's plot to drop the liquor of love-in-idleness on Titania's eyes so that

> The next thing then she waking looks upon—
> Be it on lion, bear, or wolf, or bull,
> On meddling monkey, or on busy ape—
> She shall pursue it with the soul of love. (2.1.179–82)[1]

We have seen him squeeze the juice on her eyes with the invocation,

> What thou seest when thou dost wake,
> Do it for thy true love take;
> Love and languish for his sake.
> Be it ounce, or cat, or bear,
> Pard, or boar with bristled hair,
> In thy eye that shall appear,
> When thou wak'st, it is thy dear.
> Wake when some vile thing is near. (2.2.33–40)

More recently, we have seen Robin Goodfellow moving invisibly among the mechanicals at their rehearsal, looking for mischief—'I'll be an auditor— | An actor too, perhaps, if I see cause'—and then following Bottom off-stage with the threat that at his re-entry he will appear 'A stranger Pyramus than e'er played here'. Bottom, in training to translate himself into Pyramus, has gone supposedly into the hawthorn-brake that serves him and his fellows as a tiring-house, but presumably, in Shakespeare's theatre, into the actual tiring-house. He re-enters a few moments later *'with the Asse head'*, as the Folio direction has it, and speaking the ironically appropriate words, 'If I were fair, fair Thisbe, I were only thine' (2.2.98).

Around thirty different animals have so far been named in the play, but Shakespeare has cunningly refrained from having anyone speak of an ass until the moment of Bottom's translation. For the audience, this is a moment that permits a reaction at least partly comic: we see now where Oberon's plot is leading, it seems appropriate enough that Bottom, like his close relative Dogberry, should be writ down an ass,[2] and we have the pleasure of observing the theatrical mechanics of the transformation. A history of asses' heads in *A Midsummer Night's Dream* would form an entertaining chapter of theatre history in itself. Trevor R. Griffiths provides a concise survey in his 'Shakespeare in Production' edition,[3] and the variety of expedients that have been adopted, ranging from realistic full heads with working ears and mouths to mere skull caps with ears attached, bears witness to the fact that this is not an easy moment to bring off effectively. Partly this is because Shakespeare, as often in his early plays, does little to integrate action into dialogue. The translation of Bottom into an ass is abrupt; nor is it total. Bottom needs to look enough like an ass for us to sympathize with those who believe him to have been transformed, but at the same time the actor has to be perceptible enough for us to register facial expression.

William C. Carroll, in his excellent study *The Metamorphoses of Shakespearean Comedy*, describes Bottom's translation as 'the only onstage physical man-to-beast trans-formation in all of Shakespeare's plays',[4] but of course it is not an 'on-stage transformation', which would be impossible to achieve in the theatre, at least without technical means that were not at Shakespeare's disposal. Bottom has to go off-stage to don the ass's head, and from the neck downwards he remains the actor playing Bottom. At the moment of his reappearance everything depends on visual effect, and although for the audience the effect may be comic, for Quince and his fellows it is one of consternation. A nice balance needs to be struck. If we are to have any sense that Bottom's colleagues have reason to be frightened we must at least momentarily share their fear. In their simplicity, Bottom's friends believe that he truly has been metamorphosed as the result of supernatural agency. 'O monstrous! O strange! We are haunted. Pray, masters; fly, masters: help!' says Quince on first seeing the man-ass, and he and his fellows (possibly but not certainly with Bottom too[5]) run off in a fear which will be all the more genuinely funny if it also seems real. And then Robin exults in his success in words which portray himself as the arch shape-changer; for him, translation is effortless:

> I'll follow you, I'll lead you about a round,
>   Through bog, through bush, through brake, through brier.
> Sometimes a horse I'll be, sometime a hound,
>   A hog, a headless bear, sometime a fire,
> And neigh, and bark, and grunt, and roar, and burn,
> Like horse, hound, hog, bear, fire at every turn. (3.1.101–6)

As the bolder of the mechanicals recover their nerve, they lurk back to test the evidence of their eyes. First is Snout:

> O Bottom, thou art changed. What do I see on thee?

And then Quince:

> Bless thee, Bottom, bless thee. Thou art translated.

There is an element of potential paradox in the wording of this reaction. Quince does not say, 'Bless me, here's a donkey, where has Bottom gone?', but unequivo- cally addresses what he sees as 'Bottom'. Bottom may be 'translated', but he is not transmuted. Just as a passage of prose or verse translated into a different language both is and is not what it originally was, so, to Quince, Bottom is still recognizably Bottom; similarly, the volumes of Ovid's *Metamorphoses*, both in the original Latin and in Golding's English version which no doubt lay open on Shakespeare's desk as he wrote, were recognizable to him as things that both are and are not the same.

The word 'translated' would have had a range of possible meanings for Shake- speare's early audiences. Of course it could mean 'rendered from one language into another', as on Golding's title-page—'translated oute of | *Latin into English meeter, by*

A-r | thur Golding Gentleman', but that is only metaphorically appropriate here. It could signify simply 'changed' in one way or another, but the fact that Snout has already used that word suggests an element of intensification in Quince's usage. The word could also have more elevated senses, including 'transformed' or 'transmuted', and even 'carried or conveyed to heaven without death', and the hint of the supernatural would have been supported by Quince's exhortation to his companions to pray, and by his words 'Bless thee, bless thee', which might well have been heard as more than a conventional expression of good wishes, and might indeed have been emphasized by Quince's making the sign of the cross and/or falling to his knees. The brief episode may then have been given—may still be given—a quality of awe and wonder as the result of the verbal and gestural reactions of those who witness it.

The fact is that more than one sense of the word 'translated' is felt simultaneously here. To Bottom's fellows, he is changed yet remains Bottom, rather as the story of Pyramus and Thisbe is still the same story whether it is told in Latin or in English, or in narrative or dramatic form. On one level Bottom is, we might say, a simile rather than a metaphor. To himself, he is a bilingual edition, with the original at the foot of the page and the translation at the head: he is Bottom to the extent that he has recognized his friends and can apparently speak to them in their own language (though there may be some question about this, since Shakespeare cannot avoid using this language if he is to remain in communication with his audience, and Bottom's fellows do not respond directly to what he says); but he is an ass to the extent that on his next appearance he has a longing for 'good dry oats' and a 'bottle of hay'. And out of this incongruity much mirth comes.

For Titania, however, Bottom is translated in the most elevated sense of the word: roused from her drugged sleep by his singing, she asks what angel has woken her from her flowery bed, while acknowledging that he has enough dregs of mortality in him for her to need to 'purge' his 'mortal grossness' so that he may 'like an airy spirit go'. For her, his translation resembles that of a literary work which so far transcends the original as to constitute an entirely new creation, like, perhaps, *The Rubáiyát of Omar Khayyám*. And Bottom, too, readily accepts a sense of new identity, very much as does Christopher Sly in the Induction to *The Taming of the Shrew*; just as Sly is ministered to by the Lord's servants, so Bottom yields to the pleasurable attentions of Titania's attendant fairies, Peaseblossom, Cobweb, Mote, and Mustardseed. But Titania belongs to the world of spirits, not of mortal beings, and Bottom, thus translated, enters her exalted sphere. Though Titania and her fairies address him still as a mortal he enjoys immortal privileges. Paul Hardwick beautifully conveyed this in Peter Hall's 1962 Stratford production, of which *The Times* wrote that he was 'quietly discovering unexpected truths about life, as when he accepts modestly but with respectful rapture the embraces of Titania and the homage of her fairy attendants'.[6]

Whether Bottom's privileges include physical union with the fairy queen has been a debating point among critics. David Young thought not,[7] but Carroll, citing Titania's words 'Tie up my lover's tongue, bring him silently', remarks, 'I find this last line explicit: Titania is tired of Bottom's voice, and wants him now to perform.'[8] Directors of recent productions—some taking their cue from Jan Kott's well-known assessment of the sexual equipment of the ass: 'Since antiquity and up to the Renaissance the ass was credited with the strongest sexual potency and among all the quadrupeds is supposed to have the longest and hardest phallus'[9]—have been only too ready to agree. Perhaps the best-known image of Peter Brook's famous production is the photograph of David Waller as Bottom with another actor's forearm, fist clenched, rampant between his legs, a moment which in the theatre brought the first part of the play to an exultant conclusion as confetti fluttered down and the band played a snatch of Mendelssohn's wedding march.

Later directors have been even more explicit, representing before the tiring-house wall action which Shakespeare's audience was at the most expected to imagine happening behind it. In Adrian Noble's Stratford version of 1994, for example, Titania beckoned Bottom into the large upturned umbrella that represented her bower, and as it ascended we were treated to the sight of Desmond Barrit's ample posterior lunging energetically up and down in a manner that left the relationship unequivocally sexual. Critics have taken the same tack, to such an extent that 1994 saw the publication of an article by T. B. Boecher entitled 'Bestial Buggery in A Midsummer Night's Dream' and beginning with the words 'Although no one has paid much sustained attention to the fact, A Midsummer Night's Dream is patently about bestiality.'[10] This substantial, well written, and scholarly piece is supported by an Appendix, 'Bestiality and the Law in Renaissance England', providing statistical tables on 'Indictments for bestial buggery in the reigns of Elizabeth I and James I' and 'Animals abused in English Renaissance bestiality indictments'. (The author manfully suppresses any disappointment he may have felt that the list includes no asses.)

The emphasis upon sexuality has no doubt occurred as the result of a reaction against sentimentalizing interpretations, but perhaps it is not unreasonable to suggest that the winsome phrase 'Bestial buggery' affords, to say the least, an imprecise response to the text's tonal register. Even critics heavily committed to a post-Freudian approach have demurred. Though there is truth in Boecher's claim that 'the spectacle of Titania and Bottom embracing and sleeping together comes as close to enacted sexual intercourse as any scene in Shakespearean comedy', intercourse is at most to be inferred; we should perhaps remember that Bottom is not really an ass and that Titania is a fairy, and that she has declared her intention to turn Bottom into the likeness of 'an airy spirit' by purging his 'mortal grossness'—words not quoted by Boecher. And, whatever Titania's fantasies may be, Bottom gives no signs of actively sharing them. He may acquiesce in her embraces, but even Jan Kott has dissociated himself from Brook's emphasis upon sexuality, remarking that 'in the spectacle staged by Peter Brook and many of his followers which emphasizes Titania's sexual fascination with a monstrous phallus (*mea culpa!*), the carnival ritual of Bottom's adventure is altogether lost'. Bottom, says Kott, 'appreciates being treated as a very important person, but is more interested in the frugal pleasure of eating than in the bodily charms of Titania'.[11] And James L. Calderwood has written, 'Surely a good part of Oberon's punishment of Titania centres in the physical and metaphysical impossibility of a fairy Queen to couple with an ass.'[12] To which it is worth adding that if the coupling does occur, Oberon has connived in his own cuckolding. If Bottom and Titania do make love, they do it as fairies—or, to quote another of Titania's epithets for Bottom—as angels do. However that may be.

It is also relevant that the relationship is presented as occurring in a dream—or, to use the word that both Titania and Bottom deploy, in a vision. The actor has the opportunity to convey something of this by a shift in consciousness during Bottom's scenes in the fairy court. More, I suppose, than any other character in Shakespeare, Bottom has often been played by performers associated with music hall and popular theatre—Stanley Holloway and James Cagney, Frankie Howerd and Tommy Steele among them. There is no reason why the comic skills of such performers should not be harnessed to the role, and some of them, such as Frankie Howerd, appear to have revealed new sides to their talent in doing so. But the potential range of the role fits it also for the talents of great actors of the 'legitimate' theatre, as Ralph Richardson appears to have demonstrated particularly in these scenes in an Old Vic production of 1931. According to James Agate,

> In the fairy scenes he abandoned clowning in favour of a dim consciousness of a rarer world and of being at court there. This was new to me, and if Mr Richardson had not the ripeness of some of the old actors, his acting here was an agreeable change from the familiar refusal to alternate fruitiness with anything else. Most of the old players seem to have thought that Bottom, with the ass's head on, was the same Bottom only funnier. Shakespeare says he was 'translated', and Mr Richardson translated him.[13]

'Twenty years later', as Griffiths notes, Richardson's 'performance was still being invoked as a benchmark':

> no one before Richardson, and no one after him either, guessed that there was in this weaver so deep a well of abused poetry, such an ineradicable vision of uncomprehended wonder.[14]

For Titania, Bottom's presence at her court is a fantasy induced by Oberon's love potion, and when Oberon has achieved his aim of subduing her and persuading her to return the Indian boy, he reverses the potion's effect. Bottom, still in his (possibly postcoital) sleep, has to be translated back from ass to man, and this translation takes place on stage, as Robin removes the ass-head at Oberon's behest. For the audience the effect is instantaneous, but Bottom, like the lovers, sleeps on, receding from our consciousness through Oberon and Titania's dance of reconciliation, the formal entry of Theseus with Hippolyta and 'all his train', the awakening of the lovers, Theseus's overriding of Egeus's objections to the marriage of Hermia and Lysander, and the lovers' reflections on their dream.

When Bottom wakes it seems at first that no time has elapsed since his translation: 'When my cue comes, call me, and I will answer.' But then he remembers he has had a dream, and starts to try to recall it. He fails, as we all fail when we try to translate our dreams into language. But he knows he has had an experience 'past the wit of man' to translate. He alone among the mortals of the play has had direct communion with the inhabitants of fairyland. He alone has been translated into a higher sphere, if only temporarily.

But the lovers, if they have not actually seen inhabitants of the fairy world, have been unknowingly touched by it and, like Bottom, undergo a form of translation. Roused by Theseus's hunting horns, they have given classic poetic expression to the sensation of being suspended between sleep and waking, between the unconscious world of dreams and earthly reality, in lines that figure Quince's state of mind on beholding the translated Bottom—and which, we might also suggest, portray the state of mind of a translator struggling to formulate, in a new language, thoughts that have already reached poetic form in the language from which he is translating:

> DEMETRIUS   These things seem small and undistinguishable,
>   Like far-off mountains turnèd into clouds.
> HERMIA   Methinks I see these things with parted eye,
>   When everything seems double.
> HELENA   So methinks,
>   And I have found Demetrius like a jewel,
>   Mine own and not mine own.
> DEMETRIUS   It seems to me
>   That yet we sleep, we dream.   (4.1.186–92)

To the lover, the beloved is both a possession and something that can never be possessed, just as a poem is something that can be translated yet never loses its own perfection of identity. It is a paradox that lies at the heart of artistic creation; no wonder Benjamin Britten makes a vocal quartet based on this dialogue a highspot of his opera, dwelling repeatedly and lovingly on the phrase 'mine own, and not mine own'. Here a great composer was translating Shakespeare's portrayal of translation in an act of what Inga-Stina Ewbank has called 'collusive re-creation' which, characteristically of good translation, adds a new dimension to the original.[15]

Bottom's struggle to dredge from the ooze of his subconscious mind the jewels that lie there embedded is more effortful but no less genuine. At first he thinks no time has passed, then simply that he has slept:

When my cue comes, call me, and I will answer...God's my life, stolen hence, and left me asleep?

But then the wisp of a memory supervenes:

I have had a most rare vision. I have had a dream past the wit of man to say what dream it was. Man is but an ass if he go about to expound this dream.

Bottom's metaphorical use of the word 'ass' appears to trigger his residual memory of the state of being in which he believed himself truly to be an ass.

Methought I was—there is no man can tell what. Methought I was, and methought I had—but man is but a patched fool if he will offer to say what methought I had.

(4.1.205–6)

The effort at translation is too great, and he abandons it. But the effort has been made, and it is the sense this gives us that Bottom, for all his asininity, is—like Caliban—capable of having, and of trying to put into words, a vision which lifts the role from clownishness to greatness. At least it does if the actor lets it. It did in 1853, when Samuel Phelps played Bottom:

He was still a man subdued, but subdued by the sudden plunge into a state of unfathomable wonder. His dream clings about him, he cannot sever the real from the unreal, and still we are made to feel that his reality itself is but a fiction.[16]

In some productions, Bottom has discovered about his person a tangible reminder of his dream life—a wisp of hay or a flower, for example.[17] I remember a production in Victorian style at Nottingham when Bottom's departure after his 'dream' was most touchingly marked with that phrase from Mendelssohn's incidental music which has a dying fall symbolizing the power of dream.

But not all actors approach the speech in so romantic a fashion. Everything rests on the nuance given to the words 'methought I had' and the pause that follows. The innocent, and once traditional, interpretation is that Bottom is simply recalling his ass's ears. But directors keen to demonstrate explicit sexual awareness allow their actor, by facial expression or gesture, a leer, a wiggle, or a movement of the hand, to imply that Bottom is coyly avoiding saying 'methought I "had" Titania', or 'methought I had a penis of the proportions ascribed by Jan Kott to the ass';

Desmond Barrit's peering down the front of his pants at this point in Adrian Noble's production meant even more to members of the audience who remembered Jan Kott's remark than to those who did not. One cannot say that this is wrong; but one can say that by narrowing the focus on to the physical it denies the spirituality of Bottom's translation—renders it, so to speak, with a four-letter word.

Bottom's last speech before vanishing into the hawthorn brake is given in the character of Pyramus; his translation comes as an involuntary interruption to a willed attempt at another kind of translation on which he and his fellows were engaged at the moment of his ascent into asininity. When we first see them they are embarking on the task of translating into stage action the pre-existing script of *The Most Lamentable Comedy and Most Cruel Death of Pyramus and Thisbe*, and we are left in no doubt that they find the task difficult. The first stage is the assignment of the roles into which each of the performers will endeavour to translate himself, and this introduces the need for deliberate physical transformation. Flute as Thisbe may, Quince tells him, hide his incipient beard—if it truly exists—with a mask; and Bottom boasts of a virtuosic capacity to modulate his voice according to the varied demands of the roles, from Thisbe to Lion, that he aspires to undertake. He appears, too, to have access to a rich collection of false beards (which in some productions he has brought with him).[18]

Once rehearsals get under way, the actors discover that before the text of the play can be translated into stage action certain modifications must be made in order to fit it for performance 'before the Duke' and his ladies. There are episodes, such as Pyramus's drawing a sword to kill himself, 'that will never please'. Starveling fears that the problem can be solved only by cutting the text: 'I believe we must leave the killing out, when all is done.' But Bottom proposes instead to make an addition to the text: 'Write me a prologue, and let the prologue seem to say we will do no harm with our swords, and that Pyramus is not killed indeed.' Additional lines must be written, too, to mitigate the terror of Lion's appearance, and as the rehearsal proceeds the need becomes apparent even to write in two additional characters, Moonshine and Wall, each of them to be represented by an actor who will make adjustments to his personal appearance in the attempt to 'disfigure, or present' the character.

The rehearsal scenes in *A Midsummer Night's Dream* offer a copybook demonstration by Shakespeare himself of the instability of the dramatic text. As the Folio text of the play shows (in its changes of word and stage directions from the Quarto text, in its substitution of one character—Egeus—for another—Philostrate—in the last Act, and in its reallocation of certain lines of dialogue), in the course of its translation from authorial manuscript to promptbook Shakespeare's own text underwent exactly the same kinds of changes, if on a smaller scale, as the play within the play. This makes it all the more surprising that scholars were so long resistant to the notion that variant texts of Shakespeare's plays demonstrate theatrical revision; and the fact that we cannot be sure whether Peter Quince, who makes himself responsible for the additions to the text of *Pyramus and Thisbe*, is the original author of the play, or merely its director with a talent, like some modern directors—John Barton is the most distinguished example—for literary pastiche, reflects our uncertainty whether changes in the texts of Shakespeare's own plays were made by Shakespeare himself, by members of his company, or collectively.

The actors' attempts to translate their text into action are hampered in part by their literalism, and by their expectations of a similar literalism in their audience. The ladies, they fear, will be so totally illuded by what they see that they will take it for reality, so a prologue must assure them, not only that 'Pyramus is not killed indeed', but that Pyramus is not Pyramus 'but Bottom the weaver'; similarly Snug must tell the ladies that he is 'a man, as other men are', and 'indeed name his name, and tell them plainly he is Snug the joiner'. And their audience cannot be relied upon to imagine the moonlight by which Pyramus and Thisbe meet, and the wall through which they talk—as Shakespeare's own audience was required to imagine the moonlight by which Oberon has met Titania, and, so far as we can tell, the 'orchard wall' that Romeo is said to have overleapt in *Romeo and Juliet* (2.1.5)—but must be confronted with an actor in the person of Moonshine and Wall. This literalism is akin to that of a literary translator who, in an over-zealous effort to render a text's substance, fails to convey its spirit. It can be amended only by imagination, and Shakespeare is careful to preface Theseus's wedding entertainment with the discussion between the Duke and Hippolyta about the power of imagination. This is offered as a reaction to the lovers' account of their enchanted night, and Theseus's view—perhaps surprisingly in view of attitudes he will later express—is sceptical; it is Hippolyta who acknowledges that the transformation in the lovers bears witness, not simply to fancy, but to the transmuting power of imagination:

> all the story of the night told over,
> And all their minds transfigured so together,
> More witnesseth than fancy's images,
> And grows to something of great constancy. (5.1.23–6)

In the play's terms, then, a real-life translation has been successfully effected. We are about to see whether the fictional translation of text into performance will similarly succeed; and the omens are not good.

The potentially damaging effects of unskilful theatrical translation are made apparent even in advance of the performance in the reported reactions of Philostrate (or Egeus) to the rehearsal which he has attended as part of the auditioning procedure for the wedding festivities. The ineptitude of the writing and the unfitness of the players have resulted in an involuntary change of genre, the transformation of a tragedy into a comedy:

> in all the play
> There is not one word apt, one player fitted.
> And 'tragical', my noble lord, it is,
> For Pyramus therein doth kill himself,
> Which when I saw rehearsed, I must confess,
> Made mine eyes water; but more merry tears
> The passion of loud laughter never shed. (5.1.64–70)

In spite of this warning Theseus persists in asking for the play to be performed, and does so in lines anticipative of audience response theory in their suggestion that the spectator has a part to play in the success of the performance. Egeus warns him that the mechanicals' play is

> nothing, nothing in the world,
> Unless you can find sport in their intents
> Extremely stretched, and conned with cruel pain
> To do you service. (5.1.78–81)

But Theseus rejects the warning, with a courtly expression of charity:

> never anything can be amiss
> When simpleness and duty tender it. (5.1.82–3)

Theseus's readiness to exercise imagination may seem surprising after the long speech in which he has spoken dismissively of its powers, but the theme is insistently developed in response to Hippolyta's complaint that she loves 'not to see wretchedness o'er charged, | And duty in his service perishing'. Theseus proclaims himself as the ideal member of an audience, comparing the efforts of amateur actors to those of 'great clerks'—people, presumably, such as rectors of Elizabethan universities delivering addresses of welcome to their sovereign—who, overwhelmed by the occasion, 'Make periods in the midst of sentences', exactly as Quince is about to do in his delivery of his Prologue. Theseus can, he claims, 'read as much' 'in the modesty of fearful duty' 'as from the rattling tongue | Of saucy and audacious eloquence'. He rams home the moral with almost priggish ostentation, as if to shame the theatre audience into comparable charity. Shakespeare is preparing us for both the comic incompetence of Bottom and his fellows and the paradoxical skill of the real-life actors who will be required to impersonate incompetence. The audience, like Theseus, has its part to play in the translation process, and Shakespeare not merely tells us but demonstrates that meaning can be apprehended even in a translation so bad that on the surface it means the opposite of what is intended. Although the 'periods' that Quince, shivering and pale, makes in the midst of *his* 'premeditated' sentences cause him to say the opposite of what he means—'All for your delight | We are not here'—both Theseus and we are able to 'take' what he 'mistake[s]'. His lines simultaneously convey opposed meanings, rather as the translated Bottom both is and is not Bottom, with the result that his audience may both laugh at his ineptitude yet appreciate the good will that lies behind it.

The rehearsal scenes have revealed to us only a few lines of the text of the tragedy. As the performance progresses, it becomes clear that this text is comically inadequate as a translation into dramatic terms of the story of Pyramus and Thisbe. Layers of translation here are complex. The story is a pre-existing one both for the mechanicals and for Shakespeare. Many members of the original audience, too, would have known it. Shakespeare had certainly read it both in the original Latin and in Golding's translation. We are given no clue whether Bottom and his fellows are supposed to have created the script themselves (except for the interpolated lines) or to have purchased a script from the Athenian equivalent of Samuel French. They cannot certainly be held responsible for its ineptitudes. Nevertheless, they are responsible for using it. Part of the comedy, that is, derives from their unawareness of the bathetic inadequacies of the translation into verse drama of the tragic tale they enact—and a director may make something of this unawareness.

Shakespeare, on the other hand, is responsible for the badness of the script, and is indeed to be congratulated on it. This is good bad writing—in other words, excellent parody both of Golding's translation (which Shakespeare seems to have regarded with amused admiration, or admiring amusement) and of the literary and dramatic conventions of the interlude writers.[19] In part, the criticisms of the on-stage audience are directed at the inadequacies of the script: 'This is the silliest stuff that ever I heard', says Hippolyta. But the spectators are highly conscious, too, of the performers' failure to translate this script convincingly: 'he hath played on this prologue like a child on a recorder—a sound, but not in government.' Indeed they seem to make little distinction between script and performance, in this perhaps reflecting the Elizabethan theatrical scene, where an audience probably considered a play as a company event in which the writer was simply one member of the company, and may have been performing in his own play. Frequently, that is to say, playgoers went, not to see a group of players interpret a script with which they were already familiar, but to enjoy an entirely new event, an experience that was simultaneously literary, dramatic, and theatrical.

As the play scene progresses, the mechanicals' efforts at translation sink to ever deeper levels of ineptitude which can be salvaged only by massive doses of good humour, tolerance, and imagination from its onlookers. Primarily, it represents the mechanicals' efforts at active translation, but it climaxes in a representation of passive translation which takes us back to the point earlier in the play at which we saw Bottom turned into an ass. At that point he was rehearsing the role of Pyramus. Now, enacting that role in a manner that, Theseus is to say, might well prove *him* an ass (5.1.306), he finds himself required to represent the character in the process of a translation from the corporeal to the spiritual state, such as he had himself undergone, at least in the eyes of his fellows and of Titania, within the hawthorn brake. After stabbing himself, he describes his elevation:

> Now am I dead,
> Now am I fled,
> My soul is in the sky.
> Tongue, lose thy light,
> Moon, take thy flight,
> Now die, die, die, die, die. (5.1.296–301)

But even here the translation is not complete; before long Bottom arises from the dead to offer an epilogue or a bergomask dance.

One of Shakespeare's most striking uses of the concept of translation occurs in *As You Like It*, when Amiens congratulates Duke Senior on his capacity to 'translate the stubbornness of fortune | Into so quiet and so sweet a style' (2.1.19–20). It is striking because it encapsulates the very process of comedy itself, a process that is often, as in *A Midsummer Night's Dream*, symbolized by the overcoming of obstacles to marriage. It is a process that can be accomplished only through the exercise of imagination. The last Act of *A Midsummer Night's Dream* recapitulates in comic form the turmoils that the lovers have experienced in their efforts at translation, reminds us that fortune can be stubborn; but as bedtime approaches, Oberon and his train, in their blessing on the house, invoke for us the quietness and sweetness that can come with the translation to the married state. And at the very end Robin Goodfellow, calling for our active imaginative collaboration, invites us to think that we 'have but slumbered here, | While these visions did appear'. Like Bottom, we have been granted a vision; and also like him, we shall be asses if we try to expound it. Men cannot translate dreams into language; but in this play Shakespeare comes pretty close to doing so.

11

The Once and Future *King Lear*

Poetic plays may give much pleasure to readers, and some poets have adopted a dramatic form while not writing for the theatre. But plays written for performance are not fully realized until they reach the stage, and critics who treat such plays purely as literature are choosing to work in blinkers. Increasing recognition of these facts during the past two or three decades has resulted in the growing acknowledgement among critics of drama of the need to experience plays in performance and to read them with an awareness of the theatrical dimension, both imagined and actual. Nevertheless, readers, directors, and actors must all take the text as their starting point. To this extent, in reading and performing plays of the past they depend on the work of textual critics. Usually, the literary critic, in writing about a novel, poem, or play, can ignore textual problems. Sometimes, as Fredson Bowers amply demonstrated in his *Textual and Literary Criticism* (Cambridge, 1966), he does so at his peril. And there are some works in relation to which textual questions obtrude so insistently that even the critic most purely concerned with literary values must take notice of them. No one can write seriously about Dickens's *Edwin Drood*, or about Marlowe's *Hero and Leander*, without mentioning that they are unfinished. Criticism of Shakespeare's *Timon of Athens* has become particularly tentative in face of the hypothesis that the only surviving text is an incomplete draft. *Pericles* is self-evidently a damaged text, and for that reason resists standard critical procedures. Even in the theatre, with its many freedoms, textual problems cannot be wholly ignored. Directors may—though they rarely do—slavishly follow the edition they are working with; but editors do not solve all the problems that must be faced in the theatre; so, for example, a director must either supply the song called for by Titania in the final episode of *A Midsummer Night's Dream* or must cut the lines in which she mentions it.

Problems are especially acute when a work has survived in more than one form. It is possible to write about the 1805 text of *The Prelude* without mentioning Wordsworth's revision of it, but it is not possible to take a comprehensive view of Wordsworth's poetic art without comparing the two. Here, at least, we know what the relationship is. The textual scholar can tell the critic that the version published in 1850 represents the poem as Wordsworth finally revised it, and that the 1805 text—preferred by most readers—is an earlier, distinct version. The editor can print the texts side by side, and the critic can exercise his art with as much or as little comparison between them as he finds appropriate to his purposes. In some cases, indeed, the art of the literary critic is indistinguishable from that of his textual colleague. This is true of Keats's 'Hyperion' poems. The scholar (if for the moment I may sustain a distinction which, though unreal, is convenient) can tell the critic that 'Hyperion' was included in the volume of Keats's poems published in 1820, and that 'The Fall of Hyperion' did not appear until some thirty-five years after the poet had died, but the relationship between them is not one that can be fruitfully discussed in bibliographical terms. It is a matter in which the literary critic may discuss, and even solve, problems that are more often the preserve of the textual critic.

There are also some works, including the subject of the present volume, which pose problems that are of equal importance to the textual and the literary critic, and which can be tackled only by their joint efforts. It is perhaps relevant that the current reinvestigations of the textual problems of King Lear come at a time in which Shakespeare critics have not only become increasingly aware of the need to write about plays as works to be performed, but have also become more alert than most of them once were to the need to allow for uncertainties in the texts which they study. It is an amateurish critic who writes of a Shakespeare play without knowing something about the state of its text: which words are suspected of corruption, which are emendations, which stage directions are editorial, which passages differ significantly in collateral texts, or are omitted from one or the other of them. We all know that there are important differences between, for example, the 'good' Quarto and Folio texts of Hamlet, Othello, and Troilus and Cressida. We know, too, that there are differences between the Quarto and Folio texts of King Lear, but we have been accustomed to believe that these texts can be reconciled to produce a composite version that we can read as Shakespeare's King Lear, even if we may have to tread warily from time to time before accepting the authority of particular readings.

Nevertheless, and although King Lear is widely regarded as the greatest tragedy written by the greatest dramatist of the post-classical world, and as one of the monuments of Western civilization, good critics have from time to time expressed serious dissatisfaction with it, and sometimes with aspects of it which relate to the conflation of the Quarto and Folio texts. A. C. Bradley found the play 'as a whole ... imperfectly dramatic' and was greatly worried by what he regarded as its dramatic and structural defects.[1] Allardyce Nicoll, describing it as 'one of the finest and most comprehensive of Shakespeare's productions', was 'compelled to admit that in its function as a work of dramatic art it fails when compared with [Hamlet, Othello, and Macbeth] ... and that it is not planned with that all-pervading subtlety which characterises those others'.[2] In 1957 Margaret Webster described King Lear as 'the least actable of the four' great tragedies because of its 'lack of this fundamental theatre economy'.[3] And more recently Maynard Mack has expressed dislike of Act 4, scene 3 (found only in the Quarto), in which 'Kent and a Gentleman...wrap Cordelia in a mantle of emblematic speech that is usually lost on a modern audience's ear and difficult for a modern actor to speak with conviction'.[4] Granville-Barker, too, had been critical of this scene, regarding it as 'a carpentered scene if ever there was one', which he 'could better believe that Shakespeare cut...than wrote'.[5] It is interesting that this man of letters who was also a man of the theatre should have anticipated much recent thought in his dissatisfaction with editorial conflation of the Quarto and Folio texts. He comments that 'the producer is confronted by the problem of the three hundred lines, or nearly, that the Quartos give and the Folio omits, and of the hundred given by the Folio and omitted from the Quartos. Editors, considering only, it would seem, that the more Shakespeare we get the better, bring practically the whole lot into the play we read. But a producer must ask himself whether these two versions do not come from different prompt books, and whether the Folio does not, in both cuts and additions, sometimes represent Shakespeare's own second thoughts....Where Quarto and Folio offer alternatives, to adopt both versions may make for redundancy or confusion.'[6]

Since Granville-Barker wrote there have, of course, been advances in the textual study of Shakespeare which permit a clearer view of the situation than he was able to take, and it may be helpful at this point to offer a sketch of the basic facts as they are seen at present, before going on to discuss some of their implications.

Like most plays of the time, *King Lear* had been performed before it appeared in print. It was entered in the Stationers' Register on 26 November 1607 as 'A booke called Mr Willm Shakespeare his historye of Kinge Lear as yt was played before the Kinges Maiestie at Whitehall vppon St Stephans night at Christmas Last by his Maties seruantes playinge vsually at the globe on the Banksyde'.[7] The statement does not, of course, imply that the performance before James I was the first; rather is it a boast, designed for reproduction on the title-page, that this is a work considered good enough for the court. When the manuscript was put into print, someone was careful enough to allow for the passage of time by altering the phrase 'at Christmas Last' to 'in Christmas Hollidayes'. The resulting volume, dated 1608 and printed for Nathaniel Butter, was 'to be sold at his shop in *Pauls* Church-yard at the signe of the Pide Bull neere St. *Austins* Gate'. So it has come to be called by the picturesque label of the 'Pied Bull quarto', mainly in order to distinguish it from another quarto with a similar but not identical title-page, on which the imprint reads simply 'Printed for *Nathaniel Butter.* 1608'. Until 1866 it was not known which of these editions, both bearing the same date, was printed first, but in that year the editors of the Cambridge edition, W. G. Clark and W. Aldis Wright, demonstrated that the Pied Bull quarto was the earlier, and between 1908 and 1910 W. W. Greg, A. W. Pollard, and others showed that the second edition, though dated 1608, was one of a group of plays printed by William Jaggard for Thomas Pavier in 1619. The false date may be an attempt to circumvent an order of 3 May 1619 forbidding unauthorized printing of plays belonging to the King's Men.[8]

The first quarto is, by general agreement, badly printed even by the low standards normally applicable to Elizabethan and Jacobean play quartos. Much of what is obviously verse is set out as prose; prose is sometimes broken up as if it were verse; verse is often misaligned. The punctuation is sketchy and often misleading. As P. W. K. Stone writes in his detailed study *The Textual History of 'King Lear'* (1980), 'Questionable readings meet the eye on nearly every page, many of them obviously wrong, and some of them egregious nonsense (e.g. *accent teares*; *flechuent*; *Mobing, & Mohing*)' (p. 2). The degree to which these faults reflect the nature and state of the manuscript from which the Quarto was printed, rather than resulting from incompetence in the printing-house, is important. Are the obvious errors due to the printer's incompetence, to non-authorial corruption in the manuscript from which he was working, or to Shakespeare's own illegibility? Does the light and in many ways peculiar punctuation reflect Shakespeare's own practice or the inexperience of the printer Okes (who had never before printed a play) combined with his shortage of certain important types (full stops and colons, for instance); or might it stem from both causes?[9] Do a number of peculiar spellings reflect Shakespeare's own idiosyncrasies, or are they aural errors which might testify to unauthoritative transmission?

It is fair to warn the reader that statements about the quality of the Quarto text have often been coloured by views of its relationship to the Folio. Peter W. M. Blayney quotes a clear example of such fallacious reasoning from no less an authority than W. W. Greg, who wrote:

> When, in the line:
> That iustly think'st, and hast most rightly said: [TLN 197]
> the Quarto transposes the words 'iustly' and 'rightly', the blunder is perhaps not beyond the range of original sin latent in a copyist.[10]

As Blayney comments, 'Historically speaking, the Folio transposed the Quarto's words, and we cannot begin to suggest why it may have done so until we have decided on the nature of the text which it altered. Greg's tone shows that he has himself decided – but that decision does not appear to have been based on the evidence presented.'[11] Steven Urkowitz offers a similar instance from the same source:

> Greg ... claims that many speeches are misassigned in the Quarto (*First Folio*, p. 378). His prime example is 5.3.81, TLN 3026, where Regan, in the Folio, says, 'Let the Drum strike, and prove my title thine.' Greg argues that this 'appears absurdly perverted and

misassigned in Q as '*Bast.* Let the drum strike, and prove my title good.' But there is nothing at all absurd about the Quarto's reading. Greg confuses readings that are merely different with those that are wrong.[12]

Reprints of the Quarto are accessible;[13] it is worth reading as a text in its own right. An exhaustive study of its press variants by W. W. Greg, based on a collation of the twelve surviving copies, concludes that 148 changes were made during the printing process, resulting in variant readings between one copy and another which show that the printers were not without some sense of responsibility, and which have the incidental advantage of providing clues to the process of transmission of later editions.[14]

There is no dispute that the second quarto reprints the first without recourse to the authority of an independent manuscript, though the printers tried to improve spelling, punctuation, and lineation. They also introduced many new substantive readings, some correcting obvious misprints, some aimed at improving the style, and a few attempting to emend difficult words and phrases. At the same time, new errors crept in.[15]

The title-page of each quarto labels the play as Shakespeare's *True Chronicle Historie of the life and death of King Lear...*'. In the Folio of 1623, however, the play appears among the tragedies and is headed 'The Tragedie of King Lear'. The change in designation may or may not be significant. The Folio offers a far better-printed text, more regular and consistent in spelling and punctuation, more accurate in distinguishing between verse and prose, better in its alignment of verse, and fuller in its stage directions. It divides the play carefully into Acts and scenes. (The Quarto's failure to do this is, of course, quite normal: there are no such divisions in any of the early quartos of Shakespeare's plays.) There are other, more important differences. The most striking is the presence of short passages amounting to more than 100 lines of text which are not in the Quarto. The Folio also lacks close on 300 lines which *are* in the Quarto; several speeches are differently assigned; and there are more than 850 verbal variants, some of them obviously the correct version of manifest errors in the Quarto, others offering an alternative sense. Again, the reader should be warned that views of the relative authority of the two substantive texts appear sometimes to have caused critics to regard as corrections what may more properly be looked upon simply as alternative versions. Some of the Folio variants affect not just what is spoken on stage, but the accompanying action. Although, in those passages where direct comparison is relevant, the Folio text is generally better printed than the Quarto, it has its own obvious 'errors and problematical readings, some echoing the mistakes of Q1, others diverging with doubtful accuracy, others again arising strangely where Q is manifestly correct'.[16]

From 1623, then, two basic texts were available to editors of *King Lear*. Each text could be reprinted independently, though a conscientious editor who knew both would inevitably draw on one in the attempt to correct manifest corruption in the other. It was also possible to conflate the two, introducing into one text some or all of the passages found only in the other. For a century after the publication of the First Folio, no conflation was attempted. The second quarto was reprinted in 1655. The Folio was reprinted three times, and in 1709 Nicholas Rowe, in what is, by our standards, the first edited text of the complete works, depended entirely on the Folio. Steven Urkowitz traces the process by which the composite version established itself.[17] Pope, in 1723, basing his text largely on Rowe's revised edition of 1714, made some additions from the Quarto and omitted a few lines found only in the Folio. Ten years later Theobald added to the additions, providing the version which, with minor variants, has been standard ever since. Although Theobald's text is based on the Folio, it is evident from his note on the play's final speech that he regards this as a theatre-derived text which might well display corruption. He writes: 'This speech from the authority of the Old 4to is rightly plac'd to *Albany*: in the Edition by the players it is given to *Edgar*, by whom, I doubt not, it was of Custom spoken. And the Case was this: He who play'd *Edgar*, being a more favourite Actor, than he who personated *Albany*; in Spight of Decorum, it was thought proper he should have the last word.' We may be sure that Theobald knew no more than we do about the relative popularity of the original impersonators of Albany and Edgar, and that this is mere rationalization. Theobald's assumption is that the Quarto offers the more 'literary' text. On the so-called mock trial, not present in the Folio, he remarks that 'Mr *Pope* had begun to insert several Speeches in the mad way, in this Scene, from the Old Edition', and that he—Theobald—has 'ventur'd to replace several others, which stand upon the same Footing, and had an equal right of being restor'd'. Dr Johnson, as Urkowitz shows, was more respectful of the Folio's authority as being 'probably nearest to Shakespeare's last copy', even though he believed that revision was 'carelessly and hastily performed'; but Capell, whose edition appeared in 1767, reverted to Theobald's low view of the Folio, supposing Shakespeare quartos in general to derive from 'the Poet's own copies', however badly printed, and accusing the 'player editors' of the Folio of denigrating the quartos, and even of deliberately departing from them 'to give at once a greater currency to their own lame edition, and support the charge which they bring against the quarto's' (i. 10–11). Though he found some evidence of Shakespearean revision in the Folio text, he blamed most of its omissions of lines found in the Quarto on compositors or editors. Edmond Malone, whose edition first appeared in 1790, adopted essentially the same position; nevertheless he included all the Folio-only lines. The practice of conflation had acquired the status of orthodoxy; but it had done so by a process of haphazard accretion over half a century, with no agreement on a textual theory which would satisfactorily explain the differences between the Quarto and the Folio texts.

It is fair to notice once again that the play represented by the composite text has not been regarded as entirely satisfactory, and that objections have been raised specifically to the grafting on to the Folio text of passages found only in the Quarto. Granville-Barker, whose comments I have quoted, had been anticipated most notably by the Victorian editor Charles Knight, who believed in the integrity of the Folio text while stating that Quarto-only passages should be preserved, 'upon the principle that not a line which appears to have been written by Shakespeare ought to be lost'; so his 'copy is literally that of the folio, except that where a passage occurs in the quartos which is not in the folio, we introduce such a passage, printing it, however, in brackets'.[18] Alfred Harbage followed a similar practice in his Pelican edition (1958). Other editors from time to time betrayed some concern with the question of whether the Folio represented Shakespeare's revision. So, in 1940, Kittredge wrote 'The differences between the Quarto and the Folio by no means warrant the theory that Shakespeare ever rewrote his *King Lear* or subjected it to a substantial revision';[19] and twenty years later, G. I. Duthie in the New Cambridge edition expressed a similar view: 'There is no basis for any theory of a Shakespearian revision separating Q1 and F (apart from whatever share Shakespeare may have had in the work of abridgment)' (p. 124).

Until recently, then, the general opinion has been that Shakespeare wrote one play about *King Lear*; that this play is imperfectly represented in both the Quarto and the Folio texts; that each of these texts contains genuinely Shakespearian passages which are missing from and should have been present in the other; that comparison of the variant readings of the two texts must form the most important basis for the correction of errors of transmission; and that conflation of the two texts, along with such correction, will bring us as close as we can hope to get to the lost archetype which each is supposed imperfectly to represent. This is the position to which I and other scholars are opposed. To understand why, we need to look more closely at the question of the origins of the Quarto and Folio texts, and of the relationship of the one to the other.

I have said that the second quarto of *King Lear* is essentially a reprint of the first. It can, therefore, offer no independent information about the underlying manuscript. But such a reprint may affect the transmission of a text which draws also on a manuscript of independent authority. This has happened with *King Lear*. W. W. Greg, discerning influence of the first quarto on the Folio, believed that the Folio text was printed from a copy of the first quarto 'that had been brought into general though not complete conformity' with the (manuscript) prompt-book.[20] Other studies have demonstrated that the Folio text was influenced by the second quarto as well, and that this was the only printed text used in the setting-up of the Folio.[21] Gary Taylor argues that the specific influence of the first quarto identified by Greg came by way of the prompt-book—an argument which entails the interesting consequence that this manuscript postdates the publication of the first quarto, which itself postdated the play's earliest performances.[22] It follows that a prompt-book influenced by the quarto cannot have been used for the original performances, but must have been the prompt-book of a revised text. This argument, only recently advanced, has not yet been subjected to scholarly scrutiny. But its logic, though ingenious, seems undeniable. In any case, there is no dispute that whatever printed copy was used for the Folio had been extensively annotated and supplemented by comparison with a manuscript different from that lying behind the original quarto. The influence of such a manuscript is most evident in the one hundred or so lines not present in the Quarto, but shows itself too in the many additional and variant stage directions, as well as at numerous points in the dialogue. So it is clear that, to a considerable degree, the Folio represents actual theatrical practice. This entails the possibility of theatrical corruption, on top of whatever other corruption or unnatural sophistication the text may have suffered in the course of its transmission into print. Stone (p. 127) believes that the alterations as a whole are not by Shakespeare but, possibly, by Massinger. Though this is an extreme position, it grows out of the traditional belief that Shakespeare could not have been responsible for any of the Folio omissions, or for some of its changes in stage directions and dialogue. Many of the essays in *The Divisions of the Kingdoms* (1983) directly address the problem of possible theatrical or transmissional corruption in the Folio; they challenge not only Stone's ascription of all the changes to a hand other than Shakespeare's, but also the conventional view that many changes derive from anonymous compositors, scribes, and actors rather than from Shakespeare himself.

However, the conventional view not only denies the authority of many individual Folio alternatives; it also, more systematically, denies the authority of the Quarto by claiming that it represents, in whole or in part, a memorial reconstruction. If this is true, it would be reasonable to argue that the manuscript behind it was a version of Shakespeare's *King Lear* which had been corrupted during the memorizing or reporting process. This would give far superior authority to the Folio's variants from the Quarto, even when the Quarto made sense. Yet this hypothesis has always been open to two major objections which have not been successfully resolved. First, the Quarto text clearly differs in important ways from the other texts generally regarded as 'bad' quartos. Secondly, if the Quarto has been influenced by memories of performance, and the Folio was printed from a prompt-book, why are they so different? As Greg wrote in 1955, 'Had there been a report of a stage performance it would almost certainly have given us a garbled version of F rather than anything resembling Q.'[23]

The alternative possibility is that the Quarto derives directly from a Shakespearean manuscript. The state of the text as printed suggests that if this was so the manuscript was not a prompt-book but one which, like those deduced to lie behind many other quartos—*Love's Labour's Lost, A Midsummer Night's Dream, Much Ado About Nothing, Hamlet* (1604–5), for instance—represented the play in a more-or-less final state of composition, before the author handed it over to his company of players. If this were so, the editor's position would be very different. In some ways, the Quarto's status would be raised. Those of its variants which make sense would have independent authority. But if they were not seen as corruptions of the text that lies behind the Folio, we should have to explain how it came about that equally intelligible variants found their way into the Folio text. The most obvious hypothesis would be that they represent a deliberate rewriting of the text printed in the Quarto. Whether the reviser was Shakespeare or someone else might be debated, but we should clearly be faced with two versions of the play, each consciously and distinctly fashioned, which it would be wrong to confuse. And we should be justified in an initial assumption that the Folio alterations were Shakespeare's own. As with all the other texts printed in the First Folio, the burden of proof rests upon those who wish to deny Shakespeare's authorship. We should thus have a first *King Lear* and a second one, as we have an 1805 *Prelude* and an 1850 *Prelude*. The first would be a text representing the play before it was acted. We should not know for certain whether this script had been put into production; it would be possible that Shakespeare's revisions, resulting essentially in the text as printed in the Folio, were made before the play reached the stage, and that the Quarto title-page's statement of performance referred to the revised state. Steven Urkowitz makes this assumption in his book (pp. 146–7). It seems inherently unlikely to me. If Shakespeare were revising before performance I should expect him to have used the papers of his earlier draft in the process, not to have released them (voluntarily or not) for publication. And Gary Taylor persuasively argues that the play did reach performance in its earlier version, that the revision was made on a copy of the Quarto that had been printed in 1608, and that it can be dated 1609–10.[24]

The importance of the nature of the printer's copy for the Quarto makes it particularly regrettable that this has proved to be one of the most intransigent problems in textual scholarship. A. W. Pollard, in the first systematic study of good and bad quartos, published in 1909, counted *Lear* among the good quartos, and maintained this view later.[25] But in 1930 E. K. Chambers wrote 'I think that the characteristics of Q point to a reported text', and since then many scholars, including some of the most distinguished textual critics of this century, have laboured mightily in the attempt to solve the problem.[26] So far, no consensus has been achieved, and some even of those who, having worked intensively on the problem, have arrived at a hypothesis have later abandoned it. Thus W. W. Greg, in 1933, endorsed Chambers's view of the Quarto as a reported text, stating that 'If it is indeed a reported text it must have been taken down by shorthand'.[27] He repeated this opinion in 1942, though with less confidence: 'I cannot but conclude that some kind of shorthand was employed, however little I like the conclusion.'[28] In 1949 G. I. Duthie demonstrated to Greg's satisfaction that no contemporary system of shorthand could have been responsible for the Quarto text, and by 1955 Greg thought that 'any theory that Q is essentially a report of a stage performance, however obtained, has to meet objections as formidable in their way as the theory of revision'.[29]

Duthie had argued that the Quarto was still a reported text, made not from shorthand but from the memories of actors: in the Cambridge edition of 1961 he wrote that he had 'thought of the company as being in the provinces, temporarily deprived of its prompt-book, and desirous of producing a new one; and I imagined its personnel gathered round a scribe, each actor dictating his own speeches in a kind of performance without action' (p. 131). But by 1961 he had abandoned that theory in favour of a modified version of Alice Walker's hypothesis that the text had been arrived at by 'transcription from foul papers by dictation, the persons involved having had some memorial knowledge of the play' (Duthie, 1961, p. 135). Specifically, Dr Walker had suggested, somewhat tentatively, that the boys playing Goneril and Regan provided the manuscript and that 'the scenes in which both were on the stage are most heavily contaminated because their joint recollection of the matter enabled them to concoct the text without constant reference to the foul papers'.[30]

The manner in which opinion has fluctuated is illustrated by the fact that in one book published in 1980 Steven Urkowitz could write that the 'only two theories... now seriously considered as possible explanations for the derivation of the Quarto' were 'Alice Walker's proposal that the Quarto is printed from a surreptitiously made copy of Shakespeare's foul papers' and 'the theory that it was derived from his foul papers' in a confused state (pp. 8–9), yet in the same year P. W. K. Stone, in his long and ambitious study, produced yet another version of the reported-text theory, claiming that 'It cannot but be concluded, upon any thorough examination of the evidence, that the text of Q1 derives from a theatrical report', and postulating a reporter who wrote out the play in longhand after 'attending repeated performances of the play, acquiring more of the text on each occasion until, presumably, he judged it complete, or as nearly so as he could make it' (p. 35).

The alternative theory, that the Quarto derives from Shakespeare's foul papers, received a notable statement in 1931, in an intensive study by Madeleine Doran; in The Text of 'King Lear' (Stanford), she argued that the Quarto was printed from Shakespeare's autograph, a manuscript already confused and illegible from much correction and alteration, and thrown aside as worthless when, as a result of a further thorough revision, the play had taken final shape in the prompt-book. In 1941, however, Miss Doran expressed doubts about her position, though she has continued to maintain that 'the text of Q...must represent an earlier form of the play than the Folio'. Alice Walker's theory, already mentioned, is an ingenious attempt to combine the 'reported-text' theory with the 'foul-papers' theory. More recently, there has been support for a return to Miss Doran's original position. G. K. Hunter writes that 'in the main it [Q] gives the impression of being quite closely derived from an authoritative original' while giving qualified assent to Alice Walker's theory to account for 'the film of corruption' which keeps the Quarto 'from being satisfactory'.[31] Urkowitz, arguing against Greg's and Alice Walker's interpretations of the evidence, uses Miss Doran's hypothesis to 'justify a working presumption that the Quarto text is at least an approximation of Shakespeare's draft of the play before it was adapted for the stage' (p. 11). Peter W. M. Blayney, in the prospectus to his two-volume study *The Texts of 'King Lear' and Their Origins*, concludes that copy for the Quarto 'was a much altered autograph manuscript containing the "unpolished" but probably near-final text of a play differing in some important respects from the play as we know it'. Blayney's study is announced by the publishers as 'without exception, the most exhaustive bibliographical investigation of a Shakespeare Quarto ever to have been attempted'. Certainly the first volume, *Nicholas Okes and the First Quarto* (1982), in itself represents a unique and valuable account of the printing of the Quarto of *King Lear* and, more generally, of the working methods of a Jacobean printer. The publication of Blayney's second volume, which will directly address the problem of the printer's copy for the Quarto, and its relationship to the Folio, must be awaited with the keenest interest. But already, even in advance of the publication and assessment of Blayney's evidence, it is fair to claim that those who regard the Quarto as a reported text have, by their own admission, not yet offered a satisfactory explanation of how such a report came into being; that Urkowitz has persuasively challenged much of the supposed evidence for that position; and that several essays in *The Division of the Kingdoms* contribute new arguments and evidence to support the hypothesis that the Quarto derives directly from a holograph manuscript.

Even if their arguments are not accepted, so long as the problem remains open there is no logical obstacle to pursuing the hypothesis that the differences between the Quarto and the Folio arise because the Folio represents Shakespeare's revision of the text printed in the Quarto. Essentially this is not a new position. It resembles that stated by Granville-Barker which I have already quoted. It is adumbrated by E. A. J. Honigmann in *The Stability of Shakespeare's Text* (1965), when he remarks that if Alice Walker and Duthie are right in proposing 'that Q, though contaminated by knowledge of the play as performed, goes back not to the prompt-book but to a copy taken by dictation from Shakespeare's foul papers...some QF variants could ...represent first and second thoughts' (p. 121). But the 'revision' theory was not seriously pursued in public until 1976, when Michael Warren delivered to the International Shakespeare Congress in Washington a paper, 'Quarto and Folio *King Lear* and the Interpretation of Albany and Edgar', which has proved to be of seminal importance.[32] It is worth quoting at some length the assumptions upon which he works, because they are those of all the contributors to the present volume. He writes 'that in a situation where statements about textual status are never more than hypotheses based upon the current models of thought about textual recension, it is not demonstrably erroneous to work with the possibility (a) that there may be no single "ideal play" of *King Lear* (all of "what Shakespeare wrote"), that there may never have been one, and that what we create by conflating both texts is merely an invention of editors and scholars; (b) that for all its problems Q is an authoritative version of the play of *King Lear*; and (c) that F may indeed be a revised version of the play, that its additions and omissions may constitute Shakespeare's considered modification of the earlier text, and that we certainly cannot know that they are not' (pp. 96–7). Most of Warren's essay consists of an examination of the differences in characterization of Albany and Edgar which, he claims, 'go beyond those which may be expected when two texts descend in corrupted form from a common original; they indicate that a substantial and consistent recasting of certain aspects of the play has taken place' (p. 99). He precedes this with an example of variant dialogue which it will be useful to cite here as an illustration of the problem.

In the Quarto, it reads thus:

> *Lear.* No.   *Kent.* Yes.
> *Lear.* No I say,   *Kent.* I say yea.
> *Lear.* No no, they would not.   *Kent.* Yes they have.
> *Lear.* By *Iupiter* I sweare no; they durst not do't, (E3ᵛ)

In the Folio, thus:

> *Lear.* No.
> *Kent.* Yes.
> *Lear.* No I say.
> *Kent.* I say yea.
> *Lear.* By *Iupiter* I sweare no.
> *Kent.* By *Iuno*, I sweare I.
> *Lear.* They durst not do't: (TLN 1291–7)

Normal editorial procedure is to conflate, so that the dialogue then runs:

> LEAR   No.
> KENT   Yes.
> LEAR   No, I say.
> KENT   I say, yea.
> Q { LEAR No no, they would not.
>   KENT Yes, they have.
> LEAR   By Jupiter, I swear no.
> F { KENT By Juno, I swear ay.
> LEAR   They durst not do't... (2.4.15–22)

Indisputably this produces, as Warren says (p. 98), 'a reading that has *no* authority'. If the Folio simply included words not in the Quarto the theory of a lost archetype would be tenable: reporters might easily omit such speeches. But the fact that the Folio also lacks words that *are* in the Quarto would suppose coincidentally independent omissions in both texts, or invention by the alleged Quarto reporters in a passage that did not require it, and this, though not impossible, is inherently less likely. Another example of the same problem occurs early in Act 3, scene 6. The Quarto reads:

> *Foole.* Prithe Nunckle tell me, whether a mad man be a Gen-
> tleman or a Yeoman.
> *Lear.* A King a King, to haue a thousand with red burning
> spits come hiszing in vpon them.
> *Edg.* The foule fiend bites my backe,
> *Foole.* He's mad, that trusts in the tamenes of a Wolfe, a hor-
> ses health, a boyes love, or a whores oath. (G3ᵛ)

In the Folio this is changed to:

> *Foole.* Prythee Nunkle tell me, whether a madman be
> a Gentleman, or a Yeoman.
> *Lear.* A King, a King.
> *Foole.* No, he's a Yeoman, that ha's a Gentleman to
> his Sonne: for hee's a mad Yeoman that sees his Sonne a
> Gentleman before him.
> *Lear.* To have a thousand with red burning spits
> Come hizzing in vpon'em.
> *Edg.* Blesse thy five wits. (TLN 2007–14)

The Quarto is coherent in itself. Lear does not offer a direct answer to the Fool's question so, after Edgar's marginal interjection, the Fool answers it himself. The Folio alters this so that the Fool picks up directly on the King's indirect answer, but omits the Fool's illustrations of mad behaviour. Conflation results in the following:

> FOOL   Prithee, nuncle, tell me whether a madman be a gentleman or a yeoman?
> LEAR   A king, a king!
> FOOL   No, he's a yeoman that has a gentleman to his son; for he's a mad yeoman
> that sees his son a gentleman before him.
> LEAR   To have a thousand with red burning spits
> Come hizzing in upon 'em—
> EDGAR   The foul fiend bites my back.
> FOOL   He's mad that trusts in the tameness of a wolf, a horse's health, a boy's
> love, or a whore's oath. (3.6.9–19)

This offers no motivation for the Fool's second statement, which is rendered redundant by the fact that he has already responded to the King's answer. In the absence of certainty that the Quarto is a reported text it is more in accordance with genuine conservatism of editorial principle to print one or the other version of both these passages than to create a passage of dialogue which there is no evidence that Shakespeare ever wrote.

When Warren's paper appeared in print he remarked in a footnote (p. 95) that as a consequence of delivering it he had learnt that three other scholars—Georgia Peters Burton, Steven Urkowitz, and Peter W. M. Blayney—were working on 'dissertations arguing for the distinction of the Quarto and Folio texts', and that each had 'arrived at the same major conclusion independently of the others'. Clearly a zeitgeist was at work, and it has manifested itself with increasing liveliness and substantiality in the years since 1976. In 1980 at the Cambridge, Massachusetts, meeting of the Shakespeare Association of America the issue was keenly debated during a seminar chaired by G. Blakemore Evans. One of the papers presented was Gary Taylor's 'The War in *King Lear*', later published in *Shakespeare Survey* 33 (Cambridge, 1980), which demonstrates that the two texts 'present coherent but distinct accounts' of the military actions of the fourth and fifth Acts. It provides an excellent introduction to the critical implications of the debate by illustrating within a short space that conflation muddies our understanding of Shakespeare's artistry and that textual disentangling must increase our respect for it. Later in the same year Steven Urkowitz's dissertation, to which Michael Warren had referred, was published in revised form as *Shakespeare's Revision of 'King Lear'*. Although Urkowitz does not offer a systematic and comprehensive discussion of variants, he tilts vigorously against Greg's and Alice Walker's arguments that the Quarto was not set entirely from author's papers. He offers a spirited defence of the Folio version as a revision which is also, theatrically, a great improvement on the Quarto text. Though not everyone has been persuaded,[33] George Walton Williams, reviewing the book in *Shakespeare Survey* 35, writes: 'The logic of Urkowitz's thesis is undeniable. It is impossible to disagree with his basic premise that there are two texts, that the effects in each are distinguishable, and that "the script of *King Lear*...in the Folio is Shakespeare's final version" (p. 147); the corollary is abundantly clear: "The modern composite version diminishes the intensity of the action...confuses the plot line...makes trivial the relationship [between characters]...and blurs the delicately indicated expectations" (p. 78).' In short, 'this is not *Lear*'.[34]

As the published work of Warren, Urkowitz, Blayney, and Taylor is supplemented by additional studies—including those collected in this volume, and those forthcoming from Blayney—the shift in attitude to *King Lear* which is already apparent is bound to become more general and to take various forms. Past criticism based upon the composite text will not, of course, be generally invalidated, but it will need to be read with some caution, especially when it concerns the plays' scenic structure and episodes not included in the Folio. Future criticism must acknowledge the existence of two authoritative texts. It need not be primarily comparative, but when it is not it will have to base itself upon one or the other—though, as with other plays, responsible literary criticism will take account of textual variants or uncertainties which might affect its argument.

Opinion about the relative merits of the two texts will vary, for agreement does not entail endorsement of the superiority of the revised text. Some readers may prefer the earlier version just as most readers prefer the earlier version of *The Prelude*; but they will find it hard to deny that the second, Folio *King Lear* gives us Shakespeare's later thoughts, just as readers of Wordsworth must agree that, however misguidedly, the author preferred the 1850 version of *The Prelude*. So far, most of those who have studied the two versions of *King Lear* in detail are agreed that the later is the better play, even though it omits admired passages from the earlier version.

The work of the critics will wait to some degree on that of the editors. New editions must be prepared—are, indeed, already in preparation—attempting to restore each text to an authentic, independent state. It will not be easy, for many individual variants will be disputed. But this is no new situation. It is true already of—to name only the most conspicuous examples—*Richard III, Hamlet, Troilus and Cressida, Othello*, and indeed *King Lear*, for editors presenting a composite text differ in the respective authority they allow to the primary sources of evidence for variants in passages common to both texts. In some ways, indeed, editors will find it an advantage to be required to make sense of each text in its own terms rather than to bring a conflation into conformity with a non-existent, hypothetical ideal.

Among those who accept that the Folio is a revised text—and who thus align themselves with no more revolutionary a figure than Granville-Barker—heart-searchings may be felt about the Quarto passages omitted in the Folio. A text based upon the belief that the revisions in the Folio are Shakespeare's, and in particular that its omissions from the Quarto were not, as has often been supposed, forced upon the author by vulgar theatrical exigencies—length, censorship, theatrical practicality—would deprive us of such passages, admired by many, as the Gentleman's description of Cordelia's grief at her father's plight ('her smiles and teares | Were like a better way ...'), the compassion of Gloucester's servants after his blinding (which Peter Brook was castigated for omitting from his 1962 production), and Lear's mock trial of Goneril and Regan. But these passages would not be lost for ever. They could still be read—and acted—where they belong, and where, it may be argued, they make their fullest and most proper impact, in the Quarto text, properly edited in its own right. This text, indeed, may be the more attractive to those who like their Shakespeare as close as possible to the point of conception—and, on the evidence of recent editions, this includes a number of his editors. For this reason, it seems proper that editions of the complete works should include both texts.

The two works may then be independently enjoyed, just as music-lovers may enjoy both the original and the revised version of Bach's *Magnificat* or (to take a more Shakespearean example) Tchaikovsky's *Romeo and Juliet*, recently recorded in an earlier and substantially different form from that which we know and love. If the play is to be presented for reading in a single text then, on the principle that an editor should seek to represent his author's final thoughts, it should be in a text based on the Folio, though it would seem proper for the editor to make the more substantial Quarto-only passages available in notes or appendices, since there is no reason to doubt that they are by Shakespeare. It would not, however, be fair to the reader to include them within the text, even within square brackets (as Harbage does) and even if the text otherwise were Folio-based; for this would represent an implicit subversion of the Folio's integrity. An analogy is presented by a very different play, Oscar Wilde's *The Importance of Being Earnest*; Russell Jackson, basing his text on the edition of 1899 prepared by Wilde himself, adds as appendices three substantial episodes which Wilde wrote but did not finally include (New Mermaids edition, 1980).

We must also hope that the new attitudes will be represented in theatre practice. It would probably be over-optimistic to expect professional directors to give us either the Quarto or the Folio text uncut, but it would be perfectly easy for a director to base his production on one or the other text, not admitting any degree of conflation. And it would be especially valuable to have such a production based on the Folio as a way of testing, in the only way that is ultimately valid, the belief that the revisions are theatrically justified, and that *King Lear* is a better drama in its later state.[35] A director who took this course would be following Granville-Barker's recommendation: 'On the whole then—and if he show a courageous discretion—I recommend a producer to found himself on the Folio. For that it does show some at least of Shakespeare's own reshapings I feel sure' (p. 332).

Those of us who have lived long with the traditionally conflated text of *King Lear* are likely to experience a subconscious resistance to what may appear to be a disintegrationist movement. Acceptance of its implications requires a mental adjustment that may prove painful. But we must, if we really care about what Shakespeare wrote, ask ourselves whether our resistance is logical or whether it proceeds, perhaps, from mental inertia, from mere dislike of change. Even in writing these paragraphs I have found that my natural tendency was to write of reversion to the Folio text as involving the 'omission' of passages found only in the Quarto, whereas the truth is that we have good reason to believe that they were never there. The case, it seems to me, is established. The Quarto and Folio texts of *King Lear* are distinct. There is no valid evidence that they derive from a single, lost archetype. The burden of proof rests not upon those who would keep the two texts asunder but upon those who would merge them into one. If those who support the eighteenth-century practice of conflation can prove that the Quarto and Folio texts are based upon a lost archetype, then a composite text is what we should read. But just as those who wish to emend a single word must first establish that the original requires emendation, so those who wish to produce an editorial conflation of *King Lear* must first demonstrate that both of the original documents seriously misrepresent Shakespeare's intentions. Until then the proper, conservative scholarly procedure is to suppose that the Quarto gives us Shakespeare's first thoughts and the Folio the text in its revised state. The matter of whether any of the Folio's revisions are not by Shakespeare may remain a topic for debate. Debate is likely to continue, too, about the merits of the revisions and about their philosophical implications. The process of investigation will disturb our reactions towards a greatly loved masterpiece; but it may vindicate the plays against some of the adverse criticisms based on the conflated text which I have cited. To split asunder the two texts of *King Lear* is a work of restoration, not of destruction. We shall lose by it no more than a wraith born of an unholy union; we shall gain a pair of legitimate— though not identical—twins.

12

Problems of Stagecraft in *The Tempest*

The Tempest is a play that commands great admiration as a poem in dramatic form. As is well known, the editors of the First Folio gave it pride of place in that volume; and as Shakespeare's last unaided play, it is often regarded as the culmination of his career as a poetic dramatist: a final, highly personal, even visionary utterance concerned at least in part with the relationship between life and art, and having at its centre a figure who has often been regarded as Shakespeare's shadowing forth of himself.

Its plot is comparatively slight, having none of the density and complexity of the plays that immediately preceded it in Shakespeare's output such as the immensely intricate *Cymbeline*. Its language, on the contrary, is very substantial—far more so than would have been necessary to project the story in naturalistic terms; the poetry is rich, dense, suggestive, complexly resonant; wonderfully integrated yet also, because of the way the play is constructed, falling often into set-pieces (Prospero's 'Our revels now are ended' is only the most obvious example) that are detachable and can almost be considered as poems in their own right.

Nevertheless, in spite of all its poetical power, the play has often 'proved curiously resistant to successful theatrical realization',[1] and indeed has been subjected over the centuries to various kinds of adaptation in the attempt to increase its theatrical viability; and when it is performed in relatively unadapted form it often fails to live up to the expectations raised by the impression it creates, in reading, on the theatre of the mind. In short, this is a play that exemplifies more than most the tensions between literature and drama.

In this paper I want to examine certain aspects of the play in the light of the various kinds of problems posed by their theatrical realization: not simply practical problems such as may be posed by any playscript, but problems that derive particularly from features of dramatic style which, if they are not unique to this play, are at least characteristic of the mode in which it is written. And I will start with the opening scene, which in practice has proved one of the most problematical.

The opening scene

Representing a shipwreck caused by a storm at sea, this scene provides obvious opportunities for theatrical spectacle, opportunities which the theatre has not been slow to exploit. The opening stage direction of the original text, written to be performed on the bare boards of the Globe or the Blackfriars, refers only to sound: 'A *tempestuous noise of thunder and lightning heard.*' No doubt the actors entering upon the stage would have been able to convey through gestures and bodily movements the impression that they were reeling around on a storm-driven vessel, and conceivably some properties were used to add to the atmospherics, but there could have been nothing like the visual effects demanded half a century later when the play was given at the Duke of York's theatre in an adaptation by Dryden and Davenant.

There, as the overture played, a curtain rose to reveal a new, emblematic 'frontispiece' with behind it 'the Scene, which represents a thick Cloudy Sky, a very Rocky Coast, and a Tempestuous See in perpetual Agitation. This Tempest (suppos'd to be rais'd by Magick) has many dreadful Objects in it, as several Spirits in horrid shapes flying down amongst the Sailors, then rising and crossing in the Air. And when the Ship is sinking, the whole House is darken'd, and a shower of Fire falls upon 'em. This is accompanied with Lightning, and several Claps of Thunder, to the end of the Storm.'

The scene that follows, though it retained much of Shakespeare's dialogue, made lengthy additions to it, including a lot of nautical language indicating stage business designed to increase the impression of a storm at sea. At the end of the scene, in the midst of a shower of fire, the scene changed, the theatre darkened, and 'when the Lights return discover that Beautiful part of the Island, which was the Habitation of Prospero'.[2]

The emphasis on spectacle inaugurated by the Dryden–Davenant adaptation reached its apogee in Charles Kean's production at the Princess's Theatre in 1857, in which the shipwreck was represented with extraordinary vividness but in which not a word was spoken. Shakespeare was being translated into a different medium from that in which he wrote: drama was replaced by spectacular mime; the play came close to the condition of ballet.

As this production continued, one triumph of spectacular staging succeeded another, but the text throughout was so severely shortened as to incur the condemnation even of the theatre historian G. C. D. Odell—no purist in these matters—who remarked that 'the Shakespearian enthusiast must have left the theatre with a feeling of disappointment, not to say resentment and disgust, resolving hereafter to seek his poetry at Sadler's Wells, where scenery was less in evidence'.[3]

Those are the terms in which Odell writes about the production when he is discussing the text; but when he comes to describe the production itself he reveals a distinct ambivalence in his reactions to it, describing it as 'probably the most beautiful and astonishing ever put on the stage'. 'Purists then, like purists now', he writes—implicitly aligning himself with those who are not purists—'lamented their lost fragments of Shakespeare; but the average theatregoer simply revelled in the show for a long succession of performances.'

Text versus spectacle?

These conflicting judgements are symptomatic of a constant ambivalence in the reactions of audiences to poetic drama: a feeling on the one hand that the text is what most matters, that the highest pleasures offered by the play are those that come through language, and at the same time a somewhat guilty feeling that in the theatre other values may supervene, even that the play's poetic integrity may be subverted by the more physical pleasures provided in its theatrical realization.

In recent times we have perhaps become a little more tolerant of adaptation, more receptive to the notion that each attempt to put a play on the stage must differ from every other one, and that it is ultimately impossible to define an essence which only is the play itself; we may respond to the pleasures of productions that alter the text, that substitute theatrical for verbal effects, that use the text as a jumping-off ground for an experience very different from that conveyed by reading alone, even a reading that is fully informed by consciousness of theatrical values.

Nevertheless there are many directors who work with full texts, and many audiences who are interested in the efforts that can made to be faithful to these texts; they present a challenge, and even if the challenge is finally evaded it is worth discussing the nature of this challenge and the terms in which it may be faced.

To return to scene 1 of The Tempest: although the theatres of Shakespeare's time offered far less opportunity for spectacular staging than those of later ages, the mode in which this scene is composed is not conspicuously poetical. Most of the dialogue is written in prose. This may seem a mere technicality, because Shakespeare's prose can itself be very poetical, but here the prose is relatively naturalistic, colloquial in diction, often subservient to the bustling action that it serves: 'Hey, my hearts! Cheerly, cheerly, my hearts! Yare, yare! Take in the topsail. Tend to the master's whistle . . .' and so on. In spite of a few antiquated expressions, it conveys an impression of modernity; and much of it could stand without alteration in, for instance, a television script.

If this were all, nothing might be lost by submerging it by action, or even by abandoning it altogether in the manner of Charles Kean. But if we look at it closely, and especially in the light of what is to come in later scenes, we may begin to feel that the impression of naturalism is illusory, that the dialogue is not simply atmospheric in the manner that spectacular productions (of any age) emphasize, and that neither is it simply expository of action, setting up the initial situation of the plot.

Rather, the scene is one in which what is represented has emblematic as well as narrative significance, and in which what is said is no less important than what is represented: it is expository of the play's ideas as well as of its plot, and introduces us to what it is perhaps too unfashionable to call the 'themes' of the play—to those ideas that enrich its texture and that have caused it to be regarded not just as a stimulus to theatrical effect but also as one of the more important documents in our literary as well as our theatrical heritage. Let us try to look at the scene not from a single point of view but as a whole, a piece of poetical drama.[4]

The ship as microcosm

We may note first that, as the play is to take place on an island, so this scene takes place upon a ship—itself a kind of island, giving the scene some of the aspects of a microcosm of the whole play. As I have remarked, it opens not with dialogue, but with sound—the ominous sound of thunder and of lightning (I'm not entirely clear what lightning sounds like). In the shorthand of drama, this sound of the elements threatening human life can immediately establish a mode in which symbol is important, in which anything that is heard or seen has significance beyond the mundane. The opening dialogue of the scene, and therefore of the play, gives us an image of authority—the authority exercised by the master of a ship as he gives orders to his crew: it introduces us to the concept of authority as an instrument of control: the master is controlling the crew's efforts which themselves are directed to control the ship so as to withstand the onslaught of forces mysteriously inimical to human life.

Having given us a glimpse of one kind of authority, Shakespeare rapidly juxtaposes it with another. On the ship the master has the kind of authority that a king exercises over the country that he rules. And the next characters to enter are a king—Alonso, King of Naples—and members of his court. It must be one of the minor problems in producing the play that these characters are not named in the dialogue of the scene, and that their offices, so important to our understanding of what is happening, are only implicitly alluded to: this is something that can be at least partially solved by costuming, but it is symptomatic of one of the more awkward aspects of the play's technique.

The King, having entered upon the scene, immediately starts trying to exert an authority that is irrelevant to the circumstances in which he finds himself. On board, the ship's master is king: Alonso's assumption of authority is irrelevant, is indeed subversive of the authority of the true ruler of this little kingdom: and the play that follows is to be much concerned with usurpation, both in the past and in the present.

The Boatswain's rebukes of Alonso and his fellows—at first polite ('I pray you, keep below'), then more insistent ('You mar our labour. Keep your cabin—you do assist the storm')—show two kinds of authority in collision, resulting in danger to each, as the Boatswain points out: 'you do assist the storm'. We are shown vividly and verbally that in some circumstances the higher power may be at the mercy of a lesser one; a parallel image might be that of a king having to submit to a medical authority. We are shown this through words: 'What cares these roarers for the name of king?' asks the exasperated Boatswain, in a simple, direct, and memorable sentence that epitomizes the situation—and that has resonances characteristic of the play in that the word 'roarers' could mean not only roaring winds and waves but also rioters, that is those who try to subvert authority. Significant too is the formulation 'the name of king'; the power of a king derives partly from the name of the office that he occupies, from a word which in itself has no power to quell the inimical forces of thunder and lightning—a theme that Shakespeare had already memorably explored in both *Richard II* and *King Lear*.

The Boatswain expands upon his rebuke in response to Gonzalo's injunction 'yet remember whom thou hast aboard'. 'None that I love more than myself,' he replies; 'You are a councillor; if you can command these elements to silence, and work the peace of the present, we will not hand a rope more—use your authority. If you cannot, give thanks you have lived so long, and make yourself ready in your cabin for the mischance of the hour, if it so hap.'

As the brief scene progresses, we see that the clash between two systems of authority produces reactions that are expressive of character. Sebastian and Antonio are harsh, insolent, and uncharitable—everything that they themselves accuse the Boatswain of being. Gonzalo, on the other hand, is good-humoured, tolerant, and humane. In the face of increasing disaster both the mariners and the more sympathetic members of the King's party abandon all claims to authority and resort to prayer—and if we know the play in advance we will remember that it is to end with a request for the audience's prayers. But two characters—Antonio and Sebastian—seem entirely resistant to the idea that their fate depends upon any power beyond that of the sailors: 'We are merely cheated of our lives by drunkards', says Antonio—and we may remember that there will be drunkenness, a condition in which self-control is as it were voluntarily abnegated, in the play, too.

So far as we know at the end of the scene, as the ship splits apart, the storm has won, though Shakespeare cunningly provides a transition with Gonzalo's closing words:

Now would I give a thousand furlongs of sea for an acre of barren ground—long heath, brown furze, anything. The wills above be done, but I would fain die a dry death.

There are, then, several different sorts of problem in this scene. One is for the actors to establish the characters in the audience's imaginations on the basis of relatively little information. Another is to determine the appropriate balance between naturalism and stylization. And most important, at least for a director who seeks (granted the changes in theatrical conditions between Shakespeare's times and ours) to achieve Shakespeare's effects in his own way, is to allow the ideas that the scene articulates to make themselves apparent: if elaborate sound effects are used, and if visual spectacle is to play its part in the presentation of the scene, the orchestration of these effects must be such that the words carrying the scene's ideas are not lost.

The problem is similar to that of the storm scenes in *King Lear*, though there it is more apparent because Lear so obviously must be heard: even Charles Kean—assuming he was playing Lear himself—would not have totally eliminated words there.

Problems of narrative and character

The opening scene shows us something of the struggle that man has to exert to impose order on his universe, and at the beginning of the next scene we see a man who does literally have power, albeit a limited power, to exert control over the forces of nature. I say at the beginning of the second scene, but directors have frequently chosen to bring Prospero—and even (as in Sam Mendes's 1993 Stratford production) Ariel too—on stage at the very beginning of the play to show us that the storm is of Prospero's making. To do this runs the risk of diminishing the impact of the storm; foregrounding narrative over symbol, it suggests from the start that man *can* control the elements, and so reduces the scene's emblematic quality. It also adds yet another unidentified character to the scene, at least for audiences who are unfamiliar with the play.

The second scene is very much of a contrast with the first in both verbal style and dramatic mode, and taken together the two scenes represent a variation upon a technique of double exposition that Shakespeare uses elsewhere—notably in, for instance, *Hamlet* and *Macbeth*, where too a vividly atmospheric scene or episode is followed by one that lays out information essential to our understanding of the action in a more leisurely, amplificatory style.

In *The Tempest* Prospero's narrative is so long, so relatively free from interruption, so obviously literary, that it is often seen as undramatic and in need of theatrical pepping up; but this perhaps underestimates the theatrical force of spoken narrative. An actor inevitably imbues the lines with his own personality, and, as he relives it, Prospero's account of his past can compel our interest.

Prospero's long narration, addressed to Miranda, and his subsequent inter-changes with Ariel and Caliban, firmly establish him as the play's central charac-ter; indeed there is even a sense in which he might be described as the play's only fully realized human character. I don't mean by this that, as some have main-tained, the entire play takes place in Prospero's mind; but it does seem to me that one of the major theatrical problems of the play lies in Shakespeare's use of what we might call foreshortening and symbolical techniques in his presentation of certain characters.

Shakespeare's techniques of characterization vary from play to play, even from phase to phase of his career. In some plays, such as *Coriolanus* and *Antony and Cleopatra*, he is clearly very much interested in the quirks of individual personalities; in others, characterization tends to be more stylized, projecting only selected aspects of a personality and leaving the actor freedom either to maintain some detachment from the character, or to suggest hidden depths not apparent in the dialogue. One may think for example of Don John in *Much Ado About Nothing*, who can be played as a melodramatic villain but for whom some actors try to supply psychological motivation; or of the good and bad Dukes in *As You Like It*, defined largely by contrast.

The plays in which this technique predominates tend to be those in which the emphasis is on ideas rather than on human psychology. Shakespeare is particularly inclined to use such devices in his late plays (especially *Cymbeline* with, for example, its wicked, Snow White-type Queen), but there is no other play in his output in which they are so predominant as *The Tempest*. In the storm scene Shakespeare rapidly establishes a contrast between Gonzalo on the one hand and, on the other, Antonio and Sebastian—this play's Rosencrantz and Guildenstern, or Tweedledum and Tweedledee—by juxtaposing the idealism of the former with the cynicism of the latter.

Dramatizing moral contrasts

These are the tips of the icebergs of their personalities, all the actor has to work with at this stage of the play. And as the action continues the same techniques may be observed at work in both these and other characters. It causes particular problems, I think, in the court characters. Prospero names the more important of these in his narration, and it was perhaps in response to the shadowiness of their textual characterization that Mendes, in the production I have referred to, caused each of them to step forward from behind a screen as he did so, helping to fix their identities in our mind. Directorial devices like this, while they may sometimes seem like unnecessary impositions on a play, may also represent relevant and justifiable criticisms of it.

The difficulties with the courtiers come to a head in Act 2, scene 1, in the first part of which we witness their reactions to the shipwreck and to the island on which they find themselves, and in which contrasts between these reactions help to define them: Gonzalo again, and the very subsidiary lord Adrian—a dramatic nonentity if ever there was one—are full of idealism, especially in Gonzalo's Montaigne-inspired description of an ideal commonwealth; whereas Antonio and Sebastian take a jaundiced, cynical view of all they see.

In my experience, the audience's attention is all too liable to sag during this scene, with its somewhat obscure dialogue, its arid witticisms, and its two-dimensional characters. Roger Warren writes of it that 'It is...one of the most difficult for actors to perform and for audiences to concentrate upon', while feeling, nevertheless that its problems are soluble—and were solved in Peter Hall's National Theatre production of 1988, largely as the result of subtle acting that found a psychological subtext to motivate the apparently stylized utterances. The actors, we may feel, were bailing Shakespeare out; but of course a playwright can legitimately expect help from his interpreters. Another way of tackling the problems, however, might be to accept the scene's artificialities and to play it in a consciously stylized fashion.

The dramatic mode of romance within which Shakespeare is working in this play encourages the presentation of moral absolutes, and this is very apparent in *The Tempest*. The moral contrasts within the court party are mirrored in other relationships in the play, most strongly perhaps in that between Ferdinand, the King's son, and Caliban. Here Shakespeare employs a symbolical method of characterization which helps both to distinguish between the two characters and to point to similarities between them. Before we see Caliban, Prospero tells Miranda

> He does make our fire,
> Fetch in our wood, and serves in offices
> That profit us,

and Caliban's first words, spoken 'within', are 'There's wood enough within.' The carrying of wood is a symbolical burden, in Caliban's case a punishment imposed on him for the crime of attempted rape. The uncontrolled sexual urge is easily seen as part of that destructive disorder of which thunder and lightning had been the initial symbols. And it is a clear aspect of the play's self-conscious design that Shakespeare immediately follows the exit of the lustful figure of Caliban with the entrance of the play's romantic lover, Ferdinand.

Where Caliban resists control, Ferdinand, who enters under the magic control of Ariel (and thus of Prospero, whose agent Ariel is), willingly accepts it as a means of winning Miranda. For him love is a power, a bondage, but one that illustrates the Christian paradox that in some kinds of service lies perfect freedom:

My spirits, as in a dream, are all bound up.
My father's loss, the weakness which I feel,
The wreck of all my friends, nor this man's threats,
To whom I am subdued, are but light to me,
Might I but through my prison once a day
Behold this maid. All corners o'th'earth
Let liberty make use of—space enough
Have I in such a prison.

The love-test and betrothal

And Prospero imposes on Ferdinand a love-test, a task such as those to which heroes of chivalric romances were customarily subjected. In some stories, such love-tests involved heroic feats such as the subjugation of giants. Ferdinand's is less arduous: like Caliban, he has to fetch and chop Prospero's firewood. The opening stage direction of Act 3 reads 'Enter Ferdinand bearing a log', and his subsequent soliloquy, followed by the dialogue between him and Miranda, bases itself on his attitude towards his task, along with Miranda's concern that he 'Work not so hard'. Whereas the first words we have heard Caliban speak are a complaint against his task—'There's wood enough within'—Ferdinand accepts his 'mean task' gladly because 'The mistress which I serve quickens what's dead, | And makes my labours pleasures.'

One of the problems in staging the play is to determine the nature and quantity of the wood to be carried by Ferdinand; it may seem a small enough point, but the decision will have a considerable effect on the tone of the scene and on the way we react to Ferdinand. If the logs are too heavy, Miranda's offer to relieve him of the task will seem absurd, and Prospero will seem to be punishing rather than testing him; if they are too light, the scene will be trivialized.

Nicholas Hytner hit the right note, I thought, when, placing this scene after the interval, he showed us Ferdinand repeatedly going to and fro in a spirit of rueful acceptance of his lot, bearing logs weighty enough to cause him moderate discomfort, before the house lights went down. The audience's amusement was channelled off before the play proper resumed. The significance of the symbolism is brought home at the end of the scene when Ferdinand, betrothing himself to Miranda, declares himself her husband 'with a heart as willing | As bondage e'er of freedom'.

Prospero has been an unseen witness of the conversation between the lovers, and at the end of the scene declares his satisfaction at their betrothal. But he is constantly concerned to sustain the distinction—not always an easy one to maintain—between lust and love, as symbolized in Caliban's uncontrolled desire and Ferdinand's acceptance of the need for self-restraint. Giving Miranda to Ferdinand, he says:

> All thy vexations
> Were but my trials of thy love, and thou
> Hast strangely stood the test. Here, afore heaven,
> I ratify this my rich gift.

Yet still he insists on the importance of control:

> If thou dost break her virgin-knot before
> All sanctimonious ceremonies may
> With full and holy rite be ministered,
> No sweet aspersion shall the heavens let fall
> To make this contract grow,

and again,

> Look thou be true; do not give dalliance
> Too much the rein. The strongest oaths are straw
> To th' fire i' th' blood.

The explicit moralizing here is unusual for Shakespeare, though it has its parallels in other late plays; it may be seen as an aspect, perhaps even an unpleasant one, of the characterization of Prospero, but it certainly also relates to the play's overriding concern, adumbrated in the opening scene, with man's attempts to control and tame the potentially anarchic forces of nature both within and outside of himself. Thus, both the importance of sexual self-control and the rewards that it may reap are the very themes of the masque that Prospero conjures up as his entertainment for the lovers.

Masque as medium—and as message

No one would question, I suppose, that the staging of the masque ranks high among the problems that this play presents to modern interpreters. In his essay on *The Tempest* Jan Kott speaks of Shakespeare's plays as 'a system of mirrors, as it were, both concave and convex, which reflect, magnify, and parody the same situation'.[5] In more than one respect the masque mirrors the opening scene of the play. It is Prospero who conjures up both the storm and the masque; both episodes represent an exercise of the powers he has learnt from his books, and both are ultimately beneficent in effect. Both present technical problems to their performers; but for present-day performers the most difficult aspect of the masque rests not in the mechanics of its staging but in the outdatedness of the conventions upon which it draws.

The problem is both literary and theatrical. Even the more highly educated members of a modern audience are likely to be less familiar than their Jacobean counterparts with either the mythological or the poetical traditions on which Shakespeare draws in his representation of Iris, Ceres, and Juno. And the framework in which he presents them, the formal structure of a masque, is one that, highly topical at the time of the play's first performances, went out of fashion during the next few decades and now requires a major exercise of the historical imagination before it can convey anything of the excitement that it must have had in the early seventeenth century—the great age of the court masque, represented at its finest in the collaborative work of Ben Jonson and Inigo Jones.

In *The Tempest* Shakespeare provides for the audiences of the public theatres at least a shadow of the glory that the form achieved at the court of King James, where it stood at once as a symbol of power and wealth—frequently used as such in the game of power politics—and as a celebration of the highest achievements of civilization, in which the arts of music, dancing, painting, poetry, and acting combined in entertainments whose splendour was enhanced by their folly—for immense amounts of money were lavished upon a single evening's entertainment by those who did not have the good fortune, like Prospero, to be able to command unpaid spirits to enact their fancies.

An attempt on the part of a modern director to reproduce the conventions of the Jacobean masque is likely to mean little or nothing to members of a modern audience, and is rarely attempted. More commonly an effort is made to reproduce the effect of these conventions through other means. It is not particularly difficult to convey a sense of the splendour of the masque, as a 'vanity' of Prospero's art designed to divert the lovers. Often it has been sung, sometimes adopting the musical and theatrical conventions of a particular operatic style of the past—that of Monteverdi or Cavalli, for instance. Sam Mendes, in his 1993 production, flew down a large model of a Victorian toy theatre and represented the goddesses almost as mechanical figures.

The difficulty, as with the storm, is to convey the sense of the words that the goddesses utter, to convey the moral message that underpins the spectacle and that relates it to the system of ideas embodied in the play. Prospero is certainly present throughout this performance, and we see him here in multiple functions—as father to Miranda, as an artist capable of devising this show, as a kind of surrogate playwright, as a magician, and also as a monarch with power (like James I) to create a lavish entertainment to be attended only by his personal guests.

But we see him also as teacher. Just as Ben Jonson's masques, for all their splendour, often carried a moral message—the 'more removed mysteries' of which he speaks in the preface to *Hymenaei*—so Prospero's is very much designed to reinforce the injunctions to pre-marital chastity that precede it. Iris alludes explicitly to the temptations with which Venus and Cupid have beset the lovers, and praises the strength of will—the self-control—with which these temptations have been resisted:

> Here thought they to have done
> Some wanton charm upon this man and maid,
> Whose vows are that no bed-right shall be paid
> Till Hymen's torch be lighted; but in vain.
> Mars's hot minion is returned again;
> Her waspish-headed son has broke his arrows,
> Swears he will shoot no more, but play with sparrows,
> And be a boy right out.

The masque will lose its point unless the director ensures that its message is not submerged in spectacle. In the printed text of *Hymenaei*, Jonson says:

> Nor was there wanting whatsoever might give to the furniture or complement, either in richness, or strangeness of the habits, delicacy of dances, magnificence of the scene, or divine rapture of music. Only the envy was that it lasted not still, or, now it is past, cannot by imagination, much less description, be recovered to a part of that spirit it had in the gliding by.

Here Jonson describes his awareness of the transience that Prospero is soon to acknowledge: if the masque is a fitting symbol of the greatest splendour that man can achieve, it is a fitting symbol too of the impermanence of all human effort; the visions of a Prospero are at the mercy of the Calibans of this world; power that can create can also destroy, and so, when Prospero recalls 'that foul conspiracy | Of the beast Caliban and his confederates' against his life, the vision vanishes, leaving not a rack behind.

Crisis, calculation—and renunciation

One last problem that I want to mention briefly is a matter of interpretation rather than of stagecraft in the more limited sense, but it is crucial to the presentation of the play. While the masque is being performed, the King and his followers are prisoners, unable, as Ariel says, to 'budge' until Prospero releases them. Prospero finds himself in a position of complete power over his enemies, and Ariel tells him:

> Your charm so strongly works 'em
> That if you now beheld them, your affections
> Would become tender.

It is a moment of crisis in the portrayal of Prospero, and it is also a moment that is subject to varied interpretation. 'Dost think so, spirit?' asks Prospero, and Ariel replies: 'Mine would, sir, were I human.' Prospero may well pause for thought before his next speech.

> And mine shall.
> Hast thou, which art but air, a touch, a feeling
> Of their afflictions, and shall not myself,
> One of their kind, that relish all as sharply
> Passion as they, be kindlier moved than thou art?
> Though with their high wrongs I am struck to th'quick,
> Yet with my nobler reason 'gainst my fury
> Do I take part. The rarer action is
> In virtue than in vengeance. They being penitent,
> The sole drift of my purpose doth extend
> Not a frown further. Go, release them, Ariel.

This is certainly a speech of self-examination. The interpretive question is whether it also represents a moment of crisis at which Prospero's intentions towards the shipwrecked men undergo a radical change.

Is it only now that Prospero decides upon forgiveness? Or, at the other extreme, can the whole action of the play be seen as essentially benevolent, the result of a desire to bring his enemies to a state of self-awareness which could naturally lead on their part to penitence and reconciliation? Or does the truth lie somewhere between these extremes? Or has Shakespeare deliberately left the question open?

Many arguments could be adduced on both sides of the question, and I doubt if any definitive answer can be found. I would ask only that the style in which the speech is written be taken into account. To me, Prospero does not sound here like a man going through a crisis of the soul, being wrenched from one course of action to another that is fundamentally different. There is not here the sense of anguish that we hear in, for example, Macbeth's 'If it were done when 'tis done . . .'. If the actor is going to suggest conversion, he will have to do so not through the words he speaks but between the lines—in, perhaps, the silence between Ariel's 'Mine would, sir, were I human' and Prospero's 'And mine shall'.

In any case, it is after this final test, or demonstration, of his self-mastery that Prospero is able to describe his intention to renounce his supernatural powers. The speech in which he does so—'Ye elves of hills, brooks, standing lakes, and groves'— is remarkable for the way it offers a verbal re-creation of the powers that Prospero has been able to exert at the very moment that he renounces them. 'But this rough magic I here abjure'—it's as if, in some paradoxical way, the greatest of his achievements was not the exercise of power but the capacity to give it up. It is an acknowledgement of limitation, of humanity, and of mortality. In exercising, not vengeance, but virtue, Prospero is able to reveal to Alonso that his son, Ferdinand, is alive, and to bring about their reunion. When he reveals the lovers, they are playing chess—yet another symbol, surely, of self-control.

The final paradox of a play that has been so deeply concerned with control and restraint is that it ends in liberty. Ariel, who has done the services required of him, is freed. All the travellers are freed from the island to which they came unwillingly; and finally Prospero himself, freed from the responsibility of exerting his power, appeals to the audience to free him from the stage.

There are of course many more problems in the staging of *The Tempest* of which I could have written—problems in the visual representation of Ariel and Caliban, for instance, or in the integration into the masque of the nymphs and reapers, in the staging of the magical banquet and the 'spirits in shape of dogs and hounds' who torment Caliban, Stephano, and Trinculo. But whichever I had chosen, they would all need to be related to questions of interpretation, to the projection through theatrical means of the significances that we can derive from the play's text.

It is in the nature of the transmission of Shakespeare's plays that we can conjecture far more about the literary than the theatrical impact that they made in their own time, whether in reading or in performance. Critics and scholars may be inclined to over-emphasize the literary; though the theatre can do something to redress the balance, it can never hope to arrive with any certainty at the solutions found in Shakespeare's day; but it may at least find ways of projecting the text which will work in terms of today's audiences.

13

'My Name is Will':
Shakespeare's Sonnets and Autobiography

I once wrote on Twitter that the more I read Shakespeare's sonnets, the more difficult I find them. To which an unknown follower, flatteringly assuming that I was an undergraduate, responded with 'Finals are going to be fun, then.'

There are many reasons for the difficulties that I experience with the Sonnets. It is partly that many of them are highly intellectual poems written in an exceptionally dense and demanding style. I have problems too with the complex interrelationships among the sonnets and with the challenge of reading consecutively a large number of short poems, some clearly interrelated, whether in subject matter or by syntactical links, some not. Continually one has to make a fresh start after the apparent finality of a couplet. But many of my difficulties relate directly to the poems' origins and their originality.

The vexed question of their origin—where they came from—may be asked in what we might call the geographical, or physical, sense of 'Where did Thomas Thorpe get the manuscript that lies behind his 1609 publication?' Did Shakespeare himself negotiate its publication—possibly for ready money—or did Thorpe somehow acquire a manuscript (or possibly two manuscripts, one containing the sonnets, the other 'A Lover's Complaint') from someone other than Shakespeare who may not have had the author's permission to part with it? It is an important question because if Shakespeare authorized the publication, that would imply that he had signed off on the collection, regarding it as a finished and publishable work, whereas if publication was unauthorized the volume could more rationally be thought of as an open-ended collection of poems which had accumulated over the years, which might have continued to grow after 1609, and which the author might even have regarded as too personal to be published. The ordering may be Shakespeare's—I think there are good reasons to suppose that it is—but the numbers could have been inserted by a scribe or by someone in the printing house.

The Arden editor, Katherine Duncan-Jones, is one of the primary exponents of the belief that publication *was* authorized. She addressed the question in her wonderfully well-researched 1983 article 'Was the 1609 *Shake-speares Sonnets* really unauthorized?'[1] There she demonstrates that Thorpe was not, as had been suggested, an unscrupulous publisher who would have been likely to print a surreptitiously obtained manuscript against its author's wishes, and concludes that it is reasonable to suppose that he received a finished manuscript from Shakespeare himself. She has sustained this position, writing in the 2010 revision of her 1997 Arden edition that 'there is good reason to believe that the 1609 Quarto publication was authorized by Shakespeare himself'.[2]

An obvious objection to this is the fact that the dedication appears over Thorpe's initials, not over Shakespeare's name (as in the narrative poems). To get round this, she hypothesizes that Thorpe wrote the dedication on Shakespeare's behalf because plague had driven the poet out of London. Thorpe, it would seem, had more boldly—or foolhardily—stayed behind. 'The hasty departure of the author', she writes, 'and his prolonged absence, rather than any kind of conspiracy or deception, probably account for Thorpe's being the signatory of the dedication.'[3] In her biographical study, *Ungentle Shakespeare*, too, she writes confidently that Shakespeare sold 'the valuable and much laboured-over text ... surely for a good sum', to Thorpe, and that the dedication was 'signed by Thorpe, but authorized by Shakespeare'.[4]

Colin Burrow, in the Oxford edition published in 2002 (between the two versions of the Arden), is less confident about the state of the manuscript that Thorpe printed and of its provenance. Certain 'features of the printed text', he notes, 'suggest that the copy from which Eld's compositors worked may have been hard to read or that it may not have been finally revised'.[5] And whereas Duncan-Jones is willing to believe that 'The "book" sold to Thorpe may have taken the form either of an autograph manuscript or of an authorially corrected scribal transcript',[6] Burrow thinks the manuscript was a scribal copy, possibly written in more than one hand.[7]

My own view is that publication was not authorized. This is partly because the title-page (like the Stationers' Register entry) is written, as it were, in the third person—'Shakespeare's Sonnets, never before imprinted'. 'Shakespeare's Sonnets' is also the running title, and the volume bears a dedication followed by the initials of its publisher, not of its author. All this makes me believe that Thorpe published the poems without Shakespeare's authority. I see no reason to suppose that Shakespeare chose the dedicatee. And the theory, which has also been advanced, that 'Mr W. H.' is a misprint for 'Mr W. S.', standing for Master William Shakespeare, is surely absurd—why should a publisher, then or now, dedicate a book to the man who wrote it?

This does not, however, require us to doubt that Shakespeare is responsible for the order in which the sonnets are printed. To judge by the most reliable dating studies, that order does not correspond to their dates of composition. That is a crucial factor in discussion of whether the Sonnets were conceived as a whole. The fact that the collection includes a number of clearly interconnected groups of poems, such as those encouraging a young man to procreate, and the last twenty-six, which contain all those with female addressees, along with a number of other subsections such as those poems that have been supposed to refer to a rival poet or poets—all this favours the supposition that someone who knew the poems extremely well put them in their present order. This is most likely to have been Shakespeare himself, rearranging them for his own satisfaction (like a boy with a stamp album), for perusal by one or more private friends, or, just possibly, with the thought in mind that he might eventually offer them for publication. I am not greatly attracted by the theory that he was inhibited by shyness from doing so until after his mother died, in September 1608, but I do suspect that he regarded the collection as a whole as something that he preferred to keep under wraps. The posthumous publication of John Donne's *Songs and Sonnets* in 1633 suggests itself as a parallel. I am happy to believe that Shakespeare wrote 'A Lover's Complaint' and that he would not have objected to its appearing along with the sonnets, though I am not convinced that it is integral to the collection.

A different aspect of the poems' origin is their relationship to sonnet sequences written during the 1590s in the wake of the publication of Sir Philip Sidney's *Astrophil and Stella*. In the book that I co-authored with Paul Edmondson ten years ago we argued that Shakespeare's sonnets do not form a unified sequence but that they are a collection of disparate poems, some of them closely interrelated, though written (as chronological studies show) over a long period of time. As I have said, studies of chronology (as well as common sense) also show that they were not written in the order in which they are printed; so they are more properly regarded as a miscellany than as a sequence.[8] This view is surely supported by the indisputable fact that not all the poems in the volume are love sonnets. Indeed, 146—'Poor soul, the centre of my sinful earth...'—would not be out of place among Donne's Holy Sonnets. It is, says Duncan-Jones, 'Shakespeare's only explicitly religious poem'.[9] And 129, 'Th'expense of spirit in a waste of shame', is a philosophical meditation on love and lust written in the third person which, though it can be related to other poems in the collection, can stand entirely on its own and would, moreover, seem completely out of place in a conventional sonnet sequence of the 1590s.

Furthermore, although we concur that all the sonnets clearly addressed to or written about a male person occur among the first 126 of the poems in order of printing, we dispute the common assumption that they are addressed to only one young man (or boy—'sweet boy', 108, 'my lovely boy', 126), supporting our argument (which had been notably anticipated by Heather Dubrow[10]) by demonstrating on the evidence of pronouns and forms of address that only twenty of these poems can confidently be said to be addressed to a male, and that many of the earlier-printed poems, including some of the most intensely amatory, could equally well relate to either a male or a female. I do not find it easy to overcome my own preconceptions about this. Just as it is difficult to get out of the habit of referring to the sonnets as a sequence (which, in the most basic, etymological sense of a series of poems that follow one another, they are) rather than as a collection or a miscellany, so also I often need to make a conscious effort in reading many of the first group of poems to think hard about whether the gender of the addressee, or of the person referred to, is ascertainable. Take for example Sonnet 27, in which the poet tells how, exhausted after a hard day's work, he lies awake thinking and writing in absence to a loved one:

> For then my thoughts, from far where I abide,
> Intend a zealous pilgrimage to thee,
> And keep my drooping eyelids open wide,
> Looking on darkness which the blind do see.

Traditionally this poem, and the subsequent sonnet, which links with it in sense—'How can I then return in happy plight, | That am debarred the benefit of rest ...'—are regarded as poems addressed to the supposed male friend, but there is nothing in them to gender the addressee; Germaine Greer is fully justified in suggesting not merely that they do not have to be addressed to a male but that they could even be expressive of what she calls 'the loneliness and anxiety, the frustration and disappointment' that Shakespeare may have felt as he rode away from his wife and family.[11] (The same may be true of Sonnets 50 and 51, both of which take place, as it were, on horseback.)

These propositions seem to me to be self-evident—but old beliefs die hard. It is still all too common to hear reputable scholars and critics rolling out the old fallacies about 'the young man of the sonnets' and basing whole arguments on the totally erroneous assumption that there is undisputably only one young man, whether fictional or not. This idea is encouraged by Thorpe's dedication to 'the only begetter of these ensuing sonnets', whatever 'begetter' may mean and on whatever authority he may have said it, but is refuted by the contents of the volume. It permeates Hyder Rollins's monumental New Variorum edition of 1944,[12] and afflicts many currently circulating editions. Even in the revised Arden of 2010 (which does not refer to our study) Duncan-Jones writes that 'more than four-fifths of the sequence [sic] is devoted to celebrating a [sic] fair youth', and she devotes a large part of her introduction to identifying William Herbert, Earl of Pembroke 'as the dedicatee and addressee [sic] of Sonnets'.[13] Colin Burrow, who allows that many of the earlier printed poems 'carefully skirt around even giving a fixed gender to their addressee', nevertheless also slips into referring to 'poems to the young man'.[14] David Ellis, in a book, The Truth About William Shakespeare (2012), which aims pugnaciously to take a hard-headed attitude to Shakespeare biography, writes of the sonnets as 'a story in which the poet is continually contrasted with *a beloved male* younger than himself' (p. 75) and of '*the man* to whom most of the sonnets were predominantly or exclusively addressed' (p. 79).[15]

These questions are of the highest importance to an understanding of the sonnets both as poetry and as the most personal of all Shakespeare's writings, the only ones that might give us direct access to his private thoughts and perhaps even to his daily existence. Are they indeed, as Wordsworth wrote in 'Scorn not the Sonnet', the 'key' with which 'Shakespeare unlocked his heart'? To liberate the sonnets from the notion that individual poems in the collection are necessarily subordinate to an overall design enables us to examine individual poems, or small groups of clearly interrelated poems, in their own right. To acknowledge that Shakespeare might have written love poems to and about a variety of persons, including past lovers, has fascinating consequences for biographical studies. And it is supported by the statement in Sonnet 31 (which is ungendered), 'Thou art the grave where buried love doth lie, | Hung with the trophies of my lovers gone.' Many critics have protected the poet's reputation (thus implicitly acknowledging that the poem may be autobiographical) by saying that the word 'lovers' 'need not', as Duncan-Jones puts it in her note on this poem, 'carry any erotic charge', but doesn't the word 'trophies' imply some form of amatory conquest? Burrow seems to think so. In his fascinating note on the same poem he suggests 'there is something at once resurrective and vampiric in the way the beloved makes life from buried former loves'. To recognize, however, that not all the poems are straightforward love poems is also to extend the potential breadth of reference of the volume. An example is Sonnet 26, beginning

> Lord of my love, to whom in vassalage
> Thy merit hath my duty strongly knit,
> To thee I send this written embassage
> To witness duty, not to show my wit.

Duncan-Jones glosses 'this written embassage' as the sonnet itself but it might equally refer to a written gift which the sonnet accompanied. Capell, in 1780, when the Sonnets were only just beginning to be taken seriously, remarked on the resemblance between this poem and the dedication to *The Rape of Lucrece*.[16] Both the poem and the dedication refer to the poet's 'love' for the person addressed, and to his 'duty', and indeed Rollins finds that this resemblance became the starting point for the theory that Southampton is not only addressed in this poem but is the addressee of all the male-oriented sonnets. To my mind abandonment of the concept that the sonnets have a single male addressee gives strength to the theory that Shakespeare wrote this sonnet to accompany the manuscript of *Lucrece* when he sent it to the Earl.

There are also at least three sonnets which make me suspect the existence of a portrait of a lover of the poet as an external reference, and which embolden me to make an association again with Southampton. One such sonnet is 20, 'A woman's face with nature's own hand painted | Hast thou, the master-mistress of my passion', which is immediately followed by the poem beginning 'So is it not with me as with that muse | Stirred by a *painted* beauty to his verse'. And three poems later comes 24, beginning 'Mine eye hath played the painter, and hath steeled | Thy beauty's form in table of my heart. | My body is the frame wherein 'tis held, | And perspective it is best painter's art.' ('Table' could mean the canvas or board on which a painting was done.) The poem continues with references to 'the painter', his 'bosom's shop', and other words associated with painting: 'glazed', 'drawn', 'art', and 'draw'. The sonnets' order of printing does not of course necessarily correspond to their order of composition, but it is at least suggestive that only two poems later comes 26, which may have accompanied the presentation manuscript of *Lucrece*. Anyone who has seen the portrait of the Earl of Southampton identified in 2002 and looking singularly androgynous can surely be forgiven for suspecting a connection between the sonnets that reference painting and the Earl. It has to be emphatically said, however, that to associate *some* of the poems with Southampton does not require us to suppose that he is the only male presence behind the poems.

In 1598—before many of the poems in the 1609 volume were composed, if we accept chronological studies by Macdonald P. Jackson and others—Francis Meres wrote of Shakespeare's 'sugared sonnets among his private friends'. Did he mean simply that Shakespeare let some of his friends read poems that he had written purely out of an impulse to create pleasing verbal artefacts, or might Meres have meant that the poet was showing intimately personal poems only to friends who would recognize their links with Shakespeare's closest personal relationships? The phrase 'sugared sonnets' had been used in a cryptic poem published four years previously by Richard Barnfield, whom Meres calls his friend, which forms part of Barnfield's sequence *Greene's Funerals*. There, curiously referring, it would seem, to Marlowe as 'Malta's poet'—i.e. the author of *The Jew of Malta*—Barnfield writes that his muse 'seldom sings' 'sugared sonnets'.[17] The association of this phrase with the two best-known homoerotic poets of the period is intriguing; might 'sugared sonnets' have implied poems that were homoerotic in tone? And perhaps we should remember that the word 'sonnet' did not necessarily mean poems in the fourteen-line form with which it is now most generally associated.

Writers on the Sonnets often invoke a dichotomy between literary convention and personal experience, simplistically suggesting that the poems are either 'literary exercises' on the one hand or autobiographical documents on the other. If we think of them as a series of individual poems or groups of poems written over a long period of time—perhaps as much as twenty-seven years—we may gain insights into the range of reasons why in any given poem Shakespeare may be seen to be writing as a professional poet concerned to create a verbal artefact either for its own sake, or as a literary exercise, or for fun, or as a professional task—and perhaps to make money—or on the other hand in order to work out for himself in poetic form matters of deep and essentially private personal significance.

There is of course an element of poetic convention behind all these poems in the very fact that they adopt the conventions of sonnet form deriving ultimately from Petrarch and Dante. Shakespeare plays with this point of origin in 130, 'My mistress' eyes are nothing like the sun', as if to imply the existence of a poem which makes that comparison. Sonnet 21, too, beginning

> So is it not with me as with that muse
> Stirred by a painted beauty to his verse,
> Who heaven itself for ornament doth use,
> And every fair with his fair doth rehearse

similarly defies poetic convention in its claim that the poet's beloved—whether male or female—though 'as fair | As any mother's child', is nevertheless 'not so bright as those gold candles fixed in heaven's air'. The first of these poems, 'My mistress' eyes', is printed among the late-numbered group and is clearly about a woman, whereas 'So is it not with me...', which is ungendered, is printed among the earlier group.

In spite of the undeniable literariness of the form, there are remarkably few identifiable specific literary sources for Shakespeare's sonnets. The two most derivative are 153 and 154, both based on a single Greek epigram. Here unquestionably Shakespeare is writing with a literary model before him, but where he read the epigram, and whether he read it in Greek, in Latin translation, or even in someone else's English version, remains a mystery in spite of numerous attempts to solve it. Burrow (p. 117) writes of these two sonnets as 'alternative versions of each other and of a poem (which Shakespeare might have encountered in any one of a multitude of disguises)' without, however, identifying any of these disguises. And Duncan-Jones in her edition (p. 422), conjecturing that they may be based on a lost English version of the epigram translated by Ben Jonson, nevertheless admits that they 'seem closer to the Greek original than to any of the [surviving] Latin or vernacular adaptations of it'. A simple, possibly simplistic explanation would be that Shakespeare translated it himself from the Greek, but neither Duncan-Jones nor Burrow allows for this possibility. In my lecture to the World Shakespeare Congress in 2011 I made what seems to be the original suggestion that these two poems might even be 'schoolboy exercises in translation undertaken by a young man who was obliged to study Greek at school but did not take it much, if any, further than classroom level'.[18] This would place them close in date to the Anne Hathaway sonnet, 145. Whether this is so or not, it seems to me that the derivative nature of these two poems invalidates any attempts to link them to Shakespeare's life, such as the common suggestion that the references to baths, which are present in the original poem, show that he visited the city of Bath to be treated for a venereal disease, or that he took mercury baths in London.

Beyond this, identifiable literary sources for the sonnets are confined to a few echoes of Ovid, especially in the opening lines of 60—'Like as the waves make towards the pebbled shore...'—a generalized debt to Erasmus's 'Epistle to Persuade a Young Gentleman to Marriage' in those of the sonnets that encourage procreation, and a surprisingly small number of classical allusions, such as the references to Adonis and Helen in 53 and to Mars in 55. In sheer density of literary allusiveness the Sonnets are surely less obviously 'literary' than most, perhaps any, of the plays.

Let me now embark on a kind of taxonomy of the sonnets. Some of them may be thought of as generalized love poems which, though they might spring from personal emotion, nevertheless would not be out of place in a collection that either had no identifiable personal referent or that was written as it were for public consumption, the poet wearing his heart on his sleeve—or appearing to do so—like the professional sonneteers. Examples are: 29, 'When, in disgrace with fortune and men's eyes...'; 39, 'O, how thy worth with manners may I sing...'; 40, 'Take all my loves, my love, yea, take them all...'; 53, 'What is your substance, whereof are you made...'; 60, 'Like as the waves make towards the pebbled shore...'; and, among the later printed group, 128, 'How oft, when thou, my music, music play'st', and 107, beginning

> Not mine own fears, nor the prophetic soul
> Of the wide world dreaming on things to come,
> Can yet the lease of my true love control,
> Supposed as forfeit to a confined doom...

This is a magnificent declaration of love that even readers not in the know about its ungendered addressee, or about the 'peace' to which it appears to refer, may enjoy; the points of reference in the lines beginning 'The mortal moon hath her eclipse endured', lost to us, may have been intelligible to at least some general readers at the time.

All these poems are romantic in tone. Another, which also is intelligible without special knowledge on the part of the reader, is the determinedly anti-romantic 151, 'Love is too young to know what conscience is'. Like 146 it has as its topos the contrast between soul and body, but whereas that poem treats its subject matter in spiritual terms, this one does so with explicit, not to say lewd frankness:

> My soul doth tell my body that he may
> Triumph in love; flesh stays no farther reason,
> But rising at thy name doth point out thee

As his triumphant prize. Proud of this pride,
He is contented thy poor drudge to be,
To stand in thy affairs, fall by thy side.
  No want of conscience hold it that I call
  Her 'love' for whose dear love I rise and fall.

The final couplet gives power of speech to the poet's penis.

As you might expect, the Variorum commentary on this poem makes intriguing reading. In a 1937 book entitled *The Sonnets of Shakespeare: A Psychosexual Analysis* one H. McC. Young wrote that the poem is 'so frankly physiological as to violate even the shreds of taboo that Professor Freud has left us'. Hyder Rollins comments: 'The majority of readers pass this sonnet by in silence, and probably most readers fail to understand it.'[19] There are of course parallels to its sexual frankness in the plays, as for example in the scene in *Love's Labour's Lost* in which Boyet and the ladies of the court jest bawdily about pricks and masturbation of a man by a woman, provoking Maria to say, understandably, 'you talk greasily, your lips grow foul' (4.1.131–6). Shakespeare might have written the sonnet for publication as a corrective to sentimentalizing poems. In any case it demands to be taken into account in any investigation into Shakespeare's mind and imagination.

Other poems, while not being especially intimate, invite us to identify the poet with Shakespeare himself because of what we know about aspects of his life. Sonnet 23, for instance, beginning 'Like an imperfect actor on the stage' and including reference to 'my books', does not have to have been written by a bookish actor, but our knowledge that Shakespeare was such a man personalizes it for us. And the obvious pun on Hathaway identified by Andrew Gurr, and the somewhat less obvious one on Ann suggested by Stephen Booth,[20] in the couplet of the octosyllabic Sonnet 145—

'I hate' from hate away she threw,
And saved my life, saying 'not you'

are surely enough to identify this as a private poem written in Shakespeare's youth, and therefore also, incidentally, as evidence that he had ambitions as a writer well before he left Stratford.

Attempts to link the sonnets to Shakespeare's life sometimes hinge on decisions as to whether language is being used metaphorically or literally. Obvious examples are what might be interpreted as allusions to physical disability in Sonnets 37, 66, 89, and (possibly) 90. Should we believe that Shakespeare was literally 'made lame by fortune's dearest spite', and did he actually 'halt' because of lameness (89)—an interpretation which might lead to the suggestion that he wrote Richard III as a role for himself to play? René Weis is the most recent biographer to accept this reading.[21] I suspect the allusions are metaphorical, not literal, but there is no definitive answer. I feel less diffident about dismissing a suggestion by Martin Green referring to the sonnet beginning 'Why didst thou promise such a beauteous day | And make me travel forth without my cloak?' Green took this to mean that Shakespeare had contracted a venereal disease as a result of not wearing a condom—a 'cloak'—during a 'brief intimacy' with his friend—'he was not one hour mine' (Sonnet 33)—and suggests that John Shakespeare manufactured such items out of leather and sold them under the counter of his glover's shop.[22] He writes: 'The puns on quondam in Shakespeare's plays reveal this familiarity with the condom', undeterred by the fact that the word 'condom' is not recorded until c.1706.

The first seventeen of the poems as printed (one has to say this because it is all too common for scholars to slip into writing as if the order of printing were also the order of composition) are perhaps also the most clearly interrelated group in the collection. They all play loving, sometimes rapturously eloquent (but occasionally irritable) variations on the theme of persuading a young man to marry and beget a child—or even, in Sonnet 6, to beget ten children:

> That use is not forbidden usury
> Which happies those that pay the willing loan—
> That's for thyself to breed another thee,
> Or ten times happier, be it ten for one.

(Am I alone in finding the notion that a young man might wish to multiply himself by the going rate of usury rather funny?) There is an element of technical virtuosity here, as if Shakespeare were flexing his poetical muscles in a series of exercises in creating variations on a theme. But that does not preclude their being strongly personal poems. It has been suggested that they might have been written to commission from a parent anxious that his or her son was not getting down to the task of perpetuating the family line, and various potential aristocratic candidates for this position have been suggested. Indeed in the television film *A Waste of Shame*, scripted by William Boyd with the Arden editor as adviser, we see Shakespeare visiting the Countess of Pembroke, played by Zoë Wanamaker, and carrying a sheaf of sonnets, identified ingeniously as 'one for each of [her son's] years', which the poet hands over to her for ready cash even before he has met her beautiful and flirtatiously seductive son, who enters the room as Shakespeare is about to leave. But the idea that the impetus to write poems addressed to a young man he had never met came purely as the result of a commission is surely negated by the intensity of personal affection displayed in the poems, which express admiration not just of the addressee's beauty but of his 'gracious and kind [presence]', which address him as 'love' and 'dear my love' (13), and in which the poet speaks of himself as 'all in war with time' for love of the youth (15). And would it have been seemly for a commissioned poet to advise the young man, who 'buries his content' within his 'own bud', and who has 'traffic with [him]self alone' (4), to stop masturbating and start copulating?

> Thou that art now the world's fresh ornament
> And only herald to the gaudy spring,
> Within thine own bud buriest thy content,
> And, tender churl, mak'st waste in niggarding.

For me, all this adds up to the belief that these opening sonnets spring from a strongly personal impulse, that they were not written either to commission or for publication, that they could have been written to or about more than one young man, and that they are essentially private poems.

These so-called 'procreation' sonnets are at least fully intelligible without a specific point of reference. Other sonnets are not. An obvious example is 125, beginning 'Were't aught to me I bore the canopy', where the point of reference is lost to us. It is not, however, so obviously intimate that the poem might not, in its time, have been intelligible at least to Shakespeare's 'private friends' if, for example, he had actually borne a canopy in a court procession.

This is not true, it seems to me, of the poems generally taken to refer to rivalry between their author and another poet. Why, putting it crudely, should people have been expected to pay good money for a book in which they would be puzzled by references to the 'proud full sail' of some unidentified poet's 'great verse', to 'a better spirit' (80) and to 'some affable familiar ghost' (86), references which must have been as unintelligible to most people in Shakespeare's time as they have been to generations of subsequent commentators? I suppose you might say that this is coterie verse, which the poet knew would have only limited intelligibility but which readers not in the know might have enjoyed puzzling over, but at the very least this is clearly poetry with strong autobiographical content.

A rather similar air of mystery arises from the sub-group opening with 'Full many a glorious morning' (33), where the poems appear to allude to an unexplained series of shifts in an emotional relationship. First the poet forgives his 'sun' for withdrawing some unexplained favour; then it appears that the friend has apologized, that the poet still feels aggrieved—'I have still the loss'—but finally the friend's tears of penitence bring him round—'ransom all ill deeds'; then the poet 'brings in sense' to account for some intriguingly unexplained 'sensual fault'; then even more opaquely he refers to a 'separable spite', also unexplained but sometimes identified as a penis, that 'steal[s] sweet hours from love's delight'; then consoles himself for his own 'lameness' but takes pleasure in the friend's 'abundance'; then expresses gratitude that the friend inspires his 'muse'; then says it is acceptable for them to be apart because that means he can 'entertain the time' with 'thoughts of love'; and then segues into a poem (40) which in conjunction with 41 starts a new thread implying that the friend (or should we say 'a friend'?) has stolen the poet's (female) lover: 'when a woman woos, what woman's son | Will sourly leave her till he have prevailed?' If these poems were written for public consumption, all one can say is that the poet is singularly incompetent as a storyteller.

In speaking of Sonnet 129, 'Th'expense of spirit in a waste of shame', I said that it would seem completely out of place in a conventional sonnet sequence of the period. This is even more true of some of the last-printed group of poems—it's tempting to call them a group, as they include all that are clearly addressed to a woman, but this is true of only seven of them. The poet speaks of his mistress—if indeed there is only one mistress—in conflicting and conflicted terms. The parodic 'My mistress' eyes'—taking up a phrase in Sonnet 127, 'My mistress's eyes are raven black'—denies her the conventional attributes of a poetical love object but ends with a declaration of love which is all the more powerful for the volte-face that it expresses:

> And yet, by heaven, I think my love as rare
> As any she belied with false compare.

But other poems in this group are cryptic in allusions to a love triangle—'Beshrew that heart that makes my heart to groan | For that deep wound it gives my friend and me'—and expressive of a love–hate relationship that is totally at odds with conventional love poetry.

Even more explicitly autobiographical are those poems which pun on the poet's own name. 'My name is', he declares, not Christopher, nor Henry, nor Edward, not even Mary or Elizabeth Regina, let us note, but 'Will'. Nowhere else does Shakespeare identify himself so emphatically. And nowhere else—not even in 151 with its reference to an erection—does he write with such unabashed sexual frankness. Sonnet 133, pretty clearly addressed to a woman, speaks of an anguished triangular affair:

> Me from myself thy cruel eye hath taken,
> And my next self thou harder hast engrossed.
> Of him, myself, and thee I am forsaken—
> A torment thrice threefold thus to be crossed.

Then 135, beginning 'Whoever hath her wish, thou hast thy Will', uses the word 'will' thirteen times, and does so, sometimes with grotesquely lewd punning, in at least five distinct senses: object of desire, the poet's own name, desire, vagina, and penis. The poem that follows it, 136, uses the word five times and ends 'my name is Will'. The two poems that follow, though they do not pun on 'will', continue the theme. In

137 the poet castigates himself for thinking that 'a several plot' which his heart knows 'the wide world's common place' and, in 138, admitting that he suppresses truth by believing his mistress's lies, he bitterly acknowledges his folly:

> Therefore I lie with her, and she with me,
> And in our lies by lies we flattered be.

* * *

I have suggested that Shakespeare's sonnets fall into several main categories. The last two in the collection as printed are literary exercises in the purest sense. Two of the poems parody the sonnet convention. One sonnet—146—is a religious meditation, another—129—a philosophical study. Some of the poems display no necessarily personal reference but would be at home in any collection of love poetry of the period. Others may be more or less identifiably related to Shakespeare's personal experience but would nevertheless have been intelligible and enjoyable to contemporary readers who did not know him. One—the Hathaway poem—is identifiable as a personal love poem. The sonnets advocating marriage seem to me to be poems written altruistically to a young man whom Shakespeare loves deeply but with no expectation of physical reciprocity. And finally there are some poems that seem so intimately personal, not to say confessional, that I find it difficult not to see them as highly original poems that are autobiographical in origin and which Shakespeare wrote primarily for himself, to help him to clarify his mind and emotions about personal dilemmas and rivalries in love.

These poems reveal a man who was at various times of his life caught up in emotional and sexual entanglements with more than one male (man or boy, one of whom was also a poet) and with more than one woman; a man of conscience who experienced transcendent joy and happiness in love but who suffered as the result of other people's infidelities, and who was tormented with profound jealousy, guilt, and remorse about his own behaviour. 'She that makes me sin | Awards me pain', he writes in 141; 'Love is my sin', and his mistress's lips 'have sealed false bonds of love as oft as mine, | Robbed others' beds' revenues of their rents' (142).

In other words I, like Wordsworth, and whatever Browning may have thought, see some of these poems as keys with which Shakespeare did indeed unlock his heart—though I suspect he intended the keys to remain in his own pocket.

14

Shakespeare Without Sources

I

W e are accustomed to the study of Shakespeare's plays by way of his sources. It is a common, and often rewarding, critical technique. But there are a few plays in which Shakespeare did not adapt existing sources. These are, chronologically, *Love's Labour's Lost*, *A Midsummer Night's Dream*, and *The Tempest*.[1] Other plays might almost be included in this list, and even these three show the influence of his reading, though in them the influence is local rather than pervasive. But in these three plays Shakespeare seems himself to have been responsible for the main story line, however much he may have drawn on his reading for points of detail. In this essay I want to look at these plays as a group, and to explore the ways in which Shakespeare's mind worked when he was inventing plots rather than adapting them.

Though some scholars would assign a very early date to *Love's Labour's Lost*, there is fairly general agreement that it was written only shortly before *A Midsummer Night's Dream*, probably about 1594 or 1595. So it would not be surprising that these two plays should have much in common. *The Tempest* is probably Shakespeare's last non-collaborative play, but it is perhaps a mark of the essential unity of his achievement that structurally the play with which it has most in common is an early one, *The Comedy of Errors*. The irregular spacing of my three plays among the canon may warn us against attaching excessive significance to resemblances among them. If they were more evenly spaced, we might more reasonably look in them for an index to Shakespeare's development. But they are not.

The simplest resemblance is that they are all comedies. We may remember Dr Johnson:

> his disposition, as Rymer has remarked, led him to comedy. In tragedy he often writes, with great appearance of toil and study, what is written at last with little felicity; but, in his comic scenes, he seems to produce, without labour, what no labour can improve...in comedy he seems to repose, or to luxuriate, as in a mode of thinking congenial to his nature...his comedy often surpasses expectation or desire. His comedy

pleases by the thoughts and the language, and his tragedy for the greater part by incident and action. His tragedy seems to be skill, his comedy to be instinct.[2]

This pronouncement might seem to receive support from the observation that Shakespeare's three most original plays are comedies. It would be fair to object that he could hardly have invented the plots of history plays, and that in his time tragedies, too, were generally based on historical events (though of course *Macbeth*, for example, is further from its main source than *Richard II* or *Julius Caesar*, and the events of *Titus Andronicus* seem, happily, to have little basis in recorded fact). But comedies form the bulk of his output, and Johnson is arguing partly on the basis of style, so perhaps the evidence in relation to sources does indeed support the view that Shakespeare's natural instincts led him towards comedy.

II

The resemblances among the three plays I am considering seem to hinge on *A Midsummer Night's Dream*. *Love's Labour's Lost*, that is to say, is closer to *A Midsummer Night's Dream* than to *The Tempest*; and *The Tempest* resembles *A Midsummer Night's Dream* more than it resembles *Love's Labour's Lost*. The two earlier plays offer obvious points of comparison. Both have a highly patterned structure. The characters fall neatly into groups. In *Love's Labour's Lost* we have the King of Navarre and his three courtiers, balancing the Princess of France and her three ladies, attended by Boyet; Armado and his foil, Moth; Holofernes and Nathaniel with their foil, Dull; and the clowns, Costard and Jaquenetta. The principle of division is partly social; but it is also, more importantly, conceptual. Armado, Holofernes, and Sir Nathaniel represent a kind of polarization of some instincts of the lords: a pushing to the extreme of their tendency to verbalization and their pedantry. They provide an *exemplum horrendum* of the destination to which the course the lords have adopted is likely to lead. Costard and Jaquenetta delightfully represent a simplification of the lords' (and ladies') baser selves, the all-too-natural instincts that they are over-anxious to quell. The characters are not entirely static. In particular, Armado's fall from his ideals provides an example no less horrendous than the intensity with which he pursues them. But it is clear that in constructing this play Shakespeare has created his characters in order to embody a set of ideas.

In *A Midsummer Night's Dream* the characters are equally obviously grouped. There are the fairies, the two groups of lovers (Theseus and Hippolyta on the one hand, and the four younger lovers on the other), and the mechanicals. It is not as easy to think of the characters of this play in conceptual terms as it is in *Love's Labour's Lost*. But it is clear that Theseus and Hippolyta show greater maturity than the younger lovers, and that this relates to the disjunction of reason and love on which Bottom remarks. If the play had been much simpler than it is, the fairies might have been more idealized than they are, and the mechanicals cruder; but Shakespeare has chosen to give his fairies some all-too-human characteristics. In doing so he perhaps emphasizes the humanity of his play, the fact that human life can be confounded by misfortune, that happiness is dependent partly upon chance, the fortunate conjunction of accidental circumstances (represented by the reconciliation of Oberon and Titania), as well as upon the will of man, that is by his reason swayed. But let me not try to abstract a scheme when Shakespeare has taken obvious pains to conceal it. It is enough to notice that the characters fall clearly into homogeneous groups, and to suggest that the overruling characteristics of each group are designed to contribute to the play's intellectual coherence.

The patterned structure of the two plays is further dependent upon the disposition of scenes involving the character groups, and the layout of the incidents. This could be demonstrated by means of a structural analysis of both plays, but it seems unnecessary. The plays have a different overall structure, of course; but they are equally neat. Love's Labour's Lost is the more original, with its curious ending that projects a happy resolution into a future which stretches well beyond the time-scheme of the play. Before this it has moved to a climax of complication in the overhearing scene (4.3), in which much of our pleasure derives from the gratification of our expectations as each character is successively exposed. The corresponding scene in A Midsummer Night's Dream is the night scene in the forest, in which Puck plays his tricks upon the lovers, followed by the separate episode of their awakening (3.2 and 4.1). The patterning of A Midsummer Night's Dream is very prominent at this stage of the play, with the awakening in turn of Titania, the lovers, and Bottom.

An obvious structural parallel between the two plays is the giving over of most of the last Act of each to a play-within-the-play. Again Love's Labour's Lost might be felt to be the more sophisticated, since in it the play-within-the-play is enclosed within the main action, whereas in A Midsummer Night's Dream it is rather an appendage to the action, having a celebratory function. If one were presented simply with a structural analysis of the two plays one might be forgiven for deducing that Love's Labour's Lost was the later. In both plays the play-within-the-play has the structural function of bringing groups of characters together, though to different effect. In both it has, also, common though not identical thematic functions. In Love's Labour's Lost there are in effect two plays-within-the-play, the first, and simpler, being the masque of Muscovites which provides the discomfiture of the lords, and a consequent adjustment of their relations with the ladies, which is a necessary preliminary to their forming together an audience for the entertainment that is to be offered to them by their social inferiors. As in some of Shakespeare's other comedies, notably All's Well that Ends Well, embarrassment is a prime source of comic effect in this play; and, as also in other plays, it is succeeded by an improvement in the relations of the embarrassed and their observers. After the ladies have embarrassed the lords, they settle down together to embarrass those who are performing for them the patently ludicrous pageant of the Nine Worthies. That it is patently ludicrous helps us to preserve sympathy with the mockers as well as the mocked. The same is true of *A Midsummer Night's Dream*, where the noble characters, their own differences resolved, together form a somewhat restive audience for a performance by their social inferiors.

The characters of both plays are obviously concerned with right behaviour. Those of *Love's Labour's Lost* repeatedly fail to achieve it. This is why the happy ending has to be deferred. And one of their areas of failure is in courtesy. The lords' interruptions of the pageant eventually provoke Holofernes' rebuke: 'This is not generous, not gentle, not humble.' The line strikes with more force in its dramatic context than its phrasing might seem to merit, partly perhaps because it is likely to embarrass the theatre audience as well as the one on the stage, causing both to reflect on the quality of their laughter. In *A Midsummer Night's Dream* the aristocratic characters similarly mock the play that is being performed for them, and in that play the interruptions are more fully developed. But they are also less disruptive because, while in *Love's Labour's Lost* the comments are addressed directly to the actors, in *A Midsummer Night's Dream* they are almost always made by one member of the stage audience to the others, even though they are sometimes overheard by the actors. Relations become strained, and Moonshine has his moment of exasperation, but good will triumphs, and the play reaches a conclusion which its actors, at least, can feel to be successful. In *Love's Labour's Lost*, however, the play becomes a fiasco with the climax of Armado's embarrassment, when he is 'infamonized among potentates' by the revelation that Jaquenetta is quick with child by him. The stage is, designedly, a shambles before the moment of total embarrassment; a moment that, in successful performance, embraces the audience as well as everyone on stage, when the wordless, sombre figure of Marcade rebukes our laughter.

Marcade's entrance forces the characters of the play not merely into seriousness, but into a level of seriousness deeper than any they have shown so far. The Princess apologizes on behalf of the ladies if they have been guilty of lack of courtesy. She asks that the lords will

> excuse or hide
> The liberal opposition of our spirits,
> If over-boldly we have borne ourselves
> In the converse of breath. (5.2.720–3)

Berowne makes a similar apology on behalf of the men, and the play draws to an end with the lords' promise to undergo a more serious kind of retreat than that to which they had committed themselves in the play's opening lines, one which involves not merely restraint and moderation but also the active pursuit of good works. Rosaline's reply to Berowne's protest 'Mirth cannot move a soul in agony' is a marvellous expression of an ideal of courtesy that, once it is made, can be seen to have underlain the whole action of the play:

> A jest's prosperity lies in the ear
> Of him that hears it, never in the tongue
> Of him that makes it; then, if sickly ears,
> Deaf'd with the clamours of their own dear groans,
> Will hear your idle scorns, continue then,
> And I will have you and that fault withal.
> But if they will not, throw away that spirit,
> And I shall find you empty of that fault,
> Right joyful of your reformation. (5.2.849–57)

It is a moralistic speech, however lightened by the intelligence of style in which it is expressed. It is paralleled by Armado's vow to 'hold the plough' for Jaquenetta's sake for three years, and it is surely not too much to say that the play ends by recommending the virtues of restraint, moderation, penitence, generosity, and courtesy. Unfortunately the text is uninformative about just how the action should end, but I think it is significant that the final dialogue of the cuckoo and the owl is not interrupted by its stage audience. It seems desirable that the noblemen, their ladies, and the yokels should join together to respond to the performance of the songs with generosity, gentleness, and humility.

A Midsummer Night's Dream shows a similar concern with courtesy, and with moderation and restraint. The ardour of Theseus and Hippolyta in their opening exchange is a controlled one. Soon afterwards, Hermia is warned of the harsh external restraints that will be imposed upon her if she fails to moderate her desires in obedience to her father. As Hermia and Lysander lie down in the wood, she bids him,

> for love and courtesy
> Lie further off, in human modesty;
> Such separation as may well be said
> Becomes a virtuous bachelor and a maid. (2.2.56–9)

Helena, thinking that her companions are mocking her, says:

> If you were civil and knew courtesy,
> You would not do me thus much injury.
> Can you not hate me, as I know you do,
> But you must join in souls to mock me too? (3. 2.147–50)

An ideal of courtesy is implied in this play, as in *Love's Labour's Lost*, even though none of the characters finds that he can easily live up to it. Mockery is a denial of the ideal, a failure of the imagination. However bad the play they are watching, says Theseus, 'in courtesy, in all reason, we must stay the time'. And this goes along with an ideal of married chastity without which all is strife and dissension, but which, observed, will earn Oberon's blessing:

> So shall all the couples three
> Ever true in loving be. (5.1.396–7)

A Midsummer Night's Dream is not as heavily moralistic as *Love's Labour's Lost*, but I think it shows similar moral concerns.

III

The Tempest, too, has a highly schematic structure which, in its neo-classical concern for the unities, seems a deliberately far cry from the episodic freedom of the other romances. In this play, again, the characters fall into obvious groups. As in *A Midsummer Night's Dream*, though not in *Love's Labour's Lost*, some of the characters are supernatural. They bear, however, some resemblance to the subsidiary character groups in *Love's Labour's Lost* in that, more easily than the fairies in *A Midsummer Night's Dream*, they can be seen as a polarization of characteristics of the main characters. Even Berowne, in the overhearing scene, feels 'like a demi-god'. Oberon, Puck, and Titania all have power over the elements, and all influence the lives of the human characters. In *The Tempest* Shakespeare creates a kind of amalgamation of these three figures in one human being—Prospero, who is possessed of limited supernatural power; and one wholly supernatural one—Ariel, who, as the agent of Prospero's power, has affinities with Puck. The supernatural aspects of Caliban have no parallel in the earlier plays, but Bottom seems to be one of his less harmful ancestors, and there are stronger resemblances with another of Shakespeare's invented characters, Barnardine in *Measure for Measure*, in which play the Duke also affords parallels with Prospero.

Obviously, the use of the supernatural in itself amounts to a denial of naturalistic intent, if not a declaration of the symbolic, and this seems to link with the general absence from these plays of detailed psychological characterization.[3] Often the function of the character in the overall design seems of more significance than his individual reality. In making his characters expressive of general attitudes, Shakespeare creates special problems for his interpreters. The actors, and their director, have to decide to what extent they should emphasize the representative aspects of their roles, and to what extent they should attempt to invest them with personal characteristics. Not, of course, that Shakespeare himself cannot when he wishes provide an abundance of individualizing touches, as he does especially among the low-life characters such as Costard and the mechanicals. This faculty is less apparent in *The Tempest*, in which Trinculo and Stephano are less fully developed than some of their comic forebears, and in which some of the lords seem to be pushed close towards abstraction—or not to emerge very strongly from it. Miranda and Ferdinand are not perhaps much less real than the lovers of the other plays, but they are certainly no more so, and in the log-carrying episode, for instance, Shakespeare risks incredulity in pursuit of his symbolic purpose—it is not, after all, likely to do Ferdinand much harm to spend an hour or two carrying wood, yet this is imposed on him as a probationary task of almost as much significance as Berowne's year-long sick-visiting.

There is a real parallel between the tasks that Prospero requires Ferdinand to perform in order to make sure that he does not underestimate his good fortune in winning Miranda and the closing episodes of *Love's Labour's Lost*. One reason for this obviously symbolic action in *The Tempest* is that Shakespeare is here attempting the difficult task of compressing the material of romance—usually highly episodic in form—into the tight structure of a play that, instead of rambling in both space and time as most romances do, is set in a single locality within a very few hours. In such stories it is conventional for the hero and heroine to be separated by misfortune, and to demonstrate their love by remaining true to one another in spite of the perils and temptations set before them in their wanderings. Ferdinand's log-bearing is a rather lightweight substitute for the trials usually experienced by heroes of romance, and Prospero's homilies on chastity, along with Ferdinand's reassuring responses to them, though they seem uncharacteristically explicit in their moralization, serve their purpose as a substitute for the assurances of virtue that a narrator can convey in a prose or verse romance. Anyhow, it is clear that Shakespeare, for whatever reason, felt a desire to stress this theme, since he does so at the expense of credulity. Chastity finds its highest celebration in the masque, in which Ceres and Juno, the products of Prospero's art, virtually repeat the teaching that he himself has just given.

The masque is *The Tempest's* play-within-the-play, coming at a much earlier point of the action than in the two previous plays. It is performed by characters of higher social status than its audience—spirits, no less; it is heard with respectful attention until its presenter himself puts an end to it; and it provides not a test of the audience's courtesy, but rather an ideal, and an exhortation. It does not involve all the character groups of the play, and its interruption is the result of Prospero's memory of one that it does not, 'Caliban and his confederates'. The interruption is reminiscent of that in *Love's Labour's Lost*. In that play, Costard's news about Jaquenetta discomposes the performers, while Marcade's news discomposes the audience. The moment of interruption in *The Tempest* is, perhaps, technically less well managed. Prospero's awareness of evil comes from within himself; there is no objective correlative to strike the audience. Though he composes himself enough to speak comfortingly to Ferdinand and Miranda, he then has to turn his thoughts to his preparations to 'meet with Caliban'. Though misfortune and evil were felt in the earlier plays, it is only in this one that a confrontation and resolution are arranged, and this is one of the reasons why *The Tempest* seems a more deeply serious play than the other two.

The blessing that Ceres and Juno invoke on the virtuous lovers recalls Oberon's blessing on the house in *A Midsummer Night's Dream*. It also looks forward to at least two works of art written later than any of these plays—Jonson's masque, *Pleasure Reconciled to Virtue*, and Milton's *Comus*, which seems to have been influenced by both *A Midsummer Night's Dream* and *The Tempest*, and also by the Jonson masque. *Pleasure Reconciled to Virtue* ends with a firm recommendation of virtue addressed to Prince Charles, and *Comus* of course is much concerned with chastity. This resemblance might be held to support the hypothesis that has been put forward in relation to all the Shakespeare plays I have been discussing, especially *A Midsummer Night's Dream*, that they are 'occasional' plays written, as masques were generally written, to celebrate—and perhaps to influence—a special occasion. *A Midsummer Night's Dream* is often said to be a play for a wedding as well as about weddings, and it has been suggested that the masque in *The Tempest* was an addition for performance during the wedding celebrations of the Princess Elizabeth in 1613. If this were so, the emphases on virtue might be regarded as tributes to the occasion. The hypotheses lack evidence to support them. If they were true, the plays would be likely to look out to their intended real-life audiences in the way that the masque in *The Tempest* does to Ferdinand and Miranda. It is possible that the moral attitudes discernible in the plays are attributable to dramatic decorum and literary convention; but it is also possible that they reflect Shakespeare's own convictions, and that he believed deeply in the importance of the virtues implied in *Love's Labour's Lost*, demonstrated in *A Midsummer Night's Dream*, and virtually preached in *The Tempest*. The plays do not suggest that the virtues are easily attained, or that failure to attain them automatically entails damnation. The moral attitudes the plays seem to endorse are straightforward, traditional ones; but at the same time the plays reveal a sensibility that is aware of the complexity of moral issues, that can allow sympathy with Caliban's sense of injustice even while it approves the values that have created this sense.

IV

One of the most characteristic devices in Shakespearean comedy is the adaptation into dramatic form of the pastoral myth, using what is sometimes called 'the place apart', often a forest, as a symbol of a set of circumstances in which the characters are able to free themselves from their past and achieve a development which seems to release their true, so far repressed, selves. *As You Like It* provides the most obvious example, and *King Lear* shows a tragedy borrowing the same device. So far as my three plays are concerned it is only lightly adumbrated in *Love's Labour's Lost*. Appropriately, the action of this play takes place in a park, not a forest. The formality of a park suggests the artificiality, and essential unnaturalness, of the decision the lords have forced upon themselves. The device is fully present in *A Midsummer Night's Dream*, with its escape of the lovers into the forest at night. *The Tempest* extends the idea still further, for here, except for the preliminary scene of shipwreck, the entire action is set in a place where, Gonzalo will say—perhaps over-optimistically—all the characters found themselves 'when no man was his own'. The other plays, too, are concerned with self-discovery and self-realization. We may remember the climax of Berowne's marvellous speech on love:

> Let us once lose our oaths to find ourselves,
> Or else we lose ourselves to keep our oaths.
> It is religion to be thus forsworn;
> For charity itself fulfils the law;
> And who can sever love from charity? (4.3.357–61)

With these lines the lords together recognize their folly, and decide to 'lay these glozes by'. The moment was well marked in John Barton's Stratford-upon-Avon production (1965) by a casting aside of their academic gowns (though it suggested an unusual gloss on 'glozes'). But the lords have a long way to go before they will be completely cured.

In *A Midsummer Night's Dream* a parallel moment is the awakening of the lovers, when there comes a 'gentle concord' into the world, and when Helena finds Demetrius,

> like a jewel,
> Mine own, and not mine own. (4.1.188–9)

(Benjamin Britten, in his opera based on the play, seizes on these words and makes of them a complete quartet, each of the lovers using them of his or her partner. It is the emotional climax of the work.)

In the association, then, of the 'place apart' with the theme of self-discovery, Shakespeare in these plays uses and develops a technique that he made peculiarly his own.

V

The resemblances among these plays, in point of technique and also of content, on which I have commented may seem no more revealing than the information that there are salmons in the rivers of both Monmouth and Macedon. But they may, more usefully, suggest characteristic workings of Shakespeare's mind. Obviously these workings might be sought in other plays in which Shakespeare was more dependent on sources. But this is beyond my present scope. More relevant to my purpose is an idea that has been propounded about all these plays: that, to a rather exceptional degree, they betray a preoccupation on the part of the dramatist with his own art. In this way, too, they may be unusually personal documents. Writing about *Love's Labour's Lost*, F. P. Wilson says, 'One of his special preoccupations in the play is the function of language in society.'[4] It is surely undeniable that in constructing this play Shakespeare was strongly motivated by his interest in the means of communication, in the fact that words can obscure meaning as well as reveal it, that an excessive concern with the means of communication may inhibit true expression, that feeling can communicate itself in spite of words rather than through them. (The interest is especially strongly felt also in *Much Ado About Nothing*.) It is no accident that the most important communication in *Love's Labour's Lost* is the ostentatiously wordless one made by Marcade's mere presence.

If *Love's Labour's Lost* is largely about words, it is also noticeably conscious of itself as a play. Perhaps the harshness of the final episode is softened for us by the way the play draws attention to its own mode, helping us to detach ourselves from the action. 'Our wooing doth not end like an old play', says Berowne, acknowledging from within the action that the postponement of the happy ending for a 'twelvemonth and a day' (and thus possibly for ever) is 'too long for a play'.

A *Midsummer Night's Dream* shows an even broader concern with Shakespeare's own art. On a simple level, this is evident in the fact that all the mechanicals' scenes show the preparation and performance of a play. That it is an amateur performance is rendered the less significant by Theseus' remark 'The best in this kind are but shadows ...'. But on other levels, too, the play shows concerns which relate to the endeavours of the imaginative artist, to such an extent that David P. Young, in his full-length study of the play, can conclude that this 'is Shakespeare's *ars poetica*, embedded in a perfected example of his art', and that it must therefore 'be regarded as one of his most important plays and a touchstone for the understanding and interpretation of others'.[5] If this is so, it is not surprising that Shakespeare should have felt the need to shape the play from within rather than work through an existing story. Young amply demonstrates Shakespeare's concern with the imagination, made most explicit in Theseus' well-known lines (5. 1.2–22). Hippolyta's reply is even more important, admitting that

all the story of the night told over,
And all their minds transfigured so together,
More witnesseth than fancy's images,
And grows to something of great constancy;
But howsoever, strange and admirable. (5.1.23–7)

These speeches are strategically placed just before the performance of the mechanicals' play, which is to provide both an illustration of its actors' own imaginative failures and a test of the imaginative capacities of their betters. The play firmly, though with a wise gaiety, asserts the basic importance of the imagination in human life, the fact that a world of dreams can grow 'to something of great constancy', and the constant though shifting harmonies of the last Act demonstrate the need for imaginative tolerance in successful relationships. On these the forces of nature bestow their blessings.

In *The Tempest*, too, Shakespeare's concern with his own art emerges most clearly from the play-within-the-play, especially in the great speech of Prospero which has become the best-known of all celebrations of the glorious transience of theatrical art. But just as, in that speech, the theatrical imagery serves as a metaphorical expression for an experience which, actually theatrical, is fictionally supernatural, so in the play as a whole Shakespeare's concern with his own art is subordinated to a much broader concern with the opposition between constructive good and destructive evil, whether in the individual human consciousness or on any scale up to the cosmic. That Shakespeare was to an unusual degree working to a conceptual pattern in this play is suggested by its peculiar susceptibility to allegorical interpretations. That none of these interpretations seems satisfactory is a measure of the success with which he has effected the sea-change of the bare bones of his concepts into something richly suggestive and strangely elusive. Whether we see Prospero as animal-tamer, employer, father, probation officer, magistrate, theatre director, colonial administrator, creative artist, Shakespeare, an embodiment of the imagination, a Christ-figure, God, or even (as Wilson Knight does) as 'a matured and fully self-conscious embodiment of those moments of fifth-act transcendental speculation to which earlier tragic heroes, including Macbeth, were unwittingly forced',[6] we see a figure whose power to do good is real, but always limited both by his own imperfections and by circumstances over which he has no control. The splendours of his vision vanish at the remembrance of the need for action against his adversaries. Lacking at last both the spirits that have helped him and the art with which he was able to enchant, he is doomed to despair unless the audience grants him its prayers. It is natural to see in Prospero a reflection of his human creator, and to see in the play a concern with the creations of the artistic imagination, creations which at their strongest have a power of transfiguration, yet which are terrifyingly dependent for their power upon the sympathetic imagination. *The Tempest* at its first performance might have held its audience spellbound: it might have been hooted off the stage. So, Shakespeare seems to say, with all the works of man; their value has no absolute existence. Nothing is but as 'tis valued. Gonzalo may enthuse, Sebastian and Antonio may mock; Ferdinand may adore, Caliban may try to violate. And the response of the audience, upon which all that Shakespeare has to say depends for its effect, is equally uncertain. In *The Tempest* Shakespeare wrote not only about his own art, but about that of all who work through the mind.

VI

The Tempest is a wonderful, infinitely subtle, if enigmatic play. *A Midsummer Night's Dream* is one of Shakespeare's most popular plays. *Love's Labour's Lost* is handicapped by its topicalities, but with judicious abbreviation is capable of highly successful performance. Still, if we considered these three plays in relation to the remainder of Shakespeare's output, we should not necessarily regard them as the height of his achievement. One or other might happen to be a favourite of ours. We might, like Frank Kermode, 'be prepared to maintain that *A Midsummer Night's Dream* is Shakespeare's best comedy'.[7] We might easily feel that *The Tempest* is a personal utterance of unparalleled intimacy, related to the great tragedies in the same way that a late Beethoven quartet is related to the greatest of his symphonies. But obviously these plays do not have the grandeur of *King Lear*, the elemental passion of *Othello*, the emotional range of *Hamlet* or *The Winter's Tale*. The artist who betrays a preoccupation with his own art may seem a little limited, even if at the same time he relates his art to a wide range of human activity, as Shakespeare does in *The Tempest*. If these plays only had survived, I think we should not rate Shakespeare so highly as if, for example, we had only *King Lear* by which to judge him. And it is possible that Shakespeare realized this. Perhaps it is significant that *Love's Labour's Lost* and *A Midsummer Night's Dream* were, so far as we can tell, written at about the same time. If *A Midsummer Night's Dream* really is 'Shakespeare's *ars poetica*', it would be very natural that, having written it, he should go on to put his art into practice in very different ways. The resemblances among these three plays may suggest that, left to his own inventive powers, Shakespeare was apt to confine himself to a comparatively narrow range of techniques and themes. And I wonder if, aware of this, he made a wholly conscious effort to extend his range by compelling himself to work through stories not of his own making, set often in civilizations other than that to which he belonged, expressive even of moral attitudes that were not his own. He is highly derivative; perhaps the most literary of great dramatists. Paradoxically, this might help to explain why he is also the most wide-ranging, the most personally elusive, the most original in the fullest sense of the word. Perhaps one of the reasons why we find it so difficult to pin Shakespeare down is that he so often wears other men's clothes and speaks with their accents.

But even when he does so, we can often see him using methods and expressing ideas similar to those I have discerned in his invented works. I have suggested that in them we can often see him working to a predetermined scheme; and I have pointed to his use in these plays of highly patterned structural devices. On the whole, and particularly in his later plays, we do not think of Shakespeare as a specially tidy-minded dramatist. Sometimes he seems not fully to have subjugated recalcitrant source material to an overriding creative concept, with the result that he produces a structure of more grandeur than regularity. In some of his greatest plays he seems to have started with an idea of character—as in Coriolanus or Cleopatra—rather than based a character on an idea. In the three plays I have been discussing the idea seems often to have come first, as in Holofernes and, more complexly, Caliban. An awareness derived from his sourceless plays of his capacity to body forth a structure of ideas in character and action should lead us to exercise caution before assuming absence of preconceived design in plays in which a superficial neatness of structure is not apparent. Shakespeare may have sometimes accepted an existing narrative and elaborated it in such a way as to produce episodes that have the function of cadenzas rather than elements of a fully integrated design. At one time Launce's soliloquies in *The Two Gentlemen of Verona* might have been felt to belong to this category. Most modern critics would not support this view. Certainly the speeches show Shakespeare's ability to improvise with wonderful inventiveness upon a basic theme. But to over-emphasize his improvisatory powers may take us too far back to the concept of a Shakespeare warbling his woodnotes wild with no thought for where the next tune was coming from. There is ample evidence in the plays of Shakespeare's early maturity that he could, and did, sometimes lay out a play with intense consciousness of design in both the larger structural elements and the verbal detail. Apart from the two earlier plays on which I have been concentrating, we may think of *Richard III*, with its highly formalized disposition of historical-based material, or of the patterns created in *Romeo and Juliet* by the counterpointing of the attitudes of Mercutio and the Nurse alongside those of the hero and heroine. Later in his career, too, Shakespeare writes scenes in which a conceptual basis is evident. The graveyard scene in *Hamlet*, for instance, is probably Shakespeare's addition to his source. In the apparent spontaneity of the gravediggers' prose it might seem a prime illustration of his improvisatory faculty; yet it is not difficult to discern behind the easy movement of the scene a carefully programmed series of confrontations with death, mounting from the gravediggers' unimpassioned handling of anonymous remains through increasingly familiar encounters until Hamlet is in the grave with the dead Ophelia. Our appreciation of Shakespeare's developing capacity to hide his framework, to weave a pattern so complex that it resembles a work of nature rather than one of art, should not lead to scepticism about the presence of his artistry.

Although I have temporarily isolated three of Shakespeare's plays, I do not wish to make exaggerated claims for them either in themselves or as keys to the understanding of Shakespeare. But I suggest that in them Shakespeare does, as Dr Johnson put it, repose in 'a mode of thinking congenial to his nature'; that they reveal something of his personal concerns, especially in relation to his art; and that, by remembering how his mind worked in them, we may be helped in our approach to plays where he owed more of his narrative material to other writings.

15

Shakespeare and Romance

Though in Shakespeare's day the word 'romance' had been in the language for two centuries,[1] it occurs in none of his writings. The Elizabethans generally found little use for it, and so far as I know it was never used to describe a play. To the editors of the First Folio, *The Winter's Tale* and *The Tempest* were comedies, *Cymbeline* was a tragedy, and *Pericles* was—for reasons that we can only surmise—beyond the pale. Modern critics, discerning common characteristics in these plays, have grouped them together, sometimes non-committally as 'last plays', sometimes as 'romances'—and the term is genuinely descriptive. But it has been increasingly recognized that the final romances are in many ways directly descended from Shakespeare's earlier comedies. These are often called 'romantic' comedies; are they not, then, also romances? It depends, of course, what you mean by a romance. The very word is shadowy, having associations with literature of various kinds, forms, and periods; with modes of sensibility; with languages; and with love. It can be spoken with an auspicious or a dropping eye; with a sob, a sigh, or a sneer; with the aspiration to define or with a defiance of definition. It means so much that often it means nothing at all.

If the literary genre of romance can be defined—or described—it is not by formal characteristics. Rather perhaps is it a matter of certain recurrent motifs, and also of a recognizable attitude towards the subject-matter. Romancers delight in the marvellous; quite often this involves the supernatural; generally the characters are larger than life size. All is unrealistic; the logic of cause and effect is ignored, and chance or fortune governs all. Characteristic features vary somewhat from one sort of romance to another; and attempts at definition are bound to be circular—we can only decide what makes a romance by looking at works to which the label has been attached and seeing what they have in common. But it is fair to say that Shakespearean romance frequently includes the separation and disruption of families, followed by their eventual reunion and reconciliation; scenes of apparent resurrection; the love of a virtuous young hero and heroine; and the recovery of lost royal children. In this essay it will be my purpose first to sketch the background of material such as this, then to say something of Shakespeare's use of it in certain of his earlier comedies, and finally to discuss the romantic characteristics of *The Winter's Tale* and *The Tempest*.

Elements of romance can be traced far back in the history of the world's literature. *The Odyssey* itself is (like *Pericles*) the story of a voyage and its hero's reunion with his wife. Oedipus, like Perdita, was cast away in infancy; and Euripides' *Alcestis* is often cited as an analogue of *The Winter's Tale*—both tell of a wife restored to her husband from apparent death. Romance elements are found in greater concentration in classical comedy—a form we are apt to think of as the antithesis of romantic. The common features of Greek New Comedy, we are told, are 'loss of children, far wanderings over many years, fortunate recognition at a moment of imminent peril, and final happy reunion of parents and children'.[2] Menander's *The Girl with Shorn Hair* tells—as do Plautus's *Menaechmi* and its derivative, *The Comedy of Errors*—of the reunion with each other and with their father of twins separated in infancy. That the plays of Plautus and Terence include this sort of material is the more interesting since, of course, they were standard textbooks in Elizabethan schools. But it would not do to exaggerate their romantic characteristics, which in most of these plays are rather treated as plot-mechanism than elaborated for their own sake.

Far more important are the Greek romances, prose tales whose influence on later literature has been incalculable. They date from the post-classical period—most of them from the second and third centuries AD. Perhaps the three most important are *Daphnis and Chloe*, by Longus; Heliodorus's *Aethiopica*; and *Clitophon and Leucippe*, by Achilles Tatius. Here the familiar motifs abound. *Daphnis and Chloe* tells of a pair of abandoned infants who are brought up together, tend flocks, and in adolescence fall in love with each other. Daphnis is captured by pirates, but escapes in circumstances of wild improbability. Chloe too is carried off, but is restored to Daphnis as a result of Pan's direct intervention. Finally their true identity is revealed, they are reunited with their families, and they marry. This is the most pastoral, and the least eventful, of the Greek romances.

Perhaps the most influential was the *Aethiopica*. Again the story centres on a pair of lovers—Theagenes and Chariclea. Many episodes could be paralleled at least in outline from Shakespeare's last plays. There is a wicked stepmother on the same pattern as the Queen in *Cymbeline*; there is more than one shipwreck; there are oracular dreams; insistence is placed on the heroine's virginity; the lovers are several times parted; and there is a scene of grief over a dead body mistakenly believed to be the beloved's—it is difficult not to think of Imogen with Cloten's body when we read how 'Theagenes, as though by violence one had thrust him down, fell on the dead body and held the same in his arms a great while without moving'.[3] Our memories of the same play must be still stronger when we read of the lovers' reunion; Chariclea

> ran to him like a mad woman, and, hanging by her arms about his neck, said nothing, but saluted him with certain pitiful lamentations. He, seeing her foul face (belike of

purpose beblacked) and her apparel vile and all torn, supposing her to be one of the makeshifts of the city, and a vagabond, cast her off and put her away, and at length gave her a blow on the ear for that she troubled him in seeing Calasiris. Then she spake to him softly: 'Pithius, have you quite forgotten this taper?' Theagenes was stricken with that word as if he had been pierced with a dart, and by tokens agreed on between them knew the taper and, looking steadfastly upon her, espied her beauty shining like the sun appearing through the clouds, cast his arms about her neck.[4]

In the final book there is a protracted reunion scene, as well as an episode in which the hero, under sentence of death, performs deeds of great valour—again one is reminded of the last act of *Cymbeline*.

Some of Heliodorus's comments, too, are interesting in relation to Shakespeare. Towards the end of the last book he describes the rejoicing at the satisfactory conclusion of events in terms that could be paralleled from a number of Shakespeare's plays, and that might indeed almost serve as an epigraph to the last plays:

The people in another place rejoiced and almost danced for joy, and with one consent were all glad of that which was done; marry, all they understood not, but gathered the most part of Chariclea. Perhaps also they were stirred to understand the truth by inspiration of the gods, whose will it was that this should fall out wonderfully, as in a comedy. Surely they made very contrary things agree, and joined sorrow and mirth, tears and laughter, together, and turned fearful and terrible things into a joyful banquet in the end; many that wept began to laugh, and such as were sorrowful to rejoice, when they found that they sought not for, and lost that they hoped to find; and to be short, the cruel slaughters which were looked for every moment were turned into holy sacrifice.[5]

The third Greek romance to have some importance in the Elizabethan period is *Clitophon and Leucippe*. Achilles Tatius, imitating Heliodorus, tells of a pair of lovers who pass through many dangers and narrow escapes from death to final reunion. Again the story includes features reminiscent of Shakespearean romance, such as oracular dreams, shipwreck, mourning over the wrong body, and scenes of apparent resurrection; and again the heroine's virginity is heavily emphasized.

The Greek romances were written well over a thousand years before Shakespeare's time. In the interim, many subspecies of romance developed and flourished—it is noticeable how often we need to qualify the noun. We hear of chivalric and heroic romance; epic and pastoral romance; courtly love romance; and even religious romance.[6] Malory's translation of French Arthurian cycles into the English *Morte D'Arthur* was known in late-Elizabethan England; so were chivalric romances such as those of the Palmerin cycle (written in Spanish in the sixteenth century) and the slightly earlier tales of Amadis de Gaule (also written in Spanish but probably based on lost French originals). And there was *Huon of Bordeaux*, the French *chanson de geste* of the thirteenth century which, translated by Lord Berners, suggested to Shakespeare at least the name of Oberon.

To compile a list of romances written up to Shakespeare's time would not of course take us far; but merely the widespread currency of romance in the period has significance. It is true that stories, especially plays, using this material were often scorned. Gosson attacked the artifices of recognition. Sir Philip Sidney (in a well-known passage of the *Apology for Poetry*) and Ben Jonson (in the Prologue to *Every Man in his Humour*) mocked at the violation of the neo-classical unities often necessitated by the adaptation of romance material. Nashe scorned those 'from whose idle pens proceeded those worn-out impressions of the feigned nowhere acts of Sir Arthur of the Round Table, Arthur of Little Britain, Sir Tristram, Huon of Bordeaux, the Squire of Low Degree, the Four Sons of Aymon, with infinite others'.[7] But the irritated utterances of literary and moral reformers should not suggest that romance was ever less than popular. Certain specimens went out of fashion, but others came in. It was during the later part of the sixteenth century that the Greek romances first began to be translated, and they immediately exercised a profound influence especially on the development of prose fiction. First came Heliodorus: a brief extract in 1567, and the full translation by Thomas Underdowne in 1569, with reprints in 1577, 1587, 1605, and 1622. Underdowne worked from the French of the invaluable Amyot, from whose version of *Daphnis and Chloe* Angel Day made the first English translation in 1587. Achilles Tatius was translated by William Burton in 1597.

We cannot prove that Shakespeare used these works directly; but the related tale of Apollonius of Tyre, on which *Pericles* is based, was of great importance to him. Though the earliest known version is a Latin manuscript of the tenth century, the original appears to have been another Greek romance. The story had a wide and long-lasting circulation—over a hundred medieval Latin manuscripts, in both prose and verse, are known—and was popular in many languages; it was translated, imitated, adapted, versified, and dramatized. (In Greece, we are told, it is still passed on by word of mouth.) Shakespeare of course can have known only a few of the versions extant in his time. He certainly knew Gower's (in *Confessio Amantis*), and also Lawrence Twine's *The Pattern of Painful Adventures*. For the student of Shakespeare these obviously are the important versions; but it is helpful to be aware of the others—to know that Shakespeare was telling a story of great antiquity, familiar to many of his audience. The 'mouldy tale', as Jonson described it, must have seemed to his less censorious contemporaries rather to be part of their folklore; a tale they would no more consider rationally than we should question the motives of Cinderella or examine the psychology of the three bears.

Of Shakespeare's romances, only *Pericles* is wholly based on a traditional tale; but all the others employ equally conventional motifs. Obviously Shakespeare, in employing the material of romance, must have been well aware that many other writers of the time used similar conventions. Some (such as Greene and Lodge) we remember mainly for their connections with Shakespeare; others (such as Emanuel Forde and Henry Roberts—both very popular in their day) we remember hardly at all. And a few survive with the status of 'classics'; Spenser's *The Faerie Queene* (much influenced by Italian romantic epic) and Sidney's *Arcadia* (on which Heliodorus was an important influence) have been declared 'outstanding epitomes of all that was most vital at the time in the romance tradition'.[8]

These two works no longer enjoy the popularity that was once their lot. 'The *Arcadia*', T. S. Eliot has said, 'is a monument of dulness';[9] and S. L. Wolff wrote, 'one who reads for pleasure simply cannot understand the *Arcadia*'.[10] Scholars and critics have tried to help the modern reader to understand them, partly by assuring us how serious they are. The *Arcadia*, we are told, 'is as sage and serious as Spenser, or as anything Milton himself could have wished'. It is 'a study in Christian patience'—like *King Lear*.[11] This attitude can be overstressed. Undoubtedly many romances raise, or touch on, serious intellectual issues; at the same time they tend to resist intellectual schematization. The Elizabethans themselves, nervous lest their fictions be considered corrupting, tended to make exaggerated claims for their moral and ethical value. Defending romance, Sidney wrote: 'Truly I have known men that even with reading *Amadis de Gaule* (which God knoweth wanteth much of a perfect poesy) have found their hearts moved to the exercise of courtesy, liberality, and especially courage.' Clearly he expected moral benefits to come as a result of enjoyment and admiration rather than of any intellectual process induced by the work. No doubt he expected to confer similar benefits upon *Arcadia*'s readers. But no doubt either that he expected people (or at least his sister) to *read* his book, and to do so with enjoyment. And this happened: 'for a century and a half', writes John Buxton, it 'remained the best-loved book in the English language.'[12] Indeed, most prose romances, including some very poor specimens, were read much more widely than works for which the modern reader tends to have a higher regard. 'Today', we are told,[13] 'the most widely read work of Elizabethan fiction is *The Unfortunate Traveller*' of Thomas Nashe; a book which, though reprinted in the year of its publication (1594), had to wait till 1883 for its next edition. Of the far longer *Arcadia* on the other hand there were seventeen issues between 1590 and 1638. Clearly people read it—largely, we must assume, for pleasure, undeterred either by its great length or by the fact that parts of it are unfinished. Romances have a habit of being left unfinished; it is a symptom of their inclusive nature. Most of the motifs common in romance encourage copiousness, a virtue more admired perhaps in the Renaissance than at present. As Dr Johnson put it, 'In romance, when the wide field of possibility lies open to invention, the incidents may easily be made more numerous.' There is no real reason why romances should not go on for ever. This is not to say that romance material cannot be combined with a classical respect for form and economy, as certain of Shakespeare's plays clearly show. But the inclusive quality of the genre may warn us that to seek in examples of it for a single dominant purpose or theme is to risk denying its very nature. Spenser, in his letter to Raleigh printed with *The Faerie Queene*, says that most men 'delight to read...an historical fiction...rather for variety of matter than for profit of the example'. Readers expected variety as one of their rightful pleasures.

It is important, then, that the romances were written, not to be studied, but to be read primarily for enjoyment—or 'entertainment', if the word may be allowed. I quoted the remark that 'one who reads for pleasure simply cannot understand the *Arcadia*'. It would be truer to say that *until* we can read it for pleasure we cannot understand it. Sidney, Spenser, and Shakespeare all had serious purposes; but this does not necessarily imply that they were consciously didactic in any way. It is serious to create images of the joys of reunion after long parting, of the loneliness of the parted, of the fears that assail men to whom, as to Marina, the world is 'like a lasting storm, whirring me from my friends'. To construct a verbal or dramatic structure that can stimulate our imaginations to a keener apprehension of these matters requires no further justification. The full response to the works of the romancers comes only when we find ourselves reading for pure pleasure, caught up in the swirl of the story, rapt in wonder and tense with anticipation—reading in fact as children read. Sidney, Spenser, and Shakespeare appeal primarily to our imaginations, not our brains; and the standard motifs and conventions of romance were invaluable raw material to them.

Conventions can of course be both an advantage and a disadvantage. They enable an artist to establish a basis of communication; but they can all too easily harden into clichés, in which the intention of communication is mistaken for the act. Some situations can be relied on to produce an automatic response without much help from the author. This is particularly true of the theatre, where something can always be left to the performers. The romantic situation of recognition and reconciliation found in the last Acts of many of Shakespeare's plays recurs at other stages of our drama; but not always so well handled. An instance is the last page of *Lovers' Vows*, that play translated by Mrs Inchbald from the German of Kotzebue, and rehearsed with such dire consequences at Mansfield Park. The once wicked but now reformed Baron is reunited with the mistress he has wronged, and their bastard. The tender scene is presented with remarkable verbal economy. Indeed the stage directions are more eloquent than the dialogue.

> *Anhalt leads on Agatha—The Baron runs and clasps her in his arms—Supported by him, she sinks on a chair which Amelia places in the middle of the stage—The Baron kneels by her side, holding her hand.*
>
> BARON   Agatha, Agatha, do you know this voice?
> AGATHA   Wildenhaim.
> BARON   Can you forgive me?

AGATHA   I forgive you (*embracing him*)

[*Enter Frederick (their son)*]

FREDERICK   I hear the voice of my mother!—Ha! mother! father!

Frederick throws himself on his knees by the other side of his mother—She clasps him in her
arms.—Amelia is placed on the side of her father attentively viewing Agatha—Anhalt stands
on the side of Frederick with his hands gratefully raised to Heaven.—The curtain slowly drops.

In its day this was a perfectly successful piece of dramatic writing, even though the
convention behind it had already been burlesqued by Sheridan in *The Critic*. The
convention will stand up to burlesque. In the once popular farce *Box and Cox* (1847),
the conventional mark of recognition is similarly parodied:

BOX   Cox! You'll excuse the apparent insanity of the remark, but the more I gaze on
    your features, the more I'm convinced that you're my long-lost brother.

COX   The very remark I was going to make to you.

BOX   Ah—tell me—in mercy tell me—have you such a thing as a strawberry mark
    on your left arm?

COX   No.

BOX   Then 'tis he!

They rush into each other's arms.

We recognize the absurdity of the bare husk of the convention, but this need not
prevent us from responding with genuine emotion to a properly devised use of it.
The great writer can invest a stock situation with the weight of reality, illumining the
commonplace. He can even call upon our awareness of the convention to produce a
complex reaction in which the literary trick is transmuted into a symbol of the
archetypal quality of a situation. In *Twelfth Night* there is a version of the 'strawberry
mark' convention. 'My father had a mole upon his brow', says Viola, reunited with
Sebastian. 'And so had mine', he replies. The exchange is sometimes cut in the
theatre, presumably lest it arouse the wrong kind of laughter. Yet it can be spoken in
such a way as to expand the stage situation until it becomes an image of a timelessly
recurrent experience. At the same time, and paradoxically, our subconscious awareness of the weight of convention behind the situation may awaken just enough
disbelief to arouse a sense of pathos that men should so often have needed to create
such an image.

Shakespeare employed the conventions of romance to different effect at different
stages of his career, and it is my purpose in what follows to explore some aspects of
his use of romance material. In the romantic comedies, comedy is more to the fore
than in the last plays. That the conventions of romance are not incompatible with
comedy he could have learned from many sources: from, for instance, his reading of
Daphnis and Chloe, *Arcadia*, or Greene's *Menaphon*. And the presence of comic elements in works such as these may well have been an encouragement to him in view of

the dramatic convention of the comic underplot. In *The Two Gentlemen of Verona* he added comedy to a serious romance story; the result, in my view, is not altogether satisfactory. In *The Comedy of Errors*—perhaps the most interesting of the early comedies in relation to the late plays—he romanticized a mainly comic source, Plautus's *Menaechmi*. This he complicated in a number of ways. Some of his alterations, especially the addition of twin servants—the Dromios—increase the possibilities of comic confusion. Others are clearly designed to redress the balance by giving greater emotional weight. These latter are derived from seeds found in Plautus with the addition of material probably taken from the story of *Apollonius of Tyre*. The twins' father, merely mentioned in *Menaechmi*, appears before us in *The Comedy of Errors*, and in a peculiarly poignant situation—he is about to have his head chopped off. The tale he tells is pure romance, involving the birth of two pairs of twins 'in the self-same inn' (Egeon admits by implication that it is surprising) and a shipwreck much out of the ordinary. To be shipwrecked once might have been regarded as a normal enough misfortune in Elizabethan times; but that a family, having escaped together from shipwreck, should then be separated when the mast to which they were tied was 'splitted in the midst' by 'a mighty rock' might well have been regarded by a contemporary Lady Bracknell as carelessness. Certainly it lifts this story out of sordid reality into the realms of romance. Opening in this way, Shakespeare prepares us for improbabilities such as the fact that two pairs of identical twins who share not only the same name but even, it seems, identical clothes should be chasing each other around Ephesus. He prepares us too for some of the other variations he is going to play on the Plautine farce, especially for the multiple reunions with which he is to end.

The influence of romance is felt in this play not only in the development of the clearly romantic elements implicit in the structure of *Menaechmi* but also in the modifications made in the treatment of that play's comic substance. The comedy remains, but is given added weight and humanity by the interweaving of more serious material. Some of this is to be linked with the romance aspects of the play only because of the capacity of romance to include a wide variety of material—one thinks for instance of the theme, explored in a seriously comic way, of the proper relationships of husband and wife. Another theme that runs through the play, and that is both related to this previous one and also more clearly appropriate in itself to romance, is that of family relationships in general, involving the separation of the brothers, the apparent estrangement between Adriana and her husband, and the reunion of father, mother, sons, and servants in the last scene.

Also characteristic of romance is the notion, frequently stated or implied, that the events in the world of the play are subject to forces other than those of normal cause and effect; that there is some magical reason for the errors of the action. This serves a useful dramatic purpose in diverting our attention from the central personages' failure to deduce the true reasons for their mishaps; it provides a comic heightening of some of the situations; furthermore, by arousing a sense of wonder and even of fear, it helps to keep us in touch with some of the drama's more serious issues—that there is indeed a mystery about the human personality; that we depend for our sense of identity very much upon the reactions of those around us; that if everything familiar to us is taken away we are deprived of something inside as well as outside us (an idea prominent in *King Lear*); and that, more specifically, separation is a form of bereavement—'partir c'est mourir un peu'.

Conversely, of course, reunion is a renewal of life; and in this play both the poignancy of separation and the joy of reunion are concentrated on—though not confined to—Egeon. He had been condemned to death on the principle of strict tit-for-tat justice; it is perhaps no mere chance that the character who effects the happy resolution is an abbess, an explicitly Christian figure who brings with her the softening influence of a mercy that seasons justice—a redemptive mercy replacing death by life.

The last scene, with its multiple reunions so characteristic of romance, is no mere untangling of a farcical knot. Egeon's emotion on being rejected by the man whom he believes to be the son he has tended from birth is given full and wholly serious expression, and stands as the high emotional point. The background of suffering that has been genuinely if economically presented, along with the background of anticipated joy in union stated in Antipholus of Syracuse's declarations of love for Luciana, gives depth and reality to the joyful climax. It is still a climax appropriate to a comedy; there is enough improbability about the Abbess to keep us on the cheerful side of pathos; but pathos there certainly is. It is a romantic climax; comedy is subsumed in joy, bewilderment in rapturous wonder, the wonder of a dream—'If I dream not, thou art Emilia'—'If this be not a dream I see and hear'. The play ends with images of birth; on a serious level in the Abbess's final lines:

> Thirty-three years have I but gone in travail
> Of you, my sons; and till this present hour
> My heavy burden ne'er delivered.
> The duke, my husband and my children both,
> And you the calendars of their nativity,
> Go to a gossips' feast, and go with me.
> After so long grief, such nativity![14]

and more lightly from Dromio, in the final couplet:

> We came into the world like brother and brother;
> And now let's go hand in hand, not one before another.

It is unnecessary to labour the point that rebirth is a prominent theme of the last plays.

The conventions of romantic love are only one element in romance literature. In *The Comedy of Errors* the romance of courtship is present only between Antipholus of Syracuse and Luciana. The love of husband and wife is of course important; but equally important as a driving force in most of the major characters is a non-sexual love; the love of father for son, brother for brother, mother for son. Love in this sense is a major value of the play. None of the characters can feel complete in himself as long as he is apart from those he loves (the theme is particularly appropriate in a play so much concerned with twins, about whose psychology Shakespeare had more reason than most of us to be concerned). This emphasis on love that extends far beyond the romance of courtship is responsible for much of the emotional richness of Shakespeare's romantic comedies, including perhaps the greatest, *Twelfth Night*.

In one respect the plot of *Twelfth Night* is very close to that of *The Comedy of Errors*: twins—brother and sister this time—have been separated by shipwreck. The separation is recent, and Viola's grief is keen because she thinks her brother is dead. In some ways she resembles Antipholus of Syracuse, but she seems to be of a more buoyant temperament; also she is forced into a more practical state of mind by the necessity to earn her living. During the course of the action she does not, so far as we are told, spend much time thinking of her brother. But the possibility of reunion is built into the play to a much greater extent than in *The Comedy of Errors*. There it is always latent; is indeed by all dramatic laws inevitable; but it is scarcely made explicit after the opening scene. In *Twelfth Night* on the other hand we are explicitly reminded of the separation several times during the action. At the end of Act 3 Viola is permitted to reveal the sort of deductive intelligence denied to the Antipholuses when, hearing Antonio mistake her for her brother, she says:

> Prove true, imagination, O, prove true,
> That I, dear brother, be now ta'en for you!

And:

> He named Sebastian: I my brother know
> Yet living in my glass; even such and so
> In favour was my brother, and he went
> Still in this fashion, colour, ornament,
> For him I imitate: O, if it prove,
> Tempests are kind and salt waves fresh in love.

(Here too Shakespeare builds in an excuse for the similarity of costume that is presumed but unexplained in the earlier play.) These are not extended passages, but they are prominent, partly because they are in soliloquy, and partly because they are in a higher style than the rest of the scene. (Anyone who saw Dorothy Tutin's Viola will remember the moving radiancy of renewed hope with which she delivered these lines.)

Her brother, Sebastian, is reflected to us largely through his friend Antonio, perhaps the most seriously drawn figure in the play. Antonio regards Sebastian with unmistakable depths of selfless devotion. When the young man apparently denies him, he breaks into generalized remarks on the deceit of appearances comparable with, for instance, Claudio's anguish on hearing that Hero is false, or Othello's false judgement on Desdemona:

> But O how vile an idol proves this god!
> Thou hast, Sebastian, done good feature shame.
> In nature there's no blemish but the mind;
> None can be call'd deform'd but the unkind:
> Virtue is beauty, but the beauteous evil
> Are empty trunks o'erflourished by the devil. (3.4.399-404)

It is Antonio who suffers most as a result of the confusion of identities. In defending himself to Orsino he stresses the selflessness of his love:

> for his sake
> Did I expose myself, pure for his love,
> Into the danger of this adverse town.

This outburst of Antonio's is functionally very similar to Egeon's in the last scene of *The Comedy of Errors*. Both reveal a depth of suffering that casts into higher relief the joy to come. The twins' forthcoming reunion is invested with heavy emotional significance. Those who look for *Twelfth Night*'s climax in the coming together of Viola and Orsino are disappointed. The climax, effected in true romance fashion by chance and time, lies not in the union of lovers but in the reunion of brother and sister—the triumph of pure love. The radiancy that this sheds provides the emotional solvent in which all obstacles to understanding and union are dissolved. The long scene of reunion strikes with all the wonder and rapture of an achieved impossibility. Across a stage crowded with people, many of them deeply affected by the reunion, brother and sister confront each other. Each believed the other was drowned; the truth comes like a slow dawn:

> SEBASTIAN Do I stand there? I never had a brother;
> Nor can there be that deity in my nature,
> Of here and every where. I had a sister,
> Whom the blind waves and surges have devour'd.

> Of charity, what kin are you to me?
> What countryman? what name? what parentage?
> VIOLA Of Messaline: Sebastian was my father;
> Such a Sebastian was my brother too,
> So went he suited to his watery tomb:
> If spirits can assume both form and suit
> You come to fright us.
> SEBASTIAN   A spirit I am indeed;
> But am in that dimension grossly clad
> Which from the womb I did participate.
> Were you a woman, as the rest goes even,
> I should my tears let fall upon your cheek,
> And say 'Thrice-welcome, drowned Viola!'
> VIOLA   My father had a mole upon his brow.
> SEBASTIAN   And so had mine.
> VIOLA   And died that day when Viola from her birth
> Had number'd thirteen years.
> SEBASTIAN   O, that record is lively in my soul!
> He finishèd indeed his mortal act
> That day that made my sister thirteen years.
> VIOLA   If nothing lets to make us happy both
> But this my masculine usurp'd attire,
> Do not embrace me till each circumstance
> Of place, time, fortune, do cohere and jump
> That I am Viola. (5.1.233–61)

The style is measured, grave, requiring an adjustment in tempo. As at a comparable point in *The Comedy of Errors*, there is a suggestion of the supernatural; but the spirit becomes flesh, and brings a benediction with it.

Academic critics rarely give much prominence to this passage;[15] its importance is much more likely to be recognized in the theatre. Virginia Woolf wrote of an Old Vic performance:

> Perhaps the most impressive effect in the play is achieved by the long pause which Sebastian and Viola make as they stand looking at each other in a silent ecstasy of recognition. The reader's eye may have slipped over that moment entirely. Here we are made to pause and think about it; and are reminded that Shakespeare wrote for the body and for the mind simultaneously.[16]

And Alan Downer, writing of a performance in which the play had been translated and adapted by Jean Anouilh, and in which one actress played both Viola and Sebastian, made a similar point:

For four and a half acts the complex structure of *Twelfth Night* prepares the audience for the confrontation of the twins. Shakespeare rewards our patience with seventy lines of anagnorisis, a long and gratifying tribute to the comic view of life. It is a *necessary* scene, and Shakespeare does not cheat even when improbability might have tempted him to do so. To share in the triumph of the improbable is the true delight of *Twelfth Night*, but Anouilh will be tinkering.[17]

Properly played, the scene creates a vision of harmony and concord in which are celebrated many aspects of human love; and at the end Feste remains to remind us that the romance vision is only, though beautifully, a dream.

When we turn from Shakespeare's romantic comedies to his last plays, we find much similar material. There are, however, important changes of emphasis in the way it is treated. *The Winter's Tale* is perhaps best approached by way of its main source. Here, Shakespeare was working closely from a prose romance written a generation earlier—Robert Greene's *Pandosto* (1588). No single source of real importance has been found for *Pandosto*, though many have been proposed. There are many analogues, not necessarily because Greene knew or remembered any or all of those that have been put forward, but because he was a conventionally minded writer who picked up his material where he could find it, with no concern for originality. *Pandosto* is a fabric woven from the common stuff of romance literature; predominant in their influence upon it are the Greek romances.[18] The romance background to *Pandosto* is relevant to a consideration of *The Winter's Tale* because it may remind us of some of the overtones that the play would have aroused in its own time, but that are no longer audible nowadays.

Although *Pandosto* is crudely constructed and on the whole badly written, it was popular for a phenomenally long time. It had been reprinted four times by the time Shakespeare wrote his play, and went on being read and reprinted regularly for at least a hundred and fifty years. It seems to have appealed especially to a not very highly educated class of reader. In Shakespeare's lifetime for instance it was said that a typical chambermaid 'reads Greene's works over and over', and it is a girl of the same class who is shown reading it, a hundred and fifty years later, in Richardson's *Clarissa*. Probably no Elizabethan novel had as long a natural life as *Pandosto*.[19] Its popularity can be explained only on the assumption that its readers enjoyed its presentation of basic human situations in an undemanding manner. The same quality may well have recommended it to Shakespeare as a source. A fully realized work of art would have left him no room to work in. *Pandosto* is a collection of clichés, of the well-worn themes and stock situations of pastoral romance. Greene had done Shakespeare an initial service by organizing these stereotyped elements into a pattern. In taking them over Shakespeare was of course well aware of their unoriginal nature and improbable aspects. During the play we are reminded of the old-fashioned nature of the story we are watching. By a sort of alienation technique

Shakespeare draws our attention to the nature of the fiction. Time the chorus says he will

> make stale
> The glistering of this present, as my tale
> Now seems to it;

and within the play itself, especially towards the end when marvellous events crowd upon each other, we have such remarks as the comment upon Antigonus's death:

> Like an old tale still,

and Paulina's remark that the fact that Hermione is still alive would be 'hooted at like an old tale'. It appears not only that Shakespeare was fully aware of the unrealities of the story, but that he deliberately played upon the audience's awareness too, inviting them to recall similar situations—even perhaps their memories of the source story itself, and also the centuries of tradition that lie behind it.

Shakespeare's handling of *Pandosto* is characterized at once by extreme freedom and by a remarkable willingness to turn to account even minute details of the original. He both takes over the episodic structure and draws attention to it in the long speech of Time as chorus. This emphasis seems designed to stress the romantic nature of the tale: in the non-dramatic romances, time is commonly the ally of chance and fortune in bringing about the changes of the actions. Time's speech is pivotal to the play. Shakespeare may have got the idea for it from Greene's subtitle, which is *The Triumph of Time*; and Greene's title-page bears the tag 'temporis filia veritas'. Certainly Shakespeare makes of the time element a poetic complex that helps in giving the play a richness of harmony without parallel in the novel. Showing how human beings can achieve at least the illusion of having triumphed over time, Shakespeare creates that illusion for us.

Leontes' comparatively unmotivated jealousy may be thought of as an intensification of the play's romance characteristics—motivation is not the strong point of most romancers; but the first scene is less than typical in the emotional intensity that it generates. Leontes' sexual obsession is portrayed as a self-consuming, almost fanatical state of mind; impervious to suggestion, completely incapable of admitting the possibility of error. This makes it appropriate that Shakespeare should have changed the business of the oracle. In Greene, the Queen asks her husband to send to the oracle, for the sake of their child. In the play Leontes sends of his own accord, merely to help to convince others of the truth of his suspicions:

> Though I am satisfied and need no more
> Than what I know, yet shall the oracle

> Give rest to the minds of others, such as he
> Whose ignorant credulity will not
> Come up to the truth. (2.1.189–93)

Whereas Pandosto penitently accepts the oracle's pronouncement, Leontes at first denies it, pursuing his wilful course to the point of blasphemy:

> There is no truth at all i' the oracle:
> The sessions shall proceed: this is mere falsehood. (3.2.141–2)

Immediately there arrives the report of his son's death from an illness that Leontes had earlier attributed to shame at hearing of Hermione's disgrace—which was as if Leontes blamed himself. The news strikes home. 'Apollo's angry,' he says, 'and the heavens themselves | Do strike at my injustice.' Thus Shakespeare greatly increases Leontes' implied responsibility for his son's death.

This emphasis on personal responsibility diminishes to some extent the part played in the action by those typical romance agents, chance, fate, fortune, etc. Shakespeare is humanizing his source, giving it greater relevance to normal life, making it a story of human beings rather than of puppets. To this extent the play is less of a romance than *Pandosto*. Shakespeare makes the baby Perdita's fate, too, less dependent on chance than in Greene, where she is simply left floating. Antigonus sails with the baby; we see him depositing her on the shore of Bohemia. But all evidence of where the baby is must be destroyed as otherwise it would be possible for the penitent Leontes to find his daughter. This no doubt is at least partly responsible for Shakespeare's introduction of the notorious bear that chases and devours Antigonus, and also for the less spectacular deaths of the sailors on his boat.

Shakespeare plays down too the element of chance in the matter of the lovers' return to Leontes' court. In *Pandosto* they are intent simply on getting away from the land ruled by the prince's father, who disapproves of their match; it is only because of a typical romance shipwreck that they land in Pandosto's country. In the play on the other hand the journey is carefully planned by Camillo, who suggests to Florizel that he may well be very welcome in Sicily, and says (in words that sound like a criticism of the lack of planning in *Pandosto*) that this is

> A course more promising
> Than a wild dedication of yourselves
> To unpath'd waters, undream'd shores. (4.4.576–8)

In such ways does Shakespeare give greater credibility to his original. 'There is a strong web of realism running through the warp of the romance.'[20] But 'realism' is an even more dangerous word than 'romance'. It could be argued that Shakespeare's love scenes are more realistic than Greene's. In another sense they are far more romantic; they are suffused by a passion that is real in a poetic, not an everyday, sense. Certainly the sheep-shearing scenes represent an almost total transformation of the original. Greene's lovers are largely preoccupied by social considerations: the prince constantly astounded that he can feel anything remotely resembling affection for a lowly shepherdess, the girl equally shocked by her presumption in loving a prince. In Shakespeare of course all is on a much higher plane; and it is all much more deeply related to the main plot. It is significant for instance that Florizel's admiration finds expression in a sense of the timelessness of Perdita's actions:

> When you speak, sweet,
> I'd have you do it ever; when you sing,
> I'd have you buy and sell so, so give alms,
> Pray so; and, for the ordering your affairs,
> To sing them too: when you do dance, I wish you
> A wave o' the sea, that you might ever do
> Nothing but that; move still, still so,
> And own no other function. (4.4.136–43)

We remember Polixenes' description of the time when he and Leontes, the fathers of this pair, were 'Two lads that thought there was no more behind | But such a day to-morrow as to-day, | And to be boy eternal.' The lines look forward too to the illusion created by the last scene, that time the conqueror has been conquered: an illusion created partly by the presence of this same Perdita.

In the final episodes of Greene's novel, Pandosto is no different from his earlier self. He is violent and lustful; he throws the fugitives into prison and condemns all but the young prince to death. Leontes however is still penitent and intensely conscious of the wrong he did his wife. With terrible concentration he remembers her virtues and her beauty. This constancy of penitence may be regarded as a change in the direction of romance; certainly it is in line with, for instance, the inconsolable grief displayed by Pericles and by Posthumus. And it leads to the most important departures from the source. Greene has a tacked-on tragic ending—Pandosto, suddenly smitten once more with repentance, kills himself. Leontes of course remains alive, and, more important still, is reunited with his wife in the amazing statue scene, surely one of the most daring in Shakespeare. Here Shakespeare invests the familiar motifs of reunion and apparent resurrection with exceptional poetic and dramatic force. The scene is essentially of the theatre; the long wait before the statue moves is unfailing in its hold upon audiences. And Leontes' realization that Hermione lives, when art melts into nature, is one of those moments of silence in which in a sense Shakespeare leaves everything to the actor, yet in another sense has done everything for him. 'Silence', says Claudio, 'is the perfect'st herald of joy'; and here (as in the *Alcestis*) husband and wife do not address each other. But there must be (as the First Gentleman says of the reunion of Leontes and Camillo) 'speech in their dumbness, language in their very gesture'. If one considered the scene in purely literary terms it might seem perfunctory, especially when Hermione tells Perdita that she has preserved herself in order to see whether the oracle was right in suggesting that Perdita might be alive (this does not suggest any great affection for Leontes). But there is no danger of this in the theatre, at any rate when Leontes is performed with the intensity with which, according to Helena Faucit, Macready played the scene:

At first he stood speechless, as if turned to stone; his face with an awe-struck look upon it.... Thus absorbed in wonder, he remained until Paulina said, 'Nay, present your hand.' Tremblingly he advanced, and touched gently the hand held out to him. Then, what a cry came with, 'O, she's warm!' It is impossible to describe Mr Macready here. He was Leontes' very self! His passionate joy at finding Hermione really alive seemed beyond control. Now he was prostrate at her feet, then enfolding her in his arms. I had a slight veil or covering over my head and neck, supposed to make the statue look older. This fell off in an instant. The hair, which came unbound, and fell on my shoulders, was reverently kissed and caressed. The whole change was so sudden, so overwhelming, that I suppose I cried out hysterically, for he whispered to me, 'Don't be frightened, my child! don't be frightened! Control yourself!' All this went on during a tumult of applause that sounded like a storm of hail.... It was such a comfort to me, as well as true to natural feeling, that Shakespeare gives Hermione no words to say to Leontes, but leaves her to assure him of her joy and forgiveness by look and manner only.[21]

It is appropriate to the suffering we have witnessed during the play that there should be a strongly elegiac tone here. Shakespeare's changes of his source have increased the marvellous—or the miraculous. There is joy in the scene; but it is pregnant with sorrow:

> In the very temple of delight
> Veil'd melancholy has her sovran shrine.

Deep emotions have been stirred, and will not be satisfied by a conventionally cheerful ending. In the romantic comedies we are accustomed to final scenes that stress the restoration of the social order, of which the dance or feast is an appropriate symbol. In *The Winter's Tale* there are no macrocosmic implications. Emphasis is placed not on the group but on individuals whose suffering we have closely followed. The ending is not a vision of ultimate unity, as that of *Cymbeline* might be considered. There is sobriety as Leontes in his closing lines suggests how each may heal the wounds 'Perform'd in this wide gap of time since first | We were dissever'd'. It is not in fact a high romantic climax. The emphasis is not on the lovers, but on the older generation. We are reminded that Antigonus is dead, that Leontes has 'in vain said many | A prayer upon' Hermione's grave, and that he needs pardon from both Polixenes and Hermione. The individuals must salvage what they can.

A late seventeenth-century edition of *Pandosto* is adorned with a crude woodcut illustrative of the story; one of the things represented is a cradle floating upon what appears to be a river but is presumably intended for the sea. It is a fitting emblem of the helplessness of humanity often implied in romance literature. Sometimes the forces against which mankind is helpless are external, sometimes internal. The baby Perdita is helpless in the face of her father's unreasonable passion; so is her mother; and so in a sense is Leontes himself—he is swept away by jealousy as a child might be swept away by the ocean. And the end of the play, focusing upon a few figures in their newly poised adjustments to each other, stresses the importance of human relationships as bulwarks against the forces of disaster. In his adaptation of *Pandosto* Shakespeare has produced a work that is far more powerful as a human document. He has done so not by denying the romance elements in Greene's book but by readjusting them— sometimes adding to them, sometimes toning them down with a modified realism, and always investing them with a poetic rather than a mundane reality.

That *The Tempest* employs basic romance material requires little demonstration. It begins with a shipwreck; Prospero and Miranda had themselves been cast up on this island after being exposed to wind and waves like the heroine of *Pandosto*; in the past Prospero had been separated from his brother; now Alonso is separated from his son and believes him dead; Miranda and Ferdinand are the handsome hero and pure heroine typical of romance; the supernatural plays its part; an air of deliberate unreality pervades the play; the story works towards reunion, reconciliation, and the happy conclusion of the love affair. But in form the play is very different from a typical romance. Shakespeare has chosen to begin his story at the end. The action is concentrated into a small space and a few hours. The sea-voyages and land-travels of *Pericles*, *Cymbeline*, and *The Winter's Tale* here can only be told in retrospect, or at most symbolized by the wanderings of the shipwrecked men around the island. Instead of being moved from a present which in the later Acts becomes the past, we are throughout required to be conscious of the past in the present. The 'wide gap' of time in which we imagined the coming to maturity of Marina and Perdita has here become 'the dark backward and abysm of time' into which Miranda gazes with her father. The method is closer to that of *The Comedy of Errors* than to that of the other last plays; but Prospero is the centre of this play, whereas Egeon is present only in the framework of the earlier one. The tension that results from this combination of romantic material with 'classical' form helps to give this play its peculiar dynamic. The characters, as well as the audience, are often bidden to remember the past; our minds move with theirs. The result is perhaps, paradoxically enough, a more consistent and deeper consciousness of the effects of time than in plays in which a wider time-span is directly presented.

By sacrificing the large dimensions of space and time common in romance, Shakespeare clearly gains much in concentration. Nevertheless, it is a sacrifice. The romancer, typically writing a story in which little attention is paid to the sequence of cause and effect, depends a good deal upon time, and also chance or fortune (sometimes conceived of as an active god-figure) in order to render plausible those turns of the action or changes of character for which no explanation is given. In *Cymbeline*, for instance, Iachimo's sudden last-Act penitence goes psychologically uninvestigated but is the more easily accepted in that we last saw him some time ago and in a different country. The story of *The Tempest* demands similar changes. Alonso has to be shown in penitence for his usurpation; and the penitence has to come about as the direct result of his experiences on the island. Shakespeare can (and to some extent does) hint that the Alonso we see at the beginning of the action is not as objectionable as he was twelve years before, but the actual process of conversion has to take place within the brief time-span of the play. This is made convincing primarily by being made the result of a conscious purpose. In a normal romance story, chance would have caused the shipwreck that puts Prospero's enemies at his mercy. In this play, though fortune plays her part (and Shakespeare is most subtle in his constant shifting of responsibility), it is Prospero himself who by his 'art' brings about the shipwreck. He is partly dependent on fortune, partly master of it. In a sense he is the 'god of this great vast' on whom Pericles calls. He has superhuman power, yet remains human. He is both god and man, a worker of miracles who finally accepts the full burden of humanity. At times it is difficult to distinguish him from a supernatural controlling force. It is partly by creating the wholly superhuman Ariel to act as the semi-independent agent of Prospero's will that Shakespeare has been able to keep Prospero human—perhaps the most remarkable technical feat of the play.

As the controlling agent of the play in which he has his being, Prospero himself resembles the narrator of a romance story. This is true not merely of the second scene, in which he tells Miranda of her childhood (with results, it would seem, resembling those of many romancers) but also of the methods by which he exercises his influence. Frequently and deliberately he tries to create a sense of awe, mystery, and wonder in the minds of those he is trying to influence. His use—generally through Ariel—of music is part of this. So is Ariel's tricksiness, such as his appearance to the mariners causing them to feel 'a fever of the mad', and the living drollery that reminds Gonzalo of the romantic travellers' tales he heard in boyhood. It is after the wonder induced by the appearance of the 'strange shapes bringing in a banquet' that Ariel makes his great speech of accusation against the courtiers; and in the last scene Prospero remarks:

> I perceive, these lords
> At this encounter do so much admire
> That they devour their reason and scarce think

> Their eyes do offices of truth, their words
> Are natural breath: but, howsoe'er you have
> Been justled from your senses, know for certain
> That I am Prospero.

To justle them from their senses has been part of his aim; but not all are responsive to this—just as Antonio and Sebastian had not responded to Ariel's sleep-inducing music. The cynical pair deny the wonder expressed by the perhaps over-credulous Gonzalo (e.g. 2.1 *passim*).

If Prospero resembles a spinner of romance tales, his daughter is even more clearly the ideal audience for such tales. Belarius (in *Cymbeline*) describes such a person:

> When on my three-foot stool I sit and tell
> The warlike feats I have done, his spirits fly out
> Into my story: say 'Thus mine enemy fell,
> And thus I set my foot on's neck;' even then
> The princely blood flows in his cheek, he sweats,
> Strains his young nerves and puts himself in posture
> That acts my words. (3.3.89–95)

Miranda too has all the open-mindedness, the willingness to be impressed, the capacity for wonder, that a story-teller could desire. She is all sympathy and eagerness to believe the best:

> O, I have suffered
> With those that I saw suffer: a brave vessel,
> Who had, no doubt, some noble creature in her,
> Dash'd all to pieces. (1.2.5–8)

Her first sight of Ferdinand arouses similar awe:

> I might call him
> A thing divine, for nothing natural
> I ever saw so noble. (1.2.417–19)

And the climax comes as Miranda looks up from her game of chess and sees the assembled group:

> O, wonder!
> How many goodly creatures are there here!
> How beauteous mankind is! O brave new world,
> That has such people in't! (5.1.181–4)

By this time in the play we know a number of these people rather well, and Miranda's innocence has a deep pathos, all the more pointed by Prospero's quiet comment, 'Tis new to thee'. But though Prospero's words provide an implied criticism of Miranda's attitude, they do nothing to destroy it. It is one of Shakespeare's greatest achievements that he can show the coexistence of opposed attitudes, making us aware of the tension between them but not forcing us to decide in favour of one or the other. Miranda's naïve innocence and Prospero's mature wisdom are both part of the truth; to counterpoint one against the other is to create a harmony that more than doubles the effect of each alone.[22]

Another quality typical of romance that Shakespeare might appear to have sacrificed by his decision to cast his play in an approximation to classical form is discursiveness: the provision of that 'variety of mirth and pastime' that Elizabethan romancers were so fond of advertising in their wares. But in fact he manages to cram a remarkable amount of material into this, the second shortest of his plays. He does so not by the multiplication of incident, the copiousness, the sheer length of many of his predecessors, but rather by an extraordinary multiplicity of suggestiveness—his power of creating a structure which looks different from every angle—his myriad-mindedness, as Coleridge put it. The enchanted island reverberates with sounds hinting at tunes that never appear fully formed. We can follow one strand through the work, but only by shutting our ears to the others; what we gain in line we lose in depth. It is this of course that has made the play so happy a hunting ground for the symbol-seekers. 'Any set of symbols moved close to this play', wrote Mark van Doren, 'lights up as in an electric field.'[23] Prospero has frequently been seen as a self-projection of the author; the notion has been handled sensibly and persuasively by some, less so by others. Most critics find themselves driven to speak of Prospero in terms other than those in which Shakespeare has written of him. For some he is God; for others, the imagination. One sees him as Hymen or a masque-presenter; another as 'the genius of poetry'; yet another as both 'a close replica of Christ' and 'a matured and fully self-conscious embodiment of those moments of fifth-act transcendental speculation to which earlier tragic heroes, including Macbeth, were unwillingly forced'.[24]

Criticism of this play has its excesses; but we must recognize that the variety of available interpretations is the result of its extraordinary suggestiveness. The play invites consideration on different levels. Partly this comes from the resonance of the verse, which often takes us far beyond the immediate situation. Intimately connected is the fact that the characters lack the strong individuality of some—though by no means all—leading figures of the great tragedies. Depth of characterization is not a normal feature of romance. Generally this is because the emphasis is on event. The figures of the story are conventionalized. What happens to them is more important than what they are. In The Tempest there is less emphasis on event; there is indeed less event; but the characters also are representative rather than individual.

They are comparatively little distinguished by variety of style. Miranda is not a Viola, a Rosalind, or an Imogen. But though she may lack these girls' vibrantly immediate impact, she gains in representativeness. Being less of a particular time and place, she becomes more of all time and everywhere. In this context, actions the more easily take on a symbolical value. It is not necessary to go outside the play to see Ferdinand's log-carrying as an expression of a theme that crops up at many points. On a realistic level, it is no hardship for a healthy young man to spend a few hours carrying firewood; but any hint of this attitude in performance is ruinous. Ferdinand's task must appear as one of the complex of actions and statements connected with the idea of control; a complex that begins in the first scene where the voyaging noblemen are seen powerless against the force of (as it seems) nature; which is further adumbrated in Prospero's control over nature, over Ariel, and over Caliban; in Caliban's failure to achieve self-control; in the falsely based power that Stephano and Trinculo achieve over Caliban; in their joint attempt to overcome Prospero's authority, which parallels Sebastian's and Antonio's plot to kill Alonso, which itself parallels Antonio's and Alonso's earlier usurpation of Prospero; in Prospero's ability to conjure up the masque, and in the explicit themes of the masque itself, which are clearly related to the self-control that Prospero regards as so important in his future son-in-law; and finally in Prospero's ultimate renunciation of power. By a variety of juxtapositions, hints, and poetic devices, Shakespeare makes his romance story a carrier of what might be regarded as a scheme of ideas on a philosophical topic.

And he even introduces contemporary matters. It is not fanciful to see in the play a whole set of correspondences to what for its original audience was a burning question of the day—the matter of colonization; it is no accident that among the few accepted minor sources are pamphlets on voyaging. There is little explicit reference to the topic; but there is enough for us to be sure that it was present in Shakespeare's consciousness. Caliban complains against Prospero's enslavement of him; and there is a kind of justice in his complaint. We are shown the totally irreconcilable situation that arises when civilizations clash. It is parallel to the situation of Shylock and Portia; and though we cannot but feel that Shylock and Caliban must be overcome, yet we feel too something of the anguish involved in a complex moral impasse.

While the unreality of The Tempest contributes towards the play's high suggestive power, it would be false to suggest that the total effect is unreal. The first scene is in prose so vivid and colloquial that with a few changes it could stand in a television script. But the opening lines of the next scene suspend reality as we learn that the storm was the effect of Prospero's art, and for the remainder of the play the alternation and balance between the palpably unreal and the illusion of reality is maintained. The romance is toughened by a strain of anti-romance. The unrealistic idealism of Gonzalo is countered by the callous cynicism of Antonio and

Sebastian—just as, for instance, Autolycus adds astringency to the pastoral scenes of *The Winter's Tale*. The virtue of Ferdinand and Miranda is not taken for granted; it is thrown into relief by what we know of Caliban, by his suggestions that Stephano should make Miranda his queen, and by the care with which Prospero guards the lovers' virtue. Even Prospero's own virtue is not without its strains. It is easy to lay too much emphasis on the scene in which Ariel recommends him to have mercy on his enemies; the style does not suggest severe internal struggle. Nevertheless, we are reminded that he might have taken vengeance, that the travellers are in fact his enemies. He does not bear his responsibilities lightly; he is one of Shakespeare's worried rulers, for whom the burden of power is greater than the rewards.

In ways such as these the vicissitudes commonly undergone by inhabitants of the world of romance come to be seen, not so much as random happenings that they survive by the help of fortune, as events designed to test and, during the course of the action, to define them. The play has a moral seriousness uncommon in most romance literature—though least uncommon, perhaps, in Shakespeare's greatest immediate predecessors, Sidney and Spenser. *The Tempest* is a romance containing a built-in criticism of romance; not a rejection of it, but an appreciation both of its glories and of its limitations. Romance is associated with all that brings man nearer to Ariel than to Caliban. Responsiveness to nature and to art, the capacity for wonder, the ability to sympathize with those that suffer, the desire to shape experience in accordance with an imaginative and moral vision, the value of an attitude to life that denies cynicism even to the extent of creating a somewhat naïve credulity such as Gonzalo's—all these are included. When art guides nature, when the civilizing forces of self-control are dominant, then Gonzalo's vision may be realized—a vision that looks forward to the masque:

> Earth's increase, foison plenty,
> Barns and garners never empty,
> Vines with clustering bunches growing,
> Plants with godly burthen bowing;
> Spring come to you at the farthest
> In the very end of harvest!
> Scarcity and want shall shun you;
> Ceres' blessing so is on you. (4.1.110–17)

It is indeed 'a most majestic vision', and it is fitting that it should be celebrated in the form of a masque-like performance enacted by the spirits over whom Prospero has power. This was the great age of the masque—nothing could have been more suitable as an image of the results that man can achieve by the exercise of mind and imagination. The masque was at once a symbol of power and wealth—frequently used as such in the Jacobean game of power politics—and also of the highest achievements of civilization, in which the arts of music, dancing, painting, acting, and poetry combined in entertainments whose splendour was enhanced by their folly. Many thousands of pounds were lavished upon a single evening's entertainment by those who could not command unpaid spirits to enact their fancies. Thus the masque was an apt symbol too of the vanity of human greatness. The glittering bubble is easily pricked. The visions of a Prospero are at the mercy of the Calibans of this world. Power that can create can also destroy, and so, when Prospero learns of the evil being plotted against him, the vision vanishes, leaving not a rack behind. Prospero's famous reaction is one of acceptance rather than mourning. Though he is momentarily angered, he controls himself and consoles Ferdinand. The dream is recognized for what it is, but allowed the reality that belongs even to a dream—or to any other product of the imagination—a play, poem, or romance.

The Tempest takes the familiar material of romance but adopts to it an attitude firmly though sympathetically judicious. The creations of the fancy are subjected to the scrutiny of the imagination; and they do not emerge unscathed. The ending thus disappoints those who ask for a full romantic climax. It is true that Prospero's forgiveness, though nominally extended to all, lacks warmth, at any rate when he speaks to his brother Antonio:

> For you, most wicked sir, whom to call brother
> Would even infect my mouth, I do forgive
> Thy rankest fault. (5.1.130–2)

But perhaps we should have the right to be disappointed by this only if Prospero had been presented as wholly superhuman. Since Antonio is not shown as penitent, it is not easy to see why Prospero should be expected so soon to show any warmth towards the man who had behaved to him somewhat as Macbeth had to Duncan. The Tempest is austere, and its final moments are muted; but it is not harsh in its total effect. Antonio's impenitence is balanced by Alonso's contrition; Prospero's world-weary emotional exhaustion by Gonzalo's ebullient recognition of the good that has come out of these events and also, in the younger generation, by the satisfactory conclusion of the love affair of Ferdinand and Miranda. If Caliban remains in bondage, he is at least temporarily the wiser for his folly; and after Prospero has taken care to ensure that the royal party will have 'calm seas, auspicious gales | And sail so expeditious that shall catch | Your royal fleet far off', Ariel is finally freed to the elements. One might even see a touch of humour in this reversal of the play's opening situation.

It would seem then that though the two 'last plays' on which I have concentrated make more use of the conventions of romance literature than do some of the romantic comedies, their total effect is by no means unqualifiedly romantic. In discussing romantic aspects of earlier plays I have had to omit much. These plays are of course more comic than the romances; but they are also more romantic, in the sense that their attitude towards the conventions of romance is less critical. Feste may cast his shadow over the bridal couples at the end of *Twelfth Night*, and Jaques has his sardonic contribution to make to *As You Like It*; but the mature Leontes, Hermione, and Prospero need no external safeguards against illusion; and the young lovers in both *The Winter's Tale* and *The Tempest* are surrounded by older and wiser friends and relatives. The world of romance is both tested against reality and itself shown to be a part of reality. The realization of the romance vision has involved suffering, self-discipline, even death. There is here none of the irresponsibility with which romance literature is often charged. But neither is there any of that portent-ousness with which it is only too easy to invest these plays. They are entertainments; that is to say, the response they demand is primarily imaginative.

The mood most characteristic of Shakespeare's later handling of romance mater-ial is perhaps o;ne that fuses extremes of emotion. It can be felt in plays that are not predominantly romantic—in Cordelia's 'smiles and tears' on hearing news of her father, in Menenius's 'I could weep | And I could laugh' when he welcomes home the victorious Coriolanus. In the romances, Pericles has to call on Helicanus to 'Give me a gash...Lest this great sea of joys rushing upon me | O'erbear the shores of my mortality'; when Leontes and Polixenes were reunited, 'their joy waded in tears'; and every third thought of Prospero, his purpose accomplished, will be his grave. But more important than such formulations is the pervasiveness of this mood in the climaxes. These plays suggest a Shakespeare who has been able with clear eyes to contemplate extremes of imaginative experience. At the same time, each play has its own uniqueness; there is great variety within each, and within the romances as a group. Nothing is more indicative of the total control that Shakespeare maintained over his inherited material.

PART III
SHAKESPEARE IN THE THEATRE

16

Boys Should be Girls:
Shakespeare's Female Roles and the
Boy Players

In recent years transgendered performances in Shakespearian roles have become common in both England and America. Women have played men: at the National Theatre (and on television) Fiona Shaw was Richard II, and at the Globe it has been possible to see Vanessa Redgrave as Prospero as well as several plays performed entirely by women. Complicite offered Kathryn Hunter as King Lear, and in the West End Dawn French played Bottom in *A Midsummer Night's Dream*. In Kenneth Branagh's film of *Love's Labour's Lost* Geraldine McEwan gave us a Holofernes translated into Holoferna. Conversely, men have been cast in women's roles: Adrian Lester was a fine Rosalind for Cheek by Jowl, and Mark Rylance played Olivia and Cleopatra at the Globe.

This kind of thing is not new. Female Hamlets have abounded, going back as far at least as Sarah Siddons, in the late eighteenth century.[1] In a Danish film of 1920, Hamlet was played not merely by but as a woman. Probably the finest of nineteenth-century Romeos was the American Charlotte Cushman, often playing against her sister Susan's Juliet; Charlotte excelled too as Shylock, Henry VIII, and Cardinal Wolsey. Millicent Bandmann-Palmer played male roles around the turn of the nineteenth century and even achieved mention in James Joyce's *Ulysses*. Just as Ellen Tree—Mrs Charles Kean—played the Chorus to *Henry V* (in the guise of Clio, the Muse of History), in her husband's production at the Princess's Theatre in 1859, so in 2003 Penny Downie played the Chorus at the National Theatre—though this is hardly a gendered role in the first place.

Reasons for these phenomena vary from case to case and period to period; they may be ideological, sociological, psychological, political, marital (as with Mrs Kean), practical, whimsical, and a mixture of any or all of these. During the past twenty or so years they have been underpinned by academic criticism. Feminist critics and performers have demanded equal rights for women in playing the great roles; queer theory has made much of Shakespeare's blurring of gender distinctions, of ways in which consciousness of the male gender of the actors lurks beneath his presentation of female characters such as Viola and Rosalind; sexual ambivalence has been discerned in Richard II and in Hamlet, in Pandarus and Iago. And gender switches may appear to be supported by history: by the fact that male actors exclusively played female roles in the professional English theatre from its beginnings to the Restoration.

It may therefore seem to be for historical reasons that in Wanamaker's—or, as it is now known, Shakespeare's—Globe all performances labelled as conforming to original practice cast adult male actors in the female roles. They do so with varying success. Rylance's Cleopatra was outstanding, but the casting of males in the happily not very prominent female roles of *Richard II* in 2003 was less successful. Heavily rouged, bewigged, and wearing silly hats, gliding over the stage in an excessively stylized manner, the Queen and her women looked like something out of a pantomime or a circus. This kind of caricature was condescending to women as well as to the audience.

The question of the 'adult' women

But I am not concerned here with the success or otherwise of individual perform-ances. What worries me is that the casting of adult males in female roles at, especially, the Globe, is creating in many persons' minds the impression that this is indeed a return to original practice. This is not a new attitude. It has too often been said that, though 'boy' actors played, for instance, the romantic heroines, the maids, and of course the boys in early performances, nevertheless older female roles must have been played by adults. Marvin Rosenberg, in one of his last publications, an article published in *Shakespeare Bulletin* in 2001, repeated arguments that he had used earlier, writing:

> When I first began to study Shakespeare's plays, with my own experience of the theatre in mind, I simply could not accept the image of a stripling, however precocious, sustaining Shakespeare's increasingly complex, weighty women's roles against experi-enced male players in perhaps the greatest acting company the world has known. It would be as if an ultimately designed racing vehicle were to be run on three full-size wheels and a half-size one—the half-size replaced every few years. The Globe's playwright and actors—artists all—would never have tolerated this restriction on their creativity. Nor would their audiences. It made no sense. I was sure we had to look for a veteran male actor—of the kind we see acting so entrancingly in the cross-dressing theatres of our own day.

And Rosenberg quoted Janet Suzman on Cleopatra:

I find it hard to think he wrote [the role] for a boy. I think he must have written it for a man, perhaps a kind of Shakespearean Danny La Rue—there must have been some kind of prima donna in his company playing women's parts. It could never have been acted by a boy.[2]

'Would never have', 'could never have', 'must have', and 'must have been': the appeal is not to evidence but to common sense. Adult males were available, so they 'must have' played 'heavy' roles, such as Volumnia, Lady Macbeth, Tamora, Cleopatra, the Nurse in *Romeo and Juliet*, for which, from our modern perspective, they appear to be more readily suited. G. E. Bentley recognized this long ago when he wrote that 'the only evidence for such assignments has been the individual scholar's conception of the requirements of such a role and his assumption of the inadequacy of any boy to carry it off'.[3]

Evidence about theatre practice in Shakespeare's time is sketchy. We do not have lists of all the actors in any of the companies at any given time, let alone their dates of birth. It is impossible to assign most of the roles in Shakespeare's plays to specific actors—we know that Richard Burbage was the original Richard III, Hamlet, Lear, and Pericles, that Will Kemp played Dogberry, and we feel fairly sure that Robert Armin was Feste and Lear's Fool, but we can't with any confidence assign specific actors to any of the female roles.

There is also a problem in defining exactly what we mean by a 'boy'. When do boys stop being boys? The most obvious answer is 'when they reach the age of puberty'. The age at which that in many ways desirable condition is reached varies greatly from one individual to another, and historians tell us that it was likely to be later in Shakespeare's time than it is in ours. One of the most apparent symptoms of approaching manhood is the breaking of the voice, and this is the characteristic that might have seemed most important in actors. Greeting the players who come to Elsinore, Hamlet says to his 'young lady and mistress', 'Pray God your voice, like a piece of uncurrent gold, be not cracked within the ring' (2.2.427–31). And in *Cymbeline* Arviragus regrets that his and his brothers' voices have 'got the mannish crack' (4.2.237)—suggesting that they were played by young men rather than boys.

In spite of Flute's compunctions about playing a woman because he 'has a beard coming', it is possible to remove or to disguise facial hair, and even, as Bottom suggests, to 'speak in a monstrous little voice', but for the possessor of a broken voice to adopt falsetto tones throughout a long role would impose damaging vocal strain. It is also possible to argue that, since theatre (like opera) is a conventionalized medium anyway, we may—as Japanese audiences have long done—just as easily accept a bass or baritone heroine as a woman in her thirties playing the 13-year-old Juliet, and that we have been able to accept similar practices in modern productions. The corollary of this would be that the Elizabethans might just as well have accepted them on their stage.

The scant surviving evidence

This attitude would be tenable if we had no evidence that boys ever took female roles in the Elizabethan theatre; but we do have such evidence, all over the place. What is at issue is whether they always did so: whether in Shakespeare's time anyone going to the theatre would as a matter of course have expected to see every female role played by a male actor who could reasonably be defined as a boy.

Bits and pieces of evidence survive about the ages of actors, and David Kathman, whose knowledge of the acting profession in Shakespeare's time is unrivalled, finds no evidence that any young person over the age of 18 ever played a female before the Restoration. He tells me that the documentary evidence supports the conclusion that the actors who played female roles in the adult companies ranged from around 10 to 17 years of age, concentrated around 14 to 16, sometimes extending into the late teens.

But absence of evidence, however suggestive it may be, does not constitute proof. I want to approach the problem from a different angle, by looking at the number of roles in Shakespeare's plays that may reasonably be regarded as having been written for boys. My simple premise is that as there were boys in Shakespeare's company it would have been unprofessional of him not to write parts for them.

We don't know exactly how many boys that company included. The number may well have fluctuated from time to time. Kathman writes:

> The best evidence I know of is the surviving 'platt', or plot, of 2 *Seven Deadly Sins*, which dates from the Chamberlain's Men in 1597–98. There were six boys in that cast, three of whom (Saunder, Ro. Go., and Nick—i.e., Alexander Cooke, Robert Gough, and Nicholas Tooley) played substantial roles. One of them, Will, played Itis, a child's role, though we can only speculate how old the actor was. Obviously, plays varied in the number of boys they would require, and doubling is a factor. But six would seem to be close to the upper limit, with probably two or three of those being accomplished boys able to take on a major role (such as Portia or Beatrice).[4]

Examining the number of women's and boys' roles in each play may indicate how many boys were normally available to Shakespeare, and also the extent to which this conditioned the gender balance of his casts. And in the process we may also test the assumption that women's parts were sometimes played by grown men, remembering that one player would often play more than one role in a production. And boys may have played walk-on roles.

Some plays are very undemanding. By my calculations, and allowing for doubling, thirty of Shakespeare's plays—well over two-thirds of the total, written from the beginning to almost the end of his career—call for no more than four boy actors. Some—*Julius Caesar* and *Troilus and Cressida* are examples—could easily be performed with only two. Others, including *The Merchant of Venice, Hamlet, Twelfth Night*, and *Othello*, need three. Some demand four.

In *The Comedy of Errors* Adriana, Luciana, the Courtesan, and the Abbess are all on stage in the final scene, just as in *Coriolanus* Volumnia, Virgilia, Valeria, and the boy Martius appear together in 5.3. In *Much Ado About Nothing* Hero, Beatrice, Margaret, and Ursula are all present in 3.4; the play also has Benedick's Boy (easily doublable), and the silent Innogen, Hero's mother, present only in stage directions. Shakespeare may have expunged her for fear of running out of actors.

Indeed the reason that, as is often remarked, there are few mothers in the plays may have more to do with practical than with sociological reasons. The unexpected demise of one of them, Lady Montague in *Romeo and Juliet*, may derive from the need for the boy who played her to take on the role of Tybalt's page. In *Macbeth*, which can be played with four boys, Shakespeare actually draws attention to an apparent breach of convention by giving the Weird Sisters beards, so indicating that characters whom the audience might have expected to be played by boys are in fact played by grown men.

Some of the history plays, with their enormous cast lists, may appear particularly demanding, but the size of the casts can mislead. *2 Henry VI*, with over seventy characters, has only four women—Queen Margaret, Eleanor Duchess of Gloucester, Margery Jordan, and Simpcox's Wife—along with a number of young men's roles which might have been played by boys: Young Clifford and the two Princes, Edward and Richard. In one scene three of the women appear together, and the boys (if boys they are) appear with Queen Margaret in 5.1. So these seven characters could have been played by three boys.

3 Henry VI has well over forty characters but only three are women, and York's sons seem pretty certainly to have grown up, except for the newly introduced Earl of Rutland (one scene only, so available for doubling with e.g. Lady Grey). 'Young Henry Earl of Richmond' (among a number of instances where the phrase 'the young' in early stage directions may indicate that a boy is called for) appears in only one scene in which no other boys are needed. The entrance of the infant Prince Edward in the final scene does not require a paid-up member of the company.

What about plays that seem to call for more than four boys? *All's Well that Ends Well* has five women. Doubling is not easy, as Helen, Diana, Mariana, and the Widow all appear in one scene, 3.5, which opens immediately after the Countess has exited. It looks as if Shakespeare expected to have five boy actors for this play, one of them playing the tiny role of Mariana, who appears in only one scene. *Love's Labour's Lost* needs four women—the Princess, Rosaline, Maria, and Katherine—on stage together for much of the time, and also has the page Mote, and Jaquenetta. All are present at the end of the final scene, so this play needs a minimum of six. *The Merry Wives of Windsor* has Mistress Page, Mistress Ford, Mistress Quickly, and Anne Page, along with the boys William and Robin and some 'children of

Windsor'. William appears in only one scene and could easily be doubled with Robin. (The presence of children of Windsor may give support to the idea that the play was written for a special performance, or perhaps supernumerary children were drafted in as required.)

The late plays

For most of Shakespeare's career, then, he calls upon between two and six boy actors per play. Several of the late plays give opportunities for more than the standard number of boys without actually demanding them. *Pericles* seems to call for an unusual number in the tournament scene, which has five knights entering and exiting separately and in succession, each attended by a page, and Thaisa too is on stage. It is no wonder that, as the direction has it, Pericles himself has no 'page to deliver his shield', though possible I suppose that more than one of the pages was played by the same boy exercising a nifty bit of footwork and costume changing to give the impression that he differed from the one who had last appeared. Otherwise there is no scene that requires more than three or four boys to be on stage simultaneously, and the episodic nature of the play makes doubling particularly easy.

Although *The Tempest* has only Miranda as a female human being, we may need to count Ariel (also playing Ceres) and the Spirits Iris and Juno in the masque (which would only add up to four altogether). But there are also an unspecified number of nymphs, so perhaps we should list this play among those that can make use of more than four boys. The last of the history plays—and another late play—*All Is True* (or *Henry VIII*) has an exceptionally large cast in which however women and boys play a relatively small part. The main female roles are Queen Katherine and Anne Boleyn, along with an Old Lady who appears in two scenes and the Queen's woman Patience (in one scene only, 4.2).

There are however opportunities for a number of boy extras, in for example the banquet scene's 'Anne Boleyn and divers other ladies and gentlemen' (1.4), an unspecified number of women attendants on the Queen (e.g. 3.1), 'certain ladies or countesses', and the silent Duchess of Norfolk for the coronation procession, and a page (5.1). Again we have a hopefully silent infant, this time Princess Elizabeth herself. It would seem fair to say that this play calls for as many boy actors as the company can muster, though it might at a pinch be played with no more than the six that Kathman regards as 'close to the upper limit'.

Another late, collaborative play, *The Two Noble Kinsmen*, is especially demanding. The first scene needs a singing boy, three nymphs, Hippolyta, Emilia, and three Queens—nine characters, each of whom we should normally expect to have been played by a boy, on stage at once. There are five wenches, the Jailer's Daughter, and after they have left the stage, Hippolyta and Emilia and six female participants in the dance called for in 3.5; and in 5.3 Emilia is attended by two maids. Lois Potter, in her Arden edition, interestingly suggests that this play, like Middleton's *A Chaste Maid in Cheapside*, of around the same date, which requires nine females to be on stage at once, may have been performed by an amalgamated company.[5]

The case of the *Dream*

The most potentially anomalous play is *A Midsummer Night's Dream*, written relatively early. The major question here is whether fairies are played by adult or boy actors. The play has only three human female mortals: Hippolyta (if an Amazon is human), Hermia, and Helena. They appear together in the awakening scene and in the play scene (where, curiously, Hermia and Helena say nothing), so the play needs at least three boys. If to the female mortals we add Robin Goodfellow and Titania, the absolute minimum rises to four. It is quite possible too that Flute, who has 'a beard coming', was played by a boy.

The number then rises according to doubling possibilities. The First Fairy could be doubled with one of the female lovers. Peaseblossom, Cobweb, Mote, and Mustard-seed could in theory be doubled with the boys playing Hippolyta, Helena, Hermia, and one other boy; on the other hand they could be played by actors playing the mechanicals; the title-page of the droll *Bottom the Weaver*, the heavily abbreviated version of *A Midsummer Night's Dream* published in 1661, anticipates Peter Brook and others by suggesting that the actors playing Oberon and Titania may double Theseus and Hippolyta, and that those who enact Pyramus, Thisbe, and Wall 'likewise may present three fairies'. This could reflect pre-Commonwealth practice. The possibility that the play requires an exceptionally large number of boys has been used to buttress the theory that it was written for private performance at an event such as a wedding. I disbelieve this theory, but the fact that the play needs at least three boys is more relevant to my present purposes.

A conclusion

What I hope I have established is that throughout his career Shakespeare must have had available to him at the very least three boy actors, but that he very rarely expected to have more than six. No play, I think it is fair to say, has more than four boys' roles of great substance. Shakespeare was extremely professional in plotting his plays so that he did not exceed the number of actors available to him, or make demands that he could not expect to be met. Surely the obvious corollary of this is that, conversely, he would not waste the resources of his company by calling upon adult males to play parts that made use of the talents of his boys. What would the boy star of the company be doing if the leading female roles in *Antony and Cleopatra* and *Coriolanus* were given to adults? Having a hell of a tantrum in the tiring-room,

I should think. If a man were playing the Nurse in *Romeo and Juliet*, there would be a decent role in the play for only one boy.

I propose, then, that a survey of the boys' roles in Shakespeare's plays supports the contention that women's roles were always played by boys, and that it also demonstrates Shakespeare's professional skill in cutting his coat according to his cloth.

17

Staging Shakespeare's Ghosts

S tudy of the arts of performance in Shakespeare's time takes on practical as well as academic significance as the likelihood grows that before long a reconstructed Globe theatre will become available for experimentation; and the discovery of remains of both the Globe and the Rose may do something to increase confidence in the authenticity of such a structure. If we are to make good use of a third Globe we shall need to think afresh about many matters extending from relatively straightforward ones such as exits and entrances, sightlines, use of upper levels, and stage furniture, to costumes, make-up, blocking, acoustics, music, and acting styles. Scholars and theatre practitioners jointly will seek to establish a range of possibilities which may be regarded as normative, but will also be conscious that certain kinds of character or types of action call for a differentiation that will set them off from the norm. One may think of happenings such as dumbshows, plays (or masques) within plays, processions, theophanies, and the like, and characters such as witches, jesters, and spirits, who by no stretch of the imagination can be expected to behave like even the theatrical manifestations of ordinary human beings.

I want to look at the ghosts in Shakespeare's plays with the aim of raising questions about styles of performance that may have been associated with their portrayal in the theatres of Shakespeare's time. Ghosts are so closely related to other supernatural manifestations such as spirits and apparitions as to raise problems of definition. Although *OED* traces the word 'ghost' back to the ninth century, its first instance under the definition 'an apparition, a spectre' is, surprisingly, in Shakespeare's *Venus and Adonis* (1593), when Venus 'chides...death' as 'Grim-grinning ghost, earth's worm' (line 933). But it is difficult to see how this differs from 'The soul of a deceased person, spoken of as appearing, in a visible form, or otherwise manifesting its presence, to the living', said to be 'Now the prevailing

Dates of plays are from Alfred Harbage's *Annals of English Drama 975–1700*, rev. S. Schoenbaum (London, 1964). Quotations from Shakespeare are from *The Complete Works*, gen. eds Stanley Wells and Gary Taylor (Oxford, 1986). Quotations from other early printed sources are modernized from reputable editions. I am grateful for assistance from Dr R. V. Holdsworth and Professor Marvin Rosenberg.

sense' and traced back to the fourteenth century. It seems distinctive of a ghost to appear of its own volition, not (like the apparitions in *Macbeth*) at the behest of others. Although its appearance may be associated with abnormal states of mind in those who see it (as is Banquo's ghost) it must have some claims to objective, non-hallucinatory reality; though (like the ghosts in *Richard III* and *Julius Caesar*) it may be associated with sleep, it must be not simply a dream vision (like that of Queen Katherine in *All is True*, or *Henry VIII*). The ghosts in *Richard III* escape disqualification under this clause on the grounds that for two men simultaneously to dream the same dream must be regarded as more than coincidence. So I shall restrict myself here to the ghosts in *Richard III*, *Julius Caesar*, *Hamlet*, and *Macbeth*, leaving their close relatives to another occasion.

Ghosts had entered English drama by way of translations of Seneca several decades before Shakespeare started to write, and a number of allusions to theatrical ghosts in the sixteenth and early seventeenth centuries have fostered preconceptions about them and have suggested that their representation may have been governed by convention. One of the principal pieces of evidence for the existence of a play about Hamlet before Shakespeare's is the allusion in Thomas Lodge's pamphlet *Wit's Misery* (1596) to one who 'looks as pale as the vizard of the ghost which cried so miserably at the Theatre, like an oyster wife, "Hamlet, revenge."' (p. 56). 'Vizard' has many meanings; a common one in this period was 'mask', though it could also mean a part of a helmet or simply a face. The allusion has helped to suggest that stage ghosts may have worn masks, but there is no clear evidence for this. The miserable crying clearly implies the wailing kind of vocal delivery traditionally associated with ghosts, who in *Julius Caesar* are said to 'shriek and squeal about the streets' (2.2.24), and in the Induction to the anonymous play *A Warning for Fair Women* (1599) to come 'screaming like a pig half sticked' (line 56). Ideas about the appearance of ghosts are often related to the concept that they have broken directly from their graves (*Contention*, 1.4.20, *Measure for Measure*, 5.1.432) and can return 'to their wormy beds' (*A Midsummer Night's Dream*, 3.2.385). So they may be represented in their burial clothes (like Elizabethan grave sculptures), as is implied in the sarcastic reference, also in the Induction to *A Warning for Fair Women*, to

> a filthy whining ghost,
> Lapped in some foul sheet, or a leather pilch. (lines 54–5)

(A pilch was 'a leathern or coarse woollen outer garment'.) Use of a sheet is additionally substantiated in Middleton's play *The Puritan* (1606): 'we'll ha' the ghost i'th'white sheet sit at upper end o'th'table' (4.3.90–1)—often taken to refer directly to the apparition of Banquo's ghost in *Macbeth*, though R. V. Holdsworth has shown that Middleton had already had a ghost 'Sit...at the upper end of a tavern-table' in *The Black Book* (1604), before *Macbeth* was written.[1] And in Tourneur's *The Atheist's*

Tragedy (1609), Languebeau Snuffe, preparing to disguise himself as a ghost, 'pulls out a sheet, a hair [that is, a wig], and a beard' (4.3.55). On the other hand some ghosts are explicitly stated to wear costumes of the living, not of the dead; Hamlet's father is the most obvious example, and later Brachiano's Ghost in Webster's *The White Devil* (1612) appears 'In his leather cassock and breeches...boots, a cowl' (5.2.120). The idea that ghosts are 'pale' (*1 Henry VI*, 1.2.7) may refer either (or both) to the colour of their costume or to their bloodlessness; 'hollow' (*King John*, 3.4.84) suggests decay and would be more difficult to represent on the stage. In *The Knight of the Burning Pestle* (1607) a ghost's pallor is comically simulated when Jasper enters with 'his face mealed' (5.1.4)—a primitive kind of make-up.

Ghosts sometimes simply 'walk' (*Winter's Tale*, 5.1.63, 80) but are often thought of as having a particular style of movement; in *Julius Caesar* we hear of 'gliding ghosts' (1.3.63), and Macbeth compares Tarquin, with his 'ravishing strides', to a ghost (2.1.55–6). But Macbeth's comparison may be rather to Tarquin's efforts to remain unheard than to his gait; certainly in later stage tradition it became important for a ghost to move noiselessly: a nineteenth-century performer of Hamlet's deceased father was advised, 'if thou didst never that dear father play before, see that your boots or shoes creak not. Macready, when he played the Ghost to Charles Young's Hamlet, wore list or felt slippers under his mail-clad feet. You have no carpet on the platform, recollect.'[2] There is some evidence that the appearance of ghosts may have been enhanced atmospherically by the use of special effects. In *Locrine* (1591), for instance, is the stage direction *Enter the ghost of Corineus, with thunder and lightning* (5.4.0), and according to the Induction to *A Warning for Fair Women*, when the ghost cries 'Vindicta! Revenge, revenge!', 'a little rosin flasheth forth, like smoke out of a tobacco pipe, or a boy's squib' (lines 59–60). (Powdered rosin could be blown through a candle flame or torch to simulate lightning.[3]) Nevertheless, extant plays in which ghosts appear do not justify the assumption that they were conventionally accompanied by thunder and lightning. I have found no evidence for the use of music to increase the eeriness of a ghost's appearance, but this is not to deny the possibility.

Surviving allusions to the appearance of ghosts in Shakespeare's theatre certainly indicate distinctive styles of performance, but they cannot be regarded as prescriptive, and one has only to think of the difference between, say, the ghost of Hamlet's father and Banquo's ghost to realize that Shakespeare was not bound by predetermined convention, even though he may have drawn upon it. I want now to examine the dramaturgy of Shakespeare's ghost scenes in an attempt to discover how he made his ghosts ghostly and to consider some of the options open to those trying to reconstruct the early performance of those scenes. I shall assume the agreed basics of the Globe stage—a tiring-house wall with at least two apertures, a thrust stage which may have held a trap, and an upper acting level.

The first unequivocal ghosts in Shakespeare's plays are those in *Richard III*—eleven of them—and a fine body of men and women they are. They are associated with retribution, and their appearance is an important factor in making the closing scenes of *Richard III* the climax not only of the play but of the whole sequence of plays concerned with the Plantagenets, since they include the ghosts of two people—Henry VI and his son, Prince Edward—who have not appeared in the play and refer to events (such as the Battle of Tewkesbury) that reach backward into its pre-history. Shakespeare could have got the idea for these ghosts from either his reading or his playgoing. In *A Mirror for Magistrates* Richard says that he thought he saw the ghosts of all he had killed crying for vengeance around his tent, and in the anonymous *True Tragedy of Richard III* (surviving in a corrupt text printed in 1594) Richard has a long speech in which thirteen out of seventeen lines end in the word 'revenge', and in which he says

> Methinks their ghosts comes gaping for revenge,
> Whom I have slain in reaching for a crown.

The traditional association of ghosts with demands for revenge had been firmly established in English popular drama by the appearances of Revenge in person along with the ghost of the murdered Don Andrea in Kyd's *The Spanish Tragedy* (1587), and there are numerous other examples: in George Peele's *The Battle of Alcazar* (1589), for example, we find the direction 'Three ghosts crying Vindicta'—apparently just a sound effect—and in the anonymous *Locrine* (1591) the ghost of Albanect cries 'Revenge! Revenge for blood!' and exits declaiming 'Vindicta, vindicta' (3.6.41, 54). Pre-Shakespearean ghosts betray their Senecan origins and have all benefited from a classical education; as F. W. Moorman remarks, 'though the ghosts of Richard's victims are Senecan in character, in that they are represented as spirits of vengeance …they depart from Seneca's manner in making absolutely no reference to the underworld of classical mythology'.[4] This in itself may warn us against associating them with conventional modes of presentation, and so may their style of speech, for there is nothing to suggest that these ghosts should shriek, squeal, or scream. They are dream-spectres, and Shakespeare sets the scene carefully for them.

Before they appear the pace of the action has been slowing down, the focus of the audience's attention narrowing, but we have also been made increasingly conscious of the duality of the action and of the division of the characters of the play into two parties, one headed by Richard, the other by Richmond, each associated visually with one of the stage doors. A mood of concentration and stillness is set up in preparation for the ghosts' arrival. The mood could be either sustained or broken by the method of their appearance.

It is commonly assumed that convention would have required them to arrive from under the stage through a trap-door. So, for example, Julie Hankey, in her 'Plays in Performance' edition of *Richard III*, writes in her note on the entry: 'Elizabethan stage ghosts customarily rose up through the trap-door from under the stage, which represented the "kingdom of perpetual night"—where Queen Elizabeth knew King Edward had gone.'[5] It is true that in later performances they customarily did so, that the directions to Colley Cibber's popular adaptation (1700) require them to do so, and that one of them is shown emergent (or descendent) in Rowe's frontispiece (1709), where seven ghosts, some dressed in winding-sheets, most with open mouths as if in the act of speech, and all with uplifted hands, are lined up around an understandably grumpy-looking Richard sitting asleep, his head propped on his hand, at a table.

But early texts of Shakespeare's plays require the ghosts simply to 'enter', there is no reference in their speeches to the classical—or any other—underworld, and the absence of directions for covering noises such as would be provided by thunder combines with the inappropriateness of such effects to the tone of the scene to suggest that traps were not used. As Gary Taylor writes in the Oxford *Textual Companion*, use of a trap 'might suggest that they all (including the innocent princes and "holy Harry") came from hell, and would create problems with exits if one ghost were going back down the trap while another was rising'.[6] Each ghost is required to address both Richmond and Richard who sleep on the main stage. The effectiveness of their speeches would be enhanced if the ghosts were placed above the sleepers; for this reason the Oxford edition conjectures that they should appear on the upper level, an arrangement that would be worth experimenting with.

The effect of the ghosts' speeches is cumulative; their heightened formality of both speech and action resembles that of a play within the play. In the Folio text they enter in the order approximating to that of their deaths; in the Quarto (which may be closer to performance) the Princes come on before Hastings—who died first—perhaps because one of the boy actors had to reappear as Lady Anne and could scarcely do so instantly. Each is required to address first Richard, then Richmond, which suggests that, whether on the main stage or on an upper level, they would be placed centrally. The unreal formality of this episode is emphasized by the fact that the ghosts of Rivers, Grey, and Vaughan appear together and speak their last speech in chorus, and the ghosts of the Princes speak the whole of their eight-line speech in concert. There is nothing to indicate how they were costumed except that each speaks a few words of self-identification, which would be particularly helpful if they were ghostlily garbed. A declamatory, perhaps even 'wailing' method of delivery is suggested by their incantatory, repetitive style: every ghost except Grey ends its apostrophe to Richard with the words 'Despair and die' (and even Grey says 'Let thy soul despair'); their speeches to Richmond, by contrast, dwell on themes of life and success, stress the idea of 'comfort', and associate him with virtue and heavenly protection. As W. H. Clemen, who examines the style of this scene in great detail, remarks, 'the recurring pattern of incident and phrase emphasises the ritual and ceremonial, the supra-personal quality of the sequence and thereby heightens its effectiveness'.[7] The episode reaches a climax in Buckingham's speech—the longest—'in which rhyme and an accumulation of rhetorical devices help bring about a moment of heightened intensity at the close of their ghost scene' (p. 213). Although most of the speeches have been in the play's prevailing blank verse there have been occasional rhymes, and Buckingham's climactic speech ends with three couplets. All these stylistic features provide cues for the actors.

The ghosts in *Richard III* serve to exemplify awakening aspects of Richard's conscience and to offer supernatural confirmation of Richmond as God's agent in a virtuous task. So far from being Senecan figures of vengeance, they never mention revenge (though their presence may implicitly suggest the concept). The originality of their function may have been matched by an absence of conventionality in their presentation.

In *Julius Caesar* the ghost of Caesar is presented even more subjectively. Shakespeare read about the ghost in North's translation of Plutarch, where the tale is finely told:

> So, being ready to go into Europe, one night very late, as he was in his tent with a little light, thinking of weighty matters, he thought he heard one come in to him, and, casting his eye towards the door of his tent, that he saw a wonderful strange and monstrous shape of a body coming towards him, and said never a word. So Brutus boldly asked what he was, a god or a man, and what cause brought him thither. The spirit answered him, 'I am thy evil spirit, Brutus, and thou shalt see me by the city of Philippi.' Brutus, being no otherwise afraid, replied again unto it, 'Well, then I shall see thee again.' The spirit presently vanished away, and Brutus called his men unto him, who told him that they heard no noise, nor saw anything at all.

In dramatizing this incident Shakespeare is, as in *Richard III*, careful to arouse the audience's receptivity. The emotional tumult of Brutus's quarrel with Cassius is past, and the scene goes through successive slackenings of tension signalled initially by Brutus's call (like Richard before him) for 'a bowl of wine' (4.2.194, 220). Lucius brings wine and tapers, the reconciliation between the two leaders is strengthened by the news of Portia's death, and the need for sleep begins to be felt:

> The deep of night is crept upon our talk,
> And nature must obey necessity,
> Which we will niggard with a little rest.

Brutus calls for his nightgown and bids an affectionate farewell to Cassius, Titinius, and Messala. Harmony is succeeding discord, and is symbolized by Brutus's request for music. Lucius speaks 'drowsily'; Brutus, acknowledging that everyone is 'o'erwatched', calls on Varrus and Claudio to sleep in his tent. The focus is contracting, there is more talk of sleep, Lucius plays and sings himself to sleep, Brutus considerately takes the boy's instrument away from him and opens the book that he has found in the pocket of his own gown. Everything is done to concentrate attention on a single spot on the stage—the book that the seated Brutus is reading—before the ghost appears. Presumably the audience should see it first, before Brutus complains 'How ill this taper burns'—alluding to a superstition drawn, according to Moorman, from folklore and reflected also in Richard III's 'The lights burn blue' after his ghosts have gone. It seems quite certain that for this ghost to emerge head first from a trap would destroy all Shakespeare's careful preparation for the mystery of its appearance. Brutus at first doubts its reality:

> Ha! Who comes here?
> I think it is the weakness of mine eyes
> That shapes this monstrous apparition.

The word 'monstrous' comes from Plutarch—'a wonderful strange and monstrous shape of a body'—and Brutus's 'It comes upon me', echoing Plutarch's phrase 'coming towards him', suggests a walking rather than an ascending figure.[8]

If it is to do anything to live up to Brutus's description of it as a 'monstrous apparition' its appearance must differ from that of the living Caesar—and, incidentally, a ghostly sheet would make more difference to an actor in Elizabethan costume than to one wearing a toga. Its monstrousness might lie specifically in its resemblance to the murdered Caesar: it might even have been shown 'pointing unto his wounds' as Agamemnon's ghost was to do in Thomas Heywood's 2 *The Iron Age* (1612); though the absence of explicit allusion to the assassination, and of guilt in Brutus's reactions, makes this unlikely.

Brutus's brief conversation with the ghost is remarkably close to Plutarch, and the ghost's style of speech is not strongly characterized; indeed, it says nothing but 'Thy evil spirit, Brutus', 'To tell thee thou shalt see me at Philippi', and 'Ay, at Philippi'. The one major change is that whereas Plutarch's Brutus sees simply a 'spirit', Shakespeare's sees unequivocally the ghost of Caesar: this is not stated in the dialogue of their encounter, but the Folio's direction reads *Enter the Ghost of Caesar* and later Brutus is to speak of it as precisely that—'The ghost of Caesar'—seeing in its appearance a premonition of death (5.5.17).

The ghost departs quietly; and again there is no suggestion that machinery was involved. True, Brutus says, 'Now I have taken heart, thou vanishest', but the word 'vanish' is used in a later play—Barnabe Barnes's *The Devil's Charter* (1607)—in a direction that refers explicitly to an exit through one of the stage doors:

> *He goeth to one door of the stage, from whence he bringeth the ghost of* Candie *ghastly haunted by* Caesar *pursuing and stabbing it; these vanish in at another door.* (lines 1952–5)

Later theatre practice has tried to turn Caesar's ghost into a spectacular rather than a mysterious figure: in the eighteenth century, for instance, its promise to see Brutus at Philippi is fulfilled; in added lines it boasts 'my three and thirty wounds are now revenged' and sinks down a trap saying

> The Ides of March Remember—I must go.
> To meet thee on the burning Lake below.[9]

Some twentieth-century directors, too, have brought the ghost into the final scenes: J. R. Ripley writes that John Barton, at Stratford in 1968,

> gave his ghost, in addition to the tent visit, two further appearances. Just after the farewells of Brutus and Cassius, his wrathful presence crossed the battlefield, and finally, as Brutus lay dead at the end of the play, he stood, gleaming, over the body, the last thing visible as the lights faded.[10]

Treatments such as these bring the ghost closer to the Senecan revenge figure; but although the naming of Plutarch's 'spirit' as Caesar's ghost introduces an element at least of conscience—for this is the spirit of a murdered man appearing to his murderer—Shakespeare's ghost is essentially premonitory rather than vengeful, a fact that should be reflected in the style adopted for its performance.

Of all Shakespeare's ghosts, the most Senecan is the ghost of Hamlet's father, who comes straight from the underworld (and talks of it graphically) to incite his son to take vengeance on his murderer. We know that this ghost had appeared on the English stage before Shakespeare's play was written, and the loss of the earlier Hamlet play makes it particularly difficult to assess the originality of Shakespeare's treatment. Its most obvious extant dramatic forebear is Kyd's Ghost of Andrea, but Shakespeare's ghost is far more closely integrated into the dramatic structure. Unlike the ghosts in *Richard III*, *Julius Caesar*, and *Macbeth*, it is the ghost of a character we have not previously seen, and like Kyd's ghost it has things to tell us that are essential to the play's exposition, but its first appearance is atmospheric rather than expository, and again its entry is carefully prepared. As in *Richard III* and *Julius Caesar*, the characters to whom it first appears are seated; it is night time, but no one is asleep or even close to sleep. On the contrary, it is the duty of Barnardo and Marcellus to stay awake, and Horatio has been summoned specifically to see the Ghost. Its appearance is both expected and dreaded, and the first reference to it—'What, has this thing appeared again tonight?'—establishes it as something beyond ordinary human experience, and consequently difficult to name. Horatio, Marcellus tells us, refuses to believe in its existence, and Horatio confirms this with 'Tush, tush, 'twill not appear.' The dialogue moves into the narrative mode as Barnardo prepares to repeat his account of the Ghost's previous two appearances, creating a sense of expectation rather in the way that a conjurer will distract our attention from something he does not want us to see by telling us of something irrelevant to it; and expectation that we are about to hear a long story is increased by the way the narrator and his hearers settle down to it: 'Sit down a while', says Barnardo, and 'Well, sit we down', agrees Horatio. Where do they sit? Stools could have been set out in advance; or, if a throne of state was already in position (perhaps unlikely for a scene on the battlements), it could supply steps on which they might settle down; but perhaps they would sit on the front of the stage, focusing attention as far as possible from the tiring-house façade. W. J. Lawrence argued that the Ghost's entry must have been through a trap and that the three men would see it rising in front of them;[11] others have followed him (for example, Sprague: 'The Ghost's entrance, in Elizabethan productions, was unquestionably through a trap'[12]). Certainly anyone experimenting with a reconstructed Globe might wish to put this theory to the test. My own opinion is that it rests partly on a conditioned faith in the theatricality of the use of stage machinery for supernatural entries deriving from post-Restoration theatre practice and partly on an excessively condescending attitude to Elizabethan audiences; thus Lawrence writes: 'There can be little doubt that stage effects of this order were hugely delighted in by the mob and could have been omitted by the players only at their peril.'[13] More genuinely theatrical, to my mind, and more consonant with Shakespeare's use of an interrupted narrative, would have been the Ghost's silent appearance at one of the apertures in the tiring-house wall, initially unobserved by most of the audience as Barnardo directed their attention to 'yon same star that's westward from the pole'. In the text (Q2) closest to Shakespeare's manuscript the entry direction breaks Barnardo's narrative after the phrase 'The bell then beating one' ('tolling one' in Q1). Only the time that it takes to speak thirty-one lines has elapsed since we were told, ''Tis now struck twelve'—and modern productions, at least, often use this as a sound-effect to still the audience for the play's opening words—but since Marcellus is later to remark that the Ghost's previous appearances have been 'just at this dead hour' (1.1.64), it seems likely that an apparently coincidental stroke on a bell would have broken the listeners' concentration and signalled the Ghost's presence. Coleridge, commenting on Barnardo's 'elevation of style', remarks on 'the interruption of the narration at the very moment when we are most intensively listening for the sequel, and have our thoughts diverted from the dreaded sight in expectation of the desired yet almost dreaded tale—thus giving all the suddenness and surprise of the original appearance'.[14]

The dialogue seems to imply that (as we might expect) the onlookers do not approach particularly close to the Ghost, which does not speak to them; it would be worth experimenting here, too, with an upper-level entry, which might thereby be the more unobtrusive.

If there was indeed a convention of costuming ghosts so that they appeared to have risen directly from the grave, the convention must have been broken here, for the onlookers immediately remark on the Ghost's resemblance to 'the King that's dead' and on its 'fair and warlike form': after its departure Horatio will refer directly to its costume: 'Such was the very armour he had on | When he the ambitious Norway combated.' Even if the Ghost is dressed in everyday clothes, it must be visually impressive if there is to be any correlation between its appearance and what is said about it. It apparently looks grim—'So frowned he once . . .'—yet Horatio later claims to have discerned more sorrow than anger in its countenance, which was 'very pale'; it apparently carries a truncheon and must walk in a stately, dignified manner if it is to justify Barnardo's statement that 'it stalks away' and Marcellus's later reference to its 'martial stalk'. It is not impassive, for Marcellus can see that 'It is offended', presumably at the peremptoriness of Horatio's 'I charge thee speak'. (A recent Stratford ghost was walking towards Horatio at this point, then suddenly turned on its heel and stalked away rather more rapidly in a distinctly huffy manner.)

Horatio interprets this first appearance as premonitory—it 'bodes some strange eruption to our state'. After it has gone the onlookers sit again and Horatio embarks on an expository narration which again focuses attention and is again interrupted by the Ghost's appearance. The Folio omits Horatio's description of how, shortly before Julius Caesar's fall,

> The graves stood tenantless, and the sheeted dead
> Did squeak and gibber in the Roman streets.

Shakespeare may have felt that it was unfair to confront the actor playing a very different kind of ghost with such images; this ghost is not sheeted and does not 'squeak and gibber'; indeed its very silence on its first two appearances is among its most mysteriously impressive features. Here too it has been argued that the Ghost would have entered by the trap.[15] DeLuca's argument against this raises unnecessarily naturalistic considerations: 'Why should the Ghost have returned below at this time—especially when it is known to have been walking the battlements?'—but there is nothing in the text to suggest that its entrance is anything but unobtrusive, and it apparently approaches the onlookers—'lo where it comes again!'. Horatio declares that he will 'cross it', a daring thing to do since it was supposed that anyone crossing a ghost's path was asking for trouble. Or perhaps he means that he will make the sign of the cross.[16] The 'good' Quarto's stage direction *It spreads his armes* has caused problems. Dover Wilson among others took 'It' as a mistake for 'He', that is Horatio, but there is no evidence for this; Hibbard suggests that the Ghost's 'spreading of its arms is interpreted by Horatio as preparation for flight and leads to his cry, "Stay, illusion."'

The cock crows—an actual sound effect according to Q2's direction—before Horatio has finished questioning the Ghost, provoking its departure; W. J. Lawrence writes that 'from the producer's standpoint, no greater puzzle is presented anywhere in the entire Shakespeare canon than the difficulty of determining what was the exact "business" arranged for the situation developing out of Horatio's command, "Stop it, Marcellus."' The dialogue reads:

> MARCELLUS   Shall I strike at it with my partisan?
> HORATIO   Do, if it will not stand.
> BARNARDO   'Tis here.
> HORATIO   'Tis here.
> MARCELLUS   'Tis gone.

This is substantially the same in all three early texts. The good Quarto—the one nearest to Shakespeare's manuscript—has no direction for the Ghost's departure. The 'bad' Quarto directs *exit Ghost.* after Barnardo's "Tis here'; the Folio has a similar direction after Marcellus' "Tis gone'; but of course the placing of such directions in early printed texts is no reliable guide to the exact timing of the actions to which they refer.

Whether, as he wrote these lines, Shakespeare knew exactly what stage movement would accompany them we cannot tell. The closest parallel in the Shakespeare canon is probably the vanishing of the Witches in *Macbeth* (1.3.77–8: 'The earth hath bubbles, as the water has, | And these are of them. Whither are they vanished?') The fact that the *Hamlet* passage is exactly the same in all three early printed texts, two of them palpably influenced by performance, suggests that the lines were made to work. Lawrence, influenced by the actor Louis Calvert, proposes that 'a double for the Ghost was adroitly provided'. He imagines the first Ghost disappearing 'at one of the two widely separated entering doors' as Barnardo cried 'Tis here' while the double simultaneously 'came forth from the other door'—like figures on a weather clock—then 'took a step forward and flung itself down the suddenly yawning grave trap'.[17] Current beliefs about the area of the stage would require the Ghost to have taken a running jump rather than a single step to reach the grave trap, and Lawrence himself realizes that if the Ghost 'had been arrayed cap-à-pie in real armour, considerable danger would have attended the jump, a constant risk of bruises and broken bones', and then demonstrates with characteristic learning that imitation armour might have been used. McManaway, in an even more farcical scenario, imagined a single Ghost jumping into the trap—'to the delight of the groundlings'—as Marcellus tried to stop it, then immediately rising 'through another trap' only 'to vanish again through a trap to the bewilderment of all the onlookers',[18] and scarcely justifying Marcellus's later statement 'It faded on the crowing of the cock' (1.1.138) and Horatio's that 'it shrunk in haste away | And vanished from our sight' (1.1.219–20). It has even been suggested that at this point the ghosts were 'figures painted upon canvas, stretched over a wooden framework' which 'could have been mounted upon poles and merely thrust into view from beneath the stage through a narrow slot'.[19] Sabbatini describes the construction of such a device in his *Pratica di fabricar Scene e Machine ne' Teatri* (Ravenna, 1638, p. 20), and if its use in *Hamlet* seems improbable to us, that may serve as a useful reminder that the acceptable conventionalities of one generation may become the outdated absurdities of the next. To me it seems that Shakespeare has provided Marcellus's offer to strike at the Ghost with his partisan, as well as the dispute between Barnardo and Horatio about the Ghost's whereabouts, as a cover for the Ghost's quick exit through a stage-door or arras.[20] (Similar, though wordless, action is needed at a later moment in the play when Hamlet escapes from his captors on 'Hide fox, and all after': 4.2.29–30.) But Lawrence's theory has appealed to some modern directors; indeed Peter Hall used three outsize ghosts in his 1965 Stratford production. Certainly the dispute leaves ample opportunity for experimentation in a reconstructed performance, and it raises the fundamental question of principle as to the degree to which actors attempting reconstructions of early performances should feel free to elaborate on the evidence supplied by the early texts. The scholarly nature of the enterprise would appear to dictate an austere rejection of stage business for which there is no evidence, yet it is difficult to believe that the Elizabethans would have been similarly austere. If, to cite an example from *Hamlet* itself, only the 1604 Quarto and the Folio texts had survived—as might easily have happened—we should lack the evidence supplied by the 1603 Quarto that Ophelia entered *playing on a Lute* in her mad scene.

By the time the Ghost makes its third appearance we are more accustomed to it, and its entrance is less impressively built up. We are on the battlements, 'it is very cold', and the time 'draws near the season | Wherein the spirit held his wont to walk.' (1.4.6–7). Horatio sees it first—'Look, my lord, it comes' (line 19), and there is no evidence for (or against) the use of a trap. The Ghost's impressiveness is created for us by the vehemence of Hamlet's reaction (in the speech beginning 'Angels and ministers of grace defend us!', lines 20–38), by its continuing silence in the face of Hamlet's demands and questions, by the 'courteous action' (line 41) with which it repeatedly—at least four times—but still silently beckons Hamlet to follow it, and by Horatio's fear that it may 'tempt' Hamlet 'toward the flood', change itself into 'some other horrible form', and drive Hamlet mad, culminating in Horatio's and Marcellus's unsuccessful attempts to hold Hamlet back before he throws them off— 'By heaven, I'll make a ghost of him that lets me' (line 62)—and leaves the stage with the Ghost (even Lawrence did not suggest a trap for their joint exit).

On their re-entry, doubtless by a different stage-door, the Ghost quickly satisfies Hamlet's and our desire to hear him speak. Responsibility for the impression that he makes passes now from the director to the actor. An adequate analysis of the style of the Ghost's speeches would form a study on its own; suffice it here to note that their formality, their long sentence structures and frequent enjambments, their intensity of utterance and the momentousness of their content cumulatively both justify and are enhanced by the Ghost's earlier silences.

The Ghost's final words in this sequence are (in the Folio):

Adieu, adieu, Hamlet. Remember me.

After having for so long been seen but not heard, he will shortly be heard but not seen as he calls upon Hamlet from the cellarage, so here if anywhere there might be a case for his descending down a trap. His final words vary in the Quartos and the Folio; Lawrence, accepting Q2's

Adieu, adieu, adieu! Remember me

suggests that the line 'was uttered while standing on a trap, and that with each *adieu* the spectre sank a little, and disappeared rapidly on saying, "Remember me."'[21] This is shown happening in drawings by C. Walter Hodges in the New Cambridge edition of the play,[22] and Harold Jenkins supports the use of a trap here. Varying Lawrence's suggestion, DeLuca proposes that 'The ghost may actually descend a portable stair well moved up under the trap and take one step down as it utters each of the syllables of the final line'.[23] To me, either of these suggestions would seem more appropriate to a travesty of *Hamlet* than to a serious production, yet there is no way of firmly refuting them. I find more sympathetic G. R. Hibbard's note: 'The Ghost's lingering farewell sounds far better suited to one making his exit through a door than to one about to disappear through a trap.'[24] And in practical terms, as he points out, the actor 'has ample time in which to make his way into the cellarage from backstage before he has to speak again...'. It will be interesting, in a reconstructed Globe, to know whether the Ghost's cries from the cellarage will be muffled or resonated by the wooden sounding chamber.

The Ghost's final appearance is in the Closet scene (3.4), dressed, so the 1603 Quarto tells us, *in his night gowne*, which appears to mean some kind of dressing gown. By this point in the play the Ghost is, as it were, becoming internalized. The fact that it is not seen by Gertrude might be held simply to indicate her guilt. Partial sighting of a ghost also occurs in Thomas Heywood's 2 *Edward IV* (1599), though there innocence is the reason that a messenger fails to see the ghost of Friar Anselm:

thy untainted soul
Cannot discern the horrors that I do. (Sig. V2v)

But it seems significant that it is only at the height of Hamlet's supremely eloquent and passionate invective against Claudius that the Ghost appears, as if it were truly, as Gertrude claims, 'the very coinage of [Hamlet's] brain' (line 128). (See Anthonisen: 'what we see here described is an episode of visual hallucinosis that hardly could be represented any better'. Anthonisen also remarks 'the difference between Hamlet's hallucinatory experience in his last encounter with the ghost and the "epidemiological", shared experiences at the opening of the play'.[25]) Still, there is no question that Shakespeare intended it to be represented objectively. Again Lawrence argues for the use of a trap, and again a sudden appearance through a door or arras would seem more appropriate, if only because the precise timing of an entry in mid-sentence, on 'A king of shreds and patches—', would be virtually impossible to achieve by hand-operated machinery. (It seems astonishing, nevertheless, that as recently as 1973 DeLuca could object to the use of the trap on the grounds that 'Gertrude's closet must be in the upper levels of the castle, meaning that the Ghost must rise through the floors and walls of several stories of the castle'.[26]) Even Lawrence admitted that the Ghost should walk off, on the evidence of Hamlet's

> Look how it steals away.
> My father, in his habit as he lived.
> Look where he goes even now out at the portal. (lines 125–7)

As A. C. Sprague put it, 'If the Ghost really did descend here—out of habit, as it were—one can only say that he should have known better.'[27]

The hallucinatory elements in the final appearance of the Ghost of Hamlet's father seem premonitory of the last unequivocal ghost in the Shakespeare canon, that of Banquo in *Macbeth*. We have already seen Macbeth experiencing, and analysing, a hallucination,

> a false creation
> Proceeding from the heat-oppressèd brain. (2.1.38–9)

We have inhabited a world in which the boundaries between natural and supernatural are easily crossed and uncertain of identification. We have witnessed the murder of Banquo and moved with ironic speed to a scene of festivity for which a table and stools must be set. Macbeth has told us that 'Both sides of the table are even', which presumably means that both sides are full (though G. K. Hunter takes Macbeth to refer to the guests' 'even' (equivalent) response to the Queen[28]). He himself will sit 'i'th'-midst', which I take to mean at one end of the table. We have seen and heard Macbeth in surreptitious conversation with the First Murderer, who has said of Banquo

> Safe in a ditch he bides,
> With twenty trenchèd gashes on his head,
> The least a death to nature.

A degree of stylization is inescapable in the presentation of this scene. The on-stage characters must ignore the Murderer's presence—as they must later ignore the Ghost's—and must seem not to hear his conversation with Macbeth; it would seem best to play this episode close to the stage-door by which the Murderer comes and goes. After he has left, Lady Macbeth urges her husband to 'give the cheer', and we have the direction *Enter the Ghost of Banquo, and sits in Macbeth's place*. If the Ghost enters by a door it must be a different one from that through which the Murderer has left, and Macbeth must be looking away from it as the Ghost enters and sits with its back to him—for as Ross invites him to sit, all Macbeth can see is that 'The table's full'. The place reserved for him is occupied by a ghost; it is the ghost of an unburied man, so there is no naturalistic reason why it should wear grave clothes, though it might well be made up in such a way as to suggest the 'twenty trenchèd gashes' and to justify Macbeth's 'Never shake thy gory locks at me'. Its ghostliness is created principally by its trick of sitting in Macbeth's place, its silence, and the vehemence of Macbeth's reactions combined with the bewilderment of the other onlookers. It may reasonably 'glide', 'stalk', or move 'like a ghost' (as Macbeth has earlier said) 'With Tarquin's ravishing strides', but traps, thunder, or lightning effects seem inappropriate to a ghost that can create so devastating an effect on Macbeth by its mere presence and a shake of its head. Its exit is unmarked in the Folio, but must occur between Macbeth's 'If thou canst nod, speak, too!' (line 69) and his 'If I stand here, I saw him' (line 73). In Davenant's adaptation of 1663 *The Ghost descends*. The direction deserves respect, since Davenant's printing of the songs shows that he must have had access to a manuscript of the King's Men; still, he may have adapted its staging as much as its dialogue.

The Ghost enters for a second time as Macbeth drinks a health to Banquo and wishes for his presence at the feast. This second appearance of the Ghost is one of the few moments in Shakespeare's plays of which we have an eyewitness account of a performance in the Globe itself. Simon Forman saw *Macbeth* there on 20 April 1611 and wrote:

> The next night, beinge at supper with his noble men whom he had bid to a feaste to the which also Banco should haue com, he began to speake of Noble Banco, and to wish that he wer ther. And as he thus did, standing vp to drincke a Carouse to him, the ghoste of Banco came and sate down in his cheier behind him. And he turninge About to sit down Again sawe the goste of Banco, which fronted him so, that he fell into a great passion of fear and fury....[29]

The Folio's direction for the Ghost's entry is merely *Enter Ghost*; Davenant has *The Ghost of Banquo rises at his* [Macbeth's] *feet*. Perhaps a trap was used in the Globe, too, but Forman's 'came and sate down...' does not imply this. There is no indication to the effect that the Ghost should sit on its second appearance, but equally no reason why it should not do so. As Forman does not describe the Ghost's first appearance, when it unquestionably does sit, we may allow for the possibility that he has conflated the two, but his account deserves to be taken seriously, and is a testimony to the power of the actor (presumably Burbage) playing Macbeth; as Dennis Bartholomeusz remarks, 'The reactions observed, fear, the impulse to retreat, and fury, the impulse to attack, indicate that the Elizabethan [sic] actor was bringing complex feelings to the surface.'[30] We cannot claim a certain allusion to *Macbeth* in the passage in *The Knight of the Burning Pestle* (1607) in which Jasper, disguised as a ghost, threatens the Merchant:

> When thou art at thy table with thy friends,
> Merry in heart, and filled with swelling wine,
> I'll come in midst of all thy pride and mirth,
> Invisible to all men but thyself,
> And whisper such a sad tale in thine ear
> Shall make thee let the cup fall from thy hand,
> And stand as mute and pale as Death itself. (5.5.22–8)

Still, the business of dropping the cup sounds entirely natural and has been adopted by many subsequent actors.[31]

Modern productions frequently leave this ghost to the audience's imagination— an idea that goes back at least to the mid-eighteenth century.[32] Those that bring it on often engineer matters so that the audience is unaware of its presence until Macbeth sees it, but this would have been difficult on Shakespeare's stage and does not seem consonant with the Folio direction. If we wish to see the play as Shakespeare's audiences saw it, Banquo's ghost must enter in full view of the audience and must be as visible to us, and to Macbeth, as the Murderer who has killed him. Earlier in the play, before Macbeth had embarked on his life of crime, he had hallucinated a dagger; now the presence that accuses him should seem as real as the Witches that had tempted him.

It is perhaps too easy to assume that the apparent simplicities of the Elizabethan stage mean that a presentation of the plays in an Elizabethan style will be a comparatively straightforward matter. But although editors of the plays have examined their dialogue with minute care they have rarely paid equal attention to their stage directions, and as a consequence many of the problems related to their staging have gone unexamined. This is a result in part of the study of Shakespeare's plays as literary rather than as theatrical artefacts, and in part a recognition of the fact that the plays belong to the theatre of all ages subsequent to Shakespeare's own, and that later performances will require staging methods different from those of Shakespeare's time. Perhaps my discussion of Shakespeare's ghosts will suggest that the detailed examination of the texts necessitated by reconstructed performances is likely to throw up many theatrical cruces just as detailed examination of the plays' dialogue has thrown up literary cruces. An examination of the plays in the light of theatrical conventions of Shakespeare's time may be illuminating but is likely to show too that Shakespeare departed from convention, and re-moulded it, as often as he followed it. Reconstructed performances are bound to be experimental, and their results provisional; but they will be no less exciting for that.

18

Staging Shakespeare's Apparitions and Dream Visions

Introduction

The First Annual Shakespeare Globe Lecture was held in St Etheldreda's Church, Ely Place, London, 7 March 1990 in memory of Professor Philip Brockbank, who had been Chairman of the International Academic Council advising Shakespeare's Globe.

The evening began with 'Staging Shakespeare's Apparitions and Dream Visions' a lecture given by Professor Stanley Wells, Professor Brockbank's successor as Director of the Shakespeare Institute.

Following the lecture, Sam Wanamaker read two extracts from *Richard II* and the evening concluded with 'Brockbeasts: A Menagerie of Beast Verses by Brock', read by Barbara Leigh-Hunt and Richard Pasco.

Patrick Spottiswoode
Director, Globe Education

It is an honour for me to be invited to give the first Annual Shakespeare Globe lecture, and I am particularly happy that it is to be dedicated to the memory of Philip Brockbank, my predecessor as Director of the Shakespeare Institute and a good friend to me in his late years—years in which his courage in the face of debilitating illness, his unfailing intellectual vigour, his wit, his courtesy, and his constant determination to make the best possible use of the time left to him were an inspiration and an example to all who encountered him. His own predecessor in this office, Terence Spencer, was among the first academics to support Sam Wanamaker's plans to reconstruct Shakespeare's Globe in Southwark; Philip was no less enthusiastic for the project, which owes much to him. He was a great believer in what he called festive scholarship, and he was a practitioner of literature as well as of literary criticism, so it seems fitting that we should pay tribute equally to scholarship, to literature, and to the festive spirit.

When Sam Wanamaker's dream comes true, when the reconstructed Globe is a reality, we shall have to learn to use it. We shall need to think in the closest practical detail about the staging requirements of the plays we want to perform in it, and about the performance styles that are appropriate. We shall have to try to establish both normative performance styles and exceptional ones. The normative style will be for the bulk of each play—and it will vary according to the distinct demands of each individual play. The exceptional styles will be for those parts that require to be set off from the norm. The clues for this lie frequently within the literary texture of the plays themselves. In *Love's Labour's Lost*, *A Midsummer Night's Dream*, and *Hamlet* Shakespeare clearly sets off the plays within the plays by employing distinct verbal styles for them, and these styles call out for an equal degree of difference in the manner in which they are projected. Similarly some of Shakespeare's characters need to be acted in a manner that will set them off from their fellows—we may think of the fools, the clowns, the witches, and the ghosts.

It is true that these matters have not gone uninvestigated by editors and other scholars. But in working on an edition of Shakespeare's Complete Works[1] I became increasingly conscious that editors have tended to neglect considerations of staging, with the result that the texts from which actors work offer them little help in the areas that are most important to them. This is partly because editors have tended to be preoccupied with literary values and so have concentrated on the dialogue at the expense of the stage directions. Perhaps also it has resulted from their knowledge that directors and actors using their texts would be engaging with the theatre of their own time, not in historical reconstruction, and so would be interested almost exclusively in the dialogue, and not particularly concerned with the details of the plays' original staging. Though this may be a more creditable explanation of the neglect of theatrical values, it rests on a fallacious assumption. The meaning of a play lies not simply in its dialogue, in the words spoken, but in its entire action, the complete dramatic experience. Inevitably this varies from production to production, performance to performance, and no editor or scholar can hope to provide more than a fraction of the evidence relating either to a play's original performance or to later performances. But if the task of an editor or, more generally, of any dramatic scholar is to retrieve the past, to create a sense of the dramatic experience that lies behind the surviving documents, then it is the editor's task to endeavour to investigate in detail the staging methods implied by the play's dialogue and action.

This belief is fundamental to the entire Globe enterprise, which has always represented an acknowledgement of the necessary collaboration between the worlds of scholarship and the practical theatre. This was the ideal that led Allardyce Nicoll to found the Shakespeare Institute in Stratford-upon-Avon at the time that his friend Sir Barry Jackson became Director of the Shakespeare Memorial Theatre. It is not a belief in mere antiquarianism. Neither I nor many of my colleagues would be interested in supporting the Globe enterprise if there lay behind it the belief that

Shakespeare's plays should only ever be performed in circumstances as close as possible to those for which they were conceived. What I do believe is that scholars and theatre folk may learn more about those plays by exploring their original staging as well as their vocabulary, their imagery, their topical allusiveness, their symbolism, and their characterization. The provision of a reconstructed Globe with a high claim to authenticity will provide a laboratory in which such explorations can be conducted more rigorously than ever before.

A necessary prelude to theatrical investigation is a re-examination of the texts themselves with practical considerations in mind. I have chosen two related examples of the type of scene that needs to be set off from the norm, scenes involving apparitions and dream visions. These take us from one of Shakespeare's *Henry VI* plays, on which Philip wrote his thesis, to the late romances, about which he wrote and spoke with particular sensitiveness and subtlety. These scenes tend not to appear in the central Globe plays but in ones written before the Lord Chamberlain's Men acquired the Globe, or in plays written by the time the Company had acquired the Blackfriars playhouse, whose facilities may have influenced the staging implied by the texts, or, in *Macbeth*, in a text that gives every indication of having been adapted after its first performance. So I shall not discuss the plays in the light of the stage resources at the Globe but will look at them more generally in relation to agreed features of the theatres of Shakespeare's time, drawing attention to particular problems as they arise.

Shakespeare's ghosts may be best defined as spirits that appear of their own accord. Apparitions, in contrast, are spirits that have to be summoned, most often from the nether regions or, as Glyndŵr puts it in 1 *Henry IV*, from 'the vasty deep' (3.1.51). What is probably the earliest spectral scene in Shakespeare is also one of the most elaborate, and investigation of its staging is complicated by the survival of divergent texts which may be more or less closely related to actual theatre practice. The play known in the First Folio of 1623 as 2 *Henry VI* is printed there in a text that seems to derive primarily from its author's working papers, or possibly from a fair copy of such papers, but in any case representing the play before it had been put into rehearsal. A different, and much shorter, version had appeared in 1594 as *The First Part of the Contention betwixt the Two Famous Houses of York and Lancaster*, presumably the title by which it was presented in London's theatres. Most scholars over the past sixty years have believed this to be a reported text, based on performance, which may therefore represent, however imperfectly, a later stage in the play's composition than the later-printed Folio text. This hypothesis is supported by investigation of the staging requirements of the two versions.

In Act 1, scene 4 a spirit is conjured up with elaborate ritual and to the accompaniment of impressive effects of thunder and lightning. The 'cunning witch' Margery Jordan and 'Roger Bolingbroke the conjuror' have promised to show to Dame Eleanor, the ambitious Duchess of Gloucester:

A spirit raised from depth of under ground
That shall make answer to such questions
As by your grace shall be propounded him. (1.2.75)

In the Folio the ritual is referred to as an 'exorcism', and the OED cites this among its examples of the improper use of the word to mean 'The action of calling up spirits; the ceremonies observed for that purpose; conjuration'. It is presented very much as a performance, and forms a kind of miniature play within the play with Hume and the Duchess as an on-stage audience, witnessing the ceremony from 'aloft'—clearly the dramatist had in mind a stage with an upper level.

Whereas in the Folio the only word relating to the Duchess's elevated position is 'aloft' (which occurs both in the dialogue and in a stage direction), in the quarto she says 'I will stand upon this tower here' (1.4.3), and the direction says '*She goes up to the tower*'. The word 'tower' may merely indicate an imaginative fictionalizing of the action on the part of a reporter, but it assumes potential significance in the light of Herbert Berry's recent study of documents relating to the Red Lion playhouse at Mile End and dating from 1567.[2] They are exceptional in that they specify all the main dimensions for the stage—five feet high, forty feet long, thirty feet broad—but their most intriguing feature is the provision of a turret thirty feet high from the ground and twenty-five feet from the stage. Berry writes, 'Within, it was to have a "convenyent" floor "of Tymber & boords" seven feet under its top. The top seven feet, that is, were to be a room.'[3] This raises the interesting possibility that the word 'tower' in the theatrical text of *The Contention* is a direct allusion to a feature of the building in which the play was acted.

Arranging the encounter, Hume has told the Duchess that the spirit 'shall make answer to such questions | As by your grace shall be propounded him', and Eleanor has promised to 'Think upon the questions' (1.2.80). In the Folio, Bolingbroke asks the questions with no indication of how he has come to know what it is that he should ask; the quarto, interestingly, supplies the gap: at the beginning of the scene Eleanor says, 'Here, Sir John, take this scroll of paper here, | Wherein is writ the questions you shall ask' (1.4.1). It is easy to see this as the kind of clarification of action that might have been made during rehearsals.

In the play's chronicle sources the Duchess's 'aiders and counsellors...had devised an image of wax, representing the King, which by their sorcery a little and little consumed, intending thereby in conclusion to waste and destroy the King's person and so to bring him death'.[4] In the play the Duchess certainly desires the King's death but there is no suggestion that she is trying to bring it about in this scene, which is very similar to that of the apparitions in *Macbeth* in that the spirit is asked questions about the future and replies to them in riddling terms. It is clear from the Folio that the dramatist expected properties to be brought on in order to enhance the impressiveness of the occasion. Told that the Duchess 'expects performance of your promises', Bolingbroke replies, 'Master Hume, we are therefore provided' (1.4.3); and later the Duke of York commands, 'Lay hands upon these traitors and their trash' (1.4.41). The quarto makes no direct reference to the use of properties, but there is no doubt that a ritual of conjuration is called for in each version, or that the episode calls for a heightened style of performance. Margery Jordan is required to prostrate herself and *'grovel on the earth'* (the quarto's wording is *'She lies downe upon her face'*), and Bolingbroke is given an impressive conjuration:

> Deep night, dark night, the silent of the night,
> The time of night when Troy was set on fire,
> The time when screech-owls cry and bandogs howl,
> And spirits walk, and ghosts break up their graves—
> That time best fits the work we have in hand. (1.4.17)

Bolingbroke impresses himself enough to fear that he may have unduly disturbed the Duchess: 'Madam, sit you', he says, 'and fear not', assuring her that 'Whom we raise | We will make fast within a hallowed verge' (1.4.22), i.e. within a circle to which the spirit will be confined. Characteristically of a pre-performance text, the Folio's direction for the ceremony is permissively vague: *'Here do the ceremonies belonging, and make the circle, Bolingbroke or Southwell reads, "Conjuro te etc."* It thunders and lightens terribly, then the spirits riseth.' The quarto, though curter, is also more specific: *'Bolingbroke makes a circle'*; this direction precedes the conjuration, which may represent the way it was performed.

The *'ceremonies'* called for by the Folio direction are not precisely specified, and according to the Folio either Bolingbroke or Southwell reads *'Conjuro te etc.'*; Bolingbroke has instructed Southwell 'read you' (1.4.13), so the Oxford editor assigns the function to him.[5] The 'etc.' would have to be filled in in performance. There seems to be at least a remnant of it in the quarto's lines that replace Bolingbroke's Folio invocation:

> Dark night, dread night, the silence of the night,
> Wherein the Furies masque in hellish troops,
> Send up I charge you from Sosetus' lake
> The spirit Askalon to come to me
> To pierce the bowels of this centric earth,
> And hither come in twinkling of an eye.
> Askalon, ascende, ascende.[6] (1.4.14)

We know something from other sources of the paraphernalia that would conventionally be employed in such conjurations. The conjuror—like Prospero in *The Tempest*—would put on 'magic robes' which might be black or coloured, and which would often be decorated with mystical signs. He would carry a wand or staff. In *The Discovery of Witchcraft* Reginald Scot directs that 'If you wish to make a contract with hell', it is written in the Book *Sanctum Regum*:

> Two days before the conjuration you must cut a bough from a wild hazel tree with a new knife that has never before been used. It must be a bough which has never carried fruit, and it must be cut at the very moment when the sun rises over the horizon.[7]

In the theatre, we may take it, any old stick would do but it would have to be substantial enough to be struck upon the ground in the ritualistic gestures needed to summon up the spirits. With the wand Bolingbroke would trace a circle, as both the quarto and the Folio texts require, in order to circumscribe the limits within which the spirit could move; other figures, such as a triangle or two triangles forming a star, might be inscribed within the circle—there is plenty of scope for ritualistic mumbo jumbo. The conjuror might carry a vessel of incense which he would burn on a fire placed within the circle and would produce a book from which to declaim his spell. These are the properties that the Duke of York, breaking in at the end of the ceremony, will order to be confiscated.

Shakespeare's ghost scenes seem to have used a stage trap rarely, if at all. Here, however, use of the trap seems clearly called for. Both the quarto and the Folio agree that the spirit '*riseth*' to the accompaniment of the thunder and lightning that frequently accompanied use of the trap, in part no doubt to distract attention from the creaking of its machinery. Thunder could be imitated either by the battering of drums or by the rolling of stones or cannonballs down a thunder run—'Are there no stones in heaven but what serves for the thunder?' asks Othello (5.2.241). The call for lightning would make its customary demands upon the theatre's pyrotechnics experts. Elizabethan dramatists seem to have assumed that characters consigned to the underworld spent their time in improving their classical education; here, for instance, the spirit has at least a smattering of Latin—'*Ad sum*' it says as it rises, in the Folio text (1.4.24), and in the quarto it responds to the call '*ascende*' (1.4.20). It speaks in an oracular fashion that would need to be reflected in the actor's mode of delivery. Its disappearance again clearly calls for the trap—'Descend to darkness, and the burning lake' (1.4.39) says Bolingbroke in the Folio, which again has a direction for '*Thunder and lightning*'. This is followed in the Folio only by '*Exit Spirit*', but the quarto makes the mode of exit more explicit, specifying '*He sinkes downe againe*', and supplying Bolingbroke with additional lines in pseudo-classical style which the Oxford editor suggests may have been 'added in rehearsal to the prompt-book to cover the spirit's descent'.[8] In the quarto too Bolingbroke instructs 'Rise, Jordan, rise, and stay thy charming spells' (1.4.36), which may suggest that Margery Jordan should be seen to be in at least partial control of the spirit, like a spiritualist medium, throughout its appearance. Our view of these episodes, and consequently the tone of their presentation, would be affected if we had any reason to suppose that genuine witchcraft was not being employed; but, although later in the play Margery Jordan is condemned to be 'burned to ashes' and her accomplices to be 'strangled on the gallows' (2.3.7), there is nothing to suggest that their witchcraft was faked.

The scene in *The Contention* is an obvious forerunner of the better-known scene in *Macbeth* in which apparitions appear at Macbeth's behest. In this later play the boundaries between the human and the spirit world are less clear. Margery Jordan is described in the Folio direction and speech prefixes as a witch, and presumably her costume and manner should do something to suggest this; otherwise she is scarcely characterized. The Witches in *Macbeth*, on the other hand, have been vividly presented to us as creatures 'That look not like th'inhabitants o'th'earth | And yet are on't' (1.3.39). Margery Jordan was a human medium enabling Bolingbroke to raise a spirit to whom he could address the written questions that Eleanor had given him in advance; Macbeth poses his questions directly to the Witches, and we have seen them engaged in incantations before he arrives to question them. It is as if they themselves had enough supernatural power to know that he has already said 'I will tomorrow, | And betimes I will, to the weird sisters' (3.5.131). If we take it that the two songs from Middleton's *The Witch* whose first lines are cited in the Folio text of *Macbeth* were presented in full—and really they are quasi-operatic scenas rather than simply songs—then at this point the Witches have already been seen in the company of unambiguously otherworldly spirits. In any case, they have certainly been seen performing 'A deed without a name' (4.1.65) as they cast gruesome ingredients into the cauldron at the opening of the scene, before Macbeth arrives. The cauldron may have been carried on to the stage at the opening of the scene; if so, it is likely to have been placed directly on the trap, since it is later to descend. Alternatively, and more probably, it may have arisen, with or without the Witches, from a trap.

Although the episode that follows resembles the incantation scene in *The Contention*, it is more fully integrated, less of a play within the play. In the earlier play a surrogate had spoken '*Conjuro te*' on the Duchess's behalf while she watched '*aloft*'. Here Macbeth himself has a marvellously eloquent speech beginning similarly 'I conjure you' (4.1.66) which he addresses directly to the Witches, as if the spirits that will supply the answers to his questions were extensions of themselves. In terms of stagecraft his conjuration serves, like the 'ceremonies' of *The Contention*, to compel the audience's heightened attention, arousing expectation even beyond that which the stage can provide:

> I conjure you by that which you profess,
> Howe'er you come to know it, answer me.

Though you untie the winds and let them fight
Against the churches, though the yeasty waves
Confound and swallow navigation up,
Though bladed corn be lodged and trees blown down,
Though castles topple on their warders' heads,
Though palaces and pyramids do slope
Their heads to their foundations, though the treasure
Of nature's germens tumble all together
Even till destruction sicken, answer me
To what I ask you. (4.1.66)

There is still further heightening with the Witches' spell as they add more horrible ingredients to their cauldron, but after this the apparitions themselves are liable to appear anti-climactic. The cauldron provides a focal point for the audience's attention, and presumably the apparitions were contrived to rise either through a trap behind the cauldron or from within the cauldron itself, by means of a false bottom providing access from under the stage.[9] The Folio simply names the apparitions before they speak, not marking an entry, but each is heralded by thunder and after speaking '*descends*'. Considering the nature of the apparitions—'*an armed head*', '*a bloody child*', and '*a child crowned, with a tree in his hand*'—it seems likely that they were represented by artificial figures manipulated, and ventriloquially assisted, from the cellarage: work for the property makers.[10] By now Shakespeare has thrown off the classical colouring that was part of his Senecan heritage in 2 *Henry VI*, but the spirits in *Macbeth* are oracular in utterance in a manner that is far more central to the scheme of this play than in *The Contention* and that leads us forward to the play's resolution.

After the apparitions have descended Macbeth again addresses the Witches as if the apparitions had merely been their mouthpieces:

Tell me, if your art
Can tell so much, shall Banquo's issue ever
Reign in this kingdom? (4.1.117)

And now the cauldron itself sinks—'Why sinks that cauldron?' asks Macbeth—to the accompaniment of another covering noise, the shrill sound of 'Hautboys' (the closest the Scottish play comes to using bagpipes) and we have the direction '*A show of eight kings, the last with a glass in his hand; and Banquo*'. This is an editorial variant on the Folio's '*A show of eight Kings, and Banquo last, with a glasse in his hand*', which is at odds with Macbeth's subsequent speech. There is no telling how this was originally staged. Certainly we should be made to feel that the Witches are responsible for this 'show' and that it remains to some degree under their control, as if they were uttering commands to spirits who bring it to pass: 'Show...Show...Show' they say before it appears, 'Show his eyes and grieve his heart, | Come like shadows, so depart' (4.1.123); and during the show Macbeth addresses the Witches: 'Filthy hags, | Why do you show me this?' (4.1.131).

The sinking of the cauldron sounds like a preparation for the use of the trap for the appearance of the kings. If so, they seem likely to have emerged one by one— there is nothing to suggest that stage traps of this period were big enough to carry nine actors simultaneously. It would surely have been far too cumbersome for the trap to descend and rise again nine times, so perhaps the actors could have used a ladder in the cellarage to climb up on to the stage one after another. Some commentators suppose that the show of kings would have taken place on the inner stage—Cranford Adams, for instance, imagines them walking 'in single file through the passageway behind the study, coming successively into view as each moves at a dignified pace past an opening in the middle of the rear wall of the study made by drawing aside the rear hangings'—but this depends on an outmoded concept of the 'inner stage'.[11] This seems to be denied by Macbeth's command to Banquo, 'Down', and would have required a regrouping of the characters already on stage that would have been difficult to motivate.

Certainly the kings must eventually all be on stage at once; as Beckerman remarks, 'The apparitions do not pass over the stage immediately, but assemble upon it until Banquo's ghost "points at them for his"'.[12] This would impose a strain on the company's manpower unless they were all played by actors who played other roles or by supernumeraries. This in turn would encourage anonymity of costuming—Macbeth identifies one of the apparitions as a king by his crown and another by his 'gold-bound brow' (4.1.130), so all that is needed for each of them is a cloak and a crown. It is interesting, and slightly curious, that Macbeth's first words are 'Thou art too like the spirit of Banquo' (4.1.128), although the original direction explicitly states that Banquo appears last. There is a contradiction, too, between the original direction's 'Banquo last, with a glass in his hand', and Macbeth's words 'And yet the eighth appears, who bears a glass | Which shows me many more' (4.1.135). The direction probably reveals Shakespeare's original intention, revised (during composition?) as he felt the need for 'the blood-baltered Banquo' to smile upon Macbeth and point at the ghosts 'for his'. The 'glass' may be not a mirror but rather (as Watkins and Lemmon put it) 'the crystal ball traditionally used for divination, like the "glassy globe" devised by Merlin for King Ryence in The Faerie Queene (Book III, Canto II, 21)'.[13]

There is even more uncertainty about how the apparitions and Banquo should leave the stage than how they should enter. Beckerman comments that 'The lines that follow being of doubtful authenticity, they offer no assistance in determining how the apparitions depart, though nothing in the text conflicts with the conventional manner of staging ghost scenes'.[14] Whether there was a 'conventional manner of staging ghost scenes' is arguable and in any case the authenticity of the lines is irrelevant to the contribution they make to our understanding of the play's Jacobean staging (though perhaps not to its first staging, which is Beckerman's prime concern). Beckerman's remarks elsewhere imply that he does not think the trap would have been used: 'there is no evidence that the stage machinery was employed in the staging of ghost scenes at the Globe'.[15] Peter Thomson also discounts the use of traps for the original staging of *Macbeth* at the first Globe, taking the Folio's demands for stage machinery to arise from adaptation of the play for the Blackfriars or the second Globe.[16] Departure through one or more of the stage-doors seems more likely to produce an appropriately dignified effect than a possibly unseemly scramble through a trap, and there is no indication of any covering noise for the use of stage machinery. But use of the trap cannot be confidently discounted.

Absence of even a minimal stage direction for the departure of Banquo and the apparitions combines with the violent discrepancy in tone between the closing lines of Macbeth's speech and the Witch's response to cast doubt on the authenticity of the latter:

> MACBETH   Now I see 'tis true,
> For the blood-baltered Banquo smiles upon me,
> And points at them for his. What, is this so?
> [HECATE].   Ay, sir, all this is so. But why
> Stands Macbeth thus amazedly?
> Come, sisters, cheer we up his sprites,
> And show the best of our delights. (4.1.138)

So they prepare for their 'antic round'—'The Dashing White Sergeant' perhaps. The stage direction for their exit is *'The Witches dance, and vanish'*. In the text as printed Macbeth's next words, 'Where are they? Gone? Let this pernicious hour | Stand aye accursed in the calendar' (4.1.149) refer to the disappearance of the Witches, but they could equally refer to the departure of the apparitions, and in stage practice regularly do so.[17]

The apparitions so far discussed are spirits who have been conjured up from the underworld. Even Banquo falls into this category in the cauldron scene because the Witches bring about his appearance. Shakespeare seems regularly to have used the stage trap for such appearances, but to have been much less inclined to use it for ghosts appearing of their own accord. Otherworldly figures also appear in his plays to the living in the form of dream visions. The distinction is not always clear cut. The figures who appear to Richard and Richmond in the climactic scene of *Richard III* can be counted as ghosts mainly on the grounds that, although Richard and Richmond are asleep at the time, it is too much of a coincidence that two men should simultaneously dream the same dream. Some dream visions are merely narrated, not staged; conspicuous among these is Antigonus's account in *The Winter's Tale* of how the weeping Hermione appeared to tell him what to do with her baby, and what to call her. All the staged dream visions—i.e. those in which we see actors representing the dream of a character asleep on the stage—are in late plays, and all—like the appearance of the ghosts in *Richard III*—occur at a climactic point either in the structure of the play or (in one possibly non-Shakespearean case) in the life of the character concerned.

The first of them is preceded by an effect which itself poses a staging problem. In scene 21 of *Pericles* the hero, at the height of his happiness at being reunited with his daughter Marina, attires himself in 'fresh garments' and calls for a blessing on Marina—'O heavens, bless my girl!'—and suddenly hears mysterious music—'But hark, what music?' (21.210). A few moments later he asks again:

> PERICLES   But what music?
> HELICANUS   My lord, I hear none.
> PERICLES   None, the music of the spheres! List my Marina. (21.213)

It is clear from Lysimachus's next line—'It is not good to cross him. Give him way'—that no one else on stage hears this music, which rapidly induces sleep in Pericles:

> I hear most heavn'ly music.
> It raps me unto list'ning, and thick slumber
> Hangs upon mine eyelids. Let me rest. (21.219)

The 'exposition of sleep' that comes over Pericles is oddly parallel to that experienced by Bottom in *A Midsummer Night's Dream*, but in that play it is induced by the all-too-earthly sounds of the tongs and bones, pretty certainly played on stage. It is not clear whether Pericles speaks literally or metaphorically when he claims to hear the 'music of the spheres'; more importantly from the performers' point of view, it is not even clear whether music should be heard in the theatre or should be supposed audible to Pericles alone. McDonald P. Jackson writes in the Oxford *Textual Companion*:

> Some editors refuse to supply a stage direction for music, arguing that (a) it is heard by Pericles alone among those on stage, and that (b) attempts to simulate the heavenly harmonies will inevitably be bathetic. But (a) it is surely Pericles' blissful state of mind that the audience is invited to share in this scene, not the normality of Helicanus and Lysimachus, and (b) an imaginative musical accompaniment will aid rather than hinder the process of emotional identification.[18]

This is cogent. It might be added that the heavenly music played in *1 Henry IV* by musicians who a moment earlier were hanging 'in the air a thousand leagues from hence' (3.1.211) was unquestionably meant to be heard in the theatre, as was the 'music i'th'air'—or 'Under the earth'—directed to be played under the stage on hautboys in *Antony and Cleopatra* (4.3). In *Cymbeline* we are to hear the '*solemn music*' of Belarius's 'ingenious instrument' (4.2.187), and in several non-Shakespearean plays too, some written before some after *Pericles*, there are clear directions for the performance of miraculous music. Instrumentation is rarely specified, though in *The Two Noble Ladies* (*c.*1620) recorders provide the 'heavenly harmony' to accompany the appearance of an angel.[19] Certainly Shakespeare and contemporary dramatists expected their composers to accept the challenge of supplying celestial music, though we cannot say for certain that it would have sounded in *Pericles*.

After Pericles has fallen asleep he is left alone on stage to experience the dream vision in which Diana directs him to visit her temple in Ephesus and to make a sacrifice upon her altar. As with the appearance of Hymen in *As You Like It* the text provides no lead in to Diana's appearance, which cries out for some kind of transition. Perhaps—as certainly in the earlier comedy—it was provided by music. In the quarto text, Diana's speech is preceded not by an entry direction but simply by her name, leaving even more than usual latitude for her presentation. Malone's direction, '*Pericles on deck asleep; Diana appearing to him as in a vision*',[20] adopted by most subsequent editors, is no help to a director. It seems certain that Diana should appear to the audience as well as to Pericles; a descent from the canopy over the stage, with an ascent into the same regions after she has spoken, would be consonant with Shakespeare's practice for celestial visitants in *Cymbeline* and *The Tempest*. Beckerman, however, referring to the absence of directions for ascent or descent for both Hymen in *As You Like It* and Diana in *Pericles*, speculates 'that the company lacked means for flying actors until it moved to Blackfriars',[21] so perhaps in the play's earliest performances Diana simply walked on to the upper level. Such requirements were always liable to be tempered by practicalities; we may recall Robert Greene's opening direction in *Alphonsus, King of Aragon* (*c.*1587, printed in 1599), '*After you have sounded thrice, let Venus be let down from the top of the stage*', followed at the end of the play by '*Exit Venus. Or if you can conveniently, let a chair come down from the top of the stage and draw her up.*' In *Pericles* Diana speaks in oracular fashion in lines, clearly mangled in the quarto, that appear originally to have been composed in a form resembling that of the last ten lines of a sonnet. Emblematic costuming, such as had been described in Samuel Daniel's masque *The Vision of the Twelve Goddesses*— 'Diana, in a green mantle embroidered with silver half moons, and a crescent of pearl on her head' (line 75)—seems to be called for; a designer might also draw on the Inigo Jones sketch of Diana made probably for Ben Jonson's masque *Time Vindicated* (1623).[22] Pericles' description of Diana as 'goddess argentine' (21.236) is another— rather obvious—clue to her costume. Clearly Shakespeare (and his collaborator) were doing all they could to create a climactic effect with this episode; as Philip Brockbank wrote, 'By the theatrical device of a vision the story is formally given what the poetry and the music have already conferred upon it—a supernal and subliminal authority';[23] the authors' efforts need to be matched by those of their interpreters.

The most elaborate of all Shakespeare's dream visions is the one in Act 5, scene 5 of *Cymbeline*. We believe that this play was written after his company had started to use the indoor Blackfriars playhouse, and it may therefore employ techniques of staging that had not been available to him in the Globe. Ever since Pope relegated it to the margin of his edition of the plays, refusing to believe in its authenticity, the vision has been one of the most maligned passages in Shakespeare. In spite of Wilson Knight's eloquent and thorough defence of its authenticity as well as its quality in 1947[24] Dover Wilson found it necessary to add a Prefatory Note to J. C. Maxwell's New (Cambridge) Shakespeare edition of 1960, taking issue with Maxwell's acceptance of the vision's authenticity and expressing incredulity 'that, being the poet he was, whatever else he wrote or did not write in this play, he could possibly have written what Granville-Barker calls "the jingling twaddle of the apparitions"'. (Granville-Barker, in fact, had gone so far as to suggest that their speeches were written by the prompter 'kept in between rehearsal and performance, thumping the stuff out and thumbing it down between bites and sips of his bread and cheese and ale'.[25]) Such aesthetic judgements are ultimately subjective, and argument about the quality or even the authenticity of the episode is irrelevant to my present purpose. The proper criterion for the quality of dramatic verse is its effectiveness in performance, and I was deeply moved by this 'jingling twaddle' in, particularly, William Gaskill's Stratford production of 1962. I still recall the pathos of:

> Lucina lent me not her aid,
> But took me in my throes,
> That from me was Posthumus ripped,
> Came crying 'mongst his foes,
> A thing of pity. (5.5.137)

The vision is heralded by 'Solemn music'—a direction that Shakespeare uses only in very late plays—as the fettered Posthumus lies asleep. Then we have the direction:

Enter, as in an apparition, Sicilius Leonatus (father to Posthumus, an old man), attired like a warrior, leading in his hand an ancient matron, his wife, and mother to Posthumus, with music before them. Then, after other music, follows the two young Leonati, brothers to Posthumus, with wounds as they died in the wars. They circle Posthumus round as he lies sleeping. (5.5.123)

It seems natural to assume that the representatives of the older and the younger generations should enter separately, probably through different entrances, each group preceded by musicians. The attendant musicians have no further function to perform unless to enhance the effectiveness of the vision with on-stage music.

The most cryptic phrase in the direction (though editors do not comment on it) is '*as in an apparition*'. It seems to imply some device that would convey a sense of otherworldliness. The '*Solemn music*' would have helped; perhaps no more was needed. But conceivably Shakespeare's company could have summoned up an early version of the dry ice so dear to the present Royal Shakespeare Company: there is evidence for the simulation of mist and fog in theatres of the time, as in the directions '*Night rises in mists*' in *The Maid's Tragedy* and '*Delphia raises a mist*' in *The Prophetess*, both Blackfriars plays not too distant in time from Cymbeline.[26] White clothes tend to be associated with visions—when the living Hermione's spirit appeared to Antigonus it wore 'pure white robes' (3.3.21), Diana in *Pericles* was 'argentine', and the figures who appear to Queen Katherine in the play about Henry VIII reveal their spiritual status by entering '*solemnly tripping one after another ... clad in white robes*'—but in *Cymbeline* we have unusually precise (though still far from full) directions implying that the characters wear everyday dress.

Perhaps the fact that the Leonati are visionary figures would have been conveyed by their mode of entry, even their gait. Granville-Barker supposed that they would enter through curtains—but he had old-fashioned ideas about the 'inner stage'—and form a stationary circle around Posthumus. But '*They circle Posthumus round*' may mean that they move in the shape of a circle, which would permit each to adopt the most effective position—centrally behind Posthumus, I take it—for his or her speech. In the modern theatre a revolve can be used to achieve this effect; Roger Warren describes how, in William Gaskill's production, 'As Posthumus's dream began, the revolve slowly started to move and, in a hazy half-light, the ghosts of Posthumus's family moved slowly, in a series of turns, against the motion of the revolve, an aptly weird physical accompaniment to their bizarre speeches'.[27] The archaic artifice of these speeches, based on rhyming fourteeners, demands an incantatory style of delivery but it must also be imploratory since the spirits of the Leonati are calling upon Jupiter and indeed are somewhat petulantly rebuking him for the way the gods have treated their family. The last five speeches call directly upon Jupiter to appear from the heavens: 'Thy crystal window ope; look out' (5.5.175) and 'Peep through thy marble mansion' (5.5.181), and he responds dramatically and spectacularly in the direction '*Jupiter descends in thunder and lightning, sitting upon an eagle. He throws a thunderbolt*', at which '*The ghosts fall on their knees*'.

The allusions to Jupiter's 'crystal window' and his 'marble mansion' clearly relate in some way to the area above the stage from which he was to descend, perhaps simply through an aperture in the floor of the hut that held the flying apparatus, perhaps through a suitably decorated trap-door which would need to be heaved open just before his descent. After his departure, according to Sicilius, 'the marble pavement closes, he is entered | His radiant roof' (5.5.214), which leads Granville-

Barker, in a section of his Preface on 'The Play's First Staging', to say that if Jupiter 'could descend through an actual marble pavement of a ceiling, so much the better';[28] but perhaps the epithets are intended simply to give an impression of the splendour in which the god lives. Granville-Barker also suggests, plausibly, that Jupiter 'can hardly come all the way down. As a god he must hold the centre of the stage; and if he did come all the way he would then obliterate the sleeping Posthumus, who...would almost certainly be in the centre, too.'[29] I am less convinced by his suggestion that Jupiter's 'best resting place would be on the upper stage', but this is a decision that the precise design of the theatre would determine. The thunder and lightning that accompany Jupiter's descent would make their customary calls upon the theatre's thunder run and its pyrotechnics experts, and the eagle that carries him would tax the skills of the property makers; this was probably an overbudget production.

There is reason to suppose that the eagle would have come as even more of a surprise to its first audience than to later ones. According to Cranford Adams 'The use of the eagle...broke with the tradition of actors sitting in or upon some more or less conventional car',[30] so in addition to its spectacular effect it would have provided the thrill of novelty. The device occurs also in Thomas Heywood's Red Bull play The Golden Age and it is uncertain which came first. It is related to the staging methods of court masques, and there is an Inigo Jones sketch of Jupiter mounted on his eagle for a much later masque, Aurelian Townshend's Tempe Restored of 1632. In this, a cloud obscures the wires needed for the flying apparatus. Adams also refers to 'an early seventeenth-century Italian theatre print illustrating Jupiter descending upon an eagle' and showing four wires, 'two on either side (to keep the bird from rotating and from rocking)'.[31] Clearly the aperture in the floor of the hut must have been quite large. There is no doubt that the construction and manipulation of the eagle would have posed major technical problems in the theatres of Shakespeare's time as it also does in ours; indeed, modern directors all too often chicken out of the eagle's challenge.[32] If there is any thought that Cymbeline may be among the earlier plays to be presented in either the reconstructed Globe or the Inigo Jones theatre, then I strongly advise the organizers to make an early start on thinking about how to set about it.

The climax comes as Jupiter 'throws a thunderbolt'. It is I think the only thunderbolt required in any of Shakespeare's plays, and one wonders how it was done. The technique most commonly referred to is described by Serlio in a book first published in 1545 and clearly relating to Italian stage settings. This was translated into English in 1611, the year in which Simon Forman appears to have seen Cymbeline, providing the first recorded allusion to the play. Serlio writes that 'A thunderbolt is made by letting down a rocket or ray ornamented with sparkling gold on a wire stretched at the back of the scene. Before the thunder has stopped rumbling the tail of the rocket is discharged, setting fire to the thunderbolt and producing an excellent effect.'[33] 'Fireworks on lines' are called for in an English play of the same period as *Cymbeline*, Dekker's *If it be not Good, the Devil is in it*, performed at the Red Bull, so the same effect may also have been used in Shakespeare's play. The direction, however, says specifically that Jupiter 'throws' the thunderbolt, so perhaps something more portable, like the explosive caps with which schoolboys delight to surprise their friends, would have been used.

After Jupiter has thrown his thunderbolt the spirits fall to their knees and he addresses them in a superbly sonorous piece of rhymed rhetoric ('pedestrian' according to Granville-Barker),[34] towards the end of which he requires them to 'Rise, and fade'. They rise so that he can present them with '*a tablet which they lay upon Posthumus' breast*', but are not required to 'fade' until after Jupiter '*ascends into the heavens*', urging on his steed (and on a more practical level supplying a cue for the stage hands in the hut) with 'Mount, eagle, to my palace crystalline' (5.5.207). Sicilius covers the ascent with six lines of verse during which he somewhat insultingly declares that Jupiter's 'celestial breath | Was sulphurous to smell' (5.5.208); later Pisanio is to refer to thunderbolts as 'stones of sulphur' (5.6.241). It is perhaps over-literal to interpret Sicilius's words as an allusion to the actual smell of the fireworks used in the theatre, but his statement 'The marble pavement closes, he is entered | His radiant roof' certainly fuses the theatrical with the fictional situation, and it is difficult not to take 'The marble pavement' as a reference to a trap-door in the floor of the hut way above the stage at which the spirits have been gazing. Jupiter has instructed the spirits to 'fade'; the Folio direction is '*Vanish*'; whether in Shakespeare's theatre they would simply have glided off through the stage-doors or whether some more spectral mode of departure would have been devised, there is no way to tell. After the apparition scene in *Macbeth* the Witches, too, are said to 'vanish'; the word occurs in Shakespeare's stage directions only in *Macbeth* and the late romances—another scrap of evidence that the surviving text of *Macbeth* is a late adaptation.

Posthumus's vision has faded, but—as in all the best children's stories—tangible evidence of his dream remains in the 'tablet' (5.5.203), or 'book' (5.5.227) (which could mean a single leaf), or 'label' (5.6.431) in which Posthumus reads the oracular prophecy which, interpreted by the Soothsayer, will bring about the final interpret-ation of the play's action. This Soothsayer had pre-echoed Posthumus's dream vision when, shortly after Innogen's awakening over what she believed to be Posthumus's body, he had told Lucius of his own vision:

> I saw Jove's bird, the Roman eagle, winged
> From the spongy south to this part of the west,
> There vanished in the sunbeams. (4.2.350)

Now, in the play's penultimate speech, his recall of this vision gains in resonance from our memory of the vision that only we and the sleeping Posthumus have seen:

The vision,
Which I made known to Lucius ere the stroke
Of this yet scarce-cold battle, at this instant
Is full accomplished. For the Roman eagle,
From south to west on wing soaring aloft,
Lessened herself, and in the beams o'th'sun
So vanished; which foreshowed our princely eagle
Th'imperial Caesar should again unite
His favour with the radiant Cymbeline,
Which shines here in the west. (5.6.468)

I have referred in passing to the one later dream vision in the canon, the appearance of 'six personages clad in white robes'—to the accompaniment, incidentally, of 'Sad and solemn music'—to Queen Katherine (in Henry VIII, or All is True, 4.2), but this is in part of the play that is commonly ascribed to Fletcher. Apparitions and dream visions—spirits of health or goblins damned, bringing with them airs from heaven or blasts from hell or, to put it in practical terms, descending from above to the sound of solemn music or emerging from the cellarage accompanied by thunder and lightning—all form part of the challenge of making proper use of the Wanamaker Globe once it is there.

19

Shakespeare in Planché's Extravaganzas

James Robinson Planché (1796–1880) was a man of varied talents: on the one hand, a Fellow of the Society of Antiquaries, instrumental in the founding of the British Archaeological Association, Rouge Croix Pursuivant of Arms and later Somerset Herald, author of books on heraldry, *A History of British Costumes* (1834) and *A Cyclopaedia of Costume* (1876–9); on the other hand a practical man of the theatre—musician, designer, translator, and adapter of many plays from the French, and author of innumerable pantomimes, burlesques, burlettas, melodramas, and other stage works. His output was prodigious; but scarcely a line of it is remembered. If we hear anything that he wrote, it is as likely as not to be in the German translation of his libretto for Weber's opera *Oberon*. True, he has his place in theatrical history; but he is remembered less for his original writing than as a campaigner for reasonable copyright laws for the protection of the rights of librettists and playwrights, and as the man whose work on the history of costume had a profound influence on the staging of Shakespeare and other 'historical' dramatists. His best work for the stage is undoubtedly in the forty-four extravaganzas, published in a Testimonial Edition in 1879.[1] A number of writers have demonstrated W. S. Gilbert's indebtedness to these works,[2] but Planché was a Gilbert without a Sullivan. The extravaganzas are no longer read or performed. Indeed they, along with the rest of his output, have been declared unreadable.[3] But this is a harsh judgement; I feel more sympathy with that expressed by Allardyce Nicoll, who describes some of Planché's earlier writings as 'among the most delightful things the early nineteenth-century theatre produced. Trivial they may be, but they have a grace and a lightness of touch which makes us esteem more highly this prolific Somerset Herald.'[4]

Those who condemn and those who praise have alike recognized that Planché's writings are highly informative about the stage of his time. As Dougald MacMillan has shown, his intentions were not always trivial.[5] He was genuinely concerned about the future of the English theatre, anxious to raise the standards of both the 'legitimate' and the 'illegitimate' drama, and this concern is evident even in many of his lightest works. Writers such as Allardyce Nicoll and George Rowell[6] have quoted from Planché's works in general surveys of the Victorian stage. My object here is the more limited one of looking at the extravaganzas to see what they have to tell us about Shakespeare.

I

In the preface (published in 1879) to the first of his works to be called an extravaganza—*High, Low, Jack, and the Game*, first performed in 1833—Planché explained that he had used blank verse instead of the rhyming verse normal in pieces written, as this was, for the Olympic Theatre: 'There was some risk in departing from a style which had become identified with the popular little theatre; but it was favourably received by the audience, the ears of the play-going public being more accustomed to the heroic measure in those days than they are at present, and thoroughly familiar with all the quotations from, or parodies on, passages in Shakespeare and other of our elder dramatists with which the dialogue was copiously interlarded.' There seems no need to question the assumption that his public would recognize allusions to Shakespeare.[7] Indeed it might reasonably be argued that Shakespeare's plays—in however debased versions—were more truly a part of the living theatre a century ago than they are today. Henry Morley, for instance, wrote of a production in 1853: 'The "Midsummer Night's Dream" abounds in the most delicate passages of Shakespeare's verse; the Sadler's Wells pit has a keen enjoyment for them; and pit and gallery were crowded to the farthest wall on Saturday night with a most earnest audience, among whom many a subdued hush arose, not during, but just before, the delivery of the most charming passages.'[8] And the actor John Coleman, writing of the early Victorian theatre, says that even 'country audiences were as familiar with the standard plays as the actors themselves; indeed, it is upon record that in his youth, when [Charles] Kean broke down in the last act of *Macbeth* at Newcastle-on-Tyne, the "King of the gallery" "gave him the word" in the euphonious dialect of the district, and that Charles readily accepted the help of his rough and ready prompter, bowing his grateful acknowledgment'.[9] The reason for this familiarity is a matter of theatrical rather than educational history. Familiarity with Shakespeare was bred in the theatre, not in the classroom. This was the age of the Great Actor; and the prevailing repertory system made it possible for a regular theatregoer to become a connoisseur of performances in a way that is scarcely possible today. For instance, *Who's Who in the Theatre* (1961) lists eight *important* revivals of *Richard III* in London between 1833 and 1838: Warde, Vandenhoff, Denvil, Wallack, J. B. Booth, Edwin Forrest, Phelps, and Charles Kean played the title-role; and between 1850 and 1855 you could have seen, among others, Phelps, C. Kean, Wallack, G. V. Brooke, and James Anderson as Macbeth. If you were a keen theatregoer you probably did see them all, and discourse on their relative merits, just as a music-lover of today will compare different conductors' inter-pretations of a Beethoven symphony.

No precision is possible, of course, in the attempt to determine the degree to which Victorian audiences were familiar with Shakespeare: and it seems fairly clear that as the 'long-run' came to prevail over the repertory system this familiarity gradually diminished. But it is certain that Planché felt able to slip in a Shakespearian allusion or quotation with the assurance that at any rate a fair proportion of his audience would recognize its aptness. True, some of the quotations that he used are very obvious ones. In *The Drama's Levée* (1838), for instance, 'Drama', exasperated by the quarrelling of Legitimate and Illegitimate Drama, exclaims:

> Hence both and each who either cause espouses!
> You'll drive me mad! a plague on *all* your houses! (ii. 13)

No great familiarity with *Hamlet* would be required to give point to the exclamation 'Dead for a ducat, dead' in *Fortunio* (1843; ii. 208) when a dragon is killed. Only slightly less obvious, though entirely unforced in its application, is another allusion to *Hamlet*, also in *Fortunio*:

> BOISTERER. Lightfoot has hit upon a rare invention.
> FORTUNIO. What is't?
> FINE-EAR.   A flying steamcoach!
> FOR.   Ha!—indeed!
> STRONGBACK. Built on a principle that must succeed.
> MARKSMAN. Just like a bird—with body, wings, and tail.
> TIPPLE. Or like a fish—
> FOR.   Aye—very like a whale.
> MARKS. You think we're joking, sir.
> FOR. In truth, I do. (ii. 217)

But it may be doubted whether many members of a modern audience would know *Richard III* well enough to see the point of the following:

> DUKE. ...what's o'clock?
>   Who's there?
> STAFFHOLD. 'Tis I! the early village cock
>   Hath thrice done salutation to the morn!
>   (*The Prince of Happy Land*, 1851, iv. 200)

Somewhat elusive, too, is the reference to *The Merchant of Venice*, 2.2, in *The King of the Peacocks* (1848):

> POO-LEE-HA-LEE.   I am a chap—chap fall'n—with Fortune out,
>   Who's conscience hanging his heart's neck about,
>   Like Gobbo junior's, would the owner strangle,
>   If at the yard-arm he'd no right to dangle. (iii. 303)

These allusions are not, it is true, of the first importance. They are made in passing; they would raise hardly more than a smile of recognition, and if they went unnoticed little would be lost. More important, and far more extensive, are those passages in which Planché consciously parodies lines, speeches, and sometimes whole scenes from Shakespeare. The brilliant pun in the following lines from *Once Upon a Time there were Two Kings* (1853) would be quite lost if the audience did not remember its *Hamlet*:

> PASTORA.   ...a piano you're not born to play.
>   Oh, there be misses, I have here and there heard,
>   Play in a style that quite out Erard's Erard.
>   Pray you avoid it.... (iv. 343)

A longer passage from *High, Low, Jack, and the Game*, in which the characters are members of a pack of playing cards, is based on *Macbeth* (with a glance at *Hamlet*), and gains its point from the witty and sustained word-play linking card-terms with the original:

> *The Ghost of the* King of Hearts *appears.*
> KING OF SPADES. (*starting*). Mother o'pearl! What *carte-blanche* have we here?
> GHOST.   I am the *ombre* of the King of Hearts.
> QUEEN OF HEARTS.   My husband!
> KNAVE OF HEARTS.   My late King!
> KING OF SPADES.   Avaunt and quit my sight—let the earth hide thee!
>   There is no speculation in those eyes
>   That thou dost glare withal!
> GHOST.   I do not play
> At speculation.
> KNAVE OF HEARTS.   (No; he plays at fright.)
> KING OF SPADES.   What game is now a-foot?
> GHOST. Whist! whist! oh whist! (i. 131)

Planché's own definition of the extravaganza was a 'whimsical treatment of a poetical subject' as distinguished from 'the broad caricature of a tragedy or serious opera, which was correctly termed a "Burlesque"'.[10] But this did not prevent him from including in a 'fairy extravaganza' passages, at least, of 'broad caricature'. In *The Fair One with the Golden Locks* (1843), for instance, King Lachrymosa is rejected by his beloved, Queen Lucidora; he bemoans his fate in lines obviously inspired by *Othello*:

Haply, for I take snuff, she thinks me dirty;
Or, for I'm on the shady side of thirty.
But that's not much, I'm only thirty-four. (ii. 260)

However, he decides that in order to improve his chances he will take a draught of
an 'elixir, that can youth restore!' He goes to get it, slightly misquoting *Macbeth*, 4.1:

This deed I'll do before this purpose fail.

And at his next appearance the hint of *Macbeth* burgeons into a full-scale burlesque
of the dagger soliloquy:

Is this a corkscrew that I see before me?
The handle towards my hand—clutch thee I will!
I have thee not—and yet I see thee still!
Art thou a hardware article? or, oh!
Simply a fancy article, for show.
A corkscrew of the mind—a false creation
Of crooked ways, a strong insinuation!
I see thee yet, as plain as e'er I saw
This patent one, which any cork can draw!
(*shewing patent corkscrew*)
Thou marshal'st me the way that I should choose,
And such an instrument I was to use!
There's no such thing; 'tis what I steal to do,
That on my fancy thus has put the screw.
I go, and it is done. (*going*) Confound it! there's
That stupid Mollymopsa on the stairs. (ii. 262)

He drinks poison by mistake, and *Macbeth* is further recalled in a few slight and
subtle echoes of wording and dramatic technique:

KING (*WITHIN*).   Help, there, ho!
  (*Exit* Viscount)
QUEEN.   What voice was that?
GRACE.   My royal master's surely.
                         Re-enter Viscount.
VIS.   Run for a doctor, the King's taken poorly.
  Exeunt Officer *and* Viscount.
QUEEN.   The cramp has seized his conscience, I presume.
  What business has he in my dressing-room?
                      Re-enter Viscount, *with bottle.*
VIS.   Oh, horror! horror! Madam—

> *Enter* Courtiers *from different entrances.*
> QUEEN.   Well, proceed.
> VIS.   His Majesty is very ill, indeed. (ii. 263)

Many examples of this sort of thing could be cited: *Fortunio* has a parody (ii. 223) of a speech from *Macbeth*; in *Graciosa and Percinet* there is a lengthy parody (ii. 324–5) of the closet scene from *Hamlet*; *King Charming* has a long sequence (iv. 100–11) based, often closely, on *Romeo and Juliet*, as well as references to *Macbeth, 1 Henry IV, Hamlet,* and *Twelfth Night*; in *Once Upon a Time There Were Two Kings* (iv. 329–31) there are parodies of speeches from *Hamlet* and *Romeo and Juliet* (quoted by Granville-Barker, pp. 114–16); and *The Yellow Dwarf* has a wooing scene (v. 59–60) based on that in *Richard III*, as well as parodies and quotations of parts of *Othello, Macbeth, The Merchant of Venice, A Midsummer Night's Dream,* and *Romeo and Juliet*. Many of the parodies are still entertaining; Planché punned with less strain than many of his contemporaries. Even the skit, in *The Island of Jewels,* on a scene of *King Lear* is inoffensive and sometimes funny. Laidronetta's father, a King, is wandering in a storm in a Rocky Pass, with his Queen, Tinsellina; his son, Prince Prettiphello; his daughter, Princess Bellotta; and Count Merecho:

> PRINCE.   As to the King, who thought such wealth to sack,
>   The blow has given his cranium quite a crack;
>   His talk is all of money, but so queer,
>   I really think he must have seen King Lear.
> *Enter* King, Queen, *and* Count.
> KING.   Blow winds and crack your cheeks, the clouds go spout!
>   To raise the wind, and get a good blow out.
>   Rain cats and dogs, or pitchforks perpendicular,
>   The sky's not mine, and needn't be particular.
>   I tax not you, ye elements, you pay
>   No duty under schedules D or A,
>   You owe me no subscription. Funds may fall,
>   It makes no difference to you at all.
> BEL.   Gracious, papa! don't stand here, if you please.
> QUEEN.   'Things that love night, love not such nights as these.'
>   Persuade him to move on, Prince Prettiphello.
> PRINCE.   Are you aware, sir, you have no umbrella? *(rain)*
> KING.   A thought has struck me, rather entertaining,
>   I am a King more rained upon than reigning.
>   My wits are going fast!
> QUEEN.   I fear 'tis so.
> PRINCE.   Take comfort, ma'am, there are so few to go.
>   Would that our loss was nothing more, alas!
> KING.   What, have his daughters brought him to this pass?

COUNT. He has no daughters, sir.
KING. 'Sdeath! don't tell fibs!
He must have one who won't down with the dibs,
Although she's made of money! Nothing I know
Bothers your gig so much as want of *rhino*.
PRINCE. His head's quite turned with losing all that pelf.
KING. For coining they can't touch the King himself.
QUEEN. Here's a dry cavern, if he would but cross over.
KING. I'd talk a word with this philosopher!
What is the price of stocks?
PRINCE. Mine are but low.
Suppose you just walk in, some here may know.
KING. A famous dodge! For ninety millions draw
A bill at sight upon my son-in-law,
And then—bolt—bolt-bolt-bolt.
(*Exeunt* King *into cavern, followed by* Queen, *&c.*) (iv. 41–2)

It is interesting to learn that in performance some of Planché's parodies retained a measure of the force of their originals. The following lines from *The Yellow Dwarf* (1854) read like a vulgarization of their model in *Othello*:

HARIDAN. Monster, what means this tragical tableau?
You've killed the little King on whom I doted.
DWARF. And caused her death to whom I was devoted.
Oh heavy trial! Verdict—Serves me right!
Whip me ye devils—winds come, blow me tight!
Roast me in flames of sulphur—very slow!
Oh Allfair—Allfair!—Dead—O, O, O, O! (v. 72)

But the dwarf was played by that very remarkable actor, Frederick Robson, of whose performance Planché wrote: 'So powerful was his personation of the cunning, the malignity, the passion and despair of the monster, that he elevated Extravaganza into Tragedy. His delivery of the lines, slightly parodied from the wail of Othello over the dead body of Desdemona, moved Thackeray, "albeit unused to the melting mood", almost to tears. "This is not a burlesque," he exclaimed, "It is an idyl!"' (v. 37). *The Illustrated London News* in its review confirms this, saying that the Shakespeare parodies 'told exceedingly well, and proved, what has often been asserted, that, notwithstanding his minute size, Mr Robson's power in a legitimate tragic part would be great indeed'. The work was 'not merely a burlesque, but a poem'.

Planché's light-hearted variations upon Shakespeare suggest a less solemn attitude than might be inferred from the general trend of Shakespearian production during the century. The comic effect of some Shakespeare skits of our own time is based upon incomprehension: our sympathetic laughter is invited for someone who is trying unsuccessfully to master a seemingly confused plot, to understand half-forgotten allusions, or to explain in realistic terms the conventions and motives of poetic drama. This is not Planché's way. Nor does he write critical burlesque; his is not the searching parody of a Beerbohm, drawing attention by imitation and concentration to the stylistic mannerisms of the author parodied. Planché's is the humour of the consciously absurd; he plays tricks with the original, he exercises his ingenuity upon it, but he leaves it intact. He felt able as it were to say to his audience, 'You all know Macbeth's dagger soliloquy; let's see how we can apply it to this ridiculous situation.' The audience's respect for, and understanding of, the original is urbanely taken for granted; consequently, there is no cheapening.

II

Besides providing general evidence on the attitude of Planché and his audiences to Shakespeare, the extravaganzas also yield interesting information on specific points of the staging of Shakespeare's plays over a wide period of time.

In *Olympic Devils, or, Orpheus and Eurydice*, first performed on Boxing Day 1831, Orpheus and Eurydice are pleading to Pluto:

ORPHEUS. I kneel to you—the son of great Apollo
    Kneels—who ne'er knelt before—I—me—like Rolla.
EURYDICE. I kneel—like Miss O'Neill—in Desdemona,
    'Let me go with him.'
ORPHEUS. Oh, be mercy shown her!
    To ransom her I'd give my best Cremona. (i. 75)

In his first speech, Orpheus refers to a climactic moment in Sheridan's *Pizarro*, 5.2; the mention of Eliza O'Neill's Desdemona is particularly striking in that she had retired from the stage in June 1819—eleven years before this was written. True, her name is introduced partly for the sake of a pun; but the quotation from *Othello* suggests that Planché had in mind a particular theatrical effect. I know of no evidence that Miss O'Neill knelt on the line 'Let me go with him' (1.3.260); but Oxberry's acting edition dated 1822, which lists her as Desdemona at Covent Garden, makes her kneel at her father's exit in the same scene:

BRABANTIO. Look to her, Moor; have a quick eye to see;
    She has deceived her father, and may thee.
(Desdemona follows her father and kneels to him, he puts her from him.—The Moor raises her.
    Brabantio and Gratiano go off, R.H.)

Planché's reference to this kneeling[11] may suggest that it was a memorable effect, worthy of record.

In *The Camp at the Olympic* (17 October 1853) Planché goes into more detail in a scene (iv. 304–6) that reflects his interest in the costuming of historical drama. Tragedy enters 'in the costume of Lady Macbeth, 1753'—there is no especial significance in this date, which is simply a century before the date of Planché's work. Fancy says:

> First in the field, old English Tragedy
> In stately hoop and train 'comes sweeping by'!
> As in the British Drama's palmy day,
> When people took an interest in the play!

It is only by the letter in her hand that she is recognized as Lady Macbeth. Mrs Wigan (she and her husband were playing themselves) exclaims, 'Lady Macbeth! In Dollalolla's dress!', and her husband comments

> That must have been a hundred years ago,
> To judge from a costume so rococo!

Tragedy delivers an impassioned attack on the degeneration of the stage that has occurred since her time. In retaliation Fancy speaks:

> The times have changed; but there is still a stage,
> And one on which Macbeth has been the rage.

There is then discovered '"The Blasted Heath", same as at the Princess's Theatre, with the Three Witches—Macbeth *and* Banquo *in the costume worn at that theatre—Temp.* 1853'. Charles Kean's production of *Macbeth* in February 1853 had been attended by some controversy about the costumes used. Kean, with his usual passion for archaeological accuracy, had been worried by 'the very uncertain information ... which we possess respecting the dress worn by the inhabitants of Scotland in the eleventh century'. He therefore 'introduced the tunic, mantle, cross gartering, and ringed byrnie of the Danes and Anglo-Saxons, between whom it does not appear any very material difference existed; retaining, however, the peculiarity of "the striped and chequered garb", which seems to be generally admitted as belonging to the Scotch long anterior to the history of this play; together with the eagle feather in the helmet, which according to Gaelic tradition, was the distinguishing mark of a chieftain'.[12]

This spectacle astonishes Tragedy:

> ...'Great Glamis! worthy Cawdor!'
> Can that be he?

> *Fancy.* In heavy marching order.
> > Not as when Garrick used to meet the witches—
> > In gold-laced waistcoat and red velvet breeches...

whereupon 'Garrick *appears as* Macbeth *with the daggers*'. Fancy continues:

> > Nor as in Kemble's time, correct was reckoned,
> > Accoutred like 'the gallant forty-second',

and 'Kemble *appears as* Macbeth, *with target and truncheon*'. An officer of 'the forty-second' wore 'bonnet, plaid, red jacket faced with blue, the philibeg [kilt] and tartan hose'.[13] Fancy concludes her speech with:

> > But as a Scottish chieftain roamed scot-free—
> > In the year one thousand and fifty-three.

There follow various comments on what has been seen. Mr and Mrs Wigan with Fancy sing, to the tune of 'Auld Lang Syne':

> > My auld acquaintance I've forgot,
> > If ever he was mine;
> > Is that the way they clad a Scot
> > In days o' Lang Syne.

Tragedy expresses her surprise in words aptly chosen from *Macbeth*:

> TRAGEDY. 'My countryman—and yet I know him not!'
> MR W. More like an antique *Rum'un* than a Scot!
> TRAG. A Scotchman, and no kilt?
> MRS W. Don't Macbeth say,
> > 'We've *scotch'd* the snake, not *kilt* it!'

And finally Fancy sings:

> > Through their habits conventional managers broke,
> > To make old plays go down they new habits bespoke;
> > The old-fashioned Scotchman no longer we see,
> > Except as a sign for the sale of rappee.
> > So pack up your tartans, whatever your clan,
> > And look a new 'garb of old Gaul' out, my man;
> > For the stage in its bonnet has got such a bee,
> > It's all up with 'The Bonnets of Bonny Dundee'.

This curious piece of dramatized stage-history reflects the surprise of Kean's audiences at his break with tradition: it also shows Planché's own awareness of the rapid changes in theatrical fashion over the preceding century—changes he himself had helped to bring about. It was perhaps a little unfair to suggest that the new costumes were adopted 'to make old plays go down'; though Kean's productions were on the whole very popular, his innovations were not universally approved, and he complained in his farewell speech that he had 'been blamed for depriving Macbeth of a dress never worn at any period, or in any place, and for providing him instead with one resembling those used by the surrounding nations with whom the country of that chieftain was in constant intercourse'.[14] Nearer the mark was Planché's reference to the bee in 'the stage's' bonnet.[15]

III

Planché's concern with the staging of Shakespeare is a reflection of his faith in Shakespeare as the cornerstone of the British stage, a faith which finds expression in a *Tableau Vivant* at the end of *The New Planet* (1847). Juno sings:

> See of Britain's stage the splendour;
>   Not for ages, but all time,
> Wrote the bard whose form we render;
>   Who shall reach his height sublime?
> Till the earth to circle ceases,
>   Till no eye his scenes can trace,
> Spite of fashion's wild caprices,
>   He will ne'er be out of place. (iii. 179)

A similar note was heard in a patriotic passage of *The Drama's Levée* first performed on 16 April 1838. Victoria had come to the throne in the previous year and, as Planché notes, 'was a constant visitor to the theatres, and at this period attended nearly all the farewell performances of Charles Kemble at Covent Garden'. Her interest in the theatre seemed like a portent of better days ahead.

> . . .whatso'er may be the moment's rage,
> The British public love the British stage,
> And days as bright as when thy [i.e. Drama's] birth was seen,
> Are dawning 'neath another British Queen.
> To thine old temples she hath led the town,
> With garlands fresh thy Shakespeare's bust to crown;
> Richard, Coriolanus, Hamlet, Lear,
> In splendour worthy of themselves appear;
> And by their Sovereign's gracious smile inspired,

> Shall British bards with nobler ardour fired,
> Strike chords which find their echoes in the heart,
> And make the muses from their slumber start. (ii. 22)

As things turned out, the muses had their full quota of sleep for some considerable time after this was written; and it is not long before Planché is complaining that Shakespeare's heroes do not 'in splendour worthy of themselves appear'.

The Drama at Home (8 April 1844) presents a vision of Drury Lane: 'as soon as the building is up, the portion beneath the portico opens, and the stage is seen with a tableau from the play of "Richard III", as lately performed there [by Charles Kean].' Drama is delighted at the sight.

> Vision of glory!—I'm at Drury Lane
> With Shakespeare—'Richard is himself again!'

But the statue of Shakespeare over the portico speaks, Commendatore-like:

> Awake! Beware of fibbers!
> That Richard's none of mine—'Tis Colley Cibbers!

Puff, who has been trying to impress Drama, is annoyed:

> Rot that Shakespeare, he always speaks the truth! I wonder what the devil they stuck him up there for. There was a leaden Apollo, with a lyre in his hand, on the top of the old building—much more appropriate to the new one—where William Tell[16] draws more than William Shakespeare. (ii. 297–80).

Planché's voice may thus have been one of those that encouraged Samuel Phelps, less than a year later, to stage Shakespeare's, instead of Cibber's, *Richard III*—not, as it happened, with any lasting result.

In the same piece is a passage in which we see famous Shakespearian characters out of work: Othello is a sandwich-man advertising Warren's Blacking; Macbeth has 'set up a cigar divan, | And stands at his own door as a Highlandman', and Shylock has 'opened a slop shop in the Minories' (ii. 284–7). But again the note of hope is sounded. Portia and Nerissa enter and tell Drama, who feels that 'they've ceased to care for me at home': 'Then you've not heard the news—the Drama's free!' The allusion is, of course, to the Theatre Regulations Act of 1843, by which the monopoly of the patent theatres had been abolished. As a sign of what has already been achieved, the principals from *The Merry Wives of Windsor* and *The Taming of the Shrew* appear, representing the important Haymarket productions of these plays: the first had an exceptionally long run, and the second was a very remarkable, and successful, attempt, suggested and designed by Planché himself,[17] to produce a full text of Shakespeare's play (instead of Garrick's *Katherine and Petruchio*, which went on being performed throughout the century), and to present it in conditions approximating to those of the Elizabethan theatre. There were, then, fair reasons for hope.

One of the results of the Theatre Regulations Act was that the serious drama tended to move out of the large patent theatres, to which it had been for too long confined, into smaller theatres in which an actor had a better chance of making an effect without coarsening his style. This was in many ways a good thing; but naturally some regret was felt at the consequent degeneration in the state of Covent Garden and Drury Lane. Planché reflects this regret in *The Camp at the Olympic* (1853) where Tragedy asks how she can fail to be in a passion

> when I see the State
> Of Denmark rotten! When I hear the fate
> Which hath befallen both the classic domes,
> 'Neath which my votaries once found their homes!
> Where Garrick, monarch of the mimic scene,
> His sceptre passed from Kemble down to Kean;
> Where Cibber's silver tones the heart would steal,
> And Siddons left her mantle to O'Neil!
> The Drama banished from her highest places
> By *débardeurs* and 'fools with varnished faces',
> Sees foreign foes her sacred ruins spurning,
> Fiddling like Neros while her Rome is burning. (iv. 304)

The author's own awareness that there is another side to the question is suggested by Fancy's reply, which begins 'The times have changed'.

The move to smaller theatres did nothing to lessen the increasing emphasis on the spectacular in Shakespearian productions. Planché deplored this. In *Mr Buckstone's Ascent of Mount Parnassus* (28 March 1853) he has a dig at the elaborate productions of Shakespeare then being given by Phelps at Sadler's Wells and by Charles Kean at the Princess's Theatre. Melpomene asks for news of Shakespeare, and Mr Buckstone replies:

> Shakespeare! We call him the illustrious stranger;
> He has been drooping—but he's out of danger,
> And gone to Sadler's Wells and the Princess's
> For change of air—I may say scenes and dresses. (iv. 289)

Later in the same year, in *The Camp at the Olympic*, a similar complaint is voiced in more general terms. The somewhat didactic tone suggests that Planché is here expressing strong personal feelings:

> TRAGEDY.   Has not immortal Shakespeare said 'tis silly,
> 'To gild refinèd gold—to paint the lily?'
> SPECTACLE.   Immortal Shakespeare! come, the less you say
> The better on that head. There's not a play
> Of his for many a year the town has taken,
> If I've not buttered preciously his bacon. (iv. 317)

And a few lines later Fancy says:

> What's to be done when the immortal names
> Of Shakespeare and of Byron urge their claims
> In vain to popularity, without
> Spectacle march all his contingent out?
> Not mere Dutch metal, spangles, foil, and paste,
> But gems culled from authority by Taste;
> Until, reflecting every bygone age,
> A picture-gallery becomes the stage;
> And modern Babylon may there behold
> The pomp and pageantry that wrecked the old! (iv. 318)

It is worthy of note that Planché is attacking, not merely tawdrily decorated productions, but also those which employ 'gems culled from authority by Taste'. He had culled such gems himself. We may remember his work with Charles Kemble, his pride in the 'roar of approbation, accompanied by four distinct rounds of applause', which in 1823 greeted the sight of 'King John dressed as his effigy appears in Worcester Cathedral, surrounded by his barons sheathed in mail, with cylindrical helmets and correct armorial shields, and his courtiers in the long tunics and mantles of the thirteenth century'. Charles Kean was to some extent his disciple. But half a century later he wrote:

> if propriety be pushed to extravagance, if what should be mere accessories are occasionally elevated by short-sighted managers into the principal features of their productions, I am not answerable for their suicidal folly.... I can perfectly understand 'King John' or any other historical play being acted in plain evening dress without any scenery at all, and interpreted by great actors interesting the audience to such a degree that imagination would supply the picturesque accessories to them as sufficiently as it does to the reader of the play in his study.[18]

He wrote similarly of his revival of *The Taming of the Shrew*; it was 'eminently successful, incontestably proving that a good play, well acted, will carry the audience along with it, unassisted by scenery; and in this case also, remember, it was a comedy in *five* acts, without the curtain once falling during its performance'.[19] This production was fifty years before the founding of the Elizabethan Stage Society. It is paradoxical that Planché has claim to be remembered as the forerunner of both the elaborately pictorial school of Shakespeare production and of the simplicity of William Poel.

IV

During the fifties the rage for burlesque drama was at its height, and Planché depicts what he saw as the battle between burlesque and tragedy. In *The Camp at the Olympic* he hints, rather subtly, that the decline of tragedy is due to a lack of great actors: on Burlesque's approach, Tragedy calls for support, but Mr Wigan asks, 'where's the actor strong enough?' 'Then I shall fall!', says Tragedy, sinking into a chair (iv. 308). It is somewhat curious that Frederick Robson was playing Burlesque; curious because he was probably the greatest English burlesque actor, and curious too because a common reaction to his performances in travesties of Shakespeare was a comment deploring the fact that he was not playing the role 'straight'. Burlesque sings:

> Your Hamlet may give up his Ghost,
> Your Richard may run himself through,
> I'm Cock-of-the-Walk to your cost,
> And I crow over all your crew!
> For Burlesque is up! up! up!
> And Tragedy down! down! down! O!
> Pop up your nob again,
> And I'll box you for your crown, O!

In the words of Macbeth to Banquo's ghost, Tragedy bids Burlesque depart, but is met with a seriously argued self-defence:

> ...I fling your follies in your face,
> And call back all the false starts of your race,
> Shew up your shows, affect your affectation,
> And by such homoeopathic aggravation,
> Would cleanse your bosom of that perilous stuff,
> Which weighs upon our art—bombast and puff.

He cites *Tom Thumb*, *The Critic*, and *Bombastes Furioso* as evidence that burlesque can have a serious purpose, and claims that

> When in his words he's not one to the wise,
> When his fool's bolt, *spares* folly as it flies,
> When in his chaff there's not a grain to seize on,
> When in his rhyme there's not a ray of reason,

> His slang but slang, no point beyond the pun,
> Burlesque may walk, for he will cease to run.

He begs however that his claims to sense will not be spread abroad:

> If once of common sense I was suspected,
> I should be quite as much as you—neglected. (iv. 309)

This is admirable dramatic argument; Planché triumphantly succeeds here in presenting a serious case with urbanity and wit. The pun in 'for he will cease to run', for instance, lightens a passage that might without it have appeared unduly homiletic.

In *Love and Fortune* (1859) comes Planché's final defence of the liberties he and other dramatists have taken with Shakespeare. The piece was presented at the Princess's Theatre, in which Charles Kean's Shakespeare productions had been so successful. Augustus Harris had just followed Kean in the management of the theatre, and Fortune says:

> Oh, don't name Shakespeare—of his awful shade
> The new lessee is horribly afraid.
> Here in such state he lately wore his crown.
> His spirit on us fatally may frown.

But Love reassures him:

> What, gentle Shakespeare? pleasant Will, who'd run
> Through a whole page to make a shocking pun!
> Who shed a glory round things most grotesque?
> Who wrote for Grecian clowns the best burlesque?
> He look on harmless mirth with angry eyes?
> No, no, he is too genial and too wise.
> His heart was e'en his matchless mind above—
> He nothing owes to Fortune, much to Love! (v. 203)

The extravaganzas preserve for us something of the Victorian attitude to Shakespeare; they should also remind us that their author, in his vigilance for high standards of production, a vigilance which often rose above the prevailing standards of his time, served Shakespeare well. The Victorian attitude has developed into our own, and Planché was one of its shaping forces.

20

Shakespeare in Max Beerbohm's Theatre Criticism

In May 1898 Bernard Shaw gave up his post of theatre critic of *The Saturday Review*. He was ill. His doctor, he explained, had discovered that 'for many years [he had] been converting the entire stock of energy extractable from [his] food...into pure genius'. He was 'already almost an angel', and would complete the process if he wrote any more articles. So, on 21 May, he wrote an essay headed 'Valedictory'.[1] He cannot justify the fact that he has spent four years on dramatic criticism. He has

> sworn an oath to endure no more of it.... Still, the gaiety of nations must not be eclipsed. The long string of beautiful ladies who are at present in the square without, awaiting, under the supervision of two gallant policemen, their turn at my bedside, must be reassured when they protest, as they will, that the light of their life will go out if my dramatic articles cease. To each of them I will present the flower left by her predecessor, and assure her that there are as good fish in the sea as ever came out of it. The younger generation is knocking at the door; and as I open it there steps spritely in the incomparable Max.

Shaw was 41 years old; Max Beerbohm was 26. *The Saturday Review* was edited with great success by Frank Harris, who was already developing an unhealthy interest in Shakespeare. He had published his essay 'The True Shakespeare' in March of this year. The following year, Oscar Wilde was to write in a letter from France, 'Frank Harris is upstairs, thinking about Shakespeare at the top of his voice.'[2] The thinking eventually bore ripe fruit in Harris's sensational book *The Man Shakespeare and His Tragic Life-Story*, published in 1909, and its sequel, *The Women of Shakespeare*, of two years later. Max Beerbohm knew Harris, and had already contributed to *The Saturday Review* before becoming its theatre critic. Lord David Cecil tells the story of a luncheon party in 1896:

> During a moment of silence Harris's voice was heard booming out. 'Unnatural vice!' he was saying, 'I know nothing of the joys of unnatural vice. You must ask my friend

Oscar about them. But,' he went on, with a reverential change of tone, 'had Shakespeare asked me, I should have had to submit!' Max went home and drew a cartoon of Harris, stark naked and with his moustache bristling, looking coyly over his shoulder at Shakespeare who shrinks back at the alarming prospect. Underneath was written, 'Had Shakespeare asked ...'. This was a very daring cartoon for 1896; and Max showed it to few people. It is not known if Harris was one of them. He is unlikely to have minded if he did see it; he was remarkably impervious to Max's teasing.[3]

It was with no great enthusiasm that Max accepted Harris's invitation to succeed Shaw. He needed the money: £5 a week at the start. He held the post for twelve years, until two weeks before his marriage, soon after which he left England to live in Italy. It was the only regular work he ever did; and he disliked it. In his own valedictory essay he wrote: 'Had I been told that I was destined to write about plays for twelve weeks, I should have shuddered. Had I been told that I was destined to write about them for twelve years, I should have expired on the spot, neatly falsifying the prediction.' He admits that he 'acquired a vivid interest' in the task. But the writing itself was uphill work, 'mainly because I am cursed with an acute literary conscience ... And thus it is that Thursday, the day chosen by me (as being the latest possible one) for writing my article, has for twelve years been regarded by me as the least pleasant day of the week.'[4] He locked himself in his room, the household observed a nervous silence, and Max spent much of the time gloomily staring at the paper and doodling in the effort to get started.[5] Nevertheless, he fulfilled his duties with great success, and admitted that the discipline was good for him.[6] A selection of his reviews was published in two volumes in 1924 under the title of *Around Theatres*. It was reprinted as a single volume in 1953. A second selection, *More Theatres: 1898–1903* appeared in 1969, and the reprinting of his theatre criticism was completed in 1970 with the publication of *Last Theatres: 1904–1910*.[7] Between them, the volumes run to well over 1,700 pages. Most of the essays are straightforward reviews of plays, but there are occasional departures in the form of reviews of books on theatrical subjects, more general essays on the theatre, and obituaries. These volumes are, of course, an invaluable commentary on the theatre of their time. Max was, he claimed, more interested in literature than in the theatre, and much of his criticism reflects this. There is, for instance, a brilliant essay on Pinero's prose style (i. 286–90). Bernard Shaw, released from the bonds of weekly composition, entered into a fruitful period of playwriting on his own account, and Max's reviews of the first productions of some of Shaw's plays include still some of the most thoughtful criticism they have received. Max was writing at a time when the music-hall was rich in talent, and this too he was able to enjoy and to communicate in words.

Still, it was not simply out of a delight in paradox that Max headed his first essay as a dramatic critic 'Why I Ought Not to Have Become a Dramatic Critic' (i. 1–4). He admits that of the arts he loves literature best of all, and claims that he is 'not fond of the theatre'. He has not read his distinguished predecessors such as Hazlitt, Lamb, and Lewes, though he has 'a fragmentary recollection of Aristotle's fragment on the drama', on which he once wrote an examination paper for which he was awarded the mark of 'gamma-minus query'. He cannot even claim the virtue of coming fresh to the theatre, because, having been born into the theatrical world, he is over-familiar with it. He was half-brother to Sir Herbert Beerbohm Tree, one of the leading actors of the day.

> One well-known player and manager is my near relative. Who will not smile if I praise him? How could I possibly disparage him?...Most of the elder actors have patted me on the head and given me sixpence when I was 'only *so* high'. Even if, with an air of incorruptibility, I now return them their sixpences, they will yet expect me to pat *them* on the head in the *Saturday Review*.[8]

In fact, Max wrote so urbanely that such considerations never have the appearance of troubling him. Reviewing his half-brother as Falstaff in *The Merry Wives of Windsor*, for instance, he was to write:

> It is difficult for us, to whom Mr Tree's personality is so familiar through photographs in the illustrated papers, to accept him as a perfect Falstaff. But...if we project ourselves into the state of knowing nothing whatsoever about Mr Tree as he is, we get, I think, the true impression of a fat mind in a fat body. (ii. 473)

In his first article there is a Shakespeare allusion: 'The Editor of this paper has come to me as Romeo came to the apothecary, and what he wants I give him for the apothecary's reason.' And later Max was to draw a cartoon illustrating this, with Frank Harris as a florid Romeo, and Max as the apothecary, handing him a phial marked 'Dramatic Criticisms'. The caption is 'My poverty, but not my will, consents'.[9] Still, Max tries to cheer himself up:

> I daresay that there are many callings more uncomfortable and dispiriting than that of dramatic critic. To be a porter on the Underground Railway must, I have often thought, be very terrible. Whenever I feel myself sinking under the stress of my labours, I shall say to myself, 'I am not a porter on the Underground Railway'. (i. 4).

The proportion of Shakespearean comment in Max's theatre criticism is relatively small. This is not the result of any shortage of productions of Shakespeare's plays while Max was reviewing. It is because he was far more interested, in general, in the art of his own time than in that of the past, and also because he was temperamentally unresponsive to much in Shakespeare. He admits as much in the Epistle Dedicatory to *Around Theatres*. He has had to select the articles as in themselves they were. 'Whether the play I had criticised were by Shakespeare or by Mr Tomkins must not matter to me...And I fear I had always preferred Mr Tomkins, as a theme, to Shakespeare. I felt more at home with him, and wrote better about him. That is a drawback of the satiric temperament; and I deplore it.'

The 'satiric temperament' is also something of a drawback for us in so far as it makes it difficult for us always to know how seriously to take Max's statements about his lack of knowledge. He certainly had an educated person's familiarity with at least those Shakespeare plays that were in the popular repertory, and of the general background. Shakespeare allusions are scattered through his writings. There are several in *Zuleika Dobson*, for instance, including the exquisitely humorous one in which Gertrude's account of Ophelia's death introduces a description of Zuleika in her morning bath.[10] Sotheby's catalogue of the sale of Max's books in 1960 records a copy of Dowden's edition of the Sonnets in which, we are tantalizingly told, Max has supplied irreverent endings to three sonnets. It records too a collected Shakespeare containing eight limericks on the characters of Shakespeare.[11] The one on Othello is reproduced:

> No doubt you have heard of Othello—
> An African sort of a fellow.
> > When they said 'You are black'
> > He cried 'Take it back!
> I am only an exquisite yellow.'

The theatre review in which Max displays most familiarity with Shakespeare scholarship is one of *Macbeth*, dating from October 1898 (i. 8–11). In this, he makes an excursus into stage history. He recalls Aubrey's account of the performance of the play at Hampton Court in 1606 from which we learn that the boy taking the part of Lady Macbeth fell sick, as a result of which 'Master Shakespeare himself did enacte in his stead.' Combating the fallacy that the play has 'hitherto been acted only in the blood- and-thunder convention of Mrs Siddons', he quotes also a passage from Pepys's diary which seems to suggest, he feels, that Mrs Knipp's performance in the autumn of 1667 was not essentially different from Mrs Patrick Campbell's.

Methought Mrs Knipp did never play so fine, specially in the matter of the two daggers, yet without brawl or overmuch tragick gesture, the which is most wearisome, as though an actress do care more to affright us than to be approved. She was most comickal and natural when she walks forth sleeping (the which I can testify, for Mrs Pepys also walks sleeping at some times), and did most ingeniously mimick the manner of women who walk thus.

Max's use of these passages of historical evidence is impressive enough when one considers how little known they were in 1898. It is even more impressive when one realizes that they are entirely of his invention. Here Max is the total ironist, employing his gifts as a parodist in a completely straight-faced manner which may easily go undetected and, indeed, appears to have done so. The spoof is a careful one; Pepys did in fact see *Macbeth* in October 1667. Max was indulging here the strange impulse that led him to spend so many hours in his later years decorating his books with incongruous but totally convincing additions, like the mock-inscription in a copy of Ibsen's *When We Dead Awaken*, which reads 'For Max Beerbohm | critic of who | the writings fills | with pleasure me. | H. Ibsen.'[12] Had there been any dishonesty in his nature, Max could have completely overshadowed Chatterton, Ireland, and Collier. He was so clever it is even possible that he has.

In a letter to his future wife, Max acknowledged his temperamental unresponsiveness to Shakespeare. 'You shall teach me to enjoy, as well as respect and bow to, Shakespeare.'[13] But at many points in the theatre reviews he shows no respect and makes no obeisances, but rather offers reasoned criticisms. Early in his career, in the notice of *Macbeth* from which I have quoted, he writes:

> Shakespeare had his shortcomings. Love of him does not blind me to his limitations and his faults of excess. But, after all, the man is dead, and I do not wish to emulate that captious and rancorous spirit—inflamed, as it often seemed to me, by an almost personal animosity—in which my predecessor persecuted him beyond the grave.

Max's discussions of Shakespeare's limitations and faults are certainly not rancorous. But they are often sharp. He blames Shakespeare for pandering to his public, using 'stupid stories conceived by stupid writers as a quick means of catching a stupid public'. He censures him for his 'plagiaristic method', inviting his readers to conceive the possibility that the twentieth century should produce a dramatic poet as great as Shakespeare who nevertheless was 'so weak or so modest as to found his plays on the farces of the late Mr H. J. Byron, and on the melodramas of the late Mr Pettitt, and on the romantic dramas of the late Mr Wills and the present Mr Henry Hamilton'. The result of such a method in Shakespeare, says Max, is that 'throughout the fabric of his work you will find much that is tawdry, irrational, otiose—much that is, however shy you may be of admitting that it is, tedious' (ii. 342–3).

This general criticism underlies much of Max's comment on particular plays. He is, indeed, so unappreciative of some of them that I prefer to pass over his remarks as rapidly as possible. *Henry V* as produced by Benson is 'just a dull, incoherent series of speeches, interspersed with alarums and excursions' (i. 63) (though when it was performed by Lewis Waller at the Lyceum Max enjoyed it 'very much indeed' (ii. 341)); '*Coriolanus* is a bad play we all agree' (ii. 366); in reading, *King John* had seemed 'insufferably tedious' (ii. 193); *Richard III* 'is very tedious indeed' (ii. 186); *The Merchant of Venice* 'is a particularly sad instance of the way in which Shakespeare wasted so much of his time' (ii. 343); *The Merry Wives of Windsor* 'is the wretchedest bit of hack-work ever done by a great writer' (ii. 473); and even *Twelfth Night* is 'perfunctory and formless', though 'in some degree redeemed by its accessory characters' (ii. 347). Once, his criticism is bodied forth in parody of one of the areas of Shakespeare which, in our bardolatrous age, it is still permissible to find tedious. Reviewing Shaw's *The Admirable Bashville*, Max laments the absence of Shakespearean comic relief, and imagines what it might have been like:

SECOND POLICEMAN: Canst tell me of this prize-fight? Is't within law?

FIRST POLICEMAN: Aye! To't. For what does a man prize highest? A fight. But no
    man fights what he prizes, else is he no man, being not manly, nor yet unmannerly.
    Argal, if he fight the prize, then is not the prize his, save in misprision, and 'tis no
    prize-fight within the meaning of the Act.

SECOND POLICEMAN: Marry, I like thy wit, etc., etc. (ii. 582)

An often repeated theme of Max's criticism is that Shakespeare's plays should be performed less frequently than they are. This would be a natural reaction to the plays that Max finds tedious; but he applies it even to those that he most admires. Even Shakespeare's 'best work should not be laid before us so often as to rob us of the capacity for being freshly affected by it. And his second-best and third-best work should not be laid before us at all' (ii. 339). He complains that 'Hamlet has long ceased to be treated as a play. It has become simply a hoop through which every very eminent actor must, sooner or later, jump' (i. 36). His most serious attempt to grapple with the question of how he can both enormously admire a play yet not wish to see it performed comes in a discussion of Benson's *Hamlet* written in March 1901 (ii. 359–63). He admits that 'To see *Hamlet* is one of our natural functions, one of our needs'. He finds that 'every time I hear it, the language in *Hamlet* seems lovelier, comes with a new thrill'. Nevertheless, 'As drama, *Hamlet* has no power to affect me at all.' His analysis of why this should be so is revealing about his own conception of drama. Partly it is expressed in those terms of light-hearted irony with which he often veils his fundamental seriousness.

> I am too much at home in Elsinore. I seem to have stayed there so often, to have written so many letters on its notepaper, helped the son of the house so often with his theatricals, talked so cordially about him to his *fiancée*, tried so sympathetically to reassure his mother as to his sanity, been so very sorry when he was called away to England.

But clearly also Max finds that *Hamlet* does not conform with his view of a well-made play. 'In modern times dramaturgy has become a strict art-form. A play has to be a concise exposition and development of a theme, and to be consistent in its manner throughout.' To Shakespeare, dramaturgy was a go-as-you-please affair, in which any amount of time might be spent in divagations from the main theme, and in which one manner of treatment might be alternated with another, and in which the characters might, from time to time, and without warning, become the mere mouthpiece of the author.

It may seem that Max here is judging Shakespeare by the standards of Pinero. But perhaps this is not an altogether false description of Shakespeare's technique. Its implicit criticism, like that which lies behind Max's scorn of the 'stupid stories' that Shakespeare uses, and his belief that Shakespeare was pandering to a 'stupid public', anticipates points that Robert Bridges was to make in his essay 'On the Influence of the Audience'[14] in 1907, and that were to be discussed also by, notably, Stoll and Schücking during the next few decades. It is not so much that the analysis of Shakespeare's technique is mistaken as that, in general, our attitude has changed, and we are now encouraged to admire these features of his art as indispensable means to a higher end.

Max's views on Shakespeare's methods of composition—his 'plagiaristic method' (ii. 343)—are coloured by beliefs about Shakespeare's sources that would now have to be much modified. He envisages Shakespeare working over 'crude farces and melodramas' (ii. 518), letting 'his genius gallop lightly over the ready-made material, glorifying it, but leaving it, essentially, much as it was before' (ii. 361). More recent scholarship suggests that there are fewer dramatic sources for Shakespeare's plays than Max seems to have believed, and that Shakespeare put far more preliminary thought into his design. Criticism may have gone too far in the opposite direction, but it is not necessary to believe that Shakespeare's normal method was to have an idea and then to embody it in character and plot—something which I think he did only quite infrequently—to feel that still he was not at all as haphazard in his methods as Max suggests.

It will be apparent that though Max could speak so disparagingly of Shakespeare as even to be able to say that 'as a dramatist, in the narrow sense of the word, Shakespeare has had his day' (ii. 518), nevertheless he found much to admire in the plays. It is understandable that a play he particularly admired, The Tempest, is one in which he felt that Shakespeare was not writing in a haphazard way but to an idea. In a review published on 7 November 1903 (i. 293–7), he suggests that no sources have been found for this play because 'Shakespeare, at the close of his career, wished to write an epilogue to his work, an autobiography, in allegorical form. . . . And what more natural than that he should proceed to evolve from his own brain, now at leisure for the task, a story after his own less quickly-pulsing heart?' For this reason, The Tempest is the only play 'that satisfies the modern standard of art'. Max fully accepts the belief, current in his time, that the play is an allegory of Shakespeare's own career, and that 'he who impersonates Prospero impersonates also the creator of Prospero'. His view that this play is 'essentially the work of an elder', in which art has triumphed over 'impoverished vitality', seems to be approaching Lytton Strachey's view, first propounded less than three weeks after this review appeared, of the last plays as the products of boredom.[15]

It is not surprising that one possessed of the satiric temperament should respond most easily to comedies. Although by comparison with *The Tempest* Max found *A Midsummer Night's Dream* a 'debauch of uncontrolled fancy', still it was a favourite play.

> Shakespeare fulminating, Shakespeare pontificating, has never been surpassed, but Shakespeare in his slippers has never been approached by any poet in *his*. Throughout the *Midsummer Night's Dream* we see him in his slippers—exquisitely embroidered slippers, which, in sheer gaiety and lightness of heart, he kicks up into the empyrean and catches again on the tip of his toe upturned. (ii. 113–16)

The theme is reiterated in another notice (ii. 230–3), in which he describes this as 'the most impressive of all Shakespeare's works, because it was idly done, because it was a mere overflow of genius'. *As You Like It* is praised in somewhat similar terms: 'It is less like a play than like a lyric that has been miraculously prolonged to the length of a play without losing its airiness and its enchantment' (i. 478).

To the tragedies Max responded less easily. *Hamlet* was a great favourite, and drew from him an interesting paragraph about the subtlety of character-portrayal in Hamlet himself. Finding that H. B. Irving does not give us 'a wholly consistent or wholly intelligible picture' of Hamlet, he says

> We must blame Shakespeare. Or, rather, we must praise Shakespeare. None of us is wholly consistent or wholly intelligible—at any rate to himself, who knows most about the matter. To his acquaintances a man may seem to be this or that kind of man, quite definitely. That is only because they know so little about him. To his intimate friends he is rather a problem. To himself he is an insoluble problem. Shakespeare, drawing Hamlet, drew him from within ... drew him in all his complexity and changefulness.... We must not ask of any actor that he shall explain Hamlet to us. The most we can expect is that he shall give unity to the divergent characteristics and moods. (iii. 150)

In *Hamlet*, as in many of the plays, Max finds the chief interest to lie in the portrayal of the central character. So it is with *Macbeth*, *The Merchant of Venice*, and *Othello*. He writes well on Iago and the problems that he poses for the actor (ii. 518–21). *King Lear* was a difficult play for him to face. The unnaturalness of behaviour in the early scenes is too much for him; there is 'too much that Shakespeare did not transmute in the crucible of his brain'. But he recognizes that 'Shakespeare's great imagination certainly did begin to work at high pressure so soon as he got Lear out upon the storm-swept heath with the clown, and in the hovel where Poor Tom gibbered' (iii. 483–7).

Max's most sustained piece of analytical Shakespeare criticism comes in relation to *Julius Caesar*, and is spread over a series of reviews. Beerbohm Tree had revived the play successfully after a long period of neglect, which Max attributed to the lack of love-interest. Max reviewed the production in September 1900 (ii. 285–8). He admires *Julius Caesar* as a 'man's play', ranging 'between a sphere where the appeal is merely intellectual, and a sphere where emotion is strictly divorced from sex'. In the course of his notice he suggests that 'its idea—how finely developed!—is the vanity of idealism in practical affairs'. Two weeks later, he refers at the end of a review of another play to a 'long interesting letter' printed in the same issue by one H.H. trying 'to show that the moral drawn by me from *Julius Caesar*—the vanity of idealism in practical affairs—was never pointed by Shakespeare himself, for that his Brutus was not an idealist but a self-seeking humbug.' Max 'cannot swallow' this. Shakespeare was a professional dramatist who knew perfectly well how to guide his audience's reactions; he could and would have made Brutus's hypocrisy apparent if this was what he had intended. Max does not object to H.H.'s finding the moral elsewhere. 'A masterpiece can be seen rightly from many aspects.' But he sticks to his own point of view. There the matter rested. But five-and-a-half years later Max devotes an entire essay to comment on an article by Harold Hodge which had just appeared in *Harper's Magazine*. Mr Hodge is, of course, H.H., who had written up his views on Brutus into a 'critical comment'.[16] He was, in fact, Max's editor, having succeeded Frank Harris in 1898; he remained editor of *The Saturday Review* till 1913. So there may be more than meets the eye in this controversy. Max's article of 17 February 1906 is a developed objection to Hodge's developed version of his earlier point of view. It is an entirely serious and forcefully expressed piece of close criticism. It provoked a reply from Hodge, to which Max devotes yet another entire article the following week, replying carefully and with some warmth to each of Hodge's points. These articles reveal Max's capacity to enter wholeheartedly into a critical debate. The issue is still live. Hodge's point of view has become a powerful one; it resembles, for instance, that of T. S. Dorsch in his new Arden edition. Max's articles form a well-argued defence of Brutus and make a real contribution to the history of the criticism of *Julius Caesar*.

Of the English history plays Max had a generally low opinion, though he was several times surprised to find that he enjoyed performances of them far more than he had expected. Writing about a performance of *King John* leads him into an admission that there is a difference between reading plays and seeing them.

> I had never seen the play acted before, and I must confess that, reading it, I had found it insufferably tedious. I had found many beautiful pieces of poetry in it, but drama had seemed to me absolutely lacking. That was because I have not much imagination. Lengths of blank verse with a few bald directions—enter A, exeunt B and D; dies; alarums and excursions; are not enough to make me *see* a thing. (And, I take it, this is

the case with most of my fellow-creatures.) Therefore, when I go to a theatre and find that what bored me very much in the reading of it is a really fine play, I feel that I owe a great debt of gratitude to the management which has brought out the latent possibilities. I can imagine that a bad production of *King John* would be infinitely worse than a private reading of it.... But a good production, as at Her Majesty's, makes one forget what is bad in sheer surprise at finding so much that is good. (ii. 193)

Max is quite clear that, if he is to see the plays performed, it should be with modern staging methods. He saw a number of William Poel's productions with the Elizabethan Stage Society, but the only one he seems to have enjoyed was of the first Quarto of *Hamlet*, and that was because it 'came almost as a new play.... The verbal and structural differences between the First and Second Quartos were just enough to create for me a new Hamlet. And so I was grateful to Mr Poel' (i. 64–5). But in general he found that the professedly 'educational' aims of the Society were fulfilled only in so far as Poel succeeded 'in teaching us to pity the poor Elizabethans and to be thankful for the realism of the modern theatre' (i. 61). He had no objections to the Society's productions 'as object lessons in a branch of archaeology' (ii. 223); he respects the Society's 'enthusiastic scholarship'; himself, he finds their activities owlish, but they enjoy themselves, so 'Long may they blink and flutter and hoot.' But he resents claims made by 'some authoritative persons' that Poel's way is 'the one and only dignified mode of presenting Shakespeare's plays' (i. 258–9). 'To compare these revivals with the ordinary modern productions is to be convinced that if Shakespeare could come to life again he would give Mr Poel a wide berth, and would hurry to the nearest commercial theatre in which a play of his happened to be running' (ii. 222). 'Shakespeare wrote at a time when the science of scenic production was in its infancy, and he himself, as he has told us, was conscious and resentful of the limitations' (i. 258). Max admits that the Elizabethans must nevertheless have found the productions satisfactory, but feels that 'we, in the twentieth century, cannot project—or rather retroject—ourselves into their state of receptivity' (i. 258). In the 1970s we have to admit that this feeling still lies behind most modern productions of Shakespeare. But we might not wish to go quite so far as Max in his praise of productions in which 'everything...contributes to illusion' (ii. 222). He reviewed his half-brother's famous production of *A Midsummer Night's Dream* (ii. 230–3), now regarded as a notorious climax in naturalistic presentation, and thoroughly enjoyed it.[17] He found himself

really and truly illuded by the Wood near Athens. All the little fairies there gambolled in a spontaneous and elfin way; the tuition of them had been carried so far as to make us forget that they were real children, licensed by a Magistrate, and that 'at break of day' they were going to meet, not Oberon, but a certificated Board School teacher.

In this notice he makes gentle fun of Sidney Lee, suggesting that he would have been likely only to enjoy the moment in the play-scene when Quince came on 'bearing a board with the inscription "THIS IS A WOOD"'. This quip was no doubt provoked by Sidney Lee's article 'Shakespeare and the Modern Stage'[18], printed in *The Nineteenth Century* in the same month as Max wrote his review. This is a well-considered plea that 'lovers of Shakespeare should lose no opportunity of urging the cause of simplicity in the production of the plays of Shakespeare'. Max may well have regarded it as an implicit attack on his half-brother's production methods.

Max felt similar admiration for his half-brother's production of *Twelfth Night*, in reviewing which he again defended the point of view that the plays 'are not at all degraded by a setting of beauty, that they deserve such setting, and by it are made more beautiful, and that anyone who by it is distracted from their own intrinsic beauty betrays in himself a lack of visual sense' (9 February 1901; ii. 346–50).

Beerbohm Tree's elaborate productions seem, from our vantage point, the last, climactic fling of scenic extravagance in Shakespeare presentation. On *A Midsummer Night's Dream*, says Odell, 'Tree lavished the very last possibilities of stage craft', and with it he produced for the last year of the century the 'utmost scenic marvels toward which that century had steadily progressed'.[19] *The Athenaeum* was even more affirmative: 'In presenting the poetic aspects of a Midsummer Night's Dream, Mr Tree has not only gone beyond precedent and record, he has reached what may, until science brings about new possibilities, be regarded as the limits of the conceivable.'[20] It is only fair to Max to remark that his insistence on visual beauty was not limited to the purely representational. He praises Charles Ricketts's pioneering designs for *King Lear* (1909; iii. 485), and writes with high admiration of Gordon Craig's scenery for *Much Ado About Nothing* (1903; ii. 573–6), which was quite beyond the understanding of many who saw it.

On acting-styles in Shakespeare, Max declared his hand in an early notice (i. 24–7) in which he discusses what he calls the new and the old schools of acting. The new school, he finds, triumphs in modern comedy or modern tragedy, but the old school comes into its own with romantic melodrama, a form which is old-fashioned, not in the sense that it is no longer popular, but that 'it is no longer a form to which any vital English dramatist devotes himself'. The old method still flourishes in the provinces, where 'one finds infinitely better acting in romantic melodrama than one ever finds in London. There, too, Shakespeare's plays are performed much better than in London, for in Shakespeare's plays the poetry and the rhetoric are of far greater importance than the psychology' (i. 27). This theme is repeated and developed in a number of notices. Max does not crudely suggest that 'the poetry' should be emphasized all the time. Shakespeare 'was both a dramatist and a poet', and 'the best Shakespearian acting is a kind of compromise between poetry and drama' (i. 72). Thus, 'the ideal interpreter of a Shakespearean part is one who effects an exactly fair compromise between the poetry and the drama, giving to the words as much of the beauty of their rhythm as is compatible with their reflection of mood and character' (i. 260). This seems very fair, though we might not always agree with its interpretation. For example, to Max 'Ophelia's mad-scene is mere poetry'. It should not be played for an effect of realistic lunacy, as Mrs Benson plays it, 'who groans and gasps, glares, shrieks and gesticulates, so indefatigably as to make havoc of every beautiful line the poet has put into her mouth' (i. 72–3). Similarly

> Miss Brayton is very pleasant in the sane scenes of Ophelia, but one would hardly be surprised if at any moment she entered springing off a bicycle. In the mad scenes of Ophelia she tries hard not to be so pleasant, and manages to give a realistic represen-tation of lunacy.

Max thinks this a mistake, and that 'The only right way for an actress to interpret these mad scenes is through her sense of beauty.' This is questionable, though his discussion in the same notice of the speaking of Gertrude's description of Ophelia's death makes admirable sense:

> 'There is', says lyric Shakespeare, 'a willow grows aslant a brook', and he proceeds to revel in the landscape, quite forgetting (to our eternal gain) that he speaks through the lips of an agonised lady. What is the agonised lady to do? . . . . She must forget that she is an agonised lady, and speak the words as beautifully and as simply as she can. Then there will be no absurdity. But what could be more absurd than to hear a lady talking, as Miss Maud Milton talks, about 'crow-flowers, nettles, daisies, and long purples' with tragic gasps and violent gestures of woe, and dwelling with special emphasis on 'long purples' as though they were quite the most harrowing thing of all? Here the passion for naturalness leads to sheer nonsense.

H. B. Irving, in the same production, is also unsatisfactory because he sacrifices 'beauty . . . to exact realism' (iii. 149, 151).

Max explicitly dissociates himself from 'those who would have dramatic expres-sion, in poetic plays, utterly subordinated to the rhythm of the verse' (i. 479). He does not wish meaning to be sacrificed to rhythm; but he does ask that in both prose and verse, rhythm should be 'recognisably preserved'. This did not happen in Oscar Asche's 1907 As You Like It, perhaps because the players ate too many apples.

> According to the modern doctor, apples are a splendidly wholesome diet, and I should not like the players to risk their health by abstaining. But I suggest that two-thirds or so of the fruit consumed on the stage might with advantage be consumed in the dressing-rooms. No doubt it is very natural that Jaques, for example, should be engaged on an apple while he describes the seven ages of man. No doubt the thoughts in that speech are not so profound that their thinker would have had to postpone his meal because of them. But I maintain that the speech is a beautifully written one, very vivid, quaint, and

offering scope for great variety in enunciation. It ought to be given for all it is worth, and not in a series of grunts between mouthfuls. (i. 479–80)

Max could praise good speaking as well as make fun of bad. Lewis Waller as Henry V has 'an elocution which wrings the full value out of every syllable. His innumerable long speeches…stir one in virtue of their delivery' (ii. 341). Forbes-Robertson's famous Hamlet evokes praise for a mode of speaking which shows Hamlet for the first time 'as a quite definite and intelligible being'. 'In face, and in voice, and in manner, Mr Robertson is a heaven-born Hamlet' (ii. 487). But as Othello he fails, even though he so declaims the poetry 'that every phrase and cadence has its due beauty' (ii. 521).

Some of the best passages in Max's theatre criticism are ones in which he writes about an actor or actress in a manner that conveys an impression of their quality, not necessarily by direct description of their acting. His obituary of Irving (i. 396–401) provides an excellent example. It is one of the best of English essays, and a wonderful tribute to the power of personality in acting. Here, as elsewhere, Max uses the word 'beauty' quite often, and it would be easy to accuse him, with his predilection for comedy, his insistence on the need for visual beauty, his demands that verse and prose should both be spoken with a due sense of rhythm, of a shallow over-emphasis on the superficially pleasing at the expense of the serious. It would not, I think, be fair. He can write eloquently on *Othello* as well as of *A Midsummer Night's Dream*; he can appreciate the avant-garde designs of Gordon Craig as well as the traditional settings for Tree's productions; and although he finds that Irving could not declaim, could not give Shakespeare's verse its 'true music and magic', yet he could pay noble tribute to Irving's speaking, to 'the meanings that he made the verse yield to him', even though these 'subtle and sometimes profound meanings were not always Shakespeare's own'. Irving's 'prime appeal was always to the sense of beauty'. This obviously suited Max. But 'it was not…to a sense of obvious beauty. It was to a sense of strange, delicate, almost mystical and unearthly beauty' (i. 397–8).

Of course, Max's 'satiric temperament' finds its natural outlet in reviews of performances that he found less than satisfactory, and especially in those that he found positively ridiculous. He was averse to intellectual pretension, which he found very prominent in the spectacle of playgoers watching Shakespeare being performed in a language that they did not understand. A natural target was Sarah Bernhardt's Hamlet. He heads his notice 'Hamlet; Princess of Denmark' (i. 34–7), and opens it with the admission that he cannot take the performance seriously. He deploys his wit and his irony.

Sarah ought not to have supposed that Hamlet's weakness set him in any possible relation to her own feminine mind and body. Her friends ought to have restrained her. The native critics ought not to have encouraged her. The custom-house officials at Charing Cross ought to have confiscated her sable doublet and hose.

The only compliment he could pay her was that her Hamlet 'was, from first to last, *très grande dame*'. Yet even this essay, masterpiece of comic prose as it is, includes a serious and perceptive passage on the difference between the French and the English languages. No less brilliant in its satirical effect is Max's well-known essay (i. 61–3) on the Benson company in the light of their sporting interests.

> Every member of the cast [of *Henry V*] seemed in tip-top condition—thoroughly 'fit'. Subordinates and principals all worked well together. The fielding was excellent, and so was the batting. Speech after speech was sent spinning across the boundary, and one was constantly inclined to shout 'Well *played*, sir! Well played *indeed!*' As a branch of university cricket, the whole performance was, indeed, beyond praise. But, as a form of acting, it was not impressive.

The virtues displayed in passages such as these are in part those of the essayist who happens to have chosen a theatrical topic. But then, many of our best theatre critics have also been among our best essayists. The most memorable theatre criticism, it seems to me, is not that which aims at abstract discussion or displays analytical power. It is rather that which tells us what actually happened, which gives us a sense of watching the performance described. It is not purely objective description, because it may use stylistic devices to give us a sense of emotional involvement as well as simply informing us about what was seen. This is something that Lichtenberg does brilliantly in his descriptions of Garrick as Hamlet. Hazlitt does it, especially when he is writing about Edmund Kean; Leigh Hunt does it, on Kean's Timon, for instance; and Max does it, too. He does it of a real-life situation, when he tells us how he caught a glimpse of Irving on his way to Windsor to receive his knighthood (i. 400). He does it of Dan Leno in an essay (i. 349–52) that does more to convey to us what it was like to be a member of the great comedian's audience than any of Dan Leno's gramophone records or photographs. And he does it occasionally, too, in his descriptions of Shakespearean acting. The best example in the classical style is perhaps when he describes a wordless episode in Beerbohm Tree's *Twelfth Night*.

> As the two topers reel off to bed, the uncanny dawn peers at them through the windows. The Clown wanders on, humming a snatch of the tune he has sung to them. He looks at the empty bowl of sack and the overturned tankards, smiles, shrugs his shoulders, yawns, lies down before the embers of the fire, goes to sleep. Down the stairs, warily, with a night-cap on his head and a sword in his hand, comes Malvolio, awakened and fearful of danger. He peers around, lunging with his sword at the harmless furniture. One thinks of Don Quixote and 'the notable adventure of the wine-skins'. Satisfied, he retraces his footsteps up the staircase. A cock crows, and, as the curtain falls, one is aware of a whole slumbering household, and of the mystery of an actual dawn. Pedants might cavil at such imaginative glosses in a production of

317

Shakespeare. To me the question is simply whether the imagination be of a good or bad kind. In this instance the imagination seems to me distinctly good. (ii. 349)

Finally, it is worth mentioning a review in which Max uses an unusual technique with considerable success. It is closely related to that of *Twelfth Night*, but differs in that the first five hundred words or so consist of a series of what Max himself calls 'disjointed sentences' aiming to preserve his own impressions of Tree's production of *King John*. It was a characteristically elaborate production, including a spectacular interpolated tableau of the granting of Magna Carta. Max enjoyed it greatly, though, as he admits, most of what he describes is 'points of "business" and stage management'. He responds to it very much as a visual experience. Here he is on the last scene:

> The dying king is borne out in a chair. He is murmuring snatches of a song. The chair is set down, and with weak hands he motions away his bearers. 'Ay, marry', he gasps, 'now my soul hath elbow-room; it would not out at windows nor at doors. There is so hot a summer in my bosom, that all my bowels crumble up to dust.... And none of you will bid the winter come, to thrust his icy fingers in my maw.' The bastard comes in hot haste, and the king, to receive his tidings, sits upright, and is crowned for the last time. He makes no answer to the tidings. One of the courtiers touches him, ever so lightly, on the shoulder, and he falls back. The crown is taken from his head and laid on the head of the child who is now king. The bastard rings out those words in which poetry of patriotism finds the noblest expression it can ever find...'. (ii. 192)

It is a somewhat self-conscious style. Spontaneity was not among Max's virtues as a writer. But it is an expressive and informative style which might have been valuably applied to other productions.

A survey of Max's theatre criticism reveals him as a serious critic of Shakespeare, no wider in his response than most cultured playgoers of his time, but with a capacity for thoughtful analysis and a genius for expressing his personal reactions to theatrical experience. He was not a leader of taste, but neither was he entirely reactionary. We can value him as a recorder, an observing eye, ear, mind, during a period of transition from the high naturalism of his half-brother to the symbolism of Gordon Craig. He is, of course, more to be valued as a master of English prose than as a Shakespeare critic; but it is a happy fact that Max's hard labour in his profession provided the circumstances for a fruitful reaction between his mind and the Shakespeare productions of his time. It is fortunate for us, as it was fortunate for Max, that he was not a porter on the Underground Railway.

21

Shakespeare in Leigh Hunt's Theatre Criticism

L eigh Hunt was only 20 years old when, in May 1805, his brother John started a paper called *The News* and asked him to be its theatre critic. He wrote regularly for it until the end of 1807. This makes him the first of our distinguished theatre critics to have engaged in regular criticism of performances shortly after they were given. In his *Autobiography* (1858) he writes interestingly about the state of theatre criticism at the time.[1] It was customary 'for editors of papers to be intimate with actors and dramatists'. The result was a good deal of corruption.

> Puffing and plenty of tickets were ... the system of the day. It was an interchange of amenities over the dinner-table; a flattery of power on the one side, and puns on the other; and what the public took for a criticism on a play was a draft upon the box-office, or reminiscences of last Thursday's salmon and lobster-sauce. The custom was, to write as short and as favourable a paragraph on the new piece as could be; to say that Bannister was 'excellent' and Mrs Jordan 'charming'; to notice the 'crowded house' or invent it, if necessary; and to conclude by observing that 'the whole went off with *éclat*'.

The Hunt brothers decided that 'independence in theatrical criticism would be a great novelty. We announced it, and nobody believed us; we stuck to it, and the town believed everything we said.' Writing many years later, Hunt clearly finds something pompous about his younger self: 'To know an actor personally appeared to me a vice not to be thought of; and I would as lief have taken poison as accepted a ticket from the theatres.' He admits to feeling shame at his own presumption in undertaking so responsible a task while still so young and inexperienced, though he seems more concerned with the problems that he had found in criticizing new plays than with his treatment of revivals of the classics. And he admits that he does not feel these early criticisms had no merit at all. They showed an acquaintance with the style of Voltaire, Johnson, and others; were not unagreeably sprinkled with quotation; and, above all, were written with more care and attention than was customary with newspapers at that time. The pains I took to round a period with nothing in it, or to invent a simile that should appear offhand, would have done honour to better stuff.[2]

In other words, he was writing literary essays, and may at times have been tempted to sacrifice truth to effect.

Early in 1808, Hunt published a volume called *Critical Essays on the Performers of the London Theatres*, made up of many essays on individual performers, written not as notices of separate performances, but as retrospective studies based on his own theatre-going. The volume includes a long Appendix, reprinting extracts from the criticisms first printed in *The News*. It is one of the main sources (other than the original newspapers) for a study of Hunt's theatre criticism. Another is *Dramatic Essays by Leigh Hunt*, edited by William Archer and Robert Lowe, published in 1894 and now difficult to come by. It includes an excellent introduction by Archer, and a selection of the essays from *The News*.

In January 1808 the Hunt brothers launched a new periodical, *The Examiner*, which appeared every Sunday. Again Leigh Hunt undertook the theatre criticism. Archer feels that he did so in a generally less censorious frame of mind than he had displayed in *The News*, but Hunt himself wrote that 'The spirit of the criticism on the theatres continued the same as it had been in the *News*.'[3] Certainly Hunt did not abstain from making personal remarks about leading actors. Praising Kemble for his good taste in keeping Shakespeare before the public, he wrote,

> The other Managers of the present day have so little taste, with the exception of Sheridan who cares for no taste but that of port, that were it not for Mr Kemble's exertions the tragedies of our glorious bard would almost be in danger of dismissal from the stage;

and Mrs Faucit cannot have been pleased to be told, in relation to her performance as Volumnia, that

> A Roman matron did not think it essential to her dignity to step about with her head thrown half a yard back, as if she had a contempt for her own chin.[4]

Hunt made enemies by his outspokenness, and one of his weekly essays is largely given over to a defence of himself against charges of over-severity. At least this quality had the merit of increasing respect for him in those whom he praised. There is evidence for this in the biography of the famous comic actor, Charles Mathews, written by his wife, who says that 'the success' of one of Mathews's performances in 1808 'was recorded by the greatest dramatic critic of that day, Mr Leigh Hunt, whose judgment was universally sought and received as infallible by all actors and lovers of the drama'.[5] Hunt's notices in *The Examiner* give the impression of having been written with time to spare. They are little essays, including literary criticism as well as analyses of performances. Hunt went on writing for *The Examiner* until it ceased publication in 1821, though with a gap of two years spent in prison because of his excessive outspokenness on non-theatrical matters, which resulted in legal action against him for libelling the Prince Regent. A selection of the criticisms written during these years is printed in *Leigh Hunt's Dramatic Criticism 1808–1831* (1949), edited by L. C. and C. W. Houtchens, the most scholarly edition of any of our theatre critics.

In 1830, impelled by poverty, Leigh Hunt began to write, almost single-handed, a daily newspaper of four folio pages called *The Tatler*, which lasted until 1832 and included a high proportion of theatre criticism. Hunt himself considered that he never wrote 'theatricals so well, as in the pages of this most unremunerating speculation'.[6] Understandably, these notices are usually briefer than those written for the weekly *Examiner*. They sometimes include comment on the plays performed, but consist mainly of discussion of the performances of the principal actors. A few are reprinted in the Houtchens volume; a larger selection forms the second part of the Archer and Lowe collection.

Leigh Hunt's theatre criticism extends, then, over a quarter of a century. In discussing its relevance to Shakespeare I shall treat it as a single body of work, while drawing attention to chronological considerations when it seems desirable to do so. Hunt was, throughout his life, an omnivorous reader; and this fact shows in much of his writing. He refers often to Dr Johnson's Shakespeare criticism, but most of his references end in disagreement. Hunt defends Shakespeare's ending for *King Lear* against Johnson's criticism of it; he finds that Johnson's remarks on *King John* are 'in the usual spirit of the Doctor's criticism, consisting of assertions very well founded, but careless of all proof'; similarly, quoting Johnson on *Julius Caesar*, he writes, 'this is a sorry piece of criticism: it is, at best, like most of his criticisms, only so much gratuitous opinion without analysis, without argument'; he even goes so far as to assert that it is a 'betrayal of his absolute unfitness for poetical criticism, at least with regard to the works of a higher order'; and he praises Hazlitt's *Characters of Shakespear's Plays* by saying that 'it must inevitably supersede the dogmatic and half-informed criticisms of Johnson'.[7] In reacting against Johnson, Hunt reveals himself as a child of his time, at one with the other, greater proponents of Romanticism with whom he had many associations. Of the essay in which Hunt defends Shakespeare's decision to show the death of King Lear, L.C. and C. W. Houtchens write,

This review is historically significant in romantic Shakespeare criticism. It appeared in the same spring [of 1808] that Schlegel was lecturing on Shakespeare in Vienna, and Coleridge on Shakespeare at the Royal Institution. Hunt's sympathy with the romantic point of view is apparent here in his attack on Dr Johnson and the neo-classical objection to Shakespeare's disregard of poetic justice....Through this review and certain of his later articles on the drama, Hunt added impetus to the English romantic movement by his adoption of romantic criteria . . .[8]

The extent of Coleridge's indebtedness to Schlegel in his Shakespeare criticism is still a matter for debate, though it seems now to be agreed that it was considerable but unacknowledged. Hunt expresses his admiration for Schlegel in his review of Hazlitt's *Characters of Shakespear's Plays*, where he describes Schlegel as the 'critic, who, with the exception of a few scattered criticisms from Mr Lamb, had hitherto been the only writer who seemed truly to *understand* as well as feel him [Shakespeare]'. Hunt praised Hazlitt as the first Englishman to have done 'justice to Shakspeare's characters in general'.[9] He had little to say about Coleridge, whose criticism he seems to have underrated, although he attended at least one of Coleridge's Shakespeare lectures of 1811.

Anyhow, members of the literary circles of the Romantic period held so many ideas in common that it is often impossible to determine who thought of what first. It is perhaps more important to observe the community of ideas and their distinctive features. It seems significant that Hunt praised Hazlitt as the first in England to show thorough appreciation of Shakespeare's *characters*. Hunt shared the characteristic Romantic concern with individuality, as is clear from his strong emphasis upon the actor's realization of idiosyncratic character traits. This is reflected partly in the kinds of acting that he admired. He has a number of interesting discussions of tragic acting, expressing admiration for what he regarded as a 'natural' style, and dislike of the evidently artificial. For example, on his first visit to the theatre after his imprisonment, in 1815, he saw for the first time Edmund Kean, who had had a meteoric rise to success the previous year. He was rather disappointed. He had, he says, 'been in the habit, for years, of objecting to the artificial style of the actors lately in vogue', and had hoped that in Kean he would see all that was 'natural and desirable in theatrical representation'. But even Kean in *Richard III* appeared 'nothing but a first-rate actor of the ordinary, stagy class, and to start only occasionally into passages of truth and originality'. Hunt has a long and interesting analysis of the artificial and the natural styles, and complains that Kean

> dealt out his syllables, and stood finely, and strutted at the set off of a speech, just as other well-received performers do; and he is much farther gone in stage trickery than we supposed him to be, particularly in the old violent contrasts when delivering an equivoque, dropping his voice too consciously from a serious line to a sly one, and fairly putting it to the house as a good joke.

Here he is complaining that the actor seemed to be standing somewhat outside the role, nudging the audience into noticing his artistry. But at other times Kean had 'touches of nature' such as Hunt was hoping to find. He had a manner of 'rubbing his hands' when Richard thought that he was succeeding in his aims, which Hunt found proper to the character. This, and 'other gestures . . . and the turns of his countenance [tended] in a very happy manner to unite common life with tragedy—which is the great stage-desideratum'.[10]

This is a recurrent theme. Hunt recognized that tragic acting required a certain elevation, but demanded that it should be intermingled with the familiar. Reviewing Fanny Kemble's Juliet in 1830, he found that she played in

> the regular conventional tragic style, both in voice and manner, which was maintained with little variation the whole evening, and which has certainly left an impression on our minds that this young lady is entirely an artificial performer . . . She wanted real passion throughout, and variety of feeling.[11]

Hunt's *bête noire* among the greatest actors of his time was John Philip Kemble; and long after Edmund Kean's *début*—indeed, in the last stages of Kean's career—he wrote a comparison of Kemble and Kean which sums up his ideas on this head, as well as showing that over the years he came to feel much more favourably about Kean. He admits 'a certain merit of taste and what is called "classicality"' in Kemble. He admits the truth of Kemble's feeling that 'a certain elevation of treatment' was due to tragedy, but he finds that with him all was 'external and artificial . . . It was not the man, but his mask.' Kean, on the other hand, 'the finest tragic actor we ever beheld', was full of passion. His

> face is full of light and shade, his tones vary, his voice trembles, his eye glistens, sometimes with withering scorn, sometimes with a tear: at least he can speak as if there were tears in his eyes, and he brings tears into those of other people.[12]

This distinction between the natural and the artificial is one that Hunt frequently makes; predictably, his preference is always for the natural.

This attitude towards acting is paralleled by Hunt's views on Shakespeare's plays. Often he takes their greatness as understood, but he has a number of panegyrics on Shakespeare's genius. He recognizes the impersonality of the dramatist's art:

> The difficulty of getting at the real opinions of dramatic writers is notorious . . . there is no more reason to imagine that he thought with *Iago* than that he did with *Falstaff*, or *Romeo*, or *Sir Andrew Aguecheek*. The character thought like itself, and that was enough for him.[13]

Again we observe the Romantic emphasis upon character. Hunt was writing in 1814. In the community of ideas to which I referred, it is interesting to find that this is essentially the view expressed three years later by Hazlitt in his lecture on 'Shakespeare and Milton': Shakespeare 'was the least of an egotist that it was possible to be. He was nothing in himself; but he was all that others were...'.[14] And Keats, who heard Hazlitt's lecture, is nevertheless in some ways closer to Hunt in his letter of 27 October 1818 to Richard Woodhouse: 'the poetical character ... has no self ... It has as much delight in conceiving an Iago as an Imogen.'

A nineteenth-century phenomenon in relation to Shakespeare's characters is the adulation given to his women. Whereas until the time of Sir Walter Scott it was conventional to praise Beaumont and Fletcher above Shakespeare for their women characters, it was, wrote Terence Spencer in an essay on 'Shakespeare and the Noble Woman',[15] 'Coleridge's great discovery (which was exploited throughout the nineteenth century) that Shakespeare's women-characters were remarkable in that you felt like marrying them'. Shelley spoke of

> A wonder of this earth,
> Where there is little of transcendent worth—
> Like one of Shakespeare's women.
> (*Julian and Maddalo*, lines 590–2)

And Leigh Hunt joined in this chorus, particularly in his later writings. In 1830 he has a whole paragraph of exclamations about them—'How poor do the women of almost all other dramatic poets (which they intend to be attractive or seducing) appear by the side of them! How unlovely their virtues, how vicious and unvoluptuous their love!' In the following year he is moved to rhetorical questions instead of exclamations: 'What notion of sweetness can be too great for such a character as Imogen? What perfect love and ingenuousness ought we not to look for in a Desdemona? What an union of cordiality with court shrewdness in Rosalind?'[16] and so on. No wonder he often found that actresses could not measure up to his expectations.

A curious sidelight on Hunt's views about the women characters is his interest in their legs. In Hunt's time ladies' legs were far less frequently displayed in public, or indeed anywhere other than in the most intimate surroundings, than now. Even on the stage, actresses normally wore long dresses—except, of course, when they were playing what were known as breeches roles. Shakespeare's disguised heroines, such as Viola and Rosalind, were popular partly for this reason. Hunt's comments suggest a natural attraction combined with a degree of that pre-Victorian prudishness which is the obverse of the Regency image. When Mrs Jordan played Rosalind, 'you admire the shape of her leg'; but Mrs Henry Siddons was even better because you admired her with 'a chastened feeling, you love the very awkwardness with which she wears her male attire, and you are even better pleased with her shape because you are left to fancy it'. Rather more than legs seems to have been on potential display when Miss Meadows played Ariel: 'We very much admired the air of modesty which this young lady preserved in a dress necessarily light and thin.' That was in 1807. By 1820 he was somewhat less concerned about modesty. Of Miss Tree's Viola, 'we must be allowed to say that her leg is the very prettiest leg we ever saw on the stage'. And he goes into analytical detail:

> It is not at all like the leg which is vulgarly praised even in a man, and which is doubly misplaced under a lady—a bit of balustrade turned upside down; a large calf, and an ankle only small in proportion. It is a right feminine leg, delicate in foot, trim in ankle, and with a calf at once soft and well-cut, distinguished and unobtrusive. . . . It is impossible not to be struck, as an Irishman would say, with a leg like this. It is fit for a statue; still fitter for where it is.

The rest of the performance was less satisfactory. Ten years later he was still remembering Miss Tree's legs, in spite of the competition offered by the 'light smartness' of Miss Taylor's.[17]

A more general virtue in Shakespeare which rouses Hunt to rhetorical panegyric is his humanity. Comparing *The Merchant of Venice* with *The Jew of Malta*, he finds that 'up rose Shakspeare in the complete wisdom of his humanity'; and he apostrophizes him with full Romantic fervour: 'Blessings on thy memory, thou divinest of human beings . . .', continuing in a single rhapsodic sentence of over 200 words.[18]

But when it came to particular plays, Hunt was not always blindly adoring. Although he defended *King John* against Dr Johnson's strictures in a manner to which his editors apply the term 'romantic idolatry', other history plays, now more highly valued, were less to his taste. Reviewing 1 *Henry IV* in 1830, he wrote, 'the historical plays of Shakspeare certainly do not tell, as they used to do', though this one was at least partly redeemed by the character of Falstaff. *Henry V* pleased him still less: 'It is not a good acting play—at least not for these times.' His excuse on Shakespeare's behalf is that the play 'was written to please the uninformed subjects of a despotic government two hundred years ago, and as it comprises little of the everlasting humanity that fills most of the plays of Shakspeare, it falls flat on the ears of an audience in these times of popular spirit!'[19] No doubt Hunt's radical political opinions influenced his assessment of the history plays. Nor was he entirely sympathetic with the comedies. The improbabilities of *The Comedy of Errors* were too much for him; and in 1811 he found *Twelfth Night* 'perhaps the last in rank of Shakspeare's more popular dramas'. However, when he saw Frederick Reynolds's heavily adapted musical version in 1820—the one that displayed Miss Tree's legs so satisfactorily—he wrote a little panegyric on it: 'What a good-natured play was not this, altogether, to close his dramas with! for *Twelfth Night* was the last work of Shakspeare.'[20] (In this opinion, he was simply following Malone.)

It cannot be claimed that Hunt shows any strongly Coleridgean concern for the organic quality of Shakespeare's art. Admittedly, he joins in the protests, increasingly common at this time, against the continuing use in the theatre of the most flagrant adaptations, such as the Dryden–Davenant *Tempest* (which he found morally objectionable), Tate's *King Lear*, and Garrick's *Romeo and Juliet*. But he was tolerant of other alterations, such as Reynolds's musical versions of *The Comedy of Errors* and *Twelfth Night*; and he mentions with no apparent consciousness of its impropriety that in *As You Like It* Miss Taylor, as Rosalind, 'sang the cuckoo-song with great good taste and effect, closing the stanzas well . . . and was ardently encored in it'. Clearly this was in a much adapted version. Hunt's reviews do not suggest a serious concern for overall interpretation. He shows some signs of the interest in the beginnings of the movement to present the plays with a historical accuracy that would be educative as well as effective. Of Kemble's *Julius Caesar* in 1812 he writes that 'an impression is left upon us of Roman manners and greatness, of the appearance as well as intellect of Romans, which to a young mind in particular must furnish an indelible picture for the assistance of his studies'. This seems a prim view of a notably spectacular production. He remarks of 1 *Henry IV* (in 1830) that

> we must dress up the historical play with plumes, and decorations, and real costume, in order to amuse the eye, because the other interest languishes. And we dress it very well, yet it languishes still.

And he observes that the scenery of *As You Like It* was

> very beautiful. When we did not like any actor who was speaking, *we took a walk in it*; and found ourselves in the midst of glades and woods, 'and alleys leading inward far'.[21]

But in general Hunt's interest centres firmly on the actors, and on the problems of performers interpreting particular roles. This reflects both the theatrical and the intellectual fashions of his time. This was an actors' rather than a directors' theatre. Audiences hoped above all to be impressed and thrilled by great individual performers. Theatre-goers were connoisseurs of acting, seeing the great classic roles played by a variety of actors and avidly comparing the 'points' that they made. That which surrounded the leading actors was, in most theatres, a matter of comparative indifference. Only a few managers, Kemble among them, were beginning that process of reform in the overall staging of plays which was to lead to the carefully managed productions of Samuel Phelps, Charles Kean, and Henry Irving, and finally to the directors' theatre as we know it today. The emphasis on star actors is itself a manifestation of Romanticism, with its fascination with individual personality.

Hunt had a keen sense of the difficulty experienced by actors in the attempt to encompass the full range of Shakespeare's major roles. This emerges strongly from his comparison (1819) of Edmund Kean and Macready as Richard III. He found that Kean's portrayal has 'more of the seriousness of conscious evil in it, the other [Macready's] of the gaiety of meditated success'. And he continues:

If these two features in the character of *Richard* could be united by any actor, the performance would be a perfect one: but when did the world ever see a perfect performance of a character of Shakspeare's? When did it ever see the same *Macbeth's* good and ill nature work truly together, the same *King John* looking mean with his airs of royalty, the same *Hamlet* the model of a court and the victim of melancholy? ... The union of such a variety of tones of feeling as prevails in the great humanities of Shakspeare seems as impossible to be found in an actor, as the finest musical instrument is insufficient to supply all the effect of a great writer for a band.[22]

This theme recurs. As early as 1807, he had said,

The character of Hamlet . . . seems beyond the genius of the present stage, and I do not see that its personification will be easily attained by future stages, for its actor must unite the most contrary as well as the most assimilating powers of comedy and tragedy, and to unite these powers in their highest degree belongs to the highest genius only.[23]

Twenty-three years later, in 1830, he says something very similar in reviewing Macready's Hamlet:

We never yet saw a Hamlet on the stage, nor do we expect to see one. It is a character, though quite in nature, made up of too many qualities to be represented by any but a Hamlet himself.... We have seen parts of Hamlet represented, but we never saw the whole.

And he goes on to discuss 'what Hamlet was' in a little character-sketch in line with many other examples of this kind of writing. (One could make a little anthology of character-sketches from Hunt's criticism.)

But more often than offering a self-contained sketch of an important character, Hunt tends to discuss the character in terms of the problems that it poses for the actor. This results in passages of analytical criticism which can be genuinely illuminating. For example, finding that Macready was sometimes too noisy as Hamlet, he excepts one loud passage:

His most warrantable loudness (indeed there it is desirable, because Hamlet is bullying his own indecision into action) was where he makes the stab through the arras, crying out 'Dead for a ducat!'[24]

That Hamlet is here 'bullying his own indecision into action' is a good perception. And sometimes Hunt passes from observation of the way a character is portrayed to generalized remarks about human behaviour which one imagines might still be valuable to actors studying certain roles. He has such a passage on Cassio's drunkenness. He praises Charles Kemble for the way that he makes Cassio's remorse appear

> so much the stronger from his inability to rid himself of the debauch which he abhors. There is no actor who imitates this defect with such a total want of affectation. All the other performers wish to be humorous drunkards, and by this error they cannot help showing a kind of abstract reasoning which defeats their purpose. They play a hundred antics with legs which a drunkard would be unable to lift, they make a thousand grimaces which the jaws of a drunkard could not attempt from mere want of tone; they roll about from place to place, though his whole strength is exerted to command his limbs; they wish, in short, to appear drunk, when the great object of a drunkard is to appear sober.[25]

There is a curious echo of this in an anecdote told in F. W. Hawkins's *Life of Edmund Kean* (1869, ii. 360),

> ... he was asked by a friend when he studied? Indicating a man on the other side of the room, who was very much intoxicated, but who was labouring to keep up an appearance of sobriety, he replied, 'I am studying now. I wish some of my Cassios were here. They might see that, instead of rolling about in the ridiculous manner they do, the great secret of delineating intoxication is the endeavour to stand straight when it is impossible to do so.'

Hunt's interest in individual character has a natural corollary in the prominence he gives to particular actors. It is significant that the only volume he himself published about the theatre is called *Critical Essays on the Performers of the London Theatres*. Each essay is about a particular actor; indeed, Hunt tells us in his Preface that his original plan was to write an essay about each and every actor on the list of the only two 'legitimate' theatres in London, Covent Garden and Drury Lane, and that 'it was not till the tragic section had been printed that I discovered the nameless multitude which this plan would have compelled me to individualize'. He hoped to excite 'an honourable ambition in the actors, who have hitherto been the subjects of mere scandal, or at best of the most partial levity'. He hoped, in other words, by taking them seriously to encourage them to take themselves seriously. He defends the art of the actor by saying that 'If the knowledge of ourselves be the height of wisdom, is that art contemptible which conveys this knowledge to us in the most pleasing manner?' (It is rather touching, in the light of the present enterprise, that Hunt ends his Preface by saying that 'Upon so perishable a subject I cannot enjoy the hope of talking to other times.')[26] Many of his reviews, too, as I have suggested, centre firmly on the performance of the leading actor or actress. Their interest is, therefore, commensurate with our interest in the actors about whom he is writing. His notices of forgotten actors may have incidental interest in relation to the play in which they performed or because of the vigour of the prose in which Hunt discusses them. His notices of actors who continue to hold the attention of posterity are part of the reason they do so, an essential aspect of the record.

Of all the performers of his lengthy career as a theatre-goer, the one who achieved the most unanimous chorus of praise is the great Sarah Siddons, Sir Joshua Reynolds's 'Tragic Muse'. Her career was well advanced by the time that Hunt began going to the theatre, in 1800, and she officially retired in 1812. She was regarded as rather prudish (exceptionally, for actors in those days), and in view of what I wrote about 'breeches parts', it is interesting to read that 'she jibbed at the breeches in Rosalind, appearing in a costume which was that neither of a man nor of a woman, and extremely unbecoming'. Hunt's *Critical Essay* on her begins, 'To write a criticism on Mrs Siddons is to write a panegyric, and a panegyric of a very peculiar sort, for the praise will be true.' He praises her for absorption in her roles: 'Mrs Siddons has the air of never being the actress.' He finds that she has a power of which he often deplores the absence in other performers: the power to balance exactly the expression of human nature with the technical skill of the actor: she could seem natural while most powerfully projecting her art. Thus, in a later review of her Volumnia, he writes, 'Mrs Siddons knows when to lift her countenance into commanding majesty, and when to fall into the familiarity of domestic ease.' (Yet in his *Autobiography*, written long afterwards, he admits to feeling that even in her 'something of too much art was apparent'.) The late date of Hunt's criticism means that when he writes of her it is usually in retrospect. He decided not to attend her farewell performance, but wrote an essay on the occasion, praising her Queen Katherine, Constance, and Lady Macbeth as 'almost perfect pieces of acting'. She excelled in portraying 'regality and conscious dignity', and

> it was in *Queen Katherine* that this dignity was seen in all its perfection; never was lofty grief so equally kept up, never a good conscience so nobly prepared, never a dying hour so royal and so considerate to the last. That was a beautiful touch with which she used to have her chair and cushions changed, during the wearisome pain of her resting body! And her cheek too against the pillow![27]

Here Hunt is praising touches of the nature which he found all too lacking in the performances of Mrs Siddons's distinguished brother, John Philip Kemble, about whom he is often remarkably and extendedly rude. Kemble, he says, should study such effects, and

> not the clap-provoking frivolities of ending every speech with an energetic dash of the fist, or of running off the stage after a vehement declamation, as if the actor was in haste to get his pint of wine.

When a role demanded the familiar touch, Kemble was—still Mr Kemble, as in Coriolanus's lines:

> I will go wash:
> And when my face is fair, you shall perceive
> Whether I blush or no.

The word fair might positively have been measured by a stop-watch: instead of being a short monosyllable, it became a word of tremendous elongation. We can describe the pronunciation by nothing else than by such a sound as fay-er-r-r. Luckily for our fastidious, or as Mr Kemble would say, our fastijjus ears, we had no opportunity of hearing bird for beard; but it was in vain to expect any repose in orthöepy, when Mr Kemble had gotten such a word as Aufidius to transmogrify. This he universally called Aufijjus, like a young lady who talks of her ojus lover, or the ojus month of November. The name too of Coriolanus is divided by Mr Kemble with syllabical precision into five distinct sounds, though the general pronunciation, as well as Shakspeare himself, shortens the rio into one syllable, as in the word chariot: the alteration is of no effect, but to give a stiffness to what is already too stiff, and to render many of the poet's lines harsh and unmetrical.

Hunt seems to have felt strongly about Kemble's faults of pronunciation, which he ascribes to misplaced pedantry, and is unmercifully scornful about them on several occasions. He praised him in some roles, especially Prospero, but admits in his *Autobiography* that he thought him overrated: 'He was no more to be compared to his sister, than stone is to flesh and blood.'[28]

Probably the greatest male tragic actor about whom Hunt wrote was Edmund Kean, before whom, says Hunt, Kemble faded, 'like a tragedy ghost'. When Hunt saw him first, as Richard III, he was disappointed, probably because he had expected to find him the very antithesis of Kemble, whom he so much disliked. But he was profoundly moved by Kean's Othello, which he summed up as 'the masterpiece of the living stage'. He has interesting and touching notices of some of Kean's late performances, when some, but far from all, of the old magnetism had gone. It is sad to find him regretting, in 1831, that audiences do not applaud Kean as they once had:

Their shouts do not leap forth, as they used to do, at every turn and bidding of his genius, and we could not help thinking last night that some of his very finest passages met with a very ill and a very *ungrateful* reception, and that he felt it; and was the worse for it.[29]

While Leigh Hunt's overall estimates of leading actors offer valuable evidence to the stage historian, perhaps the most striking passages of his theatre criticism in relation to Shakespeare's plays are those in which he describes and comments on the way particular actors handled specific, limited areas of the texts. In the best of these he reveals, along with an analytical capacity on which I have already commented, a sensitive response both to the sound of the lines and to visual effects of appearance, stage business, and the like. On speaking, for instance, he has an excellent close analysis of Fanny Kemble's delivery of Juliet's lines beginning 'Come, gentle night', which he finds that she treated far too solemnly rather than in the manner he feels to be appropriate,

> with a joyous tone throughout; with an undiminished hilarity; with her heart dancing in her eyes; nay, even with an enthusiastic pacing down the stage lamps, looking the audience rapturously in the face, as if she breathed out her soul to the air and to all nature.[30]

He is fine on Macready's handling of King John's last moments, and on a passage in Charles Mayne Young's Macbeth:

> His apostrophe to the imaginary dagger was impressive, but it wanted, what I never saw given to it yet, a variety of countenance approaching to delirium; and he spoke its first lines with his face turned away from *Duncan's* chamber door *directly toward* the side scenes: this appears to me an erroneous position: his face should at least have been a three-quarter one, for to give a most impassioned expression a profile only, except in cases which absolutely require it, is to cheat the audience of the full fancy of the scene.

Here Hunt shows himself to have that connoisseur's appreciation of the finer points of acting which must have inspired many of his contemporaries in their frequent revisits to a small number of classical plays; and in describing another moment of the same performance he shows a knowledge of traditional stage business:

> The imprecatory action of lifted arms with which he repulsed the ghost off the stage, according to custom, at that passage 'Hence horrible shadow! Unreal mockery hence!' was too violent and dictatorial.[31]

Understandably, some of Hunt's best writing is evoked by performances which particularly excited him, and I should like to quote two of these, both about Edmund Kean. The first refers to his death scene as Richard III, which must stand with Mrs Siddons's sleepwalking scene, in *Macbeth*, as one of the most powerful of all passages of Romantic acting. After seeing one of Kean's late performances, in 1831, Hunt wrote

> the crowning point was the look he gave Richmond, after receiving the mortal blow. This has been always admired; but last night it appeared to us that he made it longer and therefore more ghastly. He stood looking the other in the face, as if he was already

a disembodied spirit, searching him with the eyes of another world; or, as if he silently cursed him with some new scorn, to which death and its dreadful knowledge had given him a right.[32]

Finally a description of Kean in his prime which, perhaps more than any other passage in Hunt's criticism, gives one a sense of feeling what it was like to be there. It is from a review of *Timon of Athens* (1816).

Timon, digging in the woods with his spade, hears the approach of military music; he starts, waits its approach sullenly, and at last in comes the gallant *Alcibiades* with a train of splendid soldiery. Never was scene more effectively managed. First, you heard a sprightly quick march playing in the distance; Kean started, listened, and leaned in a fixed and angry manner on his spade, with frowning eyes, and lips full of the truest feeling, compressed but not too much so; he seemed as if resolved not to be deceived, even by the charm of a thing inanimate; the audience were silent; the march threw forth its gallant note nearer and nearer; the Athenian standards appear, then the soldiers come treading on the scene with that air of confident progress which is produced by the accompaniment of music; and at last, while the squalid misanthrope still maintains his posture and keeps his back to the strangers, in steps the young and splendid *Alcibiades*, in the flush of victorious expectation. It is the encounter of hope with despair.[33]

At least in passages like this, surely. Leigh Hunt can 'enjoy the hope of talking to other times'.

22

Shakespeare in Hazlitt's
Theatre Criticism

Our two first important theatre critics are also two of the best: Leigh Hunt[1] and William Hazlitt. Hazlitt, born six years before Hunt, started to write theatre criticism after Hunt, and ended before him. So his career is, in a sense, included within Hunt's; and it touches his at some points. Hazlitt started as critic of the *Morning Chronicle*, a daily paper, in 1813, by which time he was already a seasoned playgoer. He had settled in London the previous year, and had been writing parliamentary reports and political articles for that paper. He stayed with the *Morning Chronicle* till May 1814, and from August of that year till the following January wrote regular theatre criticism for a weekly paper, *The Champion*; in March 1815 he became the regular theatre critic for the Hunts' paper *The Examiner*—Leigh Hunt was in prison. He continued to write frequently for *The Examiner*, sharing the task with Hunt after his release, till June 1817. He then wrote for *The Times* from June 1817 till about April 1818. This five-year period is the most fruitful and important in his career as a theatre critic, though in 1820 he wrote a series of monthly articles about the drama for the *London Magazine*. These are long essays which include only a comparatively small proportion of immediate (as opposed to retrospective) theatre reviewing. Hazlitt's career as a reviewer ends with a short spell on *The Examiner* again in 1828.

In 1818, Hazlitt published a selection of his own theatre criticisms as a volume to which he gave the title *A View of the English Stage; or, A Series of Dramatic Criticisms*.[2] This includes a high proportion of all his criticism written up to the date of publication except for that published in *The Times*, which he may have had to omit for copyright reasons. The reviews are reprinted as written, with only a few omissions. Hazlitt's theatre criticism is more accessible to the modern reader than Leigh Hunt's. An ample selection was reprinted by William Archer and Robert Lowe in 1895, and although that volume itself is scarce, it was reprinted in the Dramabooks series published by Hill and Wang (New York, 1957). This can be supplemented from the twenty-volume complete edition of Hazlitt's works by P. P. Howe (1930–4).

In his Preface to *A View of the English Stage*, Hazlitt speaks of the curiosity felt about actors of the past: 'the player's art is one that perishes with him, and leaves no traces of itself, but in the faint descriptions of the pen or pencil'. Knowledge of the past 'serves to keep alive the memory of past excellence, and to stimulate future efforts'. For this reason a detailed account of the stage of his own time—'a period not unfruitful in theatrical genius'—may be useful. He has interesting remarks about the effects of his criticism. He was the centre of a controversy over the merits of Edmund Kean, whose first London performance was the occasion of one of Hazlitt's earliest reviews. Hazlitt was profoundly impressed, and said so. 'I am not', he says, 'one of those who, when they see the sun breaking from behind a cloud, stop to ask others whether it is the moon.' And he has gone on acclaiming Kean's merits, though not, as he justly points out, without attending to his faults as well. He does not repent of anything that he has said in praise of certain actors; but he wishes he 'could retract what I have been obliged to say in reprobation of others'. There is no denying that Hazlitt could be severe. On Charles Mayne Young's Prospero, in 1815, he wrote: 'His Prospero was good for nothing; and consequently, was indes-cribably bad . . . Mr Young did not personate Prospero, but a pedagogue teaching his scholars how to recite the part, and not teaching them well' (*View*, p. 236). Of an over-enthusiastic Romeo, Alexander Rae: 'When this "gentle tassel" is lured back in the garden by his Juliet's voice, he returns at full speed, like a Harlequin going to take a flying leap through a trap-door. This was, we suppose, to give us an allegorical idea of his being borne on the wings of love, but we could discover neither his wings nor his love' (*View*, pp. 300–1). In 1816, Stephen Kemble, John Philip's brother, played Falstaff; he has become famous as one of the few actors who could play the part without padding. Hazlitt was not impressed. 'We see no more reason why Mr Stephen Kemble should play Falstaff, than why Louis XVIII is qualified to fill a throne, because he is fat, and belongs to a particular family. Every fat man cannot represent a great man. The knight was fat; so is the player: the Emperor was fat, so is the King who stands in his shoes. But there the comparison ends.' Falstaff was not—as, by implication, Stephen Kemble is—'a mere paunch, a bag-pudding, a lump of lethargy, a huge falling sickness, an imminent apoplexy, with water in the head' (*View*, p. 340).

In his Preface, Hazlitt points out that acting is 'an arduous profession', in which failure is 'only a misfortune, and not a disgrace'. Those who put themselves upon their trial, must, however, submit to the verdict; and the critic in general does little more than prevent a lingering death, by anticipating, or putting in immediate force, the sentence of the public.' And he claims, very much as Leigh Hunt also claimed, that he has refrained from cultivating the acquaintance of actors, and has never been motivated by personal considerations. Interestingly, he defends himself not merely against the severity of some of his criticisms, but also against accusations of caricaturing the objects of his criticism. The actor may 'caricature absurdity off the Stage', so 'Why should not the critic sometimes caricature it on the Stage?... Authors must live as well as actors; and the *insipid* must at all events be avoided as that which the public abhors most.' Newspaper readers have generally shown a taste for pungent criticism rather than insipid, whatever the merits of the case.

To look at Hazlitt as a critic of Shakespeare by way of his theatre reviews is, of course, a partial exercise. His reputation as a Shakespeare critic rests to some extent on his lecture 'On Shakespear and Milton' but mainly on his book *Characters of Shakespear's Plays*. However, the distinction between the theatre criticism and the book is by no means as clear-cut as might appear. Hazlitt was working on the book while he was a theatre critic; it was published in 1817, a year before *A View of the English Stage*. In both bodies of work he reveals the same attitudes, and he even takes over into the book many paragraphs that he had first used in his reviews of plays in performance, sometimes adapting them, but more often reprinting them unaltered. Indeed, at times Hazlitt's reviews are rather in the nature of literary essays on the theatrical interpretation of certain roles than immediate reviews of a particular performance. This is especially likely to be so when the review is of a performance that he has seen more than once. For instance in 1814 he has first a brief notice of Kean as Iago; then, two months later and after seeing the performance again, he writes a long essay on the role—published in *The Examiner* in two parts, the second a fortnight after the first—which occupies twenty pages in *A View of the English Stage*. Hazlitt made economical use of this essay. He reprinted it in 1817, in a volume of essays by himself and Leigh Hunt called *The Round Table*; in the same year he worked much of it into his essay on *Othello* in *Characters of Shakespear's Plays*; and then in the following year he reprinted it all again in *A View of the English Stage*. Clearly, then, there is no clear-cut distinction between Hazlitt the reviewer of Shakespeare in the theatre, and Hazlitt the literary critic of Shakespeare.

On the whole, it would seem that Hazlitt enjoyed reading Shakespeare's plays more than seeing them performed. He certainly shared in the Romantic adoration of Shakespeare, though his scholarship was shaky and he did not respond with equal enthusiasm to all the plays. He writes best on the tragedies, which he most admired. He writes as an enthusiast, carried away by his subject; like Leigh Hunt, he reacts against Dr Johnson's judiciousness. In his theatre reviews he is, naturally, more limited in scope than in the book, so the reviews tell us less about his views on Shakespeare in general. In them he more often confines himself to the play under discussion, and quite often to the leading role alone. But even in the reviews he sometimes opens out into more generalized remarks. In the essay on Kean's Iago, for instance, commenting on Iago's character, he commits himself to the general statement that Shakespeare was 'quite as good a philosopher as he was a poet' (*View*, p. 213), and goes on to justify this in a piece of discursive writing which has reference to Iago but in fact is itself of a strongly philosophical trend. He has some particularly interesting remarks on Shakespeare's morality. (Incidentally, all the ones to which I shall refer were later incorporated into *Characters of Shakespear's Plays*.) While Dr Johnson had found fault with Shakespeare for being 'so much more careful to please than to instruct, that he seems to write without any moral purpose', Hazlitt praises him for this very characteristic.[3] Remarking that the 'moral perfection' of Hamlet 'has been called in question', Hazlitt writes: 'It is more natural than conformable to rules; and if not more amiable, is certainly more dramatic on that account.' Shakespeare 'does not set his heroes in the stocks of virtue, to make mouths at their own situation. His plays are not transcribed from the Whole Duty of Man! We confess, we are a little shocked at the want of refinement in those, who are shocked at the want of refinement in Hamlet' (*View*, p. 186). He pursues the theme in a review of *Measure for Measure*, in which he quotes at length from Schlegel and castigates him for being 'so severe on those pleasant persons Lucio, Pompey, and Master Froth, as to call them "wretches"'. From this he moves into a general disquisition on Shakespeare and morality.

> Shakespear was the least moral of all writers; for morality (commonly so called) is made up of antipathies, and his talent consisted in sympathy with human nature, in all its shapes, degrees, elevations, and depressions. The object of the pedantic moralist is to make the worst of everything; *his* was to make the best, according to his own principle, 'There is some soul of goodness in things evil.' Even Master Barnardine is not left to the mercy of what others think of him, but when he comes in, he speaks for himself. We would recommend it to the Society for the Suppression of Vice to read Shakespear. (*View*, p. 283)

Here, as in the passage on *Hamlet*, Hazlitt is partly indulging his love of paradox, his republicanism, his moral unconventionality in a manner that provokes the kinds of epigrammatic turn of phrase which often make him so literally memorable a writer. Many of his phrases stick in the mind. But he is also stating something which he felt as an important truth, and which must have seemed excitingly liberating to those trained to take a morally judicial view of the characters of literary works. As with Leigh Hunt, those familiar with Keats's views on Shakespeare as expressed in his letters will recognize a theme which Keats may have derived partly from his conversations with Hazlitt, but to which he gave expression with even greater subtlety in his remarks on 'the poetical character'.[4]

Hazlitt's emphasis on Shakespeare's sympathy 'with human nature' forms an obvious link with the interest in character displayed also by Leigh Hunt. The very title of Hazlitt's book reflects this interest (though there the word *Characters* is ambiguous, referring to the overall 'character' of the individual plays as well as to the characters portrayed in them). Certainly Hazlitt has a predominant interest in

Shakespeare as a delineator of human character. This finds notable expression in his review of Kean's Hamlet, which opens with the statement:

> That which distinguishes the dramatic productions of Shakespear from all others, is the wonderful variety and perfect individuality of his characters. Each of these is as much itself, and as absolutely independent of the rest, as if they were living persons, not fictions of the mind. The poet appears, for the time being, to be identified with the character he wishes to represent, and to pass from one to the other, like the same soul, successively animating different bodies. By an art like that of the ventriloquist, he throws his imagination out of himself, and makes every word appear to proceed from the very mouth of the person whose name it bears. (*View*, p. 185)

This last sentiment, which seems so romantic in its attitude, is in fact very close to something that Pope had said almost a century before, in the Preface to his edition of Shakespeare, where he wrote that if Shakespeare's plays were printed without the names of the characters it would be possible to supply the names simply on the basis of the varying styles of the speeches.[5] Hazlitt's statements reveal an apprehension of one important feature of Shakespeare's genius, even though his generalizing expression of it leads him into extravagance. We can agree that, as he continues, Shakespeare's 'characters are real beings of flesh and blood; they speak like men, not like authors' in the sense that Shakespeare does often seem to be showing us the 'quick forge and working-house of thought', nowhere more vividly than in Hamlet's soliloquies. We can endorse, too, and admire Hazlitt's perception that Shakespeare's imagination must have been able to work simultaneously on many different planes, like that of the composer of a piece of intricately contrapuntal music: as he puts it, 'Each object and circumstance seems to exist in his mind as it existed in nature; each several train of thought and feeling goes on of itself without effort or confusion; in the world of his imagination every thing has a life, a place and being of its own.' We can admire his application to Shakespeare of the phrase 'magnanimity of genius'. But surely he lets himself down badly with what is intended as an emphatic conclusion: 'The whole play is an exact transcript of what might have taken place at the Court of Denmark five hundred years ago, before the modern refinements in morality and manners' (*View*, p. 185). Shakespeare seems to be lowered with a bump from being a transforming genius to a kind of retrospective newspaper reporter. Hazlitt continues with a memorable character sketch of Hamlet which, like much of the review, was taken over into *Characters of Shakespear's Plays*.

The interest in character, in the way people behave in real life, is naturally linked with an interest in acting, the way that human behaviour is imitated on the stage. Hazlitt's attitude to the theatre is very ambiguous. He was obviously fascinated by it, and towards the end of his life, in his essay 'The Free Admission', wrote with intensely romantic nostalgia about his theatre-going, remembering his 'beloved corner' in Covent Garden as a 'throne of felicity', a 'palace of delights' (Howe, vol. 17, p. 367). Nevertheless, he often expresses a preference for reading Shakespeare's plays rather than seeing them performed. In the essay on *Hamlet* in *Characters of Shakespear's Plays* he writes: 'We do not like to see our author's plays acted, and least of all, *Hamlet*. There is no play that suffers so much in being transferred to the stage' (pp. 92–3). Reviewing an adaptation of *A Midsummer Night's Dream* at Covent Garden, he writes, 'Poetry and the stage do not agree together'. He finds that while

> Bottom's head in the play is a fantastic illusion, produced by magic spells: on the stage it is an ass's head, and nothing more; certainly a very strange costume for a gentleman to appear in . . . Fairies are not incredible, but fairies six feet high are so. Monsters are not shocking, if they are seen at a proper distance. When ghosts appear in mid-day, when apparitions stalk along Cheapside, then may the Midsummer Night's Dream be represented at Covent Garden or at Drury-Lane; for we hear, that it is to be brought out there also, and that we have to undergo another crucifixion. (*View*, p. 276)

A Midsummer Night's Dream, with its frequent use of the supernatural and its magical effects, might seem a particularly severe test, but Hazlitt is no less emphatic in reviewing *Richard II*. 'The representing of the very finest [of the plays] even by the best actors, is . . . an abuse of the genius of the poet, and even in those of a second-rate class, the quantity of sentiment and imagery greatly outweighs the immediate impression of the situation and story.' Subtleties are lost on the audience, even 'the most striking and impressive passages . . . fail comparatively of their effect', the 'parts of the play on which the reader dwells the longest . . . are hurried through in the performance', and 'the reader of the plays of Shakespear is almost always disappointed in seeing them acted; and, for our own part, we should never go to see them acted, if we could help it' (*View*, pp. 221–2).

It is difficult to assess the extent to which this is an absolute judgement rather than a reaction against the way the plays were presented in his own time. Undoubtedly Hazlitt had much fault to find with the way in which London's only two legitimate theatres, Covent Garden and Drury Lane, were run, and the manner in which plays were put on to their stages. He has a number of attacks on the managers, for making Kean play one part over and over again instead of demonstrating his versatility in a range of parts, for allowing unqualified actors to play major roles, and for their excessive emphasis on spectacle. Thus, the spirit of *A Midsummer Night's Dream* 'was evaporated, the genius was fled; but the spectacle was fine: it was that which saved the play. Oh, ye scene-shifters, ye scene-painters, ye machinists and dress-makers, ye manufacturers of moon and stars that give no light, ye musical composers, ye men in the orchestra, fiddlers and trumpeters and players on the double drum and loud bassoon, rejoice! This is your triumph; it is not ours' (*View*, p. 275). The version of *A Midsummer Night's Dream* performed on this occasion was in fact heavily adapted, with many omissions, interpolations, rearrangements, and added songs, so it was a poor basis on which to form a judgement of the suitability of the play for the stage. Hazlitt quite often attacks the continuing use of corrupt old stage versions of certain plays, just as Leigh Hunt, also, does. He refers to the 'miserable medley acted for *Richard III*', and on another occasion calls it 'a vile jumble' (*View*, p. 181; Howe, vol. 18, p. 255); he deplores an adaptation of *Antony and Cleopatra* with cuts, transpositions, and additions from Dryden (*View*, pp. 190–2); like Hunt several years before him, he castigates the continuing use of the Dryden–Davenant adaptation of *The Tempest* after seeing a performance which so sickened him that as he returned home, he says, he 'almost came to the resolution of never going to another representation of a play of Shakespear's as long as [he] lived; and [he] certainly did come to this determination, that [he] would never go *by choice*. To call it a representation, is indeed an abuse of language: it is travestie, caricature, any thing you please, but a representation' (*View*, p. 234). And he attacks the managers 'for reviving Nahum Tate's Lear, instead of the original text' (Howe, vol. 18, p. 318).

However, Hazlitt, also like Hunt, was not a total purist in textual matters. Like Hunt, he remarks that an actress playing Rosalind 'sung the *Cuckoo* song very prettily, and was encored in it' (Howe, vol. 18, p. 249), without pointing out that she ought not to have been singing it at all. He observes that 'The manner in which Shakespear's plays have been generally altered, or rather mangled, by modern mechanists, is in our opinion a disgrace to the English Stage. The patch-work Richard which is acted under the sanction of his name, is a striking example of this remark.' Nevertheless, he finds that the original play is 'too long for representation, and there are some few scenes which might be better spared than preserved'. And he commits himself to a general statement of principle that 'The only rule … for altering Shakespear, is to retrench certain passages which may be considered either as superfluous or obsolete, but not to add or transpose any thing' (Howe, vol. 18, p. 191). Thus he can speak with moderate approbation of the version of *Richard II* in which Kean appeared as the best alteration of the play 'that has been attempted; for it consists entirely of omissions, except one or two scenes which are idly tacked on to the conclusion' (*View*, p. 224). However, reference to the text of this adaptation suggests that Hazlitt's impression on such matters is not entirely to be trusted, since in fact there were very extensive cuts, including the tournament and Aumerle's plot against Bolingbroke; the adapter added a number of lines of his own, the Queen's part was fattened out by the addition of lines from *Richard III*; and, still more startlingly, at the end of the play, Richard having been killed, the Queen mourned over his body in the following words:[6]

> Never will we part! O, you are men of stone,
> Had I your tongues and eyes, I'd use them so,
> That heaven's vault should crack! O he is gone forever.

A plague upon you! Murderers—Traitors all!
[to Bolingbroke] You might have saved him—now he is lost forever.
BOLINGBROKE.   What words can soothe such aggravated woes!
QUEEN.   O dearest Richard, dearer than my soul,
  Had I but seen thy picture in this plight,
  It would have madded me—what shall I do,
  Now I behold thy lovely body thus —
  Plot some device of further misery,
  To make us wondered at in time to come.
BOLINGBROKE.   Be comforted, and leave this fatal place.
QUEEN.   Why should a dog, a horse, a rat, have life,
  And thou no breath at all? O, thou will come no more,
  Never, never, never!
  Pray you undo my lace—Thank you.
  Do you see this, look on him, look on his lips,
  Look there, look there. [Falls]

These are the scenes 'idly tacked on to the conclusion'. The use of Lear's dying speeches was, perhaps, more easily justified in that they had not been spoken on the stage in performances of King Lear for 150 years; one might have expected Hazlitt to remark on their use here, even if he could not be expected to notice that a few lines from Titus Andronicus were spliced into them. Similarly, although he observes that Juliet's scene in the tomb with Romeo 'is not from Shakespear'—it is by Garrick—he lets it pass since it 'tells admirably on the stage' (View, p. 200).

Also like Hunt, Hazlitt does not often refer to the ways in which the plays were put on—or, as the expression was, 'got up'. There is a kind of basic acceptance—albeit a weary, reluctant acceptance—of the system, a system which meant generally that the stock companies using stock scenery and standard, corrupt acting versions provided a setting—often a very shabby setting—for the performances of star actors. Occasionally Hazlitt comments briefly on the staging. He wishes that 'the introduction of the ghosts through the trap-doors of the stage' in Richard III 'were altogether omitted' (View, p. 184). He goes to see Kean play Iago, and describes it as 'the most faultless of his performances', yet has to add that the Othello of Mr Sowerby 'was a complete failure, and the rest of the play was very ill got up' (View, p. 190). But never do we have the sense that he had any concept of the 'production' of a play in the modern sense of the word, of the attempt, that is, to put on—or 'get up'—a performance that would be articulated in all its parts, that would present an overall view, or interpretation, of a play such as Hazlitt might present in literary terms. He was stuck with an actors' theatre. He knew it, and he did not entirely like it. He knew that he would never see a Shakespeare play presented on the stage in the way he could imagine it as he read it. He knew that he was often bitterly disappointed when he saw Shakespeare acted, and that, much as he loved the theatre, he would prefer not to see performances of the plays that he most admired. Perhaps he did not see quite deeply enough to realize that this was not the fault of the plays, or of theatre as a medium, but rather of the theatrical conditions of his age. It is even possible that if he, and others like him, had displayed in their writing a stronger sense of the structure of the plays, of their overall design and their basic stage-worthiness, the theatre might have been pushed into getting up the plays in a fashion that showed more awareness of these qualities. But, though he was highly conscious of many of the faults of the theatre of his time, he was himself of his time. It was the age of the actors' theatre, and, in a sense, of the characters' Shakespeare. Hazlitt's book is called *Characters of Shakespear's Plays*; the literary critic places his emphasis on the characters, and the theatre critic, correspondingly, places *his* emphasis on the individual actors.[7]

Nevertheless, Hazlitt does not feel that the theatre can succeed completely even in the presentation of Shakespeare's characters. Even in this limited area, reading is better than seeing. It is ridiculous 'to suppose that anyone ever went to see Hamlet or Othello represented by Kean or Kemble; we go to see Kean or Kemble in Hamlet or Othello'. Shakespeare's characters are no more powerful on the stage than other characters in far less well-written plays. The reason we wish to see actors perform them is that they offer more of a challenge to the actor: 'It appears . . . not that the most intellectual characters excite most interest on the stage, but that they are objects of greater curiosity; they are nicer tests of the skill of the actor, and afford greater scope for controversy' (*View*, p. 223). They are, in other words, vehicles for virtuosity. There is no doubt that this is still part of their appeal. Theatre-lovers collect performances of the great roles as music-lovers collect performances of the great concertos.

Hazlitt discusses the difficulties that the great roles present particularly in relation to Hamlet, which, he thinks, is probably the most difficult—'It is like the attempt to embody a shadow. . . . The character is spun to the finest thread, yet never loses its continuity. It has the yielding flexibility of "a wave of the sea." It is made up of undulating lines, without a single sharp angle' (*View*, pp. 186–7). This is, for its date, a curiously impressionistic way of writing. We can see what Hazlitt means without, perhaps, feeling that he has fully explained himself. Even though on this occasion 'Mr Kean's representation of the character had the most brilliant success', still the character 'did not . . . come home to our feelings, as Hamlet (that very Hamlet whom we read of in our youth, and seem almost to remember in our after-years)'. Hazlitt seems often to have felt an irritating yet inevitable dislocation between his own imaginative vision of a character and the actor's embodiment of it, so that even the best performances represented an adaptation of the role to the actor's personality. He knows, in general terms, what he wants an actor to do. 'Our highest conception of an actor is, that he shall assume the character once for all, and be it throughout, and trust to this conscious sympathy for the effect produced' (*View*, p. 184). But even the best actors rarely, if ever, achieved this. Even the greatest actor about whom Hazlitt writes, Edmund Kean, 'is not a literal transcriber of his author's text; he translates his characters with great freedom and ingenuity into a language of his own', producing 'dramatic versions' which are 'liberal and spirited' and therefore preferable to the 'dull, literal, commonplace monotony of his competitors' (*View*, p. 190). Using one of the favourite concepts of his age, and one which is for this very reason often difficult to define, Hazlitt asks in acting for truth to nature. Shakespeare is true to nature in his writing. He is like the ideal actor that Hazlitt desiderates. Shakespeare '*becomes*' his characters, 'His imagination passes out of himself into them...His plays can only be compared with Nature—they are unlike everything else' (*View*, p. 191). This resembles the view that *Hamlet* is like an 'exact transcript of what might have taken place at the Court of Denmark...'. We know that it is not true, except in the most specialized sense. So actors, too, must seem like nature: 'executive power in acting...is only valuable as it is made subservient to truth and nature' (*View*, p. 201). By itself, this might seem like a simplistic demand for naturalism. But another review helps to clarify it. After seeing an actor fail badly as Richard III, Hazlitt wrote:

> We suspect that he has a wrong theory of his art. He has taken a lesson from Mr Kean, whom he caricatures, and seems to suppose that to be familiar or violent is natural, and that to be natural is the perfection of acting. And so it is, if properly understood. But to play Richard naturally, is to play it as Richard would play it, not as Mr Cobham would play it; he comes there to shew us not himself, but the tyrant and the king—not what he would do, but what another would do in such circumstances. Before he can do this he must become that other, and cease to be himself. Dignity is natural to certain stations, and grandeur of expression to certain feelings. In art, nature cannot exist without the highest art; it is a pure effort of the imagination, which throws the mind out of itself into the supposed situation of others, and enables it to feel and act there as if it were at home. (*View*, p. 299)

I am not sure that even here Hazlitt has completely solved the problem which seems often to have perplexed him. And indeed it is a perpetual problem in acting—the maintaining of the balance between rhetoric, conscious and visible control of the audience, the deployment of highly-developed skills, on the one hand, and on the other hand the maintaining of integrity, of faith to nature, to the way human beings actually speak, act, and feel. No human beings, even at the court of Denmark 500 years ago, have ever spoken naturally in blank verse. The actor has to employ his art to resolve the tension between the dramatist's artifices of language and stylized action, and the audience's illusion that they are watching real people. He has to use his art to create an illusion of naturalness within a strictly controlled framework. Hazlitt recognizes this when he says that 'In art, nature cannot exist without the highest art'; and his statements of the importance of 'nature' in acting need to be seen in the context of this admission. To achieve the semblance of naturalness is the highest achievement of art; or, as Hazlitt says in yet another review, 'Art may be taught, because it is learnt: Nature can neither be taught nor learnt. The secrets of Art may be said to have a common or *pass* key to unlock them; the secrets of Nature have but one master-key: the heart' (*View*, p. 355). Given this full context, we can understand Hazlitt's opinion, expressed in a review of Kean's Richard III, that once an actor has perfected his interpretation of a role he should vary its execution as little as possible. 'He should make up his mind as to the best mode of representing the part, and come as near to this standard as he can, in every successive exhibition.' This may sound like a preference for artificiality rather than naturalness; but Hazlitt is ready for the objection. 'All acting is studied or artificial. An actor is no more called upon to vary his gestures or articulation at every new rehearsal of the character, than an author can be required to furnish various readings to every separate copy of his work' (*View*, p. 202).

While feeling that the execution of a great role is only a poor substitute for a reading of the play in which the role occurs, Hazlitt seems nevertheless to have found a great fascination in watching actors at work, and there are a few passages in his reviews which give us hints of why this should have been so. Writing of a fine actress, Eliza O'Neill, he says that, for all her merits, she did not make the same impression on him as Kean did. And speculating on the reason for this, he says that her acting 'adds little to the stock of our ideas, or to our materials for reflection, but passes away with the momentary illusion of the scene' (*View*, p. 211). Great acting was a stimulus to Hazlitt's imagination; watching actors intensely portraying intense emotion, he felt that he was learning about humanity, and some of the best passages in Hazlitt's criticism are ones that give us a sense that he has been stimulated to explore his response to the character and personality of the actor by the performance he has watched.

Although he lived at a time when the English drama was at a low ebb, he was fortunate enough to see many times two of the greatest of all English actors, Sarah Siddons and Edmund Kean, on both of whom he writes much. Mrs Siddons officially retired in 1812, one year before Hazlitt began his career as a theatre critic. But he had often seen her act before then, and she made one or two appearances on special occasions after her retirement. Hazlitt felt that she was mistaken to come out of retirement. When she played Lady Macbeth again in both 1816 and 1817, he found her slow, ponderous, and laboured. But his memories of her in her best days are a frequent source of inspiration to him, and produce some of the nostalgic, retrospective criticism in which he excelled. To her, along with Edmund Kean, he pays the highest tribute that he pays to any actor: that, whereas all other actors in Shakespearean roles have interfered with his 'conception of the character itself', they alone 'have raised' his 'imagination of the part they acted'. When he writes of Mrs Siddons at her best he makes one feel that not to have seen her performances in tragedy is to have missed one of the wonders of the world.

She raised Tragedy to the skies, or brought it down from thence. It was something above nature. We can conceive of nothing grander. She embodied to our imagination the fables of mythology, of the heroic and deified mortals of elder time. She was not less than a goddess, or than a prophetess inspired by the gods. Power was seated on her brow, passion emanated from her breast as from a shrine. She was Tragedy personified. She was the stateliest ornament of the public mind. She was not only the idol of the people, she not only hushed the tumultuous shouts of the pit in breathless expectation, and quenched the blaze of surrounding beauty in silent tears, but to the retired and lonely student, through long years of solitude, her face has shone as if an eye had appeared from heaven; her name has been as if a voice had opened the chambers of the human heart, or as if a trumpet had awakened the sleeping and the dead. To have seen Mrs Siddons, was an event in one's life. (*View*, p. 312)

Perhaps no more eloquent a tribute has ever been paid to an actress. We can only regret that it is couched in general terms, telling us nothing about the precise manner of her acting.

Hazlitt's other idol was Edmund Kean. One of Hazlitt's earliest professional visits to the theatre was to see Kean's London début, and he saw many of his performances when Kean was at his best and when he himself was writing most freshly. Never, perhaps, has there been so happy a conjunction of critic and actor. They seem to have been made for one another. Kean is remembered partly because Hazlitt wrote so well about him; Hazlitt's theatre criticism is read partly because Kean stirred him to such eloquence. Hazlitt seems to have felt something of this himself, since in reprinting his reviews he grouped together at the beginning of the volume the ones dealing with Kean's early performances. And in his Preface he recounts how he was asked by his editor to attend Kean's first performance, of Shylock. 'The boxes were empty, and the pit not half full.' Hazlitt 'had been told to give as favourable an account' as he could, but, he says, he 'gave a true one'. He defends himself against the suggestion that he has overpraised Kean, and if we are tempted to suspect him of doing so, we should remember that many other excellent judges thought equally highly of Kean. Moreover, Hazlitt does not write as a blind worshipper. He sees faults in Kean's performances, and analyses them with what seems like objective care. His outbursts of eulogy are the more convincing for being juxtaposed with passages of cool criticism. Kean's main physical deficiencies lay in his short stature and a voice that often gave the impression of hoarseness. In Hazlitt's very first notice of him, he finds that 'The fault of his acting was . . . an over-display of the resources of his art', that his pauses were occasionally held for too long, and that he placed too great a reliance 'on the expression of the countenance, which is a language intelligible only to a part of the house' (*View*, pp. 179–80). The large theatres of the time seem often to have caused actors to exaggerate and coarsen their effects, and in a later review Hazlitt says that one reason why Leigh Hunt had been disappointed on first seeing Kean was probably that he was sitting too far from the stage (*View*, p. 224).

344

Hazlitt does not find that Kean is equally good in all his roles. He was not a lyrical actor. His Hamlet, for all its virtues, was a little too close to his Richard III, too vehement, too harsh. This characteristic seems to have been the obverse of his virtues. Coleridge said that to see him was like reading Shakespeare by flashes of lightning, a method which suits some roles better than others. Kean made Richard II 'a character of *passion*, that is, of feeling combined with energy; whereas it is a character of *pathos*, that is to say, of feeling combined with weakness'. Apropos of this performance, Hazlitt says that 'the general fault' of Kean's acting is 'that it is always energetic or nothing. He is always on full stretch—never relaxed' (*View*, p. 223). Predictably, he was not an ideal Romeo. 'His Romeo had nothing of the lover in it. We never saw anything less ardent or less voluptuous. In the Balcony scene in particular, he was cold, tame, and unimpressive.... He stood like a statue of lead' (*View*, p. 209). Nevertheless, Hazlitt writes still early in Kean's career, 'In every character that he has played, in Shylock, in Richard III, in Hamlet, in Othello, in Iago... and in Macbeth, there has been either a dazzling repetition of master-strokes of art and nature' or a remedying of any deficiency 'by some collected and overpowering display of energy or pathos, which electrified at the moment, and left a lasting impression on the mind afterwards' (*View*, pp. 208–9).

Hazlitt's eulogies of Kean tend towards the generalizing in their method. On the whole he seems more concerned to convey an impression of the manner in which Kean played a role, and the effect he created, than to give a moment-by-moment commentary. For example, the first time he saw Kean play Othello he wrote that, though Kean did not succeed in portraying a 'noble tide of deep and sustained passion', nevertheless there were

> repeated bursts of feeling and energy which we have never seen surpassed. The whole of the latter part of the third act was a master piece of profound pathos and exquisite conception, and its effect in the house was electrical. The tone of voice in which he delivered the beautiful apostrophe, 'Then, oh farewell!' struck on the heart and the imagination like the swelling notes of some divine music. The look, the action, the expression of voice, with which he accompanied the exclamation, 'Not a jot, not a jot;' the reflection, 'I felt not *Cassio's kisses* on her lips;' and his vow of revenge against Cassio, and abandonment of his love for Desdemona, laid open the very tumult and agony of the soul. (*View*, p. 189)

I quote this rather substantial passage because it is the whole of what Hazlitt says in praise of this particular performance. It is the kind of criticism that makes one wish one had seen the performance—which is something—but does not reach the excellence of almost making one feel one *has* seen the performance. In a later notice of the same role (*View*, p. 271), Hazlitt calls Kean's Othello 'his best character, and the highest effort of genius on the stage', and writes well on Shakespeare's portrayal of

Othello, but does not tell us much more about what Kean did. Indeed, it seems perfectly clear that in writing this review, Hazlitt looked up what he had said previously, since some of the same phrases recur. In 1814, he had said that 'The tone of voice in which he delivered the beautiful apostrophe, "Then, oh farewell!" struck on the heart and the imagination like the swelling notes of some divine music.' This sentence is precisely repeated in 1816, except for the omission of the phrase 'and the imagination' and the addition at the end of the sentence of the words, 'like the sound of years of departed happiness'. In 1817 he concentrates on the actor playing Iago, and can only say of Kean that his performance 'is beyond all praise. Any one who has not seen him in the third act of Othello (and seen him near) cannot have an idea of perfect tragic acting' (*View*, p. 357). Seven months later he sees the performance again, and this time takes the trouble to rethink his reactions to it. He still writes partly in metaphors: 'His lips might be said less to utter words, than to bleed drops of blood gushing from his heart.' He illustrates this, but in a tantalizingly uninformative manner, saying 'An instance of this was in his pronunciation of the line "Of one that loved not wisely but too well"'. No doubt this comment was interesting to its original readers, who could go to Drury Lane a few days later and listen to the way Kean said the line, and have the pleasure of finding that they agreed with Hazlitt, or the distinction of finding that they did not. But it does little for posterity. More useful is his statement that Othello's 'exclamation on seeing his wife, "I cannot think but Desdemona's honest", was "the glorious triumph of exceeding love"; a thought flashing conviction on his mind, and irradiating his countenance with joy, like sudden sunshine'. The main impression conveyed by his notice is that Kean's Othello was above all a masterly portrayal of suffering; and Hazlitt's final sentence shows that the grotesque was an element in the composition. 'The convulsed motion of the hands, and the involuntary swellings of the veins of the forehead in some of the most painful situations, should not only suggest topics of critical panegyric, but might furnish studies to the painter or anatomist' (Howe, vol. 18, p. 263). This is Hazlitt's best notice of Kean's Othello. He obviously knew it, as he reprinted the whole passage (with acknowledgement) in 1820, and then again in 1828.

Even when Hazlitt is only writing generally he is still capable of stirring eloquence. And at times he does come closer to the object, often with thrilling effect. One of the most memorable of all pieces of theatre criticism is his description of Kean's death scene as Richard III: 'He fought like one drunk with wounds: and the attitude in which he stands with his hands stretched out, after his sword is taken from him, had a preternatural and terrific grandeur, as if his will could not be disarmed, and the very phantoms of his despair had a withering power' (*View*, p. 182). That is wonderfully evocative prose, implying a deeply imaginative view of Richard as a desperately, if evilly, courageous figure. Hazlitt was interested in the actor as a commentator on the role, as an interpreter who should be taken seriously. In *Hamlet*, for instance, he finds that Kean introduced 'a *new reading*, as it is called, which we think perfectly correct. In the scene where he breaks from his friends to obey the command of his father, he keeps his sword pointed behind him, to prevent them from following him, instead of holding it before him to protect him from the Ghost.' In the same performance, he describes and praises a piece of business on Kean's part which seems to us quintessentially romantic. The scene with Ophelia— the 'nunnery' scene—was over-emphatically acted: 'But whatever nice faults might be found...they were amply redeemed by the manner of his coming back after he has gone to the extremity of the stage, from a pause of parting tenderness to press his lips to Ophelia's hand. It had an electrical effect on the house. It was the finest commentary that was ever made on Shakespear. It explained the character at once (as he meant it), as one of disappointed hope, of bitter regret, of affection suspended, not obliterated, by the distractions of the scene around him!' (*View*, p. 188). It was also highly influential. Sheridan Knowles felt that Kean had preserved 'one of Shakespeare's noblest characters' from 'the conduct of a coward and a savage'.[8] Others might feel that it sentimentalized the role and represented rather a romantic gloss upon it than a legitimate deduction from, and extension of, the text. But clearly it is the sort of stage business that is almost irresistible to an actor who wishes to regain his audience's sympathy after a scene in which he has been required to behave rather brutally.

Hazlitt has a more general discussion of such matters in a later review of Kean's Richard III, where he says that 'Mr Kean's *bye-play* is certainly one of his greatest excellences, and it might be said, that if Shakespear had written marginal directions to the players, in the manner of the German dramatists, he would often have directed them to do what Mr Kean does' (*View*, p. 202). This reveals an awareness of the unwritten dimension in Shakespeare's plays, the fact that Shakespeare necessarily and consciously left something to his actors, or to rehearsals during which he might himself give them their instructions. So Hazlitt can praise Kean for the intensity with which he fleshes out the bare words in, for example, Macbeth's scene after the murder. This was one of Kean's greatest episodes. 'The hesitation, the bewildered look, the coming to himself when he sees his hands bloody; the manner in which his voice clung to his throat, and choked his utterance; his agony and tears, the force of nature overcome by passion—beggared description. It was a scene, which no one who saw it can ever efface from his recollection' (*View*, p. 207).

One could go on for a long time quoting from Hazlitt's reviews of Kean. He wrote best when he wrote admiringly; and above all other actors he admired Kean. There were of course other performers whom he would praise, such as Eliza O'Neill and the young Macready. And there was the actor whom Leigh Hunt found it so difficult to praise, Mrs Siddons' brother, John Philip Kemble. Hazlitt summed up his feelings about him in an article headed 'Mr Kemble's Retirement', written after seeing his farewell performance as Coriolanus in June 1817. In this essay, which Hazlitt's biographer, Herschel Baker, calls 'one of the peaks of English drama criticism',[9] Hazlitt draws on some of his earlier, 'immediate' criticism in a retrospective review of great power. He felt the pathos of the occasion:

'There is something in these partings with old public favourites exceedingly affecting. They teach us the shortness of human life, and the vanity of human pleasures.' Happily, Kemble's final performance showed 'no abatement of spirit and energy'. But Hazlitt approves of his retiring because he does 'not wish him to wait till it is *necessary* for him to retire'. He surveys Kemble's best performances, delineating his special characteristics and also referring to his weaknesses. As Hamlet he had failed because he played the role, in Hazlitt's memorable phrase, 'like a man in armour, in one undeviating straight line'. His manner 'had always something dry, hard, and pedantic in it'. But his distinguishing excellence was '*intensity*', 'and in embodying a high idea of certain characters, which belong rather to sentiment than passion, to energy of will, than to loftiness or to originality of imagination, he was the most excellent actor of his time' (*View*, pp. 374–9). In Hazlitt's peroration there is perhaps something a little self-conscious, as of one who writes an obituary; but it is a noble essay which must have helped Kemble to forgive Hazlitt's earlier remark that his 'supercilious airs and *nonchalance*' as Coriolanus 'remind one of the unaccountable abstracted air, the contracted eyebrows and suspended chin of a man who is just going to sneeze' (*View*, p. 350).

Hazlitt is, of course, one of the finest of English essayists. The art of the theatre critic is closely, perhaps inextricably, related to that of the essayist. As an essayist, Hazlitt is rightly held in greater esteem than Leigh Hunt. The prose style of the best of his theatre criticism is finer and more eloquent than Hunt's. Nevertheless, there are indications that ideally Hazlitt needed more time to produce his best effects than 'immediate' reviewing permitted him. This shows itself in the frequency with which he repeats himself, and in his liking for nostalgic, retrospective criticism. There is truth in the assessment later made by his friend Thomas Noon Talfourd, who wrote:

> his habits of mind were unsuited to the ordinary duties of the critic. The players put him out. He could not, like Mr Leigh Hunt, who gave theatrical criticism a place in modern literature, apply his graphic powers to a detail of a performance, and make it interesting by the delicacy of his touch....Hazlitt...required a more powerful impulse; he never wrote willingly, except on what was great in itself, or, forming a portion of his own past being, was great to him; and when both these felicities combined in the subject, he was best of all—as upon Kemble and Mrs Siddons.[10]

But to attempt a comparative assessment of Hazlitt and Leigh Hunt is not particularly fruitful. It is fortunate that two such fine writers, with somewhat complementary virtues, have left us such detailed impressions of the English theatre in the first three decades of the nineteenth century.

23

Peter Hall's *Coriolanus*, 1959

In 1959 the Shakespeare Memorial Theatre had an anniversary to celebrate. It was mounting its one-hundredth season. Celebrations were called for. Stratford likes celebrations. It celebrates Shakespeare's birthday every year; it celebrated his four-hundredth birthday for months on end; it celebrated for two weeks the two-hundredth anniversary of the celebrations that David Garrick organized in 1759; in 1975 it celebrated the centenary of the granting of the charter to the theatre; and undoubtedly in 1979 it will celebrate the centenary of the first season to be performed in that theatre. The celebrations for the hundredth season took place only eighty years after the first season; but they were justified, if justification was needed, by the fact that in some of the intervening years, when seasons sometimes lasted no longer than a week, there had been two of them: one, traditionally, around Shakespeare's birthday, the other in the summer. Glen Byam Shaw had announced in October 1958, that he would retire from his position as Director of the theatre at the end of 1959, and that he would be succeeded by Peter Hall. His final season was to bring an exceptional number of specially distinguished actors to Stratford. Paul Robeson was to play Othello; Dame Edith Evans was to play the Countess in *All's Well That Ends Well*, directed by Tyrone Guthrie; Charles Laughton was to play King Lear, and Bottom in *A Midsummer Night's Dream*; and Sir Laurence Olivier was to play Coriolanus, with Edith Evans as Volumnia, in performances directed by Peter Hall.

Coriolanus was an especially exciting prospect. Dame Edith had not appeared at Stratford since 1913, when, newly recruited to the stage from the millinery business, she had acted Cressida under the direction of William Poel, one of the formative influences on the twentieth century's attitude to the staging of Shakespeare. In the meantime she had become a great name in the history of the English stage, the leading comic actress of her time, famous above all for roles in comedy of manners, in Congreve and in Wilde. Her Lady Bracknell, which she once said she had played in every possible way except under water, was legendary. In Shakespeare she had excelled as Rosalind, as the Nurse in *Romeo and Juliet*, and as Queen Katherine in *Henry VIII*. But her Cleopatra had not been particularly successful; she had yielded the palm in tragic roles to her older contemporary, Dame Sybil Thorndike, who had in fact played Volumnia to Olivier's previous Coriolanus, at the Old Vic in 1938.

Olivier in 1959 was at a high point in his career. He was in his fifty-second year and had behind him a wide range of Shakespearian triumphs, in roles as diverse as Henry V, Justice Shallow, Hotspur, Macbeth, Malvolio, Richard III, and Titus Andronicus. In 1957 he had taken the bold step of appearing at the Royal Court Theatre in the entirely unheroic role of the broken-down comedian, Archie Rice, in John Osborne's *The Entertainer;* and he had been brilliantly successful in this unexpected encounter with the new wave of younger dramatists. He was in fact to be engaged in filming this role during the day while playing Coriolanus in the evenings. Peter Hall, who was to have the responsibility of directing these two great performers in one of Shakespeare's less popular and more difficult plays, was only 28 years old. But he had already directed some distinguished productions, including the first of *Waiting for Godot*, and at Stratford had directed *Love's Labour's Lost* in 1956, *Cymbeline* in 1957, and before *Coriolanus* opened, *A Midsummer Night's Dream* in 1959.

At the time of this production, I was a student at the Shakespeare Institute in Stratford. I had seen Olivier's Richard III in London in 1949, and counted it as my first, most exciting encounter with great acting. I had seen Edith Evans, too, in some of her finest parts, and thought of her with awe. (We were an impressionable lot in those days.) I was excited at the idea of the *Coriolanus* production. I was hoping to be bowled over by it. I have to say this because it may help to explain why indeed I *was* bowled over by it. I saw it the first night, and I saw it again several times—whenever I could spare the time from my thesis and the money from my grant. In talking about it, then, I can call upon personal memories, some of them still very vivid. But memory is fallible. I have also been able to consult documents that are available for public study—the programme, the very detailed prompt-book, with ancillary documents, which is in the library of the Shakespeare Centre; a number of photographs; and the reviews. These last, I may say, are less extensive than usual. The first night appears to have coincided with a period of what is now euphemistically called 'industrial action', which unfortunately means inaction, in the printing industry. The reviews in newspapers and periodicals are therefore scantier than usual. Easily the best piece that has appeared on the production is an essay by Laurence Kitchin in his *Mid-Century Drama* (1960). It is remarkable that although both *Shakespeare Survey* and *Shakespeare Quarterly* at this period were carrying reviews of Shakespeare productions, neither of them considered this one. The explanation seems to be simply that it opened inconveniently late in the season for their press-dates. It is a measure of the swing towards a theatrically-orientated approach to the study of Shakespeare that we can scarcely imagine a comparable academic neglect of so obviously important a production at the present time.

Coriolanus must have presented both the director and his actors with many problems. It is not one of Shakespeare's most popular plays. The leading role, moreover, is one in which few great actors have succeeded. At least two—Edmund Kean and Henry Irving—failed badly. The most successful was John Philip Kemble; but he had played in a heavily rewritten version, and his merits of statuesque and heavy dignity seem a long way from those of the volatile Laurence Olivier. Of course, Olivier himself had already succeeded in the role; but that was in 1938, when he was only 31 years old—a factor of some importance, since so much is made of Coriolanus's physical prowess. The play has appealed especially at times of political turmoil. Kemble first played the role in 1789, the year of the French Revolution. His contemporary, William Hazlitt, wrote about it in political terms, finding that Shakespeare 'seems to have had a leaning to the arbitrary side of the question, perhaps from some feeling of contempt for his own origin; and to have spared no occasion of baiting the rabble'.[1] In 1934 a version was performed in Paris with the direct intention of provoking revolution and with the actual effect of inciting at least demonstrations and riots in the streets.

Though certainly the play is seriously concerned with political issues, they are continuously bound up with personal ones. Coriolanus's political failure is the result of personal characteristics, and his personality is a preoccupation of many of the play's other characters; taciturn as he is, he might be described as a man more talked about than talking. It is, as Peter Ure says, 'an irony of the play that in it most of the characters spend most of their time discussing a hero who cannot bear to be talked about'.[2] This interest in character reflects Plutarch's emphasis on the combination in Coriolanus of 'many good and evil things together', and it presents the actor of the central role with challenging opportunities.

The play's lack of general appeal has sometimes been attributed partly to its lack of love-story; 'but then,' as A. C. Bradley points out, 'there is none in *Macbeth*, and next to none in *King Lear*'.[3] More to the point, perhaps, are the frequent difficulties in Shakespeare's language; his late style makes no concessions, and the verse has little obvious lyricism. The play presents an apparently unremitting seriousness of purpose, an absence of the concern to entertain which is so much to the fore in *Hamlet*, for instance, with its great variety of theatrical appeal. But Olivier is a great comic actor, and he found a surprising amount of comedy in the role of Coriolanus. I shall say more about this later; for the moment it is worth recalling that Bradley, a far-from frivolous critic, also found comedy in the play:

When the people appear as individuals they are frequently more or less comical. Shakespeare always enjoyed the inconsequence of the uneducated mind, and its tendency to express a sound meaning in an absurd form. Again, the talk of the servants with one another and with the muffled hero, and the conversation of the sentinels with Menenius, are amusing. There is a touch of comedy in the contrast between Volumnia and Virgilia when we see them on occasions not too serious. And then, not only at the beginning, as in Plutarch, but throughout the story we meet with that pleasant and wise old gentleman Menenius, whose humor tells him how to keep the peace while he gains his point and to say without offense what the hero cannot say without raising a storm. (p. 233)

What Bradley does not remark, however, is the humour that Olivier was able to find in Coriolanus himself.

A final problem worth noting is the play's sheer length. It is one of the five longest of all Shakespeare's plays. In his recent (1975) production of *Hamlet* at the National Theatre, Peter Hall used the full text and spoke out against cutting; but this was not his policy, nor that of the Stratford theatre in general, in 1959. Line counts of the play vary of course, according to the way that prose is spaced out on the page. The prompt-book uses Dover Wilson's New Cambridge edition. By my reckoning this has 3,325 lines, of which almost 800 were cut, a little less than a quarter of the play. The cuts are fairly distributed among the characters; this is not an example of star roles being emphasized at the expense of lesser ones. Coriolanus loses about 115 lines and Menenius 95. Volumnia loses only about 20, but of course hers is not a long role. It would be easy to disturb the balance of sympathies in this play by selective cutting, but a distinct effort was made to avoid this.

Two scenes were omitted entirely. One is the short scene between a Roman spy and a Volscian soldier (4.3). This has been a frequent casualty. It is a pity, especially because the Roman spy's unconcerned treachery forms an effective contrast with Coriolanus's heart-searchings. But the scene does not further the plot, and the fact that it is set in some unidentified locality between Rome and Antium is no doubt an embarrassment when, as here, the production is given on a permanent set. The other scene that was sacrificed is much longer: Act 2, scene 2, which takes place in the Capitol, and begins with an interesting discussion of Coriolanus by two officers, while they are laying cushions, concluding with the verdict, 'He's a worthy man.' The scene continues with a formal entrance of the patricians and the tribunes, Menenius's request that Cominius be allowed to speak in favour of Coriolanus's election to the consulship, Coriolanus's refusal to stay while he is praised, Cominius's oration praising Coriolanus's valour, Coriolanus's recall and his request that he be allowed to 'o'erleap' the custom of begging for the people's votes, and the tribunes' insistence that he be compelled to do so. It is a strong scene, and its loss must be regretted. The prompt-book shows that whereas Act 4, scene 3 was never put into rehearsal, this scene was. Thus it may be assumed that the original intention was to include the scene. The actor most likely to regret its omission is the performer of Cominius, who loses 83 lines of verse. It is fruitless to speculate on the reasons for the omission.

These scenes account for 260 of the 800 omitted lines. The remaining 540 are made up of what are known as internal cuts, that is, of short passages within individual speeches. These include some lines that offer obvious difficulties of vocabulary or syntax to a modern audience, others that amplify what has already been expressed, and some that might be regarded as repetitious. Some of the cuts seem more regrettable than others. I am sorry, for instance, to lose the climax of Aufidius's tribute to Coriolanus at the end of Act 4:

> But he has a merit
> To choke it in the utterance. So our virtues
> Lie in th' interpretation of the time;
> And power, unto itself most commendable,
> Hath not a tomb so evident as a chair
> T'extol what it hath done.

This is a generalizing comment of a kind that is particularly liable to be cut by a director who is concentrating on the play's story line. But it is an interesting remark in relation to the play's insistence on fame and on the relativity of judgement. The virtues of Coriolanus 'lie in th' interpretation of the time'; Shakespeare is distancing us, holding us back from judgement, not simply by including this statement, but also by using it as the climax of a tribute to Coriolanus from his greatest enemy. The phrase epitomizes the subtlety of Shakespeare's method. There is something free-standing about his portrayal of Coriolanus which leaves it open to the interpretation of actors and spectators.

On the whole, the cutting seems judicious. Most important, it appears in general to be practical rather than interpretative. The director is not trying to shape our interpretation by manipulating the text. At this time, the Stratford theatre still managed without state subsidy. It is perhaps a measure of the shift from commercial to subsidized theatre that whereas this production had a playing-time of two and a half hours (plus an interval) the following Stratford production of this same play, by John Barton, took three hours (with two intervals), and the most recent, by Trevor Nunn, three hours and ten minutes (with one interval plus a three-minute break).

Peter Hall's handling of the text also included a few minor revisions. In the crowd scenes, for instance, speeches indicated to be spoken by 'all' were sometimes allocated to a single actor, no doubt for the sake of clarity. The revised text gives instructions for laughs and noises from the crowd, who are also given a few additional phrases, such as 'Yes, yes!', 'To the Capitol!' (1.1.12), and so on.

Coriolanus is not a text that poses serious editorial difficulties, but the prompt-book shows that the director gave thought to textual matters. There are one or two apparently considered divergences from Dover Wilson's edition. For instance, in the first scene, according to Dover Wilson, the First Citizen says that what Coriolanus 'hath done famously he did it to that end; though soft-conscienced men can be content to say it was for his country, he did it partly to please his mother and to be proud'. This, however, is an emendation. The earliest printed text, in the First Folio, reads: 'He did it to please his mother and to be partly proud.' It is a small enough change, but the reversion to an emphasis on Coriolanus's desire to please his mother acquires significance in the light of the overall interpretation given to the relationship of mother and son. There are one or two other reversions to Folio readings. At a few points, the director has substituted a word still in current use for one used by Shakespeare in a sense that is now obsolete; for example, Coriolanus says: 'as high | As I could pitch'—instead of 'pick'—'my lance' (1.1.198), and in the last scene the phrase, 'betrayed your business' (5.92), is altered to 'abused our powers'. In the prompt-book I have noticed only about half-a-dozen examples of this kind of thing.

Although it is only seventeen years since this production was given, there are ways in which it would already seem dated to a modern audience. Theatrical fashions change quickly. The dominant mode in the visual presentation of Shakespeare's plays in the late 1950s was a kind of modified pictorialism deriving from the influence of the Elizabethan revival on the nineteenth-century spectacular tradition. It was a mode that was being eroded under the influence of the Festival Theatre at Stratford, Ontario; but the Stratford-upon-Avon theatre is very much a building of the 1930s. It is structurally incapable of being altered to a thrust-stage theatre, and in 1959 modifications in its basic structure were less extensive than they are now. Plays were commonly presented on a permanent set erected on the stage and having a strong pictorial quality, while nevertheless being capable of modifications during the performance in order to create varied stage pictures appropriate to the changing localities of the scenes.

The setting for *Coriolanus*, designed by Boris Aronson, was a heavy structure placed far forward on the stage. It was not strictly representative of any one place, such as the Forum in Rome, but had steps, gates, and a number of perches and platforms built on a craggy, rock-like structure. A central projection at stage level could be opened to form a kind of inner-stage. Lighting could focus on this area, but the surrounding structures remained implacably present. Some parts of the structure were movable, however. The gates could be opened, and smoke could issue from them in the scene in which Coriolanus storms the gates of Corioli (1.4).

The set attracted a good deal of comment, mostly unfavourable. Alan Alvarez was scornful: it 'looked like the first-class saloon of an old transatlantic liner... arranged so that all the action was crammed into a few feet at the front of the stage, stifling and airless' (*New Statesman*, 18 July). Kenneth Tynan said it was 'mountainous, which is fine, and full of mountainous steps, which is not', and recalled 'Alec Guinness' remark, *à propos* of Shakespearean productions in general, that he himself had very few conversations on the stairs of his own house'.[4] Laurence Kitchin wrote that it

laid down the rules of the game. This was going to be a vertical production, with coigns of vantage on steps, landings, and an isolated projection resembling the Tarpeian rock. The biggest uninterrupted plane, no bigger than a cramped provincial repertory stage, was bounded by the prompt corner, archaic subtarpeian doors and steps leading up to a city gate. There could be no ceremonial entrances between ranked guards of honour, of the kind Groucho Marx discredited in *Duck Soup* by awaiting his own entrance at the extreme end of a file, neither could a dense mob assemble nor a marching column gather impetus. An immediate effect of the arrangement was that Olivier's first appearance, on top of the rock, did none of the usual things to invite applause. There, like the apparition of an eagle, he suddenly was. (p. 143)

It is possible to offer explanations of some features of the set. In pushing the action forward, as in the fact that no front curtains were used, it was an early move in Peter Hall's efforts to break the barrier of the proscenium arch. The forwardness of the action may also have helped to overcome acoustic problems—the theatre is not easy in this respect—and the smallness of the playing area may have helped to disguise the fact that the crowds were rather small.

Coriolanus is not one of Shakespeare's more musical plays. There are no songs, and most of the original music cues are for martial instruments: for drums, trumpets, and cornets. In keeping with a fashion of the time, this production used *musique concrète*, a combination of music and sound effects pre-recorded and played on a tape during the performance. A distinguished composer, Roberto Gerhard, was responsible for this, and he achieved striking, sometimes indeed shattering, effects with unconventional instruments such as drums and tam-tams.

The music was one way in which the director dealt with one of the play's theatrical problems, its unusual form. In most of Shakespeare's plays about warfare the battle scenes come at the end, as a climax. Even in *Macbeth*, in which, as in *Coriolanus*, the hero's valour is important, the action begins at the end of a battle, not in the thick of it. But in *Coriolanus* the battle scenes come early in the play. There is a danger that the director and his actors will exhaust their energies in the early scenes, and that the rest of the play will be a long anti-climax. Peter Hall certainly did not try to minimize the potential excitement of these scenes. At the opening, the lights dimmed on the uncurtained set, to be followed by a racket of bells, shouts, crowd-noises, and beating sounds working up to a climax as the mob broke through the gates on to the stage. It was a 'thrilling opening',[5] causing Frank Granville-Barker to write: 'From the moment . . . that the Roman mob surged on to the stage—vomited, as it seemed, from the very bowels of the earth—my attention was gripped.' Sound effects were used in the scenes that followed to reinforce the noise made by the comparatively small stage armies. But Peter Hall also used musical and lighting effects as a means of articulating the scenes and effecting transitions of mood. He was careful to create a theatrical structure which would relax as well as create tension, so that the audience would not be excessively stretched. In the first Act there was an episode of domestic repose in the scene with Volumnia and her ladies, introduced by soothing music. The battle scenes that followed were undoubtedly noisy, but there was some effectively peaceful and eerie music for the return to Rome at the beginning of the second Act. The scenes of Coriolanus's begging for the people's voices were a relaxed interlude before the mounting climax of his banishment, and the first movement of the play as performed came at the end of Act 4, scene 2, in which Volumnia berates the tribunes. It was a powerful and emotional scene. Volumnia's strong exit was usually greeted with applause, leaving Menenius to give the first part a quiet ending with his words 'Fie! fie! fie!' spoken slowly and thoughtfully as he made a slow exit.

This placing of the single interval means that it was followed by several comparatively relaxed scenes. The beginning of Act 4, scene 6 was calculated as an idyllic glimpse of Rome at peace. As the critic of *The Scotsman* (14 July) put it, 'We are given a glimpse of the happiness which follows his banishment, when the mob leader passes over the stage carrying his youngest child on his shoulders, and followed by the rest of his family, as if he were bound for a day at the seaside.' It was a calculated point of repose, with Sicinius and Brutus, the uncles of the people, complacently and patronizingly benevolent, as if the achievement were theirs. But the peace was soon disturbed by the breathless entrances of messengers with news of the advance of the Volscian armies, disturbing and angering the tribunes; and emotional tension was high through the fluctuating rhythms of the remaining episodes. The theatrical rhythm of a play is different in each production, according to the cuts in the text, the moments chosen by the actors for their climaxes, and many other factors. Peter Hall, helped by his musicians and actors, seemed to me to create a satisfying shape for this production.

I have been speaking so far mainly about matters which are the province and responsibility of the director rather than the actors. But I have laid stress on the importance in this play of individual personality within the no-less-important political framework, and no doubt this was in the director's mind when he cast his performers. The company included many actors of impressive physical appearance, manly in voice and movement, and this enabled some of the less important roles to be appropriately and strongly cast. The company included, too, some talented younger performers, who have since risen to greater prominence and were already showing their abilities. For example, Roy Dotrice and Ian Holm, both of them now star actors, played two of the servants in Aufidius's house. These are brilliantly written cameo parts, in which Shakespeare uses individualizing comic touches both to create entertainment and to show a kinship between the Volscian commoners and the Roman ones. Like the individual members of the Roman mob, these serving men are easily swayed; their engaging mutability is the reverse of Coriolanus's stern integrity and is fittingly juxtaposed with it. Holm and Dotrice were not among the more heroically-built members of the company, and this fact assisted the comedy of their feeble efforts to resist Coriolanus, and the bravado of their protestations in his absence. They were not altogether helped by the Welsh accents which they were required to adopt as a device for distinguishing the Volscians from the Romans; but they realized the potential within their roles with a sharp, well-timed immediacy that was capable of raising loud laughter.

On the opposing side, the Roman citizens were led by another actor who has since risen to greater heights, Albert Finney, now playing Hamlet for Peter Hall at the National Theatre. Then only 23 years old, he had already played Macbeth at the Birmingham Repertory Theatre. He was Olivier's understudy as Coriolanus and played the role several times. A big, brawny, barrel-chested man, he played the First Citizen with a natural authority combined with a mutinously hang-dog look, a man with a chip on his shoulder who attracted sympathy all the same. Like other actors of his generation, he retained a local accent even when playing classical parts, and the Roman citizens had Lancashire accents to oppose to the Welsh of the Volscians. The lesser women's parts were played by Mary Ure, as Virgilia, and by Vanessa Redgrave, aged 22, as Valeria.

There was strong casting, too, in the middle-range parts. Robert Hardy, later to play Coriolanus himself for BBC television, was one of the tribunes; the other was Peter Woodthorpe. Several times the action narrows to a focus on this sinister pair, and I have never been so conscious of their Rosencrantz-and-Guildenstern-like affinity. Paul Hardwick was a bluff, manly Cominius, strong of voice and physique but easily touched, and with a soldierly tenderness towards Coriolanus. In the other camp, Anthony Nicholls, no less convincing as a warrior, was suaver in speech and manner, a political realist whose admiration for Coriolanus went unquestioned, but whose treachery came as no surprise. As an upper-class Volscian, he was not required to adopt a Welsh accent—obviously he had been sent to public school over the border—but he and his officers wore furs that were occasionally more suggestive of Danny La Rue than of the barbarism they were doubtless meant to evoke.

The Menenius was Harry Andrews, who played many principal supporting roles in Stratford productions. He too is a big man, and his natural authority was helpful in his dealings with the citizens. Menenius is an ambiguous figure. When John Barton directed the play in 1967, he pointed out in a programme note that Menenius is usually played as 'a centre of sympathy, a choric figure', but suggested that we should see him rather as a 'political old-hand...motivated more by his sense of his own skill as a manipulator than by love for his country and friends'. Whichever view we take, this draws attention to a point of central interest in the play; that is, the extent to which a man may adapt himself to a situation without compromising his own integrity. Coriolanus finds this intensely difficult. The Roman spy has no problems at all. The most obvious manipulators in the play are the tribunes, who play upon the sympathies and weaknesses of the citizens like a pair of unscrupulous shop-stewards. Menenius, too, knows how to handle the citizens, and commands their sympathetic interest with his fable of the belly. But he also speaks deprecatingly,

even contemptuously, of them: 'Rome and her rats are at the point of battle…
though abundantly they lack discretion, | Yet are they passing cowardly.'

How are we to take this? Is he just a smooth operator, or rather (as Bradley
suggests) a wise, just, and statesmanlike figure? Harry Andrews certainly leaned to
the latter interpretation, playing the character very much from his own point of
view, as a sincere statesman, devoted to the cause of the patricians, and personally
devoted to Coriolanus, but genuinely concerned, nevertheless, for the citizens, and
regretful at their folly. He was impressive in his anxious but controlled attempts to
conciliate the tribunes in their rabble-rousing incitements of the crowd against
Coriolanus, as also, a scene or two later, when he has to apply similar palliatives
to Coriolanus's wrath against the tribunes. Harry Andrews can convey an impression of inner strength and calm which contrasted with Coriolanus's lack of self-
control. He did indeed seem like a wise centre in the play, emphasized by his
presence alone on-stage just before the interval. His words, 'Fie! fie! fie!' might go
for very little, but he sighed them out, well separated one from another, shaking his
head as he moved off, in a way that certainly suggested the sagacious observer,
saddened by experience. He was moving, too, in his reactions to Coriolanus's later
rejection of his pleading.

We are lucky enough to have some inside information about how one of the
leading performers approached her role. Dame Edith Evans spoke to the annual
Theatre Summer School on 21 August. Her talk was called, a little coyly and also a
little defensively, 'A Little Talk', and was concerned with her role of Volumnia. I was
present, and I remember feeling the star quality of a great actress in these circumstances as strongly as in her stage performances. The hall was crowded. Before she
began to speak she removed a wrap from her shoulders and hung it on the back of a
chair, giving the audience a sly glance which, for no easily discernible reason,
suddenly had us all eating out of her hand. The talk was reported in both *The
Times* (22 August) and the *Times Educational Supplement* (28 August). Like many actors
speaking in public, she was anxious not to seem to be giving a lecture; and, also like
many actors speaking in public, she beat most lecturers at their own game. *The Times*
reported her as saying that when she 'accepted the part she had neither seen nor read
the play—oh yes, that often happens with me, we were assured. She had, however, a
preconceived notion. Volumnia surely was a bloodthirsty old harridan. "How"—
with a glance at Mr. Glen Byam Shaw in her audience—"how could I possibly be a
bloodthirsty old harridan?" Mr. Byam Shaw…had asked her to remember that
Volumnia lived somewhere about the fourth century B.C. That was something.
There was no need to excuse Volumnia for not having heard about turning the other
cheek. She was a pagan, a Roman, and a patrician.' The *Times Educational Supplement*
varies the report: 'There was none of that "loving your enemies" nonsense: you had
enemies, and you hated them.' She 'said that she knew about Rome: she had been
there three times recently and seen all the columns'.

Still, she had to discover the woman in Volumnia, and to play her as a woman. 'After all, at her first appearance Volumnia brings her sewing, and she and the women sit at stools—"That's a friendly little opening, isn't it?" In this first scene she talks about Coriolanus' honour, and it is very strong meat. It's all very strong stuff—but they're *sewing!*'

She found Volumnia's womanliness in her love for her son, whom she described as 'a very arrogant boy. He displeases—what do you call it?—the Labour Party. She pleads with him not to antagonize them: he should get power first and afterwards he can antagonize them as much as he likes' (*TES*). She spoke about how an actress has to find in the words that she speaks a reality that is meaningful to herself. 'When she meets her son after his triumph she is almost too excited to be coherent. "What is it—Coriolanus must I call thee?" In other words "What's this thing they have pinned on you, darling? The V.C.?" She went on to stress the personal rather than the political in Volumnia. His banishment is not only a crying injustice done to him but also means that he will be completely cut off from her. That is what provokes her to anger, Juno-like, "and of course," adds Edith Evans, "one has to do the best one can with *that!*"'

Dame Edith was interesting on Volumnia's physical appearance when she goes to appeal to Coriolanus on behalf of Rome, and on her return to Rome. 'When she sees him again her raiment and state of body ought indeed to show what her life has been since Coriolanus' exile. In the eighteenth century a tragedy queen would dress like a tragedy queen for this scene. Quite wrong, thinks Edith Evans, Volumnia has in fact been wasting away. And at the end, when she has won him over, doesn't she realize that, instead of getting him back, she has lost him a second time, almost certainly for good? He will go back to Corioli to face the music, and she will go back to Rome. No wonder she has nothing to say to the Romans when they welcome her' (*The Times*).

Dame Edith's talk was amusing, and was reported with appreciation of this. We were reminded as we listened that it was given by the greatest living exponent of Restoration comedy. But it also made some brilliantly revealing points about both the play and the way in which a modern actress may approach a classical part. Dame Edith was not typecast as Volumnia. Her strength had been mainly in comic and melodramatic roles. Her style is unquestionably mannered, though it has to be said that in this very season she had played the Countess of Rousillon in *All's Well That Ends Well*, with a tranquil, elegiac beauty, as well as a queenly dignity, that was profoundly moving. Though she has a fine presence, she is not heavily dominating. In its report of her talk, *The Times* said that she 'was speaking in the Conference Hall [that is, the rehearsal room behind the main theatre] where she had begun rehearsing the part. There the producer, Mr. Peter Hall, had asked her to do just one thing: to add two feet to her stature. For that she had had to wait till they moved into the theatre itself...'. The effort, it must be admitted, was occasionally visible.

Dame Edith was a little over 70 years old. She was in very good physical shape, but, as she implied in her talk, she was not too obviously qualified to represent a 'bloodthirsty old harridan'. The effort sometimes showed. She had a habit of nervously clenching and unclenching her fists that could be distracting. The mannerisms in her wonderful voice, her capacity to colour a phrase, to suggest infinite nuances of expression, were not obviously suited to the more strident aspects of Volumnia's character. It seemed a bit like asking a born Susanna to sing Brunhilde. But the training and experience of a great actress were evident both in the way she found those aspects of the role that most suited her, and, more courageously, faced the need to act against her natural stage presence. She demonstrated the classical actress's skill in responding to the role's varied vocal demands, ranging from the chatty domesticity of the opening scene—in which she is sewing—to the fierce anger of her denunciation of the tribunes and the incantatory grandeur called for by

> Before him he carries noise, [and] behind him he leaves tears:
> Death, that dark spirit, in's nervy arm doth lie,
> Which, being advanced, declines, and then men die. (2.1.156–9)

In the later scenes the colourful extravagance of her first gown was replaced by mourning black, for the reasons explained in her talk; grief predominated to the extent that some critics found monotony in her speaking of the long plea to Coriolanus. Her return to Rome was that of a woman who knew she had failed, though she was greeted with triumph. Kenneth Tynan complained that her 'fussy, warbling vibrato swamps all too often the meaning of the lines', and the critic of the *Glasgow Herald* found that 'Her voice instead of sounding forceful and resonant, was more often querulous'. These were first-night reactions. I saw the performance several times, and felt that although Dame Edith was not always at her best, when she was, such criticisms seemed quite irrelevant. Even on the first night, *The Times* found that her 'rating of the Tribunes is quite unforgettable'. In this scene, she could suggest the womanly aspects of Volumnia simultaneously with the tyrannical ones. At its strongest, her voice here was indeed 'forceful and resonant'. The scene ends with the lines about her being provoked 'to anger, Juno-like', of which she said in her talk 'one has to do the best one can with *that*!' Her best was magnificent: profoundly strong, but never inhuman.

The production is, of course, remembered mainly for its central performance, Olivier's Coriolanus. Before talking about it, I should like to say something about his style and reputation as an actor. He was, at this time, acknowledged, along with Sir John Gielgud, as the head of his profession. Any performance by him in a major classical role was sure to arouse excitement. He also is an intensely individual and idiosyncratic actor who can create violent reactions of antipathy as well as admiration. He is famous for his athleticism and for technical self-consciousness. He looks different in every role he plays and will go to endless trouble to perfect an accent or to create appropriate make-up. He is, in short, a virtuoso; and virtuosity can create antipathy. Some members of an audience will be carried away by it; others will remain aloof, aware of technical brilliance but also somewhat repelled by it. I give way to it all the time; but the minority of critics who responded adversely to Olivier's performance seem to have been reacting against his virtuosity. Alan Brien, for instance, wrote: 'I would ask for less consciousness on Olivier's part that every word is putty and can be moulded to his whim. I would ask for less technique—instead I would like to feel that the lines are mastering him occasionally... I would ask for less decoration, less bravura, less personality, less expertise' (*Spectator*, 17 July). To me that seems ungrateful; but I can, by an effort of the imagination, understand something of the objection.

Laurence Kitchin's excellent essay on Olivier's performance is virtually a defence of it against Alan Brien's kind of accusation. Kitchin praises Olivier's 'interpretative intelligence of a very high order' which, he says, had been brought 'to bear on this role; he was not intelligent only in action, from point to point'. Kitchin's essay is so good a piece of interpretation that I cannot compete with it; but I will try to describe some of the salient features of Olivier's performance.

His make-up seemed designed to hide some of the quick intelligence of his face. He wore a black wig and was beetle-browed, heavier looking than usual. The bridge of his nose was built up, his mouth arrogantly snarled, his knit eyebrows scornfully lifted. His walk and stance emphasized the warrior. As he addressed the mob he clenched his fists, bunched his muscles, and inflated his chest, looking, as Kitchin puts it, like 'some ruggedly aggressive Roman statue'. He is a master of gesture that is both characterful and graceful; there was a strange beauty in the way he wielded his sword, or disposed his arms and hands as he invited his men to follow him through the gates of Corioli. Here he seemed in his element. Here we saw the positive side, the value, of his arrogance. In the battle scenes no less than in the scenes in Rome, Coriolanus is contemptuous of the men to whom he owes part of his success. But Olivier showed us that the scorn which he pours on his men is inseparable from the anger and energy which impel him in his fights against the common enemy, and which inspire his followers to do all they can to support him. The example of inspiring courage—even foolhardiness—which he gave in the battles of the opening Act was powerful enough to make us believe that, like many warriors after him, he could be hero-worshipped by his men in action, even though they might later lose confidence in him as a peace-time leader.

One of the attributes of a great actor is, I suppose, the capacity to suggest complexity of character. It is also, of course, one of the attributes of a great playwright. Both can make us feel contact with the richness of human experience, with the surprising inconsistencies in human behaviour, the unexpected thoughts or actions which, when they are revealed, seem much truer than the expected.

The audience's reaction to these can be one of delighted laughter, as it so often is with Falstaff, Shakespeare's greatest creation of this kind. Olivier's Coriolanus, too, often provoked this sort of laughter. I have said that he is a great comic actor, and his discovery of potential comedy in the role was one of his ways of accommodating it to his own genius, just as Dame Edith had found Volumnia's womanliness. He found comedy in his coy, bashful, perhaps vain rejection of praise for his prowess in battle, and in his affectionate hyperbole about his mother's strength of character. He roused a big laugh with

> Nay, mother,
> Resume that spirit when you were wont to say
> If you had been the wife of Hercules,
> Six of his labours you'ld have done, and saved
> Your husband so much sweat.

But the scene in which this quality was most apparent was that in which Coriolanus is shown in external conflict with his mother, Menenius, and Cominius, and in internal conflict with himself, about whether he can apologize to the people in order to improve his standing with them. The obvious way to play the scene (3.2) would, I suppose, be with a depressed earnestness, Coriolanus grimly, even despairingly, forcing himself to behave against his nature. Olivier gave it instead with a lightness of touch which amused but was, perhaps, no less essentially serious. The sense of a man trying but failing to resist domination by his mother was strong here, and was increased by Volumnia's addition of 'my son' in the line 'Prithee now, [my son,] say you will, and go about it' (line 98) and by the anger in her parting words: 'Do your will'—as it were, 'Do what the hell you like, I wash my hands of you.' Kitchin describes how Olivier 'listened to his mother's reproofs with infantile sullenness...An habitual battle of wills, fought out not so long ago about apologizing for rough words or the breaking of a companion's toy, was being reopened.' There is one particularly fine speech in which Coriolanus torments himself with a vision of the prostitution he must undergo which becomes so vivid that he rejects it with the words, 'I will not do it.' They might be spoken violently, but Olivier paused and spoke the words quietly as if with sudden acknowledgement of the truth within himself, and burst into anger against a further attempt to persuade him before the audience's delayed laughter showed that it had taken the point.

In Volumnia's ensuing rebuke of his pride, Olivier listened with a mocking appearance of deference which revealed his true feeling. Then his plea that he would do as he was told had the comic quality of a little boy seeking approval though he knows he has been naughty. At the end of the scene Menenius and Cominius are still trying to keep him in order. He will speak to the people. 'Ay but mildly,' says Menenius. 'Well, mildly be it then—mildly', replies Coriolanus. But instead of speaking the final word, Olivier, after a long pause, simply mouthed it, achieving, as Kitchin says, an 'unforgettable effect'.

Not everyone capitulated to Olivier's comic treatment of this scene; and it has to be admitted that it was accompanied by a certain amount of mouthing and tongue-rolling that perhaps too strongly recalled the music-hall vulgarities of Archie Rice. But an actor's treatment of individual scenes has to be considered in the context of the performance as a whole. In the scene following this one, Coriolanus has to deliver some of his most forceful denunciations of the people, culminating in the speech beginning, 'You common cry of curs...'. If we had already had anger in the scene with his mother, the effect might have become monotonous. The light handling of the earlier scene made for greater contrasts, and left Olivier with amazing energy for the full explosion of his pent-up rage, triggered by Sicinius's accusation, 'You are a traitor to the people.'

The air was highly charged for the rest of the scene, but for his final speech Coriolanus had regained a degree of self-control and spoke with comparative calm. Kitchin had seen Olivier's earlier performance in the role and wrote:

> Two decades had scarcely dimmed my memory of his 'You common cry of curs!'...
> Now the delivery was changed. Just before this speech Olivier leaned against the
> masonry high up on Aronson's set, head rolling from side to side, eyes mad as those
> of a Sistine Chapel prophetess while he listened to the tribunes. The head movement,
> I was amused to notice, was one recommended by Elsie Fogerty to her students for
> relaxing tension in the neck; Olivier was preparing himself. Advancing to the Tarpeian
> projection on which we had first seen him, he made the speech with less volume than
> in Casson's production, but with a terrifying concentration of contempt. People who
> think him a prose actor, because he so often breaks up lines, overlook his sustained
> power in a passage of invective like this...he gave the phrases such a charge of
> emotion that he gathered them into a single rhetorical missile, so that the speech
> had an impact like jagged stones parcelled together and hurled in somebody's face.

Edith Evans had found that much of Volumnia's motive force derived from adoration of her son. Olivier's Coriolanus derived much of its power from tension between two strong relationships: the domination of his mother, from which he could never quite escape; and his paradoxical admiration for Aufidius, his greatest enemy. The speeches before Antium were gently, quietly given. The awe he inspired in Aufidius's servants, before they knew who he was, helped him, appropriately to the text, to regain a sense of identity in the 'world elsewhere'; and with Aufidius his personality found a temporary release and wholeness that it could never command in Rome. Laurence Kitchin found that 'There was no doubt at all where the play's climax comes. It is on the sealing of their pact, or so I shall always believe after Olivier's extraordinary handshake.' But a man is not 'author of himself'. Coriolanus successfully turns Menenius away, and the episode was movingly performed. But from his mother's entry, his fall was seen to be inevitable, and his capitulation to Volumnia, as he held 'her by the hand, silent', was as moving as it should be.

Olivier kept his most startling effect of all for the moment of his death. Indeed, it is said that not even his fellow-actors knew how he would perform this scene until a very late stage in the proceedings; and this is borne out by the fact that the pencilled directions in the prompt-book overlay others that have been erased. Kenneth Tynan's description cannot be bettered:

> At the close, faithful as ever to the characterization on which he has fixed, Olivier is roused to suicidal frenzy by Aufidius' gibe—'thou boy of tears!' '*Boy!*' shrieks the overmothered general, in an outburst of strangled fury, and leaps up a flight of precipitous steps to vent his rage. Arrived at the top, he relents and throws his sword away. After letting his voice fly high in the great, swinging line about how he 'flutter'd your Volscians in *Cor-i-ol-i*', he allows a dozen spears to impale him. He is poised, now, on a promontory some twelve feet above the stage, from which he topples forward, to be caught by the ankles so that he dangles, inverted, like the slaughtered Mussolini. A more shocking, less sentimental death I have not seen in the theatre; it is at once proud and ignominious, as befits the titanic fool who dies it.

Olivier created a startling visual image of Coriolanus's downfall, the more ironically effective in that the rostrum on which he was stabbed was that from which he had berated the mob on his first entry, and from which he had cursed the 'common cry of curs'. When he fell from it with a strangulated cry, to be caught by the ankles and held dangling while Aufidius stabbed him in the belly, the magnitude and the squalor of his fall were epitomized. Philip Hope-Wallace found it 'overwhelmingly tragic' (*Manchester Guardian*, 9 July), but it had its critics. Glynne Wickham is clearly girding at it when in an essay on performances of the play he writes, 'it is easy to obliterate the tragic stature of Coriolanus in a matter of seconds by allowing him to leap to his death in the manner of a trapeze-artist for the sake of the gasp of surprise in the auditorium.'[6] But that is ungenerous. The fall was a final, climactic assertion of Coriolanus's grandeur in the moment of his death, the last of a series of strokes with which Olivier had portrayed the bewildering many-sidedness of the character. It was theatrical; but we were in a theatre. It was dangerous; but Coriolanus lived, as well as died, dangerously. It was the final shock for an audience that had been given many surprises, and it left me, at least, overcome with awe. I left the theatre, on the first night, profoundly impressed, and walked the streets of Stratford for twenty minutes before feeling I wanted to talk to anyone. That, I think, is what Aristotle meant by catharsis.

PART IV

SHAKESPEARE'S TEXT

24

On Being a General Editor

The Editor has asked me to write about being a General Editor of Shakespeare, a function which I have fulfilled—and continue to fulfil—both for Penguin Books and for Oxford University Press and to which I have devoted a significant portion of my life. I could write an entire autobiography centring on the subject, but that would not be welcome here. So let me set down some thoughts relating to the various tasks that the General Editor has to perform, and to the qualities that he (please read 'or she' throughout) needs to bring to them. And let me attempt to illustrate these from my experiences over not much less than half a century in which much of my time has been devoted to this practice. I shall confine myself largely to the general editing of a multi-volume edition rather than of the Complete Works, which is a subject in itself. And I shall not concern myself at all with the general editing of a monograph series such as the Oxford Shakespeare Topics, on which I have worked happily with Peter Holland since its inception.

The first and perhaps most important task of a General Editor is to lay down the principles to which he and his publisher wish his edition to conform. The publisher's wishes are vital. Editions have to be financed, and it is the publisher who provides the financial backing. This does not mean that an edition needs to be driven by commercial considerations alone. Shakespeare can be a status symbol. Publishing houses may feel that their lists are incomplete if they do not include an edition of his works. They—by which one has to mean a number of individuals within the publishing house who are responsible for its policy—may even acknowledge a duty to provide the scholarly community with editions which fulfil their needs but are unlikely to make a profit. This is especially likely to be true of scholarly publishing houses, though I have yet to encounter a publisher who was oblivious to financial considerations.

The first edition with which I was associated was the New Penguin. If I seem to give disproportionate space to it, that is because, although its General Editor was T. J. B. Spencer, I worked very closely with and for him from its inception, and in the process formed many of the ideas that I was later to apply both to the Oxford Complete Works and to the multi-volume Oxford Shakespeare. I edited three plays for the New Penguin and was credited as its Associate Editor. After Spencer died, in 1988, I succeeded him as *de facto* editor of the ongoing New Penguin edition, though my employment by Oxford University Press meant that this was not publicly acknowledged. Then in 2005 I was officially credited as General Editor of what is now called the Penguin Shakespeare in undertaking a major revision, with Paul Edmondson as my co-supervisory editor.

The impetus for the Penguin edition came from within the publishing house itself. It may well have been driven partly by a recognition of the high public interest in Shakespeare evinced by the celebrations in 1964 for the four-hundredth anniversary of his birth. Terence (or T. J. B., as we used to write in those more formal days) Spencer had fairly recently taken over from Allardyce Nicoll as Director of the University of Birmingham's Shakespeare Institute, which at that time had premises in both Birmingham and Stratford-upon-Avon. One of Penguin's executives, Charles Clark, approached Spencer to discuss the inauguration under his General Editorship of a new edition of the Complete Works which would conform to the image presented by that publishing house, an image which may be summed up as appealing to the 'general reader'. The politics of publishing, and the nature of editions already on the market, inevitably formed a background to the project. All the existing British editions dated from before the war—a landmark of psychological if not of logical significance. Penguin itself had on its books an edition prepared entirely by G. B. Harrison which had appeared from 1937 to 1959. It offers a chronology followed by very brief introductory essays on Shakespeare himself, the Elizabethan theatre, and the play; this amounts in total, to take *As You Like It* as an example, to no more than a dozen pages. The text is followed by idiosyncratic notes and a straightforward glossary. Based eccentrically on the First Folio, whose punctuation it generally and illogically retains while modernizing spelling, and offering relatively little help to the reader, it already seemed out of date, and I should suppose it was not selling well.

At this time two British editions with high scholarly ambitions were on the market. Cambridge University Press offered the New Shakespeare—commonly referred to then as the new, or New, Cambridge Shakespeare—which had started publication as long ago as 1921, under the General Editorship of Arthur Quiller-Couch—who dropped out in 1931 after contributing the introductions to fourteen comedies—and John Dover Wilson. In 1964 it was struggling towards completion, which it achieved belatedly in 1966 with the publication of the now half-blind but eternally sprightly Wilson's edition of the Sonnets, the Introduction originally printed independently as a mischievous riposte to A. L. Rowse's views on the biographical aspects of the poems. Though its volumes were printed in paperback the series was too recondite, and its earlier volumes were by now too old-fashioned both textually and critically, for it to compete seriously in the mass market to which Penguin aspired—and which indeed it had largely created.

To some extent the Cambridge series had been overtaken by the ongoing Arden edition—what we now know as Arden 2, begun in 1951, originally as a revision of its first series, dating as far back as 1899—which at that time was under the General Editorship of 'the Harolds'—Harold Jenkins and Harold Brooks. It was somewhat in the doldrums, and it too was forbidding in its academicism.

Moreover, competition on the paperback market, which Penguin sought to dominate, had appeared from overseas. The Pelican, under the General Editorship of the highly respected senior scholar Alfred Harbage (born in 1901), had started to appear in 1956 and was drawing close to completion, which it achieved in 1967. A little more recent was the Signet, which began to appear in 1963 under the direction of Sylvan Barnet, a good scholar with less of an independent reputation, though the fact that his paperback edition was completed within five years suggests that he was enviably efficient as a General Editor. Both the Pelican and the Signet editions differentiated themselves from the Cambridge and Arden series in clearly seeking to attract a popular market. The Pelican is unambitious in scope, offering a few pages on Shakespeare and his Stage and a very brief section on 'The Texts of His Plays' written by the General Editor, a short Introduction—roughly 2,000 words—to the play by the volume editor, and simple glossarial notes printed on the same page as the text. Harbage recruited a distinguished team of contributors but asked little of them, even though they included some of the best textual scholars of the time, some of them veterans, others at an early stage in their careers. Among them were Fredson Bowers, G. Blakemore Evans (later to edit the Riverside edition), George Walton Williams, M. A. Schaaber, Charles T. Prouty, and Charlton Hinman. In the Preface, written when the Pelican editions came to be printed together, with revisions, as a single hardback volume in 1969, Harbage notes that 'Leaders in bibliographical study in this country have edited the more difficult texts, and have generously lent their counsel in the case of the less difficult ones.'[1] This series, like others before and after it, apparently evolved as it progressed; Harbage remarks that 'At first no textual apparatus was supplied, but after the early volumes of the edition had appeared, it seemed advisable to include an essential minimum.'[2] I wonder if this was done in an attempt to keep up with the competition offered by the Signet series. Other editors selected by Harbage included scholars who were best known as theatre historians, such as Gerald Eades Bentley, Bernard Beckerman, and Richard Hosley; others were primarily critics: Northrop Frye, for instance, undertook *The Tempest*, Maynard Mack *Antony and Cleopatra*, and Harry Levin *Coriolanus*, all relatively straightforward texts. Only Harbage himself, with *Macbeth*, *Henry V*, and the textually difficult *King Lear* and *Love's Labour's Lost*, undertook more than one text—a case of the General Editor coming to the rescue: 'My original intention was to edit only *Macbeth* in addition to serving as factotum. *King Lear* and *Love's Labor's Lost* were edited by me after the persons whom I first asked to do so declined, and *Henry V*, so that its original editor could include the play in his own series.'[3] There are two women on the list, Josephine Waters Bennett (*Much Ado About Nothing*), and Madeleine Doran (*A Midsummer Night's Dream*), who had published important textual studies of *King Lear* and *Henry VI*.

The Signet, no doubt conscious of the competition, offers more: a series of Prefatory Remarks common to each volume and written by the General Editor, briefly supplying biographical information, a chronology, a short essay on 'Shakespeare's Theater', and an equally brief essay on 'The Texts of Shakespeare', the whole amounting to about fourteen pages, common to each volume. This is followed by a critical-cum-scholarly Introduction considerably more substantial than those in the Pelican edition, normally written by the volume editor. The text of the work follows, its lines numbered in fives; very brief explanatory notes, almost entirely lexical and historical, with a few referring to the staging of the play, are printed at the foot of the page. These are signalled, innovatively and, as it turned out, somewhat controversially, by bubbles in the text itself. At the back of the book comes a brief textual note, simply describing the textual situation relating to the individual work, followed by a straightforward list of departures from the substantive text or texts. Then comes an essay on the work's sources, followed by extracts from, for example, Plutarch, Cinthio, and Holinshed. The most innovative feature of the edition is its inclusion of a few selected extracts from criticism of the work, and the volumes are rounded off by a selection of 'Suggested References'—a brief bibliography. Clearly the series appears pretty comprehensive in catering for the needs of student readers, and it seems to have succeeded well in its competition with the Pelican. It drew upon a more international team of contributors, and it seems fair to say that Barnet laid more emphasis on critical than on textual expertise. Most of his editors, like Harbage's, were from America—they include Daniel Seltzer, Alvin Kernan, Mark Eccles, Bertrand Evans, Norman Holland, and Edward Hubler, with Barnet himself for *Titus Andronicus*—but also the British Frank Kermode, Kenneth Muir, John Russell Brown, and Barbara Everett (the only woman except for the British-born Barbara Rosen who shared responsibility for *Julius Caesar* with her American husband William Rosen), the Germans Wolfgang Clemen (whose edition of *A Midsummer Night's Dream* was, I am told, 'ghosted' by Dieter Mehl) and Ernest Schanzer, and the Indian S. Nagarajan.

These American editions are not textually ambitious; indeed, it is a remarkable fact that (if we except the New Variorum edition, started in 1871 and still far from complete, and which in any case is by definition rather a compendium of existing scholarship than in itself innovative) there has never been a multi-volume American edition of Shakespeare with textual and overall scholarly aspirations comparable to those offered by British publishers.

At this time, so far as I understand it, Pelican books of America and Penguin Books of England stood in a semi-autonomous relationship to each other. In his Preface, Harbage wrote that 'In 1953 Mr H. F. Paroissien, who had founded in Baltimore the

American subsidiary of Penguin Books Ltd, invited me to edit a series corresponding to *The Penguin* [i.e. the Harrison] *Shakespeare*, which could not be distributed in this country [i.e. America] owing to contractual agreements. Since there were at the time, incredible as it may now seem, only a few of Shakespeare's plays available in soft cover, a complete edition would obviously serve a useful purpose. However, it seemed to me that its value would be greatly enhanced if it represented a collaborative effort among American scholars rather than my personal enterprise. I was asked to draw up a plan, and presented this to Sir Allen Lane and his directors in London in 1954.'[4] In 1964, then, Penguin could both import books originating from its sister company in America and also embargo the sale of those books in England if they were seen as competing with their native products. (Later, for instance, they imported the Pelican *Hamlet* as a stopgap until their own edition appeared.) Additional background information to Clark's approach to Spencer is provided by the *Oxford Dictionary of National Biography* entry, written by John C. Ross, on G. B. Harrison, who had also edited the plays for the American publisher Harcourt Brace: 'When Penguin wished to extend sales of its Shakespeares to the United States, he could not agree to this, as he felt that this would violate the spirit of his contract with Harcourt. Penguin, therefore, embarked on a new series of editions by separate editors, to which American publication would not be a barrier.' This may be a bit disingenuous: when the New Penguin edition first appeared it was not sold in the States because of the existence of the Pelican edition.

The Signet editions were on sale in England. Both business acumen and national pride favoured the inauguration of a new series.

Most of those present at the meeting in Stratford were themselves experienced editors, such as Kenneth Muir and R. A. Foakes. At this point in my career I had edited Robert Greene's *Perimides the Blacksmith* and *Pandosto* for my PhD thesis, submitted in 1962. My work, supervised by Norman Sanders, was intended, along with other texts prepared by members of the Institute, to form part of a complete Oxford edition of Greene's works with I. A. Shapiro and Johnstone Parr as its General Editors. It never saw the light of day, though a number of theses on the shelves of the Institute library bear witness to the effort that a number of young scholars put into it. (In fact my thesis was eventually published in poorly reproduced photographic form by Garland, in 1988.) Also in 1964 I produced an edition of a substantial selection from the writings of Thomas Nashe as the first volume of the now defunct Stratford-upon-Avon Library, edited by John Russell Brown and Bernard Harris and published by Edward Arnold. So I was present at the meeting both as a junior lecturer working closely with and for Spencer and also by virtue of my interest in editorial work.

At this stage of the enterprise the aim was to discuss the general lines along which a new edition might be organized. One very basic decision facing a General Editor is what titles to include. Some of Shakespeare's works sell far worse than others and, over the years, it has become clear that once an edition has established its reputation, the quality of individual volumes does not necessarily correlate with their sales. We could not reasonably expect, for example, *Titus Andronicus*, *King John*, or the Henry VI plays to sell as well as more popular plays such as *Hamlet*, *Macbeth*, and *Romeo and Juliet*. We wanted an edition which could be called complete, but even this leaves certain options open. Adventurously, it was decided (possibly later) to include the collaborative *The Two Noble Kinsmen* (though at that stage no one would have considered including *Edward III*), and to publish *The Rape of Lucrece* in one volume and *Venus and Adonis* and other poems in another. In the end, partly because of poor sales of *Lucrece*, along with the death of its editor, it was eventually replaced by a volume which included all the poems except the Sonnets and *A Lover's Complaint*.

One of the most contentious issues was whether explanatory notes should be printed at the foot of the page, as in the most strongly competitive editions, or at the back of the book, as in Harrison and Dover Wilson. Students, some people argued, preferred notes to be available for easy reference at the foot of the page, as in the Arden, the Pelican, and the Signet. Others, perhaps remembering Dr Johnson's injunctions both that notes 'are a necessary evil' and that 'the mind is refrigerated by interruption',[5] favoured a clean page, with notes at the back. It was, I believe, Charles Clark, speaking on behalf of Penguin, who cast the die in favour of continuing Harrison's practice. To my mind this decision has much to do with the success of the series. For one thing, it differentiates the Penguin edition from most of those with which it has had to compete over close on forty years. (The Dover Wilson Cambridge also had a clean—and beautifully designed—page.) Certainly some readers studying the text may find it convenient to be able to glance down to the foot of the page to resolve a difficulty. But a clean page offers several advantages. It permits uninterrupted reading. It is easier for actors to use, both because it allows more text to the page and because it leaves more room for scribbling in the margins—a factor which may appeal to students too. And perhaps best of all, the fact that the editor does not feel constrained by lack of space permits a more relaxed and literate style of annotation, obviating the temptation to use uncivilized abbreviations of the 'cf. Tr. & Cr. v.3.41' variety. (Nevertheless, when, in 2002, Penguin reprinted *Hamlet*, in a larger format and without its textual apparatus, in a 'Great Books' series, the notes appeared at the foot of the page. This was the publisher's decision. It has not sold particularly well.)

As I remember it, Clark said that he liked to think that a buyer travelling from London to Stratford to see a play could read the text in a train on his way there and the introduction on the way back. This raised the question of whether the customary essay on the play might be printed as an Afterword (as was the practice in editions of some classic texts at the time) rather than at the beginning, but we settled for the traditional ordering of the contents. We spent hours discussing whether to signal the presence of notes and, if so, how. Some favoured the use of an asterisk in the text. Signet's bubbles—abhorrent to me (though as very much the junior participant I kept my opinions largely to myself)—had their supporters. Eventually we opted for elegant simplicity: to number the text in tens—some favoured fives—and allow readers to do their own counting.

We also had to decide what to do about textual issues. Wishing the editions to have full scholarly respectability we felt that textual notes were needed, but that if they were to be of any value they should be presented with more concern for the understanding of the non-specialist reader than in the Arden edition. Editors were not expected to undertake original textual investigations but were free to do so if they wished; some of them did, and their editions make fresh contributions to the editorial tradition. We wished to disembarrass the Introductions of over-technical material, particularly disliking the way in which Arden editors customarily opened their Introductions with off-putting sections baldly headed 'The Text' and 'The Date of the Play'. As a consequence we decided to print a discussion of textual issues, written as accessibly as the editor could manage, along with lists of collations, at the back. This relates to the printing of the text as well as to the inclusion of free-standing textual notes. Should we, for example, use typographical devices, such as square brackets, in the text to signal that stage directions were altered from, or added to, those of the original editions? The consensus was that we should prefer to keep the text as free from algebraical signs as possible, and to this end we decided to present conservatively edited stage directions in the text while listing the original directions among the textual notes so that an interested reader could identify changes.

There is also the matter of changes to the text itself. The second Arden series has what Tom Berger has memorably called the 'band of terror' of collations forming a barrier reef at the foot of the page between the text and the notes. We preferred to record textual changes in lists at the back, dividing them up in a way that facilitated easy reference: so for example Spencer's edition of *Hamlet* has seven separate lists; the first records departures from its copy text, the Second Quarto, deriving from the Folio; the second (with only two entries), gives readings deriving from the First (1603) Quarto (Spencer adventurously printed the passage from Hamlet's advice to the Players which 'gives examples of the silly "character" jests of the comic actors'). Next comes a list of emendations to Q2, followed by a collation of the stage directions which gives them first as they appear in the edition, then in their original form 'along with the more interesting F directions not accepted in this edition'; then a list of 'the variant readings and forms of words more commonly found in other editions' (i.e. rejected emendations); and finally a list of 'the more important passages found in Q2 but omitted in F'. This setting out of textual material exemplifies Spencer's wish to present the reader with all the material necessary to a scholarly understanding of the text's complexities with the greatest possible lucidity.

Some of the decisions I have already mentioned relate to aspects of design. The appearance of the page is only partly the province of the designer. For the Penguin we worked with the eminent typographer Hans Schmoller (who by one of history's accidents is held to merit an entry in the *Oxford Dictionary of National Biography* denied to Spencer). He was aware of the need, for example, to use a typeface narrow enough to avoid as far as possible the turn-over of lines of verse. But some aspects of design relate to scholarly issues and must concern the General Editor. At the time we were designing the Penguin edition scholars were emphasizing Shakespeare's practical involvement with the theatres of his time with missionary zeal; and some members of the Shakespeare Institute, most notably John Russell Brown, were, with the encouragement of Allardyce Nicoll, leaders of this movement. Increasing awareness of the non-representational nature of the stages of Shakespeare's time led to significant shifts in the presentation of the text. It was still common for editors to follow their eighteenth-century forebears in supplying directions for scenic location: thus Kenneth Muir's Arden 2 *King Lear* places Act 1, scene 3 in 'A Room in the Duke of Albany's Palace' and the following scene in 'A Hall in the Same'. And in J. M. Nosworthy's *Cymbeline* (at the time of writing still the current Arden edition) the long final scene is said to take place 'In Cymbeline's Tent', which must have got pretty crowded by the end of the play. To abandon this practice, while allowing editors to mention the fictional location of scenes in their notes where it seemed helpful to do so, was a purely editorial decision, but some non-substantive matters involve the designer as well as the editor. An important one goes as far back as those who prepared copy for the First Folio, or who gave instructions for the way in which it was prepared, in adapting playhouse manuscripts and early Quarto texts of Shakespeare in a manner that was probably influenced by Ben Jonson's practice in some of his Quartos and in his own Folio, by importing literary modes of presentation influenced by classical texts, especially by dividing the plays into Acts and scenes against both the printing and the theatrical practice of Shakespeare's time— none of the Quartos printed in his lifetime has any such divisions. The typography as well as the wording of Arden and the Signet editions was essentially readerly in its emphasis on breaks, each Act starting on a fresh page and headed in large centred capitals: 'ACT II', then on a new line 'SCENE I'. The largely inauthentic scene divisions are similarly prominent, with particularly unfortunate effect in for instance the Arden *Antony and Cleopatra*, where Act 3 has thirteen scenes and Act 4 fifteen, some of them only a few lines long. For the Penguin we sought to try to replicate for the reader the sense of continuous performance by minimizing the size of Act and scene indicators, and by printing them in the margin. There would of course be a case for eliminating Act divisions, at least for most of the plays, as Robert Smallwood and I were to do in the Revels edition of Thomas Dekker's *The Shoemaker's Holiday* of 1979, and as was later done for certain texts in the Oxford Complete Works; elimination of scene divisions too would approach still further to authenticity, but was discounted because it would make it impossible for the reader to use standard works of reference.

Other matters, too, were discussed: we wondered, for example, whether to follow Signet's example in printing extracts from critics, but Spencer particularly opposed this, believing that they inevitably gave the impression of a spurious orthodoxy, privileging certain views over others. It was decided instead to include a survey of writings about each work under the heading of Further Reading. We also considered including stage histories, but it was thought more appropriate to encourage editors to make critical use of such material in their introductions, which, with a recommended length of between 10,000 and 12,000 words, were to be more substantial and wide-ranging in scope than those in competing series.

Our deliberations on these and other matters led eventually to the two most important of all tasks for a General Editor: the preparation of a set of Editorial Procedures designed to inform individual editors as they go about their work, and the choice of editors themselves. I had been made especially aware of the need for the former in writing my thesis. Students working on the proposed Greene edition were asked to contribute to the compilation of a set of rules for overall guidance of editors. This was fine, but in the meantime we were also supposed actually to complete editions in order to win our degrees, which meant that we had to make up many of the rules for ourselves as we worked. Our frustration with the General Editors was great. The Procedures for the New Penguin edition resulted partly from the decisions made at the initial meeting, which were later refined and amplified by Spencer with some input from me as a result of my reading of the scripts as they came in. A major contribution came from the Penguin copy-editor, Judith Wardman, in the process of preparing the first batch of texts submitted for publication. Her meticulous eye for detail and passion for consistency contributed immeasurably to the professionalism of the edition. As a result we were able eventually to offer editors a thirty-five-page document which formed I suspect the most detailed set of guidelines thus far prepared for a Shakespeare edition.[6] In subject matter it ranges from the length and scope of the Introduction through such matters as abbreviations for the titles of plays to minutiae such as the use of round brackets (forbidden in the text) and of semicolons.

It is, of course, one thing to offer, another to receive. To persuade editors actually to absorb and act upon the advice they are given—especially if, as is likely to happen, they have already edited for a series with different procedures and so think they know already how it should be done—is not always easy. We expected editors to type their own texts from original editions, but there were cases where it became apparent to me, as I read through their typescripts when they were first submitted, that they had followed the all-too-common practice of marking up an already existing text and then having that typed.

Even with the precedent of the New Penguin edition behind me, when in 1978 I took up my position as General Editor of an Oxford Shakespeare I felt impelled to spend the first few months of my employment in the preparation of a new set of Editorial Procedures. I was especially concerned with the problems of modernizing spelling and other aspects of presentation, including capitalization, italicization, and so on. Up to that date no extended theoretical discussion of this issue had appeared in print. In many earlier editions it had been left to the haphazard practices of the printers—as indeed it appears to have been in the printing houses of Shakespeare's time. During the 1950s, particularly, there had been a tendency to conservatism, resulting in the preservation in some Arden editions of forms such as 'murther', 'burthen', and 'mo'. I was particularly impelled to action by my irritation with the practice in the Riverside edition of incorporating what its editor, G. Blakemore Evans, called 'a selection of Elizabethan spelling forms that reflect, or may reflect, a distinctive contemporary pronunciation'.[7] I remember saying, somewhat pompously, when I first saw this edition on Spencer's desk that it represented 'a retrograde step in Shakespeare editing'. He agreed. It had the practical disadvantage of calling for many more glosses than normal, most of them serving no purpose beyond reassuring readers that the weird spellings they saw before them were not ghastly errors. So for example, 'A single opening of Riverside's 2 *Henry IV* includes *kinreds*: kindreds, *idlely*: idly, *heckfers*: heifers, *Saint Albons*: St Albans, and *chevalry*: chivalry.'[8] But more importantly it created a spurious impression of an equivalence between scholarship and antiquarianism. In writing the first section of my Editorial Procedures, concerned with the spelling, I had the help and encouragement of Helen Gardner and the language scholar Norman Davis, both of whom were sympathetic with my aims. But not all linguists were even aware of the problems. I remember speaking to a distinguished Professor of English Language in the University who, on hearing I was working on a modern-spelling edition, said disdainfully that people might as well be reading Agatha Christie. When I asked him what edition he himself used, he replied that it was the Globe (which of course is modernized). That part of my Editorial Procedures which deals with spelling was published in 1979 as *Modernizing Shakespeare's Spelling, with Three Studies in the Text of Henry V*, the latter by Gary Taylor, early fruits of our joint work on the Oxford Complete Works.

When it comes to choosing individual editors for a multi-volume series, a General Editor needs to think long and hard about the qualities he should be seeking. Some are common to any kind of edition—and for that matter, any kind of scholarly publication. One of them, obviously but importantly, is reliability. The efficient completion of a series is dependent upon the General Editor's selection of editors who can respect deadlines and, if they know they are not going to be able to meet them, can be honest and realistic in their estimates of when they may be able to do so. This also means that the General Editor, in fairness to colleagues and to his publishers, must sometimes know when to be ruthless in cancelling contracts. If the editor has not so far done much work it should be easy—there are even scholars whom I have suspected of signing a contract so that they can state on their CV that they 'are editing' a work for Oxford University Press rather than having any serious intention of doing so. But to cut off a scholar who has put a great deal of effort into an edition while being unable, for whatever reason—psychological or practical—to complete it is a grave responsibility and I am conscious of not always having fulfilled it. Several editors chosen for both the New Penguin and the Oxford series fell by the wayside, for one reason or another, and had to be replaced, with consequent delays; others have taken far longer to complete their task than they—and I, and the publishers—had estimated. The New Penguin still lacked one play—*Cymbeline*—until the fully revised edition began to appear, in 2005.

Another quality that should, but cannot always, be taken for granted is accuracy. No one is perfect, but editorial work is more dependent on the capacity to get things right than many other sorts of literary endeavour. A General Editor who appoints a slapdash editor is making a rod for his own back. There are scholars whose reputations have been saved, or even made for them, by their copy-editors.

Not all series require the full gamut of skills that may be associated with the editorial function. The Cambridge Shakespeare in Production series, for example, permits the use of an already existing text and expects the editor to concentrate on supplying information derived from theatre history. Editions intended for schools require specialized kinds of pedagogical apparatus, and those intended for a non-Anglophone readership make special demands. The projected readership of the Penguin edition called for what we might call good generalists—versatile scholars with no axe to grind, and with a flair for writing for what the Procedures call 'a wide public of general readers and of students'. 'The scholarship of the New Penguin Shakespeare', say the Procedures, 'should be immaculate, but this edition is not intended as a rival to the new Arden.' This did not preclude the appointment of editors, such as Harold Oliver, G. K. Hunter, Kenneth Muir, R. A. Foakes, A. R. Humphreys, and E. A. J. Honigmann who had already edited for Arden, but it also opened the way for younger or less experienced scholars with little or no experience of editing, and for others who had made their reputation primarily as critics, such as Anne Righter/Barton (*The Tempest*), Barbara Everett (*All's Well That Ends Well*), R. L. Smallwood (*King John*), and myself (*A Midsummer Night's Dream, Richard II,* and *The Comedy of Errors*). G. R. Hibbard, who initially had little experience of editing, was to become a wonderful stalwart of the series, and later did work of equal excellence for the Oxford. Spencer himself contributed an exemplary edition of *Romeo and Juliet* to the first batch to be published; I remember Richard Hosley, who had edited the play for Yale in 1954, picking up an early copy and saying that Spencer 'had got all the hard bits right'. The relative amplitude of its annotation encouraged later contributors to write fuller notes than we had thought were expected.

The Oxford edition, on the other hand, was indeed intended to rival the Arden. In establishing its editorial principles I was much influenced by my work on the Penguin, but also—perhaps excessively—by the Arden itself. Like the New Penguin, the Oxford edition (now available in the World's Classics series, though its earlier paperback volumes did not appear under this label) aims at a high degree of accessibility while offering a more thorough covering of scholarly issues than the New Penguin. Like Arden 2 it prints both notes and collation lines on the page. I wish I had had the simple but excellent idea, later adopted in Arden 3, of printing the collation lines under, not above, the explanatory notes. In selecting contributors I have been reluctant to appoint anyone who lacked serious bibliographical training and previous editorial experience, and in at least one case I have regretted having done so. An ideal editor—if such a paragon exists—will command many different skills. For the most comprehensive kinds of edition he/she needs to be, at least, a bibliographer (in the full range of senses that the word encompasses), a lexicographer, a theatre historian, a cultural and social historian, a literary critic, and a prose stylist. It might seem that one way of coping with the need for such a multiplicity of qualifications would be to encourage collaboration between scholars who between them encompass a wider range of skills than each individually commands. I have worked in this way myself, with Robert Smallwood on the Revels *The Shoemaker's Holiday* and with Roger Warren on the Oxford *Twelfth Night*. And sometimes a General Editor has to step in when necessity prevails: when Spencer died leaving his Penguin *Hamlet* incomplete, I wrote the notes for several scenes, wrote and compiled the textual material, commissioned Anne Barton to write an Introduction, and saw the edition through the press. Nevertheless, in general, collaboration on editions is a policy of which I am wary. I think that in a fully integrated edition one and the same person will have worked through all the problems of the text, explained them in the notes, and applied his or her full knowledge of the play in writing the introduction. Especially I believe that the textual editor should be responsible for the explanatory notes. I felt this strongly when, in editing the text of *The Shoemaker's Holiday*, I found that Bowers, in his old-spelling edition, for which he did not have to write explanatory notes, had left unemended readings which I was sure he would have wished to alter if he had had to explain what they meant.

Also in question is the degree to which the General Editor should be an acknowledged collaborator. Although I have been graciously willing to accept tributes to my patience, generosity, and so on in Prefaces, the spectacle of Harold Brooks tiptoeing through the footnotes of the Arden made me resolve to keep myself out of the notes, and with few exceptions I have held to this. I was especially conscious of the need to hold back in acting as General Editor for plays of which I had myself prepared the texts for the Oxford Complete Works. In *As You Like It*, for example, I had modernized Arden to Ardenne; Alan Brissenden disagreed with me and, although I may have tried a bit of gentle persuasion, I did not impose my opinion on him. There are many other cases where I should have edited the texts differently if I had been doing them myself, and some instances where I felt a pang of regret that the editor did not accept my ideas; and I still wish I had argued rather harder than I did to dissuade Michael Neill, in his excellent edition of *Antony and Cleopatra*, from spelling the hero's name as Anthony—a source of much confusion thereafter. But there would have been no point in having a separate edition if it had merely replicated and repackaged the texts of the Complete Works. There is, as I constantly but with little success try to persuade publishers to acknowledge, no such thing as a definitive edition.

Having said this, however, it is necessary also to say that the General Editor does have a real contribution to make to the editions for which he is responsible. This comes mainly on delivery of copy. It has been my practice to read carefully through the introductory and annotative material, looking for error, making spot checks and asking for thorough checking if this reveals an above average susceptibility to error, suggesting additional (or fewer) annotations, and seeking compression of phrasing so that the notes do not take over the page. This can be laborious. I once spent three weeks over Christmas boiling down an over-zealous editor's prose. Often I have asked for changes ranging from minor rephrasing to major restructuring of Introductions. But the amount of additional work that the editor can realistically be expected to undertake is limited. There are times when I have observed with a sigh that an editor, having failed, for example, to observe the proposed word limits, has written a monograph rather than an Introduction, but not had the heart to wield the blue pencil too drastically. Above all, at this stage I check the text and collations against the copy-text, looking not only for error, but also for points at which the editor has failed to observe the conventions of this particular edition. I may feel a need to suggest, for instance, different modernization of spelling and punctuation, additional or rephrased stage directions, even new emendations. Eventually the package goes back to the editor with a request for correction and revision. If the incidence of error is high I may ask for more work to be done, but ultimately the editor has to accept responsibility for what appears over his or her name. It is always a comfort to know that the full script will be scrutinized by a copy-editor, and the Oxford edition has benefited greatly from the work in this capacity of, especially, Christine Buckley. The need to insert accurate line numbers in Introduction and notes causes us to have the text set in type and corrected first—getting line numbers right is not always easy—and I aim to read it at this stage, and then to read all the ancillary material in first proof, but when the edition is at page proof stage I generally content myself with an overall scrutiny, trying for example to make sure that notes are placed as closely as possible to the text to which they refer. Of course there are other little details to attend to, like illustrations and captions and the jacket copy and the blurb and publicity. Sadly, reviews are liable to be scarce after the first batch of editions has appeared, but *Shakespeare Survey* does its bit in telling us where we have gone wrong and even, sometimes, in patting us on the back.

The task of a General Editor has its trials and tribulations, but it has its rewards, too, as the row of books grows along the shelves and one envisages the possibility of living to see it complete—so long as no one adds yet another title to the canon.

25

Editorial Treatment of Foul-Paper Texts: *Much Ado About Nothing* as Test Case

Numerous plays by Shakespeare and his contemporaries appear to have been printed from foul papers, that is to say, from a script that had not undergone such polishing as might have been necessary before it could be held to represent a satisfactory performance. Such scripts are identified by imperfections that have survived the printing process: inadequate, inaccurate, and vague stage directions, inconsistent speech prefixes, the presence of 'ghost' characters, inconsistencies in the dialogue, and so on. The substance of the papers as delivered to the acting company must have undergone some modification before performance. To say this is not to suggest that all inconsistencies must have been removed; some may well have survived into performance. Nor does it imply that every alteration was necessarily ever recorded in a prompt-book or anywhere else; the actors may have worked out what was necessary without the book-keeper's having needed to make a note in his script of all their changes: minor inconsistencies in speech prefixes, for instance, would not be disastrous in a prompt-book. It is quite possible, then, that no script ever existed which properly represented such plays as acted.

These plays present peculiar problems to the editor. He has a text which, he must suppose, at many points represents correctly what the author wrote, but which includes anomalies that could not possibly have survived in performance, along with others that could. If he is editing a facsimile, or a near-facsimile, he is at liberty, of course, to leave all such anomalies as they stand in his copy-text. But the aim of most editors is to provide a text which presents the play in a workable form, tidying up its anomalies of presentation. In some respects, this is easy enough. There is no difficulty, for example, in giving Lady Capulet that name every time she speaks, even though in Q2 of *Romeo and Juliet* she is identified in the speech prefixes by abbreviations of Wife, Capulet's Wife, Old Lady, Lady, and Mother. Problems arise when the text shows more fundamental signs of being unfinished: when, in fact, the editor is tempted to take on the role of play reviser, making decisions which affect the action, such as would have had to be made before the script could be realized in performance. Sometimes he may feel sure that an alteration is both necessary and justifiable. If, for example, no exit is provided at the end of a scene, he can be certain that in adding one he is merely fulfilling his author's intentions by correcting an obvious oversight. Similarly, if a character speaks within the first few lines of a scene, but is not listed in its opening stage direction, the editor will be in no doubt that he should add the character's name to the direction. But even in doing this, he may go beyond representing what the author intended at the moment of writing the direction: for the inclusion of the character may have been an afterthought, rather than the direction's representing an accidental omission. And this points to the nub of the problem about foul-paper texts: that, representing the author in the act of creation, they may also demonstrate that at some points he has simply not made up his mind about what he wants; that he has visualized the action imperfectly, or changed his intentions in mid scene, and has failed to resolve any anomalies that result from this. Editors, it seems to me, have tended to write as if this were not so, as if the script before them represented the play as performed; they have therefore seen as soluble problems what are, in fact, unresolvable imperfections. Many of the editorial problems posed by a text derived from foul papers are not, of course, essentially different from those based on any other kind of copy. In this essay I shall consider the text of *Much Ado About Nothing* with particular reference to problems that raise matters of principle peculiar to foul-paper texts.

II

W. W. Greg wrote of *Much Ado About Nothing*, 'If ever there was a text printed from foul papers that still needed a good deal of correction to fit them for use in the theatre it is Q.'[1] (Presumably he was temporarily forgetting *Timon of Athens*.) E. K. Chambers[2] thought that the papers had been annotated by the book-keeper, but his main evidence is the presence of actors' names in speech prefixes, which are now thought to derive from Shakespeare himself.[3] Greg, too, thought that not all the stage directions remained as Shakespeare wrote them, and posited 'some annotation and possible alteration'.[4] In this he was, I suspect, over-influenced by Dover Wilson's theories of extensive revision, even though he rejected them. C. J. Sisson wrote that Q 'is beyond all reasonable question based upon Shakespeare's own manuscript prepared for stage use as a prompt copy'.[5] This seems like an excessively strong statement of the view more tentatively expounded by Chambers and Greg. G. Blakemore Evans, on the other hand, wrote that 'the evidence for a second hand is very slight'.[6] The case rests largely on the fact that Q's stage direction for 2.1—'*Enter Leonato, his brother, his wife, Hero his daughter, and Beatrice his neece, and a kinsman*'—repeats character descriptions already given in the play's opening direction; but, as E. A. J. Honigmann writes,[7] this could be because the later scene was written before the first; and I find it difficult to see why anyone should have troubled to add this information if it had not already been present. Still more significant, the presence of the 'kinsman' is not deducible from the text, and so must be attributed to Shakespeare himself. Chambers (p. 386) thought that the hypothetical annotator might have 'made some additions to the speech-prefixes, notably at ii. i. 89, where a scribbled "and Balthaser, Bor(achio) dun Iohn" has been read by the printer as "and Balthaser, or dumb Iohn"'; it is true that this phrase follows the words 'and Benedicke', and so looks like an addition, but it may well be an afterthought of Shakespeare's, especially as a similar repetition of 'and' occurs in the opening direction to 2.1, quoted above, and at 2.1. 186 we have '... and Borachio, and Conrade', though Conrad is not present in the scene that follows, so cannot reasonably be assumed to have been added by an annotator. In short, I do not believe that there is any evidence that the copy for Q1 bore non-Shakespearean additions.

When the play was reprinted in the First Folio it was from a copy of the quarto that had been lightly annotated as a result of what can have been only a cursory comparison with a prompt-book. I shall assume that the copy used for Q was Shakespeare's papers with no theatrical annotation; I shall refer to Folio readings when they seem relevant.

III

Occasionally, it seems, Shakespeare wrote a name in a stage direction, then abandoned his intention of writing the character into the scene, but omitted to amend the direction. Probably the most famous of these 'ghosts' is in *Much Ado About Nothing*: after mentioning 'Leonato gouernour of Messina', the opening stage direction lists 'Innogen his wife'; and at the beginning of 2.1 we again have 'Leonato ... his wife ...'. As she does not speak, is not addressed, and takes no part in the action, no director would be likely to bring her on stage, and editors from Theobald onwards have understandably regarded it as part of their duty in tidying up the text to sweep her away. But the direction to 2.1 reads, in full, '*Enter Leonato, his brother, his wife, Hero his daughter, and Beatrice his neece, and a kinsman.*' If Innogen is a ghost, the kinsman is the shade of a shade. Yet some editors, while dropping Innogen, have retained the kinsman. Grace R. Trenery, in her (old) Arden edition (1924), conjectured that he 'is probably the son of Anthonio (i. ii. 3, "Where is my cousin, your son")'. Chambers went even further, writing that 'Much of the stage-direction and speech-prefix confusion can be cleared up by realizing that the singer Balthaser is also Anthonio's son and Leonato's "cousin" and kinsman' (p. 386)—fictions which well exemplify that 'irritable reaching after fact and reason' which goes along with the assumption that the play is not itself confused.

Perhaps the kinsman's very nebulousness has helped to keep him on the page, if not on the boards: as the Cambridge editors wrote, 'It is impossible to conceive that Hero's mother should have been present during the scenes in which the happiness and honour of her daughter were at issue, without taking a part, or being once referred to.'[8] A mere kinsman may be thought more capable of being silent but present. Possibly those editors who have retained him have regarded him as an attendant. But there is no evidence elsewhere that Leonato would normally be attended; the kinsman would be a considerable embarrassment on stage during this long scene; and the fact that he is given a slightly less neutral status than that of an attendant suggests that Shakespeare did originally intend to involve him in the action. It therefore seems logical to treat him in the same way as Innogen, to regard him as the remnant of an abandoned intention, and to omit him.

Another example of the same kind of thing occurs in the direction at 1.1.79: 'Enter don Pedro, Claudio, Benedicke, Balthasar and Iohn the bastard.' Balthasar has no part to play in the ensuing episode. Editors retain him, presumably on the grounds that this is the entry into Messina as well as the play of the prince, and that Balthasar is thought of as one of his retinue (he accompanies Don Pedro again at 2.1.71). But he is a supernumerary character, and editors might well feel that his case is no different from those of Innogen and the kinsman.

Little more useful is the Sexton at 5.1.242; as he is mentioned at his entry—'Here, here comes master Signior Leonato, and the sexton too'—the editor cannot omit him from the stage direction, though as he has no function in the scene, a director might be forgiven for quietly disposing of him.

Finally in this category is one aspect of the problem posed by the direction at 2.1.186: 'Enter the Prince, Hero, Leonato, Iohn and Borachio, and Conrade.' This seems almost completely at odds with the action, since, of the named characters, only Don Pedro takes part in the ensuing dialogue with Benedick, who is already on stage. It is corrected in F to 'Enter the Prince'. This could be the result of accidental omission (common in F) or of intelligent reading of copy, but seems more likely to have its origin in the prompt-book. The error in Q is so extensive that, unless one adopts the now discarded hypothesis of continuous copy, one can only suppose that as he wrote the direction Shakespeare knew vaguely where his plot would take him but had not worked out how he would present it in dialogue. For although only Don Pedro need enter here, Hero and Leonato are needed before the scene ends, and Don John and Borachio are the speakers in the following scene. This completes the list of characters mentioned in the direction except for Conrad, whom Shakespeare may well have expected to bring on with Don John and Borachio, as they were plotting together in 1.3, but found that he need not. A few editors, including Dover Wilson (1923), Josephine Waters Bennett (Pelican, 1958), and D. L. Stevenson (Signet, 1964), retain Hero and Leonato in the entry at line 186; Grace R. Trenery, in the (old) Arden edition, justifies this on the grounds that 'Benedick's "this young lady" [l. 193] implies that Hero is on the stage', that 'After Benedick's impassioned outburst against her, the entrance of Beatrice, heralded by the prince's exclamation, "Look, here she comes", is much more effective if she is the only lady entering', and that her words in lines 255–6, 'I have brought Count Claudio, whom you sent me to seek', 'make it obvious that she is not meant to appear with Leonato and his daughter, but some little time after'. This ignores the possibility that 'this', in the phrase 'this young lady', is not demonstrative. And in practical terms it means that Hero and Leonato have to hang around while Don Pedro and Benedick joke about Claudio's love-sickness, and throughout Benedick's account of how Beatrice spoke of him during their dance together. Dover Wilson's direction shows awareness of the problem: 'DON PEDRO returns with LEONATO and HERO; LEONATO and HERO talk apart'; his note offers an elaborate defence of Q, while admitting that 'the entries in this scene... were clearly left in some confusion at the time of revision'. We do not need to accept Wilson's theories of revision to agree with him about the confusion; but if we believe that Q is printed from the foul papers of an original composition, we must also admit that Shakespeare was writing without due care and attention. He neglects to write Leonato and Hero into the episode introduced by the direction in which they are mentioned; he neglects to bring them on with Claudio and Beatrice at line 232; but then he writes a speech for Leonato at 271–2, and makes clear that Hero, too, is present, though she says nothing until line 339, her only speech between entering and departing.

Shakespeare can conjure up his characters from thin air as the plot requires them, but the director has to bring them on to the stage in some more naturalistic fashion. Luckily F brings Leonato and Hero on along with Claudio and Beatrice at line 232. As neither Leonato nor Hero speaks soon after the entry, and so would not have obtruded themselves upon the printer's attention, there is more reason than usual to suppose that this direction may have the authority of the prompt-book behind it. Grace Trenery's objection to it would be at least partly met if Claudio and Beatrice entered from one door, Leonato and Hero from another; and F's precise wording— 'Enter Claudio and Beatrice, Leonato, Hero'—is open to this interpretation. So a modern editor may follow F in the belief that this is the best place for Leonato and Hero to enter, and in the hope that F's direction represents the practice of Shakespeare's company, even if he might also be inclined to wish that Shakespeare had done more to motivate the entry.

IV

In the instance last discussed, Leonato and Hero do at least appear in a stage direction, even if at the wrong point in the action. But sometimes Shakespeare involves characters in action without mentioning them in directions, and, it would seem, without having considered at what point they should enter. Margaret and Ursula, for instance, take part in the second episode of 2.1, the dance. It is introduced by Leonato's 'The revellers are entering, brother. Make good room', but Margaret and Ursula are not named among those who enter, nor would it be appropriate for them to come in with the masquers, who initiate the dance. Nevertheless, Capell instructed them to do so, and was followed by the (old) Cambridge edition. The girls belong to Leonato's household, so might appropriately enter with him. Rowe's direction that they do so is followed by all modern editors, but this, too, has its awkwardnesses, in that they have nothing to say during the entire opening episode. Whatever decision the editor makes he will, as it were, be doing part of Shakespeare's work for him; and the result will be unsatisfactory because Shakespeare, if the difficulty had been pointed out to him, might well have felt that adjustments to the dialogue were necessary to smooth out the awkwardnesses to which I have referred. I incline to the view that in production it would be better for the girls to slip on with the revellers rather than remain silent through the opening episode; and I think that this possibility should be pointed out even if the alternative entry is marked.

Margaret and Ursula may not be the only characters who participate in this scene without being mentioned in the directions. The direction for the entry of the revellers reads '*Enter prince, Pedro, Claudio, and Benedicke, and Balthaser, or dumb Iohn.*' The last two words are usually interpreted as a misprint for Don John, and this seems right as his silent presence during the following episode is indicated by his comment on it (line 147). Dover Wilson interpreted '*Balthaser, or*' as a misexpansion of 'B or' for 'Borachio' and linked this with his belief that the character designated 'Balth.' at lines 93 and 96 is Borachio, not Balthasar. I find this more ingenious than convincing, but as Borachio has been involved with Don John in 1.3, and is to speak with him at line 136, it seems best to let them come on together, however one interprets the crux in the direction.

The direction at the opening of 4.2 is also deficient in its naming of characters. '*Enter the Constables, Borachio, and the Towne clearke in gownes*', says Q. Conrad soon speaks, and there is no question that he must appear along with the other malefactor, Borachio. Members of the Watch also have to appear in this scene. Presumably they should enter with everyone else, guarding Borachio and Conrad. But the dialogue suggests that Shakespeare was hazy about his intentions, and some directors (e.g. Bridges-Adams at Stratford-upon-Avon in 1933, and B. Iden Payne there in 1936) have delayed their entry until they are addressed by the Sexton—'Let them come before Master Constable'. Probably they should retire after bringing the offenders before Dogberry, and then come forward again when Dogberry says 'Let the watch come forth' (line 32).

Most editors bring the Watch on for a final appearance at 5.1.196. An exception is George Sampson, in his careful Pitt Press edition; unfortunately he does not explain his reasons. Q's direction is simply '*Enter Constables, Conrade, and Borachio*'. No speech is assigned to any member of the Watch, but there are several hints that they might be present: (*a*) Conrad and Borachio are bound, so it seems likely that someone should lead them; Dogberry's own opening words, 'Come you, sir', may, however, suggest that Shakespeare imagined them as being in his direct charge; (*b*) Borachio says 'What your wisdoms could not discover, these shallow fools have brought to light; who, in the night, overheard me...' (lines 220–2); we know that it was the Watch without Dogberry and Verges who did the overhearing, though the words alone ('these shallow fools') might refer simply to Dogberry and Verges; (*c*) Dogberry's speech beginning 'Come, bring away the plaintiffs...' (lines 239 ff.) includes the only clear allusion to the Watch: 'and, masters, do not forget to specify, when time and place shall serve, that I am an ass'; and (*d*) Leonato's closing words, 'Bring you these fellows on...', can conveniently be addressed to the Watch. On balance, then, it seems right to assign an entry to them, though it is likely that they were little more than a shadowy presence in Shakespeare's mind as he wrote the greater part of the scene.

V

It has long been recognized that one of the surest marks of the author in process of composition is the presence in directions and prefixes of variable designations for a single character. Sometimes there is no problem about identifying who is intended, but it is not always easy. The opening direction of 1.2 of *Much Ado About Nothing* lists '*an old man brother to Leonato*', and the prefixes to his speeches are '*Old*'. The opening direction of 2.1 lists him as Leonato's '*brother*', and he has that designation in the prefixes of the first episode. Then in the second episode, the dance, Ursula addresses her partner as 'Signior Anthonio', and he has this name in the prefixes to his three speeches. Editors have assumed that Ursula's partner is Leonato's brother, who is addressed as 'Brother Anthony', then 'Brother Anthonie' at 5.1.91. Guy Lambrechts[9] claims that there is 'nothing to support the identification: Anthonio is obviously one of the "revellers" who make their entrance at II. i. 71, while Leonato's brother has been present from the beginning of the scene and can have nothing to do with the masque.' He adduces as additional evidence that 'the two names [Antonio and Antony] are never used interchangeably by Shakespeare'.[10] Again, there is an implicit assumption that the copy for Q was a script polished free of inconsistencies. The coexistence of English and Italian forms of a name is paralleled in the case of Don Pedro, who is 'don Peter' on the first two occasions he is mentioned (1.1.1 and 8); Shakespeare seems then to have realized that he should have used the Italian form, and editors since Rowe have had no hesitation in emending to create consistency. Ursula's partner is old, like Leonato's brother; moreover, Shakespeare clearly

387

intended the brother to be present in 2.1. Besides being named in the opening direction, he speaks in the first episode, and is addressed at the end of it: 'The revellers are ent'ring brother; make good room' (2.1.71). No direction is given for the entry of a distinct Antonio (unless he is identified with Q's anonymous 'kinsman'). Lambrechts' claim that he is 'obviously one of the 'revellers' seems dubious considering his age. The evidence, if not conclusive, is overwhelmingly in favour of the traditional identification of Leonato's brother with Antonio, though obviously Shakespeare did not think of a name for him till Ursula had to address him.

I have alluded in passing to another uncertainty of identification in the same scene. The first of the duologues in which the dance proceeds is between Don Pedro and Hero. Then, if we are to believe Q's prefixes, Benedick dances with Margaret. But after three interchanges between them, the prefix *Bene.* changes to *Balth.*, which occurs twice. Theobald transferred Benedick's speeches to Balthasar, and has been followed by most editors. But Capell followed Q, trying to rationalize the action by adding the direction '*turning off in Quest of another*' after the last speech attributed to Benedick; other editors, including Malone, Collier (who offered a defence), and D. L. Stevenson have done the same. The result is, as Sisson says, that Margaret 'consequently has a conversation *à trois* with Benedick and Balthazar which reads very oddly and would be difficult to act'.[11]

Dover Wilson added an additional complication by abandoning both Benedick and Balthasar in favour of Borachio. He supposes that in the stage direction 'Shakespeare scribbled "and B or dun Iohn" (= Borachio Don John)' against a direction which he believes to derive from an earlier play. He therefore drops Balthasar from the entry. Furthermore,

> Borachio is the obvious partner for Margaret, while presumably the puzzled compositor took the detached 'B' in the stage-direction as Balthazar and an abbreviated 'Bo.' in the speech-headings first as 'Be.' (= Benedick) and then as 'Ba.' (= Balthazar).

He is supported by Sisson,[12] and is followed by Blakemore Evans in the Riverside edition.

The problem here seems to involve compositorial misreading as well as an unpolished manuscript. '*Balthaser*' might certainly derive from the compositor's misinterpretation of an abbreviated form of Borachio. And there are oddities in the last five words of Q's direction: '*and Balthaser, or dumb Iohn*'. The previous words are '*and Benedicke*'; the repetition of 'and' has aroused suspicion. But it is not difficult to believe that Shakespeare may initially have written the first part of the direction (to '*Benedicke*') and only minutes later have added the names of other characters, as the need for them came into his mind, without deleting the first '*and*'. Hasty writing is also suggested by '*or dumb Iohn*'. Lambrechts, most improbably, interprets '*dumb*' as a substantive; and Isaac Reed had regarded it as an appropriate epithet for Don

Pedro's taciturn brother. Dover Wilson's hypothesis that '*dumb*' is a misreading, followed by a respelling, of 'dun', found in 'Dun Iohn' at 3.3.101, is more plausible. I am less convinced by Wilson's belief (mentioned above) that '*Balthaser or*' is a misreading of 'B or'; I think it more likely that '*or*' is a misreading of an ampersand, or even of 'and'. Nor am I convinced by Sisson's statement, offered in support of Dover Wilson's substitution of Borachio for Balthasar, that Borachio 'is obviously of higher rank than Balthazar'. After all, Borachio is 'entertain'd for a perfumer' (1.3.49) and receives money from Don John for the trick played on Claudio; nor is his name in his favour. Admittedly, Borachio's relationship with Margaret, revealed later (2.2.11 ff.), might, as Dover Wilson suggests, support his being the speaker here; but there is no suggestion of any relationship outside this scene between Ursula and Antonio, who also dance together.

Again, no certain solution is possible. My conjectural reconstruction of what happened is this: Shakespeare's original direction named only Don Pedro, Claudio, and Benedick. Shakespeare allowed Don Pedro, the visiting Prince and chief guest, to open the dance with Hero, his host's daughter. Then he began to involve the second-ranking Benedick, but quickly realized that all was not well. Even for the three masquers, not enough women were present; and a dance was not much of a dance with only two couples. So Margaret and Ursula were conceived. Shakespeare did not add them to the direction, either because he was in too much of a hurry, or because they would come in more appropriately with the other women, at the beginning of the scene, and he intended to go back and write them into the opening dialogue, but never did so, at least in the script as we have it. Margaret could dance with Benedick. But no; a duologue between Benedick, masked, and Beatrice would make excellent comedy, and had best be reserved as a climax; so he replaced Benedick with Balthasar, whose name he added to the direction, but forgot to make the prefixes consistent. Leonato was perhaps too dignified to dance, but his brother was on stage, doing nothing in particular, and his age could be turned to comic advantage in a duologue with Ursula. Shakespeare gave Claudio no part in the dance,[12] perhaps through an oversight, or perhaps because he thought it better not to involve the young lover in the predominantly merry chat. At the end of the dance episode he thought of having Don John comment on it with Borachio in a transition passage, and remembered to add the master, but not the servant, to the direction. There was no need to write them into the dialogue; Don John was no dancer, and was established already as one who 'says nothing'.

These speculations may, of course, be mistaken. But if an editor is to make even minimal dramatic sense out of his text, he has to have a working hypothesis on which to base his decisions. The practical results of this one are that I should (*a*) add Margaret and Ursula to the direction at 2.1.0, with a note that they might equally enter at line 71; (*b*) retain Balthasar in the direction at line 71, and add Borachio; and (*c*) replace Benedick by Balthasar as Margaret's partner throughout their brief duologue.

VI

In several of Shakespeare's plays (and also in the Hand D addition to *Sir Thomas More*) there is uncertainty about the precise allocation of speeches among members of a group identified also by a generic name, such as Citizens, and also about how many people there are in the group. So with the Watch in *Much Ado About Nothing*. They first appear in 3.3, where the opening direction is *'Enter Dogbery and his compartner with the Watch'*. When Dogberry asks 'who think you the most desartless man to be constable?', 'Watch 1' replies, 'Hugh Oatcake, sir, or George Seacoal; for they can write and read.' We deduce that 'Watch 1' is illiterate, and that his more learned brethren are on stage. Dogberry calls Seacoal forth, and when he speaks he is 'Watch 2'; the next watchman to speak is also 'Watch 2', so there is some reason to give his line, too, to Seacoal. At lines 34, 41, 45, 50, and 62, speeches are allocated simply to 'Watch'. Each speech could be spoken by the same man, and he could be any one of the three who are certainly present. Equally, each speech could be spoken by a different actor, none of whom need have spoken before. Rowe allocated each speech to 'Watch 2'. But this is George Seacoal. To give him all the lines is to build up his part beyond justification, and to make mutes of all the other watchmen; it goes beyond the textual evidence, which is simply that Shakespeare intended the lines to be spoken by an unspecified member, or by unspecified members, of the Watch. Yet Rowe has been followed by many editors, including Dover Wilson, Alexander (1951), Sisson (1954), Foakes (1968), and Blakemore Evans. In other editions including (old) Cambridge, (old) Arden, and Signet, the direction is left vague, though the Signet editor's note—'neither the quarto nor the Folio differentiates again between First Watch and Second Watch until the end of this scene'—still implies that the only speakers are Seacoal and his sponsor. Perhaps the best note on the passage is George Sampson's:

> Editors usually assign them [i.e. the speeches] all to 'Watch 2', who seems to be the intelligent one; but we have followed the vagueness of the original. Readers and producers can therefore make what assignment they wish.

Producers have, in fact, been more liberal in their assignments than editors. Stratford-upon-Avon prompt-books show, for instance, that Iden Payne (1922–7), who used five watchmen, distributed their speeches among three of them (other than Dogberry and Verges), and John Gielgud (1949), who had seven, among four.

The next three speeches (lines 81, 89, and 99) assigned in Q simply to 'Watch' can with some confidence, though not with absolute certainty, be assigned to Seacoal as they come appropriately from the man in charge. The next (line 115) is uncertain. The speaker says, 'I know that Deformed...'. Dover Wilson, assigning the later speech, 'And one Deformed is one of them; I know him; 'a wears a lock', to Seacoal, does so on the grounds that Seacoal 'had first identified "this vile thief"'. This may be true, but his argument is the wrong way round; it is because there is another reason to give line 154 to Seacoal—as leader of the Watch—that line 115 may be retrospectively assigned to him.

At line 150, Q resumes its numbering. But now the speeches—lines 150 and 154—coming most appropriately from the leader of the Watch are assigned to 'Watch 1', not 'Watch 2', as before. As Dover Wilson, who seems to be the first to have noticed this, writes, 'Apparently Shakespeare, having originally labelled Seacoal "2 Watch" because he spoke second, now labels him "1 Watch" because he is the leader of the band.' Nevertheless, some editors, including Sisson and Foakes, have persisted in attributing these speeches to the illiterate, to the derogation of Seacoal's authority.

An editor has some freedom of choice in his treatment of this passage. His editorial policy may cause him to follow Q and do all his explaining in the notes. If he alters his text at all, he should, it seems to me, adopt a uniform prefix for those speeches that he assigns to George Seacoal; he might follow Q in calling him the second watchman at lines 15 and 24, and, if he agrees that the leader should speak lines 150 and 154, at these points depart from Q by reversing the numbers given to the watchman; but it would be more logical to call Seacoal the first watchman throughout. Better still, Seacoal might be named in the prefixes. Secondly, the editor should (as a few have) abandon the tradition of giving all those speeches which cannot be assigned to a specific watchman to either the first or the second, and leave them vague. This is unsatisfactory, of course; and it would not do for a producer. But at least it represents the truth of the situation—that Shakespeare had not fully worked out the assignment of speeches—and avoids the other unsatisfactoriness of implying that only two of the watchmen speak. Then Hugh Oatcake, who can write and read, may speak too.

The problem recurs in 4.2, where the watchmen's four speeches are assigned respectively to 'Watch 1', 'Watch 2', 'Watch 1', and 'Watch'. It would be natural to assume that Seacoal speaks first, and the second speaker has to be someone else. Rowe gave the fourth speech—'This is all'—to '2 Watch', and is followed by many later editors. Again, the limitation is misleading. Riverside assigns the speech to both the first and the second watchmen, an attractive innovation, but still an arbitrary interpretation of Q's reading.

VII

Lastly, I should like to discuss some uncertainties about the action of the play which seem to derive from the status of the copy used for Q.

1.2 takes the form of a brief conversation between Leonato and Antonio. It begins with one of the play's many loose ends: 'How now, brother!' says Leonato, 'Where is my cousin, your son?'; later (5.1.276), we hear that Antonio's (fictitious) daughter 'alone is heir to' the brothers. This opening seems designed mainly to create an impression of bustling preparations for the revelling. The scene's main business is the false report that Don Pedro is in love with Hero. When this is done, the bustle resumes: '…Cousins, you know what you have to do. O, I cry you mercy, friend; go with me, and I will use your skill. Good cousin, have a care this busy time.' Dr Johnson emended 'cousins' to 'cousin'. According to Dover Wilson, this

> is undoubtedly correct. In ll. 1–2 Leonato enquires after his 'cousin' (i.e. nephew) and a musician, and both enter at this point, as is clear from 'I will use your skill.' Moreover Q reads 'cosin' at l. 26. Most edd. attempt to support 'coosins' by giving a S.D. 'Several persons cross the stage' or 'Enter attendants.'

I see no justification for inferring that Leonato is enquiring after a musician in the opening lines; 'this music' must mean 'the music we have spoken of'. Nor is there need to emend 'Cousins' to the singular: in fact, to do so damages the impression of bustling activity which Shakespeare is trying to create. Surely this passage shows us Shakespeare writing sketchily, suggesting action that would need to be fully worked out either in a revision or when the episode came to be performed. Dover Wilson is seeking, and finding, certainty where none is possible. The editor should treat this passage for what it is, not do Shakespeare's revision for him. Several 'Cousins'— dependent relatives, I take it, like the '*kinsman*' in the opening direction to 2.1—enter, going about their tasks. Leonato apologizes to one of them ('I cry you mercy'), perhaps because he bumps into him, or fails to recognize him as the musician. He addresses another: 'Good cousin…'. Leonato and Antonio depart in different directions ('Go you and tell her of it'), and the stage clears. All that is needed is the addition of a direction along the lines of Capell: '*Enter several Persons, bearing Things for the Banquet.*' The precise staging of the scene must be worked out afresh each time the play is produced, according to the director's imagination and the resources available to him.

Although I have discussed the dance episode in 2.1 several times already, its problems are not exhausted. It is clear that some of the revellers wear a visor (line 138). Which, exactly? There is no doubt about Don Pedro, Claudio, Benedick, and Balthasar. Don John and Borachio must enter with these revellers, but I have argued that this decision to bring them on was an afterthought, and we have no evidence whether they should be masked. I think the editor will do better to point this out than to make a decision. Don John is not one of nature's revellers. Whether he should pretend to join in the fun, perhaps even take part in the dance with a non-speaking woman, or whether he should remain disdainfully aloof is part of the openness of interpretation which Shakespeare often permits and which here seems to be an involuntary result of his hasty composition.

Capell, who brought Margaret and Ursula on with the revellers, had them masked too, and is followed in this by many editors, including Foakes and Blakemore Evans, even though in their editions the ladies enter at the beginning of the scene. Evans, directing *They put on their masks* as the revellers enter, even implies that Leonato should be masked. Both Sampson and Dover Wilson pointed out that in revels such as these, it is those who enter who conventionally wear masks, not those who are already present. But this raises again the problem of Antonio. It is clear from the first words Ursula addresses to him that he is masked. This is, as Dover Wilson says, 'irregular', but he attributes it to Antonio's 'entertaining' character. In an impractic-ally fanciful direction, he follows Leonato's 'The revellers are entering, brother. Make good room' with the direction '*Antonio gives orders to the servants and goes out*'; then, in the immediately following entry, he includes the sentence 'Antonio *returns later, also masked*'. This implies a misinterpretation of 'Make good room', which surely means no more than 'stand aside'. Kittredge follows suit, though in sparer directions which merely emphasize the absurdity of having a character pop off and on. Once again, the problem derives from sketchy writing. There is no case for following the tradition that the girls wear masks, nor need an editor even mention it unless he is particularly concerned with editorial tradition. But Antonio must be masked, so it seems right to instruct him to put on a mask when the revellers enter.

Q's directions are frequently deficient, but in 2.3 the problem is one of redun-dancy. '*Enter prince, Leonato, Claudio, Musicke*' says the direction at line 32, followed six lines later by '*Enter Balthaser with musicke*'. The first direction seems merely to anticipate the entry of the singer, Balthasar, at line 38, though some editors call for '*Music within*'. The later entry of Balthasar is not well engineered, and in this instance we have evidence of how the episode was revised for performance. F reads '*Enter Prince, Leonato, Claudio, and Iacke Wilson*' at line 32, omitting the later entry for Balthasar. An editor has the choice of representing Shakespeare's original intention, in which case he should, I think, adopt Q's later entry for Balthasar, or of following the practice of Shakespeare's company as witnessed by F.

A good, small example of indeterminate action is at the beginning of 2.3. Benedick enters '*alone*' and calls 'Boy'. No entry is given for the boy, who replies 'Signior'. Benedick says, 'In my chamber-window lies a book; bring it hither to me in the orchard.' The boy declares, 'I am here already, sir', and is given an exit. We hear no more of him or the book. Most editors acknowledge no problem. A few try to explain why Shakespeare chose to begin the scene with this apparently pointless episode. The New Variorum editor records a hypothesis of W. W. Lloyd that the boy went off to tell 'the conspirators' where Benedick was, and was 'kept away by their management'. This is to treat fiction as if it were reality. Dover Wilson, more realistically, suggests that the point is to 'define the locality at the outset, so as to prepare the audience for the arbour-business. It is probably for this reason alone that he introduces the boy, who goes out never to return.' Peter Alexander, exceptionally, prescribes stage business that will make sense of the episode, though somewhat at the expense of credibility. He has the boy say 'Signior?' from 'within'; his next speech, 'I am here already, sir'. is marked 'above, at chamber window'; and then, after Benedick has said 'I know that, but I would have thee hence and here again', comes the direction 'boy brings book; exit'. This is a commendably conscientious, if somewhat laboured, accommodation of the dialogue to the facts of the Elizabethan stage, but it surely spoils the joke of the boy's pert reply. Some directors have brought the boy back on stage with a book during Benedick's soliloquy. John Barton, in his 1976 production with the Royal Shakespeare Company, found a way of accommodating the original dialogue and directions to the modern theatre. The play was given in a setting of nineteenth-century British India; the 'boy' was an impassive Indian servant; as he entered, Benedick was seated writing with his back to him, at a table; on Benedick's 'and here again', the servant produced a book from the folds of his garment, and laid it on the table before moving quietly away. As Benedick realized, with astonishment, that this was actually the book he had called for, there was a comical sense that the mystery of the East had asserted itself once again; Benedick's irritability was rebuked.

In this instance, it seems to me, both the editor and the director have, for the best of reasons and with great ingenuity, cheated. The director must be not merely forgiven but complimented, because he has found a way of making a difficult area of the text work within the context of his own production. The editor, on the other hand, has gone too far. Working at a time when scholars, following Granville-Barker's lead, were particularly concerned to demonstrate Shakespeare's mastery of theatrical craftsmanship, he has created an impression of coherence in an episode which, on the evidence of the text, Shakespeare had left in a sketchy state. It is not the editor's responsibility to complete the sketch, though of course, if his edition (unlike Alexander's) is annotated, he can suggest interpretations and improvements in his comments.

A final puzzle about action occurs in 5.3. The opening direction is 'Enter Claudio, Prince, and three or foure with tapers'. Speech prefixes include 'Lord'. Dover Wilson expanded the direction to 'A churchyard; before a sepulchre. Night. DON PEDRO, CLAUDIO and other lords approach with tapers, followed by BALTHAZAR and musicians.' Later editors have followed him to a greater or lesser degree; for example Kittredge adds 'followed by Musicians' to Q's wording; Sisson has 'Enter DON PEDRO, CLAUDIO, and others with tapers, BALTHAZAR and musicians'; Foakes adds Balthazar to Q's list; and the Signet and Pelican editors both add a Lord and the phrase 'followed by Musicians'. In fact, I suggest, we have no direct evidence as to who should sing the song, and in the absence of such evidence we may suppose that Shakespeare imagined that the singer, or singers, would be one or more of the 'three or foure'; so there is no justification for bringing on Balthasar in addition. The only evidence for extra musicians lies in Claudio's 'Now music sound & sing your solemne hymne', which could imply that the '*three or foure*' include one or more instrumentalists (who might sing as well), or alternatively could be a request for off-stage music. So there is no need to bring on 'Musicians'. Furthermore, the 'Lord' who speaks only one line (5.3.2) may be presumed to be one of the '*three or foure*', so he, too, should not be added.

VIII

It would be possible to add to the number of points in the text of *Much Ado About Nothing* where editorial problems are created by the nature of the copy used for Q, but I hope that the discussion of those that I have selected will help to show that the editor of this and other such texts may usefully bear in mind that he is dealing with a work of art which, however fine in some respects, has not been polished in all its details. Awareness of this fact will help him to avoid the trap, into which some editors have fallen, of treating the text as if its author must have known exactly how he wanted it to be performed. As a result it should be possible to reveal more of the possibilities inherent in the text than are suggested by editors who take the attitude that there must be a final solution to every problem.

26

Money in Shakespeare's Comedies

Although money is a topic of universal, timeless, and unquenchable interest, the theme of this conference seems particularly appropriate at a time of turbulence in international currency. Anyone concerned with the presentation of works of art of the past to modern readers and audiences is faced with problems of understanding and mediating their terminology; editors responsible for annotating Shakespeare's plays need to be particularly aware of this, and the adoption of decimal currency in Britain some years ago rendered out of date many notes in editions that are still in use. It is partly for this reason that I approached the topic of my talk today in a very literalistic manner: by simply listing all the references to actual sums of money that I could find in Shakespeare's comedies. I limited myself to these plays for reasons of both time and effort; I have no ambition to be definitive. And I chose the genre in which Shakespeare was most productive partly because it gives a full chronological spread over his career, and also because I was conscious before I started that allusions to specific sums of money in these plays can, as I shall be saying later, cause particular problems to modern readers and audiences.

I am not going to inflict my lists on you; they are merely the starting point for some more general reflections. But it is perhaps worth saying that they vary greatly in length from play to play. The shortest of all is for *A Midsummer Night's Dream*, where we have only a passing reference to the French crown along with the laments of Bottom's workmates that his apparent inability to appear before Theseus in the role of Pyramus has cost him 'sixpence a day during his life. He could not have scaped sixpence a day. And the Duke had not given him sixpence a day for playing Pyramus, I'll be hanged,' says Flute. 'Sixpence a day in Pyramus, or nothing' (4.1.18–22) (As you will remember, although in the end Bottom does play Pyramus before the Duke, there is nothing in the text to suggest that he receives any reward for doing so other than ducal compliments.) *The Tempest* is scarcely more prolific in allusions, nor is *The Two Gentlemen of Verona. As You Like It*; with its largely sylvan setting, is also low on the list. At the other end of the scale come *The Taming of the Shrew, The Merchant of Venice*, and *The Merry Wives of Windsor*. The general pattern is predictable : the less realistic and more romantic of the plays are least concerned with money, the plays with stronger bases in real life, and particularly in city life, along with those most concerned with the economics of marriage, yield much more. But of course Shakespeare was never one to be confined by generic conventions ; within the romance of *The Winter's Tale* the astringencies, not to say the pickpocketing, of Autolycus add to the count, as in *Cymbeline* do the wager plot and the need of the Britons to pay monetary tribute to the Romans. And the romance of *Twelfth Night* has a soberly realistic under pinning in the economic dependency of Sir Toby on Olivia and, especially, on Sir Andrew, and of Feste on society at large.

The listing of Shakespeare's monetary terminology over a broad spread of his plays yields some interesting results. Often it is very general. The term 'money' itself occurs quite often — 'nothing comes amiss', says Grumio of Petruccio, 'so money comes withal' (*The Taming of the Shrew*, 1.2.80–81), 'Thou hadst need send for more money', 'Send for more money, knight', says Sir Toby to Sir Andrew (*Twelfth Night*, 2.3.176–80), preechoing Iago's relationship with Roderigo ('Put money in thy purse'), and in *The Winter's Tale* the Clown naively asks Autolycus 'Dost lack any money ? I have a little money for thee.' (4.3.77–8) Only slightly more specific is the word 'gold' : 'There's gold', says Orsino to Feste (*Twelfth Night*, 5.1.25), and 'Take this purse of gold', Helen to the Widow in *All's Well that Ends Well*. (3.7.14)

There are of course many references to common English monetary units, some of them in non-specific, idiomatic or quasi-proverbial expressions ; thus, in *Much Ado About Nothing* Beatrice speaks of 'taking sixpence in earnest of the bearward' (2.1.34–6), and Claudio, joining Don Pedro and Leonato to dupe Benedick, threatens 'We'll fit the hid-fox with a pennyworth' (2.3.41); in *As You Like It* Rosalind remarks that the evils that her 'old religious uncle' 'laid to the charge of women' 'were all like one another as halfpence are' (3.2.333–341). In passages such as these, monetary terms are simply part and parcel of everyday linguistic usage. Some terms are particularly useful as a basis for wordplay ; in *The Two Gentlemen of Verona* Proteus declares to the 'lost mutton' Speed "twere best pound you', to which Speed opportunistically responds 'Nay sir, less than a pound shall serve me for carrying your letter' (1.1.94–104). More recondite (to us), in *As You Like It* Touchstone, alluding to the cross stamped on many coins including the penny, tells Celia 'I should bear no cross if I did bear you, for I think you have no money in your purse' (2.4.11–12).

In Shakespeare's time 'dollar' was a name for various coins from Northern countries, which probably explains why his only unpunning use of it occurs in *Macbeth* in a reference to Sweno, King of Norway (1.2.62). He found it more useful as the basis for a pun on 'dolour' meaning 'grief', as in both *Measure for Measure* (1.2.48) and *The Tempest* (2.1.19–20). Even more valuable to a dramatist with a penchant for wordplay is the term 'crown', a word of multiple meanings. Both English and French crowns circulated in Elizabethan England, and dramatists seized on the obvious opportunities for bawdy resulting from the use of the term 'French crown' to refer to the baldness caused by venereal disease. In *A Midsummer Night's Dream* Shakespeare uses the phrase with only a glancing monetary reference, either secondary or primary ('Some of your French crowns have no hair at all', says Quince in response to Bottom's offer to play the role of Pyramus in 'your French-crown-colour beard' [1.2.88–90]). In *Measure for Measure* he combines wordplay on dollar and crown in a passage where secondary meanings take precedence over primary ones ; the monetary theme is heralded by Lucio's use of the word 'purchased' when he says that he has 'purchased as many diseases under' Mistress Overdone's 'roof as come to —.' He leaves the sentence unfinished, but a Gentleman conjectures that the sum should be 'three thousand dolours a year', and Lucio adds 'a French crown more' (1.2.44–50). The pun occurs again, with a more genuinely monetary allusiveness, in *All's Well that Ends Well* when Lavatch claims to have an answer that will 'serve fit to all questions' and which will be 'As fit as ten groats is for the hand of an attorney, as your French crown for your taffeta punk …' (2.2.19–21). Not all of Shakespeare's monetary wordplay is easily accessible to modern readers or even to scholars ; for instance Sandra K. Fischer, in her useful book *Econolingua, A Glossary of Coins and Economic Language in Renaissance Drama* (Newark, N.J., 1985), plausibly enough suggests that, in *The Comedy of Errors*, the meaning of Antipholus of Syracuse's words 'There's not a man but doth salute me | … Some tender money to me' (4.3.1), is enhanced if we realize that the salute was a coin, but this meaning is not glossed in recent editions (including my own New Penguin). (I'm not absolutely convinced that it's right; Shakespeare never uses the word straightforwardly to mean a coin, but admittedly that sense may also be present in *King John* in the Bastard's line 'When his fair angels would salute my palm', 2.1.591).

In Shakespeare's time, of course, coins circulated far more freely between England and the mainland of Europe than in more recent times; 'Foreign coins were declared current in England and assigned certain values because of a shortage of native coins'[1] (Fischer, p. 71). As a result, Shakespeare was able to use the names of coins minted in other countries with assurance that they would be familiar to his audiences. Thus the French 'denier', described by Cotgrave in 1611 as 'a small copper coin valued at the tenth part of an English pennie' (cited *OED*), is used by Christopher Sly as the type of something of minimal value with no sense that he is using a foreign word—he will pay 'not a denier' for the glasses he has broken (*The Taming of the Shrew*, Induction 1, line 7), and the Dutch doit, valued at half of an English farthing—a coin which I am old enough to remember being in circulation, but which I now have to explain to my students was worth a quarter of a penny at a time when there were two hundred and forty pennies to a pound—is the object of a specifically English reference in *The Tempest*: in England, says Trinculo, 'When they will not give a doit to relieve a lame beggar, they will lay out ten to see a dead Indian' (2.2.31–3).

The specificity of this reference to the use of a foreign coin in England induces caution against inferring that in using the names of coins minted overseas

Shakespeare may be attempting to establish or reinforce the sense of a foreign setting, but I think there are good grounds for believing that this was sometimes his practice. *The Merchant of Venice* may provide an example. In this play there is one allusion to English currency: in the second scene Portia, discussing her English suitor Falconbridge, admits that she has 'a poor pennyworth in the English' (1.2.68–9). This is an obvious instance of the non-specific, metaphorical use of monetary terminology. All except one of the other monetary references in the play are specifically to the ducat, which originated in Italy, is often associated with Spain, and according to *OED* was 'A gold coin of varying value, formerly in use in most European countries'. Shakespeare uses it in nine plays, all of them with non-English, European settings— never, significantly, in the English histories—and there are considerably more occurrences of the word in *The Merchant of Venice* than in the other eight plays put together. It seems then particularly significant that the coin was specifically associated with Venice: Coryat, noting in 1611 that 'this word duckat doth not signifie any one certaine coyne', nevertheless remarks that 'the Venetian duckat is much spoken of' (cited in *OED*). And in the only other reference to a coin in the play, the English angel, Shakespeare carefully indicates that in the society of Belmont this is a foreign coin:

> They have in England
> A coin that bears the figure of an angel
> Stamped in gold...

says Portia (2.7.55–7). It is also of interest that some ducats bore a portrayal of Christ on the obverse, so that, as Sandra Fischer remarks, when Shylock bemoans the loss not only of his daughter Jessica but also of his 'Christian ducats' (2.8.16), he may be referring not simply 'to money obtained by a system antithetical to his own money-lending trade', but 'to these ducats as symbolic of the society that oppresses him.'[2] Conversely, in Shakespeare's only comedy with an English setting, *The Merry Wives of Windsor,* which of all his comedies is perhaps the most prolific in direct allusions to money, all the coins mentioned are English in origin—pounds, groats, mill sixpences, shillings, the tester, the penny, and again angels.

Although the names of many of the coins mentioned in Shakespeare's comedies are common enough in his work, there are a number that are unique to the play in which they occur, which in itself may suggest that he had a special reason for choosing them. *The Comedy of Errors*, for example, is the only one of his plays to mention the guilder. This was 'A gold coin formerly current in the Netherlands and parts of Germany' (*OED*); there seems to be no reason to link it particularly to Ephesus or to the Mediterranean in general. In the opening scene the Duke tells Egeon that Ephesan merchants, 'wanting guilders to redeem their lives', have been put to death in Syracuse (1.1.7–9), and later the Second Merchant, bound for Persia, expresses a need for a supply 'for [his] voyage' (4.1.4). I suspect that Shakespeare chose the coin simply as one that would sound vaguely foreign, and this belief is supported by a passage of word-play in the A-text of Marlowe's *Dr Faustus*; Wagner offers 'gilders' to the Clown, who responds 'Gridyrons, what be they?' To which Wagner replies, 'Why french crownes'.[3] Another unique usage is 'sicles', or more properly in a modernized text 'shekels', in *Measure for Measure*, where Isabella declares that she will bribe Angelo

> Not with fond shekels of the tested gold,
> Or stones, whose rate are either rich or poor,
> As fancy values them; but with true prayers,
> That shall be up at heaven and enter there
> Ere sunrise, prayers from preservèd souls,
> From fasting maids whose minds are dedicate
> To nothing temporal. (2.2.153–9)

OED's first recorded instance of the word is from Exodus; its biblical associations may have commended it for use by the novice Isabella. (Sandra Fischer suggests that 'The form *sicles* may indicate an intentional catachretic paronomasia for testicles': implausible, I think, in so far as I understand it.[4])

One of Shakespeare's unique usages antedates the first recorded instance in *OED* and its most recent supplements, though only by a year or two. This is *quart-d-écu* (or 'cardecu'), the French silver coin first issued in 1574, which occurs twice in *All's Well that Ends Well* and is clearly appropriate to the French setting of that play. The three other unique usages in the comedies are all found in a single scene, the first brothel scene, of *Pericles*. One is 'chequins', a word related to 'sequins' and used for a gold coin of Italy and Turkey; it seems to have come into the English language through Hakluyt, and is clearly suited to the play's exotic setting. Another is 'crown of the sun', an emendation first made in the New Penguin edition (4.2.107) by Philip Edwards from the quarto's 'crownes in the Sunne'; in spite of its exotic-sounding name, which may account for its use here, this golden crown was, according to *OED*, much current in England in the fifteenth and sixteenth centuries. And the third, present so far only in the Oxford edition's reconstructed text, is 'sesterces', in Boult's sentence 'I cannot be bated of a thousand sesterces' (16.49). In the quarto this reads 'I cannot be bated one doit of a thousand peeces', but as the equivalent point in Wilkins's *Painful Adventures of Pericles* refers to 'a hundred sestercies of golde' and in Twine's *The Pattern of Painful Adventures* to 'an hundred sestercies of gold', it is not unreasonable to conjecture that the phrase in the quarto, a notoriously bad text, misrepresents the original; as the Oxford editors write, 'A reporter might easily have substituted Q's less specific phrase; there seems little reason for Shakespeare to abandon his source in such a detail.'[5] The sesterce was an ancient Roman coin, not current in Shakespeare's time. So far as I can tell, this, if it is a genuine Shakespearean usage, is the only example in his comedies of the use of historical monetary terminology, paralleled by for instance the talent, used uniquely of coins in *Timon of Athens*.

It seems to me that for a modern reader or spectator the single most important factor in Shakespeare's references to money is as an indication of relative social status. It is of course notoriously difficult to express the value of money of the past in modern terms. Even in its own time the value of the various coins in circulation was not constant. As George Unwin put it, 'as the relative values of gold and silver then, as now, continually changed, the Government found itself obliged from time to time to re-state the value of its own gold coins and of the foreign coins in circulation in terms of the silver coinage. Thus the lighter sovereign of 22 carat gold was called down from 20s. to 13s. 4d. in 1561, and raised again to 20s. in 1592.'[6] Even more significant is the constant fluctuation in relative values, which renders useless any attempt to express the value of monetary units of Shakespeare's time by any simple equation (even though one still occasionally comes across attempts to do so). For the modern playgoer terms such as groats, ducats, nobles, angels, and so on are virtually meaningless, but an effort to understand the relative value of sums of money mentioned in the plays is important to their theatrical interpreters as well as to their readers, whether the plays are presented in the costumes of their own time or in those of later ages. Of course context can help. The stinginess of the 'remuneration' with which Don Armado rewards Costard—three-farthings—is thrown into relief by the 'guerdon'—a whole shilling—'elevenpence-farthing better'—that the aristocratic Biron bestows upon him for the identical service, and is relevant to the theatrical presentation of these two characters (*Love's Labour's Lost*, 3.1.128–68). In *A Midsummer Night's Dream* Flute clearly thinks that a pension of sixpence a day for Bottom would be riches indeed. In *Twelfth Night* sixpence is the sum Sir Toby gives Feste for singing 'O mistress mine', and Sir Andrew matches him (2.3.30–3). To us, even the double reward seems paltry, but when we consider that in 1587 the standard wage for a linen weaver was sixpence a day with meat and drink, or 10 pence a day without,[7] we find it easier to understand both Flute's regret and the generosity expected even of a relatively impecunious knight. Sixpence would have permitted Bottom to see six plays professionally performed at the Globe, or to buy the first printed text of the play in which he himself appears; on a more material level, at the prices prevailing in 1572 it would have bought him two small chickens or thirty eggs.[8]

Curiously enough, one of the standards of payment often used by those who have read biographies of Shakespeare is the salary paid to the Stratford schoolmaster in Shakespeare's youth, which was £20 a year, very much more than that of any of the wages stipulated by proclamation to be paid to members of the London companies in 1587—the highest paid were the brewers, at £10 a year.[9] This puts into some sort of perspective some of the larger sums of money in Shakespeare's plays. Take for example the foolish Master Froth, in *Measure for Measure*, who takes such delight to sit, gossiping, eating (save the mark) stewed prunes, and no doubt drinking in the Bunch of Grapes. He testifies before Escalus to being in possession of eighty pounds a year, which presumably classes him among the idle rich (2.1.119). The villainy of Don John (in *Much Ado About Nothing*) as well as his position in society does not become fully apparent unless we realize that the thousand ducats he pays Borachio for helping in the plot against Hero is a very large sum of money; the ducat appears to have been more variable in value than most monetary units, but at the lowest estimate the Elizabethan value of a thousand would have been around £175, and at the highest close on £500; as the Courtesan in *The Comedy of Errors* puts it, even 'forty ducats is too much to lose' (4.3.96); a thousand ducats would have paid that Stratford schoolmaster's salary for between nine and twenty-four years; he would have done far better as a crook. By this standard, too, Sir Andrew Aguecheek, in *Twelfth Night*, who according to Sir Toby 'has three thousand ducats' a year (1.3.20), is seriously rich, and our understanding of the relationship between Sir Toby and him will be inadequate unless we are made to realize this. By the same token in *Cymbeline* Giacomo's wager on Innogen's chastity of ten thousand ducats to Posthumus's ring (1.4.125) should be made to seem breathtaking in its self-confidence.

Courtship and marriage play a large part in all Shakespeare's comedies, and in Shakespeare's time money played an equally large part in these processes, as is made very clear in Ann Jennalie Cook's study *Making a Match: Courtship in Shakespeare and his Society*.[10] As she remarks, comedies by Shakespeare 'accept the monetary aspects of courtship in ways that can either elude or outrage modern critics' (p. 134). Characters such as Bassanio in *The Merchant of Venice*, Fenton in *The Merry Wives of Windsor*, and Claudio in *Much Ado About Nothing*, who indicate that their choice of a bride is governed at least in part by the amount of the dowry that she will bring with her, have, as Cook says, 'been denounced as fortune hunters even though their behavior was standard practice among non-fictional gentlemen of similar rank and in similar circumstances' (p. 134). More complex ethical questions are raised by the fact that 'When Lorenzo steals Jessica from Shylock's house, he also takes the 'gold and jewels she is furnished with' (2.4.31). This 'behavior has occasioned severe condemnation', but Professor Cook defends it on the grounds that 'a young gentleman like Lorenzo (or Bassanio) cannot afford to marry a bride with no dowry. What Jessica takes is some part of the portion that Shylock would unquestionably have denied her for this union' (p. 136). (I'm not sure that if I were in Shylock's place I should regard this as an adequate defence.)

It is of course impossible for us to think ourselves back completely into either Shakespeare's mind or that of a characteristic playgoer of his time, and his plays are open, like *Coriolanus*, to the interpretation of later times, so there is bound to be continuing argument about ethical questions raised by financial considerations. But at least it is possible for us to arrive at some sense of the contemporary values of the sums of money involved in these transactions. Sometimes no specific sums are mentioned; for instance, Claudio, in *Much Ado About Nothing*, merely enquires 'Hath Leonato any son, my lord?' (1.1.277), a question that has got him into more hot water than perhaps he deserves, especially since by the time he asks it he has already confessed to Benedick that he would like to marry Hero. At the other extreme, the thought that the entire province of Aquitaine is a fit 'dowry for a queen' (*Love's Labour's Lost*, 2.1.8) places the marriage of the Princess of France into a context in which mere money seems irrelevant. In *All's Well that Ends Well*, however, it is of interest that Helen offers to 'add three thousand crowns | To what is passed already' to Diana's dowry if she will agree to take part in the bed trick (3.7.35–6). As I have said, the crown was of rather indefinite value, but to judge by the dowries cited in Ann Jennalie Cook's book an offer such as this in real life would have given Diana every hope of marrying a prosperous member of the gentry. Admittedly it cannot compete with Baptista's offer of a dowry for Kate: 'After my death the one half of my lands, | And in possession twenty thousand crowns' (2.1.121–2). This, says Ann Cook (p. 140), is 'more than double the sum most peers offered with their daughters'; but then Baptista has special reasons for wanting to get Kate off his hands, and Petruccio has 'come to wive it wealthily in Padua; | If wealthily, then happily in Padua.' It is even more impressive that at the end of the play, after Kate has been shown to be tamed indeed, Baptista offers to add to the wager that Petruccio has won a second

> twenty thousand crowns,
> Another dowry to another daughter,
> For she is changed as she had never been.

In this scene too it is important, I think, that we should feel the sum of a hundred crowns that Petruccio, Hortensio, and Lucentio are wagering is substantial; however we define and value this elusive unit, a hundred crowns would have kept many members of the groundlings in the play's original audience in wages for several years. To appreciate this may perhaps usefully emphasize the play's romantic aspects: although to us it may seem one of Shakespeare's more realistic plays, to its early audiences the sums of money bandied about among its characters must have suggested a world of fantasy rather than real life—which may perhaps encourage the hypothesis that the tale of Kate is more appropriately seen as a dream-fulfilling fantasy of Christopher Sly than as a piece of social realism.

When Shakespeare's plays are performed in Elizabethan or Jacobean costume we are at least alerted by their setting to the fact that they take place in a society different from our own, however little we may understand its conventions. Matters become more complicated when the plays are updated. I was particularly conscious of problems in relation to money in Bill Alexander's very successful production of *The Merry Wives of Windsor* at Stratford in 1985 which in theory was set precisely in 1959. This made nonsense of, for example, the information in the first scene that Anne Page is to inherit £700 when she reaches the age of 17. In Elizabethan terms that is a fortune, precisely the sum that 'Joan Churchman's father provided at her wedding to Richard Hooker' in 1581 which 'became the core of the couple's financial security and formed a substantial part of the £1,100 estate Hooker left at his death'.[11] In 1959 it would probably not have paid for the wedding reception. Anne Page complains of the foolish suitor that her father favours on account of his income: 'O, what a world of vile ill-favoured faults | Looks handsome in three hundred pounds a year!' (3.4.31–2). Slender would have seemed rich indeed to Shakespeare's schoolmaster, with an income that would have paid his salary for fifteen years; but in 1959, my researches in the files of the *Stratford-upon-Avon Herald* tell me, Slender's annual income of £300 would have bought nothing more impressive than a small, rather old, second-hand car. It would not have been enough to pay the salary even of a 16-year old scientific assistant in the Plant Physiology section of the National Vegetable Research Station at Wellesbourne, and would have seemed laughably inadequate to someone applying for the post of fireman with the Warwickshire Fire Service, who would have been paid well over £500 a year provided he was physically fit, at least 5' 7" in height, and had a minimum chest measurement of 36" and an expansion of at least 2", as well as possessing perfect eyesight. (I think I might just have qualified, in 1959.) In a production ostensibly set in 1959, and where so much else was updated, there would have been a strong case for attempting some kind of modernization of the sums of money mentioned in the play; but if we start doing that sort of thing, where do we stop? Perhaps we must simply recognize that modern-dress productions overlay a play's original text with a metaphor of that text, and that part of their excitement derives from the constant mental adjustments that this process calls for.

27

To Read a Play:
The Problem of Editorial Intervention

M any paradoxes inhere in the concept of 'reading' a 'play'—or at least of supposing that the reading experience is to any substantial degree an effective substitute for the experience of seeing a play in performance. Indeed, current critical vocabulary permits us to speak of 'reading' a play while seeing it performed, so I should specify that by reading I mean here not 'interpreting' but literally 'reading the text of' a play, an activity that is virtually essential for those who need to learn the words they are to speak on stage, and for others involved in the production process, but that might reasonably be proscribed to anyone else. For centuries people have read the texts of plays with the expectation of the same kind of pleasure as they might receive from a novel, a romance, an epic, or a narrative poem: the pleasure of following and becoming emotionally involved in a story, of encountering interesting and amusing characters, and of enjoying the writer's literary skills; and of course it is true that dramatic texts can afford these pleasures. Many dramatic texts are perceived to be of high literary value, and the period of English drama which is most highly esteemed—the period lasting for a comparatively short time, from the late 1580s to, I suppose, the early 1620s—happens to be one in which the literary and rhetorical content of plays was particularly high.

This may seem a tendentious assertion; it might be suggested that this period of English drama has been overvalued precisely because literary rather than dramatic or theatrical criteria have been applied to it, and that correspondingly, texts of other periods which offer less to the armchair-based reader have been undervalued for that reason. But it is an important factor that Elizabethan and Jacobean drama, highly poetic and rhetorical though much of it is, is also a drama of performance. It is not, like the drama of the romantic period—the plays of Keats, Wordsworth, Coleridge, and Shelley—the drama of writers standing more or less wistfully outside the theatre and hoping to break in, or even, in some cases, simply using the dramatic form—as Shelley does in *Prometheus Unbound*—as a literary device, with no thoughts of practicable performance; on the contrary, the drama of Shakespeare and his contemporaries is rooted in performance, is poetic and rhetorical because this was the current theatrical mode, emerging from a period when all drama had been written in verse. The literary content of such a drama is ultimately inseparable from its dramatic power; its poetry and its prose are properly experienced only through performance.

Nevertheless, it is inevitable that such a drama should offer much pleasure to the literary-minded reader, and understandable that booksellers, and indeed writers themselves, should have sought an alternative market for dramatic texts, printing them so that they could be read both by those who had already seen the plays performed and by those who had not done so, and perhaps could not do so. To some writers this was a purely commercial matter, just a way of getting paid twice for a single product. Others were more scrupulous, and in differing ways. For instance, Thomas Heywood, in the Epistle to his play *The Rape of Lucrece* (printed 1608), claims that he is publishing it only because some of his plays have, without his knowledge or approval, 'accidentally come into the printer's hands' in a 'corrupt and mangled' form, 'copied only by the ear'; before this happened he had scorned those who 'used a double sale of their labours, first to the stage, and after to the press'. Elsewhere, too (in the Epistle to *The English Traveller*, printed 1633), Heywood disclaims the ambition 'to be in this kind voluminously read'. And John Marston, in the Epistle to *The Malcontent* (printed 1604), shows awareness that publication by printing of a work intended for performance may misrepresent it: 'only one thing afflicts me', he writes, 'to think that scenes invented merely to be spoken should be enforcively published to be read, and that the least hurt I can receive is to do myself the wrong' (in other words, if the play must be printed, at least it is better if this is done under the author's personal supervision); he asks his readers to forgive 'the unhandsome shape which this trifle in reading presents...for the pleasure it once afforded you when it was presented with the soul of lively action'. Other writers expressed their sense that what worked on the stage would not necessarily please the reader; so, for example, the publisher of Marlowe's *Tamburlaine*, in 1590, wrote that he had 'purposely omitted and left out some fond and frivolous gestures... though haply they have been of some vain conceited fondlings greatly gaped at what times they were showed upon the stage in their graced deformities', since for them 'to be mixtured in print with such matter of worth, it would prove a great disgrace to so honourable and stately a history'.

Other dramatists, rather than simply explaining that their plays were not meant to be read, attempted to mitigate the damage that might be done by this kind of publication by providing apparatus designed, with various degrees of thoroughness, to add to the printed text material that would go some way towards filling in for the reader the theatrical dimension that he would otherwise have had to imagine for himself. The most conspicuous example in Shakespeare's time is Ben Jonson, whose scholarly pretensions made him particularly sensitive to the impact that his printed texts—his 'works', as he was mocked for calling them when they were printed in folio—would make on the reading public. Thus, for example, he furnished the printed text of *Every Man Out of his Humour* (1600) with a list of the Persons in the Play along with neat little character sketches as well as providing more detailed indications of stage action than are found in most plays of the period. Jonson was particularly sensitive in his presentation of works that had been less well received in the theatre than he thought they deserved. On the title-page of *The New Inn* (1631) he blazes forth his anger with both performers and spectators while indicating greater faith in his readers: it is 'a comedy, as it was never acted, but most negligently played, by some, the King's servants, and more squeamishly beheld and censured by others, the King's subjects ... now at last set at liberty to the readers, his majesty's servants and subjects, to be judged'. A dedication 'to the reader' inveighs against the play's spectators at its single performance, and Jonson provides on their behalf a detailed summary of the action—perhaps itself a covert admission that, as some spectators found at the play's 1987 revival in Stratford-upon-Avon, the plot is by no means crystal-clear from the dialogue alone. Again, there are prose sketches of the persons of the play along, this time, with 'some short characterism of the chief actors', and the author provides not only the original epilogue but an additional one 'made for the play in the poet's defence, but the play lived not in opinion to have it spoken', rounding off with the ode to himself begotten, as he says, by 'the vulgar censure of his play by some malicious spectators'.

The care with which Jonson prepared his plays for the reading public looks forward to the ample Prefaces and highly literary stage directions of Bernard Shaw and other dramatists of the early twentieth century. Shaw—like Jonson—was a dramatist of ideas, a highly articulate and aggressive personality who liked to thrust himself between his interpreters and his public. He would have liked to act his plays single-handed; since even he admitted that this was impossible he had, as he put it in the Preface to *Plays Unpleasant* (1898), to 'fall back on his powers of literary expression, as other poets and fictionists do'. He was aware of—and slightly exaggerated—the originality of his methods, claiming that the presentation of plays as literary texts 'has hardly been seriously attempted by dramatists. Of Shakespear's plays we have not even complete prompt copies: the folio gives us hardly anything but the bare lines. What would we not give for the copy of *Hamlet* used by Shakespear at rehearsal, with the original stage "business" scrawled by the prompter's pencil? And if we had in addition the descriptive directions which the author gave on the stage: above all, the character sketches, however brief, by which he tried to convey to the actor the sort of person he meant him to incarnate'—the sort of thing, that is, that Jonson gives us in *Every Man Out of his Humour*—'what a light they would shed, not only on the play, but on the history of the sixteenth century! Well, we should have had all this and much more if Shakespear, instead of merely writing out his lines, had prepared the plays for publication in competition with fiction as elaborate as that of Meredith.' (Apparently Shaw had not recently read Sidney's *Arcadia*.)

Shaw has, of course, a self-centred view of the dramatist in relation to his work, one which we may feel to be at the opposite pole from Shakespeare's self-effacing trust in his interpreters, but he points usefully to the fact that for centuries the dominant way of putting a play into print, and so making it available to readers (and to performers), was to hand over to a printer the script as it had already been handed over to the actors for performance, with only minimal alterations; indeed, for some dramatists, including Shakespeare, we have reason to believe that the script given to the printer was in some cases a late draft in even less finished a condition than that from which the actors would work. Such scripts lack any kind of 'presentational' material: none of Shakespeare's plays printed in his lifetime has any dedication, epistle to the reader, list of characters, scene locations, notes, or Act or scene divisions. These scripts use abbreviations, especially of characters' names, that may be incomprehensible to a reader; sometimes (especially in crowd scenes) they do not specify exactly who is to speak particular speeches; and they give at most a bare minimum of stage directions. On the whole, the more deeply involved an author is with the company that puts on his plays, the less specific he needs to be in the script that he provides for them. What the actors need is their lines, the words they have to speak; their cues; and, preferably, knowledge of when they should enter and leave the stage. If the author is one of them—as Shakespeare was to a greater extent than any other author of his age—then he can give them more detailed instructions on the spot, and may well leave certain decisions to be worked out during rehearsals.

The situation I have outlined has created a set of circumstances that marks a distinction in function between the editor of a dramatic text and editors of most other literary texts. Editors have in practice a wide range of functions—and, of course, the very concept of 'editing' is open to a wide range of interpretation—but most people would agree that the editor's most basic task is the establishment of a workable text by the diagnosis and removal of any corruption that may have occurred in the process of transmission. Editors of non-dramatic texts such as novels and poems may be faced with complex problems arising from, for instance, authors' revisions, alternative readings, censorship, publishers' interventions, and so on, but at least they are dealing with texts in which the word is paramount. Editors of dramatic texts, on the other hand, have long seen it as part of their function to make some attempt to cope with the unwritten dimension of the dramatic script: with what happens on stage beyond the words that are spoken there. This is, however, an area of editorial responsibility which—at least so far as Shakespeare and his contemporaries are concerned—has been largely neglected by editorial theorists. Scholars such as W. W. Greg and Fredson Bowers have written volumin-ously about establishing the text of dramatic dialogue, but have said surprisingly little about anything other than the words spoken. They have concerned themselves, we might say, rather with the literary substance of the play than with its dramatic reality. This may be well for the most conservative types of editions, near facsimiles which are concerned primarily to reconstruct the manuscript lying behind the printed text, with no concern for the validity of this manuscript as a guide to performance—which, of course, was its initial function. But this kind of edition is of very limited utility; it is only the first stage in the preparation of a performance text; and the great majority of editors working on texts for the reading public— which during the present century has increasingly tended to mean an academic public—have acknowledged, usually tacitly, an obligation to attempt to present the text in a way that will convey the experience of seeing the play in performance more adequately than the original script would, even when that script was freed of corruption. To do this means, of course, that the editor is also preparing a text that would be more usable in the theatre than in its original state; he is taking upon himself some of the functions of the director—or at least of a theatre functionary responsible for preparing a prompt-book—in interpreting the text in theatrical terms. Let me give a few straightforward examples which will illustrate the problem.

Shakespeare's comedy *Much Ado About Nothing* was first printed from a manuscript which, all scholars agree, was in an unpolished state. The opening stage direction provides for the entry of 'Innogen', wife of the governor of Messina, and a later direction too calls for Leonato's wife. No one disputes that these directions stood in Shakespeare's manuscript. But that manuscript can have made no further mention, either implicitly or explicitly, of Innogen; she never speaks, is never addressed, and is never referred to. Anyone editing the text purely in its own right would have to retain her, because there can be no doubt that as Shakespeare wrote these directions he intended to provide a function for her in the drama. On the other hand, anyone attentive to the dramatic meaning of the text, to its function as a guide to performance, must expunge the lady, since clearly she went out of Shakespeare's head as he went on writing, and can have made no appearance in the play as performed. So she is normally written out of the edited text.

A number of the early texts obscure the points at which characters should come on to the stage. *The Winter's Tale* was first printed from a manuscript in which, in over half of the scenes, the names of the characters taking part are massed together at the opening of the scene regardless of the point at which they should enter. This is believed to have been a characteristic of a particular scribe, Ralph Crane, and is part of the evidence that the play was printed from a scribal manuscript, not from Shakespeare's own papers. It means that the editor who has in mind the play as performed must distribute the entries at points he thinks appropriate, and there may be uncertainty about where these points are. In the second scene, for instance, it is not clear how much of the conversation between the court party should be overheard by Leontes' cupbearer, Camillo. Furthermore, the fact that the stage directions have been obviously interfered with raises questions about whether indications of non-speaking roles may have been dropped. This is, in fact, a more general problem, because a playwright may have sometimes taken for granted that royal persons would be attended, and not have bothered to specify the fact. It can be quite important; in this very scene of *The Winter's Tale*, at which two kings and a queen are present, the eighteenth-century editor Theobald (himself a playwright, and thus, perhaps, particularly likely to have been influenced by the theatrical conventions of his own time) added a direction for attendants, and has been followed by most later editors; some modern directors, however, have preferred to treat the episode as a domestic scene, one that helps to establish a harmonious relationship between Leontes, Hermione, and Polixenes before it is shattered by the onset of Leontes' fanatical jealousy; and textually there is no reason why they should not do so. There are many other plays—*Hamlet*, for example—where similar issues arise.

Perhaps inevitably, the way in which editors set about the task of making what we might call theatrical emendations to a text—or removing obstacles to the reader's understanding of its theatrical function—has tended to be coloured by the editor's experience of the theatre of his time. Indeed, it is doubtful whether some of the earlier editors had any concept of any other kind of theatre than their own; they may well have felt that, just as they modernized spelling and punctuation, so they should also bring the presentational aspects of the text into line with contemporary conventions. This was particularly likely to happen at a time when little was known about the staging of the Elizabethan and Jacobean period—after all, the de Witt drawing of the Swan was only discovered in 1888—and when, also, theatrical methods were far more uniform than they are at present. During the seventeenth century, the eighteenth century, and much of the nineteenth century, methods of staging were pretty uniform over a wide range of theatres. Until 1843 the two centres of English theatrical life were Drury Lane and Covent Garden, and other theatres took their pattern from them. Actors could move around the country playing star roles with local companies with little extra rehearsal. Even in this century, Professor Sprague tells the story of the old actor who, invited to play Kent in *King Lear* at, as it were, Exeter, wrote in his letter of acceptance: 'Usual moves, I suppose?' Nowadays, on the other hand, editors know that productions of Shakespeare may employ an extraordinary range of theatrical techniques and may take place in widely diverse physical surroundings, and this in itself may have helped to push these editors into thinking more restrictedly of the Elizabethan theatre—a theatre of the past—as the only one that will provide a constant frame of reference, even though, of course, our knowledge of Elizabethan staging conventions is still all too imperfect. But modern editors continue to be heavily influenced by the editorial techniques of their predecessors, to accept unthinkingly stage directions that derive from, for example, eighteenth-century editors, rather than rethinking the theatrical dimension of their texts purely in terms of the theatrical conditions for which they were composed.

Let me give an example which has practical consequences for the modern editor. During what is now usually known as Act 2, scene 5 of *As You Like It*, Amiens tells us that 'The Duke' (who is not present) 'will drink under this tree', and at the end of the scene Amiens says, 'And I'll go seek the Duke; his banquet is prepared.'[1] This seems to imply that the 'banquet' has been in preparation during the later part of the scene, and is visibly ready by the end of it. But the Duke does not immediately enter; the following scene is an episode in which old Adam appears with Orlando in desperate need of food: 'O, I die for food', he exclaims, and Orlando declares, 'If this uncouth forest yield anything savage I will either be food for it or bring it for food to thee.' The Folio's opening direction for the following scene, in which the food is to be consumed, is '*Enter Duke Sen[ior]. & Lord, like Out-lawes*'. In 1709, Nicholas Rowe, the first of Shakespeare's named editors, helpfully added the direction '*A Table set out*', and this was repeated in all editions of the play until very recent years. Dover Wilson—whose directions, at least in the earlier plays in his edition, are more Shavianly helpful than those of any other editor—had directed in scene 5 '*Some of the company prepare a meal beneath the tree*', and now on the entry of the Duke varies Rowe to '*A meal of fruit and wine set out under the tree*'. He does not direct the meal to be taken off and then brought back again, and his note reveals his thoughts on the subject: 'Where was the table prepared in Shakespeare's theatre? Not on the front stage, otherwise the next scene would be ridiculous. We must suppose, therefore, that the inner-stage was not the Duke's cave but "this tree" (1.30), and that at the end of the scene the curtain was drawn to conceal the banquet, which was again revealed at the beginning of 2.7.'[2]

That note is marvellously revealing in two directions. First, it shows Dover Wilson working on assumptions about the past, about the Elizabethan theatre, that are no longer accepted. The very concept of the Shakespearian 'inner-stage' is now untenable, let alone the notion that it could be representative of a particular location—whether the Duke's cave or a tree—or that it would be alternately revealed and concealed by a curtain. Secondly, it shows Dover Wilson being unconsciously influenced in his concepts of the Shakespearian theatre by the conventions of his own time, when 'front scenes' such as the simple duologue between Orlando and Adam would be played on the forestage before a curtain which could be raised or drawn apart to show the full stage for the more elaborate and densely populated scene that follows.

Nearly forty years later Agnes Latham, in her new Arden edition of 1975, reverted to a variation of Rowe's direction—'*A meal set out*' instead of '*A table set out*'—and discussed the matter in an appendix, remarking on the outdatedness of Dover Wilson's concept of the inner stage and pointing out that 'The attendants might set up boards on trestles and carry them off at the end of scene v, were it not that nobody has yet sat down to the feast, which does not take place till scene vii.' Her comments make it clear that her own concepts of staging are essentially those of the naturalistic stage: 'Supposing the table is left visible at the end of scene v it must be set very far upstage, and the scene between Orlando and Adam must be played very far down. Even so there will be an awkwardness about their entrance and exit.' She is worried by the thought that the banquet 'could be concealed throughout scene vi only by being imperfectly visible in scenes v and vii', and arrives at the explanation 'that the attendants unobtrusively remove the feast as part of their comings and goings in the background at the end of scene v, and bring it on again at the beginning of scene vii'. Which leads her, understandably, to ask why Shakespeare should have been such a fool as to introduce 'the "banquet" at all at scene v', a question to which she provides no satisfactory answer.[3]

A couple of years later Richard Knowles, in his New Variorum edition, discussed the same subject, concluding: 'The early setting of the table seems to me thoroughly puzzling; it is totally unnecessary, for the banquet could have been carried on, as banquets usually were, at the beginning of scene 7.'[4]

Directors, too, have been exercised by the problem. In a Stratford, Ontario, production Robin Phillips rearranged the order of the scenes so that the Orlando–Adam one preceded the other two, whilst at the Royal Shakespeare Theatre Terry Hands (like others before him) cut the reference to the banquet in scene 5.[5]

When I came to edit the play for the Complete Oxford Shakespeare I too puzzled over the problem, coming eventually to the conclusion that it is one created by editors, a problem that exists only as a result of conditioning to naturalistic theatre practices; that for the banquet to be set up at the end of scene 5 and to remain on stage in full view of the audience while Adam bemoans his starving condition, and while Orlando declares his determination to find food, would make a strong ironic point in a non-illusionistic theatre. Consequently I did not add a direction for the removal of the food at the end of scene 5. Since then I have been cheered to find that Alan Dessen, in his book on *Elizabethan Stage Conventions*, makes the same point, regarding this sequence as 'a clear example of the kind of simultaneous staging often found in earlier English drama'.[6] Although the modern editor must make the point in terms of Shakespeare's theatre, the same dramatic point could be made by a director who employed entirely different conventions; even a production that introduced live rabbits into the wood and staged the banquet as a kind of Glyndebourne picnic could still have Adam and Orlando play their scene in ironic unawareness of its presence.

In the attention that editors have given to the staging of plays by Shakespeare and his contemporaries they have, to a greater or lesser degree, treated the texts as theatrical artefacts; but at the same time they have often treated them simultaneously as literary artefacts, presenting them as texts for reading rather than for performing. I mentioned that none of the texts of Shakespeare's plays printed in his lifetime—about half of his entire output—marks any divisions into either Acts or scenes. The plays are printed continuously, and so far as we can tell this reflects the way they were played. Act breaks appear not to have been customary in public theatres until about 1609, towards the end of Shakespeare's career. But as early as 1623, when his plays were gathered together in the First Folio, Act and scene divisions were imposed upon many of them—with, to the best of our belief, no authority from either theatre manuscripts or theatrical practice, except perhaps for the very late plays. It was part of the process of making them respectable as literary 'works', undertaken probably in emulation of the Jonson Folio of 1616. Later editors regularized and extended the practice, which was, of course, encouraged by the use of Shakespeare's texts as objects of study to which it is convenient to have a standard system of reference. It affects the typography and layout of editions, and is particularly conspicuous in the Arden Shakespeare, where every editorially created Act division begins on a fresh page with capitalized headings, and each scene—even tiny and wholly artificial ones such as the brief and numerous battle episodes in the last Act of *Antony and Cleopatra*—is set off from its predecessor by white space and indicated by a centred and capitalized label.

Still more 'literary' and at variance with the plays' original staging has been the provision of location markers for each scene. In the eighteenth century this may have arisen mainly out of a concern for the plays' contemporary staging, as I have hinted, but it seems to have developed rather as a result of a literary approach to the plays which saw them as fictions in which every episode had a prescribed location, a location which could sometimes be identified only by resort to the play's sources or to other external evidence. Some of these locations have passed into the plays' mythology; we easily speak, for example, of the 'heath' scenes in *King Lear*, but the word 'heath' occurs in no early text of the play, and was first introduced into the scene headings by Rowe in 1709.[7] The same is true of character lists and speech headings. In *Richard II*, for instance, Shakespeare gives no name to Richard's Queen, who nevertheless plays a part of some importance in the action. Editors, 'irritably', as Keats says, 'reaching after fact and reason', have given her the name of Richard's wife Isabel, who was married to Richard at the historical time of the events of the play, and who was not more than 12 years old when he died. In fact Isabel was Richard's second wife; the character in the play—a woman who feels more than childlike love for her husband—is closer to his first wife, Anne, to whom he had been devoted and with whose portrayal in *Woodstock* Shakespeare's Queen has much in common. Dramatically, the character should remain nameless; her function in the play is simply that of Richard's wife who is also Queen of England, and to give her a name is to slew the play in the direction of a historical fiction.

Up till, I would suggest, around 1960 (very roughly) editorial conventions seemed to be hardening. They can be seen at their most rigid in the earlier volumes of the new Arden Shakespeare, and they were the product of a period during which the division between the academy and the theatre was wide. Between the wars, performances of Shakespeare's plays still owed much to a popular theatrical tradition, still adopted traditional cuts, were only slowly responding to the semi-scholarly influence of William Poel and Granville-Barker, did not even have the opportunity to use the wide range of scholarly paperback editions that are available today. It was natural then that scholars editing the plays should see little connection between their work and the practical theatre. But the post-war period saw a greatly increased emphasis in Shakespeare studies on theatrical values, encouraged by pioneers such as Allardyce Nicoll, Glynne Wickham, and John Russell Brown, and by the development in England's more forward-looking universities—the provincial ones—of Departments of Drama. Slowly this emphasis came to be reflected in a rethinking of editorial conventions which is still going on (and still meeting with resistance). Editors have been able to draw on an increased amount of research into the resources and conventions of the Shakespearian stage, and have themselves taken more of an interest in the living theatre than many of their predecessors did. It is partly a matter of assumptions about readership. Editors who have in mind readers whose interest is mainly academic—who see the plays as primarily literary texts, or even as documents in social history or the history of the language—will feel little need to pay attention to theatrical values, whereas those who conceive that their editions will be read by theatre-goers, and by students who are encouraged to think of the plays in theatrical terms, and may even be used by actors, will approach their task with a different set of assumptions. Moreover, editors familiar with the contemporary theatrical scene are likely to be far more conscious of the wide range of options that Shakespeare's plays permit than those who either took no interest in the theatre or were able to see only performances that worked within a comparatively narrow range of theatrical conventions. We realize now, for example, that, so far from requiring a naturalistic setting, plays written for a non-illusionist theatre may actually gain from neutrality of setting. If Dover Wilson had seen Peter Brook's 'white box' setting for *A Midsummer Night's Dream* in 1970 he would have been unlikely to write directions such as '*A room in the cottage of Peter Quince*', or '*The palace wood, a league from Athens. A mossy stretch of broken ground, cleared of trees by wood-cutters and surrounded by thickets. Moonlight*', or '*Another part of the wood. A grassy plot before a great oak-tree; behind the tree a high bank overhung with creepers, and at one side a thorn-bush. The air is heavy with the scent of blossom.*'[8] Slowly this kind of thing has been abandoned. Early volumes of the Arden Shakespeare still include some locations, usually based on those of the eighteenth-century editors—directions such as, in *Antony and Cleopatra*, '*Athens. A room in Antony's house*'; for the next scene: '*The same. Another room*'; and for the next: '*Rome. Caesar's house*'; not as flowery as Dover Wilson's extravaganzas, but still indicative of a non-theatrical attitude to the text. More recent volumes in the Arden series, and more recent editions such as the New Penguin, the New Cambridge, and the Oxford, abandon directions for location altogether.

Of course, the reader of a complex play such as *Antony and Cleopatra* may be glad of guidance as to where he is in any given scene: guidance such as the theatre can provide by any number of devices, including colour-coding of sets and costumes, variations in accent, significant properties, and so on; and it is reasonable for the editor to provide similar guidance where necessary in his notes; but it seems misleading to place such information in the text itself in a manner that implies naturalistic staging.

A somewhat similar situation obtains with regard to Act and scene divisions. They are obtrusive even in later volumes of the Arden series, but more recent editions tend to downplay them, treating them simply as a convenient means of reference and presenting the text in a manner that stresses its continuity, the fluid merging of one scene into the next, rather than breaking it up into a series of apparently self-contained units. There is a notorious example in *Romeo and Juliet*. As Benvolio leaves the stage he says

> ... 'tis in vain
> To seek him here that means not to be found.

Romeo comes forward and completes the couplet:

> He jests at scars that never felt a wound. (2.1.42–3)

In the play as first printed—doubtless as in Shakespeare's manuscript—this is absolutely continuous. But editors have introduced a scene break at this point, with the result that the old Arden, for example, follows Benvolio's line with the direction *Exeunt*, the capitalized and centred heading SCENE II, the location 'The Same. Capulet's Orchard', and the direction 'Romeo advances' before Romeo breaks the suspense by completing the couplet.[9] Of course, there are some plays where the author clearly had Act divisions in mind—*Henry V* is an obvious example, though there the Choruses themselves provide the markers; but for other plays the scene is a more real unit of action. When I was editing Dekker's *Shoemaker's Holiday* I searched in vain for anything approximating to an Act structure and decided finally to mark only scene divisions.[10] In the Complete Oxford Shakespeare we provide Act and scene references, and Act markers for the plays where they are certainly appropriate: I should have been happy to abandon some of the divisions altogether, but we eventually acknowledged the need to provide a reference system.

Another editorial-cum-theatrical convention that has needed to be rethought in the light of theatrical experimentation is the aside. Early editions rarely indicate that speeches should be delivered 'aside'. Editors with expectations based on naturalistic acting frequently added the direction; more recently, in the face of stylized production methods, and also of new ideas about human behaviour, we have become more wary of doing so. Hamlet's first words—'A little more than kin and less than kind'—were marked *aside* by Theobald and in many later editions, including the recent New Cambridge, but are not so marked in for instance the new Arden or the Oxford (1987), whose editor, G. R. Hibbard, notes: 'Most editors since Theobald (1740) have marked the speech as an *aside*, but its barbed obscurity strongly suggests that it is intended to be heard by Claudius, to puzzle him, and to disturb him.'[11]

Clearly, then, there has been a movement away from prescriptive editing; editors are less inclined than they once were to assume the role of director. This shows itself even in quite small—but none the less significant—details of the text. Punctuation is getting lighter so that the editor, instead of trying to convey each nuance of his own interpretation of the lines, will leave them as open as possible, encouraging the reader or speaker to explore their potential range of meaning. In punctuating texts for the Oxford Shakespeare I found myself consciously trying *not* to add exclamation marks where previous editors had placed them. There is, however, a rather fine line between, on the one hand, editing in a manner that is not over-prescriptive, that leaves the director to do his own directing, and, on the other hand, measuring up to the theatrical dimension of the text so that it is genuinely presented as a theatrical rather than merely a literary text. So, although it seems right that editors should be on their guard against importing into Elizabethan texts notions derived from the theatrical practice of later ages, it does seem desirable to locate these texts within the theatres for which they were written. In the Oxford Shakespeare, for example, we have thought afresh about such matters as the use of an upper level which was certainly possible in Shakespeare's theatre even though modern designers often make no use of it, about the provision of music cues, and about the removal of bodies, especially at the ends of plays, which is necessary in an open-stage theatre without artificial lighting even though it may not be needed in theatres which make use of a front curtain or of lighting blackouts.

Editors have thought afresh, too, about symbolic gestures such as kissing, kneeling, and rising. Take for example a very well-known and important episode in *Coriolanus* which as it happens is already marked by one of Shakespeare's own most eloquent stage directions. Coriolanus's womenfolk, fearful of Rome's destruction, visit him in the enemy camp, hoping to persuade him not to lead the Volscian forces against Rome. His mother, Volumnia, pleads with him in a speech that is full of implicit stage directions, though none is provided by the Folio text. As she works up to a climax, she says:

> He turns away.
> Down, ladies. Let us shame him with our knees.
> To his surname 'Coriolanus' 'longs more pride
> Than pity to our prayers. Down! An end.
> This is the last. So we will home to Rome,

And die among our neighbours.—Nay, behold's.
This boy, that cannot tell what he would have,
But kneels and holds up hands for fellowship,
Does reason our petition with more strength
Than thou hast to deny't.—Come, let us go.
This fellow had a Volscian to his mother.
His wife is in Corioles, and this child
Like him by chance.—Yet give us our dispatch.
I am hushed until our city be afire,
And then I'll speak a little. (5.3.169–83)

Then comes the Folio direction '*Holds her by the hand silent*' after which Coriolanus says:

O mother, mother!
What have you done? Behold, the heavens do ope,
The gods look down, and this unnatural scene
They laugh at. (5.3.183–6)

I said that Volumnia's speech is full of implicit stage directions, so perhaps for this very reason it is not necessary to add many. There can surely be no doubt that all the supplicants must kneel soon after Volumnia has said 'Down, ladies. Let us shame him with our knees.' What is much less obvious is the point at which they should rise. Many editors provide no direction for either action. Some assume that Volumnia at least should have risen by the point at which Coriolanus '*holds her by the hand silent*'. But there is one textual indication against this which is often ignored by both editors and directors. 'The gods look down,' says Coriolanus, 'and this unnatural scene | They laugh at.' What is 'unnatural' about the scene unless, in a total reversal of expectation, the mother is kneeling to her son? And so, it seems to me, an editor who is trying to realize the theatrical dimension of the text owes it to his readers to indicate points for both kneeling and rising by means of stage directions.

The aim—not always formulated—behind directions such as these is to achieve at least one kind of purity, rather than to present hybrid texts reflecting a variety of diverse theatrical traditions, as has happened too often in the past. But even here the intervention of the editor will often be identifiable. The inadequacies, the openness to interpretation, of the original texts are such that an editor will often have to make an arbitrary decision which appears to close options even while providing a necessary clarification. There are points in the text at which the editor must add directions but where he must also exercise choice in either the precise action that he provides for, or its placing, or both. One very basic matter is the question of exits, frequently left unmarked in the original texts, presumably because, though an actor may need to be told when to get on to the stage, he can be more easily trusted to remember when to leave it. The precise point at which he does so may have interpretative consequences. For instance, in the middle of Act 4, scene 1 of *As You Like It* Jaques bids farewell to Orlando and Rosalind with the line

> Nay then, God b'wi'you an you talk in blank verse. (4.1.29–30)

Rosalind then has the following speech:

> Farewell, Monsieur Traveller. Look you lisp, and wear strange suits; disable all the benefits of your own country; be out of love with your nativity, and almost chide God for making you that countenance you are, or I will scarce think you have swam in a gondola. Why, how now, Orlando? (4.1.31–7)

The Folio, where this play was first printed, marks no exit for Jaques, but a responsible editor must provide one as he obviously has to leave the stage. But it could be placed either after the last line he speaks, so that Rosalind says 'Farewell, Monsieur Traveller' as he leaves the stage; or after her 'Farewell, Monsieur Traveller', so that the remainder of her speech up to the point at which she addresses Orlando is a comment on him in his absence; or Jaques could stay to hear what she says about him. The Arden editor adopts and argues for the last option, commenting, 'F does not mark the place at which Jaques leaves the stage. Later folios put it after *blank verse*, in consequence of the adieux exchanged then, without observing that Rosalind must have an audience for her anatomy of the returned traveller.'[12] But an actress might choose to address Jaques in his absence, so the Complete Oxford edition, while also marking Jaques' exit at this point, less prescriptively encloses it in the broken brackets that are our not entirely satisfactory means of signalling directions that are open to a variety of interpretation.

Sometimes we may doubt whether a character should be present at all, and the editor like the director will have to make a decision. For example, both early editions of *Othello* (Q, 1622, and F1, 1623) bring Cassio on with Othello in the senate scene, but as he says nothing and is not addressed, many editors since Capell in the late eighteenth century have dropped him. Yet he had earlier been sent to fetch Othello, and the fact that both early editions (which seem to be of independent origin) bring him on is a point in favour of his silent presence during the bulk of the earlier part of the scene, though the editor has to decide at what point he shall leave, since his presence is scarcely possible after the Duke's departure. So again, the editor must make arbitrary decisions. Such decisions may be intimately linked with the play's original staging. Thus, in Act 5 of *Othello*, after Iago has wounded Cassio, Othello enters and comments on the noises of the action unheard by Roderigo and Cassio; some editors mark Othello's speeches as asides; it seemed to me that in

Shakespeare's theatre they were most likely to have been spoken from the upper level, and I added a conjectural direction to this effect, but I could not assert dogmatically that this is how Shakespeare intended the episode to be played, and should certainly not wish to inhibit a modern director's liberty to play it in any way that would be effective.

Stage business is often certainly required, but we may have difficulty in deciding exactly what it should be. Take for example a crucial moment in the long speech of Innogen in *Cymbeline* when she awakes over the headless body of Cloten, taking it to be that of her husband, Posthumus. The climax of the speech is:

> O,
> Give colour to my pale cheek with thy blood,
> That we the horrider may seem to those
> Which chance to find us! O my lord, my lord! (4.2.332–4)

It is obvious that at this point blood is transferred from the body to Innogen's cheek, though it is not entirely clear how it gets there. In the Complete Oxford Shakespeare we added the direction '*She smears her face with blood.*' Roger Warren, who had been involved in rehearsals of Sir Peter Hall's production with the National Theatre, objected to the phrasing of this direction, arguing that the blood should be involuntarily transferred from corpse to cheek during an embrace rather than that Innogen should deliberately smear herself with it. This indicates the difficult position that the editor is in: in the attempt to do our duty by the theatre we added a direction for necessary action where it had not been added before, but we failed to find a phrasing for this action which would leave open the full range of possibilities that the text permits.

So far I have been discussing comparatively minor areas of editorial choice, ones which have theatrical implications but which do not individually have a significant influence on overall interpretation of the play. Recent years, however, have seen discussion of an area of editorial intervention which does indeed have such an influence. Some of Shakespeare's plays survive in variant early texts, some in Quarto, some in Folio. There are, for example, some 500 differences in wording between *Troilus and Cressida* as it was first printed in the Quarto of 1609 and the same play as printed in the Folio of 1623; the Prologue is present only in the later text. There are over 1,000 verbal differences between the text of *Othello* printed in 1622 and that given in the Folio in the following year, which also adds about 160 lines, including Desdemona's willow song (4.3) and Emilia's remarkable defence of female sexual independence (4.3.85–102), whose presence or absence considerably affects the tone and content of the play. Whereas the seemingly later text of *Othello* adds lines that are not in the earlier text, the later one of *Hamlet*, printed in the Folio, omits about 230 lines—including, for example, Hamlet's last soliloquy, 'How all occasions do inform against me'—that are present in the Quarto of 1604 while also adding some 80 lines that are not in that text, and again including hundreds of verbal variants. The most radical differences are found in the two early texts of *King Lear*. The Folio has over 100 lines that are not found in the Quarto of 1608, but it also lacks close on 300 lines, including an entire scene, that are in that text; there are over 850 other differences in wording, several speeches are assigned to different speakers, and the conduct of the action differs in the two texts.

These facts have been known for a long time, and the standard explanation of them has been that each of the variant texts inadequately represents a lost original, and that the variants are the result of various forms of corruption—printers' errors, scribal misreadings, actors' interpolations, and so on. On this basis, editors since the early eighteenth century—when interventionist editing made its first serious impact on the textual tradition—have conflated the variant texts, adding to one passages that are absent from the other, and choosing among the local variants those that they regarded as the more likely to be genuinely Shakespearian. In the process they have suppressed a great many readings that make perfectly good sense out of deference to a textual theory that has recently been undermined. Some of these can be crucial to interpretation.

A mixture of bibliographical and textual study undertaken during the 1970s suggests that the differences between the early texts of Shakespeare's plays are in many cases a reflection of conscious changes made by Shakespeare himself; that, for example, he first wrote *Othello* without Desdemona's willow song and Emilia's feminist outburst, and added them later; that he did a lot to streamline the text of *Hamlet*; and that he had very serious second thoughts about *King Lear*, making changes to the text as he first conceived it that amount to a radical revision. This thought is reflected for the first time in the recent Complete Works, and in the single-volume Oxford Shakespeare edition of *Hamlet*. It means, if accepted, that all other editions of certain plays by Shakespeare—editions which follow the eighteenth-century practice of conflating early texts—take intervention to the point of distortion, creating hold-all texts that have no basis in the theatre practice of Shakespeare's own time. Granville-Barker delivered an early warning against this practice in his Preface to *King Lear*, of 1927, in which he comments that 'the producer is confronted by the problem of the three hundred lines, or nearly, that the Quartos give and the Folio omits, and of the hundred given by the Folio and omitted from the Quartos. Editors, considering only, it would seem, that the more Shakespeare we get the better, bring practically the whole lot into the play we read. But a producer must ask himself whether these two versions do not come from different prompt-books, and whether the Folio does not, in both cuts and additions, sometimes represent Shakespeare's own second thoughts.' And he adds: 'Where Quarto and Folio offer alternatives, to adopt both versions may make for redundancy or confusion.'[13]

I am not so naive as to suppose that modern theatre directors, by and large, feel bound to adhere to the scripts that posterity has handed to them, nor am I so foolish as to suggest that they should be so bound. Theatre is a living art, and play scripts have a flexibility denied to poetry and the novel. Practice varies enormously. There are some very successful productions that depart substantively from the basic text, others—and sometimes by the same director—that adhere to it with remarkable fidelity. Peter Brook, for example, omitted over 650 lines from his 1955 production of *Titus Andronicus*, a landmark production which—partly because of Laurence Olivier's extraordinary interpretation of the title role—rehabilitated the play's theatrical reputation. The same director's 1970 production of *A Midsummer Night's Dream*, widely regarded as one of the most startlingly revolutionary post-war productions of Shakespeare, played the entire text with only a few minor rearrangements of dialogue. The revolutionary aspects of the production lay in what it did with the settings, costume, casting, and production devices. When Peter Hall was in Stratford in the 1960s he produced *Hamlet* in a text from which about 730 lines had been cut; when he directed the same play as his opening production at the National Theatre, he used a full text. John Barton, in productions of certain of Shakespeare's history plays, has earned himself the reputation of the Colley Cibber of our times by the prodigality with which he has not merely cut and rearranged the plays but has also added to them hundreds of lines of his own composition; yet his productions of the comedies have been among the most sensitive, and textually faithful, of our time. There are some signs of a trend among recent English productions towards textual fullness. This was apparent in David Hare's National Theatre production of *King Lear* (1986) and Peter Hall's of *Antony and Cleopatra* (1987), and I understand that in rehearsal Peter Hall used complete texts of *The Winter's Tale*, *Cymbeline*, and *The Tempest* for his season of the late plays, though there were some cuts in the plays as produced. The Royal Shakespeare Company, perhaps surprisingly, is less purist in general, though 1987 saw a quite exceptional production, by Deborah Warner at the Swan Theatre, of *Titus Andronicus* which—for the first time, to the best of my belief, on the English stage—used a complete text and in the process did a great deal to increase respect both for the play itself and for the audiences that made it popular in its own time.

Variations in the texts of plays are matched also by variations in the staging, a process which is made inevitable by the absence of a direct line of performance tradition from Shakespeare's time to ours. Seasoned theatre-goers are accustomed to performances in modern dress, in dress of a wide range of historical periods, in dress of no period at all, even to undress; they are accustomed to both minimalist and maximalist productions—ones that on the one hand, like the Cheek by Jowl *Macbeth* (1987), dispense with all properties, use the same performer in more than one role, and (in this case) allocate no individual performers to the roles of the Witches but present them as disembodied voices with their lines distributed among other members of the cast; on the other hand, theatre-goers know they may see productions, even in these economically distressed times, with elaborate scenery, numerous extras, and complex production devices which often play a kind of fantasy on the original text, transforming it into a performance that is, for better or for worse, more expressive of the director's than of the playwright's imagination.

The fact remains, however, that even the freest of directors, even those who seem to be using the original text as little more than a quarry from which they can hew the material that suits their own imaginative concepts while rejecting or distorting anything, such as the text's obvious implications, that gets in their way—even such directors need something to start from, and what they start from will almost invariably be a text that has been subjected to editorial intervention. It is also a fact, of course, that most directors acknowledge a responsibility to the playwright's imagination, and that some are deeply concerned with the playwright's original script, whether they attempt to perform it as faithfully as modern stage conditions will permit, or to translate it into the language of modern theatre. It is desirable that such directors should be aware that an edition is not simply a glass through which the dramatist's intentions are revealed in all their original purity; that, at least for our early drama, no such return to original truth is possible; and that in every edition one layer of interpretation has already been superimposed on the original even in the attempt to free the early texts of their corruptions and indeterminacies.

It is as well, in other words, that directors should know that other options than those suggested by the edited text under their hands may well be open to them: that, to repeat a small example, Jaques might leave before, during, or after Rosalind's speech about him, or, to give larger examples, omissions from the conflated texts of *Hamlet* of the Prince's last soliloquy, or of *King Lear* of the scene (4.3 in conflated texts) in which Cordelia tells a Gentleman of the plight of her distressed, maddened father seem to be justified by the practice of Shakespeare's own company. Both directors and actors should be aware, too, that the spelling and punctuation in all the texts that they are likely to use has been modernized, that there is no consistent editorial practice of modernization, and that consequently the very form of words that the actors have to speak is open to interpretation. Some editors, for instance, are reluctant to commit themselves to a process of thorough modernization in texts which they think of as having a primarily scholarly readership, and so offer what is to me an anomalous mish-mash of old and new forms. There was a particular fashion for this in Arden editions of the fifties and sixties, which often retain archaic forms such as 'murther' (for 'murder'), 'banket' (for 'banquet'), 'accompt' (for 'account'), 'enow' (for 'enough'), 'moe' (for 'more'), 'Norweyan' (for 'Norwegian'), 'Troyan' (for 'Trojan'), and so on, and I often notice actors conscientiously but misguidedly trying to convey such spellings through pronunciation. There might be some point in a thorough attempt to reconstruct the pronunciation of Shakespeare's time in a modern performance, but I see no point at all (except perhaps occasionally to preserve a rhyme) in introducing a selection of such pronunciations into a generally modernized text.

Actors might do well to realize, too, that punctuation is often more flexible than the editor can suggest. Shakespeare's own punctuation seems to have been very light. Elizabethan printers felt free to treat the punctuation of the manuscripts from which they worked according to the conventions of their own printing houses, and modern editions have too often been based on texts in which a heavily prescriptive system has been superimposed upon that of the early editions. I have heard of directors who work initially with texts from which all the punctuation has been removed, and I can see the virtue in such a procedure. Again, though this may seem a matter of insignificant minutiae, it can affect moments that are prominent in the action. Take, for example, Claudius's culminating reaction to the play scene in *Hamlet*. The words he speaks are 'Give me some light. Away' (3.2.257), and in both the good Quarto and the Folio texts the terminal punctuation is simply a full stop. Many editors have replaced this with an exclamation mark, and, as if in deference to this, actors have traditionally used the words as an opportunity for a great histrionic moment, a violent eruption of concealed guilt. Peter Hall's 1965 production showed that the moment could be equally effective if the interpolated exclamation mark was ignored. His Claudius simply stood, glared at Hamlet, and spoke the line with scornful calm, rather rebuking Hamlet for a lapse of taste than showing the depths of his own soul. In a curious way, it achieved a *coup-de-théâtre* by denying one. I am not, of course, saying that one of these ways of playing the moment is right, the other wrong. But editorial intervention should not be allowed to close the text's openness to variant interpretation, and both director and actor need to know how, as it were, to 'read' the text in order to feel the freedom to explore it within the appropriate limits.

The corollary of what I have been saying is not that editors should refrain from interpretation. They may do their best to be unobtrusive; for instance, it was directly because of the various ways in which I had seen the play scene in *Hamlet* acted that, in the Oxford Shakespeare, we did not punctuate Claudius's reaction with an exclamation mark. But, as I hope I have shown, conscientious editing is not compatible with a policy of total non-intervention. What I am suggesting is that readers, including theatre practitioners, need to learn how to use edited texts. Editors should not be deferred to; their decisions should be questioned, their interpretations greeted with proper scepticism; but this can be satisfactorily done only on the basis of an informed understanding of the nature of the original documents and of the editorial methods that have been applied to them. If such an understanding exists, then directors and actors may work with a more controlled freedom in their handling of the texts we offer them; if it does not, they had better choose their editors with care and then accept their guidance. In the past, scholars were often accused of paying too little attention to the theatre. There was much justice in the accusation. But things have changed. Many modern scholars are profoundly conscious of theatrical values, deeply aware that play scripts reach consummation only in performance. It would now not be entirely unjust, I suggest, for scholars to accuse the theatre of paying too little attention to their work, because I believe that theatre people, by becoming more aware of scholarly procedures, could learn something useful to themselves about the texts with which they work.

28

The First Folio:
Where Should We be Without it?

Shakespeare's death in April 1616 was marked, so far as we can tell, by no published tributes. This may seem odd. When Sir Philip Sidney died in 1586 he was given a state funeral extraordinary in its pomp and circumstance followed by the publication of numerous tributes both in England and on the Continent.[1] Edmund Spenser died in poverty in 1599, but the Earl of Essex paid his funeral expenses and he was buried in Westminster Abbey where, says William Camden, his hearse 'was attended by poets, and mournful elegies and poems, with the pens that wrote them, were thrown into his tomb'.[2] Memorial verses by a number of poets, some published soon after he died, survive both in print and in manuscript. Ben Jonson too died poor, in 1637, but he too was buried in the Abbey; a volume of memorial verses, *Jonsonus Virbius*, appeared soon after his death, and a subscription started to raise money for a memorial was thwarted only by the Civil War. Even poor Robert Greene's corpse is said to have been honored with a crown of bays, and his death in 1592 was marked by, admittedly, vituperative comments from enemies, as well as by the publication of a eulogy, *Greene's Funerals*, by one R. B. So it is natural to ask why the death of the man now regarded as the greatest artist of them all was not similarly marked.

Various answers are possible. One is that Sidney was an aristocrat with many claims to fame other than his literary achievement—which indeed was relatively little known when he died; that Spenser was a courtier and public servant as well as a poet; and that Jonson had worked extensively for the court and had achieved recognition from the royal family. It is only fair to note too that many other writers of the period now greatly admired, such as John Lyly, Thomas Dekker, Thomas Middleton, John Webster, and John Ford, have no memorial—we don't even know in what year Webster or Ford died. But Shakespeare, as principal dramatist and shareholder of the King's Men, and consequently a member of the royal household, must also have been known at court and had already in his lifetime been the subject of a number of printed and other tributes. If his death itself was not marked in the way of some of his great contemporaries', this is partly, I suggest, because he was the first great literary commuter. Playwrights naturally based themselves in London. But Shakespeare died in Stratford, not London; he could have been buried in the Abbey only with difficulty. Of course his work was necessarily based on the capital, and he certainly had lodgings there, although he seems to have changed them often enough to have been regarded as having no fixed address—certainly the tax inspectors had difficulty in keeping track of him. But I suspect that he had done a good deal more of his writing in Stratford than is generally supposed: he had bought a fine, large house there early in his career, and I should be surprised if, in spite of the difficulties of travel, he did not contrive to spend long periods of creative time in the peace and quiet of a study in New Place.

But in fact Shakespeare was commemorated; only a time lag creates a mistaken impression of indifference. He has two main memorials. One is the bust in Holy Trinity Church with its laudatory inscriptions in both Latin and English. This was in place by 1623, seven years after he died; inevitably it took time to commission, execute, and set in place in Stratford a sculpture made in a London workshop. The other, far greater memorial is the Folio volume M[aste]r William Shakespeare's Comedies, Histories and Tragedies published in the same year. This too could not have appeared rapidly after Shakespeare died. We do not know when plans to publish it were inaugurated. It is surely significant that the only theatre people mentioned in Shakespeare's will are John Heminges and Henry Condell, who signed the Epistle Dedicatory to the Folio, along with Richard Burbage, who had died before the book went to press. All three were colleagues of long standing who had worked with Shakespeare through most of his career. Shakespeare himself may have discussed with them the possibility of a collection of his plays, and the bequests to them of money to buy mourning rings may mark some kind of bond that they would memorialize as well as mourn him. It would not be at all surprising if the project took seven years to come to fruition; as anyone who has edited the Complete Works has reason to know, big books take a long time to prepare. The Folio is a very big book, and a lot of work had to go into its preparation even before a start could be made on its printing, which itself lasted for nearly two years.

It is also worth remarking that although the Folio is the first printed tribute to Shakespeare, this was an age in which poems circulated extensively in manuscript as well as in print. There is, for instance, a memorial poem to Shakespeare by William Basse which, although not printed until 1633, when it was attributed to John Donne in his Poems, survives in a large number of manuscripts—twenty-seven are recorded in the Oxford Textual Companion, with the statement that 'No doubt a further search would uncover further copies'.[3] This poem makes the suggestion that Shakespeare, like some of his illustrious forebears, might have been buried in the Abbey beside them:

> Renownèd Spenser, lie a thought more nigh
> To learnèd Chaucer; and rare Beaumont, lie
> A little nearer Spenser, to make room
> For Shakespeare in your threefold, fourfold tomb.

The lines go on to suggest that, if room cannot be found for Shakespeare in the Abbey, they may themselves appear upon 'this carvèd marble of thine own', which seems to indicate that their author was submitting his verses for possible publication by the monument makers. Although they had not appeared in print when the Folio was published, Ben Jonson had clearly read them since in his poem in praise of Shakespeare he writes:

> My Shakespeare, rise; I will not lodge thee by
> Chaucer, or Spenser, or bid Beaumont lie
> A little further to make thee a room.

Perhaps, then, there is no real reason to suggest that Shakespeare's death was less adequately commemorated than his later admirers might have hoped. And the great Folio is a monument whose importance cannot be exaggerated but is in danger of being underestimated. In this essay I should like to say something about the way that its compilers worked and the effect that this has had upon later ages' perception of Shakespeare.

II

We must consider first the situation at the time of his death. All his poems had appeared in print except for a few disputed lyrics, including 'Shall I die?' He had clearly authorized the publication of the narrative poems and 'The Phoenix and Turtle'; the *Sonnets* had appeared in 1609 under less certain auspices, and in *The Passionate Pilgrim* of 1599 William Jaggard had caused offence by ascribing to Shakespeare poems that he certainly did not write.

With the plays, the situation is different. None of his plays had appeared with the kind of authorizing documents represented by the dedications to the narrative poems; indeed it is generally supposed that Shakespeare had had nothing to do with the publication by printing of any of his plays. For him, it would seem, publication was performance. Nevertheless, quarto editions of reasonably high textual authority had appeared of thirteen plays now generally ascribed to him: they are *Titus Andronicus* (1594), *Love's Labor's Lost* (1598), *Richard III* (1597), *A Midsummer*

Night's Dream (1600), *Romeo and Juliet* (1597), *Richard II* (1597), *The Merchant of Venice* (1600), *1 Henry IV* (1598), *2 Henry IV* (1600), *Much Ado About Nothing* (1600), *Hamlet* (1604), *Troilus and Cressida* (1609), and *King Lear* (1608). *Othello* was to follow, in 1622. Another four plays—those now known as *2 and 3 Henry VI*, (1594, 1595), *The Merry Wives of Windsor* (1602), and *Henry V* (1600)—had appeared in texts that differ seriously enough from those later published in the Folio for them to have been regarded as unauthorized, 'bad' quartos. To these eighteen texts we may add *The Troublesome Reign of King John* (1594), which a few scholars have believed to be derived from Shakespeare's *King John*, although it is more generally regarded as a source play, and *The Taming of a Shrew* (1594), of which the reverse is true. Neither bears a close relationship to the texts printed in the Folio. Many of these texts had been reprinted by 1616, some several times, and *Richard II* had been reissued with the addition in 1608 of the episode of Richard's abdication that had been absent from the three editions printed while Queen Elizabeth was alive.

In addition to these texts, at the time of Shakespeare's death certain others had been printed with an ascription to him. These are *The London Prodigal*, a citizen comedy published in 1605, in which posterity has taken little interest; the short but powerful domestic tragedy known as *A Yorkshire Tragedy*, entered as Shakespeare's in the Stationers' Register in 1608 and published as by him in the same year, but now ascribed to Thomas Middleton and occasionally performed; and *Pericles*, published in 1609.

As time passed, other publishing projects materialized. The most important is Thomas Pavier's aborted attempt, along with the printer William Jaggard, to publish an incomplete collection of Shakespeare's plays in 1619. It was a shady venture, as is witnessed by the fact that some of the volumes were falsely dated, apparently in an attempt to evade copyright restrictions. Ten volumes had appeared before the Lord Chamberlain intervened, obtaining an injunction from the Stationers' company that 'no plays that His Majesty's players do play shall be printed without consent of some of them'.[4] All the volumes were reprints of existing quartos, and they included *A Yorkshire Tragedy* and *The First Part of Sir John Oldcastle*, a history play exploiting the popularity of Shakespeare's Falstaff plays, which had been published anonymously in 1600 but was now, in a falsely dated reprint of the 1600 quarto, declared to have been 'Written by William Shakespeare'.

The Lord Chamberlain's intervention was almost certainly prompted by the King's Men. This may, as Gary Taylor suggests, have been 'because Pavier's attempt persuaded them that they should oversee the publication of Shakespeare's work personally', but even more suggestive is his alternative hypothesis, that 'their plans for the Folio were already under way'.[5] There is no objective evidence for this, but my suspicion is based upon my hunch that Shakespeare's colleagues had long intended to memorialize him with a volume that would rival, if not surpass, the great Folio of Ben Jonson's *Works*—not, be it noted, simply plays—which had appeared in the year Shakespeare died. The Pavier project may have hastened their rate of progress, and it may be significant that the printer, Jaggard, was the same for both. To some extent the Folio must have been a labour of love, a pious act of memorialization; but it was also a commercial venture that could bring financial profit to the King's Men as well as to the publishers and printers.[6] We are accustomed to think of Heminges and Condell as the editors of the volume, and in the dedication they accept responsibility for its 'faults...if any be committed', describing themselves as 'a pair...careful to show their gratitude both to the living [i.e. the dedicatees] and the dead', but editing was only a sideline for them. Heminges was a founder-member of the Lord Chamberlain's company in 1594, and, like Shakespeare, stayed with it throughout his career; like Shakespeare, he made a good deal of money out of it. An actor, he seems also to have been one of the company's main businessmen. He is caricatured in verses on the burning of the Globe in 1613 as 'old stuttering Heminges' and three years later is described as 'old Master Heminges' in a masque by Ben Jonson. The last reference to him as an actor is in 1611, which may mean that he gave himself up to business after that; but literary editing can at best have been only a part-time activity. Condell too was not a young man, and appears to have gone on acting until around 1619, at least. It is not surprising that some people have suspected that a share of the editorial duties may have been undertaken by Ben Jonson, who contributed lines on the portrait and his famous, if qualified, eulogy on Shakespeare, and possibly even by Ralph Crane, who has been identified as the scribe responsible for making transcripts of some of the plays especially executed for the volume (and whom one sometimes suspects of being several different men masquerading as one).[7] In speaking of Heminges and Condell, and even of Ben Jonson, as editors of the Folio, we must be using the term to mean those who took the more important decisions rather than those who performed the more mundane but demanding tasks of, for example, transcription, copy-editing, and proof-reading, some of which were no less laborious and demanding of scholarly ability than those undertaken by the editors of scholarly editions at the present time. But it is not always easy to distinguish between decisions which might have been made by, as it were, overseers of the project and others which might have been the responsibility of the publishers and printers.

What exactly were the more important decisions? The first was to publish the book at all. It was a bold thing to do, a declaration of faith in Shakespeare's selling power as a dramatist for reading as well as performing. No Folio edition made up entirely of plays by an English dramatist had previously appeared. The closest precedent was the Folio of Ben Jonson's works of 1616. Jonson was mocked for this in an epigram entitled 'To Mr Ben Jonson demanding the reason why he called his plays "works"':

Pray tell me, Ben, where doth the mystery lurk:
What others call a play you call a work.[8]

But this is rather unfair, since the volume included non-dramatic writings as well as plays. The publishers' faith in Shakespeare was justified by the success of the volume, in spite of its high selling price of around £1 (depending on, for example, whether it was bought bound or unbound): a reprint was called for after nine years, in 1632, whereas the Jonson Folio was not reprinted until twenty-four years after first publication, in 1640.

Another important task was to decide on the preliminaries to the book, including the engraving of Shakespeare by Martin Droeshout which, along with the bust in Holy Trinity Church, Stratford-upon-Avon, provides us with our principal evidence of Shakespeare's physical appearance. Even Ben Jonson's volume had not been adorned with a portrait of the author. Probably Shakespeare's was specially commissioned; it may have been made from a pre-existent drawing that has not survived. Other tasks were the composition of the dedication, to the Earls of Pembroke and Montgomery, and the epistle 'To the great variety of readers', both signed by Heminges and Condell, as well as the assembling of the commendatory verses by Jonson, Hugh Holland, Leonard Digges, and James Mabbe. It would be interesting to know whether these, too, were commissioned; Digges, at least, had a personal association with Shakespeare and so may well have written mainly out of personal affection: his stepfather, Thomas Russell, lived at Alderminster, near Stratford, and was the executor of Shakespeare's will.

The preliminaries to the Folio are of genuine interest, but of far greater consequence were the editors' decisions about what to include and to exclude. This has had a paramount influence upon our perception of the canon of Shakespeare's work. The decision to exclude poems seems particularly perverse, in that these were the only works that Shakespeare clearly intended to be read. There may well have been problems about copyright. The *Sonnets*, published in 1609, had not been much of a success, judging by the absence of reprints, so Thorpe probably still had unsold copies; *Venus and Adonis* and *The Rape of Lucrece*, on the other hand, had been reprinted regularly since they first appeared in 1593 and 1594 respectively, so their publishers too would not wish to part with the rights. So the title chosen for the volume, *M[aste]r William Shakespeare's Comedies, Histories and Tragedies*, may reflect a desire not so much, as has been suspected, to avoid Jonson's term 'works' as to emphasize the range of Shakespeare's achievement. But, paradoxically, the decision not to include the poems in a volume that otherwise aimed at completeness had the effect for centuries of reducing the impression of Shakespeare's range by drawing attention away from his achievement as a non-dramatic poet. The poems were excluded from reprints of the Folio throughout the seventeenth century, and the content of eighteenth-century editions continued to reflect that of the Folio, with the poems issued at best in supplementary volumes, until Malone's edition of 1780. Partly, no doubt, for this reason, the sonnets were relatively little known until the Romantic period, and there is no serious critical discussion of the narrative poems before Coleridge's, in the *Biographia Literaria* of 1817.

The choice of plays for inclusion and exclusion must have reflected Heminges and Condell's familiarity with Shakespeare's production during the greater part of his career. Their omission of certain plays that had already been ascribed to Shakespeare has been taken ever since as evidence that he did not write them: it would be difficult to deny that he wrote both *A Yorkshire Tragedy* and *The London Prodigal* if they had been printed in the Folio. But Heminges and Condell's implicit testimony has not always been believed. They also omitted *Pericles* and *The Two Noble Kinsmen*, both now ascribed in whole or in part to Shakespeare. The omission of *Pericles* cannot be attributed simply to the fact that the edition printed in 1608 is corrupt; the play remained in the repertory during the 1620s, so the company should have been able to supply a good text. Perhaps Heminges and Condell omitted both plays because they knew that in them Shakespeare had a collaborator. Their decision had a damaging effect on the reputation of *The Two Noble Kinsmen*, which until recently has been treated as part of the Beaumont and Fletcher canon instead of being included in editions of Shakespeare. Shakespeare and Fletcher's joint authorship of this play is attested to in the 1634 quarto; no such testimony survives to the now largely accepted joint authorship of a play that was included in the Folio, *All is True*, or *Henry VIII*; if we believe in this (as I, for one, do), we must suppose that the anomaly is accounted for by the editors' desire to complete the cycle of plays about English history. Unfortunately, they also omitted the other play on which we have good reason to believe that Shakespeare collaborated with Fletcher, *Cardenio*, and so may well be held responsible for its failure to survive. Might they also have included a play called *Love's Labour's Won*? Probably we shall never know.

Heminges and Condell included in the Folio eighteen plays that had not previously appeared in print (if we regard *The Troublesome Reign of King John* and *The Taming of a Shrew* as independent plays). This is their single most important influence on our perception of Shakespeare. It is not possible to say with absolute certainty that if some of the most highly regarded of Shakespeare's plays, including *Julius Caesar*, *As You Like It*, *Twelfth Night*, *Macbeth*, *Coriolanus*, and *Antony and Cleopatra*, had not been printed in the Folio, they would not have survived: after all, one of Shakespeare's plays, *Othello*, appeared for the first time in print in 1622, after he died and before the Folio was published, and there is no absolute reason that other unpublished plays might not have reached the bookstalls, with or without the King's Men's permission, if the Folio had not appeared. On the other hand, there is no guarantee that they would, and it may be worth contemplating what would have been the nature of our loss if they had not.

Without the plays first printed in the Folio, Shakespeare's comedies would have been greatly depleted. We should have lacked three of the earliest: *The Two Gentlemen of Verona*, *The Taming of the Shrew*, and *The Comedy of Errors*; two of the greatest: *As You Like It* and *Twelfth Night*; the two that have been designated 'problem comedies': *Measure for Measure* and *All's Well that Ends Well*; and all the 'last plays', or romances, except *Pericles*. In addition, *The Merry Wives of Windsor* would have been represented only by the grossly inferior short quarto of 1602. The English history plays would have lacked their beginning—*1 Henry VI*—and their end—*All is True* (as we should certainly have called the lost play, though we should have had no external evidence that Shakespeare had anything to do with it); we should have lacked *King John*; Parts Two and Three of *Henry VI* would have been represented only by their anonymously printed early texts and again would have been known by the titles restored by the Oxford editors, *The First Part of the Contention* and *The True Tragedy of Richard, Duke of York*; and *Henry V* would have been known only in the truncated, garbled, and anonymously printed text of 1600, lacking, for example, all the speeches of the Chorus. Without the Folio, Shakespeare's only play about Roman history would have been *Titus Andronicus*—no *Julius Caesar*, *Coriolanus*, or *Antony and Cleopatra*; in the absence of *Macbeth* there would have been only three 'great tragedies', not four; *Timon of Athens* would have been unknown, *King Lear* would have been represented only by the badly printed quarto, and *Othello* would have lacked the willow song and other passages unique to the Folio text.

Perhaps the most impressive witness to the Folio editors' declared ambition to 'keep the memory of so worthy a friend and fellow alive as was our Shakespeare' is the care which they bestowed on the texts they printed. It is not easy to estimate how much they did to the texts unique to the Folio. They must have received manuscripts of these texts, presumably from the players (unless any of them had come directly from Shakespeare or his executors); it is clear that some, such as *The Comedy of Errors* and *All's Well that Ends Well*, were set up from the author's pre-performance manuscripts, which the company may have held. Others, such as *The Tempest* and *The Winter's Tale*, came from transcripts, usually supposed to have been undertaken by Ralph Crane, possibly at the instigation of the editors, who were perhaps unable to obtain a prompt-book for those plays still in the repertoire. The two Folio-only plays that seem closest to theatrical copy are *Julius Caesar* and *Macbeth*, but a transcript may have been used. (It is worth bearing in mind that the process of preparing a manuscript for printing, along with its treatment in the printing house, may have rendered it worthless for any purpose other than the lining of pie dishes or other such base uses. For this reason, as Peter Blayney writes, 'the manuscript supplied would not usually have been "the allowed book" then being used for performance'.[9] In other words, the theory that any play was printed directly from a prompt-book implies belief that it had been discarded by the players.)

For the plays that had previously appeared in print, on the other hand, we have points of comparison. It would presumably have been possible for the editors simply to hand over to the printers a copy of a printed text of each of these plays and tell them to get on with it. Rarely, if ever, did they do this, even though to have done so would have saved both the editors and their printers a great deal of trouble. Their normal practice seems to have been to select a printed copy (not necessarily of the first edition, which of course may not have been easily available) and to have this annotated with changes derived from a theatrical copy (probably a manuscript, but conceivably a printed text used as a prompt copy). The selection was itself an important matter. For no play did the editors choose one of those versions which twentieth-century scholars have designated 'bad' quartos. These texts are currently a matter of controversy, but the fact that Heminges and Condell avoided, for example, the 1600 quarto of *Henry V* and the 1603 *Hamlet* is enough to cast suspicion on the authenticity of these editions, though not to deny their intrinsic interest.

The task of comparison and annotation seems not always to have been executed with exemplary thoroughness. For some plays, such as *Love's Labour's Lost* and *Much Ado about Nothing*, the changes are slight and fail to make corrections or provide information about staging, which must be presumed to have existed in any manuscript from which a performance could adequately have been regulated. For others, changes are more substantial, though not pervasive. *Titus Andronicus*, for example, was printed from a copy of the third quarto of 1611, but with the addition of a scene that had not appeared in any of the quartos, (the 'fly' scene), and with other changes, some of which reflect theatrical practice after the introduction of Act intervals, around 1608. And for a few plays the process of annotation was remarkably thorough, resulting in copy that the printers must have found difficult to read. For *Troilus and Cressida*, for example, a copy of the 1609 quarto appears to have been marked up with some 500 variants, an average of between seventeen and eighteen changes on each page—or one every two to three lines—made after comparison with a scribal prompt-book on which revisions for production at the Globe had been marked. Most pains were taken over *King Lear*, for which, if we have writ our annals true (a phrase that I should not have been able to use had it not been for the Folio), a copy of the second quarto was marked up with the addition from a prompt-book of around 100 full lines that are not in the quarto. The copy was also marked for omission of close to 300 lines, including an entire scene, that *are* in the quarto, and contains over 850 verbal variants, including changes and additions to stage directions and reassignment of several speeches to different speakers. The result, with deletions, additions, interlineations, and interleaved sheets, must have been a compositor's nightmare.

It is hard to believe that the editors would have gone to all this trouble, and have caused so much trouble to their printers, had they not believed that they would have failed to do justice to the man they wished to commemorate if they had printed his plays from the quartos—even from the 'good' quartos—which many subsequent editors have preferred over the Folio texts. They must also have believed that the prompt-books that they used as a basis for what they regarded as necessary correction more closely represented the form in which their author would have wished to see them in print. The result of all their work is that for a number of Shakespeare's plays we have far better evidence of the form and manner in which these plays were actually performed than if only the quartos had survived, or if Heminges and Condell had taken the easier way out and simply reprinted quartos. The Folio is a tribute to Shakespeare the dramatist, an affirmation of the belief that his plays reached full fruition only in the theatre.

There is a corollary of this to which I should like to draw attention. Some of Shakespeare's plays are much longer than others, and than most of the other plays written around the same time. This has given rise to a belief on the part of some scholars that the longest plays could never have been acted in their entirety. Richard Dutton writes, 'There is substantial evidence of a Shakespeare who regularly wrote, with some facility, plays too long and complex to be staged in the theater of his day, plays for which the only plausible audience was one of readers.'[10] This idea seems to me to be decisively disproved by the Folio. It is true that the Folio versions of certain plays, including *Hamlet* and *King Lear*, are shorter by two or three hundred lines than their quarto counterparts, but they are still long plays, much longer than, for instance, *A Midsummer Night's Dream* or *The Tempest*; and *Troilus and Cressida*, which was also revised by comparing it with a theatre manuscript, was not shortened in the process and is the third longest of the plays, shorter only than *Richard III* and *Hamlet*. Yet if, as bibliographical scholarship has amply demonstrated, the Folio texts of these plays were prepared from theatre manuscripts, there are no grounds for arguing that Shakespeare was writing in the knowledge that any of his plays, even the longest, would necessarily be shortened before they reached the stage. We must accept the idea not merely that Shakespeare wrote long plays but that his company performed them and his audiences accepted them, even if they did last longer than the 'two hours' that the Prologue to *Romeo and Juliet* optimistically set forth as the length of the performance.[11]

Another corollary of the Folio editors' desire to bring the texts into line with theatrical practice is, of course, that the evidence most readily available to them, at least for plays still in the repertory of the King's Men, related to the manner in which the plays were presented in their time, rather than that at which the plays were first performed. It is for this reason that they print, for example, what is pretty certainly an adapted text of *Macbeth*, rather than the play as first acted.

An important effect of changes in theatre practice is the presence, in the Folio, of Act and scene divisions in a number of plays. None of the plays printed during Shakespeare's lifetime is divided into either Acts or scenes (though it is clear that in some plays he had the classically derived five-Act structure in mind as he wrote);

there is every reason to believe that until about 1608, plays in the public theatres, even the longest, were acted without interruption.[12] The editors of the Folio, however, clearly set out with the intention of dividing all the plays into Acts, although they abandoned this practice in the later part of the volume. Some of the subdivisions indicated in Folio texts undoubtedly reflect theatrical practice, but others are no less clearly editorial, and some are grotesquely inappropriate, as readers will testify who have had the experience of coming, possibly with relief, to what is marked as the end of Act 4 of *Love's Labour's Lost* only to find that they are only half way through the play. Although the Folio editors' intention to divide all the plays was not carried through—some plays, such as *Romeo and Juliet* and *Antony and Cleopatra*, were printed with no divisions, others, such as *Hamlet*, were only partially divided—what they did encouraged later editors to complete the process. Thus, the presentation of the plays was brought closer to that of classical drama, resulting in printed texts that misrepresent the manner in which most of the plays were originally given, breaking the flow of the action. Recognizing this, modern editors during the past thirty or forty years have done what they can to minimize Act and scene breaks; had it not been for the Folio, they would very likely be printing the plays continuously, as in the quartos, a policy that might well have had far-reaching effects on theatrical practice—and, indeed, on theatre economics as affected by bar receipts during intervals.

The other single most important decision facing the editors of the Folio was how to arrange the volume's contents. They might have arranged the plays according to order of composition. They might even have told their readers when the plays were written, thus saving scholars of later generations an enormous amount of trouble. Regrettably, they decided instead to group the plays according to the categories named in the title of their volume: comedies, histories, and tragedies. This was not a straightforward task, and the manner in which they approached it has had far-reaching effects. On quarto publication, only six of the plays had been assigned more or less precisely to the categories in which they were to be placed in the Folio: *Titus Andronicus* was 'A Roman tragedy', *Romeo and Juliet* an 'excellent conceited tragedy' in 1597 and a 'most lamentable tragedy' in 1599, *Love's Labour's Lost* a 'pleasant conceited comedy', *The Merry Wives of Windsor* a comedy, *Hamlet* a tragical history on the title-pages of the first and second quartos, and a straightforward tragedy on the head-title of the second quarto, and *Othello* a tragedy. You may note that this list includes none of the histories. Another five plays were assigned to no category— these are the first printed version of Part Two of *Henry VI*, the second part of *Henry IV*, and three comedies: *A Midsummer Night's Dream*, *Much Ado About Nothing*, and *The Two Noble Kinsmen*. One play, *Pericles*, was described simply as a 'play'. Two of the plays were classed as histories in both the Folio and the quarto: Part One of *Henry IV* and *Henry V* (a Chronicle History), but three of the Folio histories were called tragedies on first publication: the first printed version of *3 Henry VI*, *Richard II*, and

Richard III. One of the Folio comedies, *The Merchant of Venice* was a history on its title-page and a comical history according to its head-title, and two of the Folio tragedies started off as histories: *King Lear* was a chronicle history on its title-page and a history on its head-title, and *Troilus and Cressida* was a 'famous history'.

The most conspicuous anomalies in the Folio's classification relate to the plays there classified as histories. The word 'history' had a broad signification; it could be used of any narrative, not just a historical one. The Folio editors chose to use it only in the historical sense, and they also restricted it to plays based on medieval and Tudor English history. In doing so, they obscured the tragical nature of Shakespeare's treatment of the final part of the reign of Henry VI and the reigns of Richard II and Richard III, and ignored the historical aspects of the reign of King Lear as well as those of the plays based on Roman history that had not appeared in quarto. They were clearly intent on emphasizing the biographical aspects of the history plays— only one, *Richard III*, is described as a tragedy, and even that is 'The Life and Death of Richard III' in the running titles. To this extent, their procedure takes the plays away from the theatre in the direction of narrative history. To this end, they pretty certainly altered the titles under which some of the plays had been performed: the second and third parts of *Henry VI* seem to have been known in the theatres of the 1590s as the First and Second Parts of *The Contention betwixt the two Famous Houses of York and Lancaster* (or some equally unwieldy variant of this), and the play printed as *Henry VIII* in the Folio is three times alluded to as *All is True*, never unequivocally as *Henry VIII*, in accounts of the burning of the Globe: indeed the ballad commemorating that occasion has as the last words of its refrain the words 'and yet all this is true'.

Editorial decisions about genre affect other plays than those that had already appeared in print: the Roman tragedies and *Macbeth* are no less historical narratives than the plays centered on the lives of English kings, and *Cymbeline* is a historical as well as a comical play. Shakespeare's work is essentially eclectic, often drawing on a wide variety of literary and dramatic traditions and conventions within a single play. In attempting to confine it within the straitjacket of three categories, Heminges and Condell were less true to his memory than they might have wished.

There are, then, two principal ways in which the First Folio has affected our image of Shakespeare. One derives from its editorial procedures: its selection of editions and manuscripts to reprint, its employment of Ralph Crane as a transcriber, its imposition of Act and scene divisions on many of the plays, its groupings of the plays according to generic divisions, and its varying of their original titles to fit this grouping. For good and for ill, these and related matters have shaped the way in which succeeding generations have thought and written about their author, and in which the plays have been presented, both in print and on the stage.

But most important of all is the inclusion in the Folio of all those plays that had not previously reached print, and that might never have done so had it not been for the efforts of Heminges, Condell, and their colleagues. Without them, it is not too much to say, the history of the world would have been different. Shakespeare, shorn of eighteen of his plays, would not have been the pre-eminent dramatist that he now is. The English language would be far less rich. Countless works of art in many kinds that have been inspired by the plays could not have come into existence: Verdi, for instance, could not have composed *Macbeth*, or Schubert, 'Who is Sylvia?' and 'Hark, hark the lark'. W. H. Auden could not have written 'The Sea and the Mirror', or Marina Warner *Indigo*; for better or for worse, we should be without *The Forbidden Planet* and *Return to the Forbidden Planet*. Thomas Hardy's *Under the Greenwood Tree*, Julian Slade's musical comedy *Salad Days*, and Noël Coward's *Present Laughter* would have had different titles; so would Dorothy Sayers' *Gaudy Night*, Aldous Huxley's *Brave New World*, and R. C. Sherriff's *Journey's End*. The careers of most of our greatest actors and directors would have been different. How many young actresses could have made their mark without being able to play Perdita or Miranda, Rosalind or Viola, Isabella or Helen? Where would the reputations of David Garrick, Sarah Siddons, and W. C. Macready be without *Macbeth*, or John Philip Kemble without *Coriolanus*, Helena Faucit without *The Winter's Tale*, Laurence Olivier and Kenneth Branagh without *Henry V*, or John Gielgud without *The Winter's Tale* and *The Tempest*? Should we have had the Shakespeare Institute or the Shakespeare Birthplace Trust or the Royal Shakespeare Company if Shakespeare were known as the author of only fourteen or so plays? Would all the thousands of books on Shakespeare have been merely a lot shorter, or would they never have come into being? If not, would the University of Delaware Press have existed? Would Sam Wanamaker have wanted to reconstruct the Globe? Would Jay Halio have devoted his life to the works of Shackerley Marmion? It doesn't bear thinking about.

29

The Limitations of the First Folio

PAUL EDMONDSON AND STANLEY WELLS

Our essay in celebration of our German friend and Shakespeare scholar, Dieter Mehl, raises questions about what the First Folio text itself represents and then considers how it is currently being used by actors. Always an important volume, its reputation has never stood as high as it does now. Over a century ago it became the only book to be memorialized with a monument, in Love Lane, London.[1] The charred remains of a copy that was accidentally incinerated are preserved in a glass case in Philadelphia.[2] About eighty copies, in various states of preservation, have found their resting place in the Folger Shakespeare Library, Washington.[3] In 1964 the copy belonging to the Royal Shakespeare Company was taken to the Vatican to be blessed by the pope. He mistook it for a gift, and it had to be tactfully retrieved.[4] It has repeatedly been published in both type and photographic facsimile. The processes by which it was printed have been minutely analysed.[5] Scholarly monographs have been devoted to study of its publishing history, of the whereabouts of surviving copies—around 230 of them—of annotations scribbled in them by generations of owners, and of the prices they have raised when put on sale. A copy that came on the market in 2006 was treated to a world tour before coming under the hammer, and the sale was reported internationally. In recent years editors have preferred its texts of certain plays—*Hamlet* and *King Lear* among them—to previously printed, longer versions that more closely represent Shakespeare's original manuscripts. And now it has (more or less) been edited in its own right, with doctrinaire disregard of manifestly superior quarto readings and with shamefaced addition of non-Folio texts, including the poems, by Jonathan Bate and Eric Rasmussen under the auspices of the Royal Shakespeare Company.[6]

Is all this attention justified? Publication of the volume seems to have been the prime responsibility of John Heminges and Henry Condell, two of Shakespeare's lifelong colleagues in the King's Men. They, along with Richard Burbage, are the only former colleagues to whom he left bequests in his will of 1616. Possibly the four men had discussed memorializing him in this way, spurred on perhaps by the knowledge that Ben Jonson was already big with a folio. And Germaine Greer suggests that Shakespeare's wife, too, may have been instrumental in having the book published.[7] Burbage had died in 1619, before the Shakespeare volume was ready for the press, but its preliminaries are signed by the other two legatees. They were actors, not professional scholars, and they seem to have been motivated rather by love for their friend and by pride in their company's achievements than by the desire for monetary gain. They are often referred to as the book's editors, but we do not know how much they undertook personally of the very considerable amount of detailed work that went into its preparation for the press. This work was little less demanding of scholarly dedication than that undertaken by academic editors at the present time. Someone had to deal with the publishers; to commission the Droeshout engraving and the prefatory poems written by Ben Jonson, Hugh Holland, Leonard Digges, and James Mabbe; to assemble the texts, making decisions about what to include and what to omit; to decide on the order in which the plays should be printed; to make decisions about their titles; to determine which should be printed from manuscript and which from previously printed texts, to negotiate problems of copyright; and to commission and pay for transcripts of plays of which previously printed texts or manuscripts were not available. And someone decided that it was not enough simply to hand existing quartos of the plays over to the printers, but that some person or persons should to some degree—sometimes to a very considerable degree—collate and annotate certain printed texts in order to make them conform, with varying degrees of exactitude, to manuscripts that had been amended for the theatre.

Some plays, such as *Much Ado About Nothing, Love's Labour's Lost*, and *The Merchant of Venice*, were only lightly annotated, with the result that evident errors remain. For other plays the task was more substantial, though not all-pervasive. *Titus Andronicus* was printed from a copy of the third quarto, of 1611, but with the addition of a scene (the 'fly' scene, Act 3, scene 2) that had not appeared in any of the quartos and with other changes, some of which reflect theatrical practice after the introduction of Act intervals around 1608. And for a few plays the process of annotation was remarkably thorough and must have required many hours of taxing, detailed work resulting in a copy that the printers would have found difficult to read. For *Troilus and Cressida* a copy of the 1609 quarto was marked up with some 500 variants, an average of between seventeen and eighteen changes on each page—one every two to three lines—made after comparison with a scribal transcript of a theatre copy on which revisions for production at the Globe or elsewhere had been made. Most pains were taken over *King Lear*, for which a copy of the second, 1619 quarto was marked up with the addition from a theatre manuscript of around 100 full lines that are not in the quarto, with the marking for omission of close on 300 lines, including an entire scene, that *are* in the quarto, and with over 850 verbal variants, including changes and additions to stage directions and reassignment of several speeches to different speakers. The result, with deletions, additions, interlineations, and inter-leaved sheets, must have been a compositor's nightmare. There is no wonder that the book did not appear until seven years after Shakespeare died.

If Heminges and Condell did all the work themselves, they must have had skills far different from those normally required of actors. If they did not, who did? Ben Jonson, the most scholarly of the popular playwrights of the period, was associated with the enterprise, at least to the extent of providing verses to accompany the Droeshout engraving of Shakespeare that prefaces the volume and of writing for it the noble and deeply thoughtful, if not entirely translucent lines in Shakespeare's memory that represent the most serious criticism that his work had thus far received. Maybe Jonson helped in other ways, too. And it has been pretty conclu-sively established that Ralph Crane was commissioned to make transcripts of several plays; Trevor Howard-Hill has suggested that Crane may also have under-taken other editorial functions.[8] No doubt he would have had to be paid.

The result of all the work that went into preparing the volume is that for a number of Shakespeare's plays we have far better evidence of the form and manner in which they were performed than if only the quartos had survived, or if those who put the Folio together had taken the easier way out and simply reprinted quartos. The Folio is a tribute to Shakespeare the dramatist, an affirmation by his colleagues of the belief that his plays reached full fruition only in the theatre. Above all the volume preserved texts of eighteen plays, including some of Shakespeare's greatest, that had not appeared in print and that otherwise might have been lost forever. The world would have been a very different place without, for instance, *Julius Caesar*, *As You Like It*, *Twelfth Night*, *Macbeth*, *Antony and Cleopatra*, *The Winter's Tale*, and *The Tempest*. Also, if the Folio had not omitted *The London Prodigal* and *A Yorkshire Tragedy*, both of which had been published as Shakespeare's, it would have been very difficult to deny the claims of their title-pages that he had written them.

The work undertaken in preparing the Folio has, then, unquestionably exerted a paramount influence upon our perception of Shakespeare; but, important though it is, that influence has not always been to the good. The volume is a highly eclectic collection of variously derived texts, all plays. The decision to exclude any non-dramatic writings seems particularly perverse in that these are the only works that Shakespeare clearly intended to be read. There may have been problems about copyright. The *Sonnets*, published in 1609, had not been much of a success, judging by both the number of surviving copies and by the absence of reprints before Benson's garbled version of 1640, so the publisher, Thomas Thorpe, presumably still had unsold copies. *Venus and Adonis* and *The Rape of Lucrece*, on the other hand, had been reprinted regularly since they first appeared in 1593 and 1594, respectively, so their publishers too would not have wished to part with their rights. The decision not to include the poems in a volume that otherwise aimed at inclusiveness had the effect for centuries of reducing the impression of Shakespeare's range by drawing attention away from his achievement as a non-dramatic poet. The poems were excluded from reprints of the Folio throughout the seventeenth century, and the content of eighteenth-century editions continued to reflect that of the Folio, with the poems issued at best as supplementary volumes until Malone's edition of 1790. Partly for this reason the *Sonnets* were little known until the Romantic period, and there is no serious discussion of the narrative poems before Coleridge, in the *Biographia Literaria* of 1817. The Folio editors also omitted four plays—*Edward III*, *Pericles*, *The Two Noble Kinsmen*, and the lost *Cardenio*—in which it is now believed that Shakespeare had a hand, while including *All is True* under the title of *Henry VIII* (maybe in order to complete the English histories) and the collaborative *Timon of Athens*. Perhaps they could also have printed *Love's Labour's Won*.

It is significant that the Folio editors represented many of the plays in the state in which they were acted in the theatres of their own time—the later Jacobean period—rather than of the time at which they were first written and performed. This is why they offer, for example, adapted texts of *Hamlet*, *Troilus and Cressida*, *Measure for Measure*, *King Lear*, and *Macbeth* rather than the plays as Shakespeare first wrote them. An important effect of changes in theatre practice is the presence in the Folio of Act and scene divisions in a number of plays. None of the plays printed in Shakespeare's lifetime is divided into either Acts or scenes (though it is clear that in some of them, such as *Henry V*, he had the classically derived five-Act structure in mind). There is every reason to believe that until about 1608 plays in the public theatres, even the longest, were acted without interruption.[9] The editors of the Folio, however, clearly set out with the intention of dividing all the plays into Acts, though they abandoned this practice in the later plays of the volume. Some of the subdivisions in the Folio undoubtedly represent the ways the plays were acted during the later part of Shakespeare's career, but others are no less clearly editorial, and some are grotesquely inappropriate, as will be testified by readers who have had the experience of coming, perhaps with relief, to what is marked as the end of Act 4 of *Love's Labour's Lost* only to find that more than half of the play still lies ahead. Although the Folio editors' intention to divide all the plays was not carried through, what they did encouraged later editors to complete the process, bringing the representation of the plays closer to that of classical drama and resulting in printed texts that misrepresent the manner in which most of the plays were originally given by breaking the flow of the action. This must be regarded as a limitation of the Folio. Without it the plays would have gone on being printed continuously, as in the quartos, a policy that might well have had far-reaching effects on theatrical practice, and indeed on theatrical economics (which is affected by bar visits during intervals).

The other decision made by the Folio editors that has had far-reaching consequences is their arrangement of the volume's contents. They might have arranged the plays according to the order of composition. Presumably they might even have told their readers when the plays were written, thus saving scholars of later generations an enormous amount of trouble. Instead, and regrettably, they decided to group the plays according to the categories named in the title of their volume: *Mr William Shakespeare's Comedies, Histories, and Tragedies*. This was not a straightforward task, and the manner in which it was carried out has had far-reaching, and not entirely beneficial, consequences.

On original publication only six of the plays had been assigned more or less precisely to the categories in which they are placed in the Folio: *Titus Andronicus* was 'A Roman tragedy'; *Romeo and Juliet* first an 'excellent conceited tragedy', then a 'most lamentable tragedy'; *Love's Labour's Lost* a 'pleasant conceited comedy'; *The Merry Wives of Windsor* a comedy, *Hamlet* a tragical history on the title-pages of the first and second quartos and a straightforward tragedy on the head-title of the second quarto; and *Othello* a tragedy. Another five plays were assigned to no category.[10] Two of the plays—1 *Henry IV* and *Henry V* (a chronicle history)—were classed as histories in both the Folio and in quarto, but three of the Folio histories (3 *Henry VI, Richard II,* and *Richard III*)—were tragedies on first publication. One of the Folio comedies, *The Merchant of Venice*, was a history on its title-page and a comical history according to its head-title, and two of the Folio tragedies started off as histories: *King Lear* was a chronicle history on its title-page and a history on its head-title, and *Troilus and Cressida* was a 'famous history'.

The most conspicuous anomalies in the Folio's classification relate to the plays there classified as histories. The word had a broad signification; it could be used of any narrative, not just one based on actual events. The Folio editors chose to use it only in the historical sense, and restricted it to plays based on medieval and Tudor English history. In doing so they obscured the tragic nature of Shakespeare's treatment of the final part of the reign of Henry VI and the reigns of Richard II and Richard III and ignored the historical aspects of the reign of King Lear and also of the plays based on Roman history that had not appeared in quarto. They were clearly intent on emphasizing the biographical aspects of the history plays—only one, *Richard III*, is described as a tragedy, and even that is 'The Life and Death of Richard III' in the running titles. To this extent their procedure takes the plays away from the theatre in the direction of narrative history. This is probably also why the compilers pretty certainly altered the titles under which some of the plays had been performed: the second and third parts of *Henry VI* seem to have been known in the theatres of the 1590s as the 'First and Second parts of the Contention betwixt the two famous houses of York and Lancaster' (or some equally unwieldy variant of this), and accounts of the burning of the Globe three times allude to the play printed as *Henry VIII* in the Folio as *All is True*, never unequivocally as *Henry VIII*; indeed, the ballad commemorating this occasion has as its refrain the words 'and yet all this is true'.[11]

Editorial decisions about genre affect other plays than those that had already appeared in print—the Roman tragedies and *Macbeth* are historical narratives no less than the plays centred on the lives of English kings, and *Cymbeline* is a historical as well as a comical play. Shakespeare's work is essentially eclectic, often drawing on a wide range of literary and dramatic traditions and conventions within a single play. In attempting to confine it within the straitjacket of three straightforward categories Heminges and Condell were less true to his memory than they would have wished. In particular, their imposition on many of the plays of Act and scene divisions and their grouping of the plays according to generic categories along with their alteration of original titles to fit these categories have shaped the ways in which succeeding generations have thought and written about their author. The pagination of the volume is non-sequential, starting afresh for the printing of each new generic section. This, we suggest, may reflect an original intention to publish the work in three volumes, or at least to allow purchasers of unbound sheets to make three volumes out of them. Such breaks in the reading make plays difficult to locate by page number and suggest a devolved Shakespeare in three separate parts, in a similar way to the imposition of the five-Act structure.

So much for textual scholarship. What about the theatre? More and more actors are falling in love with the First Folio. Over many years, Dieter has brought hundreds of Shakespearians on short courses to Stratford-upon-Avon, initially to the Shakespeare Institute, University of Birmingham, and then to the Shakespeare Centre, headquarters of the Shakespeare Birthplace Trust. A highlight of those programmes has long been the question-and-answer sessions with members of the Royal Shakespeare Company. Dieter has sat through, and contributed to, scores of them, possibly even more than a hundred over the years. Increasingly actors have wheeled into their discussion of the plays reference to the First Folio. Why do they do this, and what is meant by it?

The critical assumption that the First Folio as printed is somehow both useful to actors and represents an existing through-line to Shakespeare's own intentions goes back at least as far as 1948. Richard Flatter, an Austrian who translated Shakespeare into German, produced *Shakespeare's Producing Hand: A Study of His Marks of Expression to Be Found in the First Folio*.[12] The literary scholar and theatrical practitioner Nevill Coghill wrote the introduction. Responses to the work acknowledged its usefulness for thinking about Shakespeare theatrically, but criticized its venturing into the territory of textual bibliography. Charlton Hinman's 1950 review recognized it as 'something of a landmark in Shakespeare studies generally' while commenting that Flatter's 'evidence of Shakespeare's own "hand" ... can scarcely be thought sound'.[13] The tensions then present between textual scholarship and theatrical experience are every bit as keen today, if not more so. What is at stake when actors turn to the First Folio for guidance?

First and foremost is a sense of Shakespearian authority. The title of Flatter's book suggests a real sense of presence, a presence that persists whenever an actor finds the Folio (at best) 'helpful' and (at worst) 'authentic'. At stake, too, is an approach to the

Folio text that is apparently unmediated by scholarly endeavour: reader and actor meet text and by so doing gain privileged access to Shakespeare's intentions for his own acting company. In ecclesiastical terms it represents the difference between Bible-based Protestantism and Church-based Catholicism.

Moreover, the approach that finds Shakespeare's presence actually within the text as printed on the Folio's pages should raise suspicions by proclaiming itself to be straightforward and simple. Herein lies the ongoing tension between the academy and the theatre. Donald Weingust, an apologist who argues for the pre-eminent position of the Folio in both the study and on-stage, betrays these critical assumptions in the following terms: 'The Folio orthography becomes a simple alternative means of textual study, one well suited to the temporal demands of theatrical production. Folio-based techniques provide actors not only technical assistance, but also a less tangible, though no less important, moral authority bound up with the supposed intentionality of the playwright.'[14]

Here Weingust betrays an approach that stems not from scholarly discipline, but from rehearsal room desirability, an approach which has nothing to do with historical truth and everything to do with a vague ('less tangible') morality. The desirability of 'a simple alternative means of textual study' betrays another item on the agenda of what is beginning to look like First Folio fundamentalism, an attack not only on New Bibliography but also on textual scholarship more generally, which is perceived as difficult. Experientially, the approach has everything to do with empowering actors, and nothing to do with empowering critical thought. 'Unediting' Renaissance texts might inspire a greater openness of interpretative framework—let us enjoy both the first and second quartos' 'base Indean' *and* the Folio's 'Judean' just moments before the end of *Othello*—but in Weingust's construction what might be a healthy and self-conscious pluralism becomes a case of lazy and overly simplistic indecision.

Guidance for actors using the Folio comes in many other guises, including: realizing asides through shifts in speeches, noticing that the Folio entrances might make theatrical sense in themselves, finding dramatic pauses in metrical gaps, understanding metrical irregularity to be a place where gestures can be inserted, obeying the Folio's lineation even when irregular (since this might be revealing about characterization), and finding markings akin to music notation within the rhetorical punctuation of the Folio: the colons indicate a pause, commas a shorter one, or breaks in the argument, similar to the modern dash; there is no need for the semicolon. Weingust refers us to Flatter's remarks about *Macbeth*: 'Flatter perceives *Macbeth* as perhaps the most perfectly transmitted of Shakespeare's texts. He finds the play relatively free of what might be called proto-editorial interference. The proof of its integrity, for Flatter, is the great deal of irregularity preserved in the text, much of which is represented in line division and irregular verse.'[15] But it is increasingly accepted that the Folio text of the play represents Middleton's adaptation of Shakespeare's original. A more valid interpretation in the light of current scholarship would be that the irregularity of the text as printed in the Folio probably has more to do with Middleton's habit of writing irregular verse lines than with Shakespeare's provision of implicit directions to the actors.

The First Folio-centred approach has found fullest expression in the work of Patrick Tucker's Original Shakespeare Company. Tucker's theatrical practice is based on trying to reproduce the kinds of dramatic energies experienced by the Lord Chamberlain's Men and the King's Men. Cue scripts rather than full texts are used—indeed, actors are dissuaded from reading the full text lest it gets in the way of the immediacy of experience. (As Oscar Wilde's Lady Bracknell says: 'I do not approve of anything that tampers with natural ignorance. Ignorance is like a delicate exotic fruit; touch it and the bloom is gone.')[16] But the Folio sits enshrined in Tucker's overall approach. His is a directorial method that ironically eschews direction: 'If an actor asks to what use he should put such opportunities ["the acting potential of Folio incidentals . . . "] Tucker is quick to reply, "I don't know, you're the actor, you decide." Proponents of using the Folio as an acting text make it clear that these opportunities are notes to the actor, rather than dicta for inflexibly specific interpretation.'[17]

Actually, Tucker's 'dicta' are carefully laid down in his 2002 book, *Secrets of Acting Shakespeare: The Original Approach*. His recommendation on the importance of capital letters in the Folio provides an illuminating example: 'In the final analysis, no one knows if the capitalization was what the actors' script would have had, but my work with actors reveals that it *always* gives useful and valuable acting notes to the performer. Even if the capitalization was a whim of the compositor—and the more work I do with the original script the more I find this difficult to believe— then at least it is an Elizabethan's [sic] choice of which word to highlight with the use of the capital, and therefore someone closer to the original performance.'[18]

The capital letters may or may not be 'Shakespearian', but they are still 'Elizabethan', which, Tucker supposes, gives them special authority. In another example Tucker gives to illustrate the integrity of the Folio's use of a question mark, Malvolio's 'Ile be reueng'd on the whole packe of you?'—'where Malvolio starts his exit with a threat, realizes that he is outnumbered, and leaves us laughing at the deflation of his pomposity'[19]—Tucker's dictum is not quite good enough. In fact, the Folio gives Malvolio no exit at this point. Here is a strange case of Tucker's 'dicta' not being used properly to his own advantage. Presumably, Tucker would not want his actors even to look into the corrupting influence of a Penguin, Oxford, Cambridge, or Arden text, and yet his own dissemination of the First Folio is not quite accurate enough, and certainly not unfiltered (though he gives the illusion that it is) by his own editorial and dramatic preferences.

The theatre's ever-growing fascination with the Folio text is compounded in the Royal Shakespeare Company's edition: *William Shakespeare: The Complete Works*, edited by Jonathan Bate and Eric Rasmussen (2007). The editors claim, '[A]stonishingly, the Shakespeare First Folio—unquestionably the most important single book in the history of world drama—has not been edited in its own right for about three hundred years. By "edited" we mean reproduced with the correction of presumed printer's errors and the modernization of spelling and punctuation. There have been *facsimile reproductions* and *diplomatic transcriptions* of the Folio: these, however, are not corrected and modernized *editions*.'[20] First Folio readings have been preserved, where these can be made sense of, stage directions and speech prefixes are Folio-based, or Folio-pointed, so that the 1623 text is everywhere apparent as an implied presence, whether this brings with it a Shakespearian authority or not. But quarto texts have been used for inevitable emendations, as have other historical editions. The editors have also felt the need to print 'substantial Quarto-only passages' at the end of relevant plays. What the edition represents 'aims to be simultaneously authentic and modern'.[21] Ironically, this apparently most theatrical of all current complete editions does not serve up the Folio quite as well as the actors who might wish to use it would like. Here is a Folio whimsically filtered and far removed from the fundamentals necessary to Tucker's influential theatrical approach. Actors who wish to use the Folio would find it much more beneficial to use a facsimile. The level of editorial intervention in the RSC edition itself clearly illustrates the limitations of the 1623 volume. This is and is not an edition of the Folio.

Having illustrated the tensions between the theatrical and scholarly approaches to the Folio, and having found a scholarly attempt to edit the Folio strangely compromised by its own terms, what are we left with? The First Folio is also the site where Lukas Erne's exaggerated case for Shakespeare as a purely literary author is being contested.[22] The 1623 publication is the primary touchstone for the ongoing tension over who can claim most Shakespearian authority: the reader or the actor, the academy or the theatre. The epigraph to this *Festschrift* for Dieter is of help here: Edmund Burke's 'There is a boundary to men's passions when they act from feelings; but none when they are under the influence of imagination.' The boundary of the feelings in Burke's formulation is the vanguard of any approach for which the First Folio is in any way a sentimental starting point, that is any theory based on a feeling, or a quest for Shakespeare's presence. It requires imagination to instigate a new kind of dialogue between the academy and the theatre. In this new dialogue, neither side would be intimidated by the other, and at the heart of it would be an openness to the mutual pursuit of truth and a new appetite for an exactness of interpretation. The dialogue would recognize the best that is to be found in Patrick Tucker's exploration of 'authentic' stagings and would inform this by a scholarship that could see beyond the limitations of the First Folio, rather than being hidebound by them.

The publication of the Folio represents one of the earliest critical acts in Shakespearian literary and theatrical scholarship. Its Shakespeare is every bit as constructed as the Shakespeare of successive centuries, and both actors and scholars need to take heed not to let sentiment rule when it comes properly to assessing what the Folio represents. The Folio is where 'the war of authority'[23] between the theatre and the academy begins, and where it is still going on. We owe an enormous debt to Heminges and Condell, but some of their work needs to be undone, not blindly followed, if we are to enhance our understanding of what Shakespeare wrote. Shakespeare's First Folio is of an age, not for all time.

Afterword

MARGRETA DE GRAZIA

H as there ever been a textual scholar more enamoured of the theatre than
Stanley Wells? In this collection, there are essays on the theatre in Shakespeare's
day, in our own time, and in the centuries in between. The stage looms even in his
critical essays, despite their focus on literary questions of style, structure, and
genre. More remarkable still is the key role the theatre plays in Wells's many
editions. His prioritizing of the playhouse prompt-book over the authorial manuscript revolutionized the scholarly Shakespeare edition. It then became the editor's
task to reproduce not only the playtext but also a sense of how it had been
performed. This collection is indeed well-named: throughout Wells's formidable
corpus, *Page and Stage* are in happy partnership.

Yet *Page versus Stage* would more accurately describe their relation in the long
history of Shakespeare studies. Textualists have been largely dismissive or even
hostile to the theatre. Indeed scholarship has generally assumed that from the start
the printing house and the playhouse were rivals: reading a play and seeing it on
stage were deemed to have been mutually exclusive. After the Restoration, the two
venues clearly part company: the stage takes bold liberties in adapting Shakespeare's
texts, while editors claim to have established the authentic text, expunging in the
process what are perceived as theatrical corruptions. But the strongest bias against
the theatre may well be philosophical. In the wake of the idealism of Kant and Hegel,
critics from Hazlitt on have maintained that performance adulterates Shakespeare's
transcendent genius. His high-minded conceptions are compromised by the exigencies of the theatre: the need to perform in real time and space through the
materializations of bodies, costumes, props, and sets. The prejudice runs deep. It
undergirds the discipline of literary studies itself, where for most of the twentieth
century bibliography and philology were required but theatre history or performance studies were not even on offer. As editors neglected the theatre in producing
playtexts, so did critics in interpreting them. Formalist critics were trained to read
plays as if they were poems, as were the new critics. Some have been known to have

taken pride in never seeing Shakespeare on stage or, if they did, with eyes shut, so as not to be distracted by on-stage action.

But there is hardly an essay in this volume that does not either centre on or draw on the theatre. Some consider stage practices in Shakespeare's day, especially in the light of the reconstructed outdoor and then indoor Globe theatres. Wells's special gift is in scrutinizing dialogue and stage action, as he does for indications of how special effects were achieved: ghosts might appear from any aperture, from the two stage-doors, the trap, and the upper level; apparitions and visions were staged with mist, music, and figures clad in white (17, 18). And then there are the essays on later theatre history, for example, on the simultaneous rise of celebrity actors and character criticism, both to the detriment of dramatic action (21, 22). Or on how the theatre reviews of Leigh Hunt and William Hazlitt mark a transition from promotional puffery to literary essay.

In Wells's own critical essays, surprising insights are sparked by performances, both past and present. In his essay on *Romeo and Juliet* (6), he takes theatrical cuts and alterations from the eighteenth century to the present as indices not of defects in the play but of a need to qualify its generic classification, from tragedy to romantic tragedy. Deborah Warner's 1987 production of *Titus Andronicus*, by drawing out structural and linguistic parallels formerly lost to the tragedy's violent sensationalism, compels a reevaluation of the entire play (5). After seeing Peter Hall's production of *Hamlet* in which it is not conscience but boredom that prompts Claudius to interrupt the Mousetrap play, Wells re-punctuates his line, 'Give me some light!' to read, less urgently, 'Give me some light.' (27). Too late, he admits, did a performance alert him to a possibility his own stage direction had precluded. In *Cymbeline*, Innogen after having fondled the beheaded corpse she mistakes for that of her lover, exclaims that blood has coloured her cheek. How did this occur? Wells's edition reads, '*She smears her face with blood*'. But Peter Hall's 1988 performance demonstrated that the same result could be produced by Innogen's embrace of the bloody corpse (27). These are small details, to be sure, but they reflect what with Wells is a regulative principle: editors must attend to 'the unwritten dimension of the dramatic script': to what happens on stage that may not be ascertainable either in dialogue or in the scant stage directions of early scripts. In doing so, however, they must not foreclose theatrical possibility, neither for readers nor for actors.

In the editing of Shakespeare, no greater honour has been accorded to the theatre than by the Wells and Taylor 1986 Oxford edition. In 1967, Wells had counted himself among those editors who neglected staging and followed the quarto editions deemed closest to Shakespeare's intentions. Twenty years later, his priorities changed: the Oxford edition set out to reproduce the plays 'so far as possible as they were acted' on Shakespeare's stage. Indeed a Shakespearian holograph, even if it were to exist, would be insufficient, for only after the trials of rehearsal and performance would a play have been brought to fruition. Shakespeare was to be imagined less as the solitary poet with quill in hand than as the playwright delivering to his acting company a manuscript he fully expected to be altered in the playhouse. (Perhaps he even assumed what has indeed proven the case: that his playtexts' essential provisionality would leave them open to a long future of re-renderings.)

By exploiting the adaptability of Shakespeare's plays, performance counteracts the desire of traditional editing to fix an authentic text, once and for all. As Wells affirms, 'There is no such thing as a prescriptive edition'. Indeed the final essay of the collection, co-authored with Paul Edmondson, warns against one that has been received as such (29). Actors in particular have been overawed by the authority of the 1623 Folio, especially when reproduced under the auspices of the RSC and two prominent academics, Jonathan Bate and Eric Rasmussen. Wells finds himself in the position of having to qualify his own long-time admiration for the Folio on which his own editing had been largely founded (28). With the Folio already enjoying iconic status, even before its upcoming quatercentenary, his criticism is salutary. The Folio's definition of the canon is incomplete; it does not acknowledge the hand of other playwrights; its tripartite generic division misleads, and its insertion of classicizing Act and scene divisions interrupts what in Shakespeare's theatre may well have been continuous performance. Furthermore, while the Folio may give the impression of offering direct access to Shakespeare, there is no denying the mediation of Heminges and Condell as well as the nameless others who assisted in its production. To the 1623 Folio's injunction to prospective readers, 'what euer you do, Buy', Wells supplies a salutary *caveat emptor*: all readers, including actors, 'need to learn how to use edited texts'.

The reifying of any edition deadens theatrical possibility. 'Theatre is a living art', and its vitality needs to be imparted to the playtext. As Wells maintains, flexibility is the distinctive privilege of drama, denied to poetry and the novel. A play over time changes materially, formally, conceptually through its multitudinous productions. Resistance to such change takes many forms, among them the retention of old spelling in modernized texts, as if by tossing in a few archaisms like 'murther' (for 'murder'), 'accompt' (for account), 'banket' (for 'banquet') a bit of Shakespeare's 'merrie olde Englande' might be recovered. Something of the same nostalgia might be charged to in-period productions that strive for a historical accuracy never attempted in Shakespeare's time. Wells admits a preference to such productions: at least they don't risk the absurdity of an otherwise admirable 1985 production of *Merry Wives of Windsor*, set precisely in 1959, in which Anne Page's inheritance remains at £700, a whacking sum around 1600 but barely enough for a modest wedding ceremony in 1959 (26).

Nor is it only spelling and monetary sums that require updating. As these essays demonstrate time and again, our beliefs about Shakespeare are constantly subject to revision. Throughout this collection, one can see Wells's abiding openness to new ideas and materials, a rarity in a scholar with such a mastery of all dimensions of traditional Shakespeare study. At several points, he himself notes the difficulty of giving up a deep-seated belief. It is not easy to invalidate the conflated *King Lear* that was the received edition for over two centuries in favour of two discrete *King Lears* (11). Nor to relinquish the conventional assumption that Shakespeare's sonnets should be read as a sequence addressed to two lovers rather than a miscellany written to numerous ones (13). Nor to recast Elizabethan and Jacobean Shakespeare as a pan-European Renaissance man (1). Wells's scholarship, like the theatre he loves, thrives on entertaining new possibilities. That is what keeps Shakespeare alive, and that is what Wells in the long half-century of work represented by these essays has done so consummately.

NOTES

1. Shakespeare: Man of the European Renaissance

1. E. I. Fripp, *Master Richard Quyny: Bailiff of Stratford-upon-Avon and Friend of William Shakespeare* (Oxford, 1924), 133.
2. R. E. Pritchard, *Odd Tom Coryate: The English Marco Polo* (Stroud, 2004), 17. Educated at Winchester and Oxford, Coryate also wrote verse and prose in Latin (ibid. 3).
3. Naseeb Shaheen, 'Shakespeare's Knowledge of Italian', *Shakespeare Survey* 47 (1994), 161–9.
4. Stanley Wells and Gary Taylor (gen. eds), *The Oxford Shakespeare: The Complete Works*, 2nd edn. (Oxford, 2005), p. lxix. All quotations from Shakespeare's works follow the text of this edition.
5. T. W. Baldwin, *William Shakspere's Small Latine and Lesse Greeke*, 2 vols. (Urbana, 1944).
6. Ibid. ii. 617–19.
7. 'It is thus clear that by Shakspere's day practically all grammar schools on regular foundations, as was that at Stratford, would at least hope to teach some Greek' (ibid. ii. 626).
8. Andrew Werth, 'Shakespeare's "Lesse Greek"', *The Oxfordian* 5 (2002), 11–29.
9. Colin Burrow (ed.), *Complete Sonnets and Poems*, Oxford Shakespeare (Oxford, 2002), note to Sonnet 153.
10. Stephen Booth (ed.), *Shakespeare's Sonnets* (New Haven, 1977).
11. Margaret Downs-Gamble, 'New Pleasures Prove: Evidence of Dialectical *Disputatio* in Early Modern Manuscript Culture', *Early Modern Literary Studies* 2/2 (1996), 1–33. British Library Additional MS 19268. 'A copie in imitation of' another verse complemented the 'master' exemplar.

> On his {Mtrs} Walkinge in the Snowe
> I sawe faire Cloris walke alone
> when featherd raine came softly downe
> And Jove descended from his towre
> to Court her in a sylver showre
> the wanton snowe flew on her breast
> as lithe birds unto their nests
> but overcome in whitnes there
> for grief it thawed into a feare
> when fallinge on her garments hem
> to deck her froze into a gemme.
> W. Stroud

> A copie in imitation of the former
> I sawe faire Flora take the aire
> When Phabus shinde and it was faire
> the heavens to allay the scorching sun
> sent drops of raine which gently come

the sunne retires ashamed to see
that he was bar'd from kissing thee
But Boreas then tooke such disdaine
that soone he dryed those drops againe
A cunninge trick but most divinne
to change and mix his breath with thine
H. Hide (fo. 23r–v)

12. Katherine Duncan-Jones (ed.), *Shakespeare's Sonnets*, Arden Shakespeare (London, 1997), 6.
13. Andrew Gurr, 'Shakespeare's First Poem: Sonnet 145', *Essays in Criticism* 21/3 (July 1947), 221–6.
14. Paul Edmondson and Stanley Wells, *Shakespeare's Sonnets* (Oxford, 2004), 49–51.
15. Sister Miriam Joseph, *Shakespeare's Use of the Arts of Language* (New York, 1947), 74.
16. Brian Vickers, 'Shakespeare's Use of Rhetoric', in Vivian Salmon and Edwina Burness (eds), *A Reader in the Language of Shakespearean Drama* (Amsterdam and Philadelphia, 1987), 406.
17. Brian Vickers, *The Artistry of Shakespeare's Prose* (London, 1968).
18. This excludes words such as '*ergo*' which were virtually anglicized.
19. 'Scholars have been unanimous, I believe, that Shakspere used his classics more in early years, but progressively less with time.' Baldwin, *Shakspere's Small Latine*, ii. 666–7.
20. Bryan Garner, 'Latin-Saxon Hybrids in Shakespeare and the Bible', in Salmon and Burness (eds), *A Reader in the Language of Shakespearean Drama*, 229–37.
21. These are *The Two Gentlemen of Verona*, *Titus Andronicus*, *1 Henry VI*, and *Richard III*, and the comparatively short *Venus and Adonis*.
22. James Shapiro, *Contested Will: Who Wrote Shakespeare?* (London, 2010), 307 and *passim*.
23. See Stanley Wells, '*The Taming of the Shrew* and *King Lear*: A Structural Comparison', *Shakespeare Survey* 33 (1990), 55–66, and reproduced in this volume.
24. *Romeo and Juliet*, ed. T. J. B. Spencer (Harmondsworth, 1967), 7.
25. See Stanley Wells, *Shakespeare, Sex, and Love* (Oxford, 2010), 148–67 (chapter 6, 'Sex and Love in *Romeo and Juliet*').
26. Andrea Mantegna, *The Vase Bearers from the Triumphs of Caesar* (1484–1492), Royal Collection, Hampton Court Palace.
27. Wells and Taylor (eds), *The Oxford Shakespeare*, p. lxix.
28. Leonardo da Vinci, *Vitruvian Man* (1485–1490), Galleria dell'Accademia, Venice, http://en.wikipedia.org/wiki/File:Da_Vinci_Vitruve_Luc_Viatour.jpg (accessed 21 September 2011).
29. Alison Brown, *The Renaissance* (London, 1999).
30. Ibid. 66–7.
31. William Shakespeare, *Pericles*, Oxford Shakespeare, ed. Roger Warren (Oxford, 2003), 58.
32. W. R. Elton, *King Lear and the Gods* (1966; Lexington, KY, 1988), 70.
33. S. L. Bethell, *Shakespeare and the Popular Dramatic Tradition* (Durham, NC, 1944), 54.
34. Masaccio, *The Expulsion of Adam and Eve from Eden* (1426–1428), Capella Brancacci, Santa Maria del Carmine, Florence, http://upload.wikimedia.org/wikipedia/commons/3/37/Masaccio-TheExpulsionOfAdamAndEveFromEden-Restoration.jpg (accessed 21 September 2011).

2. Tales from Shakespeare

1. *The Family Shakspeare*, 4 vols. (London, 1807).
2. Noel Perrin, 'The Real Bowdler', *Notes and Queries*, NS xiii (1966), 141–2.
3. William Jaggard, *Shakespeare Bibliography* (Stratford-upon-Avon, 1911).

4. Edwin W. Marrs, Jr (ed.), *The Letters of Charles and Mary Lamb*, 3 vols. (Ithaca and London, 1975–8; henceforth *Letters*); ii. 256 (Charles Lamb to William Wordsworth, 29 Jan. 1807).

5. *Letters*, ii. 228–9 (Mary Lamb to Sarah Stoddart, 30 May–2 June 1806).

6. *Letters*, ii. 233 (Charles Lamb to William Wordsworth, 26 June 1806).

7. *Letters*, ii. 233, 237 (Charles Lamb to William Wordsworth, 26 June 1806; Mary Lamb to Sarah Stoddart, 2 July 1806).

8. *Letters*, ii. 256 (Charles Lamb to William Wordsworth, 29 Jan. 1807).

9. 'The Chapbook Editions of the Lambs' *Tales from Shakespear*', *The Book Collector* vi (1957), 41–53, quotation on p. 41.

10. *The Family Shakspeare*, i, p. vii.

11. e.g. Alfred Ainger, Introduction to his edition (1879): Mary Lamb 'constantly evinces a rare shrewdness and tact in her incidental criticisms'. See also Edmund Blunden, *Charles Lamb and his Contemporaries* (London, 1937), 74.

12. 'Lamb on Shakespeare', *The Charles Lamb Bulletin*, NS li (1985), 76–85, quotations on pp. 76 and 84. On Lamb's implicit criticism of Shakespeare see also Joan Coldwell (ed.), *Charles Lamb on Shakespeare* (London, 1978), esp. pp. 12–15.

13. *The Anti-Jacobin Review* (26 March 1807), 298; *Critical Review*, ii, no. 1 (May 1807), 97–9; *The Monthly Mirror*, NS ii (July 1807), 39; *The Literary Panorama* (3 Nov. 1807), 294–5; *Gentleman's Magazine*, lxxviii, no. 2 (Nov. 1808), 1001; *The British Critic*, xxxiii (May 1809), 525; *The Satirist* (1 July 1809), 93.

14. *Letters*, ii. 82.

15. See e.g. F. J. Harvey Darnton, *Children's Books in England* (London, 1932), 3rd edn., rev. Brian Alderson (Cambridge, 1983), p. 192: 'They provide a defence of poesy by a kind of nursery introduction to it in prose.'

16. *A Portrait of Charles Lamb* (London, 1983), 127. An extreme reaction is that of Robertson Davies: 'Shakespeare was a poet and, if you rob him of his poetry, you reduce him to tedious stuff like Lamb's *Tales From Shakespear* (1807), which I was given as a child and which turned me off Shakespeare for many years' (Toronto *Globe and Mail*, 1 August 1987).

17. Vol. xii, *The Nineteenth Century* (Cambridge, 1915), 189.

18. Ibid.

19. *The Frolic and the Gentle* (London, 1934), 1970 edn., p. 131.

20. 'Hermione in *The Winter's Tale*', in Philip Brockbank (ed.), *Players of Shakespeare* (Cambridge, 1985), 153–65; quotation on p. 153.

21. Bertram Dobell writes briefly on Perrin in *Sidelights on Charles Lamb* (London, 1903).

22. Edith Nesbit's retellings of Shakespeare went through several stages: see the bibliography in Julia Briggs, *A Woman of Passion: The Life of E. Nesbit, 1858–1924* (London, 1987).

23. *Spectator* (8 Nov. 1879); cited by Arthur Colby Sprague, *Shakespearian Players and Performances* (Cambridge, MA, 1953, British edn., London, 1954), 116.

24. The stories had originally appeared as a series, 'Shakespeare's Plays as Short Stories', in the *Strand Magazine* (1933–4).

25. The most substantial study is by Maria Verch, 'Die Lambschen *Tales from Shakespeare* und ihre Nachfolger', *Shakespeare Jahrbuch* 1980, 90–108. The Lambs' *Tales* are critically considered in J. Riehl, *Charles Lamb's Children's Literature* (Salzburg, 1980).

26. The lecture as read concluded with a recording of a version of *Romeo and Juliet* from the cassette *One-minute Classics*, conceived and written by Andy Mayer and Jim Becker and performed by John 'Mighty-Mouth' Moschitta (1986).

3. The Failure of *The Two Gentlemen of Verona*

1. *Shakespear Illustrated* (London, 1753–4), iii. 44.
2. *Shakespeare: A Survey* (London, 1925), 49.
3. *Shakespearean Comedy* (New York, 1949), 108.
4. *Shakespeare and the Rose of Love* (London, 1960), 107–11.
5. E. K. Chambers perhaps came closest when he remarked on 'the lack of adroitness which allows the characters, as in *The Comedy of Errors*, and even, a little later, in *A Midsummer Night's Dream*, to fall into pairs'. (*Shakespeare: A Survey*, 52).
6. *Narrative and Dramatic Sources of Shakespeare*, i (London, 1957), 203.
7. *John Lyly* (London, 1962), 324.
8. *Endeavors of Art* (Madison, WI, 1954), 325.
9. *Cumberland's British Theatre* (London, n.d. [?1830]). Based on Ben Victor's adaptation (1763).
10. *Shakspere: His Mind and Art* (London, 1875), 57–8.
11. *Shakespeare* (London, 1911), 41.
12. *Shakespeare* (London, 1952), 95.
13. *Shakespeare and Elizabethan Poetry* (London, 1951), 150.
14. *The London Shakespeare* (London, 1958), i. 266.
15. *Johnson on Shakespeare*, ed. Walter Raleigh (London, 1908), 74.

4. *The Taming of the Shrew* and *King Lear*: A Structural Comparison

1. See e.g. chapter 14, 'Body and Soul', of Paul H. Kocher's *Science and Religion in Elizabethan England* (New York, 1953).
2. All references are to the *Complete Works*, ed. Peter Alexander (London and Glasgow, 1951).
3. Cf. *Love's Labour's Lost*, 5.2.212.
4. This is well argued by Cecil C. Seronsy, '"Supposes" as the Unifying Theme in *The Taming of the Shrew*', *Shakespeare Quarterly* 14 (1963), 15–30.
5. *Shakespearean Tragedy* (1904; repr. 1957), 216–20.
6. *Shakespeare in the Theatre* (Cambridge, 1978), 25.
7. *King Lear and the Gods* (San Marino, CA, 1966), 267, 270. While identifying non-Shakespearean treatments of the topic, including an interesting discussion of mind and body which occurs in Chapman's *Sir Giles Goosecap* (5.2.1–50), Elton does not remark its appearance in earlier plays by Shakespeare.
8. John Reibetanz, *The Lear World* (Toronto, 1977), 77.
9. It is perhaps relevant that the idea of the body as a prison for the soul, memorably enshrined by Marvell in his 'Dialogue between the Soul and Body', was commonplace; cf. K. S. Datta, 'New Light on Marvell's "A Dialogue between the Soul and Body"', *Renaissance Quarterly* 22 (1969), 242–55.
10. 'King Lear', *Prefaces to Shakespeare* (1930; repr. 1958), i. 277–8.

5. The Integration of Violent Action in *Titus Andronicus*

1. *Titus Andronicus*, ed. Eugene M. Waith, The Oxford Shakespeare (Oxford, 1984), 69.
2. *Titus Andronicus*, ed. Alan Hughes, The New Cambridge Shakespeare (Cambridge, 1994), 35, 47.
3. *Titus Andronicus*, ed. Jonathan Bate, The Arden Shakespeare, 3rd Series (London and New York, 1995), 69.

4. T. S. Eliot, 'Seneca in Elizabethan Translation', in his *Selected Essays*, 2nd edn. (London, 1934), 23.

5. *Titus Andronicus*, ed. Waith, pp. 68–9.

6. Alan C. Dessen, *Titus Andronicus* (Manchester and New York 1989), 57–60.

7. Ibid. 60.

8. *Titus Andronicus*, ed. Waith, note to 2.4.36–7.

9. I discuss these characteristics in 'The Failure of *The Two Gentlemen of Verona*', *Shakespeare Jahrbuch* 94 (1963), 161–73, reproduced in this volume.

10. The phrase is from a letter by Jacques Petit describing a private performance at Burley-on-the Hill: see Gustav Ungerer, 'An Unrecorded Elizabethan Performance of *Titus Andronicus*', *Shakespeare Survey* 14 (Cambridge, 1961), 102–9.

11. In *The Complete Works*, ed. Fredson Bowers, 2nd edn. (Cambridge, 1981), 3.1.184.1.

12. Dessen, *Titus Andronicus*, 91 and 13; the quotation from Gordon Crosse is from pp. 78–9 of his *Fifty Years of Shakespearean Playgoing* (London, 1941).

13. Bate (pp. 46–7) provides interesting examples of elaboration of stage business in a German version of the play printed in 1620 which represents, as he says, the staging 'of a company as close to [Shakespeare's] as one is ever going to get'. Dessen (pp. 9–10) discusses changes made by Edward Ravenscroft in his adaptation of 1678 which attempt to solve 'a series of problematic moments that continue to bedevil today's directors'.

14. Dessen, *Titus Andronicus*, 16, quoting from J. C. Trewin's *Peter Brook: A Biography* (London, 1971).

15. Ibid. 27–8.

16. In discussing Warner's production I draw on my article 'Shakespeare Performances in London and Stratford-upon-Avon, 1986–7', *Shakespeare Survey* 41 (Cambridge, 1989), 159–81.

17. Dessen, *Titus Andronicus*, 60.

18. Stanley Wells, Gary Taylor, John Jowett, and William Montgomery, *William Shakespeare: A Textual Companion* (Oxford, 1987), 113–15; no other play has so long an entry.

19. E. A. J. Honigmann, *Shakespeare: The Lost Years'* (Manchester, 1985), 128.

20. For reasons explained in my article cited at note 9 above.

6. The Challenges of *Romeo and Juliet*

1. Nineteenth-century burlesques and travesties are reprinted in *Shakespeare Burlesques*, ed. Stanley Wells, 5 vols. (London, 1977). One of the best is Andrew Halliday's *Romeo and Juliet Travestie, or, The Cup of Cold Poison*, first performed in 1859, in which Romeo and Juliet catch cold in the balcony scene: 'Swear not by the boon—the inconstant boon'.

2. John Downes, *Roscius Anglicanus* (London, 1708; Facsimile Reprint, Augustan Reprint Society no. 134, Los Angeles, 1969), sig. c3v.

3. Cited in G. C. D. Odell, *Shakespeare from Betterton to Irving*, 2 vols. (New York, 1920), i. 347.

4. From an article called 'The Religion of the Pianoforte' (*The Fortnightly Review*, February 1894), reprinted in part in *Shaw on Shakespeare*, ed. Edwin Wilson (London, 1962), 246.

5. See for example Peter Holding, *Romeo and Juliet: Text and Performance* (London, 1992), 61–2 for a description of the scene in a 1976 Stratford production directed by Trevor Nunn and Barry Kyle. In Adrian Noble's 1995 Stratford production, too, Juliet showed signs of life before Romeo died.

6. For example, Marjorie Garber, '*Romeo and Juliet*: Patterns and Paradigms', in *The Shakespeare Plays: A Study Guide* (San Diego, 1979), 50–63; reprinted in John F. Andrews (ed.), '*Romeo and Juliet': Critical Essays* (New York and London, 1993), 119–31; p. 131.

7. Jill L. Levenson, 'Romeo and Juliet': Shakespeare in Performance (Manchester, 1987), 66 and 97.

8. Cited in Alan Hughes, Henry Irving, Shakespearean (Cambridge, 1981), 160.

9. Henry James, in an article, 'London Plays', originally published in the Atlantic Monthly, August 1882, and reprinted in Allan Wade (ed.), The Scenic Art (London, 1949), 162–7; p. 164.

10. T. J. B. Spencer (ed.), Romeo and Juliet, New Penguin Shakespeare (Harmondsworth, 1967 etc.), 7.

11. Johnson on Shakespeare, ed. Arthur Sherbo, The Yale Edition of the Works of Samuel Johnson (New Haven, 1968), viii. 976.

12. Bertrand Evans, Shakespeare's Tragic Practice (Oxford, 1979), 51.

13. Judging by the prompt-book held in the Shakespeare Centre, Stratford-upon-Avon, Brook originally omitted all the text after Juliet's death (like Bogdanov after him) except for the addition of 'Brother Montague give me thy hand' from Capulet and the Prince's concluding six lines spoken by the Chorus, but restored some of the omitted dialogue, including part of the Friar's long speech, in later performances.

14. The theme is studied in its multiple international manifestations in Arthur T. Hatto (ed.), Eros: An Enquiry into the Theme of Lovers' Meetings and Partings at Dawn in Poetry (London, The Hague, and Paris, 1965); the section on English, by T. J. B. Spencer, includes discussion of Shakespeare's use of the motif.

15. From a review of Forbes-Robertson's production, The Saturday Review, 28 September 1895; reprinted in Shaw on Shakespeare, 168–74; p. 173.

16. M. M. Mahood, Shakespeare's Wordplay (London, 1968), 70.

17. Levenson, Romeo and Juliet, 7.

18. Johnson on Shakespeare, viii. 951.

19. David Leveaux's, in 1991.

20. Quoted from The Romantics on Shakespeare, ed. Jonathan Bate (Harmondsworth, 1992), 519.

21. Harley Granville-Barker, Prefaces to Shakespeare, 2nd Series (London, 1930), 26.

22. See, for example, Evans, Shakespeare's Tragic Practice, 42–3.

23. Charles Lower, 'Romeo and Juliet, IV.v: A Stage Direction and Purposeful Comedy', Shakespeare Studies 8 (1975), 177–94.

24. Holding, Romeo and Juliet, 56. Richard David also praises this device as 'a brilliant solution and one that was genuinely faithful to Shakespeare's intention': Richard David, Shakespeare in the Theatre (Cambridge, 1978), 113.

25. Confessions of a Young Man (1888); ed. Susan Dick (Montreal and London, 1972), 143; Moore was responding to Irving's spectacular production, which made him long for 'a simple stage, a few simple indications, and the simple recitation of that story of the sacrifice of the two white souls for the reconciliation of two great families'.

26. Johnson on Shakespeare, ii. 944.

27. Shaw on Shakespeare, 171.

28. Guardian, 7 April 1995.

29. John Dryden, 'Of Dramatic Poesy' and other Essays, ed. George Watson, Everyman's Library, 2 vols. (London, 1962), i. 180.

30. Granville-Barker, Prefaces to Shakespeare, 7.

31. E. Pearlman, 'Shakespeare at Work: Romeo and Juliet', English Literary Renaissance 24/2 (Spring 1994), 315–42; p. 336.

32. Pearlman summarizes arguments for the speech's relevance in his footnote 20.

33. David, Shakespeare in the Theatre, 115.

34. First published in 'Notes from Paris, 1876', in the *New York Tribune*, 5 February 1876; reprinted in *The Scenic Art*, 51–4; p. 54.
35. Holding, *Romeo and Juliet*, 44.
36. Levenson, *Romeo and Juliet*, 53.
37. Ibid. 67.

7. Juliet's Nurse: The Uses of Inconsequentiality

1. *Shakespeare's Early Tragedies* (London, 1968), 92.
2. In *The Friend*, 1818; *Coleridge on Shakespeare*, ed. Terence Hawkes, Penguin Shakespeare Library (Harmondsworth, 1969), 87–8.
3. 1955, p. xxxvi.
4. There is ample evidence that this phrase, recorded as a proverb (M. P. Tilley, *A Dictionary of the Proverbs in England in the Sixteenth and Seventeenth Centuries* (Ann Arbor, 1950), B 596) is self-gratulatory, meaning, as Isaac Reed glossed it, 'I have a perfect remembrance or recollection'; though the opposite meaning may easily suggest itself to a modern reader, resulting in George Skillan's note, in French's Acting Edition (London, 1947), 'then suddenly realising that she is getting somewhat away from her subject and admitting it'. T. J. B. Spencer seems to concede some doubt in his New Penguin (Harmondsworth, 1967) gloss: '(perhaps) I have a good memory still'.
5. Barbara Everett, in her subtle essay 'Romeo and Juliet: The Nurse's Story' (*Critical Quarterly* (Summer 1972), 129–39), writes that '"Shake, quoth the dovehouse!" has not been quite helpfully enough glossed, presumably because few Shakespeare editors are sufficiently acquainted with what might be said to a very small child about an earthquake. It does not simply mean, as has been suggested, "the dove-house shook"; it allows the unfluttered dovecote to satirise the earthquake, as in a comical baby mock-heroic—to be aloof and detached from what is happening to it' (p. 135).
6. I take it that the Nurse is saying that she was so shaken by the earthquake that she 'trudged' without having to be told to do so. Barbara Everett's comments on the passage (p. 136) seem rather to imply that the Nurse is saying that Juliet, in her tetchiness, had no call to send the Nurse packing, that the dovehouse was unimpressed equally by the fury of the earthquake and by the infant's crossness, and (possibly) that the Nurse was no more impressed by either. This seems to me to be an equally acceptable interpretation.
7. *Coleridge on Shakespeare*, 135.
8. See *William Shakespeare: The Most Excellent and Lamentable Tragedie of Romeo and Juliet, A Critical Edition*, by G. Walton Williams (Durham, NC, 1964), p. xii.
9. It is of only incidental interest that the published screen script of Metro-Goldwyn-Mayer's film starring Norma Shearer and Leslie Howard prints *all* the verse as prose, with the explanation that this helped the actors 'to speak their lines as Hamlet wished his players to speak theirs, "trippingly on the tongue"' (*A Motion Picture Version of Shakespeare's 'Romeo and Juliet'* (New York, 1936), 249).
10. 'The New Way with Shakespeare's Text', *Shakespeare Survey 8* (Cambridge, 1955), 98.
11. *Shakespeare's Tragic Sequence* (London, 1972), 40.
12. References are to the reprint in Geoffrey Bullough's *Narrative and Dramatic Sources of Shakespeare*, 8 vols. (London, 1957–75), vol. i (1957), 284–363.
13. *The Observer*, 3 November 1935.
14. New Penguin edition (1967), 184.
15. Ibid. 33–4.

16. *Coleridge on Shakespeare*, 145.
17. W. Hughes Hallett, reviewing Ben Greet's production at Ealing, in *The Pilot*, 17 May 1902, p. 528.
18. Jonas Barish cites the Nurse as the earliest specific illustration of his claim that Shakespeare 'virtually invented linguistic satire on the English stage' (*Ben Jonson and the Language of Prose Comedy* (Cambridge, MA, 1967), 284).

8. The Lamentable Tale of *Richard II*

This paper was given at the University of Kyoto in October, 1981 during a visit kindly arranged by the Shakespeare Society of Japan.

1. Quotations and references are from my New Penguin edition (Harmondsworth, 1969).
2. R. D. Altick, 'Symphonic Imagery in *Richard II*', *PMLA* 62 (1947), reprinted in Nicholas Brooke (ed.), *Richard II*, Casebook Series (Basingstoke, 1973), 101–30.
3. W. H. Clemen, *English Tragedy Before Shakespeare: The Development of Dramatic Speech* (London, 1961).
4. Modernized from Geoffrey Bullough, *Narrative and Dramatic Sources of Shakespeare*, iii (London, 1960), 401.
5. Ibid. 404.
6. *A Kingdom for a Stage* (Cambridge, MA, 1972), 117.
7. Ernst H. Kantorowicz, *The King's Two Bodies: A Study in Medieval Theology* (Princeton, 1957); extract reprinted in Brooke (ed.), *Richard II*, 175.
8. A. P. Rossiter, *Angel with Horns*, ed. Graham Storey (London, 1961, reprinted 1970), 25.
9. Nicholas Brooke, *Shakespeare's Early Tragedies* (London, 1968), 109, 113, 135.

9. *A Midsummer Night's Dream* Revisited

1. *A Midsummer Night's Dream*, ed. Harold F. Brooks, Arden Shakespeare (London, 1979); *A Midsummer Night's Dream*, ed. R. A. Foakes, New Cambridge Shakespeare (Cambridge, 1986); *A Midsummer Night's Dream*, in *William Shakespeare: The Complete Works*, gen. eds Stanley Wells and Gary Taylor (Oxford, 1986).
2. D. Allen Carroll and Gary Jay Williams, '*A Midsummer Night's Dream*': An Annotated Bibliography, Garland Shakespeare Bibliographies (New York and London, 1986), p. ix.
3. *A Midsummer Night's Dream*, ed. Stanley Wells, New Penguin Shakespeare (Harmondsworth, 1967), 14–15.
4. William Ringler, 'The Number of Actors in Shakespeare's Early Plays', in Gerald Eades Bentley (ed.), *The Seventeenth-Century Stage: A Collection of Critical Essays* (Chicago and London, 1968), 110–34.
5. Stephen Booth, 'Speculations on Doubling in Shakespeare's Plays', in Philip C. McGuire and David A. Samuelson (eds), *Shakespeare: The Theatrical Dimension* (New York, 1979), 108.
6. Steven W. May, '*A Midsummer Night's Dream* and the Carey Berkeley Wedding', in A. Leigh Deneef and M. Thomas Hester (eds), *Renaissance Papers 1983* (Raleigh, NC, 1984), 43–52.
7. Marion Colthorpe, 'Queen Elizabeth I and *A Midsummer Night's Dream*', *Notes and Queries* 232, NS 34 (June 1987), 206.
8. Paul A. Olson, '*A Midsummer Night's Dream* and the Meaning of Court Marriage', *ELH* 24 (1957), 95–119, reprinted in Laurence Lerner (ed.), *Shakespeare's Comedies: An Anthology of Modern Criticism*, Penguin Shakespeare Library (Harmondsworth and Baltimore, 1967).
9. Barbara Hodgdon, 'Gaining a Father: The Role of Egeus in the Quarto and the Folio', *The Review of English Studies*, NS 37, No. 148 (November 1986), 534–42.

10. Philip McGuire, *Speechless Dialect: Shakespeare's Open Silences* (Berkeley, 1985).
11. David P. Young, *Something of Great Constancy: The Art of 'A Midsummer Night's Dream'* (New Haven and London, 1966).
12. Stanley Wells, 'Shakespeare Without Sources', in Malcolm Bradbury and David Palmer (eds), *Shakespearian Comedy*, Stratford-upon-Avon Studies 14 (London and New York, 1972), 58–74, and reproduced in this volume.
13. Jan Kott, *Shakespeare our Contemporary* (London, 1964).
14. Stanley Wells, *Literature and Drama* (London, 1970), 93.
15. Maik Hamburger, 'New Concepts of Staging *A Midsummer Night's Dream*', *Shakespeare Survey* 40 (Cambridge, 1988), 51–61.
16. Roger Warren, *Text and Performance: A Midsummer Night's Dream* (London, 1983), 57.
17. Ibid. 46.
18. Booth, 'Speculations on Doubling', 108.
19. John Russell Brown, 'Free Shakespeare', *Shakespeare Survey* 24 (Cambridge, 1971), 127–35.

10. Translations in *A Midsummer Night's Dream*

1. Quotations and references are to the Oxford *Complete Works*, gen. eds Stanley Wells and Gary Taylor (Oxford, 1986).
2. So David P. Young, *Something of Great Constancy: The Art of 'A Midsummer Night's Dream'* (New Haven and London, 1966), 157: 'Bottom changed to an ass is but a short step, a revelation of inner qualities already familiar to us.' Bottom resembles Dogberry in his good qualities, too; both are men of good will.
3. *A Midsummer Night's Dream*, ed. Trevor R. Griffiths (Cambridge, 1996).
4. William C. Carroll, *The Metamorphoses of Shakespearean Comedy* (Princeton, NJ, 1985), 148.
5. See the note to 3.1.100 in Peter Holland's Oxford Shakespeare edition (Oxford, 1994).
6. *The Times*, 18 April 1962. I owe this reference, and helpful comments, to Roger Warren.
7. Young, *Something of Great Constancy*, 157: 'just as the "marriage" is probably never consummated, so is the transformation incomplete'.
8. Carroll, *Metamorphoses*, 152.
9. Jan Kott, *The Bottom Translation*, trans. Daniel Miedzyrzecka and Lillian Vallee (Evanston, IL, 1987).
10. T. B. Boecher, 'Bestial Buggery in *A Midsummer Night's Dream*', in D. L. Miller et al. (eds), *The Production of English Renaissance Culture* (Ithaca and London, 1994), 123–50.
11. Kott, *The Bottom Translation*, 52.
12. James L. Calderwood, *A Midsummer Night's Dream*, Twayne's New Critical Introductions to Shakespeare (Hemel Hempstead, 1992), 63.
13. *The Sunday Times*, 8 November 1931, quoted by Griffiths, *A Midsummer Night's Dream*, 53.
14. Griffiths, *A Midsummer Night's Dream*, 60.
15. Inga-Stina Ewbank, 'Shakespeare Translation as Cultural Exchange', *Shakespeare Survey* 48 (1995), 1–12.
16. Henry Morley, *The Journal of a London Playgoer, 1851–1866* (London, 1866, repr. 1891), 60–1.
17. Various treatments are discussed in Griffiths' note to 4.1.197–211.
18. Griffiths, *A Midsummer Night's Dream*, note to 1.2.71–8.
19. The burlesque elements of the play are discussed in J. W. Robinson, 'Palpable Hot Ice: Dramatic Burlesque in *A Midsummer Night's Dream*', *Studies in Philology* 61 (1964), 192–204.

11. The Once and Future *King Lear*

1. *Shakespearean Tragedy* (1904), 247.
2. *Studies in Shakespeare* (1927), 138.
3. *Shakespeare Today* (1957), 214.
4. '*King Lear*' in *Our Time* (Berkeley and Los Angeles, 1965), 9.
5. *Prefaces to Shakespeare* (1927; two-volume edition, 1958), i. 332.
6. *Prefaces to Shakespeare*, i. 328–9.
7. From the photographic facsimile in S. Schoenbaum, *William Shakespeare: Records and Images* (Oxford, 1981), 218.
8. The facts are summarized by E. K. Chambers, *William Shakespeare: A Study of Facts and Problems*, 2 vols. (Oxford, 1930), i. 133–7.
9. Peter W. M. Blayney establishes that *Lear* was Okes's first play in *The Texts of 'King Lear' and their Origins*, 2 vols. (Cambridge), 1 (1982), 10, 129. Information on Okes's punctuation is from Blayney's 'Shakespeare's Punctuation: A Study in Pointlessness', a paper given to a New Cambridge Shakespeare conference at the University of York, 5 April 1978. (Peter Alexander, in an unpublished paper dating from the 1950s, argued that the punctuation of Q resembles that of the Shakespearian 'good' quartos: see Kenneth Muir's new Arden edition (1952; rev. 1972), p. xvii, n. 2.)
10. 'The Function of Bibliography in Literary Criticism Illustrated in a Study of the Text of *King Lear*' [1933], in *The Collected Papers of Sir Walter W. Greg*, ed. J. C. Maxwell (Oxford, 1966), 287.
11. *Origins*, i. 7.
12. Steven Urkowitz, *Shakespeare's Revision of 'King Lear'* (Princeton, 1980), 131.
13. See Preface, pp. viii–ix.
14. *The Variants in the First Quarto of 'King Lear': A Bibliographical and Critical Inquiry* (London, 1940); now supplemented by Blayney, *Origins*, i. 207–57, 592–7.
15. See, for example, P. W. K. Stone, *The Textual History of 'King Lear'* (Farnham, 1980), 5.
16. Ibid. 6.
17. Steven Urkowitz, 'The Base Shall to th' Legitimate: The Growth of an Editorial Tradition', in Gary Taylor and Michael Warren (eds), *The Division of the Kingdoms: Shakespeare's Two Versions of 'King Lear'* (Oxford, 1983), 23–43.
18. *The Pictorial Edition of the Works of Shakespeare*, ed. Charles Knight, 8 vols. ([1839–]1843), vi. 392.
19. *King Lear*, The Kittredge Shakespeares (Boston, MA, 1940), p. viii.
20. *The Editorial Problem in Shakespeare* (Oxford, 1942; 3rd edn., 1954), 100.
21. Gary Taylor, 'Folio Copy for *Hamlet, King Lear*, and *Othello*', *Shakespeare Quarterly* 34 (1983), 44–61.
22. Gary Taylor, 'Monopolies, Show Trials, Disaster, and Invasion: *King Lear* and Censorship', in Taylor and Warren (eds), *The Division of the Kingdoms*, 75–120.
23. *The Shakespeare First Folio: Its Bibliographical and Textual History* (Oxford, 1955), 381.
24. Gary Taylor, '*King Lear*: The Date and Authorship of the Folio Version', in Taylor and Warren (eds), *The Division of the Kingdoms*, 351–468.
25. *Shakespeare Folios and Quartos* (1909), 76; *Shakespeare's Fight with the Pirates* (Cambridge, 1920), 50–1.
26. *William Shakespeare*, i. 465.
27. 'The Function of Bibliography', 289.
28. *Editorial Problem*, 96.

29. G. I. Duthie, *Elizabethan Shorthand and the First Quarto of 'King Lear'* (Oxford, 1949); W. W. Greg, *The Shakespeare First Folio*, 381.
30. *Textual Problems of the First Folio* (Cambridge, 1953), 49.
31. *New Penguin Shakespeare edition* (Harmondsworth, 1972), pp. 314–15.
32. In David Bevington and Jay L. Halio (eds), *Shakespeare, Pattern of Excelling Nature* (Newark and London, 1978), 95–107.
33. See the reviews of Urkowitz's book by Philip Edwards (*Modern Language Review* 77 (1982), 694–8) and by Richard Knowles (*Modern Philology* 79 (1981), 197–200). On the other hand, E. A. J. Honigmann (among others) accepts Urkowitz's thesis and argues for Shakespeare as the reviser: see 'Shakespeare's Revised Plays: *King Lear* and *Othello*', *The Library* VI/ 4 (1982), 142–73.
34. 'The Year's Contributions to Shakespearian Study, 3: Textual Studies', 180.
35. Since this essay was written a semi-professional production of the unedited Folio text has taken place in Santa Cruz, California. Playing in July and August 1982, it was directed by Audrey Stanley, with Tony Church as Lear and Julian Curry as the Fool.

12. Problems of Stagecraft in *The Tempest*

1. Roger Warren, *Staging Shakespeare's Late Plays* (Oxford, 1990), 13. Quotations from *The Tempest* are from Stephen Orgel's Oxford Shakespeare edition (Oxford, 1987).
2. Cited from the New Variorum edition, ed. H. H. Furness (Philadelphia, 1892, reprinted 1964), 392, 395.
3. G. C. D. Odell, *Shakespeare from Betterton to Irving* (New York, 1922, reprinted 1963), ii. 294.
4. The original staging of the scene is examined in detail in Andrew Gurr, '*The Tempest's* Tempest at Blackfriars', *Shakespeare Survey* 41 (Cambridge, 1989), 91–102.
5. Jan Kott, *Shakespeare our Contemporary* (London, 1964), 183.

13. 'My Name is Will': Shakespeare's Sonnets and Autobiography

1. *Review of English Studies* 34 (1983), 151–71.
2. *Shakespeare's Sonnets*, ed. Katherine Duncan-Jones, The Arden Shakespeare (London, 2010), 33.
3. Ibid. 11.
4. Katherine Duncan-Jones, *Ungentle Shakespeare: Scenes from His Life* (London, 2001), 217.
5. William Shakespeare, *Complete Sonnets and Poems*, ed. Colin Burrow, The Oxford Shakespeare (Oxford, 2002), 92.
6. *Sonnets*, ed. Duncan-Jones, 40.
7. *Sonnets and Poems*, ed. Burrow, 93.
8. Paul Edmondson and Stanley Wells, *Shakespeare's Sonnets*, Oxford Shakespeare Topics (Oxford, 2004), esp. pp. 49–51.
9. *Sonnets*, ed. Duncan-Jones, 408.
10. '"Incertainties now crown themselves assur'd": The Politics of Plotting Shakespeare's Sonnets', *Shakespeare Quarterly* 47 (1996), 291–305.
11. Germaine Greer, *Shakespeare's Wife* (London, 2007), 261.
12. *A New Variorum Edition of Shakespeare: The Sonnets*, ed. H. E. Rollins, 2 vols. (Philadelphia and London, 1944).
13. *Sonnets*, ed. Duncan-Jones, 52–69.
14. *Sonnets and Poems*, ed. Burrow, 135.

15. David Ellis, *The Truth About William Shakespeare: Fact, Fiction, and Modern Biographies* (Edinburgh, 2012).
16. See *New Variorum Edition*, ed. Rollins, note to Sonnet 26.
17. Richard Barnfield, *The Complete Poems*, ed. George Klawitter (Selinsgrove, 1990), 73.
18. 'Shakespeare: Man of the European Renaissance', in Martin Procházka et al. (eds) *Renaissance Shakespeare: Shakespeare Renaissances* (Newark, DE, 2014), 6, and reproduced in this volume.
19. *New Variorum Edition*, ed. Rollins, note to Sonnet 26.
20. A. J. Gurr, 'Shakespeare's First Poem: Sonnet 145', *Essays in Criticism* 21 (1971), 321–6; Stephen Booth, *Shakespeare's Sonnets: Edited with Analytic Commentary* (New Haven, 1977), 501.
21. René Weis, *Shakespeare Revealed: Decoding a Hidden Life* (London, 2007), 185–92.
22. *The Labyrinth of Shakespeare's Sonnets: An Examination of Sexual Elements in Shakespeare's Language* (London, 1974), 24.

14. Shakespeare Without Sources

1. These are the only three plays for which the Summary table in Kenneth Muir's *Shakespeare's Sources* (Vol. 1 (London, 1957), 255–7) gives 'Not known' under the heading 'Main Source'. In his Appendix of plays 'of which the sources are not precisely known' he adds *Titus Andronicus*, *The Two Gentlemen of Verona*, *The Taming of the Shrew*, *The Merry Wives of Windsor*, and *Timon of Athens*, and does not include *A Midsummer Night's Dream*. But of *A Midsummer Night's Dream* he says, 'There was probably no comprehensive source' (p. 31). *Titus Andronicus* may be a revision of an earlier play, or may be based on an earlier version of the eighteenth-century chapbook. *The Two Gentlemen of Verona* has, as Muir says, an 'ultimate source' in Montemayor's *Diana*, which, directly or indirectly, provided the basic narrative material. *The Taming of the Shrew* has undisputed origins in folk-tale and, for its sub-plot, Gascoigne's *Supposes*. *The Merry Wives of Windsor* may be based on a lost play. In any case, it is textually corrupt, and there is internal and external evidence that it stands outside the main stream of Shakespeare's achievement. The basic material of *Timon of Athens* is from Plutarch; Muir believes 'there may have been a dramatic source' (p. 260). Of *The Tempest*, Muir says 'There were a number of minor sources . . . but it is highly probable that there was a main source as yet unidentified' (p. 261). I feel that the resemblances, considered in this chapter, between *The Tempest* and some of Shakespeare's earlier plays encourage the belief that this play, too, is of Shakespeare's invention.
2. From the *Preface* (1765); *Dr Johnson on Shakespeare*, ed. W. K. Wimsatt, Penguin Shakespeare Library (Harmondsworth, 1969), 64.
3. Absence of detailed characterization, along with thinness of plot, has encouraged comparisons between some of Shakespeare's comedies and certain types of opera. Northrop Frye says, 'when we look for the most striking parallels to *Twelfth Night* or *The Tempest*, we think first of all of *Figaro* and *The Magic Flute*' (*A Natural Perspective* (New York, 1965), 25). Opera composers have had similar thoughts. Britten's *A Midsummer Night's Dream* is one of the best of Shakespearean operas. *The Tempest*, though it has produced no acknowledged masterpiece, has tempted opera composers more than any other of Shakespeare's plays—Winton Dean finds over thirty operas based on it ('Shakespeare and Opera', in Phyllis Hartnoll (ed.), *Shakespeare in Music* (London, 1964), 104). And *Love's Labour's Lost* and *The Tempest* are the two plays that come nearest to providing us with a Shakespearean opera by Mozart. There exists an adaptation of *Love's Labour's Lost* as an alternative libretto to *Così fan tutte*; and one of the saddest aspects of the fact that Mozart died when he did is

that he is said to have just agreed to set a text based on *The Tempest* (Dean, 'Shakespeare and Opera', 91 and 108). The thought of a post-*Magic Flute* opera by Mozart on this theme is awe-inspiring. Let us hope that it awaits us in heaven.

4. *Elizabethan and Jacobean* (Oxford, 1945), 109–10.
5. *Something of Great Constancy* (New Haven and London, 1966), 179.
6. 'The Shakespearian Superman', in *The Crown of Life* (London, 1947), 208.
7. 'The Mature Comedies', in J. R. Brown and B. Harris (eds), *Early Shakespeare*, Stratford-upon-Avon Studies 3 (London, 1961), 214.

15. Shakespeare and Romance

1. The adjective, however, is not recorded before 1659.
2. M. Doran, *Endeavors of Art* (Madison, WI, 1954), 172.
3. Heliodorus, *Aethiopica*, trans. by Thomas Underdowne, in *An Aethiopian History written in Greek by Heliodorus*, ed. Charles Whibley and W. E. Henley (London, 1895), 47.
4. Ibid. 181–2.
5. Ibid. 288.
6. In 1600 Robert Chambers, a Roman Catholic priest, published a most curious book called *Palestina*, which adapts the events of the Gospels to the conventions of romance.
7. Thomas Nashe, 'The Anatomie of Absurditie', in *The Works of Thomas Nashe*, ed. Ronald B. McKerrow, 5 vols. (Oxford, 1958), i. 11.
8. E. C. Pettet, *Shakespeare and the Romance Tradition* (London, 1949), 12.
9. *The Use of Poetry and the Use of Criticism* (London, 1933), 51.
10. S. L. Wolff, *The Greek Romances in Elizabethan Prose Fiction* (New York, 1912; reprinted 1961), 352.
11. John F. Danby, *Poets on Fortune's Hill: Studies in Sidney, Shakespeare, Beaumont and Fletcher* (London, 1952), 71 and 72.
12. *Elizabethan Taste* (London, 1963), 246.
13. W. H. Allen, *The English Novel* (London, 1954), 25.
14. 'nativity', the Folio's reading, is usually—perhaps rightly—emended. Globe reads 'festivity', Foakes, 'felicity'.
15. Cf. 'the confusion of twins which entertained us for five acts of *The Comedy of Errors* appears now as little more than an adroit device to bring about a happy ending' (Harold Jenkins, 'Shakespeare's *Twelfth Night*', *The Rice Institute Pamphlet* (January 1959), 20).
16. *The Death of the Moth* (1942; Harmondsworth, 1961), 45.
17. 'For Jesus' Sake Forbear', *Shakespeare Quarterly* (Spring 1962), 228.
18. Wolff studies this influence in immense detail. He is somewhat inclined to attribute any parallel between the romances and *Pandosto* to direct influence, without consideration of other writings that exhibit the same features. But he demonstrates beyond question that *Pandosto* has much in common with these works.
19. The scholars took over from the chambermaids in the middle of the eighteenth century; the last references to the book as popular reading coincide closely with the beginning of interest in it as a Shakespeare source.
20. *The Winter's Tale*, ed. J. H. P. Pafford, The Arden Shakespeare (London, 1963), Introduction, p. lxvi.
21. *On Some of Shakespeare's Female Characters*, new and enlarged edition (1891), 389–90.
22. Cf. F. R. Leavis: 'Shakespeare's power to present acceptingly and movingly the unironical vision (for us given in Miranda and Ferdinand) goes with his power to contemplate the

irony at the same time' ('The Criticism of Shakespeare's Late Plays: A Caveat', in *The Common Pursuit* (1952; Harmondsworth, 1962), 180).

23. *Shakespeare* (New York, 1941), 323.
24. Enid Welsford, *The Court Masque* (Cambridge, 1927), 339. D. G. James, *Scepticism and Poetry* (New York, 1937), 240. G. Wilson Knight, 'The Shakespearian Superman', *The Crown of Life* (London, 1947, etc.), 208.

16. Boys Should be Girls: Shakespeare's Female Roles and the Boy Players

1. See Tony Howard, *Women as Hamlet: Performance and Interpretation in Theatre, Film and Fiction* (Cambridge, 2007).
2. Marvin Rosenberg, 'The Myth of Shakespeare's Squeaking Boy Actor—or Who Played Cleopatra?', *Shakespeare Bulletin* (2001).
3. G. E. Bentley, *The Profession of Player in Shakespeare's Time* (Princeton, 1984), p. 114.
4. Privately communicated; the argument is fully set out in David Kathman, 'Reconsidering *The Seven Deadly Sins*', *Early Theatre*, 7/1 (2004), 13–44.
5. Lois Potter (ed.), *The Two Noble Kinsmen* (London, 1997), 65.

17. Staging Shakespeare's Ghosts

1. R. V. Holdsworth, '*Macbeth* and *The Puritan*', *Notes and Queries* NS 37/2 (1990), 204–5.
2. Arthur Colby Sprague, *Shakespeare and the Actors* (Cambridge, MA, 1944).
3. W. J. Lawrence, *Pre-Restoration Stage Studies* (Oxford, 1927), 174.
4. F. W. Moorman, 'Shakespeare's Ghosts', *MLR* 1 (1906), 193.
5. Julie Hankey (ed.), *Richard III*, Plays in Performance (London, 1981).
6. Stanley Wells and Gary Taylor, with John Jowett and William Montgomery, *William Shakespeare: A Textual Companion* (Oxford, 1987), 247.
7. W. H. Clemen, *A Commentary on Shakespeare's Richard III* (London, 1968), 211–13.
8. Bernard Beckerman, *Shakespeare at the Globe* (New York, 1962), 204.
9. G. C. D. Odell, *Shakespeare from Betterton to Irving*, 2 vols. (New York, 1920), i. 237.
10. John Ripley, '*Julius Caesar*' on Stage in England and America, 1599–1973 (London, 1980), 266.
11. W. J. Lawrence, *Pre-Restoration Stage Studies* (Oxford, 1927).
12. Sprague, *Shakespeare and the Actors*, 128; see also Diana Macintyre DeLuca, 'The Movements of the Ghost in *Hamlet*', *Shakespeare Quarterly* 24 (1973), 147–50.
13. *Pre-Restoration Stage Studies*, 105.
14. Samuel Taylor Coleridge, *Coleridge's Criticism of Shakespeare: A Selection*, ed. R. A. Foakes (London, 1989), 79.
15. Lawrence, *Pre-Restoration Stage Studies*, 106–7; James G. McManaway, 'The Two Earliest Prompt Books of *Hamlet*', *PBSA* 43 (1949), 315.
16. See Sprague, *Shakespeare and the Actors*, 132.
17. *Pre-Restoration Stage Studies*, 107–8.
18. 'Prompt Books', 315.
19. J. N. French, 'The Staging of Magical Effects in Elizabethan and Jacobean Drama', unpublished PhD thesis (Birmingham, 1964), 94–5.
20. See DeLuca, 'Movements of the Ghost', 151; Harold Jenkins (ed.), *Hamlet*, The Arden Shakespeare (London, 1982), note to 1.1.42.
21. *Pre-Restoration Stage Studies*, 110.

22. *Hamlet, Prince of Denmark*, ed. Philip Edwards, The New Cambridge Shakespeare (Cambridge, 1985).

23. 'Movements of the Ghost', 153.

24. G. R. Hibbard (ed.), *Hamlet*, The Oxford Shakespeare (Oxford, 1987).

25. Niels L. Anthonisen, 'The Ghost in *Hamlet*', *American Imago* 2 (1966), 232–49; quotes on pp. 245, 246.

26. 'Movements of the Ghost', 153.

27. *Shakespeare and the Actors*, 165.

28. G. K. Hunter (ed.), *Macbeth*, New Penguin Shakespeare (Harmondsworth, 1967).

29. Cited in Wells and Taylor, *Textual Companion*, 543–4.

30. *Macbeth and the Players* (Cambridge, 1969), 8.

31. Sprague, *Shakespeare and the Actors*, 261–2.

32. Ibid. 255.

18. Staging Shakespeare's Apparitions and Dream Visions

1. William Shakespeare, *The Complete Works*, ed. Stanley Wells and Gary Taylor, with John Jowett and William Montgomery (Oxford, 1986). All references are from this edition, unless otherwise stated.

2. Herbert Berry, 'The First Public Playhouses, Especially the Red Lion', in *Shakespeare Quarterly* 40/2 (1989), 133–48. William Shakespeare, *2 Henry VI*, ed. A. S. Cairncross (London, 1957), note to 1.4.8. Cairncross glosses *'aloft'* as 'on the upper stage, or even on the "top" or turret, representing a tower, as in Q'.

3. Berry, 'The First Public Playhouses', 138.

4. *Narrative and Dramatic Sources of Shakespeare*, ed. Geoffrey Bullough, 8 vols. (London, 1957–75), iii (1960), 101–2. Modernized here.

5. This was William Montgomery.

6. Cairncross, note to 1.4.22, conjectures that these lines 'are probably an English version of the L[atin] conjuration, which was presumably read from a scroll'.

7. Cited in J. Nathan French, 'The Staging of Magical Effects in Elizabethan and Jacobean Drama' (unpublished PhD thesis, University of Birmingham, 1964), 309.

8. Stanley Wells and Gary Taylor, with John Jowett and William Montgomery, *William Shakespeare: A Textual Companion* (Oxford, 1987), 181.

9. Anthony Harris, *Night's Black Agents: Witchcraft and Magic in Seventeenth-Century English Drama* (Manchester, 1980), 163.

10. Ibid. 'The apparitions might have been represented by artificial figures, perhaps equipped with speaking tubes ... Alternatively, they could have been portrayed by actors, suitably costumed and carrying appropriate properties.'

11. John Cranford Adams, *The Globe Playhouse: Its Design and Equipment*, 2nd edn. (Cambridge, MA, 1942; London, 1961), 190–1. R. Watkins and J. Lemmon, *In Shakespeare's Playhouse: Macbeth* (Newton Abbot, 1974), 119.

12. Bernard Beckerman, *Shakespeare at the Globe: 1599–1609* (New York, 1962), 243, n. 18.

13. Watkins and Lemmon, *In Shakespeare's Playhouse*, 119.

14. Beckerman, *Shakespeare at the Globe*, 243, n. 18.

15. Ibid. 203.

16. Peter Thomson, *Shakespeare's Theatre* (London, 1983), 153–4.

17. William P. Halstead, *Shakespeare as Spoken*, 14 vols. (Ann Arbor, MI, 1977–83), x (1979), 802c.

18. Wells and Taylor et al., *William Shakespeare: A Textual Companion*, 588.

19. French, 'The Staging of Magical Effects', 295.
20. *The Plays of William Shakespeare*, ed. S. Johnson and G. Steevens, 10 vols. (London, 1778–80), *Supplement* with notes by E. Malone and others, 2 vols. (London, 1780), xii, *Pericles*, 5.2.
21. Beckerman, *Shakespeare at the Globe*, 94.
22. See the illustrations in William Shakespeare, *The Complete Works*, ed. Stanley Wells and Gary Taylor, compact edition (Oxford, 1988), 1039.
23. J. P. Brockbank, *J. P. Brockbank on Shakespeare* (Oxford, 1989), 300.
24. G. Wilson Knight, *The Crown of Life* (London, 1947), 168–202. Wilson Knight's views were also upheld by J. W. Nosworthy in his Arden edition of the play in 1955.
25. Harley Granville-Barker, *Prefaces to Shakespeare*, 2 vols. (London 1958), i. 460. The *Preface* to *Cymbeline* first appeared in 1930, printed in London, in the second series of prefaces.
26. French, 'The Staging of Magical Effects', 238–47.
27. Roger Warren, *Cymbeline*, Shakespeare in Performance (Manchester, 1989), 58.
28. Granville-Barker, *Prefaces to Shakespeare*, i. 473.
29. Ibid. 478.
30. Cranford Adams, *The Globe Playhouse*, 338.
31. Ibid. 340.
32. Warren, *Cymbeline*, 58.
33. Bernard Hewitt (ed.), *The Renaissance Stage Documents of Serlio, Sabbatini, and Furtenbach* (Coral Gables, FL, 1958), 35 ff., cited in French, 'The Staging of Magical Effects', 214.
34. Granville-Barker, *Prefaces to Shakespeare*, i. 462.

19. Shakespeare in Planché's Extravaganzas

1. *The Extravaganzas of J. R. Planché, Esq., 1825–1871*, ed. T. F. Dillon Croker and Stephen Tucker, 5 vols. (1879). All references to Planché's dramatic works are to this edition.
2. e.g. H. Granville-Barker, 'Exit Planché—Enter Gilbert', in J. Drinkwater (ed.), *The Eighteen-Sixties* (Cambridge, 1932), 102–48; Sir St Vincent Troubridge, 'Gilbert and Planché', *Notes and Queries* 180 (22 March and 12 July 1941); H. H. Tilley, 'J. R. Planché, Reformer' (1951; unpublished MA dissertation in the library of the University of Birmingham).
3. *The Oxford Companion to the Theatre*, ed. Phyllis Hartnoll (Oxford, 1951).
4. *A History of English Drama, 1660–1900*, iv (Cambridge; 2nd edn., 1955), 151. See also G. Wilson Knight, *The Golden Labyrinth* (London, 1962), 273–6.
5. 'Some Burlesques with a Purpose, 1830–1870', *Philological Quarterly* 8 (1929), 255–63.
6. *The Victorian Theatre* (Oxford, 1956); see especially pp. 68–9.
7. MacMillan, 'Some Burlesques with a Purpose, 1830–1870', 259, writes: 'Fitzgerald says that his plays, which were full of delicate conceits and classical allusions, "supposed a too high state of culture in the audience"; and the producers cut and hacked them, inserting "wheezes" and "bits of fat". We know that there were exceptions to this rule, especially in the parts acted by Mathews and Robson, and Planché enters no complaints against his producers on this account.' This is based upon a misunderstanding of Fitzgerald, who wrote, not of Planché's 'plays', but of *one* play written at the end of his career. Fitzgerald's statement implies that an audience of the 1870s was less cultured than one of the 1840s: 'I remember him in great elation at being called upon to supply a piece for Covent Garden—the strange "Babil and Bijou" venture; and the old writer concocted one of his literary burlesques of the old pattern in the Vestris days—full of delicate conceits and classical allusions. This kind of wit seems now very ponderous, and is all but unreadable—it supposed a too high state of culture in the audience. The business men

of the speculation treated his work *sans ceremonie* [*sic*]—hacked and hewed it mercilessly, suppressed about half, and stuffed it with "wheezes" and bits of "fat"' (*The Garrick Club* (1904), 43). *Babil and Bijou* was Planché's last work for the stage.

8. *The Journal of a London Playgoer* (1866), 69.
9. *Fifty Years of an Actor's Life* (1904), i. 194.
10. Preface to *The Sleeping Beauty in the Wood*, ii. 66.
11. It is not recorded in A. C. Sprague's *Shakespeare and the Actors* (Cambridge, MA, 1948).
12. Quoted from W. M. Merchant's *Shakespeare and the Artist* (London, 1959), 102–3, where there is a longer quotation from Kean's playbill discussing this topic.
13. J. R. Planché, *A Cyclopaedia of Costume*, ii. 360. The 'target and truncheon' were also used by Macready: see Sprague, *Shakespeare and the Actors*, portrait facing p. 230.
14. Reprinted in A. M. Nagler's *A Source Book in Theatrical History* (New York, 1952), 489, from J. W. Cole's *The Life and Theatrical Times of Charles Kean F.S.A.*, edition of 1860, ii. 379–82.
15. Charles Kean is referred to again in *Mr Buckstone's Voyage Round the Globe* (17 April 1854; v. 23–4), where there is a passage concerning his rivalry, particularly as Richard III, with G. V. Brooke (cf. W. J. Lawrence, *The Life of Gustavus Vaughan Brooke* (Belfast, 1892), 142).
16. Rossini's opera *William Tell* had recently been performed with great success at Drury Lane.
17. *Recollections* (1872), ii. 83–6. Writing of the Induction, Planché says: 'My restoration of this "gem" is one of the events in my theatrical career on which I look back with the greatest pride and gratification.' An engraving of a scene from this production is reproduced by R. Mander and J. Mitchenson in *A Picture History of the British Theatre* (London, 1957), no. 262. G. C. D. Odell reprints part of *The Times*' report in *Shakespeare from Betterton to Irving* (New York, 1920), ii. 313.
18. Ibid. i. 56–9.
19. Ibid. ii. 85.

20. Shakespeare in Max Beerbohm's Theatre Criticism

1. Bernard Shaw, *Our Theatres in the Nineties*, 3 vols. (1932), iii. 384–6.
2. *Letters*, ed. R. Hart-Davis (London, 1962), 778.
3. David Cecil, *Max: A Biography* (London, 1964), 164.
4. *Around Theatres* (London, 1953), 578.
5. Cecil, *Max: A Biography*, 168.
6. *More Theatres: 1898–1903* (London, 1969), 12.
7. The three collections will be referred to in the text of this essay as i, ii, and iii.
8. Presumably because he took this passage too seriously, Riewald mistakenly says that Max 'made it a rule never to criticize a play in which his great brother appeared' (J. G. Riewald, *Sir Max Beerbohm...A Critical Analysis with A Brief Life and a Bibliography* ('s-Gravenhage, 1953), 146–7).
9. This is reproduced as the frontispiece to *More Theatres*.
10. Chapter XXI.
11. These are reprinted in *Max in Verse*, ed. J. G. Riewald (Brattleboro, VT, 1963), 31–3, with the information that they were printed in *The Mask* (Florence), July 1924, p. 119, and that there is a privately owned manuscript in California.
12. Cecil, *Max: A Biography*, 373.
13. Ibid. 296.
14. *The Works of William Shakespeare*, 10 vols. (Stratford-upon-Avon, 1904–7), x. 321–34.

15. Strachey's 'Shakespeare's Final Period', first published in *The Independent Review* in August 1906, had been delivered as a paper to the Sunday Essay Society at Trinity College, Cambridge, on 24 November 1903 (S. Schoenbaum, *Shakespeare's Lives* (Oxford, 1970), 664).

16. Harold Hodge is mistakenly identified as Herbert Hodge in Max Beerbohm's *Letters to Reggie Turner* (London, 1964), ed. R. Hart-Davis, p. 137, n. 1.

17. He does not refer to the live rabbits alleged to have appeared in this production.

18. Reprinted in Lee's *Shakespeare and the Modern Stage* (London, 1906), 1–24.

19. G. C. D. Odell, *Shakespeare—from Betterton to Irving*, 2 vols. (New York, 1920), ii. 453.

20. Ibid.

21. Shakespeare in Leigh Hunt's Theatre Criticism

1. *The Autobiography of Leigh Hunt*, World's Classics edn. (London, 1928). Leigh Hunt's theatre criticism is quoted from *Critical Essays on the Performers of the London Theatres* (1808), *Dramatic Essays by Leigh Hunt*, ed. William Archer and Robert W. Lowe (1894), and *Leigh Hunt's Dramatic Criticism 1808–1831*, ed. L. C. and C. W. Houtchens (New York, 1949). References to these volumes in this essay identify them respectively as *Performers*, Archer, and Houtchens.

2. *Autobiography*, 190–2, 197.

3. Ibid. 214.

4. Houtchens, 38, 225.

5. Mrs Anne Mathews, *Memoirs of Charles Mathews, Comedian*, quoted in Archer, p. xxx, n. 1.

6. *Autobiography*, 500.

7. Houtchens: on *Lear*, 16–17; *King John*, 38; *Julius Caesar*, 65; Hazlitt, 289.

8. Houtchens, 295.

9. Houtchens, 291, 173.

10. Houtchens, 112–14.

11. Archer, 148.

12. Archer, 222–6.

13. Houtchens, 82.

14. *Lectures on the English Poets* (1818); an extract reprinted in *Shakespeare Criticism*, ed. D. Nichol Smith (1916), 305–19; p. 306.

15. *Shakespeare Jahrbuch* (West) 97 (1966), 49–62.

16. Archer, 183–4, 204.

17. On Mrs Jordan and Mrs H. Siddons: *Performers*, 209; Miss Meadows, *Performers*, Appendix, 32; Miss Tree: Houtchens, 228; Miss Taylor: Archer, 182.

18. Houtchens, 197–8.

19. Houtchens, 301; Archer, 185, 179–80.

20. Houtchens, 327–9, 41, 231.

21. Archer, 183; Houtchens, 65; Archer, 185, 184.

22. Houtchens, 220.

23. Archer, 87.

24. Archer, 161–3.

25. Archer, 111.

26. The Preface is reprinted in Archer, pp. xxxvii–xlii.

27. *Oxford Companion to the Theatre*, ed. Phyllis Hartnoll (3rd edn., Oxford, 1967), s.v. Siddons, Sarah; Archer, 11, 13; *Performers*, Appendix, 6; *Autobiography*, 166; Houtchens, 72.

28. Archer, 15–16, 114–15; *Autobiography*, 194.

29. *Autobiography*, 193; Houtchens, 202; Archer, 227–8.
30. Archer, 157.
31. Archer, 193–5; Houtchens, 22–3.
32. Archer, 202.
33. Houtchens, 138.

22. Shakespeare in Hazlitt's Theatre Criticism

1. See my 'Shakespeare in Leigh Hunt's Theatre Criticism', *Essays and Studies* 33 (1980), 119–38, reproduced in this volume.
2. Cited in references as *View*. Page references are to volume 5 of Howe's edition. *Characters of Shakespear's Plays* is cited from the World's Classics edition (Oxford, 1917, etc.).
3. The point is made by Herschel Baker, *William Hazlitt* (Cambridge, MA and London, 1962), 308, in his valuable section on Shakespeare.
4. John Keats, letter to Richard Woodhouse, 27 October 1818.
5. Reprinted in *Shakespeare Criticism: A Selection*, ed. D. Nichol Smith (Oxford, 1916, etc.), 43. Hazlitt quotes this passage at the opening of his Preface to *Characters of Shakespear's Plays*.
6. From Richard Wroughton's version, cited by G. C. D. Odell, *Shakespeare—from Betterton to Irving*, 2 vols. (New York, 1920), 74–5.
7. Hazlitt's view of the tragic hero is investigated by Joseph W. Donohue, Jr, in 'Hazlitt's Sense of the Dramatic Actor as Tragic Hero', *Studies in English Literature* 5 (1965), 705–21.
8. Cited by Carol J. Carlisle, *Shakespeare from the Greenroom: Actors' Criticisms of Four Major Tragedies* (Chapel Hill, NC, 1969), 149.
9. *William Hazlitt*, 290n.
10. Cited by William Archer, Preface, pp. xxv–xxvi.

23. Peter Hall's *Coriolanus*, 1959

1. *The Characters of Shakespeare's Plays* (1817), World's Classics (London, 1916, etc.), 56.
2. J. C. Maxwell (ed.), *Elizabethan and Jacobean Drama* (Liverpool, 1974), 17.
3. 'Coriolanus' (1912), reprinted in Peter Alexander (ed.), *Studies in Shakespeare* (London, 1964), 219–37.
4. *Tynan on Theatre* (Harmondsworth, 1964), 94.
5. A. Pryce-Jones, *Observer*, 12 July.
6. 'Coriolanus: Shakespeare's Tragedy in Rehearsal and Performance', in Bernard Harris and John Russell Brown (eds), *Later Shakespeare*, Stratford-upon-Avon Studies 8 (London, 1966), 167–81; p. 169.

24. On Being a General Editor

1. Alfred Harbage (ed.), *William Shakespeare: The Complete Works* (New York, 1969), p. ix.
2. Ibid., p. ix.
3. Ibid., p. x.
4. Ibid., p. ix.
5. From the Preface (1765), in *Johnson on Shakespeare*, ed. Arthur Sherbo (New Haven, 1968), The Yale Edition vol. 7, p. 111.
6. In 1959 Fredson Bowers wrote that 'The guidance that single editors of recent Elizabethan series have received from general editorial instructions both in England and America has certainly been insufficient.' 'Principle and Practice in the Editing of Early Dramatic Texts',

in *Textual and Literary Criticism* (Cambridge, 1959), 180. Harbage's Pelican edition had started to appear three years earlier, though Bowers's contribution, *The Merry Wives of Windsor*, dates from 1963. (R. B. McKerrow's *Prolegomena for the Oxford Shakespeare* of 1939 is of course invaluable, but is rather an account of his own practice in the texts he prepared for his proposed edition than a set of guidelines for other editors.)

7. G. Blakemore Evans (ed.), *The Riverside Shakespeare* (Boston, MA, 1974), 39.
8. Stanley Wells and Gary Taylor, *Modernizing Shakespeare's Spelling with Three Studies in the Text of Henry V* (Oxford, 1979), 5.

25. Editorial Treatment of Foul-Paper Texts: *Much Ado About Nothing* as Test Case

1. *The Shakespeare First Folio* (Oxford, 1955), 279.
2. *William Shakespeare: A Study of Facts and Problems* (Oxford, 1930), i. 386.
3. Cf. e.g. F. P. Wilson, *Shakespeare and the New Bibliography*, rev. and ed. Helen Gardner (Oxford, 1970), 67–8.
4. *The Shakespeare First Folio*, 278.
5. *William Shakespeare: The Complete Works*, ed. C. J. Sisson (London, 1954), 143.
6. *The Riverside Shakespeare* (Boston, MA, 1974), 362.
7. *The Stability of Shakespeare's Text* (London, 1965), 147, n. 3.
8. *The Works of William Shakespeare*, ed. W. G. Clark, J. Glover, and W. A. Wright (1863–6, repr. 1893), ii. 105.
9. 'Proposed New Readings in Shakespeare: The Comedies', *Bulletin de la Faculté des Lettres de Strasbourg* (May–June 1965), 945–58, at p. 950.
10. In fact Mark Antony is called Antonio on five occasions in *Julius Caesar* (1.2.3, 4, 6, 190; 1.3. 37).
11. *New Readings in Shakespeare* (Cambridge, 1956), i. 100.
12. Ibid.
13. Chambers declares that 'Claudio, otherwise unpartnered' dances 'with Ursula' (i. 386), but this is his decision, not Shakespeare's.

26. Money in Shakespeare's Comedies

1. Sandra K. Fischer, *Econolingua: A Glossary of Coins and Economic Language in Renaissance Drama* (Newark, N. J., 1985).
2. Ibid. 32.
3. *Marlowe's Doctor Faustus, 1604–16, Parallel Texts*, ed. W. W. Greg (Oxford, 1950), 392–3.
4. Fischer, 119.
5. Stanley Wells and Gary Taylor, with John Jowett and William Montgomery, *William Shakespeare: A Textual Companion* (Oxford, 1987), 578.
6. George Unwin, *Shakespeare's England*, 2 vols. (Oxford, 1916 etc.), i. 340.
7. Fischer, 154.
8. Unwin, *Shakespeare's England*, i. 318.
9. Fischer, 154.
10. Ann Jennalie Cook, *Making a Match: Courtship in Shakespeare and his Society* (Princeton, 1991).
11. Ibid. 131.

27. To Read a Play: The Problem of Editorial Intervention

1. Quotations from Shakespeare are from *The Complete Oxford Shakespeare*, gen. eds Stanley Wells and Gary Taylor (Oxford, 1986), unless otherwise stated.

2. *As You Like It*, ed. Sir Arthur Quiller-Couch and John Dover Wilson (Cambridge, 1926), note to 2.5.60–1.

3. *As You Like It*, ed. Agnes Latham, The Arden Shakespeare (London, 1975).

4. *As You Like It*, ed. Richard Knowles, A New Variorum Edition of Shakespeare (New York, 1977), note to line 949.

5. Alan C. Dessen, *Elizabethan Stage Conventions and Modern Interpreters* (Cambridge, 1984), 101–2.

6. Ibid. 102, citing Bernard Beckerman, *Shakespeare at the Globe, 1599–1609* (New York, 1962), 159.

7. See A. H. Scouten, 'Designation of Locale in Shakespeare Texts', *Essays in Theatre* 2/1 (Nov. 1983), 41–55, and James Ogden, 'Lear's Blasted Heath', *Durham University Journal* 81 (Dec. 1987), 19–22.

8. *A Midsummer Night's Dream*, ed. Sir Arthur Quiller-Couch and John Dover Wilson (Cambridge, 1924), stage directions to 1.2, 2.1, and 2.2.

9. *Romeo and Juliet*, ed. Edward Dowden, The Arden Shakespear (London, 1900).

10. Thomas Dekker, *The Shoemaker's Holiday*, ed. R. L. Smallwood and Stanley Wells, Revels Plays: (Manchester, 1979), 63–4.

11. *Hamlet*, ed. G. R. Hibbard, The Oxford Shakespeare (Oxford, 1987), note to 1.2.65.

12. *As You Like It*, ed. Agnes Latham, note to 4.1.31.

13. H. Granville-Barker, *Prefaces to Shakespeare* (1927; two-volume edition, 1958), i. 328–9.

28. The First Folio: Where Should We be Without it?

1. Elegies in English, Latin, and Greek are reproduced in facsimile in *Elegies for Sir Philip Sidney* (*1587*), with an introduction by A. J. Colaianne and W. L. Godshalk, Scholar's Facsimiles and Reprint (Delmar, NY, 1980).

2. Quoted in the entry for Spenser in the *Dictionary of National Biography*, ed. Sir Sidney Lee, 63 vols. (London, 1895–1900), liii. 396.

3. Stanley Wells and Gary Taylor, with John Jowett and William Montgomery, *William Shakespeare: A Textual Companion* (Oxford, 1987), 163.

4. Ibid. 34–6; quotation modernized from p. 36.

5. Ibid. 36.

6. Peter W. M. Blayney, *The First Folio of Shakespeare*, Folger Shakespeare Library Publications (Washington, DC, 1991), 2.

7. '…we should recognize that his involvement with the First Folio was so extensive and of such a kind that it is Ralph Crane rather than the playwright Nicholas Rowe whom we should acknowledge as the first person to confront the problems of translating Shakespeare's plays from the stage to the study: Shakespeare's earliest editor.' T. Howard-Hill, 'Shakespeare's Earliest Editor: Ralph Crane', *Shakespeare Survey 44* (1992), 129.

8. Cited in *Ben Jonson*, ed. C. H. Herford, Percy and Evelyn Simpson, 11 vols. (Oxford, 1925–52), ix. 13.

9. Peter Blayney, 'The Publication of Playbooks', in John D. Cox and David Scott Kastan (eds), *A New History of Early English Drama* (New York, 1997), 392.

10. Richard Dutton, 'The Birth of the Author', in R. B. Parker and S. P. Zitner (eds), *Elizabethan Theater: Essays in Honor of S. Schoenbaum* (Newark, 1996), 87.

11. We have evidence, of course, that plays were sometimes shortened in performance, and that omitted passages were sometimes restored in printing; Humphrey Moseley, for instance, states in the Beaumont and Fletcher Folio of 1647 that the texts there published

include 'both all that was acted and all that was not'; what persuades me that the editors of the Folio brought their texts into line with the plays as acted is the very fact that in a number of instances they omit passages present in alternative versions.

12. The 1597 quarto of *Romeo and Juliet* marks the end of a number of scenes in the later part of the play with a type ornament; *Pericles* prints a rule after the ends of Acts 1 and 2, which of course immediately precede Choruses. In the 1622 *Othello*, the beginnings of Acts 2, 4, and 5 are marked, and the 1634 edition of *The Two Noble Kinsmen* is fully marked into Acts and scenes.

29. The Limitations of the First Folio

1. It is reproduced in Anthony James West, *The Shakespeare First Folio: The History of the Book*, vol. 1: *An Account of the First Folio Based on Its Sales and Prices, 1623–2000* (Oxford, 2001), p. xxii.

2. Anthony James West, *The Shakespeare First Folio: The History of the Book*, vol. 2: *A New Worldwide Census of First Folios* (Oxford, 2003), 316.

3. Ibid. 58–61.

4. Stanley Wells, *Shakespeare: For All Time* (London, 2002), 371.

5. Especially by Charlton J. Hinman, *The Printing and Proof Reading of the First Folio of Shakespeare* (Oxford, 1963).

6. *The RSC Shakespeare: The Complete Works*, ed. Jonathan Bate and Eric Rasmussen (London, 2007).

7. Germaine Greer, *Shakespeare's Wife* (London, 2007), chapter 21.

8. T. H. Howard-Hill, 'Shakespeare's Earliest Editor, Ralph Crane', *Shakespeare Survey* 44 (1992), 113–29.

9. Gary Taylor, 'The Structure of Performance: Act-Intervals in the London Theatres, 1576–1642', in Gary Taylor and John Jowett, *Shakespeare Reshaped, 1606–1623* (Oxford, 1993), 3–50.

10. *Pericles*, omitted by the Folio editors, was just a 'play' in the 1609 Quarto.

11. The relevant documents are reproduced in Stanley Wells and Gary Taylor, with John Jowett and William Montgomery, *William Shakespeare: A Textual Companion* (Oxford, 1987), 28–30.

12. Richard Flatter, *Shakespeare's Producing Hand: A Study of His Marks of Expression to Be Found in the First Folio* (London, 1948).

13. Cited in Don Weingust, *Acting from Shakespeare's First Folio: Theory, Text and Performance* (London, 2006), 40, 41.

14. Ibid. 7.

15. Ibid. 30.

16. Oscar Wilde, *The Importance of Being Earnest*, ed. Russell Jackson, New Mermaids (London, 1980), 1.495–7.

17. Weingust, *Acting from Shakespeare's First Folio*, 15.

18. Patrick Tucker, *Secrets of Acting Shakespeare: The Original Approach* (London, 2002), 236.

19. Ibid. 244.

20. *William Shakespeare: The Complete Works*, ed. Jonathan Bate and Eric Rasmussen (New York: Modern Library, 2007), p. liv.

21. Ibid. p. lvii.

22. The case is put forward in Lukas Erne, *Shakespeare as Literary Dramatist* (Cambridge, 2003).

23. Weingust, *Acting from Shakespeare's First Folio*, 38.

SELECT LIST OF PUBLICATIONS

Books

Literature and Drama: With Special Reference to Shakespeare and his Contemporaries (London: Routledge, 1970; reprinted 2005).

Shakespeare: The Writer and his Work (London: Longman, 1978).

Shakespeare: An Illustrated Dictionary (Oxford, Oxford University Press, 1978).

(with Gary Taylor), *Modernizing Shakespeare's Spelling, with Three Studies in the Text of 'Henry V'* (Oxford: Clarendon Press, 1979).

Re-Editing Shakespeare for the Modern Reader, Based on Lectures given at the Folger Shakespeare Library, Washington, DC (Oxford: Oxford University Press, 1984).

Shakespeare: A Dramatic Life (1994; also published as *Shakespeare, A Life in Drama*; revised as *Shakespeare: The Poet and his Plays* (London: Methuen, 1997)).

Shakespeare: For All Time (London: Macmillan, 2002).

Looking for Sex in Shakespeare (Cambridge: Cambridge University Press, 2004).

(with Paul Edmondson), *Shakespeare's Sonnets*, Oxford Shakespeare Topics (Oxford: Oxford University Press, 2004).

Shakespeare & Co.: Christopher Marlowe, Thomas Dekker, Ben Jonson, Thomas Middleton, John Fletcher and the Other Players in his Story (London: Allen Lane, 2006).

Is it True What they Say about Shakespeare? (Ebrington: Long Barn Books, 2007).

Shakespeare, Sex, and Love (Oxford: Oxford University Press, 2010).

Great Shakespeare Actors (Oxford: Oxford University Press, 2015).

William Shakespeare: A Very Short Introduction (Oxford: Oxford University Press, 2015).

William Shakespeare: The Tragedies: A Very Short Introduction. (Oxford: Oxford University Press, 2016).

Edited Works

Works by William Shakespeare

A Midsummer Night's Dream, Penguin Shakespeare (Harmondsworth, 1967).

Richard II, Penguin Shakespeare (Harmondsworth, 1969).

The Comedy of Errors, Penguin Shakespeare (Harmondsworth, 1972).

Hamlet, ed. T. J. B. Spencer, completed by Stanley Wells with an Introduction by Anne Barton (Harmondsworth: Penguin, 1980).

Sonnets and A Lover's Complaint (Oxford: Oxford University Press, 1985).

The Complete Works, ed. Stanley Wells and Gary Taylor, with John Jowett, and William Montgomery (Oxford: Oxford University Press, 1986); Original-Spelling edition, 1986; *A Textual Companion*, 1986.

An Oxford Anthology of Shakespeare (Oxford: Oxford University Press, 1987).

Twelfth Night (with Roger Warren), Oxford Shakespeare (Oxford: Oxford University Press, 1994).

The History of King Lear (the Quarto), Oxford Shakespeare (Oxford: Oxford University Press, 2000).

Other subjects

Thomas Nashe, *Selected Works*, Stratford-upon-Avon Library 1 (London: Edward Arnold, 1964).

Ben Jonson, '*Lovers Made Men*', in S. W. Wells and T. J. B. Spencer (eds), *A Book of Masques in Honour of Allardyce Nicoll* (Cambridge: Cambridge University Press, 1967).

Thomas Dekker, *The Shoemaker's Holiday* (with Robert Smallwood), Revels Plays (Manchester: Manchester University Press, 1975).

Nineteenth-Century Shakespeare Burlesques, 5 vols. (London: Diploma Press, 1977).

Shakespeare Survey (Cambridge: Cambridge University Press, 1980–99).

Shakespeare in the Theatre: An Anthology of Criticism (Oxford: Oxford University Press, 2000).

The New Cambridge Companion to Shakespeare (with Margreta de Grazia), (Cambridge: Cambridge University Press, 2001, etc.).

The Cambridge Companion to Shakespeare on Stage (with Sarah Stanton), (Cambridge: Cambridge University Press, 2002).

Shakespeare Found! A Life Portrait At Last (The Cobbe Foundation and The Shakespeare Birthplace Trust, 2009).

Thomas Middleton, *A Yorkshire Tragedy*, in *Thomas Middleton: The Collected Works*, General Editors Gary Taylor and John Lavagnino (Oxford: Oxford University Press, 2010).

Shakespeare Beyond Doubt: Evidence, Authorship, Controversy (with Paul Edmondson), (Cambridge: Cambridge University Press, 2013).

The Shakespeare Circle: An Alternative Biography (with Paul Edmondson), (Cambridge: Cambridge University Press, 2015).

The Oxford Companion to Shakespeare (with Michael Dobson), 2nd edn. (with Will Sharpe and Erin Sullivan), (Oxford: Oxford University Press, 2015).

Associate Editor, *Oxford Dictionary of National Biography*.

Associate Editor, *Oxford Companion to English Literature*.

Reviews of books and plays in *Notes and Queries, Critical Quarterly, Modern Language Review, Theatre Notebook, Review of English Studies, Yearbook of English Studies, Cahiers Elisabéthains, The Observer, Drama, Huntington Library Quarterly, Times Educational Supplement, The Sunday Times, Theatre Notebook, Shakespeare Quarterly, TLS, The Daily Telegraph, The Mail on Sunday*, and the *New York Review of Books*.

Articles

'Happy Endings in Shakespeare', *Shakespeare Jahrbuch West* (1966), 103–23.

'Shakespeare's Life, Times and Stage: A Review of Recent Studies', *Shakespeare Survey 19* (1966), 143–54.

'Shakespeare's Text on the Modern Stage', *Shakespeare Jahrbuch West* (1967), 175–93.

'The Academic and the Theatre', in J. G. Price (ed.), *The Triple Bond* (Philadelphia: University of Pennsylvania Press, 1975), 1–13.

'Directors' Shakespeare', *Shakespeare Jahrbuch West* (1976), 65–78.

'Thomas Nashe and the Satirical Stance', *Cahiers Elisabéthains*, 9 (1976), 1–7.

'*The Revenger's Tragedy* Revived', in G. R. Hibbard (ed.), *Elizabethan Theatre* (London: Macmillan, 1978), 105–33.

'Shakespeare and Revision', The Hilda Hulme Memorial Lecture (University of London, 1978).

'Television Shakespeare', *Shakespeare Quarterly*, 13 (1982), 261–77.

'Experiencing Shakespeare', *Caliban*, 21 (1984), 211–16.

'Stage Directions for Shakespeare: The Editor's Problem', in Keir Elam (ed.), *Quaderni 1984— Shakespeare Today: Directions and Methods of* Research (Florence: La Casa Usher, 1984), pp. 19–38.

'Shakespeare on the English Stage', in John F. Andrews (ed.), *William Shakespeare: His World, His Work, His Influence*, 3 vols. (New York: Scribner, 1985), iii. 603–28.

'Reunion Scenes in *The Comedy of Errors* and *Twelfth Night*', *Weiner Beiträge zur Englischen Philologie*, 80 (1986), 267–76.

'Shakespeare Scholarship and the Modern Theatre', *Bulletin of the John Rylands Library of Manchester* (1986), 276–93.

(with Gary Taylor), 'No Shrew, A Shrew, and the Shrew: Internal Revision in *The Taming of the Shrew*', in Bernhard Fabian and Kurt Tetzeli von Rosador (eds.), *Shakespeare: Text, Language, Criticism* (Hildesheim, 1987), 351–79.

'Revision in Shakespeare's Plays', in Richard Landon (ed.), *Editors and Editing, A Retrospect,* (New York: AMS Press, 1988), 67–97.

(with Gary Taylor), 'The Oxford Shakespeare Reviewed by the General Editors', *Analytical and Enumerative Bibliography* (1990), 6–20.

'Shakespeare Performances in England, 1987–8', *Shakespeare Survey* 42 (1990), 129–48.

'Shakespeare Performances in England in 1988–9', *Shakespeare Survey* 43 (1991), 183–203.

'W. H. Clemen: A Personal Memoir', in Dieter Mehl and Wolfgang Weiss (eds), *Interpretationem zur Englischen Literatur, by Wolfgang Clemen* (Münster, 1992), 11–14.

'Enjoying Shakespeare', Inaugural Lecture delivered on 8 May 1989, University of Birmingham School of English, 1994.

'Shakespeare's Lives: 1991–1994', in R. B. Parker and S. Zitner (eds.), *Elizabethan Theater: Essays in Honor of S. Schoenbaum* (Newark: University of Delaware Press, 1996), 15–29.

'Shakespeare and Human Evil', in *En Torno a Shakespeare*, ed. Manuel Angel Conejero, Valencia, pp. 167–91.

'A New Early Reader of Shakespeare', in Richard Meek, Jane Rickard, and Richard Wilson (eds), *Shakespeare and the Book* (Manchester: Manchester University Press, 2008), 233–40.

'Extremes of Passion in *King Lear*', in *Shakespeare/Adaptation/Modern Drama*, ed. Randall Martin and Katherine Scheil (Toronto, Toronto University Press, 2011), 166–82.

(with Paul Edmondson), *Coffee with Shakespeare* (London: Duncan Baird, 2008; reprinted as Q & A *Shakespeare: Off the Record* (Watkins Publishing, 2011)).

(with Paul Edmondson), 'Portraits of Shakespeare', in Sonja Fielitz (ed.), *Shakespeare, Satire, Academia: Essays in Honour of Wolfgang Weiss* (Heidelberg: Universitätsverlag Winter, 2012), 1–14.

(with Paul Edmondson), 'Shakespeare and the Horse', in Sonja Fielitz (ed.), '. . . that I wished myself a horse': The Horse as Representative of Cultural Change in Systems of Thought* (Heidelberg: Universitätsverlag Winter, 2015).

And numerous Forewords, Afterwords, Introductions, programme notes, etc.

ACKNOWLEDGEMENTS

The production of this book owes a great deal to Laura Marriott for volunteering her assistance to The Shakespeare Birthplace Trust, and for helping me to seek the agreement of the original publishers to reprint the essays. Stanley Wells and Oxford University Press are grateful to the publishers and organisations, in the list that follows, for their kind co-operation:

1. 'Shakespeare: Man of the European Renaissance' in *Renaissance Shakespeare: Shakespeare Renaissances. Proceedings of the Ninth World Shakespeare Congress*, ed. by Martin Prochazka, Michael Dobson, Andreas Hofele, and Hanna Scolnicov. University of Delaware Press, 2014.
2. 'Tales from Shakespeare', from the Proceedings of the British Academy, 1987.
3. 'The Failure of *The Two Gentlemen of Verona*', *Shakespeare Jahrbuch*, ed. by Hermann Heuer, Ernst Theodor Sehrt, and Rudolf Stamm. Quelle and Meyer, 1964 (now DigiZeitschriften).
4. '*The Taming of the Shrew* and *King Lear*: A Structural Comparison' in *Shakespeare Survey 33*, ed. by Kenneth Muir. Cambridge University Press, 1981.
5. 'The Integration of Violent Action in *Titus Andronicus*', in *Shakespearean Continuities*, ed. by John Batchelor, Tom Cain, and Claire Lamont. Macmillan, 1997.
6. 'The Challenges of Romeo and Juliet' in *Shakespeare Survey 49*, ed. by Stanley Wells. Cambridge University Press, 1996.
7. 'Juliet's Nurse: The Uses of Inconsequentiality' in *Shakespeare's Styles. Essays in Honour of Kenneth Muir*, ed. by Philip Edwards, Inga-Stina Ewbank, and G. K. Hunter. Cambridge University Press, 1980.
8. 'The Lamentable Tale of *Richard II*', Shakespeare Studies (17). Shakespeare Society of Japan, 1982.
9. '*A Midsummer Night's Dream* Revisited', *Critical Survey* (3.1). Berghahn Books, 1991.
10. 'Translations in *A Midsummer Night's Dream*' in *Translating Life: Studies in Transpositional Aesthetics*, ed. by Shirley Crew and Alistair Stead. Liverpool University Press, 1999.
11. 'The Once and Future *King Lear*' in *The Division of the Kingdoms: Shakespeare's Two Versions of 'King Lear'*, ed. by Gary Taylor and Michael Warren. Clarendon Press, 1983.
12. 'Problems of Stagecraft in *The Tempest*', *New Theatre Quarterly* (40), Cambridge University Press, 1994.

13. 'My Name Is Will': Shakespeare's Sonnets and Autobiography, in *Shakespeare Survey 68*, ed. by Peter Holland. Cambridge University Press, 2015.

14. 'Shakespeare Without Sources', *Stratford-upon- Avon Studies 14*, ed. by Malcolm Bradbury and David Palmer. Edward Arnold, 1972 (now Hodder Education).

15. 'Shakespeare and Romance', *Stratford-upon- Avon Studies 14*, ed. by John Russell Brown and Bernard Harris. Edward Arnold, 1966 (now Hodder Education).

16. 'Boys Should be Girls: Shakespeare's Female Roles and the Boy Players', *New Theatre Quarterly* (98). Cambridge University Press, 2009.

17. 'Staging Shakespeare's Ghosts' in *The Arts of Performance in Elizabethan and Early Stuart Drama: Essays for G.K. Hunter*, ed. by Murray Biggs, Philip Edwards, Inga-Stina Ewbank, and Eugene M. Waith. Edinburgh University Press, 1991.

18. 'Staging Shakespeare's Apparitions and Dream Visions', The First Annual Globe Lecture. Globe Publications, 1993.

19. 'Shakespeare in Planché's Extravaganzas' in *Shakespeare Survey 16*, ed. by Allardyce Nicoll. Cambridge University Press, 1963.

20. 'Shakespeare in Max Beerbohm's Theatre Criticism' in *Shakespeare Survey 29*, ed. by Kenneth Muir. Cambridge University Press, 1976.

21. 'Shakespeare in Leigh Hunt's Theatre Criticism', *Essays and Studies* (33), English Association, 1980.

22. 'Shakespeare in Hazlitt's Theatre Criticism', *Shakespeare Survey 35*, ed. by Stanley Wells. Cambridge University Press, 1982.

23. 'Peter Hall's *Coriolanus* 1959', *Furman Studies* (1976); repr. as *Royal Shakespeare: Four Major Productions at Stratford-upon-Avon*. Manchester University Press, 1977.

24. 'On Being a General Editor' in *Shakespeare Survey 59*, ed. by Peter Holland Cambridge University Press, 2006.

25. 'Editorial Treatment of Foul Paper Texts: *Much Ado About Nothing* as Test Case', *Review of English Studies* (31). Oxford University Press, 1980.

26. 'Money in Shakespeare's Comedies', *Actes des congrès de la Société française Shakespeare* (11), 1993.

27. 'To Read a Play: the Problem of Editorial Intervention' in *Reading Plays: Interpretation and Reception*, ed. by Hanna Scolnicov and Peter Holland. Cambridge University Press, 1991.

28. 'The First Folio: Where Should We be Without it?' in *Shakespeare: Text and Theater: Essays in Honor of Jay L. Halio*, ed. by Lois Potter and Arthur F. Kinney. University of Delaware, 1999.

29. 'The Limitations of the First Folio' (with Paul Edmondson), in *Shakespeare Without Boundaries: Essays in Honor of Dieter Mehl*, ed. by Christa Jansohn, Lena Cowen Orlin and Stanley Wells. University of Delaware, 2010.

PAUL EDMONDSON
The Shakespeare Birthplace Trust

INDEX

Adams, Cranford 279, 285
Agate, James 153
Ainger, Alfred 29, 30
Alexander, Bill 142, 404
Alexander, Peter 393–4
All's Well that Ends Well 251, 398, 400
Altick, R. D. 117
Alvarez, Alan 354
Anderson, Mary 112
Andrews, Harry 357, 358
Antony and Cleopatra 102, 282
apparitions, staging of 273–81
Archer, William 320, 333
Arden Shakespeare 369
Armin, Robert 249
Aronson, Boris 354
Asche, Oscar 315
Ashcroft, Dame Peggy 40, 89, 102
As You Like It 92, 160, 184, 213, 243, 311, 326,
     411–12, 418
Atkins, Robert 80

Bacon, Sir Francis 12
Baker, Herschel 348
Baldwin, T. W. 13
Bandello, Matteo 86
Bandmann-Palmer, Millicent 247
Barnes, Barnabe 261
Barnet, Sylvan 369
Barnfield, Richard 197
Barrit, Desmond 152, 156
Bartholomeusz, Dennis 269–70
Barton, Anne 377, 378
Barton, John 101, 147, 157, 213, 262, 353, 357,
     394, 421
Basse, William 426
Bate, Sir Jonathan 74, 437, 446, 451
Beckerman, Bernard 279, 280, 282, 369
Beerbohm, Max 6, 7, 304–18
Bell, John 109
Bellini, Vincenzo 89
Bennett, Josephine Waters 370, 384
Bentley, G. E. 249, 369
Berger, Tom 373
Berkeley, Thomas 135
Berlioz, Hector 89, 92, 100
Bernhardt, Sarah 316–17
Berry, Herbert 274

Bethell, S. L. 21
Billington, Michael 81, 99
Blayney, Peter W. M. 164, 171, 174, 432
Boaistuau, Pierre 86
Boecher, T. B. 152
Bogdanov, Michael 4, 88, 89, 92, 98, 100
Booth, Stephen 135, 146, 200
Bowdler, Thomas and Henrietta Maria 3, 24,
     25, 112
Bowers, Fredson 161, 369, 408
boy actors 5, 134, 248–54
Boyd, William 201
Bradbrook, M. C. 55
Bradley, A. C. 64, 162, 351–2
Branagh, Sir Kenneth 101, 247
Bridges, Robert 310
Brien, Alan 361
Brissenden, Alan 378–9
Britten, Sir Benjamin 137, 213
Brockbank, Philip 5, 271, 282–3
Brook, Peter 74, 76, 80, 81, 89, 92, 98, 102, 133, 135,
     142, 144–5, 146, 147, 152, 175, 414, 421
Brooke, Arthur 86–7, 92, 110, 111, 114
Brooke, Nicholas 104, 113, 131
Brooks, Harold F. 133, 135, 136, 369, 378
Brown, Alison 19
Brown, Charles Armitage 111
Brown, John Russell 146, 370, 374, 414
Buchan, Sir John, Lord Tweedsmuir 39
Buckley, Christine 379
Buckman, Irene 40
Bullough, Geoffrey 52, 111
Burbage, Richard 249, 426, 438, 439
Burke, Edmund 446
Burrow, Colin 193, 195, 196, 198
Burton, Georgia Peters 174
Burton, William 222
Butter, Nathaniel 163
Buxton, John 223

Cagney, James 153
Caird, John 142
Calderwood, James L 153
Calvert, Louis 265
Camden, William 425
Cardenio 431, 441
Carey, Elizabeth 135
Carroll, D. Allen 133, 143

Carroll, William C. 149–50, 152
Carter, Thomas 38
Cecil, Lord David 28, 304–5
Chambers, Sir E. K. 49, 135, 169, 382, 383
Charlton, H. B. 49–50
Churchill, Sir Winston 39
Chute, Marchette 40
Cibber, Colley 259
Cibber, Theophilus 87, 111
Clark, Charles 368, 372
Clark, W. G. 163
classification of Shakespeare's plays 435–6, 441–3
Clemen, W. H. 117–18, 125, 259, 370
Coghill, Nevill 443
Coleman, John 289
Coleridge, Samuel Taylor 49, 96, 105, 106, 113, 239,
    263, 322, 324, 345, 431, 441
Colthorpe, Marion 135–6
Comedy of Errors, The 15, 205, 226, 227–8, 399
Condell, Henry 426, 429, 430, 431, 433, 437, 438,
    439, 440, 443, 447, 451
Cook, Ann Jennalie 402–3
Copping, H. 30
Coriolanus 6, 308, 349–64, 416–17
Coryate, Tom 13
Coyne, William P 32
Craig, Gordon 314, 316, 318
Crane, Ralph 409, 429, 432, 436, 440
Crosse, Gordon 80
Cushman, Charlotte 87, 102, 247
Cymbeline 184, 237, 238, 282, 283–7, 402, 419

Dane, Clemence 39
Daniel, Samuel 120, 282
Daniels, Ron 145
Davenant, William 179, 269
David, Richard 65, 100, 143
Da Vinci, Leonardo 19
Davis, Norman 376
Dekker, Thomas 22, 60, 415, 425
Demeger, Robert 99
Derby, Earl of 135
Dessen, Alan 4, 76, 80, 81, 82, 412
Devine, George 143, 144
Dickens, Charles 161
Digges, Leonard 430, 439
Donne, John 93, 194, 426–7
Donno, Elizabeth Story 31
Doran, Madeline 54, 170, 370
Dorsch, T. S. 312
Dotrice, Roy 356–7
doubling 135, 144, 146–7
Dowden, Edward 37, 54–5
Downer, Alan 230–1
Downie, Penny 247
Downs-Gamble, Margaret 14
dream visions, staging of 273, 281–7
Droeshout, Martin 430

Dryden, John 100, 179
Dubrow, Heather 194
Duncan-Jones, Katherine 14, 192–3, 194, 195, 196, 198
Duthie, G. I. 106, 113, 167, 169–70
Dutton, Richard 434

Eccles, Mark 370
editorial intervention 408–24
Edmondson, Paul 14–15, 194, 368, 451
Eliot, T. S. 74, 124–5, 223
Elizabethan Stage Society 302, 313
Ellis, David 195–6
Elton, W. R. 21, 65
Erne, Lukas 445
Ervine, St John 111
Evans, Bertrand 91
Evans, Dame Edith 6, 89, 111, 349–50, 358–60
Evans, G. Blakemore 174, 369, 376, 382, 388
Evens, Bertrand 370
Everett, Barbara 370, 377
Ewbank, Inga-Stina 154
extravaganzas 288–303

Faucit, Helena 235
female roles 248–54, 324–5
Finney, Albert 357
First Folio 8, 426–37, 438–47
First Folio, and King Lear 7, 163–77
Fischer, Sandra 398
Flatter, Richard 443
Fletcher, John 22
Florio, John 13
Foakes, R. A. 133, 135, 138–9, 371
Forbes-Robertson, Johnston 112, 316
Ford, John 425
Forde, Emanuel 223
Forman, Simon 269, 285
foul-paper texts, editorial treatment of 381–95
Freedman, Gerald 81
French, Dawn 247
Fry, Christopher 40
Frye, Northrop 369
Furnivall, F. J. 30

Gardiner, Alfonzo 32
Gardner, Dame Helen 376
Garfield, Leon 3, 41–2
Garrick, David 87, 93, 102, 109, 111
Gaskill, William 283, 284
General Editor, work and role of 367–80
Gentleman, Francis 87
Gerhard, Roberto 355
ghosts in Shakespeare's plays 255–70
Gielgud, Sir John 88, 360
Gilbert, John 30–1
Gilbert, Sir W. S. 288
Glover, Julian 99
Godwin, Mary Jane 25

Godwin, William 25
Golding, Arthur 150–1, 159
Gounod, Charles 89
Granville-Barker, Frank 355
Granville-Barker, Harley 72, 96, 100, 142, 145, 163, 167, 175, 176, 283, 284, 285, 414, 420
Graves, Joseph 34–5
Greek 13–14, 198
Greek romances 220 1, 222
Green, Martin 201
Green, Roger Lancelyn 40–1
Greene, Robert 12, 15, 22, 231–2, 233–4, 236, 282–3, 425
Greer, Germaine 195, 438
Greg, W. W. 137, 163, 164, 165, 167, 168, 169, 382, 408
Griffiths, Trevor R. 149, 153
Gurr, Andrew 14, 102, 200
Guthrie, Tyrone 349

Hall, Sir Peter 6, 151, 185, 266, 349, 350, 352, 353, 355, 356, 423, 450
Hamburger, Maik 143
Hamlet 19, 20–1, 75–6, 217, 256, 262–8, 309, 311, 313, 315, 316–17, 327, 423
Hands, Terry 4, 97, 101
Hankey, Julie 258–9
Harbage, Alfred 167, 369, 370–1
Hardison, O. B. 31
Hardwick, Paul 151, 357
Hardy, Robert 357
Hare, David 421
Harris, Augustus 303
Harris, Frank 304–5, 306
Harrison, G. B. 40, 109, 368, 371
Haughton, William 22
Havel, Václav 11
Hawkins, F. W. 328
Hazlitt, William 6, 7, 49, 52, 317, 321, 322, 324, 333–48, 351
Heliodorus 220–1, 222
Heminges, John 426, 429, 430, 431, 433, 437, 438, 439, 440, 444, 449, 451
Henry IV 1 273, 281, 325, 326
Henry IV 2 59, 105–6
Henry V 16, 308, 325, 415
Henry VI 83–4, 110, 273–7
Henry VIII 252, 287, 431
Herbert, William 195
Heywood, Thomas 261, 267, 285, 406
Hibbard, G. R. 264, 267, 377, 416
Hinman, Charles 369
Hinman, Charlton 443
Hodgdon, Barbara 139–40, 141–2
Hodge, Harold 312
Hodges, C. Walter 267
Hoffman, Alice Spencer 38
Holding, Peter 97, 102

Holdsworth, R. V. 256
Holinshed, Raphael 119, 120
Holland, Hugh 430, 439
Holland, Norman 370
Holland, Peter 367
Holland, Philemon 58
Holloway, Stanley 153
Holm, Sir Ian 356–7
Honigmann, Ernst 85, 171, 382–3
Hope-Wallace, Philip 364
Hosley, Richard 369, 377
Houtchens, L. C. and C. W. 321–2
Howard, James 87
Howard-Hill, Trevor 440
Howe, P. P. 334
Howell, Jane 81
Howerd, Frankie 153
Hubler, Edward 370
Hudson, R. 38
Hufford, Lois Grosvenor 38
Hughes, Alan 74
Hunt, John 319
Hunt, Leigh 6, 7, 317, 319–32, 336
Hunter, G. K. 5, 53, 170, 268
Hunter, Kathryn 247
Hytner, Nicholas 186

inconsequentiality 5, 97, 114–15
Irving, Sir Henry 87, 90, 109, 112, 311, 315, 316, 326, 351

Jackson, Sir Barry 272
Jackson, Macdonald P. 197, 281
Jackson, Russell 176
Jaggard, William 427, 428, 429
James, Henry 90, 102
Jenkins, Harold 267, 369
Johnson, Samuel 50, 57, 91, 96, 98, 205–6, 218, 223, 321, 372
Jones, Gemma 33
Jones, Inigo 188, 282, 285
Jonson, Ben 13, 15, 22, 188, 189, 198, 212, 222, 282, 406–7, 425, 427, 429–30, 439, 440
Joyce, James 93
Julius Caesar 256, 257, 260–2, 312, 326

Kantorowicz, Ernst 129
Kathman, David 5, 250
Kean, Charles 179, 180, 183, 289, 296, 298, 300, 326
Kean, Edmund 322–3, 326–7, 330, 331–2, 334, 342, 343, 344–7, 351
Keats, John 162, 324, 336
Kemble, Charles 298, 301, 320, 327–8
Kemble, Fanny 323, 331
Kemble, John Philip 54, 323, 329–30, 347–8, 351
Kemble, Stephen 334
Kemp, Will 249
Kermode, Frank 216, 370

Kernan, Alvin 370
King John 110, 308, 312–13, 318
King Lear 4–5, 7, 17, 20, 21, 64–73, 75, 115–16, 162–77, 213, 311, 413, 439–40
Kitchin, Laurence 350, 354–5, 361, 362, 363
Kittredge, George Lyman 167, 393
Knight, Charles 29, 167
Knight, G. Wilson 143, 283
Knowles, Richard 412
Knowles, Sheridan 347
Kott, Jan 142–3, 144, 152–3, 156, 187
Koun, Karolos 101
Kyd, Thomas 258, 262
Kyle, Barry 4

Lamb, Charles and Mary 3, 24–33, 42
Lambrechts, Guy 387, 388
lamentation 4, 117–32
Lang, Andrew 29–30
Lang, Mrs Andrew 31
Laroque, François 136
Latham, Agnes 411–12
Latin 12–13, 16
Laughton, Charles 349
Lawrence, W J 263, 264–5, 266, 268
Lee, Sir Sidney 37, 314
Lennox, Charlotte 49
Leno, Dan 317
Lester, Adrian 247
Levenson, Jill 93, 95
Levin, Harry 369
Lloyd, W. W. 393
Lodge, Thomas 256
Love's Labour's Lost 16–17, 59, 200, 205, 206–10, 213, 214, 216, 251, 401
Lowe, Robert 320, 333
Lower, Charles 97
Lyly, John 12, 15, 425
Lyly, William 12

Mabbe, James 430, 439
Macauley, Elizabeth Wright 33–4
Macbeth 256, 257, 265, 268–70, 277–80, 292–3
McEwan, Geraldine 247
McGuire, Philip 140–1, 142
Mack, Maynard 163, 369
McKellen, Sir Ian 101
Macleod, Mary 37–8
McManaway, James G 265
MacMillan, Dougald 288
Macready, William 235, 257, 326–7, 331, 347
Mahood, M. M. 95
Malone, Edmond 166, 282, 388
Mantegna, Andrea 18
Marlowe, Christopher 12, 15, 16, 18–19, 20, 78, 117, 161, 400
Marshall, Frank A 109
Marston, John 406

masque 187–9, 241–2
Mathews, Charles 320–1
Maxwell, Caroline 34
Maxwell, J. C. 283
Measure for Measure 5, 115, 210, 400, 402
Mehl, Dieter 437, 443
Mendelssohn, Felix 145
Mendes, Sam 183, 188
Merchant of Venice, The 19, 22, 308, 396–8
Meres, Francis 197
Merry Wives of Windsor, The 12, 22, 136–7, 251–2, 308–9, 399, 404
Middleton, Thomas 22, 256, 425, 428, 444–5
Midsummer Night's Dream, A 4, 96, 133–47, 148–60, 205, 206–10, 212, 213, 214–15, 216, 253, 281, 311, 313–14, 338–9, 396, 401, 421
Miles, Bernard 41
Miller, Sir Jonathan 75
Milton, John 212
mind and body dualism 5, 58–73
money, in Shakespeare's comedies 396–403
Moore, George 98
Moorman, F. W. 258, 261
Morley, Henry 289
Morris, Harrison S 29
Much Ado About Nothing 184, 382–95, 402, 403, 409
Muir, Kenneth 109, 370, 371
Munro, John 55

Nashe, Thomas 15, 16, 114, 222, 223
Neill, Michael 379
Nesbit, Edith 36
New Cambridge Shakespeare 368
Nicholls, Anthony 357
Nicoll, Allardyce 55, 162, 272, 288, 289, 368, 374, 414
Noble, Adrian 4, 88, 97, 99, 100, 152, 156
Nunn, Sir Trevor 353

Odell, G. C. D. 179–80, 314
Olivier, Sir Laurence 6, 74, 88, 349, 350, 351, 360–4, 421
Olson, Paul 136
O'Neill, Eliza 295, 343, 347
Ornstein, Robert 119
Osborne, John 350
Othello 19–20, 345–6, 417–18
Otway, Thomas 87, 109
Ovid 199

Painter, William 86, 111
Parker, Patricia 11
Parrott, T. M. 49
pastoral myth 212–13
Pavier, Thomas 428
Payne, Iden 390
Pearlman, Edward 100
Peele, George 15, 16, 258

Pelican Shakespeare 369–71
Penguin Shakespeare 367–8, 371–5, 377
Pericles 19, 161, 222, 252, 281–3, 400, 431
Perrin, J. B. 3, 33
Petrarch 92, 198
Phelps, Samuel 155, 299, 300, 326
Phillips, Robin 412
place apart 212–13
Planché, James Robinson 6, 288–303
Plautus 220, 226
Plutarch 15, 18, 58, 260, 261, 351
Poel, William 302, 313, 349, 414
Pollard, A. W. 163, 169
Pope, Alexander 337
Prokofiev, Sergei 89
prose adaptations of Shakespeare 3, 24–43
Prouty, Charles T 369

Quarto text, and *King Lear* 7, 163–77
quibbles 93, 95
Quiller-Couch, Sir A. T. 36–7, 55, 368
Quiney, Richard 13

Rackham, Arthur 31
Rae, Alexander 334
Rape of Lucrece, The 21, 196, 430, 440
Rasmussen, Eric 438, 446, 451
reading plays 405–8
recapitulation 91–2
Redgrave, Vanessa 247, 357
Red Lion playhouse 274
Reed, Isaac 388–9
religion 20–1
Renaissance 2, 11–23
Renaissance Theatre Company 89
Reynolds, Frederick 325
rhetorical devices 15–16, 93–4
Richard II 4, 110, 117–32, 217, 339–40
Richard III 256, 257–60, 281, 308, 326–7, 331–2
Richardson, Sir Ralph 153
Rickett, Charles 314
Ringler, William 135, 144, 146
Ripley, J. R. 262
Roberts, Henry 223
Robeson, Paul 349
Robinson, Heath 31
Robson, Frederick 294, 302
Rollins, Hyder 195, 196, 200
romance 219–43
Romeo and Juliet 4, 5, 17–18, 86–102, 103–16, 217, 415
Rosen, Barbara 370
Rosenberg, Marvin 248–9
Ross, John C. 371
Rossiter, A. P. 131
Rowe, Nicholas 166, 411, 413
Rowell, George 289
Rowse, A. L. 368
Rylance, Mark 247, 248

Sampson, George 31, 386–7, 390
Schaaber, M. A. 369
Schlegel, August Wilhelm 322
Schmoller, Hans 374
Schoenbaum, S. 134–5
Scholasticus, Marianus 14
Scot, Reginald 276
Seltzer, Daniel 370
Seneca 256, 258
Serlio, Sebastiano 285
Serrailler, Ian 41
Seymour, Mary 35
Shakespeare, John 201
Shakespeare criticism 1–7
Shaw, Fiona 247
Shaw, George Bernard 87–8, 94, 98, 304, 305, 309, 407–8
Shaw, Glen Byam 349
Shelley, Percy Bysshe 324
Siddons, Sarah 247, 329, 343–4
Sidney, Sir Philip 12, 194, 222, 223, 425
Signet Shakespeare 369, 370
Sim, Adelaide C Gordon 35–6
Sisson, C. J. 382, 388, 389
Smallwood, Robert 374, 377, 378
Snowden, Philip 39
sonnets 13–15, 17, 59, 92, 192–204
Southampton, Earl of 12, 196, 197
Spencer, T. J. B. 17, 90, 111, 112, 271, 324, 367, 368, 375, 377
Spenser, Edmund 223, 224, 425
Spottiswoode, Patrick 271
Sprague, A. C. 268, 409
Spriggs, Elizabeth 101
Steele, Tommy 153
Stevenson, D. L. 384, 388
Stokes, Winston 31
Stone, P. W. K. 164, 170
Strachey, Lytton 311
Strode, William 14
Suzman, Dame Janet 248–9

Talfourd, Thomas Noon 348
Taming of the Shrew, The 4–5, 17, 19, 58, 59–64, 67, 151, 301–2, 401–2
Taylor, Gary 7, 85, 167, 169, 174, 259, 428
Tchaikovsky, Pyotr Ilyich 89, 176
Tempest, The 4, 17, 22, 178–91, 205, 206, 210–12, 213, 215–16, 236–42, 243, 252, 310–11
Theatre Regulations Act (1843) 299, 300
Theobald, Lewis 166, 388, 410, 416
Thompson, A. Hamilton 28, 29
Thomson, Peter 280
Thorndike, Dame Sybil 350
Thorpe, Thomas 15, 192, 193, 195, 440
Tillyard, E. M. W. 18
Timon of Athens 161, 332
Titus Andronicus 4, 74–82, 84–5, 421

Tourneur, Cyril 256–7
Townshend, Aurelian 285
transgendered performances 247–8
translations 4, 148–60
trap-doors 258–9, 262, 263, 264, 265, 266–7, 268, 276, 277, 279, 280, 281
Traversi, Derek 143
Tree, Ellen 247
Tree, Sir Herbert Beerbohm 306, 312, 314, 317–18
Trenery, Grace R 383, 384–5
Trewin, J. C. 31
Tuck, Raphael 30
Tucker, Patrick 445, 446
Twelfth Night 225, 228–31, 243, 309, 314, 317–18, 325, 401, 402
Twine, Lawrence 222
Two Gentlemen of Verona, The 3, 49–57, 105, 217, 226
Two Noble Kinsmen, The 22, 252–3, 431
Tynan, Kenneth 354, 360, 364

Underdowne, Thomas 222
University Wits 15
Unwin, George 401
Ure, Mary 357
Ure, Peter 351
Urkowitz, Steven 164–5, 166, 169, 170–1, 174

van Doren, Mark 239
Venus and Adonis 21, 92, 255, 430, 440
Vere, Elizabeth 135
Vickers, Sir Brian 15, 16
violence 4, 74–85
Vyvyan, John 49

Waith, Eugene 74, 75, 77
Walker, Alice 170

Waller, David 152
Waller, Lewis 308, 316
Walpole, Hugh 39
Wanamaker, Sam 271
Ward, A. C. 33
Wardman, Judith 375
Warner, Deborah 4, 74, 76, 81–2, 421, 450
Warren, Michael 7, 171–4
Warren, Roger 144–5, 146, 185, 284, 378, 419
Webster, John 425
Webster, Margaret 162–3
Weingust, Donald 444
Weis, René 200–1
Wells, Stanley 1, 2–8, 449–52
Werth, Andrew 13
Wickham, Glynne 364, 414
Wilde, Oscar 176, 304, 445
Williams, Gary Jay 133, 135
Williams, George Walton 109, 174, 369
Wilson, F. P. 214
Wilson, John Dover 55, 109, 136, 264, 283, 353, 368, 382, 384, 385, 386, 388, 389, 390–1, 392, 393, 411
Winter's Tale, The 17, 22, 231–6, 243, 281, 409–10
Wolff, S. L. 223
Woodhouse, Richard 324
Woodthorpe, Peter 357
Woolf, Virginia 230
Wordsworth, William 25–6, 161–2, 196
Wright, W. Aldis 163

Young, Charles Mayne 331, 334
Young, David P. 141, 152
Young, Frances Brett 39, 40
Young, Henry McClure 200

Zeffirelli, Sir Franco 89, 90